MARY

A HISTORY OF DOCTRINE AND DEVOTION

MARY

A History of Doctrine and Devotion

HILDA GRAEF

Sheed & Ward
London

" The Madonna is not pleased when
she is put above her Son."

POPE JOHN XXIII

FOREWORD

For a laywoman to write a history of Marian doctrine and devotion may seem presumptuous; is not this a task that had better be left to a professional theologian? But, first of all, what I have been trying to do is to trace a development, not to expound doctrine, and perhaps it may sometimes be useful to bring to this subject a lay mind—that is to say, a mind that has been formed in a tradition different from that of the theological schools and seminaries. And thirteen years' work as senior assistant on the staff of *A Patristic Greek Lexicon* has taught me something, at least, of the views of the Fathers which I have found useful when writing the present account. Finally, as a woman I have delighted in tracing the history of devotion to the most beloved and venerated woman in all human history.

It has truly been a joy to me to sketch this history of Mary of Nazareth, who was also Theotokos, Mother of God. Nevertheless, in the course of writing this book I have at times come across statements which have justified the remark of J. A. de Aldama, S.J., that Mariology is "a theological subject which lends itself more than many others to exaggerations and deviation".[1] I could have taken the easy way out, and either have omitted such questionable material altogether or reproduced it without comment, leaving the reader to draw his own conclusions. In the interests of truth and oecumenical understanding I have chosen another way—one which may, perhaps, disconcert some of my readers; I have frankly criticized where I felt criticism was necessary, even in the case

[1] In H. du Manoir, *Maria*, 2, p. 983.

of canonized saints.[1] For in what claims to be a history of Marian doctrine and devotion I have tried to give as much of the whole true story as is possible in the space of two not-too-unwieldy volumes, and to present the subject as objectively as I can without glossing over the deviations of which Père De Aldama speaks. For it is just these deviations which have so often turned our separated brethren away from the Mother of our Lord Jesus Christ, and it has seemed to me that there would be a much better chance of making them understand our devotion to her if we frankly admitted that it has at times outrun discretion. True, we all know and say that she is infinitely inferior to her divine Son—yet there is a certain amount of Catholic writing on her which, while admitting this in principle, loses sight of it in practice.

As Newman said, love has its own language, and when we call Mary our life, our sweetness and our hope, as we do in the *Salve Regina*, this is as natural an expression of affection as that of any lover calling his human love by similar endearments, and takes nothing away from our worship of God, who is our life and hope in quite a different sense. Now, it is one thing to surround Mary with such tokens of love and respect, but quite another to say that God obeys her, that we can appeal from God's tribunal to hers, that she rules over the kingdom of mercy while leaving to her Son only that of justice, and similar things which, as Newman says, "can only be explained by being explained away".[2] Therefore I have thought it right to criticize such statements, which can only lead to a quite mistaken idea of what the Church actually does teach about the blessed Virgin.

[1] When the Church canonizes saints she only asserts that they are in heaven and that their writings are free from serious error according to the knowledge then available. Thus, even great saints like St. Bernard, St. Thomas Aquinas and St. Bonaventure did not accept the Immaculate Conception, while un-canonized men like Eadmer and Duns Scotus taught it.

[2] *Certain Difficulties Felt by Anglicans*, new ed. (1892), vol. 2, p. 115.

This book cannot, of course, claim to be in any way complete—the subject is much too vast for that. I had to choose from the immense material, and another author might have chosen differently. My main purpose has been to give a survey of the teaching of theologians and preachers, and a bird's-eye view of some of the main liturgical developments and popular devotions, both in the West and in the East, in strict chronological order. For the age of the Fathers of the Church it has been comparatively easy to achieve this, but in the Middle Ages, to say nothing of modern times, the evidence would have become unmanageable unless I had confined myself to what I thought the most important features. This accounts for the *lacunae*, of which no-one could be more conscious than the author herself. But I hope I have at least been able to provide a survey of Christian thought on the subject of the Mother of God in readable form, acceptable especially to the interested laity. In doing so I have endeavoured to avail myself as far as possible of the findings of modern scholarship, and the reader who desires further information will, I trust, be helped by the footnotes and the—necessarily selective—bibliography.

HILDA GRAEF

ABBREVIATIONS

AB	*Analecta Bollandiana*
ACO	Schwartz, *Acta Conciliorum Oecumenicorum*
BA	*Biblica*
BKV	*Bibliothek der Kirchenväter*
BZ	*Biblische Zeitschrift*
CCSL	*Corpus Christianorum, Series Latina*
CSEL	*Corpus Scriptorum Ecclesiasticorum Latinorum*
DB	Denzinger-Bannwart, *Enchiridion Symbolorum*
EM	*Ephemerides Mariologicae*
EO	*Échos d'Orient*
ER	Ephraem of Syria, Rome edition
ETL	*Ephemerides Theologicae Lovanienses*
FS	*Franziskanische Studien*
GCS	*Die griechischen christlichen Schriftsteller der ersten drei Jahrhunderte*
GM	*Gregorianum*
MGH	*Monumenta Germanica Historica*
MM	*Marianum*
NRT	*Nouvelle Revue théologique*
OC	*Oriens Christianus*
PG	Migne, *Patrologia Graeca*
PL	Migne, *Patrologia Latina*
PO	*Patrologia Orientalis*
RB	*Revue biblique*
RBE	*Revue bénédictine*
RSPT	*Revue des sciences philosophiques et théologiques*
RSR	*Recherches de science religieuse*
RT	*Revue thomiste*
RTAM	*Recherches de théologie ancienne et médiévale*
SK	*Scholastik*
ST	*Studi e Testi*

PUBLISHERS' NOTE

Parts 1 and 2 of *Mary: A History of Doctrine and Devotion*, here for the first time published together as the unit originally conceived by the author, were first published as two separate volumes. The separate pagination of these two volumes has been preserved in order to facilitate use of the bibliographies and indexes.

Part 1

**From the Beginnings
to the Eve of the
Reformation**

CONTENTS

1

MARY IN THE SCRIPTURES[1]

THE OLD-TESTAMENT PROPHECIES

"I WILL put enmity between thee and the woman, and between thy seed and her seed: it shall crush thy head, and thou shalt lie in wait for his heel." (Gen. 3.15.) This is the most likely translation of the famous so-called Proto-evangelium, the "first good news", according to tradition the first mention in the Bible of Christ and his Mother, the Woman and her seed.

The interpretation of this passage as referring to Mary was greatly helped by a mistranslation of the Vulgate, which read "she" in the place of "it". Since Eve, far from crushing the head of the serpent, had herself been seduced by it, it seemed obvious that "the woman" must be another than Eve; indeed, it must be Mary herself, the "second Eve", who through her obedience repaired the damage done by the first. Today this wrong translation of the original Hebrew text has been generally abandoned, hence the reference to the Mother of Christ is now much less evident. The verse has, in fact, become one of the most widely discussed passages of Genesis, especially as it is not only of importance for the teaching on Mary as the Second Eve, but has also played a prominent part in the discussions about the Immaculate Conception as well as in the interpretation of the "woman" of Apocalypse 12, as will be seen at the end of this section.

Who, then, is meant by the "woman" whose seed shall crush the serpent's head? The term "seed" most likely refers

[1] This chapter considers only the modern exegesis of the Marian passages of the Old and New Testaments; their patristic and medieval interpretation will be given in the later parts of the book.

to an individual, and thus it was evidently understood by the translators of the so-called Septuagint version of the Old Testament, who wrote instead of the Greek neuter *auto*, "it" (shall crush thy head), which would have corresponded to the Hebrew original, the masculine *autos*, "he", thus giving the passage a messianic connotation.[1] There is to be a final, eschatological combat, in which the devil, here represented by the serpent, will be vanquished by his opponent, the "seed" of the woman. Nowadays the majority of Catholic theologians, following the Septuagint reading, are agreed that the "seed" envisaged by the author is the Messiah, that is to say, Christ, and many argue from this that the woman, therefore, must be his Mother, that is to say, Mary. Yet, if we remain strictly within the limits of the actual context, generally called the literal sense, the woman must refer to Eve, for no other woman has been mentioned in the text and the words are addressed to her.[2] But we should not overlook that they are not part of the ordinary narrative but a divine oracle, which the author of the so-called "Yahwist" document to which this chapter belongs, places in the mouth of God himself. Thus it is probable that they embrace far more than merely Eve and her descendants; indeed, that their meaning covers the whole of human history. In this view the serpent is the demon, the seed of the woman signifies the Messiah, the enmity ends with the crushing of the demon and the re-establishing of all God's rights in the eschatological future.[3]

Accepting this exegesis, many contemporary theologians are striking a kind of compromise; "the woman" refers to both, Eve and Mary, or the words refer to Eve in the literal

[1] See also G. Duncker, "Our Lady in the Old Testament", in *Mother of the Redeemer* (1959), p. 7.

[2] This is the view of many contemporary exegetes, for example of B. Rigaux, "La Femme et son lignage dans Genèse III, 14–15", in *RB*, 61 (1954), p. 344; so also A. Robert in H. du Manoir's *Maria*, 1 (subsequently cited only as *Maria* with number of volume), p. 35.

[3] So Rigaux, p. 343.

sense, but without excluding Mary. J. Coppens, in an important article in *Ephemerides Theologicae Lovanienses* entitled "Le Protévangile. Un nouvel essai d'exégèse"[1] wants to generalize the meaning so as to include both Eve and Mary, but also other individual women, the Mother of the Saviour being envisaged "not formally, but indirectly" in the general term *ishshah*.[2]

Complete agreement on the exact meaning of the Proto-evangelium will hardly be reached in the foreseeable future; for the text is by no means clear. It is full of implications accepted by some scholars as almost self-evident, rejected by others as fanciful. Most Catholic exegetes consider this to be an indication that the text is prophetic and messianic; so, for example, J. Haspecker[3] and Haspecker and Lohfink,[4] but there are some others who deny this. In any case, in the Old Testament the light of the final Christian revelation was perceived only through veils more or less opaque. As this applies to the figure of the Messiah himself, it is only to be expected that his mother should remain even more hidden.[5]

After this first glimpse of the Mother of Jesus we find her again in a prophecy of Isaiah. On the occasion of the threatened invasion of Juda by Syria and Israel and the overthrow of the Davidic dynasty (c. 735 B.C.) the prophet had been told by Yahweh to assure Ahaz, the King of Juda, of his divine assistance. The King, however, would not listen to the prophet, but pursued his own policy of alliances compromising the religion of Yahweh. Then Isaiah told him to ask God for a sign, and when he still refused the prophet informed Ahaz that God himself would give him a sign: "Behold, the virgin shall conceive and bear a son and she shall call his name Emmanuel." (7.14.) This verse, too, has given rise to much controversy. The discussion centres in the Hebrew word

[1] *ETL*, 26 (1950), pp. 5–36.   [2] Coppens, p. 30.
[3] *Bibel und Kirche*, 15 (1960), pp. 98–101.   [4] *SK*, 36 (1961), p. 358.
[5] Cf. Duncker, "Our Lady", p. 12.

'almah, which is not the strictly technical term of "virgin" but is roughly equivalent to our "young girl". In a much quoted article "'Alma",[1] the German theologian A. Schulz made an extensive study of the few other passages in which this rather rare word occurs, from which he argued that in each case the term must mean "virgin". New light has been thrown on the question by the discovery of a text in the Ras Shamra tablets (c. fourteenth century B.C.) in a Semitic dialect closely related to Hebrew. This is an Ugaritic poem about the goddess Nikkal which contains the line: "Behold, the young girl [galmatu, probably = Hebr. 'almah, so not strictly "virgin"] gives birth to a son."[2] Indeed, the idea was current, not only among the Canaanites but also among the Egyptians and other nations of the Middle East, that the extraordinary, even virginal birth of a child was to introduce a new era of happiness.[3] It is just possible that the prophet was acquainted with these ideas and transformed them for his own purpose. This, for example, is the view of R. Laurentin,[4] whereas Duncker[5] rejects it and Coppens[6] considers it very uncertain.

The prophecy itself, too, is difficult to explain. At first sight it seems to point either to the birth of Hezekiah, the son of Ahaz, thus guaranteeing the continuance of the Davidic dynasty, or to a child of the prophet himself.[7] Nevertheless, the whole tenor of the passage appears to indicate an extraordinary event, indeed, "a sign". So Coppens, after a careful analysis of other possibilities, concludes that the text is a prophecy of the Messiah and his mother in the strict, literal

---

[1] BZ, 23 (1935–6), pp. 229–41.
[2] G. R. Driver, Canaanite Myths (1925), p. 125.
[3] See J. Coppens, "La Prophétie de la 'Almah", in ETL (1952), pp. 668ff.
[4] Court Traité de théologie Mariale,[4] (1959), p. 141.
[5] "Our Lady", p. 17.
[6] "La Prophétie", p. 669.
[7] See A. Feuillet s.v. "Isaïe", in Pirot, Dictionnaire de la Bible, Supplément (1928–), 4, cols. 657f.

sense.[1] J. Steinmann, on the other hand,[2] considers that the literal sense is non-messianic and envisages Hezekiah, but that it nevertheless implies a more profound, messianic sense.[3] If the literal sense referred to Hezekiah (or a son of the prophet himself), 'almah would, of course, only mean "marriageable girl". Laurentin's view is similar to that of Steinmann. According to him the prophecy refers directly to the birth of Hezekiah, but it has also a second, eschatological and messianic sense, which was discovered by post-exilic Judaism. The Septuagint translated 'almah as parthenos, which Laurentin considers to mean "formally the virgin",[4] but which actually is as ambiguous as 'almah.[5] The whole prophecy gains a particular importance from the fact that it is quoted in St. Matthew (1.23) as foretelling the birth of Christ: "Now all this was done that it might be fulfilled which the Lord spoke by the prophet . . ." (1.22.)

The Isaiah prophecy is traditionally taken to have inspired also Micah 5.2f.: "And thou, Bethlehem-Ephrata, art a little one among the thousands of Juda; out of thee shall he come forth . . . that is to be the ruler in Israel . . . Therefore will he give them up even till the time wherein she who will bear shall bring forth." "She who will bear" is generally held to be the 'almah of Isaiah. This, however, is contested by Coppens[6] and others, who believe that Micah is referring to a corporate personality, the clan Ephrath of Bethlehem, from which the Messiah is to come. Duncker follows what would seem the majority of Catholic theologians in regarding the prophecy as an echo of Isa. 7.15.

The famous Jer. 31.22, femina circumdabit virum ("a woman shall encompass a man") is no longer accepted as a Marian text at all. St. Jerome was the first Father to give it

---

[1] "La Prophétie", p. 678. So also Duncker, "Our Lady", p. 27.
[2] Le Prophète Isaïe, 1950.   [3] Steinmann, pp. 88ff.   [4] Court Traité, p. 140.
[5] See A. Feuillet, "La Vierge Marie dans le Nouveau Testament", in Maria, 6, p. 25.
[6] "La Prophétie", p. 672.

this meaning, and his authority ensured this exegesis a large following. Today the passage is generally rejected as corrupt. The Septuagint has quite a different translation.[1]

There are many other Old-Testament texts, especially from the Wisdom books and the Canticle, which have been applied to Mary throughout the centuries, both in the Liturgy and by individual authors; but they refer to her only in an "accommodated sense", that is to say, they do not envisage her directly, as does the Isaiah passage. Both these and Old-Testament types of her such as the Ark of the Covenant, Judith, Esther etc., played an important part in the thought of the Fathers and later theologians, and will be mentioned in the relevant chapters.

THE ANNUNCIATION

The scene of the Annunciation, beloved by painters and familiar to us all, raises a host of problems which have exercised the ingenuity of biblical scholars, for all is by no means as clear as it appears at first sight. Above all, what is the source of the cycle of stories contained in the first two chapters of St. Luke, so different in style from the rest of his Gospel? It is now generally agreed that they originated in a Palestinian milieu and that their nucleus goes back to Mary herself, Luke being the final editor of the material. But, as the well-known French Mariologist R. Laurentin writes,[2] "Between these two limits one may seriously hold that there have been other pre-existing elements, a Hebrew version and the influence of Johannine circles on this version." We may, then, regard these chapters as a combination of Mary's own reminiscences with other early materials, worked over by St. Luke—naturally,

[1] So, among many others, *Maria* 1, pp. 24–6; Duncker, "Our Lady", pp. 28f. Nevertheless, W. Lauck, *Das Buch Jeremias* (1938), pp. 221ff., still retains the Marian exegesis. See C. Schedl, "Femina circumdabit virum", in *ZKT*, 83 (1961), pp. 431–42, for a critical discussion of the text.

[2] *Structure et théologie de Luc I–II*, Paris (1957), p. 20.

under the inspiration of the Holy Spirit. What picture emerges from this first appearance of the '*Almah* of Isaiah 7?

Again, as in our discussion of the Genesis passage, we have to discard a mistranslation. "Ave Maria"—"Hail Mary"—so millions of Catholics throughout the world recite the greeting of the angel every day. And yet the original Greek text has probably a different meaning.[1] The word the angel uses is *chaire*—the common Greek form of greeting, certainly. But if the Hebrew source used by Luke had had the ordinary Jewish form of greeting, *shalom*, "peace", he would very likely have translated it by the corresponding Greek word *eirene*. Instead he used *chaire*—and, we are told further, Mary was troubled "and thought by herself what manner of salutation this should be". Traditionally, Catholic theologians, following St. Ambrose, have attributed Mary's fear at the angel's greeting either to her virginity or to her humility, though it is not very obvious why either should have been endangered by it. Now Lyonnet, and, following him, Laurentin and most other modern scholars, give a different interpretation of the passage. On the lips of the angel *chaire* is not merely a simple greeting—indeed, it would seem absurd if he introduced his tremendous mission of announcing the birth of the divine Saviour of the world with words corresponding to our "Good morning" or "How do you do?" In the narrative of the Annunciation *chaire* retains the full force of its original meaning "Rejoice"—and this is how it is used in the great messianic prophecies of the Old Testament, especially Zeph. 3.14f.: "Rejoice with all thy heart, O daughter of Jerusalem . . . The king of Israel the Lord is in the midst of thee"; Joel 2.21: "Fear not, O land, be glad and rejoice: for the Lord hath done great things"; and Zech. 9.9: "Rejoice greatly, O daughter of Sion, shout for joy, O daughter of

[1] The following interpretation is based on the article of S. Lyonnet, S.J., "Chaire kecharitomene", in *BA*, 20 (1939), pp. 131–41.

Jerusalem: Behold thy King will come to thee, the Just One
and the Saviour."

The next word the angel uses, *kecharitomene*, is traditionally
translated as *gratia plena*, full of grace. But this, again, is not
quite correct. *Charitoo* means to favour, as in Ephes. 1.6,
". . . his grace, with which he has favoured us", the perfect
adding permanence, so that *kecharitomene* should be translated
"highly favoured [or, privileged] one". In his article
"L'Annonce à Marie",[1] J. P. Audet sees in the term the "new
name" Mary is given by the angel. The Dominican exegete
explains the scene as belonging to the *genre littéraire* of the
"message", pointing out striking analogies with the call of
Gideon. (Judges 6.12–24.) Like Mary, Gideon receives a
greeting and a "new name", "most valiant of men", like her,
he wonders about the salutation, is told about God's plan,
asks how he is to carry it out and is given a sign. If *kecharitomene* meant "full of grace" this would be something static,
whereas the term "by its very force of being a 'new name' . . .
creates, on the contrary . . . the whole occasion of the
narrative, both on the part of God, who has the initiative, and
on the part of Mary who accepts it".[2] This exegesis explains
also why Mary was "troubled" at the greeting. As Audet
suggests, the "message" normally answers to the preoccupations of the recipient, as in the case of Gideon. Mary obviously
belonged to the circle of the "just", like Zachariah, Elizabeth
and Simeon, who were expecting the Messiah, and so she was
"troubled" precisely because the words that were spoken to
her had an unmistakably messianic ring.[3] The angel therefore
quietens her by giving a more detailed explanation.

Then Mary puts the strange question, "How shall this be
done, because I know not man?" According to an ancient
tradition Mary asked this because she had made a vow of
virginity—a view still held by some Catholic scholars, notably

[1] *RB*, 63 (1956), pp. 346–74.
[2] "L'Annonce", p. 359.   [3] "L'Annonce", p. 362.

Laurentin. Nevertheless, this opinion has recently lost much ground. Mariologists such as O. Semmelroth, S.J., in Germany, and exegetes like P. Bénoit, O.P. and J. Coppens, in their important contributions to such authoritative publications as the *Revue biblique* and the Louvain *Ephemerides Theologicae*, have abandoned it. Mary's question is now interpreted either as a mere literary device to enliven the narrative or as referring to the immediate present: "How am I now to have a child, since I know not man?" Contemporary scholars give several reasons for this rejection of the old tradition. First of all, the story of the vow of virginity derives from the "Gospel of James", the so-called Protoevangelium, an apocryphal work without scriptural authority which will be discussed in the next chapter. Further, and this is the main reason for giving up the traditional interpretation, it is unthinkable that a Jewish girl in the time of Mary, when an unmarried life was considered a disgrace, should have made such a vow. The defenders of the older view reply to this that celibacy was by no means unknown in such contemporary Jewish sects as the Essenes; however, these were all men; and even though some kind of communities of women seem to have existed in the era immediately preceding Christ, it is highly improbable that a young girl not belonging to any community and who was, moreover, betrothed to a man, should have made such a vow. The question is still under discussion; but a widely accepted view today is that Mary only vowed never to belong to any man when she heard the words of the angel.

The angel then explains how the child is going to be born without a human father: "The Holy Ghost shall come upon thee and the power of the Most High shall overshadow thee." At first sight these seem strange terms to use for the conception of a child. But, as has been shown before, in these first chapters of Luke Mary does not appear simply as an individual. It should never be forgotten that the early Christian tradition was steeped in the language and imagery of the Old

Testament, and the surest way to draw out the implications of less obvious allusions of the New-Testament authors is to look for parallels in the books of the Old. Now at the end of the Book of Exodus (40: 32ff.) we read that the cloud, the symbol of Yahweh, covered with its shadow the tabernacle, "and the glory of the Lord filled the tabernacle". Thus, in the words of the angel, Mary is the tabernacle which is to be filled with the glory of God, "and therefore also the Holy which shall be born of thee shall be called the Son of God".

Then Mary gives her formal assent to the will of God manifested to her: "Behold the handmaid of the Lord: be it done to me according to thy word." No more is said, for immediately "the angel departed from her". Scripture does not lift the veil any further from the mystery of the divine conception. The 'almah has conceived, the glory of the Lord, the Shekinah, has entered—now no more a wooden but a living tabernacle; the prophecies have begun to be fulfilled.

VISITATION AND *MAGNIFICAT*

The very next event the Evangelist records is that "Mary rising up in those days, went into the hill country with haste" to visit her cousin Elizabeth, who said to her: "Whence is this to me that the mother of my Lord should come to me? . . . And Mary abode with her about three months." Compare with this the story of David taking the Ark of the Covenant to Jerusalem: "And David was afraid of the Lord that day, saying: How shall the ark of the Lord come to me? . . . And the ark of the Lord abode in the house of Obededom the Gethite three months." The similarities between these two accounts are too obvious not to be intentional: evidently the author of the narrative meant to present Mary as both the true daughter of Sion and the living Ark of the Covenant, the perfect realization of the Old-Testament types.

The *Magnificat* confirms this view. Not all Catholic

scholars admit that this celebrated hymn was composed by Mary herself. Some share the opinion of the Protestant theologians, F. Gunkel and Winter, that it is based on a Maccabaean psalm. According to contemporary literary criticism it is a later insertion into the Hebrew original worked over by Luke (so P. Gächter, *Maria im Erdenleben*, 3 (1955), pp. 44f.). P. Bénoit thinks it very probable that it originated in the circles of the "poor" and had been adapted by the first Christian community in Jerusalem before being utilized by St. Luke,[1] the main reason for this view being that there is no clear allusion to the birth of the Messiah. Gächter, on the other hand, believes it to belong to the literary species of hymns of thanksgiving after the birth of the first-born.[2] Most exegetes, following the traditional attribution of the hymn to Mary herself, think that she composed it much later in life, not on the occasion of her visit to Elizabeth. Feuillet subscribes to the traditional view: "Mary here incarnates what is best in Israel, with its eschatological hopes."[3]

Whatever the actual authorship of the hymn, the very fact that the inspired author put it in the mouth of Mary shows that it must be an authentic expression of her personality as well as her vocation. According to Laurentin,[4] the *Magnificat* deals with the question that must have profoundly disturbed the first Christians: Why did the coming of the Messiah remain such an obscure, hidden event? The answer is, because God loves the humble and poor; therefore the greatest exaltation takes place in the greatest lowliness. So the song of Mary is the song of the Daughter of Sion. It begins with her own role in God's plan, the lowly handmaid of the Lord, who yet, far more than Judith, her prototype (cf. Judith 13.31), will be called blessed by all generations. From there it goes on to praise the divine providence which scatters the proud and

---

[1] In his review of R. Laurentin's *Structure et théologie de Luc I–II*, *RB*, 65 (1958), p. 429.
[2] *Maria im Erdenleben*, pp. 134f.   [3] *Maria*, 6, p. 38.   [4] *Structure*, p. 83.

exalts the humble, to end with the Patriarchs, Jacob and finally Abraham, the recipients of the divine promises, which are now fulfilled in herself. Lowliness and glory, obedience and exaltation, these are the paradoxes of the divine election which made of the humble virgin of Nazareth the Mother of the Son of the Most High.

MARY, JOSEPH AND THE VIRGIN BIRTH

The first chapter of Luke tells the events before the birth of Christ from the point of view of Mary. For the reactions of Joseph, to whom she was betrothed, we have to turn to St. Matthew. She had told him nothing of her condition, no doubt trusting to God to reveal it to him in his own time. According to Jewish law an engaged couple were already regarded as husband and wife and a child conceived at that time was considered legitimate, though the marriage was not complete until the husband had taken his bride into his own home. This explains Joseph's attitude described in the first chapter of St. Matthew: "Joseph her husband, being a just man and not willing publicly to expose her, was minded to put her away privately."

Nevertheless, he would have had the right to expose her as an adulteress, and as a "just man" would even have had the duty to do so, or it would have meant that he connived at her sin. That he decided against this and only intended to give her back her freedom proves his high opinion of Mary, whose condition was inexplicable to him. The dream-vision reassures him: "Joseph, son of David, fear not to take unto thee Mary thy wife, for that which is conceived in her, is of the Holy Ghost." That the angel calls Joseph "Son of David" once more sounds the messianic theme, for the Messiah was to come from the house of David. And again there is the "Fear not" which the angel had also bidden Mary, taking away the distress of her betrothed as he had taken away her own. Then the Evangelist points out that thus the prophecy of Isaiah 7 has been fulfilled and the sign promised to Ahaz has been given: "Behold, the virgin shall conceive."

Thus Joseph takes Mary into his home: "And he knew her not till she brought forth her firstborn son." (Matt. 1.25.) This verse, taken in conjunction with the later mention of the "brethren" of Jesus (e.g., Matt. 12.46: Mark 6.3: John 7.3 etc.), has often been thought to imply that after the birth of Jesus Joseph did "know" Mary. This had been the opinion of Tertullian and probably also of other early writers. But when it was asserted by the fourth-century Latin theologian Helvidius, St. Jerome wrote against him his treatise "On the Perpetual Virginity of Blessed Mary", which will be discussed later. After Helvidius, however, it has been the constant teaching of both the Western and the Eastern Church that Mary always remained a virgin. Modern Catholic theologians point out that the Hebraism "till etc." does not imply that later Joseph did know Mary; it only emphasizes that he did not consummate his marriage with her before the birth of Jesus, without implying at all that afterwards it was consummated; and they refer to similar passages such as Gen. 8.7: 28.15 and elsewhere. As to the expression "firstborn", which is un-authentic here but occurs in Luke 2.7, this was a term generally given to the eldest son regardless of whether there were younger children or not. There remains, however, the question of the "brethren of the Lord". The Protoevangelium of James (8.3: 9.2 etc.) regards them as sons of Joseph from a first marriage, and this is still the opinion of the Eastern Church. In the West, however, they are considered to be relatives, most probably cousins, of Jesus, since the Hebrew has no simple term for this relationship. There are also papyrus texts which confirm this usage.[1] Today it is widely held that Joseph having died early—as there is no further

[1] Cf. *The Adler Papyri, The Greek Texts*, ed. E. N. Adler, J. G. Tait and F. M. Heichelheim (1939).

2+

mention of him in the New Testament—Mary would have joined her nearest relatives, whose children grew up with Jesus and were popularly called his brothers and sisters.

Mary's continued virginity after the birth of Jesus is traditionally believed to include also her virginity *in partu*, that is, in the very act of giving birth, when Jesus was thought to have passed through her closed womb without breaking the hymen. This doctrine, which an increasing number of theologians no longer hold to be "of faith", has been carefully investigated by A. Mitterer, in *Dogma und Biologie* (1952), because, according to present-day biological knowledge, such teaching would detract from her true motherhood while adding nothing to her virginity. Mitterer's views were considered worthy of serious discussion by, among others, K. Rahner[1] and the well-known German Mariologist O. Semmelroth, who calls them "truly an acceptable clarification. Since St. Thomas places the physical element of virginity too strongly in the integrity of the hymen, he could in fact retain Mary's virginity only at the cost of her true motherhood."[2] Mitterer's thought is reproduced by D. Ryan in *Mother of the Redeemer* in his article "Perpetual Virginity" under the heading "A New Approach".[3] The crux of the matter is that in antiquity and the Middle Ages the mother was considered almost entirely passive in the production of the child, which was believed to be formed out of her blood, the existence of the female ovum being unknown. The development of the fertilized ovum in the womb, whether this be fertilized by a man or, as in Mary's case, miraculously through parthenogenesis, necessitates certain lesions and changes in the female body without which motherhood is impossible, and which are far more important for true motherhood than the integrity of the hymen is for virginity.[4]

---

[1] *ZKT*, 75 (1953).   [2] *SK*, 20 (1953), p. 310.   [3] pp. 123–33.
[4] Mitterer, p. 112.

St. Thomas, like other earlier theologians, denied all pains and inner lesions because he mistakenly thought (following Aristotle) that motherhood only implied providing blood from the uterus and nothing else. Indeed, it would be difficult to see how St. Joseph would have known that his betrothed was with child if he had not observed the normal signs of pregnancy in her. Surely if the other, much surer signs of virginity are missing, Mitterer argues, it is hardly logical to insist on such an in any case uncertain thing as the integrity of the hymen? And Ryan pertinently remarks: "The theologians who state that our Lady's body after the birth was the same as if she had never born a child (e.g., B. H. Merkelbach) may be overlooking the fact that lactation involves bodily changes that are not normally found in a virgin".[1] Mitterer considers the perforation of the hymen through the act of birth as little a violation of virginity as circumcision, which no-one has ever regarded as prejudicing the virginity of Christ.[2] According to him, virginity is violated only by intercourse and all that pertains to it, but not by the destruction of the hymen as such. It should be remembered that Scripture itself nowhere suggests the virginity *in partu* in the traditional sense. On the contrary, on the occasion of the Purification Luke states: "As it is written in the law of the Lord: every male opening the womb shall be called holy to the Lord." (2.23.) Ryan comments that these words "are usually stated not to refer to the manner of the birth, as the phrase 'opening the womb' really only means first-born. In resorting to this explanation, the theologians give one the impression of doing what they sometimes accuse Scripture scholars of doing, viz. stating that the words of Scripture do not really mean what they say."[3] J. Galot, in his article "La Virginité de Marie et la naissance de Jésus",[4] is of the same opinion. Luke, he says, "who is at such pains to inform us about the virginal

---

[1] "Perpetual Virginity", n. 74.   [2] *Dogma und Biologie*, p. 109.
[3] "Perpetual Virginity", pp. 125f.   [4] *NRT*, 82 (1960), pp. 449–69.

conception and the miraculous operation of the Holy Spirit
. . . would have avoided this expression if he had had the idea
or had received the information that Jesus had not opened
Mary's womb at his birth."[1] Nor does he consider that the
expressions of the First Lateran Council and of Paul IV in
1555[2] that Jesus was born "without corruption", "in the
integrity of virginity" imply that the birth was a prodigy.
Galot asks, too, whether a miraculous birth would still be a
true birth,[3] and holds that this opinion would involve the risk
of a certain Docetism. On the contrary, the sign of Mary's
virginal motherhood is precisely that Jesus opened the womb
which is closed to all but God himself.[4]

This new approach to the subject has not yet been generally
accepted. Laurentin considers that "the traditional data do
not allow us to agree either with the general conception of
virginity [scil., as the absence of sexual intercourse and all
that pertains to it] as proposed by Mitterer according to
criteria too exclusively biological, or with his interpretation of
the virginity *in partu*,"[5] and in his article "Le Mystère de la
naissance virginale",[6] he says that Christ, "to redeem corporeal
man and to give back its inviolate perfection to all flesh, has
taken flesh without doing the least injury to the virginal body
of his Mother". How he could have done this except by passing
through her body as through a channel—an opinion repeatedly
condemned by the Church as heretical—is difficult to see in
view of the findings of modern biology. Perhaps the reluctance
of certain theologians to accept the view of Mitterer may be
due to an unconscious dualism or to Old-Testament influence
which sees in the female body and its natural functions
something "unclean".[7]

---

[1] "La Virginité de Marie", p. 453.   [2] Denzinger, 256 and 994.
[3] "La Virginité", p. 465.   [4] "La Virginité", pp. 466f.
[5] *Traité*, p. 112, n. 27.   [6] *EM*, 10 (1960).
[7] Cf. also M. L. Guérard des Lauriers, "Mariologie et Économie", in *RT*
(1962), pp. 205; J. A. de Aldama, "Natus ex Maria", in *Gregorianum*, 42 (1961),
pp. 37–62; G. Jouassard, "Deux chefs de file", *Gregorianum*, 42 (1961), pp. 5–36.

To return to the scriptural narrative. Even the joy of the birth story is not without the theme of rejection and hardship, which will sound like a refrain in our considerations of Mary's earthly life. She was not allowed to prepare for the birth of her child in the peace of her home at Nazareth; she had to go with Joseph "to the city of David, which is called Bethlehem: because he was of the house and family of David" (Luke 2.4), thus fulfilling the prophecy of Micah (5.2) quoted by St. Matthew (2.6). For, again, Mary is not merely an individual young girl. She is the representative of Israel, the true Daughter of Sion, though the fullness of her vocation is not immediately apparent to her. This emerges from the conclusion of Luke's account of the visit of the shepherds to the newborn Child: "And all that heard wondered . . . But Mary kept all these things, pondering them in her heart." (2.18f.) She needed time to assimilate the tremendous supernatural experience that had come to her.

The mystery of it deepened when, after the days of her purification according to the Law of Moses, she and Joseph went up to the Temple of Jerusalem to offer sacrifice and Simeon said to her, "Thy own soul a sword shall pierce." What was this sword that was to pierce her soul? It certainly portended intense suffering and is now generally understood of the poignant grief of the Mother under the Cross; but, as will be seen in the next chapter, it has not always been interpreted in this way. Indeed, it has sometimes been held that Luke himself could not very well have meant it thus, since he does not record Mary's presence at Calvary. Recent research, however, has discovered "signs of a deeper relationship than normally supposed" between the first two chapters of Luke and the Gospel of St. John,[1] and so it may also refer directly to Mary's presence under the Cross as recorded in St. John.

[1] So F. M. Braun, "La Mère de Jésus dans l'œuvre de saint Jean", in *RT*, 58 (1950), pp. 429–79; see also Feuillet, *Maria*, 6, p. 45 and Laurentin *Structure*, p. 20.

Mary's sufferings began with the flight into Egypt, after Herod had ordered the murder of the infants born at Bethlehem, and Matthew once more points to prophetic utterances: "Out of Egypt have I called my son" (Hos. 11.1) and "Rachel bewailing her children". (Jer. 31.15.) But so far it has never been her Son himself who has caused her suffering. The cycle of the stories contained in the first two chapters of Luke concludes with the strange narrative of the twelve-year-old Jesus in the Temple. Mary and Joseph had taken Jesus to Jerusalem. Without telling them he remained behind, conversing with the doctors, while his parents were anxiously seeking him. This behaviour seemed incomprehensible on the part of a loving son, and Mary certainly regarded it as such when she gently reproached him: "Son, why hast thou done so to us? Behold thy father and I have sought thee sorrowing. And he said to them: How is it that you sought me? Did you not know that I must be about my father's business [or: 'in my father's house']? And they understood not the word that he spoke unto them." (Luke 2.48–50.) Instead of apologizing for causing them anxiety, Jesus on the contrary reproaches both Mary and Joseph for their incomprehension; and the Evangelist says explicitly, "And they understood not the word that he spoke unto them." True, Mary knew that her child was the Messiah, that he was not like other children. Nevertheless, so far he had given no signs of his essential difference; she treated him as she would have treated any other son, and he obeyed her as a good son obeys his mother. His behaviour in the Temple was the first and unexpected indication of his messianic authority, of his divine nature by which he was the son of his Father in a far more transcendent sense than the son of his mother. "And they understood not the word that he spoke unto them"—because even Mary, despite her sinlessness and spiritual perfection, was subject to the limitations of the human intellect. "And he went down with them and came to Nazareth and was subject to them.

And his mother kept all these words in her heart." (Luke 2.51.)

This event had only been a sudden flash, lighting up the mystery of Jesus for an instant. When it was over, the life of the Holy Family resumed its normal course; Jesus was "subject to them" as before, while Mary continued to ponder the significance of the mysterious behaviour of her Son.

CANA

Mary appears next in a light not altogether dissimilar to that in which she has just been shown. The scene at the wedding of Cana, reported by St. John in Chapter 2 of his Gospel, has exercised the acumen of exegetes and Mariologists to a quite extraordinary degree[1] and the most varied explanations have been offered for almost every word of the story. The view still most generally held by Catholic scholars is that seeing the supply of wine had run out, Mary asked Jesus for a miracle. But they disagree widely on the meaning of his reply. The Greek words are: "*Gynai, ti emoi kai soi?*" followed by the no less mysterious statement: "My hour is not yet come." The most obvious meaning of the first sentence supported by general Greek usage is: "Woman, what have I to do with you?"—expressing a very definite, even harsh denial of any community between him and her. For this reason many Catholic exegetes have tried to give the sentence different meaning; the Douai version, following the Vulgate, translates, "Woman, what is that to me and to thee?" while Mgr. Knox paraphrases: "Nay, woman, why dost thou trouble me with that?" M. J. Lagrange, in his commentary on St. John, holds that the Greek is a literal translation of a Hebrew expression meaning "Do not worry about it",

[1] The volume of literature on the question even in the last twenty years is immense; see A. Feuillet, "L'Heure de Jésus et le signe de Cana", in *ETL*, 36 (1960), p. 5, *n.* 1.

implying that neither he nor she is concerned with the matter—though this interpretation is not without serious difficulties. First of all, the formal address "Woman" rather than "Mother" in itself expresses a deliberate withdrawal; secondly, despite the obvious refusal, Mary must not only have counted on a miracle but must even have known that it would involve the assistance of the servants, since she turned to them with the words generally translated as "Whatsoever he shall say to you, do ye."

The interpretation, however, which sees in the words of Jesus a deliberate rebuke to Mary has a respectable tradition, ranging from the early Fathers over St. Thomas Aquinas to John Henry Newman, and is admitted by most contemporary Mariologists and exegetes, such as Laurentin, F. M. Braun,[1] H. van den Bussche[2] and A. Feuillet.[3] According to this exegesis Mary had not yet understood that during her Son's public ministry the mother-son relation was, as it were, suspended; that throughout this period he belonged wholly to the work committed to him by his Father and that she had no rights over him, because his "hour"—in St. John always the hour of his passion and glorification—had not yet come. In that hour all, including her relationship to him, would be changed, but the time was not yet. For, as Feuillet[4] points out, "If we do not want to go astray, we must start with the fact that the scene is *before all Christological*."[5] For by this miracle Jesus wants to "manifest his glory" and encourage his disciples to believe in him. According to Feuillet the abruptness of his answer to his Mother ought not to be played down, because it signifies his transcendence. While Mary thinks only of the temporary embarrassment of their hosts, Jesus has in mind the messianic wine to be administered by the Church

[1] *La Mère des Fidèles*,[2] pp. 55–8.   [2] *L'Évangile de Jean* (1958), p. 79, *n.* 2.
[3] "L'Heure", p. 6.   [4] p. 15.
[5] His italics. So also R. Schnackenburg, *Das erste Wunder Jesu, Jo. 2: 1–11* (1951), pp. 25–30.

after his "hour" will have come. Despite the seeming rejection, however, Mary does not feel that her request has been refused, but trusts in her Son even though she does not quite understand his words. And so Jesus does the miracle, which now becomes a "sign" of far deeper meaning than Mary could have envisaged; nevertheless, "it has been granted by the intervention of Mary, who thus finds herself representing the Church and is intimately associated by her Son with the New Covenant between God and men which He is about to inaugurate".[1] The strange words "My hour has not yet come" imply that Mary, too, has her hour: "*The hour of the Woman will have come* (cf. Jo. 16.21) *when that of Jesus has come.*"[2] Having drawn attention to the fact that, despite the very concise narrative, Mary is mentioned in it no less than three times, Feuillet regards this as inexplicable unless a doctrinal intention was involved. He continues: "When it is a question of the mission of the incarnate Son of God, Jesus gives to understand that he depends on none save his Father, for he is the unique Saviour and Redeemer. This is the necessary limit Scripture imposes on Mariology [evidently an implied criticism of an indiscreet interpretation of Mary's part in the Redemption by certain Mariologists]. On the other hand, once the Passion has been accomplished, *comes the Hour of Mary properly so called, which is also the Hour of the Church and the Sacraments.*"[3] This is also the line taken by P. Gächter in an article in *Zeitschrift für katholische Theologie*,[4] "Maria in Kana", later elaborated in his book *Maria im Erdenleben* (1953). In his view Mary had not asked for a miracle at all. Indeed, since Jesus had not yet done any miracles, and in accordance with her own retiring nature, it would seem strange that she should have requested a display of his miraculous powers—and for such a none-too-important purpose as relieving their hosts' embarrassment. In Gächter's

[1] "L'Heure", p. 19.   [2] His italics; "L'Heure", p. 20.
[3] "L'Heure", p. 20; author's italics. [4] 55 (1931), pp. 351-402.

view, her remark, "They have no wine", did not imply the request for a miracle, but for help by natural means—for example, through Nathanael, himself a native of Cana who had just become one of her Son's disciples. This would tally with her words to the servants, "Whatever he shall say to you, do"—or an equally possible, and in this case better, translation: "In case he should say something to you, do it." For if Jesus had been going to provide wine by natural means, he would certainly have needed servants to carry it, whereas this would have been unnecessary in the case of a miracle. The address "Woman" instead of "Mother" signifies the distance between them, and this distance is emphasized precisely by the miracle, which she never expected. On the other hand, the words "My hour has not yet come" imply a promise, and are interpreted in the same way as later by Feuillet. This would seem a more probable explanation than, for example, that of M.-E. Boismard,[1] who takes the "My hour has not yet come" to be a question: "Has my hour not yet come?"—that is to say, "You ought to understand that my hour has come", and not to be disquieted about the lack of wine.

If we follow Gächter's and Feuillet's interpretation much will fall into place. At the beginning of her Son's public ministry Mary did not yet perfectly understand him, while he dropped the natural mother–son relationship which had until then united them. The distance between them, only briefly hinted when, many years ago, he had stayed behind in the Temple, had now become an established fact. As Gächter points out, Cana was an important landmark in Mary's spiritual development; while he was carrying out his public ministry, she had to stand aside and increase in detachment, a conception which is borne out by two incidents recorded in the other Gospels.

When Jesus had chosen his disciples and began to cause a

[1] *Du Baptême à Cana*, Paris (1956).

great stir by his miracles and his teaching, "when his friends had heard of it, they went out to lay hold of him. For they said: he is beside himself . . . And his mother and his brethren came and, standing without, sent unto him, calling him . . . And they say to him: Behold thy mother and thy brethren without seek for thee. And answering them he said: Who is my mother and my brethren? And looking round about on them who sat about him, he saith: Behold my mother and my brethren. For whosoever shall do the will of God, he is my brother and my sister and mother." (Mark 3.21–35.) Obviously Mary, too, had been distressed by what she had heard of the activities of her Son, else she would not have tried to speak to him, perhaps even to take him back home with her. She had not yet understood that even the closest family ties could not be allowed to interfere with his messianic work; hence his severe refusal to see them and his announcement of a new kind of relationship: "Whosoever shall do the will of God, he is my brother and my sister and mother."

It was a lesson which even Mary had to learn—and did learn, and which Christ reiterated on another occasion, when "a certain woman from the crowd, lifting up her voice, said to him: Blessed is the womb that bore thee and the paps that gave thee suck. But he said: Yea rather, blessed are they who hear the word of God and keep it." (Luke 11.27f.) As Semmelroth rightly says: "Even though the texts under consideration cannot simply mean that Christ rejects Marian devotion, a certain correction can nevertheless be detected. But what is it that is here being corrected? . . . The honour shown to Mary as an individual, as the Mother of Christ only in her historical humanity . . . The corrective word of Christ enlarges the view: Mary is venerable above all because and in so far as she represents the community of those who 'hear the word of God and keep it'."[1] In Christ's messianic work

[1] SK, 29 (1954). "Die unbefleckte Empfängnis als heilsökonomisches Zeichen", p. 162.

physical relationships had no place; all that mattered was doing the will of the Father, hearing the word of God and keeping it. If Mary was to be praised, it was precisely for this, as Luke had recorded before: "And his mother kept all these words in her heart."

No more is said of Mary during the public ministry of her Son, in which she took no active part. But she appears again at the most crucial moment of all, on Golgotha.

MARY UNDER THE CROSS

Only John mentions this meeting of Mother and Son under the Cross and, as at Cana, the narrative, though quite brief, has given rise to very different interpretations. "When Jesus therefore had seen his mother and the disciple standing whom he loved, he saith to his mother: Woman, behold thy son. After that, he saith to the disciple: Behold thy mother. And from that hour, the disciple took her to his own." (John 19.26f.) These words of Jesus have often been taken to refer only to the material provision Jesus made for his Mother; among the Fathers only Origen interpreted them differently. In modern times, however, they have been scrutinized more closely and been given a far wider interpretation, for example by F. M. Braun.[1] Gächter[2] argues that all Christ's words from the Cross have a profoundly messianic content, and that the words to his Mother cannot be an exception. Moreover, it might well be asked why he left this filial duty to the last moment, and why he entrusted her to his disciple rather than to his family. The words themselves are no less strange. All the words from the Cross are extremely brief; if he wanted to do no more than make provision for Mary it would have been enough to address only John. Instead of which he addresses her first, again with the formal term "Woman", and, as

[1] "La Mère de Jésus dans l'œuvre de saint Jean", RT, 58 (1950), pp. 429–79. See also Gächter and Feuillet.
[2] "Die geistige Mutterschaft Mariens", in ZKT, 47 (1923), pp. 391–492.

Gächter rightly suggests, placing a duty on her rather than consoling her, by asking her to act as a mother towards John. Only then does he say to John: "Behold thy mother." Thus, in the words of Gächter, "He revealed a relationship which had its starting-point in her and in which she had the principal obligation . . . a messianic motherhood of Mary towards John", and not only towards John, but towards all the faithful, "since the word of Jesus was not a private personal act but his bequest as Messiah and Saviour of the world."[1] And, in the words of Braun, "At the moment when Jesus consummated his sacrifice Mary's motherhood had acquired a new dimension."[2] Precisely by calling her "Woman", Jesus asked her to expand her physical motherhood of himself and to extend it to all his followers.

Both Braun and Gächter, however, give the words an even deeper meaning. According to their exegesis the words from the Cross are all a fulfilment of the prophecies of the Old Covenant, and the verses just discussed are immediately followed by the explicit statement: "Afterwards, Jesus knowing that all things were now accomplished, that the Scripture might be fulfilled, said: I thirst." Referring it back to the preceding verses, theologians have searched for a prophecy that has been fulfilled by the words of Jesus to Mary and have found it in Gen. 3.15. They consider the appellation "Woman" a deliberate reference to this passage. At the hour of the Passion Satan (cf. John 13.27) has been vanquished, and the "Woman" whom Jesus addresses "truly signifies the figure of the Second Eve that shines forth in the Protoevangelium, from whom salvation was to come".[3] This opinion is shared, among others, by Braun.[4] It has not, however, remained uncontradicted: and J. Michl[5] has attempted to prove that

---

[1] "Geistige Mutterschaft", pp. 409–11.　　　[2] "La Mère de Jésus", p. 475.
[3] Gächter, "Geistige Mutterschaft", p. 423.
[4] "La Mère de Jésus", p. 475.
[5] "Der Weibessame (Gen. 3.15) in spätjüdischer und frühchristlicher Auffassung", BA, 33 (1952), pp. 371–401, 476–505.

the term *gynai*, "Woman", was so widely used as a polite form of address that nothing can be deduced from its use in the present passage. M. E. Boismard, too, in his review of the books by Braun (*Mère des Fidèles*) and Gächter (*Maria im Erdenleben*) denies that the words from the Cross contain an allusion to the Genesis passage.

A. Kerrigan,[1] on the other hand, links the passage not so much with Gen. 3.15 but with the passages of Isaiah on Sion, seen as the mother of many children. (Isa. 49. 14–26: 52.1–2: 54.1ff: 61.1ff: 62.1ff.) "When . . . to fulfil the Scriptures Jesus made John Mary's son and Mary John's mother," writes Kerrigan, "it is most probable that Isa. 54.13 ('All thy children shall be taught by the Lord, and great shall be the peace of thy children') and other texts of this book about *Sion* and her children were uppermost in his mind."[2] He considers the words of Jesus to Mary and John as a formal expression of her spiritual motherhood of all Christians and even goes so far as to say "that Mary begins to exercise her spiritual motherhood at the same time that the Spirit starts his activities as a *begetter*. This coincidence, together with the fact that the Spirit and Mary ultimately accomplish the same achievements, suggests that their operations are . . . concurrent. Indeed, the Johannine texts on the whole seem to warrant our saying that by her sorrow under the Cross Mary assists the Spirit in his capacity as *begetter*, helping him in some way to transmit the gift of supernatural life to the followers of her Son."[3] Despite these varieties of exegesis it is generally agreed that the words just discussed have a wider meaning than the mere personal provision for Mary, that they should be understood in the general context of the Redemption that was accomplished on the Cross, in which Mary is given a

[1] "John 19, 25–27 in the Light of Johannine Theology and the Old Testament", in *Antonianum*, 35 (1960), pp. 369–416.

[2] "John 19, 25–27 etc.", p. 414. So also Feuillet, *Maria*, 6, p. 58.

[3] "John, 19, 25–27 etc.", p. 384; his italics.

special place. This would seem to be borne out also by the comment of the Evangelist: "The disciple took her to his own"—*eis ta idia*, an expression of wide connotation, meaning not only one's own home and property, but also all one's concerns and interests so that, as Braun points out, Mary shares henceforth both the Apostle's home and all his spiritual goods.

The Gospels are silent on Mary's share in the Resurrection appearances. But we find her again at the most important moment in the life of the nascent Church: when the Apostles are waiting for the outpouring of the Spirit at Pentecost: "They went up into an upper room, where abode Peter and John, James and Andrew . . . All these were persevering with one mind in prayer, with the women and Mary the mother of Jesus." (Acts 1.13f.) It is a very modest mention; nevertheless, it shows her in the office she was henceforth to fulfil: praying with and for the Church her Son had founded.

APOCALYPSE 12

This reference in Acts is the last explicit mention of Mary in the New Testament. There is, however, a mysterious figure in the apocalyptic visions of St. John which has often been identified with her, especially in modern times. "And a great sign appeared in heaven: A woman clothed with the sun, and the moon under her feet, and on her head a crown of twelve stars. And being with child, she cried travailing in birth: and was in pain to be delivered." But a great red dragon was lying in wait for her, "that, when she should be delivered, he might devour her son. And she brought forth a man child, who was to rule all nations with an iron rod. And her son was taken up to God and to his throne. And the woman fled into the wilderness, where she had a place prepared by God." Then there is a battle in heaven, and "that great dragon was cast out, that old serpent, who is called the devil and Satan". "And when the dragon saw that he was cast unto the earth he persecuted the woman who brought forth the man child. And there were given to the woman two wings of a great eagle, that she might fly into the desert, unto her place, where she is nourished . . . And the dragon was angry against the woman: and went to make war with the rest of her seed, who keep the commandments of God." (Apoc. 12.1–17.)

The early patristic tradition unanimously regards this woman as a symbol of the Church, whether of the New Testament or of the Old and New Testaments combined. The Marian interpretation appears first in the fifth century, in a dubious Epiphanius passage in the East, in St. Augustine's disciple Quodvultdeus in the West. The Old Testament habitually presents Israel as a woman, even as a woman in labour, as in Isa. 26.17: "As a woman with child, when she draweth near the time of her delivery, is in pain and crieth out in her pangs: so are we become in thy presence, O Lord", and similarly in Isa. 66.7f., as A. Feuillet points out in his article, "Le Messie et sa mère d'après le chapitre XII de l'Apocalypse".[1] St. Paul follows this usage in his Letter to the Galatians (4.26f.), and Hermas, the second-century author of *The Shepherd*, also presents the Church under the image of a woman. There is, therefore, nothing strange in this, nor need we go to the cult of Isis and Cybele to account for the star-imagery of her apparel, as some non-Catholic scholars have done; for the same symbolism appears in Joseph's dream (Gen. 37.9), representing the twelve tribes of Israel.

Should it therefore be said that Apocalypse 12 has nothing at all to do with Mary? Most contemporary exegetes would not go so far. The most widely held opinion is that the mysterious image may well have a twofold meaning. In the first place, the woman clothed with the sun is indeed the Church—but this does not exclude Mary, who herself represents the Church in an eminent manner. Like many other theologians such as

[1] *RB*, 66 (1959), 55–86.

Scheeben and Lortzing, L. Cerfaux[1] considers that the vision is based on Gen. 3.15. The actors in the two scenes are the same: the woman, the dragon or serpent and the male child (*autós* in the Septuagint version of Gen. 3.15). Also, the not-too-frequent term "seed", in the singular, occurs both in the Genesis passage and at the end of Chapter 12 of the Apocalypse: "And the dragon . . . went to make war with the rest of her seed." This view, however, is contested by others, e.g., J. Michl in his much-discussed article in *Biblica*, 33 (pp. 371ff.), which has been mentioned before. Though conceding the similarities between the Genesis passage and Apoc. 12, he holds nevertheless that the differences are even greater: "Both passages speak of a woman: but there [in Gen. 3.15] it is an embodied woman of the earth, here [Apoc. 12] a figure in the heavens, adorned with the stars, most probably a figure symbolizing a community—the people of God, the true Israel".[2] However, it should not be overlooked that the scene recorded by the author of the Apocalypse is a vision, that is to say, an experience in which many elements merge into each other: Genesis and Isaiah, the persecuted Church of the Messiah as well as his mother. No doubt Michl would not deny this. What he does oppose, however, together with such contemporary exegetes as A. Feuillet,[3] M. E. Boismard, A. Viard[4] and others, is the exclusive Mariological exegesis of Apoc. 12, which is held by, e.g., T. Gallus, S.J.,[5] J. B. Le Frois[6] and F. M. Braun,[7] though the last has since modified his opinion and now holds that Mary and the Church are seen together.[8]

In this view the Woman of Apocalypse 12 is Mary in the

---

[1] "La Vierge dans l'Apocalypse", in *ETL*, 31 (1955), pp. 21–33.
[2] "Der Weibessame", p. 399.   [3] "Le Messie et sa Mère".
[4] *RSPT*, 40 (1956), p. 160.
[5] "Scholion ad mulierem Apocalypseos", *Verbum Domini*, 30 (1952), pp. 332–40.
[6] *The Woman Clothed with the Sun*, Rome (1954).
[7] "La Mère de Jésus dans l'œuvre de saint Jean", *RT*, 59 (1951), pp. 5–68.
[8] "La Femme vêtue du soleil", *RT*, 55 (1955), pp. 639–69.

first and "literal" sense, and only in the second place the Church, as identified with her. D. M. Crossan[1] thinks that, owing to what he calls the "totality-thinking" of the Hebrew mind, the "Woman" is "both Mary and the Church in the one literal sense", and that the sun with which she is clothed represents Yahweh himself so that she may be enabled "to fulfil her tremendous task to bring forth in anguish and suffering the whole Christ; to be the physical mother of Christ and the spiritual mother of Christians".[2] This school of thought makes light not only of the early patristic evidence but also of the habitual Jewish and early Christian presentation of the People of God as a woman. It stresses, on the other hand, the similarities with Gen. 3.15 and the birth of a male child which, being evidently that of the Messiah, would refer most naturally not to the collective Church but to Mary, his individual human mother. Against this Boismard points out that the Woman of Apoc. 12, who is persecuted by the Beast, is opposed to the Harlot of Apoc. 17, who sits upon the Beast. As the Harlot is evidently the persecuting Roman Empire, the Woman is most naturally the persecuted Church.

Sifting the evidence dispassionately, it would seem that the exclusive Marian interpretation is untenable. In the mind of the seer the image of the persecuted Church may well have merged at certain moments with that of Mary, just as in St. Paul's vision Christ identified himself with his Church when he asked the future Apostle: "Why persecutest thou me?" (Acts 9.4.) For, as we have seen already in the discussion of the first chapters of Luke, in the New Testament Mary is not merely the individual mother of Jesus, she is also the "daughter of Sion", the representative of the People of God. Acclaimed by the angel as the mother of the long-awaited Messiah, she is almost completely eclipsed during the ministry of her Son, to reappear again under the Cross and in the midst of the

---

[1] "Mary's Virginity in St. John", *MM*, 19 (1957), pp. 115–26.
[2] "Mary's Virginity", p. 121.

disciples waiting for the coming of the Spirit. She appears once more in the visions of the Apocalypse, now, however, without the individual traits of the virgin of Nazareth, and as it were hidden under the splendour of the Church clothed with the sun.[1]

Thus Scripture presents Mary "through a glass in a dark manner". (1 Cor. 13.12.) Almost every passage referring to her can be—and has been—interpreted in quite different ways. Foretold by the Prophets, but in rather equivocal terms, praised by the angel, yet seemingly sometimes reproached by her Son, aware of her destiny, yet not quite comprehending it, becoming a mother for the second time under the Cross but mysteriously, finally appearing as a "sign" in the heavens—yet not she but the Church; we may well say that she, too, has a share in the paradoxes surrounding her divine Son. In the history and doctrine of the Church she will continue to be at his side, and gradually, in the course of the historical and doctrinal growth of Christianity, she will emerge into an ever-increasing light.

[1] A. Trabucco, in two articles entitled "La 'Donna ravvolta di sole'" (*MM*, 19 (1957), 1–58 and 289–334), reproduces the opinions of sixty-two post-Tridentine exegetes who preferred the ecclesiological interpretation and of twenty-six others who favoured the Mariological or ecclesio-Mariological exegesis.

THE EARLY TRADITION OF THE CHURCH TO THE BEGINNINGS OF THE NESTORIAN CONTROVERSY

APOSTOLIC FATHERS, APOLOGISTS AND APOCRYPHA

IN the Bible the figure of Mary remained, as we have seen, in a kind of chiaroscuro; she appeared veiled, as it were, in some prophecies, while in the New Testament she emerged into the full light of day in the first chapters of Luke, only to retire again into comparative darkness during the ministry of her Son and to merge with the figure of the Church in the Apocalypse. This changing pattern is repeated in the history of the first centuries of the Church; to understand it we have to remember what kind of atmosphere the young Church was growing up in.

The paganism of the Byzantine world round the shores of the Mediterranean was no longer the comparatively sober affair of the Greco-Roman Olympus, of Jupiter and Juno, of Minerva and Mars. It had become a syncretistic religion with very disturbing elements of ecstatic frenzy and sexual promiscuity, and one of its most prominent figures was the Mother Goddess, worshipped under many names, as the Magna Mater, the Phrygian Kybele, the Palestinian Ashtaroth, the Egyptian Isis and the Diana of the Ephesians whose devotees so violently opposed St. Paul. (Acts 19.) Her cult was extremely popular, for apart from its more undesirable aspects which pandered to the lowest human instincts, it also satisfied a deep-seated need for material protection and womanly understanding which the male gods could not fill.

When Christianity began to spread, not only among the Jewish communities of the Roman Empire but, under the leadership of St. Paul, also among the pagan population, its teachers had to make it clear that there was only one God, incarnate in Jesus Christ, who could tolerate no rivals, whether male or female, and who was both the creator and the redeemer of the world. A strong emphasis on his virgin mother would have led to unfortunate comparisons and, possibly, identifications. On the other hand, the more educated pagans, especially those who were philosophically inclined, could understand Christian monotheism, but not the reality of the Incarnation. For these the real birth of Christ from a real woman had to be stressed. And so we have on the one hand a seeming disregard of Mary, on the other a strong insistence on her complete humanity and the paramount importance of her childbirth.

St. Paul himself, who brought the Faith to such centres of pagan immorality as Corinth and Ephesus, refers to Mary only once, in his Letter to the Galatians, as a test of the reality of the Incarnation: "God sent his Son, made of a woman." (4.4.) Otherwise he is completely silent about her. The situation in the writings of the earliest Christian teachers, the so-called Apostolic Fathers, is similar. There is no mention of her in the famous letter of Clement of Rome to the Corinthians, nor in the *Didache*, the so-called *Teaching of the Twelve Apostles*, nor in the *Epistle of Barnabas*. The only author to mention her is the great bishop, Ignatius of Antioch, who suffered martyrdom in Rome about A.D. 110. At that time gnosticism, the most dangerous heresy that threatened the young Church, had already made its appearance. It taught a docetic doctrine of Christ, according to which he only appeared as man, but had not taken a real human body. It is easy to understand that the best defence against this pernicious teaching, which affected the reality of the Incarnation and hence also the Redemption, was to stress the true birth of Jesus from the womb of Mary. Ignatius therefore lays the greatest emphasis on the reality of Mary's childbirth.

"Jesus Christ . . . who was 'out of' Mary, who was truly born", he writes to the Trallians,[1] and in his letter to the Ephesians he stresses this real double birth "out of Mary and out of God". (7, 2.) In the same letter he uses the significant term *ekyophorethe*, literally "he was carried in the womb" by Mary, so that there should be no doubt that she bore him as any human mother bears her child. In the same epistle Ignatius makes the strange statement that both Mary's virginity and her childbirth were hidden from the prince of this world (19, 1), evidently to emphasize that she was completely withdrawn from any contact whatsoever with the devil, who knew nothing about her and the mystery God was working in her.

After these few scraps of information our orthodox documents are once more silent for another thirty years, but this does not mean that the figure of Mary did not occupy the minds of Christians, for she appeared comparatively frequently in the so-called Apocrypha. Towards the end of the first century she was mentioned in the *Ascension of Isaiah*, a Jewish-Christian work with strong gnostic influences. It is the first extant document to state the virginity *in partu*. The relevant passage[2] reads: "Mary straightaway looked with her eyes and saw a small babe, and she was astonied. And after she had been astonied, her womb was found as formerly before she had conceived" (11, 8f.), and *v.* 14 asserts that she gave birth without a midwife. This theme, E. Cothenet[3] suggests, was borrowed from the Jewish Haggada of the birth of Moses. The birth as described here is certainly not a true birth, taking place, as it does, without Mary knowing anything about it.

Some time before A.D. 150 we find another extraordinary description of Mary's childbirth, also emanating

---

[1] 9, 1; cf. also *Smyrnians*, 9, 1.
[2] In the translation of R. H. Charles (1900), p. 76.
[3] "Marie dans les Apocryphes", in *Maria*, 6, pp. 71–156.

from a source betraying gnostic influences, the *Odes of Solomon*.

> The womb of the Virgin caught [it], And received conception, And brought forth: And the Virgin became a Mother With many mercies: And she travailed And brought forth a Son Without incurring pain. Because it happened not emptily, And she had not sought a midwife (For He brought her to bear); She brought forth, As if she were a man, Of her own will, And she brought Him forth openly, And acquired Him in great power, And loved Him in salvation, And guarded Him in kindness, And showed Him in Majesty.[1]

This description of the majestic Mother of God, who brought forth her Son painlessly—a feature which will play an important role in later Mariology—"in great power"—differs strikingly from the portrait of the humble, retiring Virgin in the first chapters of St. Luke's Gospel, though the two are not incompatible; nevertheless, there are traits—"As if she were a man, of her own will"—which, like the famous statue of Epstein, seem to fit the goddess Isis, the mother of Horus, rather than the wholly human Mother of Jesus. However, these verses are clear evidence that even in these early times Mary was seen as a power, a "mother with many mercies" at least in certain circles open not only to mystical devotion but also to syncretistic influences.

Another work reflecting popular trends is the so-called Protoevangelium of James,[2] now assigned to the middle of the second century, which has exercised a tremendous influence both on later devotions and on controversies. It shows the impact of the figure of Mary on the imagination of these early Christians, who tried to supply what was missing in the sober

[1] No. 19, 6-10, ed. and tr. J. H. Bernard, *TS*, 8, 3 (1912), p. 86.

[2] E. de Stryker, *La Forme la plus ancienne du protévangile de Jacques*, 1961, from which I quote. There is an English translation by M. R. James in *The Apocryphal New Testament* (1924), pp. 38-49.

accounts of the Gospels. According to the Protoevangelium, Mary was born to Joachim and Anne when they were already very old. When she was six months, her mother set her down, and she walked seven (the sacred number!) steps unaided. Whereupon Anne "took her up saying: As the Lord my God liveth, you shall walk no more upon this earth until I bring you into the temple of the Lord. And she made a sanctuary in her chamber and suffered nothing common or unclean to pass through her."[1] So she never so much as touched the ground with her feet until she was presented at the Temple at the age of three. After having blessed her and prophesied that the Lord would make manifest his salvation in her, the priest "made her sit upon the third step of the altar. And the Lord caused grace to descend on her, and she danced with her feet and all the house of Israel loved her" (7, 2)—a description certainly "betraying great ignorance of Jewish conditions", as B. Altaner rightly points out in his *Patrology*.[2]

Henceforth she was nourished by angels until she was twelve years old. Then "there was a council of the priests who said: Behold, Mary has attained the age of twelve years in the temple of the Lord our God. What therefore are we to do with her so that she may not defile the sanctuary of the Lord our God?"[3] So they decided to assemble all the widowers of Israel, from whom Joseph was miraculously chosen as her husband.[4] He first refused because of his age and his sons (this was meant to account for the "brethren of the Lord" mentioned in the Gospels), but obeyed when the priest threatened him with the wrath of the Lord.[5]

Though these stories had a very great influence on Christian art as well as on preaching and the Liturgy, they were of little theological significance. The birth-story of Christ, however, received a very important addition. After Mary had brought forth her Son the midwife who had attended her met a friend, called Salome, and said to her: "Salome, I have to tell you a

[1] 6, 1.   [2] p. 68.   [3] 8, 2.   [4] 8, 3.   [5] 9.

new sight. A virgin has given birth, which her nature does not permit. And Salome said: As the Lord my God liveth, unless I place my finger and examine her nature I will not believe it." (Note the similarity of the words to those of St. Thomas about the risen Lord.) Salome consequently examined the Virgin and confirmed the statement of the midwife concerning the continuing physical virginity of Mary, which had not been violated even by childbirth.[1] This, together with the less popular *Ascension of Isaiah*, is the literary source of the "virginity *in partu*" which has been discussed in the preceding chapter. As will be seen, it was enthusiastically taken up by the majority of the Fathers, for the Platonic influence, with its scorn for everything pertaining to matter and the body, was very strong, and the relation between true motherhood and certain changes in the virginal body were not yet understood.

With the so-called Apologists of the second half of the second century, especially Justin Martyr (died c. 165), we are once more on firmer, biblical ground. He was the descendant of a pagan Greek family in Palestine who, after the Greek philosophers had left his craving for truth unsatisfied, was converted to Christianity and henceforth spent his life defending the Faith. In his famous *Dialogue with the Jew Trypho* there is a detailed discussion of the Virgin Birth, especially with regard to Isa. 7.14, which centres in the translation of *'almah*. Trypho holds the Greek *neanis* (= "young girl") to be the right translation, whereas Justin objects that the Septuagint, the Greek translation of the Old Testament accepted by the Jews, renders it *parthenos* (= "virgin").[2] In the same work Justin introduces the parallelism between Eve and Mary, which became a favourite subject of patristic teaching.[3]

---

[1] 20, 1-2. [2] chs. 43f., 67.
[3] We do not know if Justin himself discovered the parallelism; he may have received it as part of the post-apostolic tradition, when he was converted at Ephesus.

"Christ", he writes, "became man by the Virgin so that the disobedience which proceeded from the serpent might be destroyed in the same way as it originated. For Eve, being a virgin and undefiled, having conceived the word from the serpent, brought forth disobedience and death. The Virgin Mary, however, having received faith and joy, when the angel Gabriel announced to her the good tidings . . . answered: Be it done to me according to thy word."[1] Here we have Mary, her virginity and her obedience simultaneously compared and contrasted with Eve; both were virgins when the decisive words were spoken to them; but whereas Eve's reaction to them meant disobedience to a divine command and resulted in death, Mary obeyed God and so received faith and joy by becoming the Mother of the Saviour.

In this connection we would briefly mention a somewhat enigmatic passage in the last section of the *Epistle to Diognetus*, sometimes attributed to Hippolytus of Rome (d. 235) but now generally believed to belong to the last decade of the second century. There it almost seems as if Mary were called Eve without any further explanation, for in the context of the tree that bears fruit which the serpent does not touch, that is to say, of the Church, "Eve is not corrupted, but believed virgin; and salvation is shown forth"—though this interpretation is not generally received, and the text is sometimes held to refer to the real Eve.

THE EARLY THEOLOGIANS: IRENAEUS, TERTULLIAN, ORIGEN

Irenaeus was the first of the great theologians of Christendom. He was a native of Asia Minor who later went to the West and became Bishop of Lyons (in 177–8; d. c. 202). As was to happen time and again in Church history, his doctrine was developed in opposition to heretics, especially the gnostics,

[1] 100, 5.

and so his principal work is called *Against the Heresies*. It contains several important passages on Mary, which are particularly interesting when confronted with the rather exaggerated apocryphal stories about her inhuman purity, which forbade her even to tread the earth as a child or to be nourished by normal food.

Now Irenaeus takes up the motive of the Second Eve, not only greatly elaborating it but also linking it to the Pauline doctrine of the recapitulation (Greek *anakephalaiosis*, cf. Eph. 1.10) of all things in Christ, and so placing it at the very centre of man's redemption. Since Irenaeus represents the tradition of both East and West, his witness to a more developed Marian doctrine is particularly important. First of all he compares the creation of Adam from the virgin earth with its "recapitulation" or summing-up in the formation of Christ from the Virgin Mary,[1] a concept taken over by many later Fathers, and then launches out into a magnificent confrontation of Eve with Mary: "Mary the Virgin is found obedient, saying: Behold the handmaid of the Lord . . . Eve, however, disobedient: for she did not obey, even though she was still a virgin. Inasmuch as she, having indeed Adam for a husband, yet being still a virgin, became disobedient and was made both for herself and the whole human race the cause of death, so also Mary, having a husband destined for her yet being a virgin, by obeying, became the cause of salvation both for herself and the whole human race. And for this reason [namely for the sake of the parallelism between Eve and Mary] does the Law call her who was betrothed to a man, even though she was still a virgin, the wife of him to whom she was betrothed, signifying the transference [? of life: *re-circumlatio*] from Mary to Eve. Thus also was the knot of Eve's disobedience dissolved by Mary's obedience; for what the virgin Eve had tied up by unbelief, this the virgin Mary loosened by faith."[2] The trend of thought is once more

[1] *Against the Heresies*, 3, 21, 10.   [2] 3, 22, 4.

summed up in Chapter 5 (19, 1) of the same work: "And if the former [Eve] disobeyed God, yet the latter [Mary] was persuaded to be obedient to God, so that the virgin Mary might become the advocate of the virgin Eve. And thus, as the human race fell into bondage to death through a virgin, so it is rescued by a virgin; virginal disobedience having been balanced in the opposite scale by virginal obedience."

Irenaeus, like Justin before him, emphasizes both the virginity and the obedience of Mary as opposed to the disobedient virgin Eve, but he draws out the consequences much more explicitly. For through her obedience Mary became "the cause of salvation" not only for herself, but for the whole human race, just as Eve had become the cause of death; what had been bound by Eve was loosened by Mary. Further, Mary becomes the "advocate [or 'comforter'] of the virgin Eve" and so the rescuer of the whole human race; Irenaeus sees her already as the great intercessor for all mankind, and through her divine motherhood, the consequence of her obedience, she takes an even more active part in the great work of redemption, she becomes the "pure womb which regenerates men unto God".[1] Thus she is closely associated with the Church, as also in her gift of "prophecy": "Mary exclaimed on behalf of the Church, prophesying: My soul magnifies the Lord."[2]

It is all the more surprising that, despite his highly developed Mariology, Irenaeus yet considers Mary not free from all human faults. The New-Testament passage that puzzled him was Christ's remark to her at the wedding of Cana, on which he comments: "When Mary hurries to the admirable sign of the wine and before the time desires to participate of the mixed cup [of water and wine, i.e., the Eucharist], the Lord repels her untimely haste, saying: 'What have I to do with thee, woman?' "[3]

Another important theologian takes an even more serious

[1] 4, 33, 11.   [2] 3, 10, 2.   [3] 3,16, 7.

view of what he considers to be Mary's faults. Tertullian (c. 160–after 220), born of pagan parents in Carthage, was converted to Christianity in Rome about 195. He was the first Church Father to write in Latin, and though he later left the Church and joined the sect of the Montanists, because they held more rigorous views on the forgiveness of sins and practised harsher austerities than the Catholics, this act hardly affected his doctrinal outlook, which remained orthodox.

After having discussed at length the prophecy of Isa. 7.14,[1] Tertullian takes over from Irenaeus the comparison between the virgin earth from which Adam was made and the Virgin Mary, from whom Christ was born.[2] He then reproduces the parallelism between Eve and Mary: "Thy word [of the devil] which built up death had insinuated itself into Eve, then still a virgin; the word of God that built up life had equally to be introduced into a virgin, so that what through the female sex had gone to perdition should through the same sex be restored to salvation. Eve had believed the serpent; Mary believed Gabriel. What the one had done wrong by believing, the other made good by believing . . . Eve . . . finally brought forth the diabolic murderer of his brother. Mary, on the contrary, brought forth him, who was to redeem Israel, his brother according to the flesh, who had killed him."[3] Tertullian, however, attributes less influence to Mary than Irenaeus; he has nothing explicit about her being the cause of salvation for the whole race, though he, too, associates her closely with the Church; Eve prefigures both, Mary and the Church.[4]

Though, of course, accepting the Virgin Birth, Tertullian rejects Mary's virginity *in partu*. He had a good reason for denying this, which, after all, rested only on apocryphal evidence; for it might lend substance to the heretical gnostic

[1] *De Carne Christi*, 17, 2ff. [2] *De Carne Christi*, 7, 14.
[3] *De Carne Christi*, 17, 2. [4] *Adv. Marcionem*, 2, 4, 5.

view that Christ had not really taken flesh from the Virgin
Mary but had only "passed through her". Therefore
Tertullian affirmed that she was "a virgin as regards a man,
not a virgin, as regards the birth" and follows this statement
up with a wealth of physical detail.[1]

What was much more unorthodox, he also denied her
continued virginal life after the birth of Christ. In *De Mono-
gamia* (in which he opposes the remarriage of widows) he
states that she "has indeed brought forth Christ as a virgin,
but was going to be married after the birth" so that she should
be holy as mother, virgin, and the wife of one man;[2] for
why should Christ not be allowed to have brothers and
sisters?[3]

Whereas popular devotion, as expressed especially in the
Protoevangelium, had asserted her perpetual virginity, the
theologians had as yet been silent on this matter, at least as far
as we can judge from our sources, though it has been asserted
by Hugo Koch in his treatise *Adhuc Virgo*[4] that certain
passages in Irenaeus, in which he speaks of Mary being, like
Eve, *adhuc virgo*, still a virgin, must be interpreted as meaning
that later she did not remain a virgin. However, without going
into the detailed refutation of Koch by Catholic theologians,
we may say that the few applications of this term to Mary may
well be no more than echoes of the *adhuc virgo* applied to
Eve, without a deeper significance, and that very soon after
Tertullian the evidence for belief in Mary's perpetual virginity
becomes overwhelming.

Like Irenaeus, the African theologian finds imperfection in
Mary; more, where Irenaeus had only hinted at it, Tertullian
stresses it. The Gospel passages in which he thought to discover it are Matt. 12.46ff. and its parallels, and Luke 11.27f.
In the former Christ seemingly rejects his mother and his
brethren when they have come to seek him, while in the Luke

---

[1] *De Carne Christi*, 23, 2.   [2] 8, 2.   [3] *Adv. Marcionem*, 4, 19, 11.
[4] Tübingen (1929); also *Virgo Eva–Virgo Maria* (1937).

passage he corrects the enthusiasm of the woman in the crowd who calls out: "Blessed is the womb that bore thee." Tertullian draws quite unwarranted conclusions from these incidents; he not only asserts that Mary was not among her Son's followers,[1] he even compares her to the unbelieving Synagogue[2] and says that Christ rejected her and "transferred the blessedness from the womb and the breasts of his mother to his disciples".[3]

These judgements of a theologian of Tertullian's reputation will surprise the modern reader; yet, though they are certainly among the harshest to be found in patristic literature, they are not, as we shall see, the only ones.

From the stern and somewhat fanatical Tertullian we move now to the atmosphere of Alexandria, where intellectual speculation blended with mystical devotion in the so-called Alexandrian school of theology, the first great representative of which is Clement of Alexandria (d. 215). Only part of his work has survived, so we cannot be sure that the brief reference to Mary in Chapter 16 of the seventh book of his *Stromateis* is all he had to say about her. It is nevertheless important, for he affirms her virginity *in partu*, using the paradoxical form of expression that she was "a woman in childbed because of the birth of the child, yet was not a woman in childbed [*lechó*]", and then quotes the story of the midwife who found her to be a virgin, as "some say", evidently referring to the Protoevangelium. He goes on to compare her with the Scriptures, which also remain "virgins" in giving birth to the truth. And thus Mary "brought forth and did not bring forth" as "the Scripture says"—though such a quotation is not to be found in the Bible and would, indeed, detract from her real motherhood.

Strangely enough the second great representative of the Alexandrian school, Origen (d. 253) the pupil of Clement, is

---

[1] *De Carne Christi*, 7, 9.   [2] *De Carne Christi*, 7, 13.
[3] *Adv. Marcionem*, 4, 26, 13.

not so sure about the virginity *in partu*; in fact in his homilies
on Luke he denies it.[1] In his homilies on Leviticus, on the
other hand, which were delivered later, he affirms it.[2] Now,
the Greek original of both works being lost, this discrepancy
has sometimes been explained by the fact that the former was
translated by St. Jerome, who followed the actual Greek
text, whereas the latter was done by Rufinus (d. 410) at a time
when Origen's teaching had sparked off a great controversy.
So as to shield the great Alexandrian scholar, who was accused
of heresy, Rufinus smoothed down many of his more questionable statements. But it seems doubtful whether he did so also
in this case; for there is another passage, in Origen's commentary on Matthew, preserved in the Greek original, which
would seem to imply her virginity *in partu*. It occurs in a
curious reference to the priest Zachariah mentioned in Matt.
23.35 as "killed between the temple and the altar". Origen
writes: "Now Mary, after giving birth to the Saviour, went to
worship and stood in the place of the virgins. And when those
who knew she had given birth were preventing her, Zachariah
said to them that she was worthy of the place of the virgins,
because she was a virgin. Therefore, as he was evidently
transgressing the Law and allowed a woman to take her place
among the virgins, they killed him between the temple and
the altar."[3]

Though the reference to the virginity *in partu* is not
absolutely clear, it nevertheless may be implied. That Origen
believed in the Virgin Birth goes without saying, since this is
New-Testament teaching and belongs to the essentials of the
Faith (*Comm. on John*, 32, 16); he defended it against
the pagan philosopher Celsus and pointed to the prophecy of
Isa. 7.14. Like the great biblical scholar he was, he discussed
the *'almah* passage in detail, affirming that a birth from an
ordinary woman, not a virgin, could not be a sign, and that it

[1] *Homily, 14* (*GCS*, p. 90, 9).   [2] *Homily 8*, 2 (*GCS*, p. 395, 6).
[3] *Commentariorum Series*, 25 (*GCS*, vol. 9, p. 43, 5ff.).

was only suitable that Emmanuel, i.e., "God with us", should be born from a virgin.[1]

Whatever his belief with regard to the virginity *in partu*, he certainly held that Mary remained a virgin throughout her life, though the term *aeiparthenos* (= "ever-virgin") does not occur in his extant writings. His view is obvious from the passage quoted above; it is also affirmed in a Greek fragment from the *Homilies on Luke*, in which he indignantly refutes the allegations of "heretics" "who say against Mary that the Saviour had rejected her because after the birth of the Saviour she had intercourse with Joseph". The brethren of the Lord, he maintains, were sons of Joseph, but not by Mary.[2] Indeed, "Jesus became the firstfruit of men's pure chastity, Mary of women's; for it would not be pious to attribute the firstfruits of virginity to any one but her."[3]

Origen, too, has the Second-Eve motif, though in a less elaborate form than Irenaeus; he contrasts the disobedience of Eve with the obedience of Mary,[4] and, like Irenaeus, he considers her *Magnificat* a prophecy.[5]

Nevertheless, he, too, does not believe her to be without faults. First of all, she needed the ordinary purification of Jewish women after childbirth,[6] which would, of course, rule out the virginity *in partu*. Then, much more serious, she was invaded by doubts during the Passion. This is Origen's interpretation of the sword which, according to Simeon's prophecy, was to pierce her soul (Luke 2.35): "Why should we believe that, when the Apostles were scandalized, the Mother of the Lord remained immune from scandal? If she had not suffered scandal in the passion of the Lord, Jesus would not have died for her sins. But if 'all have sinned and

---

[1] *Contra Celsum*, 1, 34–7.   [2] *Homily 7 on Luke* (*GCS*, p. 43f.).
[3] *Comm. in Matth.*, 10, 17 (*GCS*, p. 22, 1ff.).
[4] *Homily 1 on Matthew*, 5 (*GCS*, p. 244, 27ff.).
[5] Cf. *Homily 8 on Luke* (*GCS*, p. 47, 4ff.).
[6] *Homily 14 on Luke* (*GCS*, p. 85, 4ff.).

3+

need the glory of God, justified by his grace and redeemed'
[Rom. 3.23], then Mary, too, was scandalized at that time.
Therefore Simeon prophesies also about the holy virgin Mary
herself; for standing beside the Cross and seeing what is
happening and hearing the voices of the killers—even after
Gabriel's witness, after the ineffable knowledge of the divine
conception, after the great showing forth of miracles, even
you, who were taught from above the things of the Lord, will
be perplexed and touched by dissension—that is the sword."[1]

In his view even Mary's faith wavered at the final test—like
that of the Apostles; an idea which many later Greek Fathers
made their own. But despite these inadequacies in his
Mariology, to Origen seems to belong the privilege of being
the first Father in whose works is found the famous term
Theotokos, Mother of God, or, more literally but rather
clumsily, "she who gives birth to God", which occurs in two
Greek fragments on Luke (numbers 41 and 80 in the Berlin
Edition), though his authorship is not absolutely certain. But
if he wrote these pieces he would inaugurate the succession of
Alexandrian theologians who used this name of honour and
later had to defend it in a bitter controversy until the divine
motherhood of Mary became a dogma of the Church.

The End of the Third Century

In the latter half of the third century our sources are comparatively silent on Mary. In the West Cyprian of Carthage
(d. 258) was the first Father to relate Isa. 7.14 to Gen. 3.14f.:
"This seed God had foretold would issue from the woman
and would crush (the seed, not the woman) the head of the
devil."[2] In the East, Peter of Alexandria (d. 311), a predecessor
of Athanasius, is believed to be the first known witness to
Mary's title Ever-Virgin (*aeiparthenos*), but the passage in
which the word occurs is doubtful; it reads: "Jesus Christ . . .
born according to the flesh from our holy, glorious Lady,

[1] *Homily 17 on Luke* (*GCS*, pp. 105–7).   [2] *Test.*, 2, 9.

Mother of God [*Theotokos*] and Ever-Virgin, Mary."[1] His contemporary Methodius, however, who taught philosophy and Scripture in Lycia, compares her only very soberly to the virgin earth from which Adam was taken, though his treatise on virginity, in which this passage occurs,[2] might have warranted a more enthusiastic approach. But he was an opponent of Origen and so, presumably, of the Alexandrian type of theology. This may account for his attitude, which we shall meet again about a century later in the so-called "Antiochene school".

But if our theological evidence of this period is scanty, we have two documents which suggest that Christian devotion to the Mother of Christ was already intense. The first is the description of a vision of the blessed Virgin, who is said to have appeared to Gregory the Wonderworker (d. c. 270). The story is told in a panegyric on the saint almost certainly written by Gregory of Nyssa. Though this work belongs to the latter part of the next century, it is quite probable that the vision may have been authentic. This, at least, is the view of M. Jugie, who, in fact, calls the testimony of Gregory of Nyssa "unexceptionable".[3] Compared with those of a later date, the description of the vision is very restrained. Mary appears to Gregory in the night, accompanied by St. John the Apostle, "a female form, more than life-size", in a blaze of light, "as if a brilliant torch had been lit", and she tells John to "make known to the young man [i.e., Gregory] the mystery of piety [i.e., the true faith]"; "and he said he was ready to do this for the Mother of the Lord, because such was her wish."[4]

---

[1] Fragment 7 (*PG*, 18, 517B).   [2] *Symposium*, 3, 4.

[3] *Irrécusable*; "Les Homélies mariales attribuées à Grégoire le Thaumaturge", in *AB*, 43 (1925), p. 95.

[4] *PG*, 46, 912. Three Marian homilies have also been attributed to Gregory the Wonderworker, but, as M. Jugie ("Les Homélies", pp. 86–95) points out, these are products of a much later age. The first two homilies reproduce the formulae of the Council of Chalcedon (451) and sometimes literally passages from Chrysippus of Jerusalem (d. 479), whereas the third shows resemblances to Proclus of Constantinople (d. c. 447).

The other evidence of popular devotion is the papyrus fragment of a prayer sometimes dated as early as the third century but more probably belonging to the fourth.[1] It is evidently a primitive form of the *Sub tuum praesidium*; the English translation of the Greek fragment runs: "Mother of God [hear] my supplications: suffer us not [to be] in adversity, but deliver us from danger. Thou alone . . .". Even if the papyrus fragment should belong to the middle of the fourth century, this is not to say that the prayer itself might not have existed earlier. It is certainly not liturgical, as in the Liturgy all prayers are addressed to God. Indeed, it uses language suggesting that the Theotokos herself can deliver (*rysai*, the same word as in the *Our Father*) us from danger. For this reason O. Stegmüller[2] assigns it to the end of the fourth century and to gnostic circles.

GREEK FATHERS OF THE FOURTH CENTURY

By the middle of the fourth century the veneration of Mary had gained much ground, particularly in the East, where the feast of the *Hypapante* (that is, Encounter, viz., of Christ and Simeon—our Purification) was kept in Jerusalem on February 14. Though it was at that time still principally a feast of Christ, Mary nevertheless must have had her share in it, and the preachers would no doubt have drawn attention to Simeon's prophecy that a sword was to pierce her heart. The feast is described in the famous account of the pilgrimage of a nun to the Holy Land, the *Peregrinatio Aetheriae*,[3] which dates from the end of the fourth century, but obviously reflects customs already well established by that time. According to this account, "the fortieth day of the Epiphany is

[1] C. H. Roberts, *Catalogue of Greek and Latin Papyri in the John Rylands Library*, 3 (1938), pp. 46f.

[2] "Sub tuum Praesidium. Bemerkungen zur ältesten Überlieferung", in *ZKT*, 74 (1952), pp. 76–82.

[3] Ch. 26, *CSEL*, 39, p. 77.

here celebrated with the highest honour. For on this day there is a procession in the Anastasis [evidently still without candles, or she would have mentioned them], and all is done in order and with the greatest joy as at Easter. All the priests, too, preach and then the bishop, always treating of that passage of the Gospel, when Joseph and Mary took the Lord to the Temple on the fortieth day . . . and afterwards, when everything that is customary has been celebrated in order, the mysteries are performed and thus Mass is offered." "Theotokos" had at that time come to be a title in general use, for Julian the Apostate taunted Christians with it: "You never stop calling Mary 'Theotokos'."[1]

As the popular liturgical veneration was gathering momentum, the preachers and theologians did not lag behind. It was above all the school of Alexandria, and the Fathers influenced by it, who began to proclaim the glories of the Theotokos with ever-increasing fervour. In his commentary on Isaiah, Eusebius, the great Church historian and admirer of Origen (c. 260–c. 340), considers without any question 7.14 as a prophecy that "a virgin shall conceive without intercourse with a man, and shall bring forth God",[2] and refers the "prophetess" of 8.3 to Mary, "because she had a share in the Holy Spirit".[3] He also calls her *panagia*, "all-holy".[4] Only a few fragments survive of the works of Bishop Alexander of Alexandria (d. 328). He, like so many of the Fathers of this time, had to defend the true manhood of Christ—and hence the true motherhood of Mary—against the gnostic and Manichean heresies. He, too, calls Mary Theotokos,[5] from whom came "in truth" the body of Christ. There was also another reason to give more emphasis to the Virgin Mother. With the official toleration of the Christian religion by the

---

[1] Quoted by Cyril in his work against Julian. (8 (*PG*, 76, 901).)
[2] *PG*, 24, 133D.   [3] *PG*, 24, 141A.
[4] *Ecclesiastica Theologia* (*GCS*, p. 174, 31; *PG*, 24, 1033B).
[5] Opitz ed., 3, 1, p. 28 (*PG*, 18, 568C).

Emperors Constantine and Licinius at Milan (313), the expectation of martyrdom ceased to be one of the main elements of the Christian life. In its place ascetism, favoured also by certain schools of Hellenistic philosophy, came to the fore, especially in the form of virginity practised as a particular Christian state with its own rules and customs. It was only natural that the Mother of God should be presented to those who had adopted this state as the great example on which they were to form themselves, and so Alexander tells them, in an address reproduced by his successor Athanasius: "You have the conduct of Mary, who is the type and image of the life that is proper to heaven [i.e., virginity]."[1]

This idea that Mary should be the example of virgins and celibates is further elaborated in a remarkable document preserved in Coptic, which belongs to the time of the Council of Nicaea (325) and is printed among the *gnomai* or proverbs of the Council.[2] "A wise virgin", it says "resembles Mary. Who could name the beauty of the Mother of our Lord, who was loved by God because of her works? Therefore his beloved Son dwelt in her . . . Mary is called the Mother of our Lord, and she is this in truth; she has borne him who created her . . . and she did not lose her virginity when she gave birth to our Saviour, but he preserved it like a precious treasure. Mary never saw the face of a strange man, that was why she was confused when she heard the voice of the angel Gabriel. She did not eat to feed a body, but she ate because of the necessity of her nature . . . She withdrew all by herself into her house, being served by her own mother. But when she went to her [mother] she could not tell her a word about her condition, because she had sworn to herself not to tell anyone in this world anything at all about it. She sat always with her face turned towards the East, because she prayed continually.

---

[1] In "De Virginitate", in *Le Muséon*, 42 (1929), p. 135.
[2] F. Haase, "Die koptischen Quellen zum Konzil von Nicaea", in *Studien zur Geschichte und Kultur des Altertums*, 10, 4 (1920), pp. 50–52.

For her brothers wanted to see her and speak to her. And she did not receive them. For the angels came many times to her; they observed her singular way of life and admired her. She slept only according to the need of sleep . . . When she put on a garment she used to shut her eyes . . . For she did not know many things of this life, because she remained far from the company of women. For the Lord looked upon the whole of creation and he saw no-one to equal Mary. Therefore he chose her for his mother. If, therefore, a girl wants to be called a virgin, she should resemble Mary."[1]

It is interesting to note how Mary is here portrayed not as she appears in Scripture, but as the ideal of the fourth-century consecrated virgin, who always stayed at home and prayed, meticulously guarded against any masculine society, whereas the Mary of the Gospels did not hesitate to visit her cousin Elizabeth, went up to the Temple for the feasts and generally behaved like a normal Jewish girl of her time. But, as we shall see again and again, every age unconsciously forms its image of the Virgin according to its own ideal; and the age of the Fathers of the Desert could not conceive her otherwise than as a solitary, leading a life of the most exemplary austerity and consorting not even with her own brothers but only with angels.

Athanasius (c. 296–373), the great defender of the divinity of Christ and the *homoousios*, "of the same substance" (i.e., as the Father) against its Arian opponents at the Council of Nicaea (325) also represents the two Mariological trends, mentioned in his predecessor Alexander, and which may perhaps be called the theological and the ascetical points of view. In his controversy with Arianism he stresses that Christ took his Godhead from the Father, but his manhood from his mother, "the unploughed earth",[2] "ever-virgin"[3] and,

---

[1] 34-5.
[2] *Oratio II*, 7 (*C. Arianos*) (*PG*, 26, 161B); cf. also II, 74 (305A) and elsewhere.
[3] *Or. II*, 70 (*C. Ar.*) (*PG*, 26, 296B).

naturally for the architect of the Nicene faith, Theotokos.[1] For—this in opposition not to the Arians, but to gnostics and Manicheans—Christ took his human body from Mary, "according to the divine Scriptures, and the body of the Lord was real; it was real, because it was the same as ours; for Mary is our sister".[2] For this reason he also did not teach the virginity *in partu*, but affirmed that "he who was born opened the womb".[3] The reality of Christ's divinity and the reality of his humanity make Mary the "Mother of God"; even as early as the first half of the fourth century, Christology and Mariology went together.

The ascetical point of view is represented in a *Letter to the Virgins*, preserved only in Coptic, and almost certainly by Athanasius.[4] It bears striking resemblances to the *Proverbs of Nicaea*, so much so that Lefort thinks that the words "as it is written" in the text (which we shall italicize) actually refer to the Nicene document which, as emanating from a general council, must have carried considerable weight even then; for there is no biblical passage to which the words, generally reserved for Scripture, could possibly apply. Athanasius emphasizes Mary's perpetual virginity and proves it by the fact that Christ entrusted his mother to St. John and not to his "brethren",[5] our first extant authority for this argument. Thus Mary is the ideal pattern of Christian virgins: "Mary therefore was a pure Virgin, with a harmonious disposition . . . She loved good works . . . She did not want to be seen by men; but she asked God to examine her . . . She remained continually at home, living a retired life and imitating a honey-bee . . . She generously distributed to the poor what was left over from the work of her hands . . . She prayed to God,

---

[1] *Or. III*, 14 (*C. Ar.*) (*PG*, 26, 349C and elsewhere); *Vita Antonii*, 36; *De Virginitate*, 3 (*TU*, 29, 2 (1905), p. 38, 21).

[2] *Letter to Epictetus*, 7.   [3] *Letter to Epictetus*, 5.

[4] Edited with French translation by L. T. Lefort, *Le Muséon*, 42, pp. 197–274, here quoted by pages in the margin.

[5] p. 86.

alone to the alone, being intent on two things: not to let a
bad thought take root in her heart and to grow neither bold nor
hard of heart . . . Her speech was recollected and her voice
low . . . She wanted to make progress every day; and she did
make progress. When she rose in the morning, she endeavoured to make her works more 'new' [cf. 2 Cor. 5.17] than
those she had already done, when she had neglected her good
works or had done them hastily . . . She was not afraid of death,
but rather was sad and sighed every day while she had not
yet crossed the threshold of heaven."[1]

Here Mary is represented as a model—but as a model
which has still some flaws: her good works are not perfect, and
"bad thoughts" come into her mind. Certainly Athanasius did
not attribute actual sins to her, and the mention of such faults
may have been due to his desire to paint a realistic picture of
a virginal life not too exalted to follow; it shows nevertheless
that the image of the spotlessly perfect, immaculate Virgin
had not yet emerged in the mind of the fourth-century
Fathers. Yet the "imitation of Mary" was by now an established way of life: "If, therefore, there is a girl who wants to
remain a virgin and spouse of Christ, it is possible for her to
consider the life of Mary and to imitate her; and the rule of
Mary's decision will suffice her to organize her life of virginity.
Therefore the life of Mary, who gave birth to God, should to
all of you, *as it is written*, be the image after which each one
should fashion her virginity. In fact, you should know your-
selves through her as by a mirror."[2] And quoting 1 Cor. 7.25,
he traces this imitation of Mary back to St. Paul, who, he
writes, "perhaps also knew the life of Mary, because he took
her as a model to introduce his opinion on virginity".[3] Apart
from the mention of her supposed imperfections, this *Letter*
might almost have been written in the Middle Ages; it shows
clearly how important a part Mary played in the spiritual life
of the ascetics of fourth-century Egypt.

[1] *Letter to the Virgins*, pp. 89–91.   [2] *Letter*, p. 88.   [3] *Letter*, p. 96.
3*

Titus, Bishop of Bostra, the capital of the Roman province of Arabia, a contemporary of Athanasius (d. before 378), also had to defend the real motherhood of Mary against the Manicheans. He did this in his *Homilies on Luke*, of which only fragments survive, and in the fourth book of his treatise against this sect. Titus speaks in much higher terms of Mary than Athanasius. In fact, he states that, "in addition to the holiness of her virginity the Virgin was specially sanctified by the Holy Spirit".[1] In his *Homilies on Luke* he introduces the *Magnificat* with these words: "Let us therefore hear, what the virgin in all respects 'new' says [cf. again 2 Cor. 5.17] and what is her marvellous prophecy; for as she is above nature mother and virgin, so she also shows herself a prophetess and speaker of God [*theologousa*]."[2] Apparently he also taught the virginity *in partu*, at least if, as seems probable, the fragments edited by G. Mercator[3] belong to him. For the Manicheans object to this teaching, saying: "If the Child was real flesh (which they deny), how did he not violate the virginity when he was brought forth? But if he preserved the virginity, how was the flesh not merely an appearance?"—to which the author replies that they evidently do not know what they are talking about, "for, hearing what belongs to the divine order, you seek conformity with nature". He certainly taught the virginity *post partum*, for he, like so many other Fathers of this time, regarded the brethren of Jesus as the sons of Joseph by a former marriage.[4]

Another contemporary and friend of Athanasius, Marcellus of Ancyra (d. c. 374), was probably the author of the *Exposition of the Faith*[5] formerly attributed to Athanasius himself,

---

[1] *Contra Manichaeos*, 4, 31, Syriac translation, ed. P. A. de Lagarde (1859), new impression, Hanover (1924).

[2] *Schol. in Luc.* 1.46 (*TU*, 21¹, p. 145, 1ff.).

[3] "Alcune note di letteratura patristica", in *Rendiconti del Real Istituto Lombardo di scienze e lettere*, ser. 2, vol. 31 (1898), p. 1201, 48ff.

[4] *Schol. in Luc.* 8.19 (*TU*, 21¹, p. 174, 5f.).   [5] *PG*, 25.

in which Mary is called *achrantos*, "undefiled",[1] and in which Jer. 31.22—in the translation not of the Septuagint but of Aquila (also sometimes used by the Fathers)—seems to be applied to her for the first time: "The Lord has created a new thing in the female [Septuagint: 'on the earth'], that is, in Mary. For nothing new has been created in the female except that which was born from the Virgin Mary without intercourse, the body of the Lord."[2] We see here how, apart from the obvious prophetic text of Isa. 7.14, other Old-Testament passages, too, begin to be applied to Mary, as they had from the first been applied to Christ, especially in the various controversies when both orthodox and heretics searched the Scriptures to find proof texts for their beliefs.

LATIN FATHERS

While Marian doctrine and devotion thus began to flourish in the Greek-speaking East, the development in the West was slower. Lactantius (d. 320), a former teacher of rhetoric, also quoted Isa. 7.14 as prophesying the Virgin Birth.[3] Hilary of Poitiers (d. 367),[4] the "Athanasius of the West", a convert from Neo-Platonism, taught the virginity *post partum*: "She is called the Mother of Christ, because this she was; not the wife of Joseph, because this she was not."[5] He does not, however, seem to have taught the virginity *in partu*; at least, his language is ambiguous. In his treatise on the Trinity he says he will not ask how Christ was born from the Virgin and whether her flesh suffered any "detrimentum",[6] and in a later passage he is even more definite: "For though he was born according to the law of men, yet he was not conceived according to this law."[7] Like the Greek Fathers, he, too, thought the brethren of Jesus were sons of Joseph of a former marriage,[8]

---

[1] (*PG*, 201B).
[2] 3 (*PG*, 205B).
[3] *Divinae Institutiones*, 4, 12.
[4] *PL*, 9, 10 and *CSEL* 22 and 65.
[5] *Comment. in Matthaeum*, 1, 3.
[6] 3, 19.
[7] 10, 47.
[8] 1, 4; cf. also 1, 20.

and like Origen he speculated on the "sword" in Simeon's prophecy; but he interpreted it not as referring to a doubt, but to Mary's liability to judgement: "If even this Virgin who was capable of bearing God [*capax dei*] will come to the severity of judgement, who will dare to wish to be judged by God?"[1]

With Zeno, a native of Mauretania who was Bishop of Verona from 363 to 372, we are in a different atmosphere. He teaches quite definitely Mary's virginity *in partu* and *post partum* which makes Mary the great example of virgins and monks: "She was virgin after marriage, virgin after conception, virgin after her Son. Finally, if anything had been better than virginity, the Son of God would rather have given that to his Mother, whereas he gave her to rejoice in the honour of divine virginity."[2] He states that "Mary conceived as an incorrupt virgin, after conception she brought forth as a virgin, after giving birth she remained a virgin", and then quotes the story of the midwives, the first of the Latin Fathers to do so.[3] Thus "Mary brings forth not in sorrow, but in joy: the Son is born without a father . . . who owes to himself that he is conceived, but gives to the Mother that he is born. She marvels that such a Son should have come forth from her, who could not be believed to have been born from her, had she not been an undefiled virgin after her conception and remained such also after the birth."[4] What the Greek Fathers had suggested in their characteristic speculatively-mystical language, Zeno expresses with Latin precision. In one interesting passage he also takes up the Eve-Mary theme, but equates Mary with the Church: "And because the devil had wounded and corrupted Eve, creeping in by persuasion through the ear, Christ entering by the ear into Mary, cuts out all vices from the heart: and he cures the wound of the woman when he is born by the virgin"; and the passage ends surprisingly: ". . . so that Adam should be renewed through

---

[1] *Tractatus in Ps CXVIII*, Gimel, 12 (*PL*, 11).   [2] *Tractatus*, 1, 5, 3.
[3] 2, 8, 2.   [4] 2, 9, 1.

Christ, Eve through the Church."[1] Zeno gives the ancient
Eve–Mary parallelism another new nuance; both corruption
and salvation enter by the ear, i.e., through hearing—an idea
which we shall also find in his Syrian contemporary Ephraem;
it became current in the fourth century. But instead of continuing the parallel Adam-Christ and Eve-Mary, he suddenly
changes to Eve-Church. So evidently the intimate relation of
Mary to the Church soon to be elaborated by Ambrose and
perhaps hinted already in the strange passage of the *Epistle to
Diognetus* discussed above, must have been realized even at this
early stage of Marian doctrine.

Syria: Ephraem

The fervour of Marian devotion at this time reached its
peak in Syria, in the person of the deacon Ephraem (c. 306–73),
the "lyre of the Holy Spirit" as he has been called. He was a
native of Nisibis, but left his home town in 363, after it had
been ceded to Persia, and went to Edessa. Most of his extant
works, nearly all of them in verse, seem to have been written
in that city. Ephraem is often held to be the first Father to
have taught the Immaculate Conception, the proof passage
being a verse from his *Nisibene Hymns* (27, 8): "You [Christ]
alone and your Mother are good [or beautiful] in every way;
for there is no blemish in thee, my Lord, and no stain in thy
Mother."[2] But his thought in this respect differs from that of
modern Western theologians; and the passage must be
interpreted in the light of others referring to the same subject.
In one of his hymns on the Nativity[3] he writes: "[9] . . .
Thou, who gavest birth to thy mother / In another birth,
from water! [10] I am thy sister of the House of David / Who
is the Father of us both. I am also mother / For I bore thee in

---

[1] I, 13, 10.
[2] The following argumentation is suggested by E. Beck, O.S.B., "Die
Mariologie der echten Schriften Ephräms", *OC*, 40 (1956), pp. 22–39.
[3] 16, 9–11 (*ER*, 2, 429E, F).

my womb. I am also thy bride; / For thou art chaste. [I am] handmaid and daughter / Of blood and water; for thou hast purchased, baptized [me]. [11] The Son of the Highest, who came and took up his abode in me / And I became his mother. And as I gave birth to him / In a second birth [i.e., in his human birth, after the eternal birth of the Son from the Father], he, too, has given birth to me / In a second birth. The garment of his mother / Which he put on, his body, / I have put on its glory."

The passage is typical of what one might call the "image-theology" of the Syrian poet. Here for the first time in Christian literature Mary is called the Bride of her Son. It also seems clear from these verses that Ephraem does not teach the Immaculate Conception in the technical sense, for he not only uses the imagery of baptism, but even the actual term: ". . . thou hast . . . baptized me". Does this mean that Christ actually baptized his Mother, as he himself was baptized by John? And what does it mean, that Christ put on the garment of his Mother and she put on its glory? The garment of his Mother is evidently the human nature which Mary gave to her Son—but not that nature which was marred by Adam's sin, but a garment of "glory". This, however, even Mary could not have given him, unless he had first given it to her—but when? In what Ephraem calls "a second birth". But for Ephraem the moment of this birth was not the moment of her conception, as emerges from a passage in his hymns on the Church. There he writes[1]: "[1] The eye is cleansed by the sun, through union with it. / It conquers by its weapon, it becomes clear through its light / And shining through its splendour and beautiful through its adornment. [2] Mary is like the eye: The Light came to dwell in her [cf. Matt. 6.22] / Purified her spirit, her considerations, / Her thought, and purified her virginity." So according to Ephraem Mary was purified when "the light came to dwell

[1] 36, 1–2 (ER, 2, 328D).

in her", that is, at the moment when the Word entered into her, when, as he says in one of his Christmas hymns: "Mary has become a heaven for us, because she bears God."[1]

Like Zeno, Ephraem says that Christ entered through the ear, and, again as in the case of the Latin Father, this passage occurs in the Eve-Mary context, worked out in the same hymns on the Church. In 35, 17 he writes: "With the eye Eve perceived the beauty of the tree / And the advice of the sly one [i.e., the devil] was fashioned in her mind. / And repentance was the end of the deed. / With the ear Mary perceived the Invisible One, who came in the voice, / She conceived in her womb the Power that came to her body."

In a later hymn (49, 7), the parallelism is even more pronounced: "For as from the womb, the small one, of that ear [i.e., of Eve] / Death entered and spread, So through the ear / The new one, of Mary, life has entered and spread." The temptation of Eve through the words of the serpent is cancelled out by the obedience of Mary to the words of the angel—both sin and salvation entered through the "womb" of the ear. The ancient comparison between the Virgin Eve and the Virgin Mary recurs in Hymn 17, 4 on the Nativity: "In her virginity Eve clothed herself with leaves of ignominy. Your [i.e., Christ's] mother has clothed herself in her virginity with the garment of glory, which is sufficient for all. A piece of clothing [i.e., the body] she has given to him who clothes all." In Eastern theology, e.g., in Gregory of Nyssa, the shining garments of Paradise are often contrasted with the "garments of skin", that is to say corruptible—and sexual—humanity as we now have it. These are the gifts of Eve, as Ephraem says in his hymns on Paradise (4, 5): "Adam was naked and beautiful. But his wife, the capable one / Made an effort and fashioned for him the garment of skins. / The Garden [i.e., of Eden] saw

[1] *ER*, 3, 604-08; No. 6.

and rejected him, because it thought him ugly. / But through Mary he [Adam] received a garment / Which adorned the thief [on the Cross]. And because he shone through the promise / The Garden saw and embraced him in Adam's place." In Eastern spiritual theology Paradise plays a prominent part; what modern mysticism expresses in the image of the ascent of Mount Carmel the Eastern Fathers saw as a return to Paradise—the treatise on perfection by the seventh-century Greek writer John Climacus, for example, is called the "Ladder of Paradise". In this return to Paradise Mary has the role of Eve in reverse; as Eve was responsible for the "garments of skin" in place of the glory with which the first men had been clothed in the Garden, so Mary, through the body she gave to her Son, gave to man a new garment, the spiritualized body of all the redeemed with Christ as its head. Thus, as he says in his hymns on the Church: "Through Eve was lost and through Mary returned the glorious, desirable splendour that had gone from Eve." (45, 3.)

As Eve is most intimately connected with the Fall and the consequent disastrous development of mankind, so Mary is closely associated with the Redemption. She "bore Christ in her virginal womb as the bush on Mount Horeb [Exod. 3.1ff.] bore God in the flame",[1] an image that seems to have become current in the fourth century and was further developed by later Fathers. In his hymns on the Church he says: [3] "It is evident that Mary is the soil of the sun / Which through her has illuminated the world and its inhabitants / Who had become dark through Eve, the cause of all evils. [4] They [i.e., men] are like a body whose one eye / Is blind and dark, the other however / Clear and bright, illuminating the universe. [5] Behold, two eyes are placed in mankind. / Eve was its eye, its blind, left one, / The right eye, the shining one, is Mary. [5] Through the eye which was darkened, all mankind was darkened, / And men, groping, thought all the stumbling

[1] *Hymn on the Birth of Christ* (ER 3, 604).

blocks, which they found / To be God; they called deceit truth. [7] But when they were illuminated through the eye and the heavenly light / Which made its dwelling in it [the eye], they found again unity [i.e., monotheism], because they saw / That what they found, was the loss of their life."[1] Thus Mary was the "soil" (this, according to Beck, is the correct reading) on which Christ, the sun, could shine on the world and mankind; and again, she was the bright, sound eye, through which the heavenly light of the divine Word could illumine the world which had become all dark through Eve, the diseased eye. Ephraem traces this parallelism even further, from the earth down to Sheol, the place of the dead into which Christ descended after his crucifixion, an event frequently treated by the Eastern Fathers. "Today [Christ's nativity] let Eve rejoice in Sheol. For lo, the Son of her daughter has descended as the medicine of life to raise the mother of his mother. The blessed child crushes the head of the serpent which had wounded her."[2] Here we have again the connection of Mary, through her Son, with the prophecy of Gen. 3.15. The combination Christ–Sheol–Eve–Mary is worked out even more fully in the *Sermon on Our Lord*.[3] "Since death could not devour him [Christ] without a body, he came to the Virgin, so as from there to guide a mount [that is, his body] to Sheol . . . With the body from the Virgin he entered Sheol . . . and came to Eve, the mother of all the living. She [i.e., Eve] is the vine, whose wall the Evil One pierced with her own hands and by whose fruit he made men taste death. And Eve, the mother of all the living, became the source of death for all the living. But Mary caused a new branch to sprout forth from Eve, the ancient vine, and in this [new branch] the new life [i.e., Christ] made its abode." This is a further development of Irenaeus' idea of Mary as the advocate of Eve. The Mother of Christ is the mother of the new life, as Eve was the mother of the old life; in the body that was taken from her

[1] *De Ecclesia*, 37, 3–7.   [2] *De Nativitate*, 13, 2.   [3] Lamy, 1, 153, 11ff.

Christ could enter Sheol and thus redeem Eve, and so once more Mary has her—indirect—share in the redemption of the world, extending even to Sheol, the underworld of the dead.

This association of the Mother with her Son in his redemptive work becomes most strikingly evident in Ephraem's treatment of Mary's share in the Eucharist, because for him the eucharistic body of Christ is identical with his human body taken from Mary. Thus he says in *De Azymis*, 6, 7,[1] again using the Eve–Mary opposition: "Mary gave us the living Bread instead of the bread of trouble, which Eve gave", and in the *Nisibene Hymns*: "And he took and broke a bread, another, unique one, the symbol of that body, the unique one, from Mary" (46, 11), and in his poems on the Crucifixion (3, 9),[2] he calls the Eucharist "Bread from the praised sheaf [i.e., Mary]" and "grape from Mary". Thus Mary is never absent from Ephraem's thought about Christ; she is inseparable from his work; by her prayers souls are preserved from evil.[3] And so the poet places a song of praise in her mouth: "More than all those who were cured he has rejoiced me; for I conceived him. / More than all those he raised up he raised me; for I gave birth to him. / I shall enter his paradise of life / And where Eve was defeated, I will praise him. / For I pleased him above all created women, / That I should become his mother; because he wanted it / And he my child, because such was his will."[4]

THE CAPPADOCIANS[5]

In the Greek-speaking East the three great Cappadocians, Basil of Caesarea (d. 379), the organizer and legislator of monastic life, his intimate friend Gregory of Nazianzus (d. c. 390), the poet and "theologian", and Basil's brother, the

---

[1] Lamy, 1, 593, 9.   [2] Lamy, 1, 659, 9ff.   [3] Lamy, 3, 238.
[4] *Nativ.*, 2, 7 (*ER*, 3, 600).
[5] A detailed monograph by G. Söll, "Die Mariologie der Kappadozier im Lichte der Dogmengeschichte", in *TQ*, 31 (1951).

mystically-minded Gregory of Nyssa (d. 394) were among the most influential teachers and preachers of the latter half of the fourth century.[1] Basil, too, teaches the virginity *in partu* in his homilies on the Creation, called the *Hexaemeron*: "The Virgin brings forth while her virginity is preserved undefiled",[2] and proves its possibility by a story of birds producing fertile eggs without copulating. In his sermon on the birth of Christ, now generally accepted as genuine, he repeats Origen's story that Zachariah had been killed between the altar and the Temple because he let Mary stand among the virgins.[3] In the same sermon he discusses Mary's betrothal to Joseph, giving as reasons for it that "virginity should be honoured, but marriage not despised", that Joseph should witness to her purity and, following Ignatius of Antioch, that her pregnancy should be hidden from the devil.[4] He then considers Isa. 7.14 and the *'almah* question. According to Basil, too, this childbearing could not be a "sign" unless *'almah* meant "virgin", and he quotes Deut. 22.25–8 in support of this translation.[5] He goes on to interpret Matt. 1.25, the "till" in the passage being frequently adduced by heretics to mean that later Joseph did "know" Mary. But, says Basil, "lovers of Christ" (*philochristoi*) refuse to accept such an exegesis, but hold that "the Theotokos never ceased to be a virgin".[6] He also discusses the term "firstborn" and states that this does not mean that other children must follow; thus he, like most other orthodox Fathers of this time, defends Mary's perpetual virginity. He does not, however, teach her absolute spiritual perfection, but accepts Origen's exegesis of the sword of Simeon's prophecy as referring to a doubt under the Cross, "when she sees what is happening and hears the

---

[1] For a brief analysis of the Marian doctrines of the divine maternity, virginity, sanctity and queenship see Sergius S. Fedyniak, *Mariologia apud Patres Orientales* (1958).

[2] 8, 6 (*PG*, 29, 180B). [3] 5 (*PG*, 31, 1469A).
[4] 3 (*PG*, 31, 1464B). [5] *PG*, 31, 1465B, C.
[6] 5 (*PG*, 1468B).

voices".[1] The commentary on Isaiah attributed to Basil is of doubtful authorship, but certainly belongs to our period. It gives the same interpretation of '*almah* as the homily with the quotation of the Deuteronomy passage.[2] It also calls Mary "prophetess" on account of the *Magnificat*,[3] and has the parallel between the earth from which Adam was taken and the "virginal womb" from which Christ took his body.[4]

Basil's friend Gregory of Nazianzus has only few references to Mary, but they are very significant indeed. He teaches the virginity *in partu*, as a matter of course,[5] and frequently calls her Theotokos[6] and "undefiled" (*achrantos*; *Carm.*, 1, 2, 1, 198): for "Christ was born from the Virgin, who had been purified before by the Spirit both in soul and body".[7] This view, that Mary was purified before the birth of Jesus, rules out any idea of her immaculate conception; it will be found also in many later Fathers and right into the Middle Ages. His most telling statement occurs in a letter directed against the heresy of Apollinarius, who, in his effort to uphold the full divinity of Christ against the Arians, taught that Christ did not take real flesh from Mary, but flowed through her as through a channel. Against him Gregory affirms that "If anyone does not accept the holy Mary as Theotokos, he is without the Godhead."[8] Here we have, as far as can be ascertained for the first time, a Mariological statement as a test of orthodoxy. Another Marian passage is of interest for belief in the efficacy of her intercession; in *Oratio XXIV*, 11 Gregory mentions a prayer of a virgin tempted by the devil to "the Virgin Mary, imploring her to help a virgin in danger".[9]

But the Cappadocian who had most to say about the Theotokos was Gregory of Nyssa, the mystical theologian. He, too, strenuously opposed Apollinarius and stressed the

---

[1] *Epistle* 260, 9 (*PG* 32,965C–968A). [2] No. 201 (*PG*, 30, 464B, C).
[3] No. 208 (*PG*, 30, 477B). [4] No. 201 (*PG*, 30, 465A).
[5] *Carmina* 2, 2, 7 (*PG*, 37, 1565A). [6] e.g., *Oratio XXIX*, 4 (*PG*, 26, 80A).
[7] *Or. XLV*, 9 (*PG*, 36, 633D). [8] *Ep.* 101 (*PG*, 37, 177C).
[9] *PG*, 35, 1181A.

reality of Mary's motherhood; saying that Christ "built for himself a house, forming the earth from the Virgin [note the parallel of Adam formed from the earth], through which he was mingled with the humanity";[1] ". . . for the man [i.e., Christ] was not before the Virgin"—as Apollinarius had taught.[2]

As an exegete well versed in the allegorical interpretation of the Alexandrian school, he applied many Old-Testament texts to Mary. In his collection of "Testimonies Against the Jews" he not only includes the obvious Isaiah prophecy, but also an unidentified passage:' 'The heifer [or 'the young girl', either translation is possible] has given birth and has not given birth" (cf. Clement of Alexandria, p. 43) and the Ezekiel text of the closed door (44.1) constantly adduced by later theologians, as well as Isaiah 8.3: "And I went to the prophetess: and she conceived, and bore a son"—Mary being so frequently called a prophetess.[3] He also sees a type of Mary in Moses' sister—no doubt on account of the identity of names—and regards the tympanum she played after the crossing of the Red Sea as a type of her virginity: "For as the tympanum, from which all moisture has been removed so that it is exceedingly dry, gives out a loud noise, so also is virginity, which receives no life-giving moisture, illustrious and renowned."[4]

Another Old-Testament type of Mary's virginity *in partu* which was to play as important a part as the "closed door" of Ezekiel, is the burning bush which Moses saw on Mount Horeb. Other theologians, including the Jew Philo and Clement of Alexandria, had seen in it a manifestation of the Logos. Like Ephraem, Gregory applies the story to "the mystery of the Virgin. For from her did the light of the Godhead shine on the life of man through the birth and preserved incorrupt the kindled bush, because the flower of the virginity was not made

[1] *Contra Apollinarem*, 9 (*PG*, 45, 1141).   [2] *Cont. Apoll.*, 53 (*PG*, 45, 1253B).
[3] *Testimonia Contra Judaeos*, 3 (*PG*, 46, 208f.).   [4] *De Virginitate*, 19.

to wither by the childbirth."[1] This theme is further elaborated
in the Sermon on the Nativity of Christ, which is now considered authentic by scholars like Bardenhewer and Jaeger.
"O the wonder!" Gregory exclaims: "The Virgin becomes
mother and remains virgin . . . the virginity does not prevent
the childbirth, nor does the childbirth destroy the virginity.
For it was fitting that he who entered human life that it might
have incorruption, should let incorruption begin with her
who ministered to his birth. For the unmarried woman is
usually called incorrupt (*aphthoros*); this seems to me to have
been foreshadowed by the theophany of Moses . . . when the
fire kindled the bush, and the bush did not wither . . . as there
the bush is kindled but not burned, so also here the Virgin
brings forth the light, but is not corrupted."[2] And he, too,
quotes the story of Zachariah, who let Mary stand among the
virgins in the Temple, which he does not consider apocryphal,
no doubt because he had found it in Origen, whom he greatly
admired. The tale of Mary's upbringing in the Temple, on
the other hand, he definitely calls "apocryphal".[3] Another
type of Mary's virginity, also taken from the events of Exodus,
is the manna that appeared on· the unploughed earth.[4]
Indeed, he insists on the virginity *in partu* more strongly than
any of his contemporaries, for he discusses it at length also
in the thirteenth of his homilies on the Canticle, where he
says that only Christ's birth was "without childbirth, just as
the construction [*systasis*] of his body came to pass without
marriage. For the bringing forth without corruption [scil.,
of virginity] and intercourse cannot properly be called childbirth . . . But just as the Son was given to us without a
father; so also the Child was brought forth without childbirth. For just as the Virgin did not know how the God-
receiving body was put together in her body, so she also did

[1] *Vita Mosis*, 2, 21 (*PG*, 44, 332D).   [2] *PG*, 46, 1136A, B.
[3] *On the Birth of Christ* (*PG*, 46, 1136A–1140B).
[4] *Vita Mosis* 2, 139 (*PG*, 44, 368C).

not perceive the childbirth, as the prophecy about her who brought forth without labour testifies [Isa. 66.7]."[1]

He refers to her perpetual virginity in several other places, delights in simply calling her "the Virgin", "undefiled" (*amiantos*, e.g., *Cont. Apoll.*, 6 (*PG*, 45, 1136; 54, 1256A)), though not in the sense of our "immaculate", as he applies the same term to the perfect soul described in the Canticle.[2]

Gregory, too, has the Mary–Eve theme, giving it yet a new nuance: as Eve had "introduced death through her sin and was condemned to give birth in sorrow and pain, it was fitting that the Mother of life should begin her pregnancy with joy and complete her giving birth in joy".[3] He contrasts the words of the curse on Eve with the words of blessing spoken to Mary, and again, Eve's pain in childbirth with Mary's joy.[4] Gregory seems to be the first Father to infer from Mary's words, "How shall this be done, because I know not man?", that she had made a promise of virginity: "Because she was bound to preserve her flesh, which was consecrated to God, untouched like a sacred offering, therefore she says . . . it is impossible for me to know a man."[5] He further calls Mary the "root of joy" in an interesting passage on the Resurrection, where he asserts that the "other Mary" of Matt. 28.1, who came to the tomb with Mary Magdalen on Easter morning, must have been the Theotokos: "For it was fitting that she, who was not absent from the Passion, but, as John tells us, stood beside the Cross, should also proclaim the good news of joy, as she herself is the root of joy."[6] He further explains that the person who is called Mary, the mother of James and Joseph, by the other Evangelists (Matt. 27.56) is actually the Mother of Christ, James and Joseph being sons of Joseph by a

---

[1] *PG*, 44, 1053A, B.   [2] *Hom. 9* (*PG*, 44, 953C).
[3] *Hom. 13 on the Canticle* (*PG*, 44, 1053B); cf. also *Virg.*, 13.
[4] *On the Birth of Christ* (*PG*, 46, 1140C).
[5] *Birth of Christ* (*PG*, 46, 1140D–1141A).
[6] *De Resurrectione*, 2 (*PG* 46, 633A, B).

former marriage; but the Evangelists pretended they were sons of Mary, because if the Jews had known that she was a virgin they might have killed her[1]—a somewhat roundabout explanation, which attempts to account for the discrepancies between the Synoptics and St. John and besides expresses the Christian feeling, which we shall also meet later, that Mary, who was present at the Passion, could not have been absent from the Resurrection. The same identification, together with the "sword of doubt", occurs in Ephraem's *Diatessaron*, but, as his editor, L. Leloir,[2] points out, these passages are almost certainly interpolations. They show, however, that, his identification was current at the time.

GREEK CONTEMPORARIES OF THE CAPPADOCIANS

CYRIL OF JERUSALEM

The Mariology of the contemporaries of the three great Cappadocians presents the same picture. Cyril of Jerusalem (d. 386) calls Mary Theotokos in his sole surviving major work, the *Catecheses* (ch. 10, 19), instructions to catechumens delivered mostly in the Great Church, the martyry built on Calvary at Jerusalem in 348 or 350. He also applies to her the prophecy of Mic. 5.3: "Therefore will he give them up even till the time wherein she that travaileth shall bring forth", and he varies the parallelism Eve-Mary to that of Mary and the side of Adam, saying that Christ was born from the Virgin just as Eve came forth from the side of Adam,[3] i.e., not in the normal course of nature. In one of the doubtful "mystagogical" catecheses (No. 26), Mary is called "bride", but in a general sense, as Israel was the bride of Yahweh. In a similar sense the word occurs also in many later Greek authors.

[1] *De Res.*, 2 (*PG*, 648A).
[2] *Corpus Scriptorum Christianorum Orientalium, Script. Armen.*, 1, Latin trans., 2, 17.
[3] *Cat.*, 12, 29.

AMPHILOCHIUS

Amphilochius, Bishop of Iconium (d. after 394), who was a friend of the Cappadocians and a cousin of Gregory of Nazianzus, reflects their teaching. Very little has remained of his works, but enough to show that he had an intense devotion to the Mother of God. "O Mary, O Mary", he exclaims in his sermon on the birth of Christ, "You who possess the Maker of all things as your firstborn".[1] He, too, quotes Isa. 7.14: "The incorrupt virgin shall bring forth bodily the incorrupt light",[2] and he exalts her purity, calling her *achrantos*, undefiled.[3] He opposes her to Eve in a passage of the same sermon, where he says that, as the world once fell under the reign of sin through a virgin, so now "the world is freed through a virgin".[4] He defends her virginity *in partu* against those who quote Exod. 13.2 ("Sanctify unto me every firstborn that openeth the womb"), quoting in his turn Ezek. 44.2, "This gate shall be shut. It shall not be opened and no man shall pass through it: because the Lord the God of Israel hath entered in by it"—a passage which in its original context refers to the gate of the Temple. Interpreting it of the virginity *in partu*, Amphilochius explains: "As regards the virginal nature, the virginal gates were not at all opened; as regards the power of the Lord who was born, nothing is closed to the Lord."[5]

DIDYMUS

The blind layman Didymus, famous teacher and head of the catechetical school of Alexandria (d. c. 398), upheld the tradition of his city in his devotion to Mary; most of his

---

[1] *Nativ.*, 4 (*PG*, 39, 41A).   [2] *Nativ.*, 2 (*PG*, 39, 37D).
[3] *Nativ.*, 1 (*PG*, 39, 37A).   [4] *Nativ.*, 4 (*PG*, 39, 41A).
[5] *Oratio in Hypapanten*, 3 (*PG*, 39, 49A). J. Galot, in his aforementioned article on Mary's virginity (p. 460), explains the passage as denying the virginity *in partu*, but it seems that it can at best be said to be ambiguous.

writings, too, are lost. In his major surviving work *On the Trinity* he has not much opportunity for speaking of her, but whenever he does mention her, it is in terms of intense veneration. It goes without saying that he calls her Theotokos[1] and ever-virgin.[2] He affirms her virginity *in partu*,[3] and he strenuously opposes those who maintain that after the birth of Christ she had marital relations with Joseph: "For the most glorious Mary, more honourable than any other, was never married to anyone, nor ever became the mother of another; but she remained after her childbirth for ever an undefiled virgin."[4]

EPIPHANIUS

The Father who made some of the most important contributions to Mariology about this time was Epiphanius, Bishop of Salamis (d. 403). He was an ardent defender of the Nicene faith, a violent opponent of the teaching of Origen, an austere ascetic who founded a monastery at Eleutheropolis and governed it for thirty years, before the bishops of Cyprus elected him metropolitan of the island in 367. His principal work is the *Panarion* ("Medicine Box"), generally known as the "Refutation of all Heresies" (written in 374–7), in which he described and refuted no fewer than eighty heresies known to him. His teaching on Mary is chiefly developed in his refutation of two diametrically opposed heresies, those of the Antidicomarianites (Opponents of Mary) (heresy 78), and Collyridians (heresy 79). The former were a sect flourishing especially in Arabia, who "dared to say that Holy Mary had intercourse with a man, that is to say Joseph, after the birth of Christ".[5] But Mary was *aeiparthenos*, ever-virgin;[6] indeed, whoever has mentioned the name of Mary and not at once added "the Virgin"?[7] Nevertheless, he does not

---

[1] *Trin.*, 1, 31 (*PG*, 39, 421B).   [2] *Trin.*, 1, 27 (*PG*, 39, 404B).
[3] *Trin.*, 3, 2, 20.   [4] *Trin.*, 3, 4 (*PG*, 832D).
[5] *Pan.*, 78, 1.   [6] 78, 5.   [7] 78, 6.

teach the virginity *in partu*, but says expressly that "only the
Only-Begotten opened the virginal womb".[1] According to
Epiphanius, reproducing the traditions that have already been
discussed, Joseph was a widower, given her for her protection,
not for marital intercourse. He was more than eighty years at
the time of his marriage to Mary and had six children from a
former marriage, the "brethren of the Lord".[2] Epiphanius
proves that Mary could not have had any children by Joseph
from the fact that Christ recommended her to John, not to his
"brethren".[3] He discusses various passages, such as the
"before they came together" of Matt. 1.18, which, he states
against the heretics, does not mean that they came together
afterwards.[4] In support of this Epiphanius adduces the fable,
known already to Herodotus,[5] that the lioness gives birth only
once; so it is also in the case of the "Lion of Juda".[6] Indeed,
it is quite impossible to believe that after the divine childbirth
Mary should have had intercourse with a man,[7] and in the
Creed Epiphanius cites in another work of his, the *An-
coratus*,[8] it is stated explicitly that Christ was born from Holy
Mary, ever-virgin, who is herself the fount and origin of
virginity.[9] Having defended Mary's perpetual virginity
against her opponents, Epiphanius concludes with words
containing what has become a principle of Catholic Mariology:
"He who honours the Lord honours also the holy [scil.
'vessel'='Mary']; he who dishonours the holy vessel, also
dishonours his Lord. Let Mary be by herself the holy
virgin, the holy vessel."[10] Epiphanius, too, has the parallelism
of Eve and Mary—which was a commonplace of Eastern
Mariology. For him not Eve, but Mary, is truly the "mother
of the living", and, like Ephraem, he compares the "material
garments woven by the first clever Eve" with the "garment of
incorruptibility" which we owe to the childbirth of Mary.
"For Eve became the occasion of death for men . . . but

---

[1] 77, 8.   [2] 78, 7.   [3] 78, 10.   [4] 78, 17.   [5] 3, 108.   [6] *Pan.*, 78, 12.
[7] 78, 12.   [8] 119 (120) (*GCS*, p. 148, 12).   [9] 78, 10.   [10] 78, 21.

Mary the occasion of life", and whereas the virgin Eve
transgressed and disobeyed, "through the Virgin [Mary]
came the obedience of grace."[1]

So far Epiphanius sums up the eastern tradition. Where he
seems to give something new—at least something not
mentioned in any of the extant works of the Fathers preceding
him—is in his ideas about the death of Mary. In 78, 23 he
suggests that she may have suffered martyrdom. This is his
interpretation of the "sword" mentioned in Simeon's
prophecy, probably directed against the theory that it referred
to a doubt arising in her heart under the Cross, first propounded by Origen, whom Epiphanius regarded as the arch-
heretic. In an earlier paragraph of the same section,[2] however,
he voices another opinion. After first stating that Scripture
tells us nothing at all about Mary's death, he suggests
that this silence may be due to "the exceeding great marvel, so
that the mind of men should not be perplexed. For I do not
dare to say it, but thinking about it preserve silence." He then
quotes the prophecy of the Woman of the Apocalypse, to
whom were given "two wings of a great eagle, that she might
fly into the desert" (Apoc. 12.14): "Perhaps this may have
been fulfilled in her." This seems the earliest identification
of Mary with this Woman. Nevertheless, he will neither
affirm nor deny Mary's death.[3]

So Epiphanius becomes our first witness to the idea of
Mary's bodily assumption into heaven, propounded, it is
true, very diffidently, but evidently reflecting a line of thought
that stems from intense devotion and much reflection on
biblical passages that might serve to lighten up the mystery of
the Theotokos. Now he, the vigorous defender of the sanctity
of the Ever-Virgin, had also to cope with another heresy,
which he describes in the following chapter of his treatise.
This deals with the Collyridians, a sect, consisting mostly of
women, which flourished in Thracia and Upper Scythia and

[1] 78, 18.   [2] 78, 11.   [3] 78, 11.

was evidently influenced by old pagan customs. "Certain women", he writes, "adorn a chair or a square throne, spread a linen cloth over it, and on a certain day of the year place bread on it and offer it in the name of Mary, and all partake of this bread"—surely an echo of the worship of the Great Mother. He first refutes this idea on the ground that no woman can exercise priestly functions, not even Mary herself.[1] Then he makes a very clear distinction between the worship we are bound to offer to God and the veneration which is due to Mary, a distinction on which the Church has insisted through the ages. He writes: "Now the body of Mary was indeed holy, but it was not God; the Virgin was indeed a virgin and revered, but she was not given us for worship, but herself worshipped him who was born in the flesh from her."[2] In this context he quotes John 2.4, where Christ calls Mary "Woman", saying that he does so that people may not think her "something superior" to men: "Honour Mary, but let the Father, the Son and the Holy Spirit be worshipped, but let no one worship Mary . . . even though Mary is most beautiful and holy and venerable, yet she is not to be worshipped."[3] He had already said, similarly, at the end of the previous chapter on the Antidicomarianites: "It is not right to honour the saints beyond their due . . . for Mary is not God, nor does she have a body from heaven."[4]

Thus in dealing with these two opposing heresies Epiphanius presents already a well-balanced teaching on the Theotokos, of whom he speaks in the highest terms, while neatly distinguishing between the veneration due to her and the worship given only to God himself; and, while extolling her perfect purity, he already likens her to the Woman of the Apocalypse—in these early centuries generally regarded only as the Church—and speculates on the manner of her death.

[1] 79, 1. [2] 79, 4. [3] 79, 7. [4] 78, 23 (24).

JOHN CHRYSOSTOM

The Fathers of the fourth century became increasingly aware of the glory of the Theotokos and lost no opportunity to praise her. But into this swelling chorus now breaks a dissentient voice—and it is the voice of a very great preacher and theologian, John, Patriarch of Constantinople, whom the Church herself calls Chrysostom, the Golden-Mouthed. To explain this "odd man out", we must say a little more about the school of thought he represents. So far we have dealt either with exponents of Alexandrian theology or with, as it were, "uncommitted" Fathers. Now we come into contact with the so-called Antiochene exegetical school.

The Fathers of the Alexandrian school emphasized the divinity of Christ and the right of his Mother to be called Theotokos; moreover, they favoured an allegorical or "mystical" interpretation of Scripture which they often carried to inordinate lengths. In the exegetical school of Antioch, on the other hand, which entered on its greatest period with Diodore of Tarsus, in the second half of the fourth century, Scripture was interpreted more soberly, in the strictly "literal" sense; Christ's humanity was stressed more than his divinity, and Mary was hardly ever called Theotokos. Now Chrysostom was a pupil of Diodore, imbued with his views, and moreover a moralist rather than a speculative theologian, a great preacher whose main object was to train his flock in the life of Christian virtue. To drive home this teaching he used scriptural illustrations wherever he found them—and this would partly explain the extraordinary statements he made about Mary, all the more extraordinary as, unlike some other Fathers, he had no doubts at all about her perpetual virginity. This point he discusses in his homilies on Matthew,[1] where he says that the text "before they came together" does not mean that they did so afterwards, and also adduces the fact

[1] Montfaucon edition, vol. 7.

that on the Cross Jesus recommended his mother to John.[1] In the same context he quotes Isa. 7.14, defending the translation of *'almah* as *parthenos* = virgin against *neanis* = young girl.[2] In his second homily on the Change of Names (Saul into Paul) he compares her with the virgin earth of Eden: "Therefore he called it Eden, which is virgin earth; for this virgin [scil., the earth of paradise] was the type of that virgin [scil., Mary]. Just as this earth, though it had not received seed, brought forth for us the Garden of Paradise; so also that virgin, though she had not received the seed of a man, brought forth for us Christ."[3] He also uses the traditional parallelism Eve–Mary: "A virgin [Eve] has cast us out from paradise, through a virgin [Mary] we have found eternal life",[4] and this occurs again in his second Easter homily where he says that, as once a virgin had become the symbol of our defeat, so again in Mary a virgin became the partial cause of our victory.[5] Thus on Mary's virginity and her relation to her antitype, Eve, he is in line with his non-Antiochene contemporaries. He parts company with them only when it comes to giving her the title "Theotokos" and acknowledging her outstanding sanctity. Indeed, he stresses her supposed faults and imperfections, the evidence for which he finds mainly in the two New-Testament accounts of the visit to Christ of her and his "brethren" (Matt. 12.46–50 and the parallel passage in Mark 3.31–5) and of her intervention at the wedding of Cana. In his exegesis of both passages Chrysostom accuses Mary of unbelief and vainglory.

In his homilies on Matthew[6] he says that Christ spoke to her on this occasion "rather mildly and pleasantly" only because she was his mother; he did not say, as he well might have done, "This is not my mother, nor these my brethren, because they do not do my will"; and in those on John,[7]

---

[1] *Hom.*, 5, 3 (77B, C).   [2] 5, 2 (75B).

[3] *Hom.*, 2, 3 (Montfaucon ed., vol. 3, 113A, B).

[4] *Expositio VII in Ps. XLIV* (vol. 5, 171D).   [5] vol. 3, 752C.

[6] 44 (45), 2 (Mont. 7, 469B).   [7] 21, 2 (Mont., 8 123A).

he asserts that his mother and his brethren "had not yet the right view of him; but because she had borne him, she regarded him after the fashion of mothers, as if she could order him about." In the course of his sermon the saint is actually growing annoyed with her; how dared she demand that he should come out and speak to her, seeing he was teaching the people? And so he spoke those words, "Who is my mother and my brethren?" not so as to put her to shame, but trying to give her a worthier opinion of her Son, because "she did not cease to think little of him . . . but thought herself everywhere worthy of the first place, because she was his mother",[1] for she did not know the mystery of his Godhead.[2] And so Christ had to reprove her also at Cana; for when she said "They have no wine", ". . . she wanted to confer a favour on the others, and render herself more illustrious through her Son."[3]

Surprisingly enough, Chrysostom finds fault with her even in his exegesis of the Annunciation story—but for the authentication of the message she might have killed herself in despair when she heard that she was going to have a son![4]

Apparently such preaching did not disturb his audiences at Antioch and later at Constantinople—but it would hardly have been possible at Alexandria or in Cappadocia. Despite her miraculous childbearing and her place in the plan of redemption as the counterpart of Eve, the greatest exponent of the Antiochene school nevertheless saw her above all as quite an ordinary woman, with typically feminine weaknesses which deserved to be reproved by her divine Son. He evidently wanted to teach the faithful that if even the dignity of Mary's motherhood did not prevent her from committing faults and being reproved for them, they themselves could even less expect to be saved without a morally blameless life.

---

[1] Mont., 123B.   [2] *Expositio I in Ps. XLIX* (Mont., 225C).
[3] *Hom.*, 21, 2 on John (8, 122C, D).   [4] *Hom.*, 4, 4, 5, on Matthew.

SEVERIAN OF GABALA

Severian of Gabala (d. after 408) was an opponent of Chrysostom, though he, too, belonged to the Antiochene school. In his Homily 6, 10 on the creation of the world[1] he opposed Mary, as "the mother of salvation", to Eve, but this can hardly be taken to be a Mariological interpretation of Gen. 3.15, as is sometimes affirmed, since the Greek Fathers did not read the feminine in their translation of the passage. The question is discussed by E. J. Soares,[2] who also interprets a Latin translation of a passage from Severian's Armenian sermons as teaching that Mary offered Christ on Golgotha: "There [scil., 'in paradise'] the woman, by whom sin entered into the world; here the Virgin who heard, 'Behold thy Mother!'"[3] But it is scarcely possible to read such a meaning into the text, which is a simple Eve–Mary parallelism such as we have frequently met before, in which there is no word of Mary "offering" Christ.

THE THREE GREAT LATIN DOCTORS: AMBROSE

While opinions were thus divided in the East, the West produced a Doctor of the Church who gave its Mariology its decisive direction.[4] Ambrose (339–97), a Roman *consularis* and legal expert, became Bishop of Milan in 374 only eight days after his baptism, for he was elected against his will while still a catechumen trying to mediate between Catholics and Arians, who were struggling for the possession of this important see. He devoted the first years of his episcopate to an intensive study of the Greek Fathers, and so we shall find in his Mariology largely the same themes as in them, but without

[1] *PG*, 56, 498, *int. opp. Chrys.*
[2] "Severianus of Gabala and the Protoevangelium", in *MM*, 15 (1953), pp. 401–11.
[3] *MM*, 15, p. 407.
[4] Cf. C. W. Neumann, *The Virgin Mary in the Works of Saint Ambrose* (1962), a work which discusses mostly her virginity.

4+

their more questionable speculations. He had to develop his teaching in opposition to two dangerous popular movements: Arianism, which denied the full divinity of Christ, and the pagan worship of Kybele, the *Magna Mater*. The former had gained a great victory when the Arian Goths invaded the Roman Empire after their victory in the Battle of Adrianople (378), whilst devotion to the Mother Goddess was still alive among the populace of the Italian cities.

Thus Ambrose places his Mariology firmly within the Christological context. In his treatise on the Patriarchs he writes: "As we understand that [divine] generation from the Father, thus, to complete our faith, we should also understand his [human] birth from Mary." (Ch. 51.) The eternal generation of the Son in the bosom of the Father *and* his human birth from Mary together constitute the central Christian mystery of the Incarnation; one must be complemented by the other. "For", Ambrose insists, "it was not that one person was from the Father, another from Mary, but he who was from the Father took flesh from the Virgin; he took the physical disposition from his mother so that he might adopt our infirmities."[1] "For the Virgin had something of her own which she transmitted; the mother did not give [him] something foreign [to her], but she conferred on him her own from her own flesh, indeed in an unusual way, but by a normal function. For the Virgin had flesh, which she conferred on the fruit."[2] Thus Mary's motherhood was completely real; Christ received from her her own flesh; and because—as against the Arians—he also was God, generated from the Father, she must be the Mother of God.

But while from the time of Origen the Greeks had freely used the term, *Theotokos*, Ambrose hardly ever uses its Latin equivalent, *Mater Dei*;[3] the danger of misunderstanding was

[1] *Explanatio in Psalm. LXI*, 5.
[2] *De Incarnationis Dominicae Sacramento*, 104.
[3] *Hexameron*, 5, 65; *De Virginibus*, 2, 7.

too great while the cult of Kybele was still flourishing. He makes it quite clear, however, that she is in fact the Mother of God, because she "had given birth to God".[1] "God was born from the Virgin"[2] and again in his Christmas hymn, still sung at Vespers, which he taught his people to strengthen their faith in the struggle against Arianism: "Come, Redeemer of the nations, show forth the birth of the Virgin; let all the world marvel, such a birth befitted God." Thus the Virgin Birth is closely related to the divinity of Christ. In his struggle with Arianism he uses Isa. 7.14 as a proof of Christ's Godhead, and he quotes this verse, asking: "Can we then not see the sign of his divinity?"[3] And he takes over the fable of the vulture's virginal birth from the Greeks.[4]

For Ambrose the Virgin Birth includes the virginity *in partu*, at least during and after his controversy with the apostate Milanese monk Jovinian; for in his commentary on Luke (2.57) he still wrote that Christ "opened his mother's womb".[5] But when he had to defend her virginity *post partum* against Jovinian and also against Bishop Bonosus of Sardica, who affirmed that Mary had other children after giving birth to Jesus, he changed his view. The reason why they denied Mary's perpetual virginity was their opposition to the celibate life as such, whose pattern and ideal was Mary. Against them Ambrose now contends that Mary's virginity *in partu* and *post partum* is part of the authoritative doctrine of the Church from New-Testament times onwards. He writes: "Christ . . . however, being God, came to earth in an unusual way, as . . .

---

[1] *Expositio in Lucam*, 10, 130.   [2] *De Institutione Virginis*, 104.
[3] *De Fide*, 5, 232; also *De Inst. Virg.*, 33.   [4] *Hexameron*, 5, 65.
[5] According to Jouassard (*Maria*, 1, p. 109), under the influence of Origen. In a painstaking analysis Neumann, however, considers that the passage does not refer to the birth of Christ, but to Mary as "a spouse at conception", and that Ambrose here quietly corrects Origen. (*The Virgin Mary*, p. 133.) From this he concludes that Ambrose regarded Mary not only as the Mother, but as the Spouse of Christ, "though", he admits, "Ambrose does not say so"—an exegesis which seems to me to interpret the thought of Ambrose from the point of view of a later age. (*The Virgin Mary*, p. 136.)

he was born from the immaculate Virgin . . . But they say perversely: she conceived as a virgin, but she did not give birth as a virgin. So a virgin could conceive, but a virgin could not give birth, though the conception always precedes and the birth follows? But if they will not believe the teaching of the priests, they should believe the sayings of Christ, they should believe the admonitions of the angels who say: 'No word shall be impossible with God.' (Luke 1.37.) They should believe the Apostles' Creed, which the Roman Church always guards and preserves . . . This is the Virgin who has conceived in the womb, the Virgin, who has brought forth her Son. For thus it is written: 'Behold, a virgin shall conceive and bear a son'; for he says not only that a virgin shall conceive, but also that a virgin shall bring forth. For which is the gate of the sanctuary, that outer gate looking towards the east, which remains shut? [Ezek. 44.1f.] . . . Is not this gate Mary, through whom the Saviour entered this world . . . who conceived and brought forth as a virgin?"[1]

Thus, under pressure from Jovinian and his followers, Ambrose applies the texts usually taken to indicate only the virginal conception of Christ also to the very birth itself.[2] He is, naturally, an indefatigable defender also of Mary's virginity *post partum*, which he had already taught before the controversy broke out. In his commentary on St. Luke and in one of his treatises on virginity he explains the various disputed texts such as " . . . before they came together" (Matt. 1.18) and, "He knew her not till she brought forth" (Matt. 1.25),[3] following his Greek predecessors in adducing the fact of her being entrusted to St. John as proof of her continued virginity.[4] Indeed, he asks indignantly: "Would the Lord Jesus have chosen for his mother a woman who would defile

---

[1] *Epistle 42*, 4–6.
[2] Cf. also *De Inst. Virg.*, 52f., *Explanatio in Ps. XLV*, 18, and frequently elsewhere.
[3] *Exp. in Luc.*, 2, 6; *De Inst. Virg.*, 35ff.   [4] *Exp. in Luc.*, 10, 130.

the heavenly chamber with the seed of a man, that is to say, one incapable of preserving her virginal chastity intact?"[1] Quite the contrary: "For how could her integrity be taken from Mary, who, when even the Apostles were fleeing, did not fear the torments but offered herself to the dangers? Indeed, her grace was so great that she did not only preserve the grace of virginity in herself, but bestowed even on those whom she visited the sign of integrity"—for example, on John the Baptist and John the beloved disciple.[2] So her virginal purity, far from being associated with sterility, even overflows on others, for it is so complete that it can reproduce itself. Ambrose sums up his teaching on Mary's virginity in his hymn for Terce, the hour of Christ's crucifixion: "From the sublime summit of his victory he spoke to his Mother: Behold, Mother, thy son: Apostle, behold thy Mother. Thus teaching that the married union only hid the mystery so that the sacred childbearing of the Virgin should not harm respect for the Mother."

The physical purity of Mary is parallelled by her moral integrity. Unlike Chrysostom, he sees no reproof for her in Luke 8.21 ("My mother and my brethren are those who hear the word of God and do it"). "Here the Mother, who is acknowledged even from the Cross, is not denied, as certain heretics say who are laying their snares, only the heavenly commandments are preferred to the physical relationship."[3] Nor does he attribute a doubt to her when she stands under the Cross. For he interprets the sword in the prophecy of Simeon quite differently from Origen and the Greek Fathers following him. In the view of Ambrose this sword is rather Mary's foreknowledge of the Passion, because she is "not ignorant of the heavenly mystery".[4] Quite the contrary:

---

[1] *De Inst. Virg.*, 44. Neumann rightly rejects the view, attributing to Ambrose the idea "that at the time of the Annunciation Mary had already vowed her virginity to God". (*The Virgin Mary*, p. 100.)

[2] *De Inst. Virg.*, 50.   [3] *Exp. in Luc.*, 6, 38.   [4] *Exp. in Luc.*, 2, 61.

"Mary behaved as befitted the Mother of Christ, for while the Apostles had fled she stood before the Cross and looked up full of pity to the wounds of her Son, because she expected not the death of her Son but the salvation of the world."[1] Indeed, the picture he draws of her bears already the features of the medieval *Mater Dolorosa*: "There stood before the Cross his Mother, and while the men were fleeing she stood fearlessly ... She looked with pity on the wounds of her Son, through whom she knew redemption was to come to all. The Mother stood, truly a worthy sight, who did not fear to be killed. The Son hung on the Cross, the Mother offered herself to the persecutors."[2] For Mary is without sin. Comparing her to the "cloud" of Isa. 19.1, he says of her: "He who was incarnate from the Virgin came in a light cloud ... and rightly he called the cloud light, because earthly vices did not burden it: Behold the cloud, on which the Holy Spirit came down."[3] In another context he says that "Christ chose for himself·the vessel in which he was to descend not from this earth but from heaven."[4] For Mary is the first of the redeemed: "When the Lord wanted to redeem the world he began his work with Mary, that she, through whom salvation was prepared for all, should be the first to draw the fruit of salvation from her Son."[5]

Does Ambrose, then, teach the Immaculate Conception? Theologians are divided on this. J. Huhn, in his searching study of the Mariology of the saint,[6] points out that when Ambrose wants to indicate freedom from original sin, as he does for Christ, his language is much more precise. He says of him that "not only had no vices stained him, but no unjust admixture of generation or conception (through which original sin is transmitted) had stained him"[7]—which he

[1] *Exp. in Luc.*, 10, 132.   [2] *De Inst. Virg.*, 49.   [3] *Exp. in Luc.*, 10, 42.
[4] *De Inst. Virg.*, 33.   [5] *Exp. in Luc.*, 2, 17.
[6] *Das Geheimnis der Jungfrau-Mutter Maria nach dem Kirchenvater Ambrosius*, Würzburg (1954).
[7] *De Poenitentia*, 1, 13.

never affirms of Mary. So it is doubtful, indeed, whether he is the first witness to the doctrine of the Immaculate Conception.

Mary, the sinless one, is the counterpart of Eve, for "through a woman came foolishness, through a virgin wisdom",[1] and "through a man and a woman the body [i.e., human nature] was cast out from paradise, through a virgin it was united to God."[2] In his exegesis of Cant. 1.4—"I am black but beautiful"—he writes: "Human nature says: I am black, because I have sinned, beautiful, because Christ loves me; what he had exiled in Eve, he took back from the Virgin, he accepted from Mary."[3] Finally, he equates the two: "Come therefore, Eve, rather Mary, who not only brought us an incitement to virginity, but also gave us God."[4]

Now, by giving us God, Mary gave us redemption. Through the Incarnation, therefore, she is most closely associated with our salvation. Through Mary "salvation was given to all".[5] "The Virgin has given birth to the salvation of the world, the Virgin has brought forth the life of all";[6] through her consent to the angel's message "Mary . . . has worked the salvation of the world, and conceived the redemption of all."[7] Indeed, "She freed John [the Baptist] in the womb, who leapt at the sound of her voice, and the child rejoiced exceedingly, animated by the feeling of devotion even before the breath of life had been infused into him."[8] Thus Mary has a very real part in our salvation; through her consent to the angel and her divine maternity she has co-operated in it—indeed, she has her share in the defeat of the devil, as Ambrose affirms in his funeral oration for Theodosius: "Mary has defeated you [scil., the devil], who gave birth to the victor, who, without her virginity being diminished, brought forth him, who was to defeat you when he was crucified."[9]

[1] *Exp. in Luc.*, 4, 7.
[2] *Ep. LXIII*, 32.
[3] *Exp. in Ps. CXVIII*, 8.
[4] *De Inst. Virg.*, 33.
[5] *Exp. in Luc.*, 2, 17.
[6] *Ep. LXIII*, 33.
[7] *Ep. XLIX*, 2.
[8] *De Inst. Virg.*, 8.
[9] *De Obitu Theodosii*, 44.

For this reason Mary is most intimately associated with the inner life of the redeemed, so that Ambrose can pray: "Adopt [*suscipe*] me in the flesh which fell in Adam. Adopt me, however, not from Sarah [the mother of the Old Covenant], but from Mary, so that it [the flesh][1] might be an incorrupt virgin, virgin by grace free from all stain of sin."[2] The term *suscipe* belongs to the terminology of Roman law, which came quite naturally to Ambrose, the legal expert. It means lifting a new-born child from the ground and so recognizing it and bringing it up as one's own. So Christ is to recognize the Christian as his child, born to him not from Sarah, but from Mary.

But if Mary is intimately associated with our salvation through her childbirth, she took no part in the redemptive work of her Son on the Cross. This idea Ambrose rejects quite decisively. In the same passage from his commentary on Luke quoted above, where he praises Mary for her compassion and fortitude under the Cross, he continues: "She, the royal palace, thought perhaps she might contribute by her own death something to his sacrifice for the people, since she knew the world would be redeemed through the death of her Son. But Jesus had no need of a helper for the redemption of all . . . So he accepted, indeed, the love of the Mother, but did not seek the help of a human being."[3] He insists on this several times, e.g., in *De Institutione Virginis*, 49 and in Epistle 63, 110. Christ alone worked the Redemption by his passion and death; Mary is associated with it only through her motherhood, not through any other personal contribution.

Now, in the theology of Ambrose this motherhood does not extend only to Christ, but also to his whole body, the Church. Indeed, Mary is the "type" of the Church—Ambrose is the first Church Father to state this explicitly: "Rightly is she

---

[1] We follow here the exegesis of Huhn, *Geheimnis*, p. 158.
[2] *Exp. in Ps. CXVIII*, 22, 30.
[3] *Exp. in Luc.*, 10, 132.

[i.e., Mary] betrothed, yet a virgin, because she is the type of the Church, which is immaculate yet married. The virgin [Church] has conceived us by the Spirit, the Virgin brings us forth without pain. And therefore perhaps is the holy Mary married to one [Joseph], but filled with another [the Holy Spirit], because the individual Churches, too, are filled by the Spirit and his grace, but are externally joined to a mortal priest."[1] So everything that is enacted in the Church was first enacted in Mary; Mary is inseparable from the Church and the Church from Mary, for in her womb the mystical body of Christ was formed together with his physical body. Commenting on the verse from the Canticle, "See King Solomon in the diadem wherewith his mother crowned him in the day of his espousals",[2] he writes: "Blessed the mother Jerusalem [i.e., the Church], blessed also the womb of Mary, who crowned so great a Lord. She crowned him when she formed him; she crowned him when she gave birth to him . . . by this very fact that she conceived and gave birth to him, she placed on his head the crown of eternal mercy, that through the faith of believers Christ should become every man's head."[3] Thus, through having borne Christ, Mary stands in a special relationship to all Christians; she is almost indistinguishable from the Church, as in his explanation of Cant. 7.1. "The birth of Christ from the Virgin, or the spread of the Church, has, metaphorically speaking, adorned the neck of the faithful with finely wrought necklaces, but actually with the spiritual signs of true virtue."[4] Thus Ambrose seems to be the first Father to have applied verses from the Canticle not only to the Church but also to Mary, the type of the Church. This becomes even clearer in his interpretation of the following verse from the Canticle: "From that womb of Mary was brought into the world the heap of wheat surrounded by lilies (that is to say, the faithful), when Christ was born from

[1] *Exp. in Luc.*, 2, 7.   [2] 3.11.   [3] *De Inst. Virg.*, 98.
[4] *Exp. in Ps. CXVIII*, 17, 19.
4*

her."[1] And her identification with the Church is completed
under the Cross: "You will be a son of thunder, if you are a
son of the Church. May Christ also say to you from the wood
of the Cross, 'Behold thy mother', may he also say to the
Church, 'Behold thy son'; for then you will begin to be a son
of the Church, when you see Christ victorious on the Cross."[2]

So while giving birth to Christ, Mary at the same time
brings forth the Christians, "the heap of wheat surrounded by
lilies". They were both formed in her womb; and when she
stands under the Cross she actually *is* the Church, because
Christ gives her John for her son, as everyone becomes her
Son when he sees Christ victorious on the Cross, that is, when
he becomes a believer. So Mary is the mother of all Christians
as the Church is our mother; both are, mystically speaking,
one; Mary is the Church in germ, as it were, because when
she conceived Christ she conceived also all who were to be
his own; Mary is the personification of the Church, an
almost heavenly figure, as Ambrose himself said in a passage quoted before: ". . . not from this earth but from
heaven."

But this "heavenliness" does not imply that she was not a
fully human woman—we have seen how careful Ambrose is to
exclude any hint of a "mother goddess"; he only wants to
express her perfect purity. And so for Ambrose, as for
Athanasius before him, she is the image of virtue, the model he
presents to Christian virgins, for, "What is nobler than the
Mother of God? What more glorious than she who was
chosen by the [divine] Glory, what more chaste than she who
brought forth a body without bodily contact? And what shall
I say of her other virtues? She was a virgin not only in body
but also in spirit, whose pure mind had never been spoiled by
any deceit";[3] then follows a description of her virtues, closely
resembling that of St. Athanasius, but without any hint of
imperfection. And he ends his picture of her: "Such was

[1] *De Inst. Virg.*, 94.   [2] *Exp. in Luc.*, 7, 5.   [3] *De Virg.*, 2, 7.

Mary, that the life of this one virgin might be the example of all."[1]

Ambrose also applied Old-Testament passages to Mary to an extent unknown before, and thus set an example which the Church was quick to follow, especially in her liturgy. We have mentioned before the cloud referred to in Isa. 19.1; in another context Ambrose equates this with the cloud that guided the Israelites in the desert (Exod. 13.21): "According to its outer form this cloud did indeed go before the children of Israel; according to its inner meaning, however, it signified the Lord Jesus, who was to come in a light cloud, as says Isaiah, that is, in the Virgin Mary, who was a cloud on account of the inheritance of Eve [this would certainly seem to rule out the Immaculate Conception], but light because of the integrity of her virginity; she was light, because she did not seek to please a man, but the Lord; she was light, because she did not conceive in iniquity, but through the intervention of the Spirit."[2] This "cloud" is a favourite image of Ambrose to which he reverts again and again; in his *Exhortation to Virginity* he says that Mary was called "a cloud, because she bore flesh, light, because she was a virgin, not weighed down by the burdens of marriage" (31); in his *De Institutione Virginis* he exclaims: "O the riches of Mary's virginity! . . . like a cloud she rained the grace of Christ on the earth!" (81.)

Thus this image of the cloud serves to express both her real humanity and her fullness of grace, while the epithet "light"[3] is at times said to indicate her sinlessness, at others her virginity. Another of his favourite symbols of Mary which made its way into the Liturgy[4] is the Rod of Jesse. (Isa. 11.1.) "She is the rod which brings forth the flower,

---

[1] *De Virg.*, 2, 15.   [2] *Exp. in Ps. CXVIII*, 5, 3.
[3] Latin *levis*, which can mean both "light" and "swift"; the latter is the real meaning in this passage, but Ambrose chooses the meaning that is better suited to his purpose.
[4] Still the responsory of Vespers of the Feasts of the Blessed Virgin in the Dominican Rite.

because pure and freely directed to the Lord is her virginity, which is not disturbed by any worldly cares."[1]

As has been seen, Ambrose also used the imagery of the Canticle for his teaching on Mary. "Let him kiss me with the kiss of his mouth" (Cant. 1.1) signifies the grace of the Holy Spirit coming over her at the Annunciation.[2] On "thy name is as oil poured out" (Cant. 1.2) he comments: ". . . with this oil Mary is anointed, she conceived as a virgin and as a virgin brought forth good odour, that is to say the Son of God";[3] and we have already mentioned that he applied Cant. 3.11 to her, "who crowned so great a Lord".

Thus Ambrose sees Mary as the perfect woman, the virginal Mother of God without the slightest stain of (actual) sin, the pattern of virgins, whose figure appears already in the Old Testament, and he cries out in admiration: "Who will not honour the mother of so many virgins? Who will not venerate the house of chastity?"[4] Nevertheless, he is very careful to distinguish between the veneration of the Virgin and the adoration due to God. When defending the divinity of the Holy Spirit against the heretics who denied it he writes: "Without doubt the Holy Spirit, too, must be adored when we adore him, who is born from the Spirit according to the flesh. But let no one apply this to Mary: for Mary was the temple of God, not the God of the temple. And therefore he alone is to be adored, who worked in the temple."[5]

Ambrose may truly be called the father of Western Mariology. He establishes with absolute certainty Mary's perfect physical and moral purity, which is, indeed, he says, necessitated by her divine motherhood, for Christ would not have chosen for his mother a woman defiled by the seed of man. But this motherhood is not confined to the "historical" Christ. Together with him she carried his whole mystical

---

[1] *Exhort. Virginitatis*, 31; cf. also *De Spiritu Sancto*, 2, 38; *Luc.*, 2, 24 and *De Patriarchis*, 19.

[2] *Exp. in Ps. CXVIII*, 1, 16.   [3] *De Virginitate*, 65.   [4] *Exh. virg.*, 27.

[5] *De Spiritu Sancto*, 3, 79f.

body in her womb, and so she is inseparable from his Church. The Old Testament speaks of her as the light, unsullied cloud that rains salvation, and as the woman who crowns the divine King Solomon by giving him her humanity. Yet she is but the vessel, the temple where he reigns; worship belongs to him alone.

JEROME

Jerome (c. 342–420), the slightly younger contemporary of Ambrose, whom he survived for more than twenty years, was above all a biblical scholar, whose Mariology was developed chiefly in his exegetical works and in his controversy with Helvidius. Helvidius was a theologian who undertook to defend the equal value of marriage and virginity against the prevailing teaching of the superiority of the latter. For this purpose he wrote a treatise (which has not survived) in which he declared Mary an example of both, of perfect virginity before the birth of Christ and of married love and motherhood afterwards; for according to him the "brethren of the Lord" were the sons and daughters of Mary and Joseph. Against him Jerome took up his vigorous and, it must be admitted, frequently even vitriolic pen in his short treatise *On the Perpetual Virginity of Mary against Helvidius*.[1] He answers point by point the various scriptural objections produced by Helvidius, such as the "before they came together" (Matt. 1.18), "Take unto thee Mary, thy wife" (Matt. 1.20) and "he knew her not till she brought forth her firstborn son" (Matt. 1.25), arguing from his immense knowledge of the Bible that even on purely linguistic grounds none of these passages affirms that Mary and Joseph lived as man and wife after the birth of Christ. (No. 2ff.) He is, however, silent on one point, despite the affirmations of the Greek Fathers and the teaching of such authorities as Zeno and his contemporary Ambrose in the

[1] *PL*, 23, 183–206, written c. A.D. 383.

West, and that is the virginity *in partu*.[1] Even when commenting on the famous Ezekiel passage of the closed door he avoids any precise statement but writes: "Rightly do some interpret the closed gate by which only the God of Israel enters . . . of the Virgin Mary, who remained a virgin before as well as after the birth . . . after he was born, she remained ever-virgin."[2]

Why does he almost go out of his way so as not to mention that she remained a virgin also during the birth itself? Jerome, as we have said, was a biblical scholar, *the* greatest biblical scholar of antiquity. As such he had no patience with apocryphal tales; and as we have seen, the evidence for the virginity *in partu* does not rest on biblical, but on apocryphal evidence, especially on the so-called Protoevangelium. Thus Jerome writes with all vehemence: "There [at the birth of Christ] was no midwife; no officious females interfered. She [Mary] herself wrapped the Child in swaddling clothes; she herself was both mother and midwife; for 'she brought forth her firstborn son and wrapped him up in swaddling clothes and laid him in a manger'—which sentence refutes the delirious nonsense of the apocrypha, since Mary herself wraps up the Infant."[3] Nevertheless, despite Jerome's rejection of it, the apocryphal story continued to be taken for an authority both in the East and the West.

Another tale from the same source was also rejected by Jerome. That was the legend that Joseph was a widower and the "brethren of the Lord" referred to his sons by a former marriage. "You, Helvidius," writes Jerome, "say that Mary did not remain a virgin: but I make the claim that even Joseph was a virgin through Mary, that the virginal Son was born from a virginal marriage. For if a holy man does not commit fornication, and as it is not written that he had another wife: but that he was rather the guardian than the husband of Mary

---

[1] See also Neumann, *The Virgin Mary in the Works of St. Ambrose*, pp. 150ff.
[2] *Commentary on Ezekiel*, 13, 44, 1ff. (*PL*, 25, 430A).   [3] *Helv.*, 8.

whom he was supposed to have had as a wife: it follows that he, who deserved to be called the father of the Lord, remained a virgin together with Mary."[1] Jerome's opinion has never been accepted in the East, where St. Joseph is still regarded as a widower. It was generally accepted in the West only from the fifteenth century, perhaps because of the growing devotion to St. Joseph which preferred to see him as a virgin.

Other Fathers had affirmed that the fullness of Mary's virginity overflowed, as it were, on St. John the Baptist and John the beloved disciple; Jerome claims—quite reasonably— that it must have overflowed especially on Joseph, now no longer seen as a decrepit old widower, such as the apocryphal story described him, but as Mary's protector and companion, suited both to her age and her purity. But if this was so, who were the "brethren of the Lord"? Here Jerome, too, pro- vided the solution that came to be generally accepted in the West. After a very careful investigation of the exact meaning of the biblical term "brother", Jerome concludes that it has the connotation of "cousin" (*consobrinus*) or "nephew", as Lot is called the brother of Abraham, Jacob the brother of Laban.[2] In his later commentary on Matthew Jerome reverts to the same theme: "Some people assume that the brethren of the Lord are the sons of Joseph by another wife, following the delirious nonsense of the apocrypha, and invent a certain Melcha or Escha. We, however, as we have already said in our treatise against Helvidius, take the brethren of the Lord to have been, not the sons of Joseph, but cousins of the Saviour, the children of Mary, the maternal aunt of the Lord ... For all Scripture shows that cousins are called brethren."[3]

Having disposed of the "delirious nonsense" of the apocrypha, Jerome praises the virginity of Mary in the highest terms—but always carefully circumventing the virginity *in*

[1] *Helv.*, 19.   [2] *Helv.*, 15.   [3] *In Matt.*, 12.50.

partu: "Holy Mary, blessed Mary," he writes in his homily on John 1.1–14, "Mother and Virgin, virgin before the birth, virgin after the birth. I am full of admiration, how the virgin is born from the Virgin, and after the birth of the virgin the mother is still a virgin. Do you want to know how he was born of the Virgin, and after the birth the Mother is still a virgin? The doors were closed and Jesus went in [cf. John 20.19] . . . You do not know how this was done, and you attribute it to the power of God. Attribute it also to the power of God that he was born of the Virgin and that yet the Virgin remained a virgin also after the birth"—and having once more quoted Ezek. 44.2f. he compares the miracle with the resurrection of Christ from the sealed tomb;[1] which, significantly, did not, however, remain closed!

The great biblical scholar naturally finds the figure of Mary in many Old-Testament passages. Several times he discusses the prophecy of Isa. 7.14, giving the term *'almah* a new shade of meaning. For, as he explains in his *Liber Hebraicarum Quaestionum* on Gen. 24.43, "It should be noted that the term *alma* is always used of a virgin, and it has the etymological meaning *apokryphos*, that is to say, hidden . . . Hence *alma*, which is to be translated 'hidden', i.e., a virgin guarded with the utmost care, seems to me an even more laudatory term than simply 'virgin'. For, according to the Apostle, a virgin can be this merely in body, but not in soul. But she who is a hidden virgin [viz., *alma*], has even an increase of virginity, because she is both virgin and hidden." He puts forward the same argument for this meaning of *'almah* in his commentary on Isaiah (7.14) and in his treatise against Jovinian (1, 32), against whom Ambrose, too, had written; the latter obviously took his theme of the "light cloud" of Isa. 19.1 from the commentary of Jerome, who writes briefly: "Some exegetes refer this whole prophecy to the times of the Saviour . . .

[1] *CCSL*, p. 521, 142ff.

because he was carried by a light cloud, that is, the body of the Virgin."[1] Jerome perhaps influenced Ambrose also in his interpretation of the "rod" of Isa. 11.1, which he combined with a passage from the Canticle: "The rod is the Mother of the Lord . . . who is fertile after the manner of the divine unity [i.e., without intercourse]. The virgin flower is Christ, saying, 'I am the flower of the field'." (Cant. 2.1.) And in his treatise against Jovinian he uses the famous passage from the same biblical book—"My sister . . . is a garden enclosed, a fountain sealed up" (Cant. 4.12)—of Mary: "Because it is closed and sealed, it has a likeness to the Mother of the Lord, both mother and virgin. Hence also in the new tomb of the Lord no-one had been laid either before or afterwards. And yet this Ever-Virgin is also the mother of many virgins."[2]

For Jerome, too, was a guide of virgins. In his letter to Laeta on the education of her daughter[3] he applies Ps. 44.14 to Mary (an application which later became a commonplace, through the psalm's being included in the Office of the Blessed Virgin), as an example of virgins: "Let her imitate Mary . . . of whom it is said: 'All the glory of the king's daughter is within'." And in another letter (52, 4) he compares her to Abishag, the young girl who was given to David to warm him in his old age (1 Kings 1.3), because she was a symbol of wisdom, and wisdom, again, was one of the principal Old-Testament types of Mary. (Cf. the later inclusion of Wisdom passages in her office.) The famous obscure text of Jer. 31.22, "A woman shall compass a man", he also interprets as a prophecy about her: "Without the seed of a man . . . the woman shall compass a man in her womb"[4]— which is the desert of Hos. 13.15, from which the Lord will bring a burning wind, because "it germinated without any human seed".[5] Indeed, Mary is the true daughter of Sion of

[1] *Comm. in Is.*, 5, 19.1: 7, 19.1.   [2] *Adv. Jovin.*, 1, 31.
[3] *Epist.*, 107, 7.
[4] *Comm. in Jer.*, 6, 31.22.   [5] *Comm. in Os.*, 13.15.

whom Isaiah says (37.22): "'The virgin daughter of Sion hath despised thee and laughed thee to scorn.' Her whom he calls daughter, he also designates as a virgin; lest if he had called her only daughter, you might think her married. This is the virgin daughter to whom it is said elsewhere: Give praise, thou barren, that bearest not [Isa. 54.1] . . . This is she about whom God says through Jeremiah: Will a virgin forget her ornament [2.32] . . ."—a view which, as we have seen, still plays an important part in contemporary exegesis.

For Jerome Scripture is full of her, and for him, too, she is the second Eve, a theme on which he touches briefly in his teaching on virginity. This he considers has been preserved in the Old Testament only in the case of some men, whereas "Eve gave birth in pains. But after the Virgin had conceived and brought forth for us a Son . . . the curse has been taken away. Death came through Eve, life through Mary. Therefore the gift of virginity flowed more profusely into women, because it began with a woman",[1] as he says in his letter to Eustochium, the daughter of his friend Paula. And he exhorts her to take "the blessed Mary, who was of such purity that she deserved to be the Mother of the Lord" as her example, for "you, too, can be a mother of the Lord",[2] as Ambrose had also said; in his letter to Laeta he calls the monastery "the chamber of Mary".[3]

AUGUSTINE

Ambrose and Jerome prepared the way for the Mariology of the greatest of the Latin Fathers, St. Augustine (354–430).

The story of his conversion—intellectually from Manicheism, morally from the sins of the flesh—is well known and is not without influence on his attitude to Mary. Like the other Latin Fathers, he avoids the title "Mother of God" on account of its pagan implications, though he clearly holds the

[1] *Ep. XXII*, 21.   [2] *Ep. XXII*, 8.   [3] *Ep. CVII*, 13.

doctrine, as is evident from passages such as this: "How could he cease being God, when he began to be man, who granted to his Mother that she did not cease to be a virgin when she gave birth?"[1]

He stresses the reality of her childbirth against the Manicheans; Christ really took flesh from Mary;[2] ". . . the Virgin Mother brought forth him by whom she herself was created through her fertile womb and her intact childbirth."[3] But real though this childbirth was, it was nevertheless different from any other, because it was virginal, for "thus it befitted God to be born"[4] says Augustine, echoing Ambrose. Mary's perfect and perpetual virginity is a doctrine he holds most dear, and which he stresses at every opportunity. Strangely enough, though, he never adduces the text of Isa. 7.14. The scriptural foundation he prefers is Mary's own question: "How shall this be done, because I know not man?" from which he infers a formal vow of virginity: "Therefore also is her virginity all the more pleasing and acceptable, because Christ did not prevent what he had preserved from being violated by a man only after he had been conceived, but had elected her from whom he was to be born after she had dedicated herself to God even before he was conceived. This is indicated by the words with which she answered the angel who announced to her that she was to have a child . . . which she would certainly not have said if she had not vowed herself to God already before. But because such a thing had until then been rejected by the customs of the Israelites, she was betrothed to a just man, not that he should rob her of what she had already vowed, but rather that he should guard it against violation",[5] and that "her husband should be a witness of her virginal purity".[6] St. Augustine is the first of the Latin Fathers to assume a vow of virginity, which had already been

---

[1] Sermo CLXXXVI, 1; also CXCV, 2; CCXV, 3.
[2] Sermo CXC, 3; cf. Serm. CCXXXVII, 1.   [3] Sermo CLXXXVI, 1.
[4] Sermo CLXXXVI, 1.   [5] De Sancta Virginitate, 4, 4.
[6] Sermo CCXXV, 2; cf. also Sermo CCXCI, 5.

suggested in the Greek Church by Gregory of Nyssa. It is significant that this idea did not appear until such a formal vow had become an established custom in the Church; it then seemed only fitting that Mary, the prototype of virgins, should have been the first to make such a promise to God.

St. Augustine also emphasizes the virginity *in partu*. Here again he does not use the favourite patristic proof passage from Ezekiel; instead he refers to the risen Christ, who entered through closed doors, and asks: "Why therefore should he, who, being full-grown, could enter through closed doors, when he was small not also be able to go out without violating the womb?"[1] "What human reason does not understand," he says, "faith accepts."[2] Nevertheless, Mary's own faith is even more important than her physical integrity: "More blessed is Mary through perceiving the faith of Christ than through conceiving his flesh . . . and the maternal relationship would have been of no profit to Mary, if she had not more happily borne Christ in her heart than in her womb";[3] ". . . for him whom Mary had brought forth by believing, she also had conceived by believing".[4] In this sense Augustine interprets Matt. 12.46ff., which had so exercised the Greek Fathers and Tertullian. "Should the Virgin Mary not have done the will of the Father, she, who by faith believed, by faith conceived, who was the chosen one from whom our salvation should be born among men, who was created by Christ before Christ was created in her? Indeed, the holy Mary obviously did the will of the Father: and therefore it is greater for Mary to have been Christ's disciple than to have been his Mother . . . The truth of Christ is in the mind of Mary, the flesh of Christ in her womb; greater is what she bears in her mind, than what she bears in her womb."[5] For Augustine, as for St. Ambrose, there is no question of a doubt of Mary under the Cross. The sword that pierced her soul was the grief by which her

---

[1] *Sermo CXCI*, 2.   [2] *Sermo CXC*, 2.   [3] *De Sancta Virg.*, 3, 3.
[4] *Sermo CCXV*, 4.   [5] *Sermo Denis*, 25, 7 (ed. G. Morin, Rome (1930)).

motherly heart was transfixed when she watched her Son's death, not daring to presume upon his resurrection, faith in which was momentarily overlaid by the suffering confronting her.[1] For "holy is Mary, blessed is Mary"—and yet, "better [*melior*] is the Church than the Virgin Mary. Why? Because Mary is a part of the Church, a holy member, an excellent member, a supereminent member—yet but a member of the whole body. If of the whole body, surely more is the body than the member. The head is the Lord, and the whole Christ is both head and body"[2]—a teaching abandoned in the Middle Ages, when the Blessed Virgin was assigned a place above the Church, between God and the highest angels.

Augustine follows his teacher Ambrose in stressing the special relationship between Mary and the Church as well as between her and individual Christians, who must be other Maries: "Consider how the Church, obviously, is the bride of Christ; and, what is more difficult to understand, yet true, how she is the mother of Christ. As her type has the Virgin Mary preceded her. Whence, I ask you, is Mary the mother of Christ, if not because she gave birth to the members of Christ? You, to whom I speak, are the members of Christ; who has given birth to you? I hear the voice of your heart: Mother Church. This mother is holy, honoured, similar to Mary, she brings forth, yet is a virgin. That she brings forth I prove through you; for you are born from her; she also brings forth Christ, for you are the members of Christ . . . let the members of Christ give birth in mind, as Mary, as a virgin, gave birth to him in her womb; and thus you will be mothers of Christ."[3] Thus we have here a very intricate mystical (in the patristic sense) relationship: the physical motherhood of Mary is the type and pattern of the motherhood of the Church, but through Christ this motherhood extends also to the individual Christian, so that both the Church as his body and the

[1] *Ep. CXXI*, 17.   [2] *Sermo Denis XXV*, 7.   [3] *Sermo Denis XXV*, 8.

Christians as his members in some way depend on Mary, because their motherhood, which also is virginal, was first realized in her motherhood. Augustine rings the changes on this subject and, again like Ambrose, he, too, considers that by giving birth to Christ Mary somehow gave birth to his faithful: "How do you not also belong to the childbirth of the Virgin, when you are members of Christ? Mary gave birth to your Head, the Church to you. For she [the Church], too, is both mother and virgin; mother through her charity, virgin through the integrity of her faith and piety. She gives birth to nations, but they are members of the One whose body and bride she is herself, and in this bears likeness to that virgin [Mary], because she, too, is the mother of unity in the many."[1] Mary and the Church are linked together, for "the Church could not be virgin, if she had not found her Spouse to whom she was to be given to be the Virgin's Son."[2] The Son of Mary renders his spouse the Church like to his mother, he makes her our mother, while preserving her a virgin to himself.[3] Thus Mary is more than a mere individual woman; she is the prototype of the Church. What was later realized in the Church was first shown forth in her; though the Church is greater than she, because even she is not above the Church, but a member of the Church (the most eminent member, however); for, as Augustine says in another of his Christmas sermons, from which most of the previous quotations have been taken: "The honour of the masculine sex is in the flesh of Christ, the honour of the feminine sex is in the Mother of Christ."[4]

Is Mary, then, without sin? The question had arisen in the Pelagian controversy. Pelagius had taught that men can remain wholly without sin by their own free will and adduced Mary as an example—the first among others. Augustine denied this possibility for all men—"except the holy Virgin

[1] *Sermo CXCII*, 2.   [2] *Sermo CLXXXVIII*, 4.   [3] *Sermo CXCV*, 2.
[4] *Sermo CXC*, 2.

Mary, about whom, for the honour of the Lord, I want there to be no question where sin is mentioned, for concerning her we know that more grace for conquering sin in every way was given to her who merited to conceive and give birth to him, who certainly had no sin whatsoever—this virgin excepted, if we could . . . ask all saints, whether they were without sin, what, do we think, would they answer?"[1] So Mary is without sin—but this is an exception, a privilege which was given her in view of the Incarnation, "for the honour of the Lord"; it was a grace, not an effect of her free will; and so Augustine has refuted Pelagius while preserving the sinlessness of Christ's Mother.

Does this sinlessness include freedom from original sin—that is to say, did Augustine teach the Immaculate Conception? This further question came up during his controversy with Julian of Eclanum, who subscribed to Pelagian views. Julian had attacked Augustine's teaching on the ubiquity of original sin, by which, he said, "you deliver Mary herself to the devil through the condition of her birth". Augustine's reply is by no means clear, and has given rise to a whole literature of diverse interpretations. Here is its literal translation: "We do not deliver Mary to the devil by the condition of her birth; but for this reason, because this very condition is resolved by the grace of rebirth."[2] It would seem from this that Mary, too, was under the empire of sin—not, indeed, by the very fact of birth, but by the sin inevitably accompanying it since the Fall, and from which she, too, had to be freed by grace. This interpretation is borne out by a passage from the *Enarrationes in Psalmos* (34, 3) where Augustine writes: "Mary [who descended] from Adam, died because of sin, and the flesh of the Lord [which came] from Mary, died for the destruction of sins." Christ alone, in his view, was free from all sin, original and actual, because he was born from the Virgin without that concupiscence which accompanies every

[1] *De Natura et Gratia*, 42.   [2] *Opus Imperf. Contra Julianum*, 4, 122.

other conception except his,[1] and through which original sin is transmitted, Mary not excepted; even though she was freed from it so thoroughly that she did not commit any actual personal sins.

With Augustine the Mariology in the ancient Christian West has reached its peak. Mary's perpetual virginity and her personal sinlessness are assured, her intimate relationship with the Church, whose prototype she is, has been recognized. Even her relation to original sin is already being discussed; only her greatest name, Theotokos—in Latin, *Dei Genitrix*— is hardly used; not, however, on theological grounds, but for the simple practical reason that it might give rise to misunderstandings on account of the pagan worship of Kybele, the Mother of Gods. Now, it was precisely this title which caused a major theological controversy in the East during the last years of Augustine's life, which was finally settled only after his death.

[1] *Opus Imp. c. Jul.*, 5, 52; cf. 6, 22.

THE COUNCIL OF EPHESUS AND AFTER

THE CONTROVERSY

THE great controversy was sparked off by a sermon delivered by Proclus (d. 446), a famous preacher at Constantinople and later its patriarch, in the cathedral of the city in the presence of its then Patriarch Nestorius. Nestorius was of Persian origin; he had probably studied under Theodore of Mopsuestia, one of the greatest theologians and biblical scholars of the Antiochene school. As we already saw when discussing Chrysostom, this school stressed particularly the manhood of Christ, so much so that its representatives distinguished very neatly between his divinity and his humanity; indeed, so neatly, that they were at times in danger of dividing him up into two separate beings, one human, the other divine. And because Mary had evidently not given birth to his divinity, because this had existed from all eternity, they refused to call her Theotokos, Mother of God. The opponents of this school, on the other hand, made no such radical division between Christ's divinity and his humanity; for the One who was born from Mary was true God as well as true man, and because he was true God, Mary could—and should—rightly be called Theotokos, that is to say, she who gave birth to God.

Now, probably on 23 December 428,[1] Proclus preached his sermon in honour of Mary. We shall quote it rather extensively, not only on account of its importance for the

[1] The date is uncertain. Some scholars also give 429 as the year, and the feast of the Annunciation as the occasion, but that feast was not then kept at Constantinople.

ensuing controversy, but also because it is a typical example of Byzantine preaching on the Mother of God.[1]

We have been assembled by the holy Mary, the stainless jewel of virginity, the rational paradise of the second Adam, the workshop of the unity of the natures [scil., of Christ], the scene of the saving contract, the bridal chamber, in which the Word espoused the flesh, the living bush, which was not burnt by the fire of the divine birth [cf. Exod. 3.2ff.], the truly light cloud that bore him who is above the cherubim together with his body, the fleece cleansed by the dew from heaven [cf. Judges 6.37ff.], from which the shepherd put on [the garment of] the lamb, servant and mother, virgin and heaven, the only bridge between God and men [a metaphor frequently used by the later Fathers], the awesome loom of the "economy"[2] on which the garment of union [i.e., of Christ's two natures] was woven in ineffable manner, the weaver of which is the Holy Spirit, the spinner the overshadowing power from on high, the wool Adam's ancient fleece, the woof the stainless flesh of the Virgin, the comb the measureless grace of the bearer [of that flesh], the artist the Word that went in through the ear.[3]

For, Proclus affirms towards the end of his sermon, the Incarnation is a mystery:

I see the miracles and proclaim the Godhead; I see the sufferings and do not deny the manhood. Emmanuel has, indeed, opened the gates of nature, because he was man, but he did not break the seals of virginity, because he was God.

---

[1] *Oratio I De laudibus sanctae Mariae*, Schwartz, *ACO*, I, I, I, pp. 103-07 (*PG*, 65, 680C-692B).

[2] *Oikonomia*, technical term for the whole complex of the Redemption, involving the Incarnation with all its consequences.

[3] No. 1 (*ACO*, p. 103).

As he had entered through the hearing, so he went out from the womb [i.e., without violating it]; he was born as he was conceived; he had entered without passion, he went forth without corruption,[1] according to the prophet Ezekiel [here follows the well-known text ch. 44.1f.] . . . Behold, an exact description of the holy Theotokos Mary!

If we would grasp the theological significance of the ensuing controversy we have to keep one thing in mind, which comes out quite clearly in the sermon by Proclus: the insistence on the title Theotokos is not due to any inclination to "Mariolatry"; its significance is wholly Christological, and as such it was regarded by both parties. Mary was called Theotokos in order to affirm that Christ, born from her, was true God as well as true man, that he was not a man who later attained to divinity, like the demi-gods of the pagans, nor a sort of hybrid, part man, part God. If Christ was truly God as well as man, then Mary, his Mother, was also truly the Mother of God.

But this was a view certain Antiochene theologians, with their sharp distinction between the Word of God and the man Jesus, just could not accept. Mary was only the mother of the man, *Anthropotokos*, or the mother of Christ, *Christotokos*, but on no account the Mother of God, Theotokos. So Nestorius, a convinced disciple of Antioch, was writhing with fury when he heard the doctrine he considered no less than heretical expounded from the pulpit of his own cathedral—and with all the appurtenances of the allegorical method of the Alexandrians, comparing Mary to bushes and fleeces, and making play with weavers, spinners and combs. It was too much altogether, and as soon as Proclus had finished Nestorius ascended the pulpit to reject the term "Theotokos" and explain the mystery of the Incarnation in his own way.[2] He

[1] I follow Bardenhewer, preferring the variant *aphthartos* (= "without corruption") to the text of Schwartz—*aphrastos* (= "ineffably").

[2] Only a Latin version of this sermon has come down to us, published in F. Loofs, *Nestoriana* (1905).

began by saying that Mary was, indeed, worthy of all praise—no-one, in fact, of whatever school of thought, had ever denied this. But, he continued, one cannot say simply that God was born from Mary, that would make Christianity ridiculous and bring it dangerously near to pagan fables. According to him one must distinguish between the divine and the human parts of Christ. "He who was born and for the normal number of months carried in the womb has a human nature, but indeed joined to God. But it is one thing to say that the God who is the Word of the Father was conjoined to him who was born from Mary, which is perfectly clear and sound and cannot give scandal to the pagans, but quite another that the Deity needed a birth involving months [of pregnancy]."[1] Thus "God the Word, who was in the temple [i.e., the body] which the Spirit had prepared, is something quite different from the temple which God indwelt. It is natural for the temple to be dissolved by death; it is also natural to him who indwells the temple to rise again."[2] So Christ is really divided into a human and mortal, and a divine and immortal part; only the human part is the son of Mary, the divine part is the Son of God and not born of her.

This is the essence of the whole controversy, which as we have said, was wholly Christological; what was at stake was not the greater or lesser devotion to Mary—though the former was a by-product of its outcome—but the unity of the person of Christ, in consequence of which Mary could be called the Mother of God, as Cyril of Alexandria was to emphasize in the course of the discussions, in the same way as God could be said to have suffered. For to Cyril the opponents of Nestorius in Constantinople now reported the statements of their bishop. And with this, as has happened so often in Church history, another element, besides the purely theological factor, was brought into play: the rivalry, almost a century old, between the two great sees of Alexandria and Constantinople.

[1] Loofs, p. 338.   [2] Loofs, p. 340.

The latter had been made the capital of the Eastern Empire by Constantine in 330. At the council held in the city in 381 its bishop was given precedence before all others except the Bishop of Rome, and this had naturally galled the See of Alexandria, which had counted such an outstanding authority as St. Athanasius among its occupants, and whose theologians had been held in the highest esteem from the times of Clement in the second century. A generation before, Cyril's uncle and predecessor, Theophilus, had persecuted John Chrysostom, when he became Bishop of Constantinople; now, with more justification, Cyril followed in his footsteps; Nestorius' suspect Christological opinions gave the autocratic Alexandrian just the material he needed to strike a stunning blow at his rival.

Cyril first refuted the arguments of Nestorius in a paschal letter in 429, and soon after in the long encyclical addressed to his Egyptian monks, in which he proved Mary's right to the title Theotokos with arguments taken from the tradition of the Church as well as from theological considerations, asking how one could possibly doubt whether the Holy Virgin was Theotokos if our Lord Jesus Christ was God? For this, he said, was the faith which the holy disciples transmitted to us, even though they did not use the term.[1] Both Cyril and Nestorius wrote to Pope Celestine to inform him of their respective views on the matter. Celestine was already prejudiced against Nestorius, because the latter had received followers of the Pelagian heresy condemned by the Pope. Besides, the full Godhead of Christ had never been questioned in the West, and though, as we have seen, the term "Mother of God" was only very sparingly used there, Mary's divine maternity had never been doubted. While Rome was considering the matter, Cyril was busy expounding his point of view. In his first letter to Nestorius,[2] written in 429, he urged

[1] *ACO*, 1, 1, 1, p. 11 (*PG*, 77, 13B).
[2] *ACO*, 1, 1, 1, pp. 23–5 (*PG*, 77, 40f.).

him to admit that Mary was Theotokos. Nestorius refused, but politely, because at that moment he had troubles in his own diocese. Early in the following year Cyril wrote a second letter, in which he cleared up misunderstandings: the term Theotokos did not, of course, mean that Mary gave birth to the Divinity, but to God, just as it could be said that God suffered on the Cross, though it was not the impassible Divinity which suffered.[1] This time Nestorius answered in a highly irritated tone: "I pass over the arrogance of your astonishing letters to us", emphasizing the difference between the humanity and the divinity in Christ, on account of which he felt himself unable to agree to the use of the term Theotokos.[2] Meanwhile Cyril, anxious to have the Court on his side, wrote no less than three treatises on the subject, one addressed to the Emperor, Theodosius II, the other two, "Ad Reginas", to the Emperor's three theologically-interested sisters and his consort, a move not particularly appreciated by Theodosius, who saw in it an attempt to sow discord in the imperial family. About the same time, in April 430, Cyril sent a big dossier of the whole case to Celestine, who called a synod in Rome which took place in the first half of August.

The outcome of this synod was the condemnation of Nestorius, and Celestine sent letters to Nestorius as well as to the priests and people of Constantinople, dated 10 August 430. He did not, however, send these direct to Constantinople, but to Cyril, charging him to communicate them to Nestorius and see to it that the sentence of the Synod of Rome was carried out. Celestine's letters were couched in the strongest terms; Nestorius' opinions were called blasphemies: "You do not only not give food in season, but even kill by poison those whom he has purchased by his blood and death", since by dividing Christ and impairing the reverence due to the Virgin Birth he endangered the faith of his people. And to the people he wrote to beware of the teaching of their bishop, who

[1] *ACO*, i, i, i, pp. 26f. (*PG*, 77, 45Bff.).   [2] *ACO*, i, i, i, p. 29.

seemed to have forgotten the right doctrine of salvation.[1] As soon as Cyril had received the Pope's letters he wrote to several bishops, including John of Antioch, who in his turn wrote to Nestorius counselling submission, since Nestorius was to be excommunicated unless he recanted within ten days after receiving Celestine's letters.

Cyril, however, was not content simply to forward the letters of the Pope, but added to these a document of his own containing twelve anathemas, the so-called "Twelve Chapters", which went much farther than the epistles of Celestine. His principal object was again to defend the unity of the one Christ, but in doing so he came dangerously near to the heresy of Apollinarianism, later developed into Monophysitism, according to which, after the union of the Divinity and the humanity, Christ had only one divine nature; for in his fourth anathema Cyril condemned those who divided the various activities of Christ recorded in the Gospels between his human and his divine nature. Now, the documents sent by Cyril did not arrive at Constantinople till December 430, and the month before the Emperors, Theodosius II and Valentinian III, had called a general council to be held at Ephesus at Pentecost 431 in order to settle the dispute. Nestorius therefore considered the Pope's ultimatum superseded and everything in abeyance until the meeting of the Council. He was, however, infuriated with Cyril's anathemas and, still in December 430, preached two sermons against Cyril which he forwarded to him with counter-anathemas. Nestorius also sent Cyril's "Twelve Chapters" to John of Antioch, who was so disconcerted by the views expressed therein, which ran counter to all the most cherished convictions of the theological school associated with his see, that he immediately changed over to the side of Nestorius. In the West, too, theologians were busy; Cassian (c. 360–c. 435), better known as the author of books on the monastic life, wrote a treatise *On the*

[1] *ACO*, I, 2 (1925–6), pp. 15-20.

Incarnation against Nestorius, and Marius Mercator, a disciple and friend of St. Augustine, wrote against the "blasphemous chapters" of Nestorius, a work based on the latter's December sermons. In the East, John of Antioch enlisted the support of a number of bishops, among them the famous exegete and theologian Theodoret of Cyrus (near Antioch), for the cause of Nestorius. Thus when in the spring of 431, the bishops prepared to travel to Ephesus, the two parties were well defined.

THE COUNCIL

Cyril had great advantages. Not only was Rome on his side, but Memnon, the Bishop of Ephesus, was a close friend of his. So, when Nestorius arrived at Ephesus, he and his entourage were treated very badly and forbidden to enter not only the basilica but all the other churches in the city. Moreover, the faithful were conditioned very carefully; without, of course, being able to go into the Christological details of the controversy, his opponents simply represented Nestorius to their congregations as a blasphemer of Christ and of the great Theotokos. By 12 June, five days after Pentecost, the appointed date for the Council, there had arrived at Ephesus Cyril with fifty bishops and Nestorius with ten, as well as the Counts, Irenaeus and Candidianus, the latter with instructions from the Emperor, whom he represented. There were, however, two notable absences; John of Antioch, with the Oriental bishops, who were on the side of Nestorius, and the papal legates. On 21 June Cyril had a letter from John telling him not to wait for him if he were delayed. Nestorius and Candidianus, however, wanted to wait for his arrival, while Cyril and Memnon were determined to open the Council forthwith. Cyril overruled his opponents, who drew up a document registering their disapproval (*contestatio*), signed by sixty-eight bishops. So on 22 June, the very next day, Cyril opened the Council, over which he presided himself—though on what authority is doubtful, indeed. Candidianus protested immediately in the name of the Emperor, whose instructions he read, but was thrown out. Nestorius had already refused to attend—so Cyril had virtually no opposition at all. Consequently the Patriarch of Alexandria had it all his own way. On that day, the first session of the Council, there were read out the Creed of Nicaea, Cyril's second letter to Nestorius, which was received with applause, Nestorius' second letter to Cyril, which was greeted with shouts of "Anathema!", Celestine's letter to Nestorius of August 430 and Cyril's third letter to Nestorius with the controversial anathemas. This last was received in silence. Besides, Cyril caused a number of extracts from the Fathers as well as from the writings of Nestorius to be read—a programme which simply cannot have left any time for proper discussions. At the end of this session Nestorius was declared deposed and excommunicated. The crowds which had been roaming the streets of Ephesus went wild with enthusiasm when they were told the verdict. They accompanied Cyril and his bishops to their lodgings with torchlights and shouts of "Praised be the Theotokos! Long live Cyril!" It sounds like a Christian echo of the "Great is the Diana of the Ephesians!" which, almost 400 years ago, had been shouted in the streets of this same city when the preaching of Paul had threatened the livelihood of the worshippers of the pagan goddess. (Acts 19.28ff.) And perhaps there is a connection between the two: for the veneration of a mother-figure is a deep-rooted human instinct, and so it is not improbable that, in the hearts of many simple people, the Theotokos should have taken the place of the ancient Diana. For the safeguards of Christian theology are not always generally understood by the crowds and the "Mother of God" may sometimes seem closer and more accessible to the hearts of the people than the incomprehensible Godhead or even the mysterious God-man, as we shall see on other occasions in the course of this study.

The people of Ephesus were satisfied—but what would the

5+

Emperor say to Cyril's high-handed action? For he was immediately informed of the proceedings, which he soon was able to read in the three versions of Cyril, Nestorius, and his own representative Candidianus respectively, who all wrote letters to him. Then, four days after the first session of the Council, on 26 June, John of Antioch, with his bishops, arrived at Ephesus. On being told that Cyril and his followers had excommunicated Nestorius, the Oriental bishops immediately held a council of their own, in the presence of Nestorius and the Emperor's envoy Candidianus, and in their turn excommunicated Cyril, Memnon, and all those who would not reject Cyril's twelve anathemas. So now Cyril and Nestorius were both excommunicated, though the excommunication of Cyril, by a furious minority, could hardly be taken seriously.

Three days after this, on 29 June, an imperial rescript arrived, in which the Emperor expressed his displeasure with Cyril's hasty proceedings and ordered the bishops to await the arrival of an imperial commissioner before taking any further steps. Finally, on 10 July, the papal legates arrived. In accordance with Celestine's instructions they supported Cyril, and at once held the second session of the Council, again presided over by Cyril, in which was read a letter from the Pope. On the following day, in the third session, the minutes of Session One were read; the legates expressed their approval and confirmed the sentence of excommunication passed on Nestorius. Five days later, on 16 July, John of Antioch and his followers refused to attend the Council; having therefore been excommunicated by Cyril's party the next day, they reported this to the Emperor. Finally, in August, the imperial commissioner arrived at Ephesus and in his turn announced the deposition of Cyril and Memnon as well as of Nestorius, and put all three in prison. There Cyril wrote an explanation of his notorious Twelve Chapters, while the Orientals drew up a "Formulary of Reunion" in which they stated that, in view of the union of the two natures in Christ, they confessed Mary to be Theotokos. In September the Emperor dissolved the Council, sent back Nestorius to his monastery at Antioch and ordered the consecration of a new Bishop of Constantinople. Cyril returned to his diocese in October. The controversy was at an end. Mary had solemnly been affirmed to be Theotokos by what came to be known as the Third Ecumenical Council. But final harmony was not restored in the Church until two years later, by the Edict of Union in 433.

POST-EPHESINE EASTERN THEOLOGIANS

Either during or immediately after the Council Cyril preached a sermon[1] which Quasten calls the "most famous Marian sermon of antiquity". As in Proclus' sermon quoted at the beginning of this chapter, Cyril, too, addresses Mary by a string of epithets: "Hail, Mary Theotokos, venerable jewel of the whole earth, never-extinguished lamp, crown of virginity, sceptre of orthodoxy, never-destroyed sanctuary, vessel of the Incomprehensible, Mother and Virgin . . ." It is particularly interesting that she should be called "sceptre of orthodoxy". Ephesus had shown that the touchstone of a true conception of Christ was the place Mary is given in Christology; soon the Liturgy will extol her for having destroyed all heresies. After these introductory praises Cyril breaks out into an enthusiastic enumeration of all that has come to pass through Mary; through her the Holy Trinity is adored on earth, through her heavens and angels are gladdened, demons are chased, the devil is cast down from heaven, fallen man is restored, all creation, once sunk in idolatry, has come to know the truth, through her the faithful have been baptized, churches have been built, whole nations have been led to do

[1] *Hom. Div.*, 4 (Schwartz, *ACO*, 1, 1, 8, pp. 102–04 (*PG*, 77, 992A–996C)); Bardenhewer doubts Cyril's authorship, but most other scholars, including J. Quasten (*Patrology*, 3, p. 131), hold that it was preached by him.

penance. It may seem surprising at first that these divine actions should be attributed to Mary; but they are predicted of her only in virtue of her divine motherhood, for Cyril continues: "Through whom the only-begotten Son of God . . . has shone forth as Light." The real cause of all these activities is Christ, her Son; but because Christ was given through her, she was the instrument through which all these things became possible.

The Council produced a tremendous increase in Marian devotion. The first church dedicated to Mary seems to have been in the valley of Josaphat, as is attested by the Coptic panegyric on Macarius of Thôu by Pseudo-Dioskuros,[1] but, as Baumstark points out,[2] after the Council churches must have been dedicated to the Theotokos in almost every important city. There was also a steadily growing flow of Marian preaching, especially on her feasts, the development of which will be traced later. Most of them follow the same pattern; they recall the fall of man, which affords an opportunity to oppose Mary to Eve, then develop the scene of the Annunciation and usually end up with the birth of Christ and the adoration of the Magi. These sermons were lavishly adorned with Old-Testament texts applied to Mary, as had already been the custom of pre-Ephesine authors. Theodotus of Ancyra (d. between 438 and 446),[3] who had been a friend of Nestorius but had become one of his most violent opponents at the time of the Council, says of Mary that she was "like the lily in the midst of thorns" (Cant. 2.2), "clothed with divine grace as with a garment"; she is "altogether beautiful" (Cant. 4.7; quotations from *Hom.*, 5, 11), and because of her Eve was redeemed. (*Hom.*, 5, 12.) In his sermon for the feast of the Purification (*Hom.*, 4), preached at the Council, he applies two passages from the Psalms to her: "The Most High has

---

[1] Cf. Baumstark, "Die leibliche Himmelfahrt der allerseligsten Jungfrau", in *OC*, 4 (1904), p. 379.
[2] *OC*, 4 (1904), p. 380.   [3] *PO*, 19, 13.

sanctified his own tabernacle" (Ps. 44.5) and "A man is born in her, and the Highest himself has founded her" (Ps. 86.5). His interpretation of these verses makes it clear that Theodotus, like other contemporary Fathers, thought that Mary was purified through the Incarnation. According to him "the stainless Virgin was, as it were, burned pure through the approach of the divine and immaterial fire . . . so that *henceforth* she remained inaccessible to any carnal corruption". This sermon also contains a string of "greetings", all beginning with *chaire* and hence called *chairetismoi*, for example: "Hail, joy whom we have so long desired, Hail, brightness of the Church . . . Hail, spiritual fleece of salvation . . . Hail, stainless mother of holiness", and so forth. We do not know whether Theodotus was the first Greek Father to introduce into his sermons this devotion,[1] which became a very popular device in later Byzantine preachers, especially after it had been taken up by the author of the *Akathistos hymn.* (See below.)

The allegorical method of exegesis would sometimes lead the Fathers to the most extravagant interpretations. For Hesychius of Jerusalem (d. after 451), who wrote commentaries on a number of biblical books, Mary was the oven in which, according to Lev. 2.4, the offering for Yahweh was baked, "because an oven receives bread and fire from above, as also the Theotokos received the bread of life, that is the Word of God, and the fire of the presence of the Spirit into her womb."[2] He also took up the traditional Old-Testament types of her permanent virginity, such as the burning bush and especially the closed door of Ezekiel; for "Mary's field has not known the plough, the virginal vineyard did not endure the digging fork."[3] Hesychius stresses her sinlessness to such an extent that one might almost assume he did not believe that she needed to be redeemed at all; for, he says, "Not for

---

[1] Cf. G. G. Meersseman, *Der Hymnos Akathistos* (1958), pp. 12f.
[2] *Comm. on Lev.*, 2.4 (*PG*, 93, 807B).   [3] *Serm. VI* (*PG*, 93, 1469B).

her the offering, [but] for all mankind, since for *us* Christ was circumcised . . . when he carries the Cross he relieves *us* from the burden of sin."[1] Through her sinlessness she also frees others: "She who has delivered Eve from shame and Adam from the threat, who has cut off the insolence of the serpent; whom the smoke of concupiscence or the worm of luxury has never touched."[2]

Nevertheless, the Alexandrian tradition of Mary's doubt under the Cross was too strong even for him to disregard it completely, but he considerably weakened it when he wrote: "The discord [*dichónoia*] is called a sword . . . for even though she was virgin, she was still a woman, and even though Theotokos, she was nevertheless of the same stuff as we."[3] In view of what he has said before, this would seem to imply no more than general human weakness.

But his was rather an isolated view at that time. Chrysippus, a native of Cappadocia who entered the monastery founded by St. Euthymius at Jerusalem and became a priest about 455, held that Mary shared in the consequences of the Fall before being redeemed. He applied to her Ps. 131.8 in a rather surprising way: "When you shall have arisen from there, then you shall seal also the ark of your sanctification [i.e., Mary], then will the Ark also rise with all men from the Fall, in which her descent from Eve has involved her."[4]

Antipater of Bostra in Arabia (d. c. 458), in a sermon on the Nativity of St. John the Baptist, says of her that she mediated the fire of the Godhead to the grass of the humanity;[5] he, too, compares her with Eve and says in his homily on the Annunciation (No. 10) that the Virgin Mary repaired the fault of the virgin Eve.

[1] *Serm. VI* (*PG*, 93, 1469B).　　[2] *Serm. VI* (1465A).　　[3] *Serm. VI* (1476C).
[4] *Sermon on the Blessed Virgin Mary*, in *PO*, 19 (1925), pp. 336–43.
[5] *PG*, 85, 1765A.

WESTERN POST-EPHESINE FATHERS

While the Theotokos controversy had been raging in the East, the West had been resting, so to speak, on the Mariological laurels of its great doctors Ambrose and Augustine. Sedulius, a native of southern Gaul or Italy, wrote both poetry and prose about the time of the Council. In his *Paschale Carmen*, which describes biblical events, he celebrates the true motherhood, which he describes in strong terms (2, 3), of the "new virgin" who has "expiated the crime of the old virgin". (2, 30f.) He then addresses her in words which became the Introit of most of the Masses of our Lady in the Roman rite: "*Salve, sancta Parens*"—"Hail, holy Mother who brought forth the King"—and he continues: "You, whose blessed womb has the joys of a mother together with the honour of virginity, No woman has ever been like to you, nor will you have an equal, You alone have pleased Christ above all others." Her virginal childbirth is praised in another of his hymns, the so-called *Abecedarius* (because its verses are arranged in alphabetical order), the first seven verses of which have become the hymn for Lauds of the octave day of Christmas.

Peter Chrysologus, Archbishop of Ravenna (d. c. 450) and a strong supporter of papal rights, was also an ardent defender of Mary's title, Theotokos. In one of his sermons he taunts the Nestorians: "Let them now come and hear, who have tried to befog Latin clarity with Greek confusion and blaspheme [Mary] as the mother of a man, the mother of Christ, so as to take from her the title Theotokos."[1] But, like the other Latin Fathers of his time, elsewhere he avoids the term "Mother of God", but rather calls Mary "the Virgin" or simply "Mary", which, he says, means "Mistress" (*domina*).[2] She is the cause of life, for "without Mary death could not have been put to flight, nor life been restored,"[3] and so the woman, "who in

[1] *Serm.*, 145 (*PL*, 52, 590B).   [2] *Serm.*, 142 (*PL*, 52, 579C).
[3] *Serm.*, 64 (*PL*, 52, 380B).

Adam had been the mother of the dead became through Christ the true mother of all the living".[1] Like his great Latin predecessors, he, too, linked Mary with the Church,[2] for Christ found the sheep that was lost in Adam, in Mary's womb.[3] However ardent his devotion to her, even in his highest rhetorical flights she is never praised for her own sake, always for the sake of her Son; in one of his sermons on the Annunciation he breaks forth into a whole litany, always beginning: "Truly blessed you", and continuing, "who are greater than heaven, stronger than earth, wider than the universe, for", he argues, "the God whom the world cannot contain, you alone have contained."[4] This is the Marian paradox on which the Fathers like to dwell with increasing insistence—that, because Mary is truly Theotokos, Mother of God, she is greater than all creation.

The contemporary official doctrine of Rome on the Mother of God came from Leo the Great (Pope 440–61). It was stated in the context of another controversy which concerned the two natures of Christ. This had been started by Eutyches (d. 454), the influential archimandrite of an important monastery at Constantinople. He carried his opposition to Nestorianism so far that he held the incarnate Christ to have had only one (divine) nature, a teaching which would have invalidated the Redemption, since this depends on the true manhood of the Son of God. In 448 he was excommunicated by his Patriarch, Flavius of Constantinople, who asked for Leo's view on the case. Leo replied by a letter (*Epistle 28*) of 13 June 449, which was subsequently given formal approval by the Council of Chalcedon (451) as the binding statement of the Catholic doctrine of the Incarnation, and is generally called the "Tome of Leo". As, two centuries earlier, Mary's true motherhood had to be defended against gnostics and Manicheans in order to uphold the reality of Christ's human body,

---

[1] *Serm.*, 99 (*PL*, 52, 479A).   [2] *Serm.*, 146 (*PL*, 52, 583A).
[3] *Serm.*, 168 (*PL*, 52, 641B).   [4] *Serm.*, 142 (*PL*, 52, 584A).

so now it had once more to be emphasized in the interests of the reality of his human nature. One of the main arguments of Eutyches was that if Christ had had a real human nature, he would also have inherited the stain of sin. Since at that date Mary's immaculate conception was unknown in the West and scarcely adumbrated in the East, Leo could not argue from it, but had to make a distinction between the nature, which Christ did, indeed, assume from Mary, and the guilt, which he did not assume, "because his nativity is miraculous".[1] But though the nativity of Christ was miraculous in that there was no human father, the human motherhood of Mary was completely real: "The conception is of the Holy Spirit within the womb of the virgin Mother, who brought him forth while her virginity remained intact, just as she had conceived him while preserving it . . . Now, the Holy Spirit gave the Virgin her fecundity; the reality [veritas] of his body, however, is taken from her body, in that flesh which he took from the human being."[2] The Pope clinches the argument against Eutyches by saying: "So that this unity of the person in both natures may be understood, the Son of Man is said to have descended from heaven, when the Son of God took flesh from the Virgin from whom he was born."[3]

Thus in the official teaching of the Latin Church Mariology and Christology remain intimately united. Once more the doctrine of Mary's part in the Incarnation protects the true doctrine of the mystery of Christ. Any idea of Mary's own preservation from original sin, however, is ruled out not only in the *Tome*, but also in Leo's sermons,[4] for example in 64, 2, where he writes: "Only the Son of the blessed Virgin is born without transgression, not indeed outside the human race, but a stranger to sin . . . so that of Adam's offspring one might exist in whom the devil had no share." Nevertheless, Mary is not only physically intact; like St. Augustine, Leo, too, holds that she conceived Christ in her mind even before she

[1] *Tome*, 4. [2] *Tome*, 2. [3] *Tome*, 5. [4] *PL*, 54.
5*

conceived him in her body.[1] Though Leo, too, avoids the Latin equivalents of the Greek "Theotokos", he stresses against the Nestorians that "there would be no hope of salvation for the human race if he had not been the Son of the Virgin who was the Creator of the Mother".[2]

So Leo confirms the traditional teaching of the Latin Church: Mary is ever-virgin, the Mother of God, perfectly pure, even though herself not exempt from the universal guilt of mankind—that was a privilege reserved for her Son alone.

The later Latin Fathers added practically nothing to Mariology. The whole Christian West was constantly troubled by barbarian invasions; all the Church could do was to preserve the Catholic inheritance intact, especially against the Arian Goths and Vandals and against the Monophysites in Africa. There the influence of Augustine continued. The most important theologian was Fulgentius (468–533).[3] Originally a member of the Roman civil service, he gave up his secular career in order to become a monk, later (c. 507) was made Bishop of Ruspe, and as such was persecuted by the Arian king, Thrasamund, who exiled him to Sardinia and to whom several of his controversial writings are addressed. Under the influence of St. Augustine's teaching on the ubiquity of sin and in order to defend against the Monophysites the true human nature which Christ took from his Mother, Fulgentius stressed Mary's subjection to original sin more strongly than most other authors of his time. He says explicitly that "the flesh of Mary, who had been conceived in the human way in iniquities, was definitely a flesh of sin,"[4] though he also emphasized her purity, because she "retained the virginity of both mind and body".[5] It was, however, not due to any merit of her own that she brought forth the Son of God, but solely to the divine condescension.[6]

[1] *Sermo XXI*, 1.   [2] *Sermo LXII*, 2.   [3] *PL*, 65.   [4] *Ep. XVII*, 13.
[5] *Ep. XVII*, 12.   [6] *Ep. XVII*, 14.

The disciple and biographer of Fulgentius, Ferrandus (d. c. 546), followed in his master's footsteps. He held that the flesh of Christ was like Mary's flesh, because it took its origin from her, but unlike it, because "it had not contracted the contagion of its corrupted origin from her . . . because it was purified by the union with the Divinity".[1] He, too, strongly defends Mary's true divine maternity against the Monophysites.[2]

The emphasis on the sinfulness of Mary's flesh seems to have been restricted to the African authors of the time, for their contemporary Caesarius of Arles (d. 542), the "Gallic Rome" as it was called, states that "she remained without the contagion or stain of sin".[3]

SYRIAN POST-EPHESINE FATHERS

Returning from this sober and somewhat jejune Western Mariology to the East, we are once more in a totally different climate.

JACOB OF SARUG

Jacob of Sarug (c. 451–521), called the "Flute of the Holy Spirit", was the best-known Syrian poet after Ephraem. He was an opponent of the definition of the Council of Chalcedon (451) on the two natures of Christ, but it is doubtful whether he can really be called a Monophysite, and in any case this question does not affect his Mariology; indeed, his poems are used both in the Jacobite (i.e., Syrian Monophysite) and in the Catholic liturgies. He has written a long *Ode on the Blessed Virgin Mary*,[4] the first part of which is devoted to the preparation of Mary for her divine motherhood, which is followed by an account of the Annunciation. All the burning devotion and

---

[1] *Ep. III*, 4 (*PG*, 67, 892A).   [2] *Ep. III*, 17 (*PG*, 67, 906A).
[3] *Serm. X* (*CCL*, 103, p. 51).
[4] Text and Latin translation in J. B. Abbeloos, *De Vita et Scriptis S. Jacobi . . . Sarugi* (1867); Syriac text in P. Bedjan, *Homiliae Selectae*, 5 vols. (1905–10); German translation by S. Landersdorfer, *BKV²*, 6 (1913).

exalted doctrine of the East are condensed in its pages. Mary is "the second heaven . . . the blessed among women, through whom the curse of the earth has been abolished and since whom the sentence of punishment has reached its end". Her poverty is contrasted with the spiritual riches she has given to the world, she is "the ship which brought us the treasures and goods from the house of the Father . . . the second Eve, who has given birth to life among mortals and has paid and liquidated the debt of her mother Eve; the child who stretched out her hand to her prostrate ancestress and raised her up . . . the daughter who wove a garment of glory and gave it to her father [scil., Adam], so that he might cover himself with it after he had been denuded under the trees . . . the mother who has remained a virgin, the glorious castle which the King built, entered and inhabited, and whose portals were not opened before him when he left it . . . How could I paint the picture of this marvellous beautiful One with ordinary colours? . . . too exalted and too glorious is the image of her beauty."[1]

Jacob stresses time and again Mary's perfect purity, and for this reason some modern theologians have claimed that he taught the Immaculate Conception, a view which might be supported by such passages as the one just quoted, according to which she paid the debt of Eve and wove a garment of glory for Adam. For, as the poet says a little further on, "she who was full of beauty both by nature and by her will [this probably refers to her virginity], and was never defiled by bad desires, had remained from childhood steadfast in stainless justice and had always walked in the right way without fault or stumbling. There remained in her daily the unblemished nature, the will that was directed towards the good, the virginity of the body and the sanctity of the soul,"[2] for "she was wise and filled with the love of God."[3]

For a Latin, reared in the Augustinian tradition on original

[1] Lines 33–60.   [2] Lines 143ff.   [3] Line 138.

sin and grace, it would be impossible to assert that Mary was "never defiled by bad desires" and had remained in "stainless" justice from childhood without having to admit that she had been immaculately conceived. In the Eastern tradition, which had not been influenced by the Pelagian controversy and Augustine's view of unredeemed human nature as a *massa damnata*, the idea that a man could avoid sin by his own effort was by no means so impossible as in the West. And so Jacob could write of Mary just before the Annunciation: "Through her own merit she had reached this step of perfection" (i.e., which fitted her for the Incarnation): "God examined her how far she was above and free from all evil; no movement towards [bad] desires arose in her, nor any thought exciting sensual pleasure; the love of the world did not burn in her, she did not occupy herself with puerilities."[1]

At this stage of perfection Mary had arrived through her own efforts. But at the Annunciation something different happened; now she was further purified by the direct intervention of God, and only then was she freed from original sin. Jacob says explicitly that Mary was purified like John the Baptist, John the Evangelist, Elijah and Melchizedek:[2] "The Spirit that came upon her made her such as Eve had been before she had listened to the advice of the Serpent."[3] Jacob returns repeatedly to this subject: "The same purity that belonged to Adam, Mary, too, acquired through the Spirit that came over her, because the Spirit sanctified her, so that the Son of God might descend into her."[4] It seems from these and other passages that Jacob assumed a twofold purity in Mary: one that she had reached by nature and through her own efforts, the other, merited, as it were, by the former, which removed also the stain inherited from Adam, but was given her only at the Annunciation as the final preparation for her divine motherhood. Thus Jacob cannot be considered to

[1] Lines 131-6.   [2] Lines 211ff.   [3] 400ff.   [4] Line 416.

teach the Immaculate Conception in the modern sense, but he certainly comes very near to the idea.

In the same poem Mary is seen as representing the Church when she asks the angel how she is to bring forth a son: "When she put this question, the wise Virgin was the mouth of the Church and heard the explanation for the whole creation."[1] Thus, through her divine motherhood, "Adam has been delivered from his servitude . . through her the heavenly powers have been reconciled with the mortals . . . Through her the closed way to paradise has again been made passable." Thus Mary is intimately connected with the Redemption, in which she has a share because she is the Mother of the Saviour, she is the link between heaven and earth; she is almost a cosmic figure, a representative of all creation.

But she is also thoroughly human. This quality comes out very strikingly in Jacob's sermon De Transitu, on the Passing of Mary, the Mother of God.[2] The description of the sorrowful Mother under the Cross sounds quite medieval, nor is there even the slightest allusion to any doubt. "Many sorrows", writes Jacob, "has your Mother borne for your sake, and all afflictions surrounded her at your crucifixion. How many sorrowing weepings and tears of suffering did not her eyes shed at your funeral . . . How many terrors did not the Mother of Mercy experience when you were buried and the guards of the sepulchre turned her away, so that she could not approach you!"

Here, in the sixth-century Syrian poet, we have already the fully-developed conception of Mary as the "Mother of Mercy", as well as of the Mater Dolorosa of medieval poetry and art, which is absent both from the Greek and the Latin writings of the time, a fact to be explained perhaps by the more emotional bent of the Syrian character. Jacob's description of Mary's death is particularly interesting, because there

[1] Line 446.   [2] Latin translation in OC, 5 (1905), pp. 91-9.

is no question of the assumption of her body into heaven, though, as we shall soon see, this belief was already gaining ground at the time. According to him she was buried on the Mount of Olives,[1] the Lord himself performing the funeral rites. After her body had been laid in the sepulchre, the angels led her soul into paradise.[2] The poem itself proves that the feast of Mary's passing was kept as early as the end of the fifth century, at least in Syria.

SEVERUS OF ANTIOCH

Severus of Antioch (d. 538) was a Monophysite who, despite his polemics, was really quite near the orthodox position; he, too, was an ardent defender of the Theotokos: for, says he, Emmanuel has shown that she who has given birth to him is truly Mother of God.[3] Her childbirth was without pain,[4] and he compares her to a vine from which Christ, the grape, has grown without seed;[5] through her woman is elevated in rank above Eve.[6] In *Homily 67*, which is a sermon preached on the ancient feast of her Commemoration, Severus asks, "What object could one contemplate that was more divine than the Mother of God, or that was superior to her? To approach her means to approach holy land and attain heaven. She belonged indeed to earth and was a part of humanity through her nature . . . though she was pure of all defilement and without stain, and she has brought forth from her own bowels as from a heaven the God who made himself flesh . . . and this childbirth did not even violate the seal of virginity."[7] He compares her with Mount Sinai, for she is a "spiritual mountain"—a comparison which seems to have been inspired by St. Paul's Epistle to the Galatians (4.25): "But there, where the spirit of bondage reigned, was a smoking mountain . . . Here, on the contrary, where the

---

[1] Baumstark (ed.) "De Transitu", *OC*, 4, p. 374.
[2] *OC*, 5, p. 94.   [3] *Homily 58* (*PO*, 8 (1912), p. 218).
[4] *Hom. 66*, (*PO*, 8, p. 331f.).   [5] *Hom. 63* (*PO*, 8, p. 297f.).
[6] *PO*, 8. pp. 302f.   [7] *PO*, 8, pp. 350f.

grace of adoption reigns, is a spiritual mountain, the Virgin to whom purity and the coming of the Spirit give brilliance and splendour."[1] For Mary brings men to the mystery of Christ: "Therefore the commemoration of the Virgin arouses our souls, because it leads them to consider from what irreconcilable enmity . . . to what divine familiarity and society we have been called through her intervention." (p. 365.) So through her childbirth Mary has an important part in our salvation; but though Severus calls her pure of all defilement and without stain, such expressions do not imply her immaculate conception, for in the same sermon he says explicitly: "The flesh of Christ . . . [was] of the same essence as ours, but it had this in addition, that it alone was free and removed from the corruption of sin."[2] It cannot be emphasized sufficiently that the Eastern Fathers simply thought on different lines from the later Western theologians; they used terms like "immaculate" or "stainless" much more loosely, taking them to imply only surpassing moral and physical purity, without intending to make any pronouncement about exemption from original sin, which to the Eastern mind meant mortality rather than a moral stain, as will be seen in our later discussion of the question. Without going into this problem, both Jacob of Sarug and Severus attributed the highest possible purity to Mary, while a special sanctification was assumed to have taken place at the time of the Annunciation.[3]

NARSES

While orthodox and Monophysite Fathers vied with each other in singing the praises of Mary, it might be assumed that the Nestorians were less enthusiastic. Now it is true that they were more cautious in properly doctrinal statements and, of course, they did not call her "Theotokos"; nevertheless, they

---

[1] *PO*, 8, p. 353.   [2] *PO*, 8, p. 357f.

[3] Thus also the orthodox theologian Leontius of Byzantium (d. c. 544), in his treatise against Nestorius and Eutyches, 2 (*PG*, 1328B); he also stresses the virginity *in partu* (*PG*, 1328D).

were intensely devoted to her. To give only one example: Narses (d. c. 502), the founder of the famous Nestorian school of Nisibis, called her a "second heaven";[1] he emphasized her purity and especially her poverty (cf. the first of the Beatitudes) addressing Christ as having "dwelt in the womb of the poor one".[2] He reproduces the traditional parallel with Eve,[3] and even acknowledges her part in the Redemption: "Today hope has come to Adam, for the Lord of the universe has resolved to descend through you, in order to release and deliver him [Adam]."[4] In his devotion to her he even seems to forget his Nestorianism at times, for he sings in the same *Sugitha*: "She was to become mother to him who created Adam and the world" (*v*. 7), whereas Nestorians hold that she was only mother of the man Jesus, not the Mother of God. And this doctrine naturally precluded any further Mariological progress.

ROMANOS

The most important orthodox sixth-century representative of our subject is the famous poet Romanos (c. 490–c. 560), who was a Syrian like Jacob of Sarug but wrote in Greek. Unfortunately there still exists no authoritative edition of his works, so I shall confine myself to the most important hymns on Mary which are definitely authentic.[5] As a matter of course Romanos follows the tradition of Mary's perfect virginity, quoting in this context also the Ezekiel passage of the closed door.[6] He reproduces the images of the cloud[7] and of the

[1] F. Feldmann, *Syrische Wechsellieder von Narses*, Leipzig (1896), p. 9 text, p. 16 trans.

[2] *Sugitha*, 2, 2 (Feldmann, p. 12).

[3] *Sugitha*, 2, 18f. (Feldmann, p. 13f.).　　　　[4] *v*. 29, p. 15.

[5] I quote according to J. B. Pitra, *Analecta Sacra*, 1 (1876) and G. Camelli, *Romanus il melode* (1930); cf. also C. Chevalier, "La Mariologie de Romanos", in *RSR*, 28 (1938), pp. 48–71.

[6] *In Hypapanten*, str. 9 (Camelli, p. 140); *Christmas Hymn*, str. 8 (Camelli, p. 98).

[7] *Ascension Hymn*, str. 13 (Pitra, p. 154).

mountain; but to him she is not a spiritual Mount Sinai but rather the "mystic mountain" from which "the corner stone [scil., Christ] has been cut".[1] She is also the ark in which was the urn containing the manna.[2] In his hymn on her nativity, the earliest extant evidence of this feast, the poet says that she was born like a holy temple.[3] Like his countryman, Jacob of Sarug, Romanos, too, described the Virgin under the Cross in a touching dialogue between her and the dying Christ. The Greek tradition of her doubt on Calvary was too strong even for him not at least to mention it in his hymn on the *Hypapante*, where he writes: "When you shall see your Son nailed to the Cross, blameless one . . . you will suddenly doubt; like a sword will be to you the parting of the Passion" (*vv.* 290f.); but in his beautiful poem on Mary under the Cross he has a somewhat different interpretation. There is no doubt in her words, which form a refrain: "Even though you endure the Cross, you are my Son and my God." But the question that troubles her is why he, who has done so many miracles and who has himself raised the dead, should have to suffer and die. Why could he not have redeemed Adam in some other way? After a lively interchange, in which Mary, "the blameless lamb", expresses her grief and distress, she finally accepts that such is the will of God and is promised by her Son that she will be the first to see him after the Resurrection. (11, 243f.)

For Romanos Mary is not, however, only the very human mother of Jesus; she is also the mighty intercessor for all humanity. She has shown man the right way,[4] and at the Last Judgement he prays: "Through the prayers of the ever-Virgin and Theotokos, spare me!" In the beautiful poem on the Nativity Mary herself affirms her universal motherhood: "I am not simply your [i.e., Christ's] Mother . . . but for all

[1] *Stich. 4* (Pitra, p. 223).
[2] That is to say, Christ: cf. Hebr. 9.4; *Stich.* 24 (Pitra, p. 226).
[3] *Nativity of the Virgin*, str. 3 (Pitra, p. 199).
[4] *Adam*, str. 11 (Pitra, p. 27).

men I beseech you. You have made me the mouth and the glory of my whole race; in me your world has a mighty protectress, a wall and a support. The exiles from the paradise of delights look to me."[1]

THE *AKATHISTOS*

According to the almost unanimous opinion of modern scholars Romanos is also the author of the most important Marian hymn of the Greek Church, the famous *Akathistos*. Formerly this had been attributed to Sergius of Constantinople, Germanus or George Pisidas,[2] for it was assumed that it had been composed in thanksgiving for a victory over the enemies of Constantinople; but the opening verses on which this assumption is based are almost certainly a later addition.

The *Akathistos* is essentially a hymn in praise of the Incarnation, hence it must have been composed either for the feast of the Annunciation, which probably dates from the middle of the sixth century,[3] or for the old feast of the Commemoration of Mary. The hymn, which is now sung standing (hence its name, *a-kathistos*= "not sitting") in the Greek Church on the fifth Saturday of Lent, consists of twenty-four stanzas each beginning with a different letter in alphabetical order. The first twelve tell the Gospel stories of the Nativity, including one episode, the Fall of Idols during the Flight into Egypt, from the apocryphal "Matthew". The other twelve sing the praises of Christ as the Saviour of the world and of the Theotokos. Every other stanza (one, three, five etc.) is followed by a string of salutations, each ending with the

[1] 1, 474ff. (Pitra, p. 11).

[2] Cf. C. Émereau, "Hymnographi Byzantini", in *EO*, 21 (1922); so still E. Wellesz, in the first edition of his monograph *The Akathistos Hymn* (1957), but in his ed. of 1960 he, too, accepted the authorship of Romanos. Meersseman, however, believes it to be earlier, see below. See also J. Quasten, *Patrology*.

[3] R. Fletcher, in a thesis, Oxford 1954, part of which was published in *Byzantinische Zeitschrift*, 51 (1958).

refrain: *Chaire, nymphe anympheute,* an almost untranslatable paradox: "Hail, unespoused Spouse!" and constituting, as it were, a compendium of Byzantine Mariology. For through Mary joy shines forth and Adam's fall is made good; she is the source and principle of the doctrines concerning Christ, she is both the heavenly ladder by which God descended and the bridge that leads from earth to heaven. As she is the admiration of angels, so she is the defeat of demons. She is also the propitiation of the whole world, the benevolence of God towards men as well as the confidence men have in God. She is the mouth of the Apostles and the invincible fortitude of martyrs, she extinguishes the flames of passion, she is the joy of all generations—"Hail unespoused Spouse!"[1] Next she is addressed by a string of Old-Testament types, some of which we have met before: she is the sea that has drowned the spiritual Pharaoh (i.e., the devil), the rock which has quenched men's thirst of life; she is the pillar of fire leading those in darkness, the land of promise from which flow milk and honey.[2] Then follow more theological, indeed almost metaphysical, epithets; she is the flower of incorruption from which the type of the Resurrection shines forth and which represents the life of the angels, she is the space of him who is infinite, and so she is the door to the mystery which has reconciled the opposites, virginity and childbirth, and has made good the transgression, opened paradise and become the key of Christ's kingdom.[3] She is the receptacle of God's wisdom, who shows the philosophers to be unwise and who illumines the many with wisdom. These salutations are followed by a series of others which praise her as the mighty intercessor, as which she appears ever more clearly now and in the following centuries. For she is the fortress of all who have recourse to her, because the Maker of heaven and earth dwelt in her womb; she is the minister of divine goodness, for she has regenerated those who had been conceived in shame.[4]

[1] *vv.* 12–96.   [2] 136–43.   [3] 180–90.   [4] 204–32.

She kindles the immaterial light, illuminating the mind with its radiance; she is the type of the font which takes away the filth of sin. All who hymn her childbirth praise her as the living Temple: she is the immovable tower of the Church, the unconquerable wall of the Kingdom, the healing of my body and the salvation of my soul—"Hail, unespoused Spouse, deliver all from every calamity and free all who call on you from the chastisement to come!"[1]

This hymn has been cited at length, because of its tremendous influence not only in the Greek Church, where it holds a place similar to the Latin *Te Deum* as a song of thanksgiving and rejoicing, but also in the West, having been translated in the ninth century at the latest.[2]

The *Akathistos* clearly shows the tendency, present already in Cyril and common among later writers, especially poets and preachers of both East and West, to attribute to Mary powers and activities which, strictly speaking, belong to God alone. She defeats demons, gives strength to the martyrs, extinguishes the flames of passion; she has opened paradise and is the immovable protection of the Church. All this she is and does because she is Theotokos, the Mother of the Creator. This must always be remembered, as well as the fact that these *chairetismoi* are a special *genre littéraire* and cannot, therefore, be taken as exact theological statements. It is noteworthy, however, that such poetical exaggerations, far from having originated in the medieval West, as is so often believed, first appeared in the East and only later influenced the originally far more sober Latins, as will be seen in the following chapters.

---

[1] 249–93. The hymn is to be found in *PG*, 92, 1335–48, among the works of George Pisidas, also in W. Christ and M. Paranikas in *Anthologia Carminum Christianorum* (1871) and E. Wellesz, *The Akathistos Hymn*, lxviii–lxxx; Eng. trans., D. Attwater, *The Akathistos Hymn* (1934) and G. G. Meersseman, with Greek text and introduction, Fribourg (1958).

[2] M. Huglo, "L'Ancienne Version latine de l'hymne Acathiste", in *Muséon*, 64 (1951), pp. 27–61; G. G. Meersseman, *Der Hymnos Akathistos im Abendland*, 2 vols., 1958 and 1960, in *Spicilegium Friburgense*, 2 and 3. It was also translated into Arabic, see *Muséon*, 53 (1940), pp. 89–104.

WESTERN POETRY AND DOCTRINE

The counterpart of Romanos in the West is Venantius Fortunatus (c. 530–c. 600), whose hymn *Quem Terra, Pontus, Aethera* has become the hymn for Matins and Lauds of the feasts of the blessed Virgin. Venantius, a native of Venetia, settled at Poitiers, whose bishop he became a few years before his death. Though in the form of his poetry he still followed the classical tradition, in mood and imagery he already shows a subtle change foreshadowing the Middle Ages. Like many of his predecessors he celebrates in his breviary hymn the great paradox that he whom earth, sea and heavens adore should have enclosed himself in Mary's grace-overwhelmed womb. Mary is called the glorious Lady, *gloriosa Domina*, exalted above the stars—accents absent from the more sober Latin devotion of earlier times—who suckled her Creator. Giving back what Eve had taken away, she becomes our window of heaven. For she is the portal of the great King and through her we are given life. A new tenderness makes itself felt in these verses, in which men turn trustingly to the powerful Lady who is also the gentle mother suckling her child, a being subtly different from (and, if it may be so expressed, somehow less "metaphysical" a figure than) the great Theotokos of the Greeks and the Virgin Mother of the earlier Latins. In his poem *In Praise of the Holy Virgin Mary*[1] he calls her "dear, benign, radiant, holy, venerable, lovely, flower, adornment, altar, splendour, palm, crown, chastity",[2] and he prefers to address her as "Mother". After praying to Christ he also begs her, "Deign to add your help, Mother, by prayer",[3] for she is the queen, the wonderful mother who is glorified by her childbirth,[4] and who is redder than roses, whiter than lilies, a new flower of matchless beauty.[5] Almost imperceptibly she has left the strictly theological sphere and

[1] *PL*, 88, 276–84.   [2] *PL*, 88, 284A.   [3] 8, 9.
[4] *PL*, 88, 282B.   [5] *PL*, 88, 281B.

become an image fulfilling men's desire for beauty and security.

Gregory the Great (c. 540–604), on the other hand, continued in the sober tradition of the Papacy. In one of his epistles[1] he explains that Mary is both handmaid and mother. She is the handmaid of the Lord, because the Word existed eternally equal to the Father, but she is also mother, because this same Word was made man of her own flesh through the Holy Spirit. In a homily on the Gospels,[2] when commenting on Matt. 12.46ff., he identifies her with the Synagogue, because she was standing "outside", an extraordinary interpretation, especially in view of the fact that from the time of St. Ambrose Latin theologians had generally regarded her as the type of the Church.

In the "Explanation of the First Book of Kings"[3] the language used about her is quite different: there she is identified with the Mountain of Ephraim, because she transcends every other creature by the dignity of her election, being superior to both men and angels and reaching up to the very throne of the Godhead. This work, often considered doubtful, has recently been attributed to the Pope by several theologians;[4] but the language here used about Mary does seem to be different from that in the definitely genuine works of Gregory.

THE FIRST MARIAN INTERPRETATION OF APOCALYPSE 12

The just-mentioned identification of Mary with the Church had its bearing on the exegesis of the twelfth chapter of the Apocalypse. The early Fathers had seen in the Woman clothed with the Sun only the Church. In the fifth century a

[1] 11, 67 (PL, 77, 1207C).   [2] In Evang. 3, 1 (PL, 76, 1086C).
[3] 1, 5 (PL, 79C, D).
[4] Cf. P. Verbraken in RBE, 66 (1956), pp. 39–62, 159–217.

short pseudo-Augustinian text, generally attributed to the saint's disciple, Quodvultdeus, identified this woman with the Virgin Mary, "who herself showed forth the figure of the holy Church".[1]

But the first completely Marian interpretation of the chapter without any mention of the Church comes from a Greek author, the philosopher Oecumenius, who lived in the first half of the sixth century and wrote the earliest extant commentary on the whole book.[2] The vision of the seer, he writes, "describes the Theotokos". After quoting the relevant passage he continues: "Rightly does the vision show her in heaven and not upon earth, as pure in soul and body, as equal to the angels, as a citizen of heaven, as having contained and given flesh to the God who reposes in heaven; for she has nothing in common with the earth and its evils, but is wholly sublime, wholly worthy of heaven, even though she shares our human nature and being."[3] Here the Theotokos appears as a perfectly pure being who has nothing in common with the evils of the earth. She is fully human, but through her very purity she belongs to heaven. The author then goes on to interpret the beings around her. The sun is Christ; but though she once contained him in her womb he is here seen as surrounding her, so as to make it clear that even "while he was being carried in the womb the Lord was the protector of his Mother and of all creation".[4] The twelve stars crowning her signify the Apostles, who preach Christ and with whom she also preaches herself. She was in travail, not in her childbirth, which was without pain, but on account of the suspicions of Joseph.[5] At the end of this explanation of the vision he once more affirms, as if to reproach those who interpret it of the Church, that it is wholly "about our common Lady, the holy ever-virgin and Theotokos Mary".

[1] *PL*, 40, 661.   [2] Ed. H. C. Hoskier, Univ. of Michigan (1928).
[3] Hoskier, p.135f.   [4] Hoskier, p. 137.   [5] Hoskier, p. 137.

THE ASSUMPTION. FEAST AND BELIEFS

The picture Oecumenius presents of the Woman clothed with the Sun calls to mind later paintings of the Assumption; and perhaps his interpretation[1] may have been influenced by the growing belief in the bodily presence of Mary in heaven. In Gaul this seems to have been accepted in the second half of the sixth century, for Gregory of Tours (d. 594), the friend of Venantius Fortunatus, repeats without questioning it the apocryphal story of her death which will be discussed presently.[2] Increasing acceptance of the bodily assumption of Mary was due to two developments starting towards the end of the fifth and the beginning of the sixth centuries: the appearance in various localities of a feast of Mary's death, and apocryphal writings describing the circumstances of her passing and her reception into heaven.

As in the case of most of the early feasts of the Church, the beginnings of the feast of the assumption of Mary or of her "falling asleep" (Greek *koimesis*, Latin *dormitio*), as it was usually called in the Greek Church, are not clear, and the opinion of scholars is divided. In the East a feast of Mary seems to have existed even before the Council of Ephesus; it was called the Commemoration (*mneme*) of St. Mary and was in many places kept on the Sunday before Christmas.[3] From the beginning of the sixth century it was celebrated in Antioch as well as in Gaul on 18 January, and was connected with her death, as the feasts of all the other

[1] Cf. also Cassiodorus, *Complexiones in Apoc.* 11.5, *PL*, 70, 1411B.

[2] *Miracula*, 1, 4 (*PL*, 71, 708B, C). His witness, however, is hardly more than a reflection of contemporary popular belief in Gaul and has no theological value, for, as Altaner (*Patrology*, p. 571) says: "In his great hagiographical collection [i.e., the *Miracula*] his credulity and lack of criticism with regard to accounts of miracles are even more evident" than in his other writings.

[3] Cf. Jugie's Introduction to the Marian Homilies of Theodotus of Ancyra and Chrysippus of Jerusalem, *PO*, 19 (1925); he thinks that Proclus' sermon before Nestorius was preached on this feast, because it begins: "Today, on the feast of the Virgin"; cf. also B. Capelle, *ETL*, 3 (1926), p. 35.

saints; elsewhere, especially in Palestine (Jerusalem) it was kept on 15 August.[1] About the year 600 the Emperor Maurice ordered its celebration in the East on 15 August.[2] The history of this feast is intimately connected with an apocryphal narrative, generally called the *Transitus* (= "passing"), which exists with greater or lesser variants in Greek, Latin, Syriac, Coptic, Arabic and Ethiopic versions. The original probably belonged to the end of the fifth century, and was attributed to St. John the Evangelist. According to the early Greek text and its Latin counterpart published by A. Wenger,[3] an angel appears to Mary bringing her a palm and announcing her death. She calls together her friends and tells them about it; then arrives John, later all the other Apostles, including also St. Paul. On the third day before she is to die Mary goes out to pray. On the day of her death, at the third hour, Jesus comes to her; she thanks him and dies, and he gives orders to Peter concerning her burial. When the funeral procession is on its way to the tomb the Jews attack it; the priest who tries to touch the bier has his hands cut off and all his companions are blinded. This miracle converts them and all are healed. The Apostles place Mary's body in the tomb; after three days Jesus returns, the angels take up the body and place it under the tree of life in paradise, where it is reunited to her soul. This tale, together with the institution of the feast of the *koimesis* or "dormition", greatly influenced the Marian literature of the following centuries.

Of special interest is a sermon only recently discovered on the feast by an otherwise unknown bishop, Theoteknos of Livias, a city on the left bank of the Jordan, opposite Jericho.

[1] Dom Capelle (*ETL*, 3 (1926), p. 38) finds a solution for the problem of the two different dates in a Coptic apocryphon, contained in M. R. James, *The Apocryphal New Testament* (1924), pp. 194–201, which states that Mary died on January 18 (21st of Tobi), but that her empty tomb was found only 206 days later, i.e., on August 15 (16th Mesore).

[2] Cf. Nicephorus Callistus, *Hist. Eccl.*, 17, 28 (*PG*, 147, 292).

[3] "L'Assomption de la Très-Sainte Vierge dans la tradition Byzantine du VIe au Xe Siècle", in *Archives de l'Orient chrétien*, 5, Paris (1955).

Wenger, who edited the homily,[1] places it at the end of the sixth century, or at least between 550 and 650. Thus it is one of the earliest Catholic affirmations of belief in the bodily assumption of Mary, if not perhaps *the* earliest of them.[2] Theoteknos, while reproducing the apocryphal legend, develops the theme theologically, giving the reasons why it was fitting that Mary should be assumed into heaven, body and soul. For Christ took his immaculate flesh from the immaculate flesh of Mary,[3] and if he had prepared a place in heaven for the Apostles, how much more for his mother;[4] if Enoch had been translated[5] and Elijah had gone to heaven, how much more Mary, "who like the moon in the midst of the stars, shines forth and excels among the Prophets and Apostles"?[6] For even though her God-bearing body tasted death, it did not undergo corruption, but "was preserved incorrupt and undefiled and taken up into heaven with its pure and spotless soul by the holy archangels and powers and is above Enoch and Elijah and all the Prophets and Apostles and the heavens, except only God".[7] Theoteknos stresses that her body was taken up together with her soul, because in some of the accounts it was asserted that Mary's body was preserved incorrupt in paradise but would not be reunited to her soul until the general resurrection. According to Theoteknos Mary is in heaven both with her body and her soul, the creature closest to God, and there exercises her great office of intercession. That Mary intercedes for mankind had been the common

---

[1] "L'Assomption."

[2] Wenger ("L'Assomption", p. 99), gives as evidence of its early date the fact that the feast is called *analempsis*, whereas its later name was *koimesis*; but this is not quite conclusive, as the word was used in this sense also by the eighth-century author Hippolytus of Thebe—see *A Patristic Greek Lexicon*, 1961, s.v. *analepsis*. Incidentally, Wenger's discovery refutes Baumstark's assertion, in his article on the bodily Assumption of the Blessed Virgin in *OC*, 4, p. 389, that belief in this doctrine remained foreign to the Jerusalem tradition until the eighth century.

[3] *v.* 2. p. 272 and *v.* 20, p. 282.   [4] *v.* 10, p. 276.   [5] *v.* 13, p. 278.
[6] *v.* 14, p. 278.   [7] *v.* 15, p. 278.

belief especially of Eastern Christendom, as is shown by the early prayer *Sub Tuum Praesidium*; but with the feast of her assumption it received a fresh emphasis and was proclaimed in all the sermons on this occasion. For she is the Mother of all the Apostles[1] and thus of all the Christians: ". . . even while she was still on earth she was a heaven and conversed with angels and was the ambassadress of mankind with the undefiled King . . . He has truly glorified her and will again glorify her";[2] while she was still on earth she watched over all, and "now being assumed into heaven she is the unconquerable wall for humanity, interceding for us with her Son and God".[3] Belief in her assumption has given her a new power; nothing can now prevail against her mighty intercession: for she is the ark and the pot of manna, she is a throne and a heaven, and ineffable mysteries are entrusted to her.[4] She is a cosmic figure like the Woman in the Apocalypse.

Not all theologians, however, accepted Mary's bodily assumption, and the feast of 15 August was often regarded as no more than the commemoration of her death. This, at least, was the opinion of John of Thessalonica, whose sermon on the Assumption, preached before 630, was published by M. Jugie.[5] Thessalonica, John tells us, was one of the last Greek cities to introduce the feast; his predecessors opposed it on account of the fantastic tales about Mary's death circulated by the heretics. Therefore he undertook to give the story of it shorn of some of its extravagances. He believed that an original account of it existed and was handed on by the Apostles to later generations. His work is not much more than a sobered-up reproduction of the apocryphal story; it is interesting because it emphasizes Mary's universal motherhood. Though she is the most glorious mistress of the whole world,[6] (a title dear to the later Byzantines), for him she is above all "the mother of all that are saved"[7] and is repeatedly called "Mary,

[1] *v.* 9, p. 276.   [2] *v.* 17, p. 280.   [3] *v.* 36, p. 290.   [4] *v.* 22, p. 282.
[5] *PO*, 19 (1925), pp. 344–438.   [6] 2, p. 375.   [7] 8, p. 388.

our mother".[1] At her death Jesus and Michael receive her soul,[2] and John is convinced that Christ will glorify those who glorify his immaculate mother.[3]

A far more theological homily is that attributed to Modestus of Jerusalem.[4] The author deliberately omits all the fanciful details of the apocryphal story; the angels surrounding Mary at her death remain invisible, nor is there any mention of the Jews laying hands on the bier and the ensuing miracles. On the other hand, while remaining silent on its manner, Modestus teaches firmly the fact of Mary's bodily assumption, which is a corollary of her divine motherhood. "Because she was the all-glorious Mother of Christ, our Saviour and God, the giver of life and immortality, she was brought back to life by him, con-corporeal[5] [or 'of the same body'] in incorruption for all eternity with him who had raised her from the tomb and taken her to himself in a manner known to him alone."[6] In heaven she is above the cherubim and seraphim, because she is the Mother of the Lord;[7] and she is not only his mother, she is also his bride, an idea that is gaining ground about this time, probably influenced by Christ's presentation of himself as the Bridegroom:[8] "Into the heavenly bridechamber entered the most glorious of brides . . . of Christ, the true heavenly Bridegroom."[9] Modestus repeats the well-known Old-Testament types; she is the ark of sanctification,[10] the mountain from which Christ was hewn,[11] the sealed fountain by which the paradise of the orthodox Church is watered;[12]

---

[1] e.g., 9, p. 390.   [2] 12, p. 396.   [3] 14, p. 402.

[4] PG, 86[2], 3277–3312; M. Jugie, in "La Mort et l'Assomption", ST, 114 (1944), p. 218, considers this to be spurious, but A. Wenger, "L'Assomption", as well as other theologians, think it is genuine.

[5] Greek syssomos, "of the same body with"; the word occurs first in Eph. 3.6, where St. Paul uses it of the Gentiles who are to belong to the same body as the Jews.

[6] No. 14 (PG, 86[2], 3312B).   [7] No. 3 (PG, 86[2], 3288B, C).

[8] Later the same conception in the West will be due mainly to the Marian interpretation of the Canticle.

[9] 3 (PG, 86[2], 3288A, B).   [10] 4 (PG, 86[2], 3289A).   [11] 6 (PG, 86[2], 3292B).

[12] 6 (PG, 86[2], 3292C).

she is also the bridge between heaven and earth.[1] She is intimately connected with our redemption, for through the most glorious Theotokos we have been mystically re-created, received forgiveness of sins, been redeemed and put on Christ.[2] And so she is the help of Christians (*he antilepsis . . . ton eusebounton*) who intercedes for us, the source of our remedies,[3] our refuge[4] and our spiritual paradise.[5]

EARLY MARIAN RELICS

With the ever-growing veneration of the Theotokos, especially in the Christian East, there emerged also a cult of her relics. Her veil was venerated in the sanctuary of Blachernae, near Constantinople, from the middle of the sixth century. This in itself is proof of the belief in her bodily assumption, as no other relics were held to exist, as is clearly stated in a later legend dating from the middle of the eighth century. According to this, in 451 the Empress Pulcheria asked Bishop Juvenal of Jerusalem for the body of Mary. He replied that they did not possess this, since an old tradition affirmed that, when the Apostles opened her tomb on the third day after her death, they did not find her body but only the funeral clothes. Thereupon Pulcheria asked for these, which Juvenal sent in a sealed casket. This legend also quotes a passage from Dionysius the Pseudo-Areopagite (c. 500) which has played a considerable role in establishing the belief, since the works of this anonymous writer were attributed to the disciple of St. Paul throughout the Middle Ages. The passage itself is obscure. It simply refers to "that mortal body, source of life, which received the incarnate God" which Dionysius and his companions "met together to behold" (*De Divinis Nominibus*, 3, 2), but it came to be regarded as proof of her bodily assumption. According to an earlier legend, which

[1] 9 (*PG*, 86², 3300B). [2] 7 (*PG*, 86², 3293A–3295C).
[3] 10 (*PG*, 86², 3301C). [4] *PG*, 86², 3304A.
[5] *PG*, 86², 3305A.

knows nothing of Pseudo-Dionysius, Mary had entrusted her veil, on which had also fallen some drops of her milk when she had fed Jesus, to two women of her entourage. It finally was handed down to a Jewish woman who kept it in a casket and performed miracles with it. When two patricians[1] heard of this they stole the casket with the veil and brought it to Constantinople. During an attack on the city by the Avari in 619 it was removed from its sanctuary; when the barbarians retreated after a few days, it was solemnly brought back to the sanctuary on 2 July by the Patriarch Sergius, who instituted a feast on the same day, which is still kept in the East.[2]

Sergius, who was a Monothelite, had a strong opponent in the orthodox Sophronius, a native of Damascus who was raised to the Patriarchal See of Jerusalem in 634. He preached a homily on the feast of the Annunciation, which was originally a feast of Christ but gradually was transferred to Mary, as had also been the case with the ancient feast of the Hypapante. The sermon for the Annunciation is for the greater part a conversation between the Virgin and the angel, a lengthy elaboration of the short scene in the Gospel. Mary is addressed as mother and fountain of heavenly joy, as the "unmarried Mother of God" exalted above all angels, who has soared above the six-winged seraphim and is purer than any other creature.[3] The blessing that had once been lost now flows to men through her,[4] a teaching adumbrating the mediation of grace; for no-one was ever purified "beforehand" like her, no-one enriched by God's gifts like her[5]—language nearer to the Western idea of the Immaculate Conception than most other Greek statements on Mary's purity. From her joy flowed not only to men, but also to the powers above,[6] for in her the eternal and infinite God was conceived in time and

---

[1] Byzantine title created by Constantine.
[2] Wenger, "L'Assomption", pp. 119–23.
[3] 18 (*PG*, 87, 3237B–D).   [4] 24 (*PG*, 87, 3245A).
[5] 25 (*PG*, 87, 3248A).   [6] 21 (*PG*, 87, 3241B).

circumscribed in space.[1] Therefore she does not need to be afraid of the angel; on the contrary, the angel ought to be afraid of her.[2] From now on this reverential fear she inspires on account of her tremendous dignity is a frequently recurring subject.

SPANISH THEOLOGIANS

Compared with the glowing language of the Eastern Fathers, the Latins of the seventh century sound almost commonplace. We must, however, remember that the West was overrun by the barbarians far more than the East, and theology, like every other aspect of culture, was in the doldrums. The only authors to say a little more about the Mother of God are the Spaniards Leander of Seville (d. c. 600), his younger brother Isidore (d. 636) and Ildefonsus of Toledo (d. 667), and even they say nothing new. Their main theme is the virginal motherhood. Leander calls her the "mother of incorruption", who spiritually brought forth his sister Florentina when she became a nun and is sure to intercede for her with her Son;[3] she is the "mother and leader of virgins" whom she has "brought forth by her example".[4] Isidore, whose *Etymologiae* supplied the medieval authors with much of their knowledge on all kinds of subjects, explains in this same work Mary's name as "illuminatrix or star of the sea" (7, 10) and in his *Allegoriae* equates her with the Church "which, being espoused to Christ, has as a virgin conceived us from the Holy Spirit and as a virgin brings us forth". (139.) In another work, *De Ortu et Obitu Patrum*, he gives her the well-known epithets of the rod of Jesse, garden enclosed, sealed fountain, sanctuary of the Holy Spirit. (111.) When discussing her death he records the opinion of "some" that she suffered martyrdom, because of Simeon's prophecy about the sword that was to pierce her soul; but this, Isidore

[1] 28 (*PG*, 87, 3252B).   [2] 26 (*PG*, 87, 3249A, B).
[3] *De Institutione Virginum* (*PL*, 72, 877B–877C).   [4] *PL*, 72, 877D.

comments, is "uncertain", because it may also refer to a spiritual sword, and besides, there are no records of it, not even of her death, though some say that her sepulchre is to be found in the Valley of Josaphat. Isidore either knows nothing of, or refuses to believe in, her bodily assumption, for this would have been the appropriate place to discuss it. Evidently the belief current in Gaul a century earlier (see Gregory of Tours) was not accepted in Spain, for even in the works of Ildefonsus of Toledo, her most fervent devotee, no mention is made of her assumption.

Ildefonsus consecrated a treatise to her perpetual virginity, directed against the heretics Jovinian and Helvidius as well as the Jews, who denied it.[1] It opens with an ardent invocation to his "lady and mistress", to her who is nearest to God, asking her to obtain for him "the spirit of my Redeemer, so that I may think about you what is true and worthy". (1.) In ever-varied terms he affirms especially her virginity *in partu*, a virginity that is superior to that of the angels, since it was not corrupted even by birth, whereas the purity of the angels could be corrupted because they could and did fall. (10.) In the final chapter he asks for her intercession in terms not so far used in the West: "And now I come to you, sole Mother and Virgin of God . . . I ask you to obtain for me that my sins be done away with, that you make me love the glory of your virginity . . . that you may grant me to cleave to God and to you . . . to him as my Creator, to you as the Mother of our Maker . . . to him as God, to you as the Mother of God, to him as to my Redeemer, to you as to the work of my redemption. For what he has effected in my redemption, he has formed in the truth of your person." The Redemption Christ has brought us is most intimately linked with Mary, because the Redeemer was truly formed in her. Therefore Ildefonsus prays to Christ "that I may serve your

---

[1] *De Virginitate B. Mariae*, ed. V. B. Garcia, Madrid (1937), also in *PL*, 96, 53–110.

6+

Mother so that from this fact you may recognize that I have served you", for the service of Mary is inseparable from the service of her Son—a theme Ildefonsus appears to have been the first to develop with such clarity and insistency, for he continues: "So that I may be the servant of her Son I desire that she may be my mistress . . . so that I may be the devoted slave of the Son of the Mother, I desire faithfully the servitude of the Parent . . ." accents which anticipate the language of the medieval "knight of Mary"; and he ends with an axiom which we have met before, but less emphatically expressed: "Thus overflows to the Son what is given to the Mother . . . thus the honour paid to the service of the Queen redounds to the honour of the King." (12.) The idea of personal service, of the mistress–servant relation between Mary and the Christian is something new; it involves a personal consecration which goes beyond theological speculation and liturgical devotion.

WESTERN LITURGICAL DEVELOPMENTS

This latter was now also developing in the West. Formerly it had been the generally received opinion that the *hypapante* (purification), assumption, annunciation and nativity of Mary were introduced in Rome during the reign of the Greek Pope Sergius (687–701). But recent research has shown that the development was more gradual. The Purification (2 February) was the first to be celebrated there, some time during the first half of the seventh century or even earlier; it was followed by the Assumption (15 August) round about 650,[1] a little later came the Annunciation (25 March), and finally, towards the end of the seventh century, the Nativity of Mary (8 September). Of these the first and the third were originally feasts of Christ, belonging to the Christmas cycle, but which were soon given a more

[1] Probably introduced in Rome by Pope Theodore (642–9), see Wenger, "L'Assomption", p. 141.

markedly Marian orientation,[1] whilst the Assumption became the principal Marian feast, commemorating the day
of her death, as in the case of the martyrs and all the
other saints. Belief in her bodily assumption is at least
implied by the ancient Latin prayer *Veneranda* for this feast,
still recited (for example, in the Dominican Mass and Office),
which states that the holy Mother of God indeed underwent
temporal death, "but could not be held by the bonds of
death". But of sermons on these feasts, which contributed so
much to Mariology in the East, there is hardly a trace in the
Latin-speaking countries about this time.

THE END OF THE PATRISTIC PERIOD

The eighth century brings us to the end of the patristic
period, and with it to the consummation of Marian doctrine
in the East and the beginnings of a fresh flowering of it in the
newly emerging nations of the West. As in the preceding
century, the feast of the Assumption was the occasion for the
most fervent sermons on the Theotokos. In 1958 A. Wenger
edited another hitherto unknown homily on the feast which
the medieval manuscript attributes to Germanus of Constantinople, but which is most probably not by him.[2]

AN ANONYMOUS HOMILY ON THE ASSUMPTION

It is particularly interesting that the author of this homily
frankly admits that the story of Mary's passing is nowhere to
be found in Scripture and that the holy Fathers have left no
records of it either, if one excepts Dionysius the Areopagite,
whose mention of it, however, is obscure. Hence the apocryphal writers were free to falsify the story as much as they
liked. (ch. 1.) In the following chapters the author explains

---

[1] See A. Chavasse, *Le Sacramentaire Gélasien* (1958), pp. 375–402 and
Laurentin, *Court Traité de théologie mariale*,⁴ Paris (1959), p. 56.
[2] A. Wenger, "Un Nouveau Témoin de l'Assomption", in *Etudes Byzantines*, 16 (1958), pp. 43–58.

how this came about. In the early days of Christianity heresy and idolatry were rife, hence the Fathers of the first centuries did not even leave precise explanations of the mysteries of Christ and the consubstantial Trinity. (The divinity of Christ and that of the Holy Spirit were not defined until the fourth century.) How much less would they have explained the mystery of Mary! In these circumstances Mary's passing remained a matter of oral tradition only, which, the author insists, expresses the same truths as Scripture and hence merits the same credence. (2–5.) He then produces what Wenger calls "archaeological witnesses" to the Assumption, namely, the tomb at Gethsemani, Mary's house in Jerusalem and a cubic monument in memory of the miracles that happened during the funeral procession. He adduces a further proof from the Liturgy: the three-night vigil before the feast and its celebration ordered by law. (6f.) The legend is scarcely touched upon; Christ comes to take his Mother, escorted by powers from on high, and as she had conceived without lust and given birth without pain, so she also gives up her wholly uncontaminated (*panakeratos*) soul without pain, being the only human being to do so. He explains why: Christ wanted to suffer for us in order to redeem us; but as Mary had never committed a sin, how could he have left her body in pain? After Eve, who had given us death as our heritage because of her transgression, Mary alone, because of her obedience, was judged worthy to die without suffering. She died because she had been conceived from the union of her parents, but she escaped from the pain of death because she had brought forth Christ without marital union. (7–10.) He then anathematizes all who will not confess Mary to be the bearer, receptacle and mother of God. At her death the world trembled, for how could the universe fail to be shaken when its mistress left it? Then follow the familiar strings of epithets, first the well-known ones from the Old Testament, such as "Ark of Sanctification" and "Sealed Fountain", then others in praise of her virtues, especially of her transcendent purity; she is without the slightest stain, glorified above all creatures, surpassingly wise and venerable, exalted above men, angels and any other rational creatures. (11–15.) And now, as her body, the source of life (*zoarchikon soma*), is taken up to heaven, she intercedes with Christ for the world, while the faithful endeavour to merit her prayers. Finally, she, the "daughter of Sion", is bidden to go to her rest and always remember us to her Son: "Depart in the body and remain with us, your slaves and clients. For we have placed all our hope in you, believing that we shall be saved through your holy prayers and the grace and merciful love of our Lord Jesus Christ." (16–19.)

We have here the same idea of service of Mary—the words *desmioi* and *prosphygoi*, "captives" and "refugees", are very strong—as in Ildefonsus. Besides the merciful love of Christ Mary's prayers, too, are needed for salvation; indeed, so great is the power of her intercession that Christians can even be said to place all their hope in her. This, again, is an expression that must not be taken too literally; for as in the interpretation of Scripture we have to take into account the various literary forms, so we must also, in the writings of the Fathers and the later Christian authors, distinguish between exact theological treatises and enthusiastic sermons and panegyrics, where exaggerations are not taken so seriously.

GERMANUS OF CONSTANTINOPLE

Germanus (d. 733), Patriarch of Constantinople, was an ardent defender of the veneration of icons, which was then first attacked by the Emperor Leo II the Isaurian. His two sermons on the Assumption[1] elaborate the same themes as the homily just discussed, but in even stronger language. The patriarch calls himself Mary's slave (*doulos*); he will praise her

---

[1] *PG*, 98, counted by Migne as three; but, as Jugie, "La Mort et l'Assomption", pp. 226f., has shown, the first two are two parts of the same sermon.

as best he can, even though she can never be praised sufficiently.[1] While she was on earth she conversed with heaven,
and so now she is in heaven, the "Mother of Life" will not
forget those whose salvation she is—again, a very strong
term.[2] She is, of course, in heaven both soul and body, for she
reclined in the tomb of Gethsemani "only for form's sake"
and immediately after her death she passed into life.[3] The
power of her intercession and her part in our redemption are
emphasized more strongly than in any Father before him. Her
assistance is sufficient for our salvation, and apart from God she
needs no other helper: "You are the mother of true life. You
are the leaven of the reformation of Adam. You are the freedom
from the shame of Eve . . . there is no limit to your help."[4]
"If you did not lead the way, no-one would become spiritual,
no man would adore God in truth; for then did man become
spiritual, when you, Theotokos, were made the dwelling of
the Holy Spirit. No man is filled with the knowledge of God
except through you, all-holy one, no man is saved except
through you, Theotokos; no man is freed from dangers, except through you, virgin and mother; no man is redeemed,
except through you, Mother of God . . ." even Mai, his first
Western editor, had to add a footnote explaining in what way
this could be said of her—namely, that unless Christ had been
born from her man would not have been redeemed; but the
language in which Germanus expressed himself was certainly
extremely strong.

It seems that he was also the first author to affirm two other
points concerning her intercession which became a commonplace in the Middle Ages, but which cannot be accepted at
their face value. Here is the exact translation of the relevant
passages in the same sermon: "But you, having maternal
power with God, can obtain abundant forgiveness even for the
greatest sinners. For he can never fail to hear you, because
God *obeys* [*peitharchei*] you through and in all things, as his

[1] 340B.   [2] 340B–345A.   [3] 364A.   [4] 349A–B.

true Mother."[1] However much allowance might be made for the enthusiasm of the preacher, it is not permissible to say that God obeys Mary as his Mother. For, first, even though Mary had authority over Christ as long as he was a child, he no longer obeyed her when he was a man, as is quite clear from the New-Testament accounts. Secondly, even less can one say that Christ in his Godhead obeys her, because she is his creature and handmaid. True, Mary's intercession is in a sense all-powerful, but for no other reason than that she invariably intercedes in accordance with God's will; she obeys him, not he her.

The other point Germanus makes is that Mary averts the wrath of God. "You turn away the just threat and the sentence of damnation, because you love the Christians . . . therefore the Christian people trustfully turn to you, refuge of sinners."[2] Here are the roots of another aberration of Marian devotion: the idea that God wants to destroy the sinner, who is saved only by the intercession of Mary—in flat contradiction to the saying in St. John's Gospel that "God so loved the world that he gave his only begotten Son, that whoever believed in him might not perish."[3] Mary certainly has a share in man's salvation, for Christ was born from her, but she acts always in complete dependence on him; the tendency to give her more and more independence, even to place her in a position of authority with regard to almighty God and oppose her mercy to God's wrath, is not compatible with a balanced theology. No wonder that many of the less well instructed preachers and devotional writers of a later age, who read these sermons in a Latin translation, stressed just these points, which would appeal to the emotions of their public, who could not assimilate the metaphysical considerations on the Trinity and the Incarnation of the golden age of the Fathers. The praises of Mary that follow in this homily on the Assumption all emphasize her relation to men as their supreme helper and

[1] 352A.   [2] 352A, B.   [3] 3.16.

reflect the language of the Akathistos Hymn. She is the unchangeable refuge, the never-sleeping intercessor, the everlasting salvation, the unconquerable wall and tower of help, the port of those shaken by storms, the return of the exiles and the commendation of the condemned.[1] When her Son comes to judge the earth, then those who would not confess her to be Theotokos will know of what treasure they have perversely deprived themselves, for she concerns herself with all our affairs, and her name is more necessary for our protection than our very breath.[2] The second sermon describes the actual assumption according to the legend, including the attack of the Jews on the body. It also gives a theological reason for it: Mary must be where her Son is. As soon as her body has been deposited in the tomb she passes into life, where her soul will see the Father, her stainless body the glory of the Son, and her pure spirit the Holy Spirit, following the Greek idea of the threefold division of man into body, soul and spirit.[3] There she becomes the mediatress (mesitis) between God and man.[4] The sermon ends with a prayer to the Theotokos asking her to unify the Church, to confirm Christians in faith and hope, to give peace to the world and to free all men from every danger and temptation.[5]

The two sermons on the Presentation contain sections that form part of the third nocturn of Matins of the feast of the Immaculate Conception in the Roman breviary. The first sermon opens with the verse of the Canticle, "Who is she that goeth up by the desert?"[6] which is attributed to the Theotokos, whose beauty surpasses all language and thought.[7] Germanus then reproduces the apocryphal story of Mary's childhood in the Temple, and her purity is praised in terms that have led Western theologians to assume that he believed her never to have been subject to original sin; for not only is Mary, when presented in the Temple, above the heavens, but

---

[1] 352C–353A.   [2] 353C–356B.   [3] 361A–364A.   [4] 365.   [5] 372C.
[6] 3.6 (292D–293A).   [7] 293D.

she sanctifies the sanctuary rather than is sanctified by it.[1] However, as has been stated before, the Greek Fathers had quite a different idea of original sin from that of the Latins and so his passage can hardly be taken in such a sense, indicating no more than her transcendent purity. As she grew up, the curse that had been pronounced against us in Eden was invalidated; hence she is hailed as the rational paradise of God in which blooms the tree of life; she is the new Sion, the divine Jerusalem, and is once more called "wholly without stain", *panamomos*.[2] Germanus repeats his conviction that her prayers are completely effective because of her maternal authority,[3] and asks her to help the orthodox emperors and their armies in time of war, and especially her own city, Constantinople, whose tower and foundation she is.[4]

The language of the second sermon is no less fervent, though it loses some of its strangeness if we reflect that the Byzantine emperors and princes, too, were commonly addressed in terms that would sound almost blasphemous to modern ears. "You alone, Theotokos," says Germanus, "are the highest on the whole earth; and we, O Bride of God, bless you in faith . . . and prostrate ourselves before you in fear, always magnifying you and reverently pronouncing you blessed."[5] Speaking to her in his own person, Germanus tells her that she is the strength of his weakness, the clothing of his nakedness, the riches of his poverty, "Lady . . . my refuge, life and help . . . my hope and my strength."[6]

His sermon on the Annunciation, with its customary long conversation between Mary and the angel, is in much the same style; she is truly the mediation (*mesiteia*, an abstract) of all sinners,[7] the "heavenly bride" before whom the angel must tremble,[8] under whose protection the whole human race will take refuge, for she is the propitiation of all Christians.[9]

---

[1] 301C.   [2] 304C–308C.   [3] 304C–308C.
[4] 308C–309A.   [5] 317B, C.   [6] 317D–320A.
[7] 321B.   [8] 321C, 328A.   [9] 329A, B.

6*

Yet another Marian sermon was preached on the feast of Mary's girdle, kept as a relic in the Church at Blachernae near Constantinople, and exalted in the most exaggerated terms. Since the Son rejoices when his mother is honoured,[1] Mary is once more called the comfort of Christians, and the preacher asks: "If we were abandoned by you, where should we go to?" For she is the breath and life of Christians, and her name is always on their lips.[2] Therefore "protect us with the wings of your goodness, be our help through your mediation, give us eternal life, unfailing hope of Christians . . . We seek God through you."

Once more, we have to allow for the exaggerations of Byzantine terminology; but it is interesting to note that the idea that Christians go to God by way of Mary originated with the Greeks.

ANDREW OF CRETE

With Germanus we have reached the high-water-mark of Marian devotion in the Church of the Fathers. Andrew of Crete (d. 740), a native of Damascus who became Archbishop of Gortyna in Crete about 692, though deeply devoted to Mary, was nevertheless more sober in his expressions. In his three homilies on the feast of her dormition he does not actually affirm her assumption into heaven with body and soul.[3] Though he himself seems to prefer this doctrine, he nevertheless leaves open other possibilities, such as that her soul is in heaven while her body was placed in some paradise situated in our own sphere, or that God devised some other special destiny for her which is unknown to us.[4] The feast itself, he says, was formerly kept only by a few, but is now honoured and loved by all.[5] In the second sermon he gives reasons for

[1] 376D.   [2] 377D.
[3] According to Jugie, "La Mort et l'Assomption", the three homilies printed in *PG*, 97, 1045–1110 should be read in the following order: (1) 1072–90; (2) 1045–72; (3) 1091–1110.
[4] 1084A.   [5] 1072B.

the silence of the New Testament and of the early Fathers on Mary's death: one was that her death came very late, so that it could not be recorded in the Scriptures; another, that the Incarnation had to be preached first.[1] The third sermon is a funeral eulogy: all the sacred writers have sung of her, Moses when he described the Burning Bush, David chanting of the Ark of the Sanctification, the Canticle, Isaiah, Ezekiel—all the Scriptures foretell her.[2] She is the mistress of all men, the leader and life of the living, holier than all the saints, the fortress of the Christian faith, for she fights for those who hope in her.

Her holiness is praised in terms that seem to exclude original sin, though not actually in the Latin sense of the Immaculate Conception. In his first homily on Mary's nativity Andrew says: "Today Adam . . . consecrates Mary as a firstfruit, and in her the unmixed [or 'undefiled'] one of the whole mixture [*holou phyramatos he me phyratheisa*, i.e., the only sinless one of sinful humanity] is made into bread for the restoration of the race."[3] He continues: "Today the pure nobility of men receives the grace of the first creation by God and thus returns to itself; and the [human] nature, which clings to the [newly] born Mother of the Beautiful One, receives back the glorious beauty which had been dimmed by the degradation of evil, and the best and most marvellous new formation. And this new formation is truly a re-formation, and the re-formation a deification, and this a restoration to the first state."[4] This means that in the newly-born Mary human nature is restored to its original purity before the Fall, that she is *born* without original sin; her conception is not visualized in this context.

In his fourth homily on the same subject, Andrew enunciates the principle that all biblical passages referring to the Church can also be applied to Mary. Discussing the "Marian" Ps. 44.11 ("Hear, daughter, and see . . .") he says: "Even

[1] 1060B, C.   [2] 1096Aff.   [3] 812A.   [4] 812A.

though this obviously refers to the Church of the Gentiles, it is not difficult to apply it to her, who has wholly been made the temple for the Bridegroom of the whole Church by the miracle of the Incarnation."[1] She is called mediatress between the Law and grace, because she is the fulfilment of all prophecies;[2] if one searches the Scriptures, there is no place where she is not to be found. For example, wherever there is mention of a virgin, a young woman, a prophetess, the house of God, an altar, a candlestick, or a host of similar things which the author enumerates at length, Mary is envisaged.[3]

Andrew of Crete is also the first witness to the feast of Mary's conception, which must have been established at the end of the sixth or in the course of the seventh century; for he wrote a liturgical piece for it, the Canon for "The Conception of St. Anne"[4] then celebrated on 9 December. As Jugie[5] rightly points out, the importance of this Eastern feast for the dogma of the Immaculate Conception has sometimes been exaggerated by Western theologians. Its institution was not due to any explicit belief in Mary's immaculate conception—as is clear even from one of its early names, "The Annunciation of Mary's Birth to Joachim and Anne"—but rather to the desire of the Eastern theologians to complete the cycle of Marian feasts by one paralleling the Annunciation, kept in the East as a feast of Christ rather than of Mary. Nevertheless, the feast of Mary's conception (in the passive, Anne's in the active, sense) presented a special opportunity to praise Mary's transcendent purity and holiness, which was an accepted belief in the Eastern Church throughout the Byzantine period. Thus Andrew affirms this belief, so clearly expressed in his homily on her nativity, also in his *Canon for the Conception of Anne*. He calls Mary "alone wholly without stain"[6] and asks her, the unpolluted one, to purify him, the sinner.[7] He repudiates, however, an idea that

---

[1] *PG*, 97, 864A.   [2] 865A.   [3] 868Bff.   [4] *PG*, 97, 1305–1316.
[5] *L'Immaculée Conception*, 1952, pp. 135ff.   [6] 1308C.   [7] 1308B.

had sprung up in his time, according to which Mary, too, was born virginally,[1] a further proof of how strong was the conviction of Mary's exemption from sin in the Byzantine world.

Andrew also wrote other liturgical pieces; the celebrated *Great Canon*, a penitential hymn sung in mid-Lent, is by him. It contains many so-called *theotokia*—short prayers to the Mother of God frequently following the invocation of the Trinity in the offices of the Greek Church, which came into use about this time. In these Mary is invoked as the Help of Christians, she is asked to take away the load of sin, to propitiate her Son, to give her servants humility and contrition; all the personal devotion of the faithful is expressed in these liturgical pieces written by men who were both poets and theologians.

JOHN OF DAMASCUS

Greek theology as it had developed throughout these last centuries is summed up in the work of John of Damascus (d. c. 749),[2] who is sometimes called the Thomas Aquinas of the East. Here we are interested only in his Mariology. John, of whose life little is known, came from a noble Christian family of Damascus, which was at that time ruled by the Mohammedan Caliph. He entered the Saba monastery near Jerusalem about 718, together with his younger adopted brother Cosmas, called Melodus, because he was a well-known hymn-writer. John, too, wrote poetry, but his principal works are in prose. In his great exposition of the orthodox faith, *De Fide Orthodoxa*, he defends the divine maternity of Mary against the Nestorians (3, 12), explaining that the Word did not, indeed, take his divinity from her, but that the Word who had been with the Father from all eternity took flesh from her when the time of the Incarnation had come. In a later chapter (4, 14), he gives an account of the other beliefs about her. After explaining her name as signifying "mistress",

[1] 1313A. [2] *PG*, 94–6.

because she "is truly the mistress of all creation",[1] he reproduces the apocryphal story of her upbringing in the Temple,
followed by the birth of Christ and the affirmation of the
virginity *in partu* and *post partum*, the conception having been
effected through the ear.

His four certainly genuine Marian homilies, one on the
nativity of Mary and three on her assumption, contain a more
detailed doctrine.[2] The sermon on her nativity gives the
clearest teaching on her immaculate conception that we have
met so far—though not, of course, in the terms in which the
doctrine was defined 1100 years later, because the Eastern and
Western views on original sin were somewhat different. Both
Mary's conception and her birth were completely ruled by
grace; she was the only child of an otherwise sterile couple;
for "nature did not dare to anticipate the fruit of grace, but
remained fruitless, until grace brought forth the fruit".[3] He
goes on to praise the "perfectly happy loins of Joachim, from
which has been ejected an absolutely stainless sperm", and he
goes out of his way to emphasize that the whole physical
process that followed was equally perfect: "O glorious womb
of Anne, in which grew, by the gradual additions received
from her, and after having been formed was born, an altogether holy babe."[4] So according to John of Damascus, even
the "active" conception of Mary was completely without
stain, *panamomos*—a view which goes far beyond the terms of
the later definition of the doctrine and was open to the objections raised against it by the schoolmen. Praising her,
John of Damascus applies to her all the well-known biblical
types; she is higher than the angels and their mistress, the
"lily among the thorns".[5] The most sacred daughter of

---

[1] *PG*, 94, 1157B.

[2] Cf. Chevalier's book, *La Mariologie de saint Jean Damascène, Orientalia
Christiana Analecta*, 109, Rome (1936), has been criticized and supplemented by
V. Grumel in *EO*, 36 (1937), pp. 318–46; it takes no account of the immediate
predecessors of John and is defective also in other respects.

[3] 2 (*PG*, 96, 664A).   [4] 2 (664B).   [5] 1 (669A).

Joachim and Anne, hidden from the fiery darts of the Evil One, was preserved without blemish, spouse of God and mother of God, formidable to the apostate powers. Whereas the first Eve had transgressed and through her death had come into the world, because she helped the serpent against the first father (i.e., Adam), Mary, obedient to the divine will, herself deceived the deceiving serpent and brought immortality to men. For God, foreknowing that she was worthy, loved her, and loving her predestined her to be Theotokos.[1]

John of Damascus teaches with equal clarity Mary's bodily assumption into heaven: "But even though, according to nature, your most holy and happy soul is separated from your most blessed and stainless body and the body as usual is delivered to the tomb, it will not remain in the power of death and is not subject to decay. For just as her virginity remained inviolate while giving birth, when she departed her body was preserved from destruction and only taken to a better and more divine tabernacle, which is not subject to any death . . . Hence I will call her holy passing not death, but falling asleep or departure, or, better still, arrival."[2] This implies that her body did not remain separated from her soul, the former being transferred to some kind of earthly paradise, as certain authors thought possible, but that Mary was taken body and soul to heaven, where she now reigns, a complete person: "Your stainless and wholly immaculate body has not been left on earth; the Queen, the Mistress, the Mother of God who has truly given birth to God has been translated to the royal palaces of heaven."[3] John of Damascus makes it very clear that all Mary's graces derive from her divine motherhood. She herself may be called the giver of all good things and the ornament of the human race only because

---

[1] 7 (672B–D). The sermon following the one just analysed in the edition of Migne and quoted by Chevalier and Grumel is not by John of Damascus, but most probably by Theodore Studites, and will be discussed in the next chapter.

[2] *First Sermon on the Assumption*, 1 (716A).   [3] 12 (720A).

he who could not be contemplated before his incarnation has now through her become accessible.[1] She is a spiritual Garden of Eden, but holier than the first Eden, since Adam sojourned in this, but the Lord in her.[2] Again, she is seen as Jacob's ladder, mediating between heaven and earth;[3] though she was God's handmaid through her human nature, he made her his mother because he loved the human race;[4] indeed, John strongly emphasizes her humanity so as to prevent any confusion with Kybele, the pagan mother goddess, as he states explicitly in his second sermon on the same subject: "Today we, too, want to celebrate a farewell feast for the Mother of God, but not by seizing flutes and drums and staging the orgies of the mother of the so-called gods of whom deceitful fables are told. Foolish people say she is a mother of many children, whereas the word of truth bears witness that the Mother of God had no [other] children." Then he distinguishes carefully between the adoration due to God and the veneration to be given to Mary: "For we adore [*latreuo*] God, a God who has not come into being from not being, but who exists for ever from all eternity . . . the Mother of God we honour and venerate, not as if affirming that the timeless generation of his Godhead was from her; for the generation of God the Word is timeless and coeternal with the Father—but we confess a second generation, his voluntary incarnation."[5] "Thus we venerate this Virgin as the Mother of God and celebrate her passing, but we do not pretend her to be a goddess—this be far from us, this is the babble of pagan deceit—since we also preach her death; but we confess her as the Mother of the incarnate God."[6] Hence the veneration of Mary is best expressed not by wild feasts but by mercy and pity upon the poor. "For", he asks, "if God is served best by showing mercy, who can doubt that this will also give particular pleasure to the Mother of God?"[7]

[1] 3 (701C).   [2] 8 (712B).   [3] 12 (721D–713A).   [4] 10 (716A).
[5] 2, 15 (744A).   [6] 2, 15 (741C–744B).   [7] 2, 15 (744C).

The preacher is aware that something happened to Mary at her assumption, that there is a difference between the simple maiden of Nazareth of the Gospels and the great queen of heaven the Church now venerates: "Angels and archangels have borne you upwards, the impure spirits of the air have trembled at your ascension. The air is purified, the ether sanctified by your passing through them . . . the powers meet you with sacred hymns and much solemnity, saying something like this: Who is she that comes forth as the morning rising, fair as the moon, elect like the sun? [cf. Cant. 6.9.] How you have blossomed forth, how sweet you have become! You are the flower of the field, a lily among the thorns [Cant. 2.1] . . . Not like Elijah have you entered heaven, not like Paul have you been rapt to the third heaven; no, you have penetrated even to the royal throne of your Son himself . . . a blessing for the world, a sanctification of the universe, refreshment for those who are tired, comfort for the sorrowing, healing for the sick, a port for those in danger, pardon for sinners, soothing balm for the oppressed, quick help for all who pray to you."[1] For in Mary more than in any other saint has been fulfilled the promise of Christ that those who have been faithful over a few things shall be placed over many things. (Matt. 25.21.) In her death and assumption she has "blossomed forth", and her influence, which was once restricted to the narrow circle of her life at Nazareth and later at Jerusalem with the Apostles, has now become a blessing for the whole world, sanctifying the universe. And because her authority and power have become so great, she has a right to the complete devotion of Christians so that the preacher can address her as a mistress (*despoina*) to whom they not only pay homage, but—a rather modern-sounding thought—to whom they "dedicate spirit, soul, body, all we have and are".[2] Therefore St. John asks her: "Good Mistress, graciously look down on us; direct and guide our destinies wheresoever you will. Pacify the storm of our wicked passions,

[1] I, 11 (716D–717B). [2] I, 14 (720C).

guide us into the quiet port of the divine will and grant us the blessedness to come."[1] All this power comes to her because of her divine motherhood, through which, as the preacher says in his second sermon on the Assumption, she has become "the rational paradise in which the judgement has been annulled, the tree of life has been planted, and our nakedness been covered".[2] And so Mary is once more opposed to Eve. She, "who listened to the message of the serpent, gave ear to the insinuation of the Evil One and let herself be taken in by the allurements of lies and deceitful lust, is punished with sorrow and grief, is subjected to the pains of childbirth, together with Adam condemned to death and placed in the depths of Hades. But this truly blessed Virgin who inclined her ear to the word of God, was filled with the energy of the Spirit and was assured of the good pleasure of the Father by an archangel; who, without any lust and sensual union, conceived the person of the divine Word, who fills all things, who brought him forth without pain and was wholly united to God—how could death devour *her*?" For in her, sin, the sting of death, is dead, and she herself is the principle of an unending and better life.[3] Through her Son Mary has become the giver of all good things for us and an inexhaustible ocean of joy.[4] Then Mary's tomb itself is made to speak, declaring that her sacred body has imparted to it divine grace, so that it has become a fountain of health for the sick and a defence against demons, and therefore it asks the nations to come and draw floods of graces from it.[5] To this the preacher replies that the power of the Mother of God is not restricted to any one place but is spread over the whole earth. "Therefore", he continues, "we will make our thoughts a dwelling for the Theotokos . . . If we preserve our thoughts pure as well as our bodies, her grace will make its habitation in us." On the other hand, Mary herself will prepare a place for her Son in our hearts:

[1] 1, 14 (721B).   [2] 2, 2 (725A).   [3] 2, 3 (728B, C).
[4] 16 (744C).   [5] 2, 17 (745B).

"If we zealously practise the virtues . . . she will come to her servants willingly and bring with her the fullness of all good things and also make a place for Christ, her Son, in our hearts."[1]

Thus John of Damascus teaches clearly that Mary takes an active part in our spiritual life, preparing us for the coming of her Son. He himself sings of her as a lover of his beloved; in his third sermon on the Assumption he asks: "What more sweet than the Mother of my God? She has captivated my spirit, she has made me dumb, she is before my eyes whether in sleep or in waking."[2] Her feast, too, became more and more elaborate, already it was preceded by a vigil;[3] soon a fortnight's fast will be added to its preparation in the East; John composed a canon for it.[4] He also wrote many *theotokia*. However, the attribution of the poems transmitted under his name is at present still so uncertain that they cannot be discussed in this context. In any case, they would hardly add anything new to his Mariology such as it appears in his homilies, and the same can be said of the hymns by Cosmas, his adopted brother.

THE KORAN

The veneration of Mary was not confined to Christianity. She is also known to the Koran, the sacred book of Islam which probably originated in Mohammed's lifetime (570–629), but which received its present form from Caliph Uthman (643–56). What is said about her in this book seems to reflect the relations of Mohammed with Christian communities in the Yemen and in Syria, and the stories concerning her are mostly taken from the apocrypha. According to the Koran her youth was spent in the care of Zachariah; she was miraculously nourished and especially protected from Satan. The angel told her that Allah had chosen and purified her particularly: "He has chosen you above all women in the

---

[1] 2, 19 (752B–D).   [2] 3, 1 (753B, C).   [3] 2, 16 (744B).
[4] Published in *Menaia* 6, Rome (1901).

world."[1] When the birth of the Messiah was announced to her she asked the question recorded in St. Luke, and the angel told her simply that such was the will of Allah.[2] So she conceived as a virgin, and her labour pains came upon her under a palm tree;[3] she was seized by great anguish, because she would be wrongly accused; but she was miraculously nourished and strengthened after the birth[4] and when her relatives insulted her the newly born child spoke to defend his mother's innocence.[5] The Koran defends repeatedly Mary's perfect virginity and blames the Jews for calumniating her,[6] and so through this book the Mother of Christ penetrated into the consciousness of the Mohammedans; of the learned, who wrote commentaries on it, as well as of the simple who frequently visited—as they still do—Christian shrines of Mary to satisfy their devotion.

CONCLUSION

By the end of the patristic period properly so called the main doctrinal and devotional lines have been traced: the fruitful opposition of Mary to Eve had appeared as early as the first half of the second century and was never lost sight of again; her perfect virginity was affirmed from the end of the same century; prayer to her is attested from the early fourth, possibly the late third century. Her intimate relationship with the Church was affirmed by St. Ambrose and St. Augustine; her divine motherhood was officially defined at the Council of Ephesus in 431. These early developments were not very different in East and West. But after Ephesus the picture changes. In the East feasts multiply and devotion becomes ever more fervent. The death and decomposition of her body seem no longer compatible with the dignity of the Mother of God; both the feast of her passing and the affirmations of contemporary apocryphal writings lead the preachers to think

[1] Surah 3.31–7.   [2] 3.42.   [3] 19.17–22.   [4] 19.23ff.   [5] 19.29–32.
[6] 4.155.

out the implications. Her purity, praised in the most glowing terms in the East, especially in Syria, finally raises the question of her exemption from original sin, which is stated with increasing clarity from the end of the seventh century. In the West, on the other hand, especially in Rome as opposed to Spain and Gaul, the language about Mary is far more restrained. Her bodily assumption seems to have been accepted only in Gaul, and the question of her exemption from original sin appears not even to have been asked. Her queenship and power of intercession, sometimes stated in extravagant terms in the East, are also treated much more soberly in the West, and there is no mention of her "mediation". Thus by the end of the patristic period the Mariology of the East has reached a far more advanced stage than that of the West, and the same applies to liturgy and poetry. Venantius Fortunatus comes nearest to the Greeks and Syrians in this respect; but even he cannot touch the Marian poems of Jacob of Sarug and Romanos, and especially the ecstatic language of the *Akathistos*.

4

THE "DARK" AND EARLY MIDDLE AGES

THERE is no well-defined demarcation line between the patristic period which has just been described and the so-called Dark Ages, especially if, as in the present study, both Eastern and Western Christianity are treated together. For while the Eastern tradition runs on practically without a break till the fall of Constantinople (1453), the West underwent the invasions of Goths, Vandals, Langobards and other Germanic tribes, which completely transformed the Italian peninsula and Gaul and culminated in the establishment of the Frankish Empire of Charlemagne and the so-called Carolingian Renaissance. In the field of Marian doctrine and devotion this difference between East and West produced very interesting results, as we shall see in the present chapter.

THE "DARK" AGES

THE VENERABLE BEDE

At the same time as Germanus composed his glowing homilies on the feast of the Assumption, the Venerable Bede (d. 735), formed by Benedict Biscop in the sober, Rome-inspired traditions of the English Benedictines, wrote about the Mother of God in a very different style.[1] In his commentary on Luke's Gospel Bede follows closely the generally accepted doctrine of the Latin Church; he reproduces a scribal misreading of Jerome's suggestion "stilla ['drop']

---

[1] I am discussing only those works considered authentic by contemporary scholars, leaving out the spurious commentary on Matthew frequently quoted in the Mariologies. The commentary on Luke and the Advent homilies are cited according to Hurst's edition in *CCSL* of 1960 and 1955, respectively, with the *PL* columns given in the margin of this edition.

maris" as "stella ['star'] maris", made popular by Isidore's *Etymologies*, and of the same word in Syriac as *domina*, "Lady",[1] mentions her proposal of virginity[2] and strongly affirms that she is Theotokos, using the Greek word in his text.[3] She is to be venerated by angels and men and to be esteemed more highly than any other woman.[4] In terms which almost suggest the Immaculate Conception he writes in the same commentary, on the words "Blessed are thou who hast believed": "It is not surprising if the Lord, when he was about to redeem the world, began his work with his mother, so that she through whom salvation was prepared for all should also be the first to draw the fruit of salvation from her child."[5] He follows the traditional Eve–Mary parallelism in opposing Mary's humility to Eve's pride,[6] and, in his third Advent homily, her life-giving obedience to the death that entered through Eve.[7] His teaching on the intimate connection between Mary and the Church echoes Ambrose and Augustine; both Mary and the Church are at the same time virgin and mother, because the Church conceives us by the Spirit and brings us forth without pain just as Mary conceived and gave birth to Jesus (Luke 2.6f. (330)), and both remain virgins in the act of birth. (2.23 (342).) The comparison is continued in the exegesis of the "sword" prophesied by Simeon; for Mary it means her pain during the Crucifixion, though she in no way doubted that her Son would overcome death—this perhaps in conscious contradiction of Origen and his followers; in the case of the Church it refers to the persecutions. (2.35 (346f.).)

In his Advent sermons Bede praises particularly Mary's humility; there is no trace of the Byzantine teaching on her queenship: he presents her in her earthly life rather than in her exalted state in heaven. The Benedictine sees her especially as an example for monks and nuns, to whom she shows the way to the fatherland through humility and chastity,[8] being

---

[1] 1, 27 (*PL*, 92, 319).   [2] 1, 34 (318).   [3] 1, 35 (319).   [4] 1, 42 (320).
[5] 1, 45 (321).   [6] 1, 48 (321).   [7] *PL*, 94, 9.   [8] *Serm.*, 4 (*PL*, 94, 15).

wholly occupied with divine and despising all earthly things;[1]
and even though Mary had a special privilege, because she was
the Mother of God, nevertheless, blessed are also all those who
have conceived God in their hearts.[2] Though Bede fully
recognizes Mary as the Mother of God, he makes a very clear
distinction between the divinity of Christ and his humanity—
the latter alone comes from his mother. This distinction is the
basis of his interpretation of Christ's words to her at the
wedding of Cana (John 2.4): "There is nothing in common
between the divinity which I have eternally from the Father
and your flesh from which I have taken [my] flesh; for my
hour has not yet come, when I shall show forth by dying the
weakness of the humanity I have assumed from you." And
he goes on to explain still more emphatically: "For suffering
the infirmities of the flesh, he entrusted the Mother from
whom he had received it . . . to the disciple whom he loved
best, though, when about to perform a divine action, he
pretends not to know her, because he does not acknowledge
her to be the author of his divine nativity."[3] Such a strict
division between the humanity and the divinity of Christ in
their reference to Mary would have been impossible in the
Greek Church after the definition of Ephesus, for it would
almost imply the Nestorian view that Mary was only the
mother of the man, *anthropotokos*, not also of Christ as God.
But, as Bede has shown himself a convinced defender of the
Theotokos, this cannot, of course, be his meaning; only he
guards more clearly than most of his contemporaries in the
East against the danger of giving Mary quasi-divine status.
This sobriety also appears in his attitude to the apocryphal
stories of her death, which he rejects, like the Gelasian
Decree before him.[4] His own hymn on her feast, *In Natali
Sanctae Dei Genetricis—On the Birthday* (as the death of the
saints was habitually called) *of the Holy Mother of God*—after

---

[1] *PL*, 94,18.   [2] *PL*, 94, 19.   [3] *Hom.*, 14, 69f.
[4] *Retractatio in Actus Apostolorum*, 8, 1 (*PL*, 92, 1014f.).

describing her life according to the biblical data, Bede ends
with an extremely simple prayer for her intercession,[1] which
shows no sign of exuberance.

AMBROSE AUTPERT

With Ambrose Autpert (d. 784), a native of Provence and
later abbot of a monastery at Benevento in southern Italy, we
are in a totally different atmosphere. This is not surprising,
for at that time several communities of Greek monks had
settled in southern Sicily to escape the persecutions instigated
by the iconoclastic emperors in the East. The influence of
Greek Mariology will emerge quite clearly in the discussion of
his work, much of which was later attributed to other authors
and influenced Latin Mariology under such famous names as
St. Augustine and Alcuin.[2] As Winandy[3] rightly says, no

[1] *PL*, 94, 631f.

[2] J. Winandy, in an important article, "L'Œuvre littéraire d'Ambroise
Autpert", in *RBE*, 60 (1950), pp. 93–119, has assigned to Autpert a Pseudo-
Augustinian homily on the Assumption in *PL*, 39, 2129–34, one on the Purification in *PL*, 89, 1291–1304 and almost certainly one on the nativity of the Virgin
in *PL*, 101, 1300–08. Winandy has also published a small book, *Ambroise Autpert,
moine et théologien*, Paris (1953), in which he discusses his Mariology, stating
that no-one in the West had ever before spoken about the Virgin Mother like
him. Though he mentions the Greek monks settled in Sicily and the influence
of the Syrian Pope Sergius (687–701), he holds that the works of Autpert show
no direct dependence on the Byzantine Fathers, but rather "belong simply to
the great current of devotion which at that time attracted Roman Christianity
to the Mother of God". (p. 48.) I cannot agree with this; for though the Mariology of Autpert certainly bears original features, there are too many striking
resemblances to, for example, the Akathistos Hymn, as well as Germanus, to
warrant Dom Winandy's denial of any direct dependence. There seems no reason
why translations of famous Greek Marian sermons and poems should not have
existed in certain monasteries at that time, since a Latin translation of the
Akathistos is attested for the ninth century, and Wenger has recently discovered
Latin translations of Greek homilies, among them those of Germanus, in the
Codex Augiensis 80, a tenth-century manuscript, which throw an entirely new
light on the influence of Greek Mariology on the early Middle Ages. There is,
therefore, no reason why such translations should not also have existed in the
monastery of Autpert, especially as this was so comparatively near to the Greek
monks of Sicily, or why personal contacts with the latter should not have
influenced his Marian thought.

[3] See preceding footnote.

Latin author had spoken in such terms of the Virgin Mother before. For his language echoes the Greeks, both in its positive borrowings and its negative criticisms. First of all, before Autpert we have no evidence of any Latin sermons devoted especially to the praise of Mary, despite the fact that her four major feasts had been introduced in Rome during the second half of the seventh century. Now Autpert has sermons on the Assumption, on the Purification—taking the latter as a feast of Mary rather than of Christ—and almost certainly also one on her nativity. What do we find in these sermons?

To take the sermons on the Assumption first. Autpert, like many of the Greek Fathers, begins with defending the introduction of this feast on the ground that, if we celebrate the feasts of the martyrs, how much more ought we to keep that of the Mother of the Prince of Martyrs.[1] He then discusses the object of the feast. Following the Gelasian Decree, he strongly rejects the apocryphal stories—in obvious opposition to most contemporary Greek authors—because no Catholic document says anything about them. Even St. John the Evangelist, who ought to have known, has left us no instruction on the matter. On the other hand, it is silly to speculate on the fate of her body (as the Greeks were doing), "seeing that no-one doubts that she is raised above the angels and reigns with Christ. It should suffice that she is truly called Queen of Heaven, because she has given birth to the King of Angels." This idea of Mary's queenship is new to the West, whereas it had by this time become a commonplace in the East.[2] Having established this, Autpert affirms, in the traditional manner of the East, that Mary can never be praised sufficiently "even if all our members were turned into tongues", for she is higher than the heavens and deeper than the abyss, because she has contained God, whom no creature can contain, in her

[1] 1 (*PL*, 39, 2130).   [2] 2f. (2130).

womb—the paradox beloved by the Byzantines. She alone has merited to be called both mother and spouse, for "she has made good the damage done by the first mother, she has brought redemption to man who was lost"[1]—the typical substitution of the secondary cause, Mary, for Christ, the first cause, which we have so frequently met in the East, but not so far in the Marian writings of the West. It is expressed even more strongly in the sermon on the nativity of Mary,[2] where he says: "The whole world rejoices, as being redeemed through her" [ut per ipsam redemptus],[3] echoing Germanus: ". . . no man is saved except through you, Theotokos." Autpert praises above all her humility, which had been somewhat neglected by the Byzantine authors, but he does so in the terms of Romanos, Germanus and the others; for, finding this virtue personified in Mary, he says that it "has purified the world, opened paradise and freed the souls of men from hell"[4]—all actions attributed to Mary by the Greeks and Syrians, but never before by the Latins. And so Autpert also uses the Greek imagery of Mary as the ladder by which God descended to earth, and the gate of paradise.[5] He elaborates the activities of this humility still further in the sermon on the Nativity, finishing his praises of the Mother of God in language that strongly recalls the Akathistos Hymn: "Mary has been made the door of heaven, the exaltation of apostles, the praise of martyrs, the jubilation of confessors, the continence of virgins, the rule of monks . . . the justice of kings . . . Mary has been exalted above the stars."[6]

The way in which her intercession is asked is equally reminiscent of the Eastern preachers: "Admit our prayers into the sanctuary of your hearing and bring us back the grace of reconciliation . . . Accept what we offer, obtain what we ask, protect us from what we fear: because we find no-one more powerful in merit to placate the wrath of the Judge

---

[1] 4 (2130). [2] PL, 101, 1300–08. [3] 1300D.
[4] Ass. 10 (PL, 39, 2133). [5] 10 (2133). [6] PL, 101, 1506A.

than you, who have merited to be the Mother of the Redeemer and Judge."[1]

This influence from the East penetrated also through the Liturgy. Aupert was in the habit of inserting liturgical pieces into his works, for example the antiphon of the Second Vespers of the Nativity of Mary ("Nativitas tua, Dei Genetrix, gaudium annuntiavit universo mundo" etc.) in his sermon on the feast.[2] It is a literal translation of the Greek *Apolytikon*;[3] and in the same sermon he quotes part of the ancient Greek prayer, *Sub tuum praesidium*.[4] Another prayer seems to have penetrated into the Liturgy from him, coming, as it did, with the authority of St. Augustine, though he may not have been its author. It is the one now beginning *Sancta Maria*, in which Mary is asked to help the miserable, assist the faint-hearted, comfort the sorrowful, pray for the people, plead for the clergy and intercede for the devout female sex, so that all may experience her help who devoutly praise her name,[5] expressing again a universality of intercession until then unknown in the West.

In his commentary on the Apocalypse[6] he explains the twelfth chapter as referring to the Church as well as to Mary, because the two are related to each other as the genus is to the species. He thus continues the Latin tradition of Mary's close relation to the Church; and when he writes that "in her blessed womb the Church merited to be united to its head",[7] this is but another version of St. Ambrose's "heap of wheat surrounded by lilies" that was brought into the world when Christ was born from Mary. Mary is the most excellent member of the Church[8] which descended with Christ into her womb[9]: "Whether we therefore sometimes say that the virgin mother Mary, sometimes that the virgin mother Church has born or is bringing forth Christ, we shall not

[1] *Ass.* (PL, 39, 2134).   [2] *PL*, 101, 1301B.   [3] See *Maria* 1, p. 226.
[4] 1307A.   [5] *Ass.*, 11 (PL, 39, 2134).
[6] *Maxima Biblotheca Patrum*, 13, Lyons (1677).   [7] 531A.
[8] 531E.   [9] 455A.

stray from the truth. For the one gave birth to the Head, the other brings forth the members."[1] Mary and the Church are inseparable, for Mary is the type of the Church.[2]

Beside the Eastern and the Latin patristic traditions, Autpert also continues a line that began with Venantius Fortunatus and was destined to increasing prominence in the West: the presentation of Mary as the tender mother suckling her child.[3] "O happy kisses," he writes in his sermon on the Assumption,[4] "pressed on the lips of the infant . . . when as your true son he played with you as his mother." This motherly love is not restricted to Christ, but extends to all Christians. In his sermon on the Purification Autpert says that, having once offered Jesus in the Temple she does not cease to offer him for us, but continues to unite him to us by her holy intercession, and does so with truly maternal affection. For, he says, "if Christ is the brother of believers, why should she, who has given birth to Christ, not be the mother of believers? Therefore I implore you, my most blessed Virgin, offer us to Christ by your merciful supplications, you who do not hate your sons nor even mind the insults of those sons who do not honour you as they ought. She even tolerates the irreverence of her sons, because she is overwhelmed by

---

[1] 532G.   [2] 530H.

[3] H. Weisweiler, in a much-quoted article, "Das frühe Marienbild der Westkirche unter dem Einfluss des Dogmas von Chalcedon", *SK*, 28 (1953) pp. 321–60 and 504–25, sees in this development of the tenderness of the mother for her child a consequence of the two-natures doctrine of Chalcedon. "The consubstantiality of the Lord with his mother", he writes, "could not but lead . . . to an ever stronger working out of the human love between mother and child." (p. 322.) It is, however, strange that the definition of Chalcedon, which dealt with the typically Eastern heresy of Monophysitism and was worked out in the terminology of Greek philosophy, should have had this remarkable effect only in the West and hardly at all in the East. To me it would rather seem that this new emphasis is mainly due to the emergence of the Germanic peoples in the West, with their more emotional approach, which we had also noticed in the Syrian Jacob of Sarug, but which now became even more marked in the new culture that was growing up in what was soon to become the Empire of Charlemagne.

[4] 5 (2131).

maternal love. Comfort therefore by your tender prayers those who are unworthy of such great favours, whom you have brought forth in your only Son."[1]

The Byzantine image of the glorious queen, interceding in heaven, is here given some quite new features; she is also the loving mother who tenderly helps her children, even the wayward ones, because they are Christ's brothers. For she has—a bold expression—brought them forth when she gave birth to him—an application to the individual Christian of the Ambrosian teaching that the Church was in her womb together with Christ. And when she stands under the Cross Autpert not only stresses her sufferings and her fortitude, by which "both the iniquity of the rejoicing Jews and the weakness of the fleeing Apostles and disciples are made manifest",[2] but also a certain share in the redemptive work of her Son, for he writes: "It was necessary [*necesse fuit*] that the tender heart of the mother should be transfixed by a sword through the passion of the Redeemer."[3]

Thus, at the beginning of the Carolingian period, Ambrose Autpert has already blended the splendour of the Byzantine *eikon* of Mary the queen and mistress of earth and heaven with the new "Germanic" image of the sweet mother playing with her child, and giving this maternal love and tenderness also to all his "brothers". Coming, as he did, from Provence and settling in southern Italy, he was particularly well placed to combine these two trends in a richness of Marian doctrine hardly equalled by later writers of the period.

THE THEOPHILUS LEGEND

That the Greek influence was much stronger than authors like Winandy are prepared to admit is also obvious from the fact that Paul the Deacon (d. c. 799), a monk from Monte Cassino who spent four years at the court of Charlemagne and was celebrated for his learning, translated the fifth-century

[1] 7 (1297B, C).   [2] 12 (1301A).   [3] 12 (1301B).

Greek legend of Theophilus into Latin.[1] This is the original source of the Faust saga: Theophilus, disappointed because he does not obtain the post he wants, gives his soul to the devil, but repents and prays to the Blessed Virgin to ask God's forgiveness. Mary hears his prayer and compels the devil to give him back the contract. This legend had a very wide distribution—we shall meet it repeatedly in the next centuries —and was one of the most powerful influences in the spread of an ever-increasing belief in the never-failing efficacy of Mary's intercession. In the legend itself Mary is called "the universal help and protection of those who look to her . . . the redemption of captives and the refuge of the afflicted".[2] She is the true bridge between God and men, and her intercession is asked in the most trustful terms: "In you hope all Christians, to you we fly, to you we lift up our eyes day and night."[3] But the most interesting point of all is that here, for the first time in Latin, Mary is called *mediatrix*: "Holy Mother of God, hope and support of Christians, redemption of the erring . . . who intercede for sinners, refreshment of the poor, mediatress between God and men."[4] The legend of Theophilus became very popular in the Middle Ages and was even turned into a play.[5]

PAUL THE DEACON

Although the title of "Mediatress" did not come into general use in the West until the twelfth century, its Greek origin can hardly be denied. Paul the Deacon's homily on the

---

[1] *Acta Sanctorum*, Venice (1725), 1 Feb., p. 486; modern ed. in R. Petsch, *Theophilus*, Heidelberg (1908), from which I quote.

[2] 9, p. 5, 16ff.   [3] 16, p. 9, 21.   [4] 12, pp. 7, 32ff.

[5] The Greek influence on the West in the early Middle Ages is also strongly emphasized by G. G. Meersseman in his previously mentioned work on the Akathistos Hymn in the West. The Greek works which were translated, especially the Akathistos Hymn, the Theophilus legend and the *Vita* of Mary of Egypt "furnished a series of Marian attributes which formed one of the chief pillars of the new Marian edifice of the twelfth century". Meersseman (vol. 1, p. vi).

Assumption [1] also reveals its Greek models; after stating that no praise can ever be sufficient for Mary [2] the preacher goes on to extol her virtues and gifts, for she surpasses not only men but angels in sanctity. [3] In a passage which is lacking in the Migne edition but contained in a more complete manuscript [4] the author envisages the possibility of Mary's bodily assumption. The sermon ends by asserting the power of her intercession. Though the language of the sermon is more restrained than that of most contemporary Greek homilies on the subject, its structure and contents are so similar to these that it is difficult to assume that they did not serve as his models.

In his poems, too, Paul the Deacon sees Mary as the powerful queen, [5] and he combines the cosmic picture of the virgin who through her chaste childbearing has made good the fall of the world with that of the mother who holds her son and her God "in her gentle arms". [6]

ALCUIN

Whereas the influence of the later Greeks is undeniable in Autpert and Paul the Deacon, the most famous scholar at Charlemagne's court, Alcuin (d. 804), who was educated at York, is quite free from it (he only quotes the earlier Greek Fathers), and his Marian texts are consequently far more sober. This does not mean that he had little devotion to the Mother of God; on the contrary. Indeed, a lack of Marian piety would hardly have been acceptable at the court of the Frankish king, who had the most important church of his realm, the cathedral at Aix-la-Chapelle, dedicated to her. Alcuin himself instituted the Marian Mass on Saturday, two

[1] *PL*, 95, 1565D–1569C.   [2] 1566D.   [3] 1567A–1571A.

[4] *Cod. Lat. Vatic.*, 615, saec. XI–XII, 209ᵛ, quoted by L. Scheffczyk, *Das Mariengeheimnis in Frömmigkeit und Lehre der Karolingerzeit*, Leipzig (1959), p. 450.

[5] K. Neff, "Die Gedichte des Paulus Diakonus", in *Quellen und Untersuchungen zur lateinischen Philologie des Mittelalters*, 35, 5 (1908), p. 149.

[6] Neff, "Gedichte", 5, 2, p. 21.

forms of which are contained in his sacramentary,[1] with the
application of the Wisdom text from Ecclesiasticus, "From
the beginning and before the world was I created" (24.14),
to her; later Prov. 8.22–35, "The Lord possessed me" etc.,
was also taken over into the Marian Office. The origin of this
innovation is uncertain, as the Greeks did not use these texts
of Mary.[2] In the prayers of this Office Mary is constantly asked
for her intercession, but never, as in Autpert's prayer *Sancta
Maria*, to give help through her own power.

Like many of his contemporaries, Alcuin defended the true
divinity of Christ against the so-called Adoptianist heresy,
which had originated in Spain in the eighth century, according
to which Christ, in his humanity, was not the true but only
the adopted Son of God. It was held especially by Elipandus,
Archbishop of Toledo, and Felix, Bishop of Urgel. As the
divine motherhood of Mary was also involved in the heresy,
the Carolingian writers had to expound it whenever they
wrote against Elipandus and Felix, as Alcuin does especially
in the sixth book of his great work against the latter.[3] There
he compares her with pure white wool, an image which he
had found in Arnobius the Younger (a fifth-century African
monk), and which he expands in his treatise on the Trinity,
where he writes of Mary: "She was the purest wool, most
glorious in her virginity, with whom none of all the virgins on
earth can be compared, of such quality and greatness that she
alone was worthy to receive into herself the divinity of the
Son of God. For as wool receives the blood of the purple
snail, so that from the same wool may be made the purple
that is worthy of the imperial majesty . . . so has also the
Holy Spirit, coming over the Blessed Virgin, overshadowed
her . . . that the wool might be made purple by the Divinity."[4]

Alcuin, too, has a very human, personal love for the Blessed
Virgin, which comes out occasionally in his poetry when he

---

[1] No. 7 (*PL*, 101, 455B–456A).   [2] Cf. E. Gotta, *Maria*, 5, pp. 695f.
[3] *PL*, 101, 210f.   [4] *Trin.*, 3, 14 (*PL*, 101, 46C–47A).

7+

prays to her: "You, my sweet love, my jewel and great hope of my salvation, help your servant, most glorious Virgin; my voice asks you with tears, my heart burns with love."[1]

PAULINUS OF AQUILEJA

Alcuin's friend Paulinus of Aquileja (d. 802), who also defended Mary's divine motherhood against the Adoptianists,[2] wrote even tenderer poetry about her. For him Mary is the "blessed Mother" who "bore in her most pure arms God veiled in his flesh and with her firm lips pressed sweet kisses on the mouth of him who was true God and man, by whose word the world was made".[3] Here the ancient paradox of the God made flesh is emphasized still further by presenting him as an infant in arms, whom his mother covers with kisses: an idyllic scene as remote from the theological thought of a St. Augustine as from the transcendent image of the Theotokos of the Byzantines.

AVE MARIS STELLA

It fits in much better with the picture of the Star of the Sea guiding the travellers into port, such as it is presented by the most popular of all Marian hymns, the Ave Maris Stella. Its first manuscript evidence dates from the ninth century, but it was probably written in the eighth. Here Mary, the ever-virgin Mother of God and Gate of Heaven, appears as the loving helper of men who frees prisoners from their fetters, brings light to the blind, drives away our ills and asks for all good things, exercising the prerogatives so often attributed to her in the Greek homilies on the Assumption. But here she helps men in her position of mother rather than of queen; for the poet asks her especially to show herself a mother by using her influence with her Son. What follows is also significant of a change of emphasis; he prays that she,

---

[1] MGH, Poet. Lat., I, 313.
[2] PL, 366B–367A.   [3] MGH, Poet. Lat., I, 139.

gentle above all others, should make us also gentle and chaste, giving us a pure life and a safe journey. The rough young Germanic tribes, full of as yet unconquered violence and sensuality, needed the influence of this gentle mother to tame them and teach them the Christian life.

WALAFRID STRABO AND RABANUS MAURUS

From now on this image of the Star of the Sea becomes a favourite theme of Marian devotion. Walafrid Strabo (d. 849), a monk of the famous Benedictine abbey of Fulda in Hesse-Nassau and later Abbot of Reichenau, also uses it; Mary is the Star of the Sea "for us who sail on the sea of this world", but, he explains, the light of this star is Christ, whom we must follow.[1] In his poem on agriculture[2] he compares her to the rose and calls her "spouse", "dove" and "queen".

His teacher Rabanus Maurus (d. 856), the greatest of Alcuin's pupils, Abbot of Fulda and Archbishop of Mainz, who was called *Praeceptor Germaniae*, also utilizes the image of the Star of the Sea in one of his sermons.[3] He follows the Latin tradition of Mary as the figure of the Church, both spouse and virgin,[4] who reigns beside her Son eternally and whose dignity surpasses that of the angels.[5]

VERNACULAR POEMS

This image of Mary the Queen, honoured by the angels, found its way into the vernacular literature through Otfrid (d. c. 870), a pupil of Rabanus Maurus. He wrote his poem, the *Christ*, in Old High German in order to replace the "obscene songs of the laymen". He also taught the people that "whoever sought salvation on earth, should implore her [Mary's] goodness in great humility". In this his work differs

---

[1] *Homily on the Beginning of St. Matthew's Gospel* (PL, 114, 859B, C).
[2] *MGH, Poet. Lat.*, 2, p. 349.
[3] 163 (PL, 110, 464C). [4] *Hom.* 29 (PL, 55D).   [5] 56A.

from the slightly earlier, more popular *Heliand*, an epic after the model of Caedmon, where Mary is presented purely as an ordinary mother watching over her child.

PASCHASIUS RADBERT

While the Mariological material afforded by the eastern part of Charlemagne's Empire, present-day Germany, is comparatively scanty, the abbeys of the western part, that is to say, of France, produced several remarkable theologians whose Marian doctrine is much more advanced. The greatest among them is Paschasius Radbert (d. c. 860), Abbot of Corbie, near Soissons, famous for his work on the Eucharist, the first of its kind. He was involved in a controversy on the Virgin Birth with his pupil Ratramnus (d. after 868). The latter had written a treatise "On the Birth of Christ from a Virgin"[1] against some errors which, he says, were prevalent in Germany, according to which Christ was not born in the normal human way "but had emerged unnaturally by an uncertain path into the light of day, which is not to be born, but to erupt".[2] This view had arisen because the womb was supposed to be something impure. Against this Ratramnus affirms most strongly that no creature was created vile: "Hence also a woman's uterus is not indecent, but honourable."[3] Christ was born from the womb, not from any other part, "and he opened it because he was the firstborn; not that he violated the integrity of the uterus, but that he left the palace of the womb", therefore Mary was subject to the law of purification.[4] But how was it possible to open the womb without violating it? Ratramnus answers: no creature can resist the Creator; but, whatever exists is open and passable to him",[5] reflecting the passage from Amphilochius quoted above (p. 69).

The subtle argumentation of Ratramnus is not always easy to grasp, and it seems that the nuns of Soissons were upset by

[1] *PL*, 121, 81–102.   [2] 83A.   [3] 85A.   [4] 92C.   [5] 86B.

it, imagining that he denied the virginity *in partu*. Hence they addressed themselves to Paschasius Radbert to ask for an explanation, which he gave them in his treatise on "The [Giving-] Birth of the Virgin".[1] Radbert denies the assertion of Ratramnus that Mary gave birth in the same way as other women, because this would mean that Christ was born under the curse.[2] "It is rash", he argues, "to assert that Christ was born according to the common law of nature", for the natural law as it is now is not the original natural law, but the law of curse and guilt. Mary therefore, being not under the law of corruption, brought forth Christ without any corruption or pain, while her womb remained closed.[3] Unlike Ratramnus, he does not rule out a birth by abnormal channels, even though he will not affirm it categorically;[4] he lays all stress on the idea of the completely closed womb which meant that Mary needed no purification but only submitted to it in order to obey the Law.[5]

In the same treatise Radbert makes statements that seem to imply if not the Immaculate Conception, at least a purification from original sin in the womb. "Because", he writes, "it [scil., her own birth] is venerated by the authority of the whole Church, it is certain [*constat*] that she was immune from all original sin, for through her is not only the curse on our mother Eve dissolved, but also a blessing given to all men."[6] Nevertheless, in the very next paragraph he affirms that "when the Holy Spirit came over her [i.e., at the Annunciation], it wholly purified and freed the Virgin from any stains, so that she was holier than the stars of heaven."[7] It is difficult to see how, if she was free from original sin, she could still have had stains to be removed at the Annunciation, unless we take these (*sordes*) to be some blemishes not derived from sin

---

[1] *PL*, 120, 1367–86. In this way Scheffczyk, *Mariengeheimnis*, pp. 221ff., explains the relation of the two works to each other, since the treatise by Radbert is not an exact answer to that by Ratramnus.

[2] 1367D–1368A.   [3] 1368D–1370A.   [4] 1374A, B; 1381C.

[5] 1376A and 1377B.   [6] 1372A.   [7] 1372B.

but from the mere fact of her humanity, which had to be removed before the Incarnation. We have seen before, for example, in the case of Jacob of Sarug, that the coming down of the Holy Spirit at the Annunciation was frequently connected with the idea of some further purifying preparation of the already perfectly pure Virgin.

A work which has played an important part in the history of the dogma of the bodily Assumption is now also generally attributed with almost complete certainty to Radbert. It is the famous letter *Cogitis Me* of Pseudo-Jerome.[1] The letter is a deliberate forgery, for it purports to be addressed to Jerome's friends Paula and Eustochium and to answer a question of theirs concerning the Assumption. In his "reply" Radbert vigorously repudiates the apocryphal story *De Transitu*, "so that you may not accept doubtful things as certain"; for nothing is certain about the passing of the Virgin except that "she left the body".[2] The empty tomb is indeed there, but in what way, or whither, the body was removed from there is unknown.[3] Though Radbert explicitly repudiates the "Greek confusion" which he opposes to "Latin purity",[4] his treatise nevertheless shows Greek influence, even though this was probably secondhand. Mary is "the Virgin who alone has destroyed all the wickedness of the heresies", a saying which, carrying the authority of St. Jerome, is still recited in the Tract of the Roman Mass of the Common of the Blessed Virgin in Lent and in certain Offices. After God, she confirms us in all truth and commends us to him by her merits,[5] for she is the Queen of the World, who reigns with Christ and "augments" salvation for us all through her intercession.[6] Radbert repeats in slightly different words the formula of Ildefonsus, which through him became a commonplace in the West, that whatever honour is paid to Mary overflows on her Son.[7] Rather in the Byzantine style, Radbert affirms that

---

[1] *PL*, 30, 122–42.   [2] 2 (123C).   [3] 2 (123D).   [4] 13 (136A).
[5] 3 (124C).   [6] 4 (126B).   [7] 126C.

he can never praise Mary enough,[1] that she transcends angels and archangels in dignity;[2] for even though these may be higher in nature, she nevertheless exceeds them in grace through the Incarnation.[3]

While these praises of the Mother of God echo the Greek sermons on the Assumption, Radbert adds to them a trait that is typical of the post-patristic West: he teaches that after the Ascension Mary was tortured by her love of Christ;[4] that, sorrowing, she visited the places where she had been together with him and embraced him in spirit.[5] Therefore she, too, is a martyr, even though she finished her life in peace; indeed, she is more than a martyr, "because she suffered in that part of her, which is supposed to be incapable of suffering", that is to say, her soul.[6]

This sermon enjoyed a tremendous prestige in the Carolingian period and after, being widely used in the Breviary lessons for the Office of the Assumption, including, for example, the Sarum Rite and the Roman Rite until the revision of Pius V in 1570. Owing to its influence belief in the bodily assumption of Mary was retarded in the West, until, about two and a half centuries later, a pseudo-Augustinian sermon on the subject opened up a new line of approach.

Three sermons on the Assumption printed among the works of Ildefonsus are also most probably the work of Radbert; they contain hardly any new ideas. Mary is presented as the star of the sea, the daughter[7] of Jerusalem and the Queen of the World to whom all prophecies point.[8] Her assumption (understood only as the assumption of her soul,[9] is also the assumption of the Church, because she herself is the temple of God and the ark of the New Testament,[10] a thought elaborated still further in connection with Apoc. 11.19, where the Ark, the Church and the Mother of

---

[1] 5 (126C). [2] 7 (128D). [3] 15 (138C). [4] 13 (136B, C).
[5] 13 (137A, B). [6] 14 (138A). [7] PL, 96, 241A. [8] 240B.
[9] 240A. [10] 248A.

God are seen together, Radbert, like Autpert, using the relation between genus and species. For in her womb the whole Church is contained as if in germ.

MINOR CAROLINGIANS

The other writers of the Carolingian period offer nothing new on our subject. There are no outstanding Marian sermons, and as the Gospel of the Assumption was the story of Martha and Mary, the preachers—e.g., Haimon of Auxerre (d. 855)[1]—frequently took as their theme the superiority of the contemplative life, represented by Mary. Indeed, such was the dearth of Latin sermons on the feast that, as Wenger has shown,[2] in the tenth century a number of Greek ones were translated and had a considerable influence in the West. During the second part of the ninth century the Mother of God was mostly praised in verse, at times in terms that recall the Byzantine tradition. The monk Milo of St. Armand (d. c. 871), a favourite of Charles the Bald, called her "the praise of the world, the glory of heaven", through whom "grace is diffused into the whole world . . . You open the gates of paradise which Eve had closed . . . You are my protectress, my mistress and helper."[3]

Hincmar, Archbishop of Rheims (d. 882), wrote a *Dogmatic Poem on Blessed Mary*[4] on the occasion of the dedication of his cathedral to the Mother of God. In it he affirms the main Marian doctrines, her painless childbirth, which he compares with that of the Church,[5] and her transcendent holiness.[6] The incorruption of her body is taught, but not her assumption,[7] an idea which was current also among the Greeks of the period, but which probably came to Hincmar through the Latin apocrypha. She, the Star of the Sea, resides with her Son in heaven and is praised by the angels together with him.[8]

[1] *PL*, 118, 765ff.   [2] "L'Assomption", p. 148
[3] *De Sobrietate II, MGH, Poet. Lat.*, 3, p. 645f.
[4] *MGH, Poet. Lat.*, 3, 410–12.   [5] p. 410, 9ff.   [6] 412, 85.
[7] 86.   [8] 87f.

Though she does not *rule like* him, "who has the empire with his Father" and in whose aspect she rejoices,[1] she is nevertheless said to *reign with* Him, *Christo conregnans*, and Hincmar asks her to be merciful when he is going to die.[2]

The most famous poet of the Carolingian period belongs to its very end: he is Notker, "the Stammerer", of St. Gallen (d. 912). He copied parts of the Greek New Testament and was at times surrounded by Greek monks, *ellinici fratres*,[3] another proof of a certain Byzantine influence during this period. Notker was too original a poet to have copied the Greeks; but it does seem likely that belief in the bodily assumption of Mary,[4] which he had found in Gregory of Tours, was confirmed for him by these "Hellenic brethren", and their influence may also perhaps be traced in his hymn for this feast in which he sees her as the Queen of Heaven, foretold by the Prophets and preached by the Apostles.[5] Otherwise his poetry is far less exuberant than that of the Byzantines, and shows the marks of Western devotion in his description of the relationship between Mother and Child. Even in his Assumption hymn there appears the picture of the Virgin suckling her Child,[6] and in the hymn for the Purification the poet bids her exult, because "your little One has smiled at you".[7]

LATER BYZANTINES

While the young peoples of the West thus found their way to an appreciation of the Mother of God suited to their needs, the East continued to exalt the Theotokos, not without adding some new ideas. The feast of Mary's conception, which, as we have already seen, had been introduced into the

---

[1] 81f. [2] 97f.

[3] See W. von den Steinen, *Notker der Dichter und seine geistige Welt*, 1, Berne (1948), 35. Vol. 1 contains the monograph, vol. 2 the critical edition of the poems.

[4] *PL*, 131, 1142A. [5] Von den Steinen, vol. 2, p. 66.

[6] Von den Steinen, 2, p. 66. [7] Von den Steinen, 2, p. 24.

7*

Byzantine Church fairly recently, played a considerable part in strengthening belief in her transcendent sinlessness.

JOHN OF EUBOEA

John of Euboea (d. c. 750), who preached what appears to be the first extant sermon on this feast, seems to have come fairly near to exempting her from original sin. For he affirms that through Mary's birth Eve's shame has been taken away,[1] for in her "the Creator himself has made from the aged earth a new heaven and an unburnable throne; he has transformed the old clay into a heavenly chamber".[2] This "palace of the celestial King has been constructed without the help of men",[3] meaning that though Mary was born from human parents, her virtues were implanted in her by God alone. Therefore Adam is bidden to rejoice, "for through a woman you were deceived by the serpent, and through a woman you shall crush it", apparently the first application of Gen. 3.15 to Mary's conception.

EPIPHANIUS THE MONK

Epiphanius the Monk (d. c. 800) is the first author to have attempted a Life of Mary, adding a generous portion of apocryphal material to the New-Testament data.[4] He not only describes her grave and dignified bearing after the manner of Athanasius and others, but also her exterior, according to the Byzantine idea of beauty. He imagines her as having a light complexion, light brown hair and eyes, black eyebrows, a straight nose, a long face and long hands and fingers.[5] When she was twelve years old, a voice came to her in prayer saying to her: "You will give birth to my Son."[6] When she was fourteen, she was betrothed to Joseph, a widower about seventy years old with several sons and daughters, according to the Eastern tradition, who was not intended to be her husband but only her protector.[7] Her purity was not like that

[1] 15 (PG, 96, 1484B).   [2] 16 (1485B).   [3] 17 (1488A).
[4] PG, 120, 185–216.   [5] 6 (192C–193B).   [6] 6 (192C–193B).
[7] 7f. (196A, B).

of other women, involving temptation and struggle, but as if derived from nature and superior to that of all other women, indeed "alien to human nature".[1] After the Crucifixion she did not go to the sepulchre, because she was prostrate with grief[2]—a view which, as we shall see, was not shared by all Byzantine writers, though it agrees with the silence of the Gospel. After the Ascension she performed many miracles. She was seventy-two years old when she died. Her body was placed in a sepulchre in Gethsemani and became invisible before the eyes of the Apostles; thus the question of the actual assumption of her body and soul into heaven was left open.[3]

TARASIUS OF CONSTANTINOPLE

Tarasius, the Patriarch of Constantinople (d. 806) who had been responsible for the convocation of the Second Council of Nicaea (787) to settle the iconoclastic controversy, preached a sermon on the Presentation which is often held to imply his belief in the Immaculate Conception.[4] For he says that Mary is Adam's deliverance from the curse and the payment of the debt of Eve[5] and that she is "the stainless offering of the human race".[6] She is so pure that, when she was a child, she was placed in the Holy of Holies in the Temple, which was inaccessible even to the priests.[7] This tendency to separate Mary from normal human life, first apparent in the apocryphal Gospel of St. James, makes remarkable progress during this period in the East, as opposed to the development in the West. For even though Tarasius, too, presents Jesus in his mother's arms—as did the icons he so vigorously defended against the iconoclasts—yet his presentation is as different from that of his contemporaries in the West as a Byzantine icon of the Theotokos is from a medieval Madonna. In the context of a series of names Tarasius proposes for her, such

---

[1] 10 (197C).   [2] 21 (209C).   [3] 22-5 (212A-216A).
[4] PG, 98, 1481-1500.   [5] 9 (1492A).   [6] 13 (1497A).   [7] 2 (1481B).

as "heaven", "sun", "moon", "throne", "pearl", "Eden", "mount", he asks whether he should not perhaps call her a table, because she has nourished Christ with her milk, or a sea, because she kissed him who assembled the waters, and continues that this is an altogether admirable mystery which is also terrifying.[1] So the Mother with the Child in her arms is not the sweet, altogether human and accessible girl suckling her Son and playing with him, who is to be found in the Carolingian period and later in the West, but rather the awe-inspiring Theotokos in whom the very transcendence of the Creator is reflected.

THEODORE OF STUDION

Theodore, Abbot of Studion (d. 826), a monastery near Constantinople which he reformed, had been ordained priest by Tarasius and became famous as a monastic legislator. A sermon of his on the conception of the Blessed Virgin is printed in Migne among the works of St. John of Damascus.[2] He teaches Mary's exemption from all (perhaps even original) sin, for he calls her "a land on which the thorn of sin has never sprouted" and soil which has not been cursed like the first, bringing forth thorns and thistles, but on which rests the blessing of the Lord.[3] For she, the daughter of Eve, has become the medicine of her mother, being "the new leaven of the divine re-formation, the all-holy firstfruits of the race".[4] Other images confirm her total purity; she is the burning bush that is inaccessible to sin, a pure rose, a lily, an incorruptible wood which has never admitted the worm of the corruption of sin, a paradise more blessed than Eden.[5]

In his homily on the Dormition Theodore stresses, as customary, especially her universal intercession; for now she has fallen asleep she has not died; she has been translated, but she has not for that reason abandoned mankind. For her

[1] 12 (1496A–C).   [2] PG, 96, 679–98.   [3] 4 (685A).
[4] 5 (685D).   [5] 7 (689B–696D).

hands that bore God have become incorruptible, and she raises them everlastingly to God in prayer. She puts the demons to flight and intercedes for us with the Lord.[1] Again we find here the tremendous awe before the Theotokos common to the Byzantines; for though Theodore says that through her intercession she makes the earth fruitful, gives peace to the Church and drives away the barbarians,[2] he also admits that his spirit trembles and his mind is terrified when he thinks about her admirable passing, because she is higher than the highest heavens.[3] He is also the first witness to the fortnight's fast before the Assumption, called "the fast of the Mother of God".[4]

COSMAS VESTITOR

Four Greek homilies on the Assumption have been discovered only recently in a tenth-century Latin translation by A. Wenger, who published them in the work from which we have frequently quoted before. They belong to Cosmas Vestitor, who lived in the second half of the eighth century and the first half of the ninth. Nothing is known about him except that he was probably a layman, since *vestitor* implies a court function. The first of his four homilies[5] is of little importance, as it borrows mainly from Germanus; but the other three are more interesting.

Though Cosmas reproduces at length the apocryphal story, he also adduces theological reasons for belief in the bodily assumption, which are very similar to those in the famous later pseudo-Augustinian sermon on the subject which has played such an important part in the history of the doctrine. Cosmas states that the bodily assumption of Mary is only fitting, "for the same flesh she gave to Christ, this Christ has made alive. Hence the Mother of God has justly been clothed with incorruption from now on." If she were to

[1] 721B, C. [2] 729A. [3] 728C, D. [4] *Doctrina Chronica* (*PG*, 99, 1697A).
[5] Wenger, "L'Assomption", pp. 315-33.

receive this only on the Last Day, she would have nothing
more than others; but because she, as his mother, gave him her
flesh, she received it back from him with an addition, because
it was now incorruptible.[1] The author repeats this argumentation in different forms in the other two homilies. Speaking
in the person of Christ, Cosmas says: "I shall transfer this
[Mary's body] to incorruptible life, re-establishing it in its
first state. For my own living body taken from her has been
restored to me, and that which has been given [i.e., Christ's
flesh] must correspond to that which has been received
[Mary's flesh]. For the vine does not produce an ear of corn,
but a bunch of grapes." As the fruit, the flesh of Christ, is
incorruptible, so also the seed, the flesh of Mary.[2] He varies
the argument once more in the fourth homily, where he says
that "from the one body of Mary and Christ there has been
one deposition and one translation to immortality, for the
flesh of the Mother and the Son is known to be the same. And
because the body of the Son sits at the right hand of the
Father, the Mother, too, has received incorruption in her
passing and is lawfully in heaven, dwelling with the Father
together with her Son before the promised [general] resurrection."[3]

His argument for the bodily assumption, then, rests on the
identity of the flesh of Mary and Christ; if Christ is in heaven
with his body, Mary must be there, too, because his flesh is
taken from hers. Cosmas even asserts that St. John the
Evangelist, too, was translated into heaven, because he was
Mary's spiritual son; but he does not labour the point.[4] She
was, he says, eighty years old or more at her death, which took
place before the destruction of Jerusalem by Vespasian (A.D.
70), since Peter and Paul were both still alive and took
part in her burial.[5] As Wenger points out, Cosmas
exercised a strong influence on the West through an anony-

[1] 2, 4 (Wenger, "L'Assomption", p. 319).   [2] 3, 11 (Wenger, p. 326).
[3] 4, 12.   [4] 4, 14.   [5] 4, 22-4.

mous homily [1] in which his work was combined with sermons by Germanus and Andrew of Crete.

THEOGNOSTUS

Theognostus (d. after 871), a Byzantine monk who, as a friend of the Patriarch Ignatius, played an important part in the latter's quarrel with Photius, wrote an "Encomium on the Dormition of the Blessed Virgin",[2] remarkable because it links her bodily assumption to her holy conception. "It was surely fitting that she who from the beginning had been holily conceived through saintly prayer in the womb of her holy mother . . . should also be given a holy passing; for as her beginning was holy, so also was her life as well as her end; indeed her whole existence was holy."[3] At her death Jesus separated her spirit from her body; but this separation lasted only a few days; then they were reunited, and this "union lasts for ever".[4] While Mary was thus in heaven, her Son also introduced her into paradise (in Greek thought frequently distinguished from the former), where the Good Thief, who had not noticed her at the Crucifixion, saw her and was filled with admiration. "Now as the all-holy Lady, dwelling in the world in goodly manner, has saved the world and illumined the earth, she now, having left the world, prays for its salvation." Therefore, he says, we will praise her conception so that we may also glorify her dormition and find forgiveness for our negligence.[5] We shall see that, two centuries later, her assumption was linked to her conception in the same way also in the West.

GEORGE OF NICOMEDIA

George, Metropolitan of Nicomedia (d. after 880) and a friend of Photius, also emphasizes Mary's perfect purity; indeed, he describes her in terms which almost place her

[1] Published by him in "L'Assomption", 337–60.
[2] *PO*, 16 (1922), 457–62.   [3] 1 (p. 457).   [4] 3 (p. 460).   [5] 5 (p. 462).

outside normal humanity.[1] His three sermons variously called "On the Conception of Anne" and "On the Conception of the Blessed Virgin" say very little about her and are, rather, eulogies on the sanctity of her parents. The next three have as their subject her presentation in the Temple. Here she is seen as the "patroness of our rebirth, the cause of our renewal, through which the disfigured image of God has been restored to its proper beauty". For through her we have cast off the garment of sin and have put on the vestment of light.[2] Her total exemption from all sin is further made clear when the bishop writes that the food with which she was nourished by angels in the Temple was a figure of the Eucharist, but did not purify her from sin, this being quite unnecessary, "because she was pure and altogether without stain",[3] for her purity was more marvellous even than that of the angels, since she had a body.[4] Not only is she exempt from all faults, but she also possesses, even at the age of three, the perfect *apatheia* (freedom from all emotions) that was the ideal of the Byzantine monks. For when she had entered the Temple and her parents had left her "she experienced nothing of the tyranny of nature" and did not even turn round to look after them. So this small girl was "free from all human habit and emotion . . . being superior to the necessity of nature".[5] This exemption extends even to the natural physiological processes, for "I hold", he says, "that none of the natural impurities could ever be discovered in her altogether immaculate body", so that there was no real necessity to remove her from the Temple when she had reached the age of puberty; this was done only to pacify the Jews.[6] Her removal greatly upset the priest, Zachariah, for how was she now to be nourished, who had only partaken of food prepared by angels?[7]

It is interesting to compare this increasing withdrawal of Mary from a normal human existence in the East with her

[1] *PG*, 100, 1335ff.   [2] 5 (1416B).   [3] 7 (1448B).   [4] 1444B, C.
[5] 1448C–1449A.   [6] 1452C.   [7] 1453A.

presentation as an almost ordinary maiden in much of the literature of the West at the same time; there could hardly be a greater difference of views than that between George of Nicomedia on Mary's physical abnormality and Ratramnus on the natural circumstances of her childbirth, or the former's idea of the complete impassivity of the three-year-old girl and Radbert's picture of Mary after the Ascension being tortured by her love for her Son and visiting all the places where they had been together. Indeed, the Byzantine bishop's exaggerated insistence on her *apatheia* leads him into obvious difficulties when preaching a sermon on Mary under the Cross. (*n.* 8.) He repeats that she was above natural human feelings; nevertheless, he cannot very well present her as looking at her tortured Son with complete Stoic indifference. So he attributes her suffering not to her motherly love, but to her zeal for her Son's work and her horror at the frightful impiety of those responsible for the Crucifixion.[1] Yet he makes her say that the pains she now suffers are greater than those of childbirth, for the childbirth she now undergoes is superior to the normal one, and the more admirable it is, the more must her heart be torn.[2] This has an obvious reference to Christ's words from the Cross, "Woman, behold thy son", through which Mary becomes a mother and mediatress to his disciples who honour her as such.[3]

In order to enhance Mary's role in the Passion George of Nicomedia takes the most extraordinary liberties with the Gospel story. Though he could not go so far as to assert her presence at the Last Supper, he at least insists that she was in the same house as Christ and the Apostles and supervised the preparations for the meal. She also followed her Son to the house of Annas and Caiaphas. After Christ's burial she did not return home, but remained at the sepulchre until Easter morning;[4] her witness of the Resurrection and her thanks-

[1] 1464C–1465B.   [2] 1472D.   [3] 1473D–1476B.
[4] 1488Cff.

giving for it are the subjects of another sermon.[1] In George of
Nicomedia the Byzantine devotion to the Theotokos has
reached one of its peaks—but at the expense not only of
historical truth but also of the true womanhood of Mary.
It is only consistent if he asserts that none of the mysteries
he recounts ought to be examined by reason, for nothing
pertaining to the Blessed Virgin (by which he means
the apocryphal stories and probably also his own inventions)
is to be doubted.[2] Her intercession, too, is all-powerful,
and the Metropolitan of Nicomedia speaks about it in
even more extravagant terms than Germanus of Constantinople. "However many sins we have committed,"
he writes, "if you only will it, they can easily be dissolved.
Nothing resists your power . . . everything is subject to your
command, everything serves your authority. Your Son has
made you higher than the heavens . . . [and God] regards
your glory as his own."[3] In her the privileges of the angelic
nature are eclipsed; she is superior to it even in intellect.

JOSEPH THE HYMNOGRAPHER

The exaltation of Mary is also celebrated in the many
poems of Joseph the Hymnographer (d. 886), a Basilian monk
born in Syracuse, who fled to Greece when the Saracens
invaded Sicily. Like Theognostus, he was a friend of Ignatius
of Constantinople. He was a very fertile poet, and here we
can do no more than emphasize a few points taken from his
so-called *Mariale*[4] to illustrate his views on the Theotokos.
Her perfect purity is strongly emphasized, she, "the altogether immaculate Lady", is herself called "the sterility of
sin",[5] whom "alone the Creator Logos found completely
without stain";[6] for she is purer than all other creatures.[7]
She is the "divine rose",[8] and the divine cloud that distilled

---

[1] 9 (1489D–1504C).   [2] 1436A.   [3] 6 (1440A, B).
[4] *PG*, 105, 984–1414.   [5] *Canon 1* (984A).   [6] 2 (993C).
[7] 3, 1000B.   [8] 1 (989B).

sweetness, taking away all bitterness from our souls. Both her conception and her birth are set apart; indeed, all that concerns her surpasses human understanding.[1] She is resplendent like the sun, the golden dove who causes the spiritual flood (of sin) to cease.[2] Joseph affirms her bodily assumption[3] into heaven, where she now reigns as queen of all created things,[4] made larger than the heavens, because she has borne the Creator,[5] and exalted above all creatures.[6] Therefore the poet places all his hope in her and entrusts himself to her mercy;[7] her slaves bend the knees of their hearts and ask her to save those submerged in affliction;[8] for she is the port of those tossed about on the sea of life[9] and the star which will not set.[10] Defiled by carnal stains, her slave flies to her, so that she may cure his passions and become for him the straight way to salvation.[11] The poet paints the typical Byzantine picture of the stainless Queen and all-powerful intercessor reigning in heaven, who surpasses human understanding almost like God himself, and as whose slave he regards himself.

PHOTIUS

Photius (d. c. 897), the Patriarch of Constantinople and opponent of Ignatius, who played such a controversial role in the great schism between East and West, was a scholar who, besides important historical and theological works, also wrote a number of Marian homilies.[12] Of his two homilies on the Annunciation the second (Hom. 7) is particularly important, since it was preached in the presence of the Emperor and is therefore more carefully worked out than the others. Homily 9

[1] 2 (993C).   [2] 7 (996B, C).   [3] 3 (1001A).   [4] 1001C.
[5] 1053C.   [6] 1109C.   [7] 2 (996A).   [8] 6 (1025A).
[9] 1024A.   [10] 1025D.   [11] 7 (1028–1029A).

[12] I quote from the most recent critical edition by B. Laourdas, Thessalonica, 1959, but with the page numbers of the older standard edition by S. Aristarchos, 2 vols., Constantinople, 1901, which are to be found in the margin of Laourdas. There exists also a recent English translation by C. Mango, Cambridge, Mass., 1958.

is devoted to the birth of the Virgin and Homily 17 to her image, on the occasion of its unveiling in Sancta Sophia on Holy Saturday 867 after the inconoclastic controversy had been settled. M. Jugie [1] claims that Photius teaches the Immaculate Conception; but it seems to me that, rather like Jacob of Sarug, he envisages a twofold purity, a general one from birth, and the particular freedom from original sin from the time of the Annunciation. For he writes in his second sermon on this feast: "Today the daughter of Adam has made good the fall of the first mother Eve and has been purified from the stain that had crept in from there." [2] If Mary was purified from the stain that came from Eve only at the Annunciation, "today", that is, on the feast that was being celebrated, then she must have been subject to it before. Jugie considers a passage from the first sermon on the same feast: "Blessed are you . . . because you have revoked [='made good'] the failing of the transgression of the woman" [3] as evidence of the patriarch's belief in the Immaculate Conception; but this, again, does not refer to the conception of Mary but to that of Christ at the moment of the Annunciation. If, however, one cannot claim Photius as teaching the doctrine of the Immaculate Conception in the Western sense, he nevertheless uses the image which has since become, as it were, its emblem, for he writes that through her "is killed, destroyed and trodden underfoot the devil who strikes the heel and is the cause of our being crushed". [4] Though Photius does not consider Mary to be free from original sin from the moment of her conception, he nevertheless speaks of her moral purity and excellence prior to the Annunciation in terms similar to those of Jacob of Sarug. In his first sermon for the feast he says that the Virgin found grace "because she rendered herself worthy of her Creator, because she had adorned her soul with the beauty of chastity"

[1] "La Mort et l'Assomption", pp. 164–9.   [2] *Hom.*, 7, 3 (p. 372).
[3] *Hom.*, 5, 7 (p. 244).   [4] *Hom.*, 7 (p. 379).

and, moreover, had also preserved her freewill pure, for from early childhood she had been sanctified for God as a living temple.[1] In his second sermon he praises the *apatheia* of "that scented and never-fading flower of the human race, that most admirable, great and divinely carved image" who from her swaddling-clothes had devoted herself to a wholly spiritual way of life. For she abstained not only from physical pleasures, but also from those of the mind; indeed, the blessed Virgin did not permit even her thoughts to incline towards any of them, showing that she had been set apart as a bride for the Creator even before her birth."[2] This, too, does not imply the Immaculate Conception, as the same was said of John the Baptist.

Mary's freedom from the passions extends even to her attitude at the Crucifixion. She uttered not a word of indignation, as mothers usually do when they see their children suffer. Her fortitude is sufficient evidence of her nobility. For she had "a matchless understanding and a pure mind", in fact, she was altogether above human measure.[3] This is the image that is also presented by the Byzantine icons, which Photius himself describes in his sermon on the unveiling of the picture of the Theotokos in Sancta Sophia. This represents "the virgin Mother holding in her chaste arms the common Creator for the common salvation of the [human] race reclining as an infant, this great and ineffable mystery of the economy [i.e., the Christian dispensation]. The virgin Mother, looking both like a virgin and like a mother, indivisibly dividing her will between both attitudes, yet doing injustice to neither because both are perfect . . . For, on the one hand turning her gaze with the love of her heart affectionately on her Son, on the other she assumes the expression of a perfectly imperturbable state in harmony with the passionless and supernatural being of her Son."[4] Photius sums up all that the Virgin meant to him and his contemporaries: "Before

[1] 5 (p. 236).   [2] 7 (pp. 372f.).   [3] 7 (p. 373).   [4] 17 (p. 299).

our eyes, holding the Creator as an infant in her arms, stands the Virgin motionless in the painting as she is also described in words and visions, interceding for our salvation, teaching us piety, a delight both to eyes and minds, by which the divine love that dwells in us is lifted up to the intellectual beauty of truth."[1] Mary has become the perfect incarnation of the Greek ideal of truth and beauty; a mother, certainly, but one that, because she is also a virgin, is somehow inaccessible, though, again, she intercedes for us and is our great teacher of Christian virtue. Her motherhood is majestic rather than tender, differing in this from the more human presentation of the West.

LEO VI

In the Byzantine Church Mariology was not only the concern of professional theologians. Ever since Constantine the emperors, too, had intervened in theological questions. Leo VI, called "the Wise" (d. 912) was particularly interested in them, even though his private life left much to be desired from the point of view of Christian morals. Leo favoured a closer relationship with the Western Church. Despite his political preoccupations—the Bulgarians appeared before Constantinople in 893, and Thessalonica was occupied by the Saracens in 904—he found time for theological writings, among which there are several homilies on the Theotokos. He follows the general Byzantine trends; in his oration on her nativity he emphasizes her birth from sterile parents, so that she, too, should not be born entirely "from the will of flesh and blood".[2] He emphasizes her sinlessness in imagery which was later applied to the Immaculate Conception in the West. In his oration on the Presentation the Emperor affirms that she appears like a lily among thorns in the wickedness of human confusion.[3] For the earth, "which so far had produced thorns because of the curse, now bears a fruit not of the accustomed bitterness, but showing forth the sweetness of

[1] 17 (p. 306).   [2] Cf. John 1.13 (*PG*, 107, 4A).   [3] 12D.

blessing", because she was chosen to be the bride (not the mother!) of the Only-Begotten;[1] through her childbearing Mary pays the debt of the first mother.[2] Like some other Byzantine authors Leo, too, teaches the double assumption; indeed Jugie calls him "the forerunner and leader of the school hostile to the true Assumption".[3] For in his speech on the feast the Emperor affirms that Christ's "hands, which contain all things, receive your stainless soul; whereas your pure and immaculate body is transported to the purest place. Because you have given birth to God clothed in flesh, you are now borne in the hands of God deprived of your flesh."[4] But this view, which does not allow for the reunion of Mary's body with her soul before the general resurrection, did not prevent the author from speaking in the highest terms of the power of Mary's intercession. Having once kept motherly guard over her Son when he entered the world, now, on leaving the world, she is honoured above all; and she alone is blessed because she has brought help to the first mother and her offspring, who have her as a stepping-stone to life.[5] She now uses her motherly power and trust in her Son, for she is estranged from the world in which she once lived, but always assists those who need her, for now she is inseparable from her Son. Leo gives a new twist to the type of the Ark, so frequently used, by opposing her to it; for Mary is a far more effective helper than the Ark of the Israelites, which often was itself in danger and could even be captured; whereas Mary's assistance never fails and all good things come to us if she wills it.[6]

EUTHYMIUS

Euthymius (d. 917), Leo's confessor and later Patriarch of Constantinople, had no doubt encouraged the Emperor's devotion to the Theotokos; for his own Marian homilies

---

[1] 13A.   [2] 17A.   [3] "La Mort et l'Assomption", p. 268.
[4] 161D–164D.   [5] 164A–165C.   [6] 165D–169C.

breathe the same spirit; though, unfortunately, there survives
none on the Assumption to show whether Leo's view of it
was influenced by that of his confessor. Like so many
Byzantine authors Euthymius, too, attributes to Mary actions
that properly belong to her Son. In his homily on the conception of St. Anne [1] he calls her "the royal throne, the incomprehensible ark who will destroy the sanctuaries of the idols
and the irrational sacrifices of the Hebrews, who will manifest
the great and hidden mystery", applying to Mary what is said
of Christ in Ephes. 2.14: "who will call back our forefathers
and every just soul from Hades . . . who will sanctify the
whole world . . . and destroy all heresies." Superior to all
heavenly and earthly creatures, she consoles those who
despair because of the multitude of their sins. [2] She is always
present to those who pray in her sanctuary, filling them with
all good things, while admonishing sinners and bringing them
back to the right way, for Christ has given her to us for our
redemption. [3] In his homily on Mary's girdle—of which we
have heard before—the patriarch's language becomes even
more enthusiastic and full of poetic imagery: Mary has
suffocated the serpent with her girdle, with which the divine
Word played when he was a small child, and through this
girdle the altars of the idols have been overthrown, bloodshed
has ceased, mountains leap, the sea smiles calmly and the
rivers water the earth. Indeed, this girdle is more powerful
than the heavens and shines brighter than the rays of the
sun. [4] The near-omnipotence attributed to Mary in Byzantine
preaching is now shared also by her relic, which, it is said, has
remained perfect, without dust or stain, through the centuries.
This is not surprising, for, as Euthymius once more affirms,
nothing can resist the Mother of God. [5] He finally prays:
"Reconcile us before our end to your merciful Judge, Son and
God"; for her prayer is especially needed in the hour of our
death.

[1] *PO*, 16, 463–514.   [2] 5f. (502).   [3] 6f. (503).   [4] 4 (510).   [5] 5 (511).

PETER OF ARGOS

Peter, Bishop of Argos (d. after 920), continues the line of Byzantine preachers who stress the initial sanctity of Mary in their sermons on the feast of the Conception.[1] When Anne conceived Mary our nature gave thanks to God, because in this conception "you have begun to remove from me [human nature] the thorns of damnation . . . Now appears from me in the womb of Anne Mary, the rose; she frees me from the evil smell that came from corruption and, giving her own perfume, imparts to me divine joy. Through a woman I have been wretched until now; through a woman I am now blessed."[2]

JOHN THE GEOMETER

The most important exponent of Byzantine Mariology in the tenth century is without doubt John the Geometer (d. c. 990). According to F. Scheidweiler,[3] he was an officer who was dismissed from military service under the Emperor John Tzimiskes and became probably first a monk, then a priest, and finally perhaps an archbishop. His tremendous devotion to the Theotokos found expression in poems in her honour and a *Life of Mary* of which only the last part, which deals with her assumption, has been edited by Wenger.[4] The Geometer sees the Theotokos above all in her heavenly glory, not only as queen of all creation, but also as co-redemptress, most intimately associated with the work of her Son. "Wearing a crown, clothed with a gold-embroidered mantle, she was proclaimed queen of all creation and placed at the right hand of her Son and King."[5] She is not only the Mother of her divine Son, she is "our common mother, and much more than our mother; for just as she has a nature that

[1] *PG*, 104.   [2] 10 (1360C).
[3] "Studien zu Johannes Geometres", *Byzantinische Zeitschrift*, 45 (1952), pp. 277–319.
[4] "L'Assomption de la très-sainte Vierge dans la tradition byzantine du VIᵉ au Xᵉ Siècle", *Archives de l'Orient chrétien*, 5 (1955).
[5] *v*. 1 (p. 364).

is above nature, so she also has for us men an affection that exceeds nature".[1] As Christ endured his passion for us, so Mary, too, has suffered for us, "so that the memory of her sufferings endured for us might always procure our salvation and she should love us not only because of [human] nature, but also because she remembers all she has done for us throughout her life".[2]

So our relation to Mary is not only governed by the fact that she is the Mother of the Saviour; John goes a step further than his predecessors and emphasizes her own personal contribution to the work of redemption. This idea is worked out even more clearly in the next paragraph, where he gives thanks to Christ, "that you have not only given yourself as a ransom for us, but, after yourself, have given also your mother as a ransom at every moment, so that you indeed have died for us once, but she died a million times in her will, cauterized in her heart just as for you, so also for those for whom she, just like the Father, has given her own Son and knew him to be delivered unto death".[3] This is an unequivocal statement of the "com-passion" of Mary; she has "given" her Son just as the Father has given him; her own long-drawn-out spiritual suffering, in John's view, obviously adds something to the sufferings of Christ; his attitude is quite different from that of St. Ambrose, who stated bluntly: "Jesus had no need of a helper for the redemption of all . . . So he accepted, indeed, the love of the mother, but did not seek the help of a human being."[4] John the Geometer holds that Mary has a share in the redemptive work of her Son; indeed, he even calls her "another paraclete" (allos parakletos); for her virtues surpass our human nature, therefore she is not only our mother but our mediatress, who reconciles us to God; she is another paraclete, who at all hours appeases his just wrath and showers her mercies upon us all.[5] It is not easy to see what, in John the Geometer's view, is the

[1] v. 7 (368).   [2] 59 (406).   [3] 60 (406).   [4] Exp. Luc., 10, 132.   [5] 63 (408).

difference between the redemption effected by Christ and the reconciliation effected by Mary; indeed, his language is far more exaggerated than that of Germanus of Constantinople, and at times she appears as a semi-divine being.

Jugie claims that John teaches the Immaculate Conception; and though, of course, he does not use expressions akin to those of the definition of 1854, it would seem that he considers her exempt from original sin—a view which certainly corresponds to his Marian teaching in general. Quoting from the first, hitherto unpublished part of the *Life of Mary*, Jugie points out that John teaches that she was specially created by God like Eve, that her nature was embellished from the beginning and established in a perfect harmony of body, soul and character.[1] In his hymns,[2] where his devotion reaches new peaks, her absolute purity is celebrated in even more telling expressions. Mary is the mother of incorruption, of grace and eternal life[3]; she is purer than the seraphim[4] and though she has given God flesh, she has not given him the uncleanness of flesh.[5] She destroys the shame of our forefathers[6] and bears nothing of the burden of our evil.[7]

Views are divided on the question whether the Geometer taught the doctrine of the Assumption in the Western sense. Some scholars—for example Jugie[8]—consider that he believed only in the double assumption of body and soul, not in their reunion immediately after her death. The relevant passage[9] is not quite clear; but shortly before,[10] the author has affirmed that in her our whole compound nature was with God, and this would be consonant with his Mariological thought in general, which emphasizes the parallelism between Mary and

[1] *L'Immaculée Conception*, Rome (1952), p. 186.
[2] Joannes Sajdak, *Ioannis Kyriotis Geometrae Hymni in SS. Deiparam, Analecta Byzantina*, Poznan (1931).
[3] 1, lines 5ff.   [4] line 28.
[5] line 34.   [6] 2, line 14.
[7] 3, line 18.   [8] *L'Immaculée Conception*, pp. 316–20.
[9] Wenger, 48f., p. 398. [10] 41, p. 392.

her Son. For as Christ rose on the third day, so Mary, too, was translated on the third day; as in the case of her Son, so also in hers the funeral linen was left folded up in the tomb, with fresh marks of the body imprinted on it, so that not only through her Son but also through herself our nature has been introduced into heaven [1]—an expression which seems to presuppose belief in the bodily assumption in the Western sense.

As Mary is so unequivocally approximated to the Godhead, she also participates in some way in the divine transcendence. Again this transcendence is expressed most strikingly in the hymns. For because Mary has given birth to One of the Trinity, the Trinity itself is her root and principle.[2] She is the radiant pole of the universe that frightens even the heavenly spirits,[3] she is far above all mind and understanding, a sight fearful, fiery, perfectly immaterial, sweet yet frightening, invisible and outshining the light of the seraphim [4]—in short, a completely transcendent figure that has hardly any connection with the young virgin of Nazareth.

SIMEON METAPHRASTES

Simeon Metaphrastes (d. end of tenth century), who owed his name to his paraphrases of earlier works, but about whose life practically nothing is known, has one interesting *Lament of the Blessed Virgin* which anticipates the medieval *Marienklagen* ("Laments of Mary"). Holding the dead body of her Son in her arms, the Mother of God realizes that this is the fulfilment of Simeon's prophecy. His death hurts her more than fire, and she cannot understand for what deed he should have died.[5] "Woe to me that you should lie dead on the stone . . . The rocks are broken, and my heart is almost broken with them." For he who is even now reviving the bodies of the dead in Hades is killing his own mother with sorrow. At his conception the immaterial fire of the Godhead did not burn

[1] 4, p. 392.   [2] 2, 5f.   [3] 2, 77ff.   [4] 3, 4–9.
[5] *PG*, 114,

her, but now another fire consumes her and is burning her heart. Then she addresses all his members, whose torture increases her pain.[1] Now she is no longer an urn of manna, because the manna has been poured out, she is no longer a golden candlestick, because her light has been placed under a bushel. Then she recalls what God has done for her in the terms of the Gospel of James; all these great deeds have shown "that I am larger than the heavens, I, from whom the sun of glory has shone forth". But now she would fain pierce her breast and make a hidden tomb for him so that she might once more receive him into her and bury him in her heart; for she is the mystical limpet that cannot be separated from the rock that bears her pearl.[2] Remembering the joys of her motherhood when Jesus was a child, she compares them with her present sorrow; once she washed him with warm water, now she does so with her hot tears; once she supported him in her arms, when he jumped about in the manner of children; now she does the same, but now he lies still, motionless in death: "Your hands and feet are pierced, but I feel the nails bringing torture to my innermost soul. Your side has been pierced, but my heart, too, has been pierced at the same time. I, too, am crucified by your sufferings, have died in your Passion and am buried together with you."[3]

Here Mary's motherly feelings are emphasized more than ever before in the East, except for the Syrian poets. The medieval mentality, with its greater stress on the human emotions, was now penetrating also into some—though by no means many—Byzantine authors, just as the later icons of the Theotokos show a less rigid and majestic, a more motherly, attitude than the earlier ones. Thus, as we saw when discussing Jacob of Sarug, even the image of the *Mater Dolorosa* was developed in the East before it was taken over by the West.[4]

---

[1] 212A–C.   [2] 213A–D.   [3] 216C–D.

[4] It should be remembered that we are now five centuries past Chalcedon, so this development can hardly still be attributed to the Council's influence, as Weisweiler suggests.

GREEK INFLUENCE ON THE EARLY MEDIEVAL
MARIOLOGY OF THE WEST

Recent research has shown ever more clearly how great is the debt of the Western Church to the East in all Mariological matters. Wenger's book, frequently mentioned in the course of this chapter, also contains an anonymous homily on the Assumption which had a remarkable diffusion throughout the Middle Ages and became the source of the story related in the famous *Legenda Aurea* of Jacob of Voragine (d. c. 1298) and in the *Stellarium* of Pelbart of Temesvar (d. 1504). This homily is a compilation of the homilies of Andrew of Crete, Germanus of Constantinople, the Euthymiac History[1] and the four homilies of Cosmas Vestitor. As mentioned before, the manuscript which contains it and nine other Greek homilies belongs to the end of the tenth century and to the extremely influential monastery of Reichenau, an island in Lake Constance. It is hardly probable that the monks should not have used it for their preaching and instructions; indeed, in the twelfth century Gerhoh of Reichersberg (1093–1169), well known for his zeal in introducing the reforms of Gregory VII in Germany, copied the sermon for the use of nuns on the feast of the Assumption. It contained all the principal features of Byzantine Mariology: Mary, who is purer than the heavens and superior to the seraphim, has abolished the curse of death introduced by Eve. As she was not corrupted by the birth of her Son, so she also escaped the dissolution of death, for Christ has called her to himself to live with him for ever in the light of heaven, for she must be where he is. She is the ark of those to be saved, the bridge and ladder by which they ascend to heaven, and Christ tells her that he will make her the "propitiation for sins". When she has ascended to him he will glorify her name even more. All things that are said about the blessed Virgin are possible and ought not to be investigated by natural reason; for these things are "truly terrifying and

[1] In John of Damascus, *Hom. II in Ass.*, Ch. 18.

tremendous", they are to be believed rather than examined—a principle frequently obeyed only too literally in the following centuries.

TENTH-CENTURY POPULAR LITERATURE

During the tenth century, which was lacking in great theologians, Mariology made little progress in the West, though Marian visions and miracles were very popular. To give but a few examples: About 945 John of Salerno wrote the life of Odo, the famous Abbot of Cluny (d. 942) under whom this monastery began to exercise its great influence on Western monasticism. In this *Vita* he tells the story of a converted robber who had become a monk. Before his death a glorious woman appeared to him and asked if he knew her. When he said No, she said to him: "I am the Mother of Mercy"—an expression we have also met in Eastern authors—and foretold his death. The monk reported this apparition to Odo, his abbot, and from this time, writes Odo's biographer John, "our father [i.e., Odo] was in the habit of calling blessed Mary the Mother of Mercy",[1] a title which spread from Cluny all over Western Christendom. The story is particularly interesting, since it sets the pattern repeated by many later Marian apparitions, including Lourdes: the beautiful unknown lady who reveals herself under a name by which she apparently desires to be known in the future. Her healing powers are emphasized in another apparition, whose recipient was a bishop of Utrecht and which was described by a cleric of the same city about 972; he reported that, when the bishop was sick, the holy Mother of God, the gate of salvation and the mistress of the world, appeared to him and told him he would get well. She left behind her a cloud of exquisite perfume, and the bishop's illness was cured immediately.[2]

---

[1] *PL*, 133, 72A, B.
[2] Mon. Germ., *Script.*, 15, 571B; quoted S. Beissel, *Die Geschichte der Verehrung Marias in Deutschland während des Mittelalters* (1909), p. 90.

Another abbot of Cluny, Maiolus (d. 994), was also favoured with visions and miracles of the "Mother of Mercy", whom he frequently invokes (reported in his *Vita* by Syrus-Aldebald).[1]

Mary's bodily assumption into heaven was discussed by Atto, Bishop of Vercelli (d. 961), a theologian remarkable for his learning in this unlearned century. He would not affirm anything positive about the question, the one thing certain being that, whether in the body or out of the body, she was in heaven, exalted above the angels. She did definitely die; nevertheless, since Christ's flesh, that had been taken from her, had risen again, it was quite possible that his filial piety led him to raise Mary's body, too. But, however that might be, it could not be doubted that he communicated his glory to her and constituted her mistress of the whole world.[2]

One of the most remarkable women of the Middle Ages was Hroswitha of Gandersheim, a very learned Benedictine nun who also wrote plays. She wrote versified versions of both the Theophilus legend and of the Gospel of St. James: so in her, again, the Greek influence is obvious. In her preface to the latter work she calls Mary the one hope of the world, the glorious mistress of heaven, who restores to the world the life that the virgin Eve had lost. She follows a later version of the apocryphal story, which was even more fanciful than the original: After her childhood, which was spent in the Temple in psalmody and fasting, Mary came to Joseph accompanied by five virgins who helped her to weave a precious curtain for the Temple;[3] the medieval imagination was beginning to flower quite unimpeded by historical fact. Hroswitha's version of the Theophilus legend, which she knew in the translation of Paul the Deacon discussed earlier, contributed to its immense popularity. Hroswitha, too, presents Mary as the powerful Queen of Heaven, who alone reconciles sinners

---

[1] 2, 11 (*PL*, 137, 759ff.).   [2] *Sermon on the Assumption* (*PL*, 134, 856f.).
[3] *PL*, 137, 1064ff.

by her intercession, consoles all Christians and takes them into her motherly arms;[1] for she promises that she will not cease to implore her Son "until I compel his tender mercy to spare you and forgive such great sins".[2]

ELEVENTH-CENTURY LATIN THEOLOGIANS

Though popular devotion grew and Mary was generally venerated as the all-powerful intercessor, a more detailed discussion of Mariological questions was not resumed until the next century.

FULBERT OF CHARTRES

The most important theologian of the early eleventh century was Fulbert of Chartres (d. 1028), under whom the building of the famous cathedral was begun. In his first sermon on the feast of Mary's nativity, which, he says, had only recently been introduced into France,[3] he reproduces the story of Theophilus which proves, he says, "that the Mother of the Lord rules everywhere in great magnificence, that she can easily send the holy angels to minister to us and cancel the pacts of hell according to her good pleasure".[4] Though he applies Gen. 3.15 to her he does not discuss her exemption from original sin, but interprets the crushing of the serpent's head as her resistance to the devil's suggestions through her virginity and humility. In the following sermon he briefly describes Mary's death in the Valley of Josaphat and states that the tomb was found empty: "Therefore Christian piety believes that Christ, the Son of God, has gloriously resurrected his Mother and exalted her above the heavens", but, following probably Cosmas Vestitor, he thinks that the same happened also to St. John the Beloved Disciple. He emphasizes, however, that this is only a pious belief; what we know

[1] *PL*, 137, 1101–10.　　　[2] 1108C.
[3] *Serm.*, 4 (*PL*, 141, 320B); only the definitely authentic Marian sermons, one on the Purification and two on the Nativity, 319B–325C, will be discussed.
[4] *Serm.*, 4 (324A).

8+

for certain is that "whatever the just ask of Christ they receive more speedily through the intercession of his mother, and that sinners, too, have received mercy [through her]".[1]

ODILO OF CLUNY

Odilo of Cluny (d. 1049), who wrote a sermon on the Assumption, is equally careful and quotes at length Paschasius Radbert, of course under the name of Jerome, to whose authority "we neither dare nor ought to add anything".[2] At Pentecost Mary received the grace of the Holy Spirit "which she certainly had in its fullness ever since the conception of Christ",[3] the same idea which we have found so often before, and which rules out the Immaculate Conception, which, however, was soon to be discussed in the West.

PETER DAMIAN

Peter Damian (d. 1072), the friend of the future Pope Gregory VII and himself an ardent reformer of the clergy, declared Doctor of the Church in 1828, became famous especially through his treatise on the Eucharist, the doctrine of which began to be studied more carefully during the Middle Ages. So it is not surprising that he should have worked out the connection between the Eucharist and the Virgin in his sermon on her nativity.[4] There he says that after God we must give thanks for our salvation to Mary: "For the same body of Christ which the most blessed Virgin brought forth, which she nourished in her womb, wrapped in swaddling clothes and brought up with motherly care: this same body, I say, and none other, we now perceive without any doubt on the sacred altar."[5] He uses the same idea for a new presentation of the Mary–Eve parallel, for "through the food which

---

[1] *Serm.*, 5 (725B).   [2] *PL*, 142, 1028A.   [3] 1027A.
[4] *Serm.*, 45 (*PL*, 144, 740Dff.). The preceding sermon on the same subject is, like many others attributed to Damian, by Nicholas of Clairvaux.
[5] 743B.

Eve ate we were punished by an external fast; but the food brought forth by Mary has given us access to the heavenly banquet."[1] Though Damian makes no explicit statement on Mary's immaculate conception, he strongly emphasizes her special creation. Before God made the world he elected and pre-elected her,[2] and before he was born he created her in such a way that he could fittingly become her Son.[3] In bold language he calls her "the fount of the living fount, the origin of the beginning, because from her he who is the head and principle of all things through the essence of the Deity came forth through the matter of the flesh".[4] His sermons are free from any apocryphal matter, which he rejects decisively; we ought not to want to know more than the Holy Scriptures tell us.[5] Like Ambrose and Augustine before him, Damian, too, sees Mary in the closest relationship with the Church, whose origin she is. For Christ took flesh from Mary, and from him the Church was born when the water and blood flowed from his side: "In this way, therefore, the Church is seen also to have come forth from Mary."[6] And because Christ came to men through Mary, they also go to him through Mary. This principle, which came to play such an important part both in theory and practice, is stated quite clearly: "We ask you, most clement Mother of pity and mercy, that . . . we may deserve to have the help of your intercession in heaven; because, as the Son of God has deigned to descend to us through you, so we also must come to him through you."[7]

Complete confidence in her intercession appears also in Damian's hymns, in which he asks Mary to "pay what we owe, avert what we fear, obtain what we wish, accomplish what we hope".[8] The same attitude is expressed in the daily Marian Office which he composed[9] where she, the queen of the world and the ladder of heaven, is asked to hear the

---

[1] 743C. [2] 747D. [3] *Serm.*, 46 (752D). [4] 753B.
[5] 754Bff. [6] *Serm.*, 63 (861A, B). [7] *Serm.*, 46 (761B)
[8] *Hymn* 61 (939B). [9] 935B–937C.

prayers of the poor and miserable and to placate the Judge. In *Opusculum XXXIII*, 4 [1] he describes a vision of Mary, who appeared to his dying brother. In the same chapter he explains why the Saturday is especially dedicated to her: because the Sabbath was the day of repose, and Wisdom (Mary) had built herself a house (cf. Prov. 9.1) and reposed in it through the mystery of humility. (Prov 9.4.) So by now the West had caught up with the East—no doubt through a good deal of direct influence, as has been shown before—and Mary, the Mother of Mercy, is beginning to play an ever-increasing part in both medieval Catholic life and doctrine.

GOTTSCHALK OF LIMBURG

Gottschalk of Limburg (d. 1098), a Benedictine monk who was chaplain to the German Emperor Henry IV, emphasized the necessity of Mary's intercession even more: "For as God did not come to man without you, so also man can never come to God without you" he writes in the *opusculum* in which he defends his poem on the Assumption. [2] It had been attacked because he had written: "The faithful people of the Lord wishes for you that the form [lit., "shell"] of your virginal body . . . be neither destroyed nor dissolved by decay." [3] His opponents objected to the word "wishes", because they preferred a definite affirmation; but he does not dare to express himself more positively, because Mary was born of human parents in the normal way, hence "in original sin" [4]— an interesting reasoning, because it shows up the intimate relation of the Immaculate Conception with the bodily Assumption, later to be worked out in the opposite way. Gottschalk goes on to argue that she was both a sinner and not a sinner; a sinner in her own birth, not a sinner in giving birth

---

[1] *PL*, 144, 566.
[2] G. M. Dreves, "Godescalcus Lintburgensis", in *Hymnologische Beiträge*, Leipzig (1897), *opusc. II*.
[3] Dreves, p. 108.   [4] p. 96.

to Christ: "For though she sinned neither by thought, word nor deed, yet she was a sinner. But in that she herself gave birth, she was not only not a sinner, but the destroyer of sin through him to whom she gave birth."[1] Because he is convinced that Mary was not exempt from original sin, owing to the prevalent opinion that this was inevitably transmitted in the normal way of generation, he does not dare affirm that she is in heaven with her body, though he would like to believe that this is so. Then he quotes St. Augustine[2] to the effect that no-one except Christ has ever risen again,[3] and finally Pseudo-Jerome, whose authority still prevented the acceptance of the belief, although it must by now have been widely held, seeing that Gottschalk had to defend his cautious language. In a sermon on the blessed Virgin (*Opusc. V*) he teaches her universal mediation, without which we could not come to God,[4] for, "Your merit alone surpasses the prayers of all the saints; more, you alone direct the prayer of all the saints to God."[5]

Here we meet both the doctrine of merit as applied to Mary and the idea that the prayer of the saints reaches God only through her. She appears as the mediatress between Christ and men even more clearly in his sequence (No. 2 on the blessed Virgin) where he asks the Mediatress, mother of the Mediator and mistress of all things, to placate her Son, for through her alone does he give life to all that are to be saved.[6]

With Gottschalk we have come to the end of the eleventh century; when he died a new age had already begun: the age of scholasticism, the era of the Crusades, of feudalism, of courtly love. All these new developments were also having their influence on Marian doctrine and devotion.

[1] p. 97.   [2] *In Ps. CXXIX* (*PL*, 37, 1701f.).   [3] p. 99.
[4] p. 159.   [5] p. 164.   [6] p. 171.

THE TWELFTH CENTURY:
EARLY SCHOLASTICISM:
ST. BERNARD AND THE GOLDEN AGE OF MARIOLOGY

EARLY SCHOLASTICISM

ANSELM OF CANTERBURY

ANSELM OF CANTERBURY (d. 1109), the author of the so-called ontological argument for the existence of God, is generally regarded as the father of scholasticism. A native of Aosta, he entered the Benedictine monastery of Bec in Normandy, whose abbot he became in 1078. In 1093 he succeeded Lanfranc as Archbishop of Canterbury. Though quantitatively Mary holds only a very small place in Anselm's work (most of the Marian writings printed under his name are spurious), his teaching on her nevertheless had an enormous influence on medieval Mariology. It is contained in three of his works, the famous *Cur Deus Homo* (on the reason for the Incarnation), his treatise on "The Virginal Conception and on Original Sin", and his *Orationes*.[1] Though a passage from Anselm which will be quoted presently was inserted in the bull *Ineffabilis*, which defined the Immaculate Conception, he himself did not teach this doctrine. In *Cur Deus Homo* Anselm says explicitly that "the Virgin . . . was born with original sin, because she, too, sinned in Adam"; she was purified only before the birth of Christ, who was assumed from "the sinning mass [*de massa peccatrice*]" which he had purified, for "his

[1] I quote from the critical edition of F. S. Schmitt, O.S.B., by chapter and section.

Mother's purity, by which he is pure, was only from him, whereas he was pure through and from himself".[1] In his treatise on the Virginal Conception Anselm proves that Christ could be without sin even if Mary was not, because original sin was transmitted by natural propagation, whereas Christ was born virginally.[2] Nevertheless, just this treatise contains the passage that exercised a decisive influence on the doctrine of the Immaculate Conception and was quoted in the bull defining it. It reads: "It was fitting [decebat] that this Virgin should shine with a degree of purity than which no greater can be imagined apart from God."[3] The logical conclusion from this principle would indeed be the Immaculate Conception; but the Augustinian tradition was too strong for Anselm to affirm it. His view of original sin, too, contributed to the later belief of Mary's exemption from it; for whereas the general opinion of theologians at that time was that concupiscence plays a decisive part in the transmission of it, tainting all persons generated in the normal way, Anselm saw in it nothing else but the "absence . . . due to Adam's disobedience, of the state of justice which they ought to possess".[4] If Mary was the purest of all creatures, and if original sin was but the absence of original justice, then no more was needed than the anticipation of the effects of Christ's passion to make the Immaculate Conception theologically acceptable.

Though Anselm did not draw this consequence from his own teaching, his Marian doctrine, as it emerges from his three great Marian prayers,[5] was exalted indeed.[6] These prayers, which became extremely popular, are written in a highly polished rhetorical style. Mary is addressed as the Virgin of admirable virginity and "amiable" fecundity,

---

[1] 2, 16.   [2] Chs. 15f.   [3] Ch. 18.

[4] *Treatise on the Virginal Conception*, 27; see J. S. Bruder, S.M., *The Mariology of Saint Anselm of Canterbury*, Dayton, Ohio (1939), pp. 62f.

[5] Composed probably between 1060, the date of his arrival at Bec, and 1078, when he became abbot. So A. Wilmart in *RTAM* (1930), p. 191.

[6] *Orationes*, 5–7 (Schmitt, 3, pp. 13–25).

excelling all others not only in dignity but also in power; she is the mother of salvation and temple of mercy before whom his miserable soul presents itself to be healed by her merits and prayers. Despite his assertion that she was born in original sin, he calls her purer than the angels and asks her to heal the wounds of his sins, for she is "mercifully powerful and powerfully merciful".[1] Mary's purity is contrasted with the sinner's impurity, and the latter's misery is emphasized in a way characteristic of medieval man: "Queen of angels, mistress of the world, mother of him who purifies the world, I confess that my heart is exceedingly impure, so that it is rightly ashamed to turn to so pure a one"; for he is a captive, he is lost, conscious only of his sins and misery,[2] and his dying spirit yearns for the sight of her goodness, while at the same time shying away from her surpassing splendour. Nevertheless, he makes bold to ask her to heal the wounds and ulcers of his sins.[3]

Even though Anselm is careful to distinguish between the office of Christ, who can spare, whereas Mary intercedes, he also calls him the "judge of the world" and her the "reconciler [reconciliatrix] of the world"; her merits, which he frequently emphasizes, are not only useful but necessary for us.[4] Indeed, as he says in the third prayer,[5] "I am sure that what I have been able to receive through the grace of the Son I can also receive through the merits of the Mother." And so she is the gate of life and the door of salvation, the way of reconciliation, whose power extends to Hades as well as to heaven, the admirable woman "through whom the elements are renewed, the netherworld is healed, the demons are trodden under foot, men are saved and angels are restored; O woman, filled with grace to overflowing, through whose abundant plenitude every creature is rejuvenated! O blessed and more than blessed Virgin, through whose blessing every creature is blessed, not only the creature by the Creator, but

[1] *Or. V.*   [2] *Or. VII.*   [3] *Or. V.*   [4] *Or. VI.*   [5] *Or. VII.*

also the Creator by the creature! . . . O you, beautiful to behold, lovable to contemplate, delightful to love, how far you exceed the capacity of my heart! Wait, Lady, for the weak soul is following you!"[1] Here again, as has been noted before, divine activities are attributed to Mary on account of her divine motherhood, followed by personal effusions reflecting the spirit of courtly love in a religious setting. The great Theotokos, who is also the tender Mother suckling her Child, now becomes the beautiful Lady, delightful to behold and to love, the spiritual counterpart of the worldly mistress of the knight.

But after the knight of Mary has had his say, the father of scholasticism reasserts himself and establishes the greatness of Mary by logical argument. "Nothing", Anselm writes in the same prayer, "is equal to Mary, nothing but God is greater than Mary." And he goes on to argue: "Every nature is created by God, and God is born from Mary. God has created all things, and Mary has given birth to God. God, who has made all things has made himself from Mary, and thus he has re-created all he created . . . Therefore God is the Father of all created things, and Mary is the Mother of all re-created things. God is the Father of the constitution of all things, and Mary is the Mother of the restitution of all things . . . For God generated him through whom all things were made, and Mary gave birth to him through whom all things were saved." So Mary's position in the divine dispensation is deduced by a logical process from her divine motherhood, indeed, her motherhood is paralleled by the fatherhood of God. If God is the Being than which nothing greater can be conceived (the basis of the ontological argument), Mary is that than which nothing is greater except God. God is the Father of all created things, Mary the Mother of all re-created things. As the ontological argument has been criticized for jumping from mental conception to real existence, so Anselm's "Mariological argument"—if we may be allowed to call it

[1] *Or. VII.*

8*

thus—may also be criticized for jumping from the divine to the human plane. For the fatherhood of God is something radically different from the motherhood of Mary, and she can hardly be called the mother of the restitution of all things, that is to say, of the Redemption, in the same way as God is the Father of the constitution of all things, that is to say, of Creation; for God is this directly, in his own right, but Mary only indirectly, through her Son. This Anselm, indeed, says himself, a few lines below; but his language is misleading at times and has influenced later exaggerations.

After these theoretical considerations Anselm once more addresses Mary herself: "As therefore, O most blessed one, everyone who turns away from you and is despised by you must perish, so also whoever turns to, and is regarded by you, cannot possibly be lost." "O blessed confidence, O safe refuge! The Mother of God is our mother. The mother of him, in whom alone we hope . . . is our mother." And he goes on to argue that, because she is the Mother of Christ and of us, we are also his brothers: "Our God has become our brother through Mary." While Athanasius, for example, had said that Christ became our Brother "through the coming down of the Logos to his creatures",[1] taking account only of the divine action and leaving out the human instrument, Anselm mentions only the latter, that is to say, Mary, while leaving out the first cause, the divine Word—a very suggestive difference between the patristic and medieval mentalities. And so in his prayer he places Christ and Mary on the same level: "Both salvation and damnation depend on the will of the good Brother and the merciful Mother."[2] Therefore "let him who is guilty before the just God flee to the tender Mother of the merciful God",[3] whom he addresses in the opening of his great prayer: "Mary, you great Mary, you who are greater than the [other] blessed Maries, you, the greatest of women; my heart wants to love you, surpassingly great

[1] *Contra Arianos*, 2, 62.   [2] *Or. VII.*   [3] *Or. VI.*

Lady . . . because with my whole substance I commend myself to your protection."[1]

In Anselm some of the principal trends of medieval Marian doctrine and devotion are already united: a scholastic argumentation working out the consequences of Mary's divine motherhood in a strict parallelism between it and the fatherhood of God, which leads necessarily to her share in Christ's work of redemption ("both salvation and damnation depend on the will of the good Brother and the merciful Mother"), and so to her being also the mother of men, whose prayers are as necessary to our salvation as the Incarnation itself. Besides, Mary appears not only as the Mother of God, but also as the beloved, beautiful Lady of her spiritual knight who places himself under her protection, because "it is incredible that you should not have mercy on the miserable men who implore you".[2]

EADMER AND THE IMMACULATE CONCEPTION

Anselm's influence was tremendous, both on the Continent and in England. The most famous of his English disciples was Eadmer (d. 1124), a Saxon by birth—a nationality which, as we shall see presently, was not without influence on his doctrinal beliefs. He was brought up at the Benedictine monastery of Christ Church, Canterbury, where he became a monk, and later, precentor. He wrote two important works on our subject, the *Book on the Excellence of the Virgin Mary*[3] and a *tractatus* on her conception.[4] The former work, obviously strongly influenced by Anselm, is remarkable for

---

[1] *Or. VII.*   [2] *Or. VI.*

[3] *Liber de Excellentia Virginis Mariae* (*PL*, 159, 557–80).

[4] A faulty edition of this is printed among the works of Anselm in *PL*, 59, 301ff.; there is a critical edition by H. Thurston and T. Slater, Freiburg i. Br. (1904), who prove that the work belongs to Eadmer, a view confirmed by A. W. Burridge, in his article "L'Immaculée Conception dans la théologie de l'Angleterre médiévale", in *Revue d'hist. eccl.*, 32 (1936), p. 580. The *Tractatus*, as edited by Thurston and Slater, is cited by section number followed by the Migne reference, as the critical edition is not easily accessible.

its often naïve views, which show clearly the trends of popular devotion which we have noticed before. Mary reigns over the whole world, for the Holy Spirit who reposed in her made her queen and empress of heaven, earth and all that is in them;[1] sun, stars, earth and all other creatures were made to serve just men, not sinners; when Mary appeared, through whom came redemption, the creatures were no longer subject to sinful men but regained the freedom of their original creation.[2] For every creature was created for the use of men, and through Mary they were all restored to their original state.[3] The medieval picture of the world with the earth in the centre and sun, moon and stars revolving around it made it easier than it is today to see Mary as the mistress of the whole universe. But Eadmer goes still further than that. In his opinion, as in that of Fulbert of Chartres, it may be even more useful to call on her than on Christ when one is in danger, for: "Sometimes salvation is quicker if we remember Mary's name than if we invoke the name of the Lord Jesus."[4] He then asks why this should be so, seeing that she is not more powerful than he, and he is not powerful through her, but she through him. "I will say what I feel", he answers: "Her Son is the Lord and Judge of all men, discerning the merits of the individuals, hence he does not at once answer anyone who invokes him, but does it only after just judgement. But if the name of his Mother be invoked, her merits intercede so that he is answered even if the merits of him who invokes her do not deserve it."[5] So we have here the naïve idea that it takes Christ some time to weigh the pros and cons of a case, whereas if we turn to his mother he no longer judges but only considers her merits and grants a man's prayer at once—a view which became quite common and explains why, in the Middle Ages and after, prayer to Mary so often almost superseded prayer to Christ in popular devotion.

[1] *Book on the Excellence*, 4 (565B).   [2] 10.   [3] 11 (578A).
[4] 6 (570A).   [5] 6 (570B).

Mary's reign, says Eadmer, began at the Ascension, when she knew she was going to rule over every creature, second only to her Son. Then he asks himself how Christ could bear to go to heaven first and to leave his mother behind; perhaps, he thinks, because the heavenly court would not have known whom to greet first.[1] At her assumption all heaven is made to give her a wonderful welcome and she is placed on a throne to reign over the whole world, "by motherly right presiding with her Son over heaven and earth".[2] Eadmer closely follows his master Anselm in drawing parallels between God's work and hers: "As God, through creating everything by his power, is the Father and Lord of all, so blessed Mary, re-creating all things by her merits, is the mother and mistress of things; for God is the Lord of all, constituting the individual things in their nature by his own command; and Mary is the mistress of things, restoring the individual things to their congenital dignity through the grace she merited. And inasmuch as God from his own substance generated him through whom all things originated, thus Mary from her flesh gave birth to him who restored all things to the beauty of their first creation."[3] The passage is an interesting example of the mixture of first and second causes: though in the second part of the quotation Eadmer says that it is Christ who restored all things, in the first half he praises Mary as doing this "though the grace she merited"; and this power of Mary is stressed more and more, especially with regard to the forgiveness of sins. For Christ will give whatever his mother wants, and so Eadmer, convinced that we cannot be saved without her, implores her: "If you, who are the Mother of God, and therefore the true Mother of Mercy, deny us the effect of the mercy of him whose mother you have been made so marvellously, what shall we do when your Son comes to judge all men with a just judgement?"[4] This view that Mary can provide salvation where Christ alone would condemn became increasingly

[1] 7 (570D–571A).   [2] 9 (574C).   [3] 11 (578A, B).   [4] 12 (579A).

popular; Eadmer argues naïvely with her that her exaltation would be of no profit if she did not help us, for this is her proper office: "Why do you not help us sinners, since for our sakes you have been raised to such heights that every creature has and venerates you as mistress?"[1] "For as we have your Son as the Saviour of the whole world, so we have you truly as his reconciler"[2]—Anselm's expression. Christ saves through his passion and death, but this salvation must be made effective through Mary, without whom we could not be reconciled to him: "Do you [Mary], see to it that we may not perish."[3]

Theologically more important is Eadmer's treatise on "The Conception of the Blessed Virgin", the first detailed exposition of the doctrine of the Immaculate Conception. As Bruder[4] points out, "Eadmer's defence of the Immaculate Conception may well have been written to justify the reintroduction of the feast of our Lady in the Abbey of Saint Edmund's, Bury, by its newly appointed abbot, Anselm, the nephew of our saint." He further draws attention to Anselm of Bury's links with the Greek monks of St. Sabas, near Jerusalem, who had fled to Rome when Palestine was invaded by the Saracens. St. Sabas, the monastery of John of Damascus, had celebrated the feast of Mary's conception for centuries, and its monks continued to do so when they came to Rome. There Anselm had been abbot before he was transferred to Bury, and as such he carried on the Greek tradition, which he then reintroduced in England, where the feast had been celebrated by the Saxons but had been abolished after the Norman invasion of England. Eadmer says that the poor and simple people rejoiced in it, whereas some learned men were against it;[5] he admits that Scripture says nothing about Mary being conceived without original sin, nevertheless, he does not think that it would be

---

[1] 12 (579B).   [2] 580B.   [3] 580B.
[4] *The Mariology of St. Anselm of Canterbury*, 1939, p. 46f.
[5] 1 (301C–303A).

against faith to consider it.[1] He is, however, very careful in proposing his view, asserting that he does not want to dissent from Catholic truth in any way—a caution probably due to the fact that his master, St. Anselm, had held a different opinion. Eadmer bases his belief on the fact that Christ came to save sinners and on Mary's co-operation in this: "She, who was created to be the palace of the Redeemer of sinners, was therefore free from the servitude of all sin";[2] if Jeremiah and John the Baptist were sanctified in their mother's womb, "Who dares to say that the unique propitiation of the whole world and the resting-place of the only Son of God was deprived of the grace and illumination of the Holy Spirit in the beginning of her conception?"[3] To show how this could be done though she was not born from a virgin, he compares her with a chestnut: "If God gives the chestnut the possibility of being conceived, nourished and formed under thorns, but remote from them, could he not grant to the human body which he was preparing for himself to be a temple in which he would dwell bodily . . . that although she was conceived among the thorns of sin, she might be rendered completely immune from their pricks? He certainly could do it; if, therefore, he willed it, he did it."[4] So Eadmer solved the difficulty which had prevented the Latins from acknowledging the Immaculate Conception by teaching what came to be known as the "passive conception", which he could do because his teacher Anselm had paved the way by regarding original sin as no more than the absence of original justice. And he based himself on the famous adage *potuit, voluit, fecit*, arguing from power to will, from will to deed, in a way that had been unknown in the age of the Fathers but was characteristic of medieval Western theology.

He uses this argument again when linking the Immaculate Conception to Mary's dominion over the world: "For [God] willed you to become his mother, and because he willed it,

---

[1] 5 (303C).   [2] 9 (305B).   [3] 9 (305B).   [4] 10 (305C, D).

he made you so . . . He made you his unique mother and so
at the same time constituted you mistress and empress of all
things. Therefore you are the mistress and empress of heaven
and earth, of the sea and all the elements with all that is in
them, and so that you might be this, you were created in your
mother's womb from the beginning of your conception with
the co-operation of the Holy Spirit."[1] For nothing is equal or
comparable to Mary; only God is above her, and whatever is
not God is beneath her.[2] Because of this surpassing excellence,
she could not be conceived like other human beings, but, "by
an extraordinary divine operation inaccessible to the human
intellect, most free from any admixture of sin".[3] So Mary's
freedom from original sin is linked not only to her dignity as
the Mother of the Redeemer but also to her position as mistress
and empress of the entire universe. As such she "presides
over angels and archangels and disposes of everything as
queen together with her Son".[4]

The relation between Mary and her Son in heaven is not,
however, worked out quite consistently. The treatise ends
with demands for her intercession. Here Eadmer argues, with
the naïvety which has been noticed before, that she cannot
fail us, because Christ has died for us; for this reason she must
have pity on us and intercede for us. Then she is told that she
ought not to love God's justice too much, because she herself
is wholly human; if she were to act according to God's justice,
she would deprive sinners of all hope. After that he tells her
that her Son desires our salvation, therefore she must want it,
too. But a little further on, having bemoaned his sins in the
exaggerated terms characteristic of the Middle Ages, he
asks her to free him from hell, if her Son should condemn
him to it.[5] So it is never quite clear whether Mary always acts
in accordance with the will of God or whether she is capable
of bending it to her own; on the one hand her Son desires our

[1] 11 (306A).   [2] 14 (307B).   [3] 12 (306B).   [4] 25 (312A).
[5] 35ff. (316Aff.).

salvation, which, apparently, cannot be achieved without her; on the other, he may condemn us to hell while she could free us from it.

Thus the West continued the line that had begun with the Greek prayer *Sub tuum praesidium* in the third or fourth century—which, incidentally, Eadmer echoes several times (e.g., in *Tractatus XL*; where Mary is called the "singulare praesidium omnium ad te confugientium", the "unique help of all who fly to you"), but in a way which presents the Mother of God more and more as an all-but-independent power ruling the whole world by the side of her Son, on whom she continues to exercise her maternal authority.

OPPOSITION TO THE FEAST OF THE
IMMACULATE CONCEPTION

Despite Eadmer, the feast of the conception of Mary met with some opposition even in England, and even more did the idea that she was conceived without original sin. This is shown by the letters of Osbert of Clare,[1] especially the seventh, addressed to Anselm of Bury, the nephew of Anselm of Canterbury, and the thirteenth, addressed to Warin, Dean of Worcester. In the former Osbert complains that some "followers of Satan" oppose the feast on the grounds that until then nothing had been heard about it and that bishops Roger of Salisbury and Bernard of St. David's tried to prevent its celebration. Nevertheless, Osbert himself kept it with great solemnity,[2] but was attacked vehemently by some who objected that it was not authorized by Rome. He then gives his reasons for keeping it, which reflect Eadmer's views: if John the Baptist and Jeremiah were sanctified in their mother's womb, how much more Mary; just as it was possible for God to create the first mother without sin from the side of Adam, "so we do not think it was impossible for him to sanctify the

[1] d. c. 1127; ed. by E. W. Williamson, Oxford (1929).
[2] Williamson, p. 65.

blessed Virgin Mary without the contagion of sin in her very conception".[1] He is determined to defend this truth against its opponents. Nevertheless, in his sermon "On the Conception of Holy Mary"[2] he does not discuss this matter, no doubt because, as he writes to Warin, "I do not dare to say what I think in my heart of this holy generation, because it is not lawful to cast the heavenly pearls before the multitude."[3]

PSEUDO-AUGUSTINE AND THE ASSUMPTION

Until the beginning of the twelfth century the Pseudo-Jerome's authority had prevented belief in the bodily assumption of Mary from gaining ground in the West. Now another treatise on the same subject, taking a different view, appeared, which came to be attributed to St. Augustine, and under his name gradually ousted the influence of Pseudo-Jerome (Paschasius Radbert).[4] Its date is uncertain; Laurentin[5] dates it towards the end of the eleventh century or the beginning of the twelfth, and places it in the milieu of St. Anselm. In the opinion of the present author it shows some remarkable affinities with Cosmas Vestitor (who was translated into Latin in the tenth century), especially in its insistence that the flesh of Jesus is the flesh of Mary and that therefore where his body is Mary's must be, too. On the other hand, the anonymous treatise shows that it belongs to the age of incipient scholasticism in that it completely disregards the apocrypha and instead relies on logical reasoning. It begins by stating that after the Crucifixion Scripture says nothing more about Mary except mentioning her presence with the Apostles at Pentecost.[6] Nevertheless, "There are truths on which Scripture is silent, but not reason. Of these is the assumption of

[1] Williamson, p. 66.　　[2] Thurston and Slater, pp. 63–83.
[3] Thurston and Slater, p. 79.
[4] Printed among the works of St. Augustine in *PL*, 40, 1140–48.
[5] *Court traité de théologie mariale*, 4, Paris (1959), p. 57.
[6] 1 (*PL*, 40, 1143).

Blessed Mary."[1] Thus reason is placed beside Scripture as a means of discovering religious truth—a principle which is valid within limits but which, as we shall see later, may also at times lead to undesirable consequences.

The author then quotes Gen. 3.19, according to which man is dust and must return to dust. "If this", he explains, "refers to death, its application is general. If, however, it is said of dissolving into dust, the flesh of Christ, which is taken from the flesh of Mary, has escaped it, because it has not suffered corruption."[2] He goes on to argue that Mary herself was exempt from the curse pronounced on women, because her conceptions were not multiplied and she was not under the authority of man.[3] Further, it is certain that Christ preserved his mother's virginity intact; if so, why should he not have willed to preserve her also from the corruption of death? The Law commanded men to honour their mothers: "Since he honoured her in her life before others by the grace of his conception, it is fitting to believe [*pium est credere*] that by a unique dispensation he honoured her also in death by a special grace", since his own glorified flesh remains the flesh of Mary.[4] It would not be fitting for this flesh to be eaten by worms—a thought repeated several times, anticipating the later medieval preoccupation with the macabre.[5] If Christ said, "Where I am, there also shall my minister be" (John 12.26), how much more will his Mother be where he is?[6] It is obvious that he *could* save her body from corruption, so why should it be doubted that he also *would* do so? Christ wills all things that are fitting; now, it is fitting that she who suffered no corruption in giving birth to her Son should suffer none in death either. Here again we have the same argumentation of *potuit*, *voluit*, *fecit* as in Eadmer's treatise on the Immaculate Conception—another pointer towards the close relation between the two doctrines, which both depend on the

---

[1] 2 (1143f).   [2] 3 (1144).   [3] 4 (1144).   [4] 5 (1145).
[5] 6 (1146).   [6] 7 (1146).

fittingness of these Marian prerogatives, and perhaps also to the possibility that the unknown author was a countryman of Eadmer.

MINOR BENEDICTINES

Bruno of Asti, Bishop of Segni (d. 1123), another Benedictine and an ardent supporter of Gregory VII's reforms, was one of the most famous medieval exegetes, and for this reason is worthy of mention, even though he adds little that is new to twelfth-century Mariology. Though he is generally more sober than many of his contemporaries, he calls Mary "the head of the whole Church after her Son",[1] and again "the queen and mistress of the Church" in his exegesis of Ps. 44.10ff., which he applies to Mary, though he admits that it is also applicable to the Church. It is all the more noteworthy that his explanation of the Canticle refers only to the Church and that his treatise in praise of Mary[2] is quite free from exaggerations—a fact due probably to his being above all an exegete and respecting the reticence of Scripture more than most other authors of the time.

His sobriety stands out all the more if his work be compared with the treatise on the same subject by his contemporary Guibert of Nogent (d. 1124), a Benedictine abbot and disciple of St. Anselm whom his mother had vowed to the blessed Virgin before his birth, and who later consecrated himself to her.[3] Though he follows his master in denying Mary's immaculate conception,[4] he attributes quasi-divine properties to her. Because she bore the omniscient God, she would have been omniscient, too, had not this gift been clouded by humility.[5] This statement harmonizes with Guibert's view that Mary enjoyed the Beatific Vision even on earth. His argument: "As she possessed more than an angel on earth [scil.,

---

[1] *On Exodus*, 15 (*PL*, 164, 266B).
[2] Bk. 5 of his *Sentences* (*PL*, 165, 1021–32).
[3] *Autobiography*, 1, 3 (*PL*, 156, 842A–843A).
[4] *De Laude S. Mariae*, 5 (*PL*, 156, 550D).   [5] 540B–D.

while bearing Christ], she ought not to have been less than an angel after the bliss of such a birth."[1] We see already here, as we shall notice even more frequently later, to what strange ideas such abstract reasoning could lead. As such prerogatives were hers on earth, Guibert naturally stresses her sovereignty over the universe: "She it is who through her Son presides over heaven, commands on earth and afflicts hell",[2] suggesting almost a "power behind the throne". She also avenges injuries done to her by heretics[3] and, being "the author of the creature of the Son of God" (i.e., of his humanity), she is not only honoured like the other saints, "but, as more than equal [*superpar*] to Christ's humanity, adored". (556D). She is the mediatress between men and God, who is almost compelled to listen to her by his own law (the Fourth Commandment) (557A): "And as a good son in this world so respects his mother's authority that she commands rather than asks, so he [Christ], who undoubtedly was once subject to her, cannot, I am sure, refuse her anything; and what (I speak humanly) she demands, not by asking but by commanding, will surely come to pass" (9 (564A)); for it behoves her not to ask but to command. (14 (577A).) And so Guibert even calls her "saviour" (*salvatricem* (577B)), for she is our only hope and salvation: "Exclude Mary from the Church, and what will the Church be except misery? For without her childbirth there would have been no Redemption." (4 (543C).) Though Guibert denied the Immaculate Conception, he was favourable to the idea of the bodily Assumption, probably under the influence of the pseudo-Augustine, because he uses his argument that it seems reasonable to believe that she whose flesh is the same as that of her Son did not share the common lot of mankind. Nevertheless, though we are allowed to believe this, we must not definitely assert it, by reason of lack of evidence.[4]

---

[1] 7 (561A).   [2] 6 (556B).   [3] 556C.
[4] *On the Relics of the Saints*, 1, 3, 1 (*PL*, 156, 624A).

Geoffrey of Vendôme (d. 1132), another Benedictine supporter of the Gregorian reforms, who later became a cardinal, also emphasizes Mary's power of intercession, the biblical basis for which he finds in the miracle of Cana,[1] and in evidence of which he quotes the Theophilus legend.[2] Indeed, so great is this power, "that she will obtain from her most merciful Son that none of those is lost for whom she has prayed even once. And this is not surprising, for she can save the whole world by her prayers, if she wills it. And she would certainly be most ready to pray for the whole world, and the whole world would be saved, if it rendered itself worthy of her prayers." For through her "mother's command" she can obtain from Christ whatever she desires, and she will never be defrauded of her maternal rights.[3] Though God is, indeed, omnipotent, he has never been able to refuse her anything.[4] For this reason Christ will also revenge an injury done to his mother more severely than one done to himself, and would never leave it unpunished unless she first prayed for the offender; more, he would rather that men doubted his own origin than her virginity.[5] Christ is both her Son and her Spouse "because he is united to her in love",[6] and in him she has also given birth to us; therefore Geoffrey asks his monks to take her for their mother,[7] for she is merciful like a mother.[8]

THE MARIAN INTERPRETATION OF THE CANTICLE:
RUPERT OF DEUTZ AND HONORIUS OF AUTUN

Rupert, the abbot of the Benedictines at Deutz (d. c. 1135), seems to have been the first to have interpreted the Canticle entirely with reference to Mary. Individual verses of it had, of course, been applied to her from early times; but the Marian

---

[1] *Sermon 8 (PL,* 157, 269A).   [2] 269C, D.   [3] 268B–D.
[4] 269C.   [5] 269B–D.   [6] 267B.   [7] *Ep. 4.* 24 (168B).
[8] *Serm.,* 7 (266B); on Mary as mother of individual Christians cf. also 265D–266A.

exegesis of the whole poem was something new.[1] In his
article on the Marian interpretation of the Canticle in early
scholasticism J. Beumer[2] gives as the reason for this the fact
that between the ninth and eleventh centuries the feast of the
Assumption had lessons from the Canticle, and that even
before the twelfth century these lessons, formerly continued
throughout August, were interrupted after the octave of the
feast, to be resumed for the Nativity of the Blessed Virgin in
September. Thus the liturgical readings brought her into close
connection with the Canticle, hence the Marian exegesis. The
contents of Rupert's work, however, reflect the traditional
Mariology of the time. Though the blessed Virgin was not
without the stain of original sin, this was wiped out through
the Incarnation.[3] She was both a faithful prophetess[4] and the
teacher of the Apostles, whose voice supplemented the instruction of the Holy Spirit.[5] Being a prophetess, she knew not
only where Jesus was when his parents had lost him in
Jerusalem—her ignorance recorded in the Gospel being only
assumed, according to the divine dispensation—she also foreknew the Passion even when she was still suckling him in her
arms.[6] She was chosen before the beginning of the world,
according to the text from Prov. 8,[7] and now she is queen of
the saints in heaven as well as of the kingdoms of the earth,
"possessing by right the whole kingdom of her Son",
according to the medieval legal idea, for she is the Mother of
the Church, being Christ's sister by faith and his spouse by
love.[8] Like many of his contemporaries, Rupert had a keen
sense of the continuity between the Old and the New Dis-
pensations, which are linked in Mary, the "true Jerusalem"
and the daughter of the Church of the Old Testament.[9] We

---

[1] PL, 168, 837–962.

[2] "Die marianische Deutung des Hohen Liedes in der Frühscholastik", in
ZKT, 76 (1954), pp. 411–39.

[3] 841C.   [4] 842A (see Isa. 8.3).   [5] 850A.

[6] 851A–856A.   [7] 867A.   [8] 891A–898B.

[9] 933B–936B.

owe it to Mary that Christ is our Brother, and so she is the mother of us all.[1]

Mary's connection with Israel is worked out in greater detail in Rupert's work on the Trinity, where he says that Mary is the spouse of the Father, for whose sake he was said in the Old Testament to have espoused the Church of his first people; she was "the best part of the first Church, who merited to be the spouse of God the Father so as to be also the type [*exemplar*] of the younger Church, the spouse of the Son of God and her own Son".[2] In his commentary on the Fourth Gospel Rupert emphasizes that Mary became our mother under the Cross, like many modern theologians connecting her "birth pangs" on Golgotha with John 16.21: "A woman, when she is in labour, hath sorrow because her hour is come"; if Christ said this to the Apostles, Rupert comments, how much more applicable are these words to the woman who stood beside his cross: "For she is truly a mother, and in that hour she had true birth pangs." "Because there were truly 'pains as of a woman in labour' [Ps. 47.7] and in the Passion of the only begotten Son the blessed Virgin brought forth the salvation of us all, she is obviously the Mother of us all."[3]

If Rupert was the first to have interpreted the Canticle exclusively of Mary, he must have been followed in this very soon by one of the most influential early schoolmen, Honorius of Autun (d. 1136). He, too, was a Benedictine, first at Regensburg, later at Canterbury, where he studied Anselm, whom he followed in his denial of the Immaculate Conception[4]: "She, too, is believed to have been born [*nata*, not only conceived!] in sins." On the other hand, he teaches her bodily assumption; the pseudo-Augustine was making his influence increasingly felt.[5] According to Honorius, Mary was left on earth for two

[1] 950D.   [2] 1.7f. (*PL*, 167, 1576B–1577D).   [3] *Comm. in Jo.*, 13 (*PL*, 169, 789C).
[4] *Sigillum Beatae Mariae*, 5, as his exegesis of the Canticle is called (*PL*, 172, 509B).
[5] 3 (505A).

years after the Ascension as an example to the faithful and in order to be herself tried like gold in the fire through her sorrow for his absence.[1] It is characteristic of him no less than of most medieval scholars that, though he wrote learned treatises on free will and grace and other theological questions, on the other hand he readily believed and transmitted the most extravagant miracle stories. In his various Marian sermons he not only repeated the stories of Theophilus and of the Jewish boy who consumed the Host, but also a great number of other legends, however fanciful, which fed both the devotion and the imagination of the common people.

LITURGICAL AND POPULAR DEVOTION

At the same time new hymns to the Mother of God, especially the so-called Marian antiphons, exercised a strong influence both in religious and lay circles. The most famous of them is the *Salve Regina*, the date and authorship of which are still disputed. It has frequently been attributed to Bernard of Clairvaux,[2] but most modern scholars believe it to have been composed earlier, towards the end of the eleventh century or the beginning of the twelfth. It was introduced into the liturgical services of Cluny about 1135 and soon taken over by the Cistercians, later also by the Dominicans, who recite it daily after Compline. The *Salve Regina* expresses to perfection medieval men's attitude to Mary; their complete confidence in her, the Mother of Mercy, to whom the exiled sons of Eve recommend themselves and whose life, sweetness and hope she is; her power as their advocate with God and her mediation between themselves and Christ, whom she will show them after the exile of this earth is over.

The *Alma Redemptoris Mater*, the Advent antiphon, often attributed to Hermannus Contractus, a monk of Reichenau

[1] 8 (517B).
[2] So still by, e.g., J. M. Canal, in *Sacris Erudiri*, X (1958), p. 183.

(d. 1054),[1] is probably of a later date (late eleventh or early twelfth century) as it appears only in twelfth-century manuscripts. It is obviously inspired by the *Ave Maris Stella*, and itself is a prayer to the Gate of Heaven and Star of the Sea to help those about to fall, and to have mercy on sinners.

The most popular of all Marian prayers also made its appearance about this time. This, of course, is the *Hail Mary*, the greeting of the angel (Luke 1.28) which was combined with that of Elizabeth (Luke 1.42) as early as the sixth century in the East; since it is quoted on a potsherd dated about 600[2] in the following form: "Hail Mary, full of grace, the Lord is with thee, blessed art thou among women and blessed is the fruit of thy womb, because thou didst conceive [Christ, the Son of God] the Redeemer of our souls." The twofold greeting, with the shorter addition, appears also in the Eastern liturgies[3] and in the Latin Offertory of the Mass for the Fourth Sunday of Advent. But it became popular only through the Little Office of our Lady. This is a shorter Office than the "Divine Office"; it consists of psalms and Marian hymns and antiphons, in which the *Ave Maria* is frequently used. It appeared first as a private devotion in the tenth century and is attested in the Life of Bishop Ulrich of Augsburg (d. 973) written by his contemporary, Gerard, Provost of Augsburg Cathedral.[4] Peter Damian recommended its universal recitation.[5] He reinforced his recommendation by various miracle stories—for example, one about a monastery which, after the recitation had been stopped, was afflicted by many calamities which ceased only when it had been resumed.[6] Its use on Saturday was

[1] So still J. Leclercq in *Maria*, 2, p. 555.

[2] W. L. Crum, *Coptic Ostraca* (1902), p. 3.

[3] F. E. Brightman, *Eastern Liturgies*: Liturgy of St. James (p. 56), Liturgy of St. Mark (p. 128), and in the Liturgy of the Abyssinian Jacobites with the addition, "Pray and intercede for us with thy beloved Son" (p. 218).

[4] *PL*, 135, 1016D.

[5] *Opusculum X, DeHoris Canonicis*, ch. 9 (*PL*, 145, 230B).

[6] *Ep.* 6, 32 (*PL*, 144, 413B–432A).

ordered by Pope Urban II at the Synod of Clermont in 1095[1] for both the regular and secular clergy in order to obtain Mary's help for the First Crusade. The Office, which soon was also said by many devout laymen, was further recommended by many legends attributing graces and miracles to its recitation. These Marian legends were collected from the beginning of the twelfth century and frequently translated into the vernacular and propagated in sermons.[2] In the first collection, containing seventeen miracles, four are connected with the recitation of the Little Office. From there, then, the *Hail Mary* spread far and wide through Western Christendom, still in its short, biblical form, without the later petition prayer, so that Abbot Franco of Affligham, writing before 1125, could say: "Of good right does every condition, every age, every degree honour Mary with the angelic salutation."[3] The *Hail Mary* was often accompanied by genuflexions or prostrations; a hermit, Aybert (d. c. 1140), for example, said daily one hundred and fifty *Hail Maries*,[4] with as many genuflections; and in the canons of the Synod of Paris (c. 1210) the knowledge of the *Hail Mary* was enjoined upon all the faithful in addition to the *Our Father* and the Apostles' Creed.

From the beginning of the twelfth century rhythmic Marian greeting hymns (*Grusshymnen*) also became very popular. According to Meersseman[5] they owe their origin to the *Akathistos*—we see how strong the Greek influence still was in the West—the salutations of which had been used in a

---

[1] Cf. *PL*, 151, 183B, C.

[2] A. Mussaffia, who made an extensive study of the subject, "Studien zu den mittelalterlichen Marienlegenden", in *Sitzungsberichte der Wiener Akademie der Wissenschaften, Philosophisch-historische Klasse*, vols. 113, 115, 119, 123, 139 (1887-98), dates the first from the beginning of the twelfth or even the latter part of the eleventh century (vol. 113, p. 918).

[3] *PL*, 166, 745; for a more detailed discussion of the subject see H. Thurston, *Familiar Prayers*, ed. O. Grosjean (1953), pp. 90-114.

[4] Surius, *Vita Sanctorum*, 2, 7 April, *Acta SS. Apr.*, 1, no. 14.

[5] *Der Hymnos Akathistos im Abendland*, 1, pp. 77ff.

Salutatio Sanctae Mariae which originated in Paris between 1050 and 1075. Under its influence these hymns became so numerous in our period that they are considered as forming a species of their own. It is, however, noteworthy that in the West their character differs from similar poems in the East in that they are far more prayers for help and protection— reflecting the insecurity of the times and the more naïve approach of the young, more recently converted nations.

Marian litanies came into being at the same time, developing from the All Saints' Litany, in the various versions of which Mary was often invoked under more than one appellation. When these began to multiply they threatened to upset the balance of the All Saints' Litany, and so independent Marian litanies were being composed. The two most famous ones are the Litany of Loreto, which is still in use, and the Litany of Venice, so called because it was for a long time used in the Cathedral of St. Mark. These litanies, too, were influenced by the *Akathistos*; they were constantly enlarged, abridged and otherwise changed; the first extant manuscript of the Litany of Loreto, which dates from the end of the twelfth century, contains no fewer than seventy-three invocations.[1]

Yet another devotion that came into use about the same time (c. 1130) was the so-called "greeting psalters" (*Gruss-psalter*). They originated from the paraliturgical recitation of the Psalms, in which the antiphons were replaced by strophes applying some verse of the relevant psalms to the blessed Virgin. The one hundred and fifty verse antiphons all began with the angelic greeting after the example of the Latin *Akathistos*. This strophic psalter was assigned to the seven days of the week, and later the psalms themselves were replaced by *Hail Maries* (in the short form, of course) and new antiphons, which had no connection with the Psalms, substituted for the original ones. Finally the antiphons, which would

[1] See H. Barré, "Prières mariales au Xᵉ siècle", in *EM*, 10 (1960), and Meersseman, 2, pp. 45–60.

have to be known by heart or be read in a book, were left out and simply one hundred and fifty *Hail Maries* were recited, interspersed with *Glorias* and divided into groups of fifty which were called *rosarium* after the Marian title of *Rosa Mystica*. They were counted on beads, which had also come into use at the latest in the first half of the twelfth century,[1] originally for counting the *Our Fathers* frequently given as penances. These were the origins of the Rosary.[2]

ABELARD AND HERMANN OF TOURNAI

The age that followed the early twelfth-century authors so far discussed is generally called in the history of the Church the age of St. Bernard of Clairvaux, the counsellor of popes and kings, the preacher of the Second Crusade, the great opponent of the new scholasticism represented by Abelard. Abelard (d. 1142), the highly critical author of *Sic et Non*, a collection of apparently contradictory statements of Scripture and the Fathers, more popularly known as the lover of Heloïse, was also a defender of the bodily Assumption, on which he preached a sermon.[3] Though, as he says himself, he well knew St. Jerome's contrary opinion—that is to say, Radbert's—he holds that what was unknown in Jerome's time may well have been revealed to later generations; and he quotes Gregory of Tours in evidence, though not Pseudo-Augustine.[4] For it was only fitting that Christ should have glorified both Mary's soul and body, as he had taken his own soul and body from her.[5] He accepts without question the apocryphal story of the Apostles' assembly at her death—but here we must take into account that this was a sermon preached before nuns, where critical remarks would have been out of place. He further asserts that Christ honoured his

[1] The first mention of them occurs in William of Malmesbury's *De Gestis Pontificum Anglorum*, 4, 4 (*PL*, 179, 1606A).

[2] Cf. Meersseman, vol. 2, pp. 12–25).

[3] In V. Cousin's edition, vol. 1, pp. 520–28 (*PL*, 178, 539–47).

[4] 453C, D.   [5] 541B.

mother's body even more than his own, because he did not leave it in the tomb for three days—though this was the time given by many apocryphal accounts—but at once placed it in paradise and resurrected it from there.[1] In the same sermon he calls Mary our mediatress with the Son, as the Son is our Mediator with the Father,[2] giving as examples of her mediation the wedding at Cana as well as the popular legend of Theophilus.[3] He expresses the same faith in her mediation in his Matins hymn for her feasts, almost in the words of Peter Damian: "Through you God has descended to us, through you we must also ascend to him."[4] Though Mary is as full of graces as any human nature could be, Abelard does not teach the Immaculate Conception but assumes that by his descent into her Christ cleansed her from all contagion of human weakness.[5] Nevertheless, all the gifts of the Church are concentrated in her.[6]

Before approaching Abelard's great adversary we must just mention one other theologian, Hermann of Tournai (d. after 1147), because he seems to have been the first to apply to Mary the metaphor of the neck, which was to play an important part in subsequent Mariology. In his treatise on the Incarnation of Christ,[7] he writes that, "Our Lady is rightly understood to be the neck of the Church, because she is the mediatress between God and men." The metaphor is obviously derived from St. Paul's image of Christ as the head and the Church as his body—Mary being the connecting link between the two, the neck. He also gave a new turn to the old Mary–Eve parallel, by applying to Mary the words of Gen. 2.18, "a helper like unto himself". This, Hermann says, though literally said of Eve, is yet more truly applied to Mary, who is both "spouse and mother of God", because (repeating Anselm) as God is the Father of all creation, so Mary is the

---

[1] 542C, D.   [2] 544B.   [3] 545B, C.   [4] 180B.
[5] *Homily on the Nativity of the Lord*, 390B, 394A.   [6] 540 B.
[7] Ch. 8 (*PL*, 180, 30).

mother of all re-created things.[1] But Hermann goes much further than Anselm when he says not, like Anselm, that through Mary God has become our Brother, but: "Through Mary God the Creator has been made our Father, because through her the Son of God has been made our Brother."[2] Since the fatherhood of God does not depend on the Incarnation (after all, God was already called "Father" in the Old Testament—for example, in Isa. 63.16 and elsewhere), it cannot be said even in the widest possible sense that God became our Father through Mary. To such exaggerations one might fittingly apply the words of St. Bernard, which he, mistakenly, used with regard to her immaculate conception: "The royal Virgin does not need a false honour."[3]

ST. BERNARD

St. Bernard, who has sometimes been called the last of the Fathers, did not like novelties but wanted to remain true to the teaching of the Bible and the Fathers. Nevertheless, his outlook is in many ways authentically medieval, as we shall see when analyzing his Marian doctrine. Compared with their influence, his writings on the subject are extraordinarily few, though very soon after his death a large quantity of works began to circulate under his name. His authentic Marian writings—$3\frac{1}{2}$ per cent of his whole literary output, it has been calculated—comprise homilies "In Praise of the Virgin Mother",[4] three homilies on the Purification (383–98), four on the Assumption (415–30), one on the Twelve Stars for the Sunday in the octave of the Assumption or, more probably, for the Annunciation in Lent (429–38), the famous sermon on the "Aqueduct" for the feast of her nativity, and the above-mentioned letter to the canons of Lyons, rejecting the Immaculate Conception.

[1] Ch. 11 (36B).   [2] 37A.   [3] *Letter to the Canons of Lyons*, no. 2.
[4] Also called *Super Missus Est* (*PL*, 183, 55–88).

Bernard opposed it precisely because he did not want to go beyond the data of the Bible and the Fathers—he obviously did not know about St. John of Damascus—and because he subscribed to Augustine's view of original sin: "Could sanctity", he asks, "by any chance have mingled with the conception in the marital embrace, so that she was conceived and sanctified at the same time? Reason does not admit this. For how could there have been sanctity without the sanctifying Spirit, or how could the Holy Spirit be in any way associated with sin? Or how could sin not have been present where concupiscence was not absent?"[1] Therefore he blames the canons of Lyons for introducing the feast of Mary's conception, which, according to him, is neither approved by reason nor recommended by ancient tradition,[2] though he believes that she was sanctified in the womb, as witnessed by the Church's celebration of her birth, and that she never committed any sin in her life.[3] Bernard knows, indeed, that the feast of her conception has been celebrated before, but only, he says, by simple people—referring probably to Bec in Normandy, where it had penetrated from England—so he had said nothing about it then. But now, discovering this "superstition" in a famous and noble Church whose special son he was, he felt that he must speak out.[4]

In the matter of the bodily Assumption the saint's attitude was less outspoken; he seems deliberately to have left it in the dark. Though we have four sermons on this feast from him, he never affirmed that he believed Mary to be in heaven with her body. St. Bernard's teaching and devotion centred in Mary's mediation between her Son and his faithful, and his tremendous influence is due not to any originality of thought, which he himself repudiated, but to the force and beauty with which he, the "Mellifluous Doctor", expressed his love of Mary. These are already apparent in the homilies on the Gospel of the

---

[1] *Letter to the Canons of Lyons*, no. 7 (*PL*, 182, 335C).
[2] No. 1.   [3] No. 5.   [4] No. 9.

Annunciation,[1] with the famous passage *respice stellam, voca Mariam*, the beauty of which cannot be reproduced in translation, on the universal efficacy of her intercession: "If you will not be submerged by tempests, do not turn away your eyes from the splendour of this star! If the storms of temptations arise, if you crash against the rocks of tribulation, look to the star, call upon Mary. If you are tossed about on the waves of pride, of ambition, of slander, of hostility, look to the star, call upon Mary. If wrath or avarice or the enticements of the flesh upset the boat of your mind, look to Mary. If you are disturbed by the immensity of your crimes . . . if you begin to be swallowed up by the abyss of depression and despair, think of Mary! In dangers, in anxiety, in doubt, think of Mary, call upon Mary. Let her name not leave your lips nor your heart, and that you may receive the help of her prayer, do not cease to follow the example of her conduct . . . If she holds you, you will not fall, if she protects you, you need not fear."[2] This impassioned plea to trust in Mary probably did as much to confirm medieval Christians in their faith in her all-powerful intercession as the legend of Theophilus, which recurs again and again in the sermons of this period.

The Annunciation itself is described in the anthropomorphic terms also characteristic of the age; they are inspired by the words of the psalm, "The king shall greatly desire thy beauty." (44.12.) Though "the King's going out is from the highest heaven, yet, his great desire giving him wings, he arrived before his messenger at the Virgin he had loved, whom he had elected, whose beauty he desired" (3, 2), a naïve description of God as the impatient bridegroom desiring his chosen spouse, such as would hardly have been possible in an earlier age.

The *Sermon on the Aqueduct*, preached on the feast of the Nativity of the Blessed Virgin, treats *ex professo* of her

[1] *Homiliae Super Missus Est* (*PL*, 183, 55–88).   [2] 2, 17.

9+

mediation between her Son and his faithful. St. Bernard compares this mediation not to the neck of the Mystical Body, but, as the title says, to an aqueduct which leads the divine waters to earth. If, Bernard says, the floods of grace did not reach earth for so long, the reason was that an aqueduct was lacking; he evidently did not take the graces of the Old Testament into account when suggesting this. But how, he asks, could the aqueduct reach so sublime a source? He answers: Through the vehemence of her desire, the fervour of her devotion and the purity of her prayer.[1] Thus Eve is justified in her daughter, and God wants us to honour Mary with the most affectionate devotion, because, "He has placed the fullness of all good things in Mary, so that we should know that all there is of hope, grace and salvation in us flows from her . . . Take away Mary, this star of the sea, of a sea so large and wide, what else is left but surrounding gloom, the shadow of death and densest darkness?"[2] God himself wants us to honour her, "who willed us to have everything through Mary"—a saying frequently quoted by later popes, for example Pius IX,[3] Leo XIII and Pius XII, which has become a principle of Mariology. Therefore Mary is the most efficacious advocate. True, God has given us Christ as our advocate, yet sinners might be afraid of him, "because, even though he was made Man, he yet remained God. Do you want to have an advocate even with him? Have recourse to Mary!" For in her human nature is pure—not only of sin, but also of all admixture of another, divine nature. She will certainly be heard by her Son, and the Son by the Father. "My children," he pleads, "this is the ladder of sinners, this is my greatest assurance, this is the whole reason for my hope." She will surely be heard, because she has found grace with God. Therefore "let us seek grace, and let us seek it through Mary, for she finds what she seeks".[4] Hence Bernard exhorts his hearers: "Whatever you are about to offer, remember to commend it to Mary, so that

[1] 4 and 5.   [2] 6.   [3] Encyclical *Ubi Primum* of 2 February, 1849.   [4] 7f.

through the same channel whence it flowed, grace may flow back to the Giver of grace." The saint knows quite well that God could have given us grace also without this "aqueduct", but in actual fact he did provide it. Therefore men should offer everything through Mary's most acceptable hands, if they do not want to risk being repelled. If they do this, their gifts will be made as white as lilies.[1]

Bernard reiterates his teaching in the *Sermon on the Twelve Stars*.[2] He applies to Mary the Apocalyptic picture of the Woman clothed with the Sun and surrounded by twelve stars, though he is careful to point out that it refers in the first place to the Church. He goes on to say that the words of Genesis, that it is not good for man to be alone, are also relevant in the context of the Redemption: "It is more fitting that, since both sexes were involved in our corruption, so both should also be present at our reparation." And he stresses again the necessity of a purely human mediator because of men's fear of Christ's divinity, which had come to play such an important part in the medieval mentality. (Ch. 1.) So he can affirm categorically that "Man needs a mediator with that Mediator, and there is no-one more efficacious than Mary." Of her no-one need be afraid, because she is "wholly sweet and gentle" (*tota suavis*). He asks his readers to search the New Testament to see whether they can find anything hard in Mary. No, she is only full of mercy and mildness, therefore "give thanks to him, who in his mercy has provided such a mediatress".[3] Naturally such language from the most famous teacher of the twelfth century made an enormous impact. Nevertheless, G. Miegge[4] is right when he points out that "we should be rendering a poor service to St. Bernard if we wanted to give to those devout paradoxes a greater importance than they really have in his complete thought. It is evident

[1] 18.   [2] *PL*, 183, 429–38.   [3] 2.
[4] *The Virgin Mary, The Roman Catholic Marian Doctrine* (1955). English translation by Waldo Smith. G. Miegge was Professor of Church History at the Waldensian Faculty of Theology in Rome.

that the reason for the mediation of Mary is turned mainly towards the timid and the weak in faith . . . St. Bernard speaking to adults does not offer spiritual Marian milk but the hard food of the Christ-centred mysticism, of which his eighty-six sermons on the Song of Songs offer an incomparable text."

The complete trust in her mediation is most strikingly expressed in the well-known prayer *Memorare*, often attributed to St. Bernard, probably through a confusion of names, since it was popularized by a seventeenth-century priest, Claude Bernard; but its central idea is certainly expressed in the saint's fourth sermon on the Assumption, where he writes: "May he be silent about your mercy, Blessed Virgin, if there should exist one who has called on you in his necessities and remembers that you have failed him."[1] In these four sermons on the Assumption Bernard says nothing directly about the bodily Assumption; but all the more about Mary's glorious reception and her powerful intercession in' heaven. The sermons are obviously influenced by the ideals of medieval knighthood. "Our queen", he exclaims, "has preceded us, and has been so gloriously received that her pages [*servuli*] can trustingly follow their Lady."[2] Bernard does not hesitate to

[1] 4, 8.
[2] 1, 1. See P. Bernard, *Saint Bernard et Notre-Dame* (1953), p. 357, on *servuli*: "This diminutive, full of affection and humility, signifies . . . the little pages who follow their lady, or men attached to the direct service of the Queen." There is a great deal of evidence for the influence of courtly love on the attitude of medieval men to the blessed Virgin. To mention only one famous legend, which inspired a picture by Van Dyck, and is printed in F. L. Surius, *De Probatis Sanctorum Historiis*, Cologne (1581), vol. 7, pp. 233–59, there is the story of Hermann of Cologne, a canon of Steinfeld, who was nicknamed Joseph because of his devotion to Mary and who resented this, thinking himself unworthy of such a name. But in a mystical marriage ceremony between him and the blessed Virgin the angel who performed it told him: "I give you this Virgin as your bride, as she was once espoused to Joseph, so that you should receive the name of the bridegroom together with his bride and henceforth be called Joseph." (p. 243.) Hermann, in his turn, called her "Rose", "because of his great familiarity" with her—*ex multa familiaritate* (p. 244)—for she frequently appeared to him as a beautiful young girl.

adapt the psalm of the Ascension (67) to the Assumption and to refer to Mary the words applied by the Church to Christ—"Ascending to heaven, you have given gifts to men"[1]—just as, in his fourth sermon, he accommodates to her words St. Paul uses of her Son: "Who could search out the length and the breadth, the height and the depth of your mercy?"[2] This tendency to assimilate Mary increasingly to the transcendence of God himself becomes even more pronounced in later writers. It results from the fact that she has the same Son as the Father.[3] It is offset, however, by Bernard's very human description of the meeting between Christ and Mary in heaven: "Blessed the kisses given by the Child whom the Mother pressed to her virginal breast; but now shall we not think even more blessed those which she receives today from the lips of him who sits on the right hand of the Father?"[4]—which, incidentally, might imply belief in the bodily Assumption.

FRIENDS AND DISCIPLES OF ST. BERNARD

PETER THE VENERABLE

Peter the Venerable (d. 1156), Abbot of Cluny, was a friend of St. Bernard, though this friendship was sometimes clouded by the rivalry that existed between the Benedictine and the Cistercian orders, and it is significant that Peter gave refuge to Bernard's opponent Abelard. The Abbot of Cluny was perhaps the most important man of the twelfth century after St. Bernard, but his influence and popularity were considerably less than those of the Cistercian saint. He did much to foster devotion to Mary in his order. In his *Statutes of the Congregation of Cluny* he ordered a daily Mass of the blessed Virgin to be celebrated at the altar dedicated to her,[5] the Little Office of Mary to be recited daily in the chapel of the sick

---

[1] 1, 2.   [2] 4, 8.   [3] *Sermon 2, 2 on the Annunciation.*
[4] *Sermon 1 on the Assumption*, 4.   [5] *Stat.*, 54 (*PL*, 189, 1040B).

which was dedicated to her[1] and the *Salve Regina* to be chanted on the feast of the Assumption during the procession.[2] All this was to be done, as is explained in the same statutes, so that she might be honoured above all other creatures, because she was the Mother of the Author of the universe.

His devotion, however, did not prevent him from criticizing some of the exaggerated ideas that had become current at the time, with which he deals in one of his epistles.[3] He doubts whether any special apostolic graces were added to Mary's fullness of grace at Pentecost, because it was not her office to preach the Faith; Peter will not, however, assert anything definite about it, as Scripture is silent on the subject. Even if she did not receive these special graces, she is nevertheless superior to the Apostles, who did.[4] He strongly opposes the idea that Mary was omniscient;[5] for it was thought that as she was so exalted she must even on earth have had more knowledge than the angels. Peter replies that the New Testament makes it quite clear that she had no such knowledge, since, for example, an angel had to instruct Joseph to take the Child into Egypt and Mary did not know that the twelve-year-old Jesus had stayed behind in the Temple.[6] Peter's correspondent, the monk Gregory, further applied to Mary St. Paul's words about Christ, that in him "are hidden all the treasures of wisdom and knowledge" (Col. 2.3) on the grounds that Christ had been in Mary's womb. Peter replies that even though this was true, it does not mean that the treasures belonging to him were given to her; omniscience, Peter says, "belongs to God alone and is not given to any mortal in this life".[7] In their devotion to Mary men "must not go

---

[1] *Stat.*, 60 (1041D).　　　　　[2] 76, (1048A).
[3] 3, 7 (*PL*, 189, 287ff.).　　　[4] 290A–291A.
[5] This was stated, for example, in the sermon "On the Ten Privileges of Mary", attributed to Abbo of St. Germain (d. c. 923), but which cannot have been written before the late twelfth century; parts of it were published by J. Leclercq in *Revue du moyen-âge latin*, 3 (1947), pp. 113–40.
[6] 291A–292A.　　　　　　　　[7] 292C.

beyond the rule of faith".[1] The angels in heaven, enjoying the Beatific Vision, knew immeasurably more than Mary did on earth: ". . . to attribute to her angelic knowledge without beatitude is . . . not a little silly".[2] This letter shows clearly to what excesses devotion unrestrained by biblical and theological knowledge could go.

ARNOLD OF BONNEVAL

Another friend of St. Bernard, the Benedictine abbot Arnold of Bonneval (d. after 1156), in the diocese of Chartres, was much bolder in his statements about Mary than Peter the Venerable. Though he did not actually teach the bodily Assumption, which he called "a most thorny question",[3] he considered the glory of the Son and the Mother indivisible.[4] Both divide the offices of mercy between them, Christ showing the Father his wounds, Mary her breast[5]: "Mary immolates herself to Christ in spirit and prays for the salvation of the world; the Son obtains it, the Father forgives." So Mary also shares in the redemptive work on the Cross, for Christ "was moved by the affection of his mother; then there was one single will of Christ and Mary, both together offered one holocaust to God: she in the blood of her heart, he in the blood of his flesh."[6] "Christ is the Lord, Mary the Mistress . . . For she is set over every creature, and whoever bends his knee to Jesus also bows in supplication to his Mother . . . Nor can the Mother be separated from the dominion and power of the Son. One is the flesh of Mary and Christ, one the spirit, one the charity . . . This unity allows no division, nor is it divided into parts, and even though one is made out of two, this cannot henceforth be divided, and I consider the glory of the Son and the Mother not so much a common glory, but the same."[7] Arnold here actually speaks of the union of

---

[1] 292D.   [2] 297D–298A.   [3] *Hexameron* (PL, 189, 1550B).
[4] *On the Praises of Holy Mary* (PL, 189, 1725B).   [5] 1726C, D.
[6] 1727A.   [7] 1729A.

Mary and Christ in a way the Fathers spoke of the Hypostatic Union between the Godhead and the Manhood; and it is hard to see how the essential difference between the divine-human Christ and his wholly human Mother can be preserved if their unity is considered indivisible and their glory identical. Towards the end of the treatise the author reverts to the sufferings of Mary under the Cross, and, having again said that what the nails and the spear did in the flesh of Christ was done by her mother's anguish in the mind of Mary, he suddenly remembers St. Ambrose, who so strongly affirmed that Christ did not need his Mother's help.[1] But it seems Arnold understands this only of the physical sufferings, in which Mary was not allowed a share, for in his treatise "On the Seven Words of Christ on the Cross" he repeats that whereas Christ sacrificed his flesh, Mary sacrificed her soul, because the bodily sacrifice was the privilege of the High Priest alone.[2] In this way he preserves the authority of Ambrose whilst affirming Mary's part in the redemption of the Cross.

AMADEUS OF LAUSANNE

Amadeus of Lausanne (d. 1159), a former novice of St. Bernard, is an even more fervent representative of twelfth-century Marian devotion.[3] His eight homilies are a veritable treatise on the glories of Mary. After an introductory sermon placing Mary in the centre between the Old and the New Testaments, the following seven link the life of the Virgin to the seven gifts of the Holy Spirit as enumerated in Isa. 11.2. The justification of Mary proceeds from the fear of God (2), the virginal conception is connected with piety (3), the birth of Christ with knowledge(4), her assistance at the foot of the Cross with fortitude (5), her Easter joy with counsel (6), the

---

[1] 1731B.   [2] 1694B.

[3] His eight Marian homilies, also in *PL*, 188, are quoted by page from the edition of G. Bavaud, J. Deshusses and A. Dumas in the series Sources Chrétiennes, Paris (1960).

Ascension and Assumption with understanding (7), and Mary's prayer in heaven with wisdom (8). These homilies already breathe a sensuous atmosphere, which will become even more pronounced in the following centuries, especially in the vernacular literature. Mary's garments are described in detail, her beauty attracts the divine majesty.[1] Her mediation between God and the Church is not described by St. Bernard's image of the aqueduct, but by that of the neck, which links Christ the Head to his Church.[2] In the third sermon the conception of Christ is seen as the union between lovers; no doubt under the influence of the concept of courtly love, Christ—or the Holy Spirit—is regarded as Mary's lover and she is his beloved as much as his mother. The descriptions are full of kisses and embraces, a tendency fostered by the application of the Canticle to Christ and Mary, but now with far less restraint than in the commentaries of Rupert of Deutz and Honorius of Autun. To give but one example: "Your Creator has become your Spouse, he has loved your beauty . . . He has coveted your loveliness and desires to be united to you. Impatient of delay, he hastens to come to you . . . Hurry to meet him, that you may be kissed with the kiss of the mouth of God and be drawn into his most blessed embraces . . . Go out, for the nuptial chamber is already prepared, and your Spouse is coming, the Holy Spirit comes to you . . . suddenly he will come to you, that you may enjoy happiness . . . The Holy Spirit will come upon you, that at his touch your womb may tremble and swell, your spirit rejoice and your womb flower . . . You, who will be worthy of such a kiss, who will be united to such a Spouse, who will be made fruitful by such a husband . . . For you, most beautiful Virgin, have been joined in close embraces to the Creator of beauty, and, having been made more a virgin, indeed, more than a virgin, because mother and virgin, have received the most holy seed by divine infusion."[3]

[1] pp. 72–78.   [2] p. 80.   [3] pp. 102–08.
9*

After this almost embarrassing description of the conception of Christ, the fourth sermon deals with his birth, which gives the author an opportunity to paint a picture of the Mother caressing her Child which reminds us of the contemporary artists: With his head sometimes on the left, at others on the right arm of his Mother, Jesus looks at her, and she presses him to her breast, kisses his hands and arms and also his lips, can never see enough of him. The presentation of Mary's sufferings under the Cross in the next sermon is equally detailed; she is seized by the pains of childbirth, sighs, groans, agonizes and grows pale—until Amadeus—like Arnold of Bonneval—remembers the authority of Ambrose and affirms that she did not cry—an interesting instance of the division of the medieval theologian between his natural feelings and his devotion to the authority of the Fathers. On the other hand, Amadeus makes Mary faint when she sees the risen Christ; [1] when he ascended in her flesh she received the sovereignty of heaven through glory, the reign over the world by mercy, and the dominion over hell through power. [2] In Sermon 7 he affirms the bodily Assumption, because "through the mediation of Christ the fullness of the Godhead dwelt in her corporeally"—yet another adaptation to Mary of words referring to her Son. (Col. 2.9.)[3]

Amadeus, too, asked himself why Christ let Mary stay on earth after his own ascension, and he answers that he did so for the consolation and education of the young Church, for although the Apostles were, indeed, taught by the Spirit, they still had to learn much from Mary, who gave them access to all her charisms. Among other marvels, a fiery river emanated from her which burned her enemies but gave pleasant warmth to her friends. [4] For she was a breath of death to the adversary, but a perfume of life to those who believed in her Son. For, once more adapting to her what St. Paul said of her Son, "as in Eve all die, so also in Mary all

[1] 6, p. 178.   [2] 6, p. 172.   [3] p. 184.   [4] pp. 184–86.

shall be made alive." (1 Cor. 15.22.) For it was fitting that the Virgin Mother should first reign on earth before she was received with glory into heaven.[1] She died in a good old age.[2] After her death she was resurrected, for "you will not give the body of your Mother to see corruption". (Cf. Ps. 15.10.) On her arrival in heaven the humble Virgin is crowned and told by the Father to occupy the throne of the most eminent glory, first after the Son, which once belonged to Satan, the chief of the fallen angels. From there she prays for the world and brings not only salvation to souls but also health to bodies; for in the places dedicated to her the lame walk, the blind see and the insane recover their reason. For she is the giver of life (*vitae datrix*), the mother and nurse of all.[3] These homilies had a great influence, as they were read at Matins on Saturday in Amadeus' cathedral at Lausanne.

LATER TWELFTH-CENTURY MARIOLOGY

GODFREY OF ADMONT

Godfrey, the abbot of the Benedictine monastery of Admont (d. 1165), is another remarkable representative of later twelfth-century Mariology.[4] He applies to her the metaphor of the neck.[5] He believes her to have been conceived and born in original sin and to have undergone a painful ascetical struggle—a very unusual idea at that time—until she was finally completely purified at the Annunciation.[6] On the other hand, he thinks that when the Holy Spirit came upon her, "all ignorance was chased away, since nothing of all the treasures of heavenly wisdom could henceforth be hidden from her".[7] Godfrey repeats the same idea in Homily 67,[8] though in another he states that she did not know in what way the

---

[1] pp. 188f. [2] p. 196. [3] 8, pp. 208–216.
[4] Cf. J. Beumer, "Der mariologische Gehalt der Predigten Gottfried von Admonts", in *SK*, 35 (1960), pp. 40–56.
[5] *Sunday Homilies*, 6 (PL, 174, 47D-48A). [6] *Sun. Hom.*, 4 (40A, B).
[7] *Homilies on Feasts*, 31 (772C). [8] 975B, C.

humanity of Christ was united to his divinity;[1] this divergence may perhaps be due to a change in his views. Though he wrote no fewer than nine sermons on the feast of the Assumption, he says nothing about her body being resurrected. He strongly affirms, however, that she is the mediatress of grace and the mistress of the whole world.[2] Like Gottschalk of Limburg, he believes that the prayers of the saints reach her Son only through her;[3] indeed, only through her are all the saints sanctified and predestined to glory.[4] She is the cause of redemption,[5] although Godfrey makes it clear in another sermon that Christ is its first cause;[6] he honours the blessed Virgin so much that he can refuse her nothing.[7] For he has elected her from all eternity to be both his spouse and his mother, so that he would have a suitable helper—as Adam had in Eve—when the time for the Redemption came.[8] Godfrey goes so far as to call the three persons of the Trinity Mary's lovers (*amatores* (77, 1025)), an idea that gave rise to some ribald and blasphemous jokes in the vernacular literature of the time.

Godfrey states explicitly that almost everything that Scripture says of Christ may also be applied to his Mother—a dangerous principle, since it tends to blur the distinction between the divine person of Christ and his wholly human mother. Another innovation is Godfrey's view that the Church is founded, not on Christ, but on Mary. "For she is the foundation laid by God the Father, on which he marvellously raised the house of his Holy Church. She is the foundation of our faith. For from her do we receive the beginning of belief."[9] Finally, Mary is not only the mistress of the world, the queen of heaven and the empress of the angels, but "the unique matter of all the sacraments" (*sacramentorum omnium materia singularis*.[10]

---

[1] *Sun. Hom.*, 4 (39B).   [2] *Homs. on Feasts*, 65 (967B) and 7B (1028D).
[3] 71 (989A).   [4] 988D.   [5] 69 (979C).   [6] 75 (1009D).
[7] 1009B.   [8] 31 (770B, C).   [9] 78 (1029C).   [10] 67 (974B).

AELRED OF RIEVAULX

The somewhat "erotic" conception of the relations between God and Mary is continued by Aelred, Abbot of the Cistercian monastery of Rievaulx in Yorkshire (d. 1167) and author of the famous treatise on "Spiritual Friendship".[1] In a sermon on the Annunciation, after saying that we may assume that Mary was most beautiful also in body, Aelred presents the biblical event as a marriage, "in which God [the Son] is the Bridegroom, the Virgin the bride, and the angel the best man [*paranymphus*]".[2] Though, like almost all contemporary Cistercians, he says nothing about Mary's conception—the influence of St. Bernard was too strong in his order to allow for independent thought on this matter—Aelred affirms her bodily Assumption, using the same arguments as Pseudo-Augustine;[3] in another sermon, which perhaps belongs to an earlier period of his life, he considers the matter doubtful.[4] He, too, applies to Mary New-Testament sayings that refer to Christ—for example: "Hail, sweet Lady, hail, you who are full of grace, and truly full, of whose fullness we have all received." (John 1.16.)[5] He has a very clear conception of Mary's spiritual motherhood: "She is truly our mother, brethren, we have been born through her, we are nourished by her, we grow through her." She is the mother of our redemption and sanctification, "therefore she is more our mother than our mother according to the flesh; for our better [i.e., spiritual] birth is from her."[6] But men must not only honour her as their mother; they must also—in the true spirit of medieval knighthood—serve her as their mistress: "The spouse of our Lord is our mistress, the spouse of our King is our queen, therefore let us serve her." The feudal conceptions of the age are simply applied to the religious sphere; the monk

---

[1] Works in *PL*, 195 and *Sermones Inediti*, edited by C. H. Talbot in *Series Scriptorum S. Ordinis Cisterciensis*, vol. 1, Rome (1952).

[2] *PL*, 254A.   [3] *Sermon 24*, p. 162.   [4] *PL*, 315B.

[5] *Serm. 11*, p. 90.   [6] *PL*, 323A–C.   [7] 324A.

serves Mary as the knight serves his mistress, for she is seen far more as the Spouse of Christ, reigning together with him, than as his mother, who once called herself his handmaid. As his queen she averts his wrath "so that she herself has often placed back into its sheath his naked sword, which was at that very moment raging against mankind".[1] Aelred's rules for anchoresses, so common in the England of his time, are particularly interesting because they contain meditations on the life of our Lady that are surprisingly modern. For example, when reflecting on the Annunciation the recluse should enter Mary's chamber together with the angel and salute the sweetest Lady with him, frequently repeating his *Ave Maria*. She should enter into Mary's feelings on hearing the greeting, follow her when she visits Elizabeth and when she gives birth to Jesus at Bethlehem; at the Passion she should unite her own to the tears of the sorrowful Mother—we see quite clearly the beginnings of the Rosary meditations.[2]

A CONTROVERSY ABOUT THE IMMACULATE CONCEPTION

About twenty years after St. Bernard's death a controversy broke out between Nicholas of St. Albans (though this identification has been contested, but it seems very probable) and Peter of Celle on the subject of the Immaculate Conception. Nicholas (d. after 1174) wrote a treatise "On Celebrating the Conception of Blessed Mary, Against Blessed Bernard".[3] He could not understand why the opponents of the feast should admit that John the Baptist was sanctified in the womb, but refuse Mary a sinless conception. He makes a subtle distinction between the "concupiscence of corruption", in which all other human beings are conceived, and "natural conception" "which is indeed natural, but has not been experienced before the Fall".[4] St. Bernard, whom Nicholas calls "a man of great fame, whom I also praise, but not in this particular

[1] 9, p. 81.
[2] "De Institutione Inclusarum", *Sources chrétiennes*, 76, pt. 3 (1961).
[3] Ed. by C. H. Talbot in *RBE* (1954), pp. 92–117.   [4] p. 94, 20ff.

matter", had objected that the feast of Mary's conception had no tradition behind it; but, asks Nicholas, why should the Church not have the right to institute something new?[1] Surely, "there is a difference between instituting something unknown to antiquity and subverting antiquity", as Bernard had asserted.[2] He answers Bernard's sarcastic question: "Whence the sanctity of the conception?" (*Ep.*, 174, 7) in two words: "From God", and adds that the saint gave no reasons for his view that there could not possibly be a holy conception. Why should marital intercourse necessarily be sinful, seeing that God himself commanded men to be fruitful and multiply? And he concludes: "Therefore she, whose conception knew neither the guilt nor the act of sin, was not conceived in sin",[3] and he gives as the reason for keeping the feast that it commemorates the foundation of the temple in which dwelt the fullness of the Godhead.[4]

This attack on the great saint of Clairvaux called forth the wrath of Peter of Celle (d. 1183), a monk of the Cluny reform and Abbot of St. Remy, who became Bishop of Chartres in 1181. He at once put the whole question on a geographical, not to say political basis—fog-bound Britain against lucid France: "Whatever is not based on the authority of Scripture", he thunders, "cannot be established with any security. Nor should English levity be irritated if Gallic maturity is more solidly established. For England is an island surrounded by water, hence her inhabitants are understandably affected by the property of this element and are often led to odd and unfounded fancies, comparing their dreams with visions, not to say preferring them to the latter. And how can they be blamed for this, if such is the nature of their country? I certainly have proof that the English are greater dreamers than the French. For the more humid brain is more quickly affected by the fumes of the stomach, and depicts certain images of its own which . . . have no relation to truth and are called phantasms

[1] p. 94, 42ff.   [2] p. 95, 2.   [3] p. 115, 25.   [4] p. 116, 3ff.

or dreams. Gaul, on the other hand, is not so cavernous nor so watery. She has rocks, where grows iron, and her land is heavy. Her inhabitants do not quickly leave their reason behind, but cling more tenaciously to the authorities of truth."[1] After delivering himself of this comparison between Anglo-Saxons and French, Peter goes on to praise his own steadfastness as opposed to Nicholas' volatile temperament, at considerable length. It is a scandal that Nicholas should have deprived most blessed Bernard of the veneration due to him; to touch him is to touch the pupil of Mary's eye.[2] Mary, too, had to struggle against sin: "Take away the struggle, and you take away the victory."[3]

Nicholas replied to this outburst in more measured tones.[4] True, Bernard had recently been canonized, but this means only that we cannot doubt his glory in heaven, it does not exempt him from all criticism. Then he reports a typically medieval legend, according to which Bernard appeared to a laybrother shortly after his death. The saint was clothed with a radiant white garment on which there was only one spot, and the brother was told that this spot was Bernard's mistaken view on the Immaculate Conception. The dream was written down, but the Cistercians burned the account at their General Chapter. Thus, Nicholas comments, the assembled abbots would rather diminish the glory of the Virgin than that of their founder.[5] Therefore Nicholas thinks that, as St. Bernard himself confessed his error in that dream, he acts in accordance with St. Bernard's own wish in defending the Immaculate Conception. "For," he continues, "as the Father and the Son are equal in heaven, so also the Mother is like the Son on earth, not that I say she was conceived by the Spirit, but that she was filled and sanctified by the Spirit from her mother's womb, just like the Son."[6] In his final reply Peter rightly objects to

---

[1] *Ep.*, 171 (*PL*, 202, 614A, B).   [2] 617C–618A.   [3] 619D.

[4] His answer is printed among the letters of Peter of Celle, as no. 172 (*PL*, 202, 622–8).

[5] 623B–624A.   [6] 624D.

Nicholas' principle of the equality of Mother and Son, since Mary herself was the handmaid of the Lord.[1]

Though Peter prided himself on the solidity of his doctrine in the matter of Mary's conception, some of his own views are highly controversial. He carried so far the habit of transferring to Mary statements made of God that he ascribed to her divine transcendence by varying her Son's own words about the Father (Luke 10.22): "In like manner it can also be said of the Mother: No-one knows the Mother except the Son, and to whom the Son will reveal her."[2] He even goes so far as to discuss the possibility of a Quaternity: "O Virgin of Virgins, what is this, where are you?" he asks. "You approach the Trinity itself in a unique and quite ineffable, almost direct manner, so if the Trinity admitted in any way an external quaternity, you alone would complete the quaternity." This, however, is not possible, and so she is the unique first creature after the Trinity.[3] One might almost believe such speculations to have arisen in the watery island of England rather than on the *terra firma* of France!

THE VICTORINES

So far almost all the authors discussed were Benedictines or Cistercians, and they were, indeed, the most prominent Marian preachers and theologians in the twelfth century. The great Victorine mystic theologians, on the other hand (so called because they belonged to the Paris monastery of St. Victor, of the Canons Regular of St. Augustine), contributed very little to our subject; indeed, R. Baron calls Hugh of St. Victor's (d. 1141) Mariology "embryonic".[4] He defended Mary's virginity against certain contemporary attacks in a treatise on the subject,[5] affirming her proposal of virginity

---

[1] *Ep.* 173, 631B.   [2] Cf. Luke 10.22; *Serm.*, 73 (866A).
[3] *Serm.*, 13 (675D).
[4] "La Pensée Mariale de Hugues de Saint Victor", in *Revue d'ascétique et de mystique*, 31 (1955), p. 268.
[5] *PL*, 176, 857-76.

before the Annunciation[1] and explaining her conception from the Holy Spirit.[2] In his Canticle for the Assumption he worked out the traditional parallelism between Mary and the Church, both being virgin, mother and spouse.[3]

Richard of St. Victor (d. 1173) wrote an *Explanation of the Canticle*,[4] ch. 39 of which is specially devoted to the blessed Virgin. In it he emphasizes Mary's likeness to Christ, whose beauty she reflects in herself and communicates to others.[5] He interprets Apocalypse 12 of her: Mary is clothed with the sun, because the Sun of the Divinity completely surrounds and penetrates her, and "after she has been illumined by it she enlightens the citizens of heaven".[6] The moon under her feet is "the triumphant Church, because she is inferior to her [Mary]", who is now placed above all the works of Christ, sitting at his right hand and exercising her office of mercy on behalf of mankind.[7]

PHILIP OF HARVENGT

Philip of Harvengt (d. 1183) was one of the first Premonstratensians (the order founded by St. Norbert in 1120). Like the Victorines, they followed the Augustinian Rule, and the influence of the great African doctor made itself felt in their attitude to Mary's sinlessness—even though St. Augustine himself had wanted Mary's name not to be mentioned where there was question of sin. In his Marian exegesis of the Canticle[8] Philip went so far as to attribute even actual sins to her; he did not even hesitate to call her "a daughter of wrath".[9] Before the Incarnation she had to purify herself and to remove internal stains,[10] and finally Christ assimilated her to himself, so that no rebellion was left in her.[11] The subject called forth the eroticism we have noticed before: Christ did not choose a plain, but a beautiful mother, with fine eyes and a white and

<hr />

[1] 857B.   [2] 872A.   [3] *PL*, 177, 1211.   [4] *PL*, 196.
[5] 516D–517A.   [6] 517B.   [7] 517C–518A.   [8] *PL*, 203, 181–490.
[9] *Cant.*, 6, 14 (459A).   [10] Bk. 1, 17 (227B).   [11] Bk. 1, 18 (228D)

rosy complexion;[1] he celebrated his marvellous and incomparable nuptials in her womb.[2] This sensuousness is most evident in Philip's description of the mutual embraces of Christ and his Spouse and Mother: "Not only does the Mother most tenderly embrace the Son," he writes, "but also the Spouse the Bridegroom; and he enjoys their mutual embraces as much as she, when he, kissing her, reposes most sweetly between her breasts. For if a kiss is lovingly and truly consummated, breast is turned to breast just as mouth is to mouth; nor has the love of the kissing couple made true progress unless the kiss that is given with the mouth is confirmed by the favour of the embrace. Hence the Virgin rightly says that her Spouse reposes between her breasts, which means that their tender love is confirmed by the glue of their embrace."[3] The climate of courtly love has indeed penetrated into the religious sphere; never before has the relationship between Christ and his Mother been described in such sensual terms.

Though Philip has attributed slight sins to Mary, he cedes to none in his devotion to her as the great mediating power between Christ and the faithful; he, too, uses the metaphor of the neck.[4] Indeed, with a naïvety resembling that of Eadmer, he says that Mary reminds her Son to attend to our prayers.[5] Even the souls of the saints cannot reach heaven unless they are helped by the holy Virgin: "Therefore the Bride is rightly called the mediatress of us all, and the Mother is not incongruously called Empress, because asking her Spouse and commanding her Son she turns his fury into grace and his wrath into sweetest love."[6]

Despite this great power of the Virgin, Philip distinguishes very clearly between her and her Son. As it was not given to John and James to sit on the right hand of Christ in glory, "so [it is] not [given] even to his Mother, who is the minister

---

[1] Bk. 2, 1 (247A, B).   [2] 2, 6 (258A).   [3] 2, 11 (271A).
[4] 2, 7 (260B).   [5] 260C.   [6] 4, 5 (360C, D.)

of the humanity of the Son",[1] and he states more clearly than many of his contemporaries that Mary's superiority to the angels is not a superiority of nature, but of grace.[2] He teaches the bodily Assumption, reproducing the argument of Pseudo-Augustine that the Mother must be where the Son is, "not only in the spirit . . . but also in the body, which does not seem at all incredible, for even though the canonical Scriptures do not provide clear evidence of it, yet pious belief is led to it by probable arguments", and supported by the treatise attributed to St. Augustine.[3]

MINOR AUTHORS

Of the many authors of sermons and treatises on Mary during this period only a few more can be mentioned. Henry, Abbot of Clairvaux and later Cardinal-Bishop of Albano (d. 1189), held that all the sacraments flow from Mary.[4] Peter of Blois (d. after 1203), a politician who had been adviser to King William of Sicily and later to King Henry II of England and who became a priest late in life, clearly taught the bodily Assumption; indeed, he held that Christ had not completely ascended into heaven until he had drawn the body of his mother after him.[5] It is characteristic of the caution of Rome that the great Pope Innocent III (d. 1216), though he echoed Bernard's teaching that no-one who invoked Mary devoutly was ever left unanswered,[6] was silent on the Assumption and, *a fortiori*, on the Immaculate Conception.

TWO MARIAN INTERPRETATIONS OF THE
CANTICLE AT THE END OF THE CENTURY

Alain of Lille, yet another Cistercian, who was called the "Universal Doctor" (d. 1202), had to defend the reality of the Virgin's body against the Albigensians, who attributed a

[1] 3, 19.   [2] 4, 1 (355C).   [3] 6, 50 (488C).   [4] *Tract. XI (PL*, 204, 332A).
[5] *Sermon 33, On the Assumption (PL*, 207, 662B).
[6] *Serm.*, 28 (*PL*, 217, 584D).

kind of celestial body to her.[1] Like Philip of Harvengt, he interpreted the Canticle of Mary; he said that it refers especially to the Church, but most especially to her,[2] but unlike Philip, he asserted her complete sinlessness,[3] though he did not affirm her immaculate conception. Though he believed in her bodily Assumption, he nevertheless would not teach it unequivocally, but left it to the Virgin herself to reveal it if and when she wanted to make it known according to the will of God.[4] Strangely enough, Alain does not identify Mary with the Church but rather with the Synagogue: "The Synagogue is called the Mother of the Virgin, from which Christ, too, descended. Hence to suck the breasts of the Virgin Mother is to suck the breasts of the Synagogue";[5] she was the Mother of Christ because she conceived him, but he does not follow the Latin tradition according to which she also became the true mother of the faithful; she was this only "by her teaching and example";[6] but the real Mother of Christ in his members is the Church.[7]

A more interesting work on the same subject is the *Explanatio Sacri Epithalamii in Matrem Sponsi* by William of Newburgh (d. c. 1199), an Augustinian canon who wrote the commentary at the request of Abbot Roger of Byland, who had asked specifically for a Marian exegesis of the Canticle. William was evidently unaware of the fact that the Canticle had been interpreted in this way before, since he says that it was unknown in the Church.[8] The author stresses particularly Mary's consent to the Incarnation, for the Almighty would not have taken flesh from her unless she had freely given it to him. The conception and birth of Christ did not happen in the same way as the creation of Eve, who was formed from Adam's side while he was asleep: "The Virgin was not

---

[1] See P. Glorieux, "Alain de Lille, Docteur de l'Assomption", in *Mélanges de science religieuse*, 8 (1951), pp. 5–18.

[2] *PL*, 210, 53B. [3] *Elucidatio in Cant.* (*PL*, 210, 80B). [4] 74B.

[5] 103C; also 94A. [6] 54C. [7] 60A.

[8] Ed. John C. Gorman, Fribourg (1960), *proem.*, p. 71.

visited by sleep, but by an angel sent from God . . . that he
might acquaint her with this great mystery . . . More, he did
not only want her to be conscious of it, but also to co-operate
and minister to it . . . that he might confer on his future
mother the greatest privilege of honour and grace."[1] This
co-operation was not confined to the Incarnation; it extended
to the Redemption. William expresses this very clearly:
"Drink therefore [the chalice]," Mary says, "and I will drink
it with you, willingly dying with you, that, as I once, by
believing, co-operated as much as was possible for me with
the mystery of your Incarnation, so now, by suffering with
you, I may as far as I can devoutly co-operate in the Redemption of mankind."[2] This share in the Redemption is
later confirmed by Christ himself, says William, in his exegesis
of Cant., 4. 8: "Come . . . thou shalt be crowned." Mary will
be crowned together with him, because she has shared his
labours: "For my passion has strongly overflowed into you,
my compassionate Mother . . . Since, therefore, by your
maternal affection you have drunk with me the chalice that I
have drunk, come and be crowned with me",[3] for she has "co-
agonized" with the agonizing Christ through her motherly
love and is rewarded by her assumption.[4] William strongly
affirms Mary's spiritual motherhood;[5] because it is her special
office in heaven to help the weaker members of Christ's
body, "that you may bring them forth in the bowels of mercy,
until Christ is more fully formed in them";[6] consoled by her,
we bear the afflictions of this life more easily.[7] Mary helps
especially sinners, but only those who repent; superficial
devotion is not enough; those who turn to her must reform
their morals, even though this process may be slow.[8] Nor
should men pray to her for the wrong things, such as riches and
honours; such prayers she will not offer to her Son, any more
than those of obstinate sinners even though they may pray

[1] Cant., 1. 1 (76f.).   [2] 1. 11–13 (104f.).   [3] p. 192.   [4] 193.
[5] 4. 13f. (205).   [6] 1. 7 (94).   [7] 1. 4f. (88).   [8] 1. 7 (96).

for the right things, for she is the Mother of Truth and does not tolerate insincerity [1]—words which anticipate the strictures of later writers such as Erasmus. William of Newburgh has a particularly touching and, as far as I can see, unique, passage on the blessed Virgin's prayer for her own people: "And we should know that the merits of the merciful Mother greatly help the salvation of the people of Israel. How insistently, do you think, does she daily pray to her omnipotent Son for her race? ... Remember, Son, she says, that you have taken your flesh from them, in which and by which you have worked salvation on earth, and that they must share in your spiritual goods, of whose flesh you have not been ashamed. For they ought to have been the first to be saved, because salvation is from them; but, as you are merciful, let it suffice for that fatal choice of Barabbas that they have lost their privileged birthright and be now at least the last."[2]

With this tender image of Mary, the great helper of Christians and of her own people Israel, we leave the Latin preachers and theologians of the twelfth century and turn to a more popular literature, which also came into being at this time and embellished the biblical and apocryphal stories of Christ and his Mother.

POPULAR MARIAN LITERATURE

The Latin *Vita Beatae Virginis Mariae et Salvatoris Rhythmica*[3] became the source of many similar works in the vernacular tongues. It reads like a versified novel. It begins with the annunciation of Mary's birth to Joachim and Anne, stating that she will be sanctified in her mother's womb—the prevailing view of the time.[4] Mary is presented at the Temple at the age of three and becomes a Temple virgin when she is seven, her duties being to keep the ornaments clean, to weave

[1] 3. 5 (153).   [2] 3. 5 (152).
[3] Ed. A. Vögtlin, Tübingen (1888); quoted by book and verse.
[4] 1, 192.

and spin and read the Bible—in fact, she is supposed to live rather like a medieval nun.[1] She is especially proficient in the knowledge of the Bible, being conversant with all the different senses of Scripture, tropological, mystical, moral, anagogical, and literal, which the schoolmen, following the Fathers, were developing at the time.[2] Both her moral and her physical beauty are described in detail: her exterior corresponds to the ideal of a German medieval maiden: she has blonde hair and blue eyes with highly curved brows, a slightly aquiline nose and red, moderately full lips; the purity of her skin and the cleanliness of her teeth and breath are particularly stressed— evidently somewhat rare assets in the twelfth century.[3] She was eloquent, but prudent of speech—a trait that differs considerably from the Byzantine emphasis on her silence and shows the different status of women at that time, when the knights delighted in the conversation of their ladies and nuns like the learned Hildegard of Bingen enjoyed a considerable reputation.[4] In due course Mary is elected Queen of the Temple virgins; her fame spreads far and wide, priests and bishops (!) venerate her, and many noble youths wish to marry her.[5] The priests ask her to choose one of them as her husband, but she refuses: her one spouse and sole lover is the King of the World, to whom she is united in everlasting love. She describes their eternal bridechamber and the marriage gifts which they have exchanged; her vow of virginity cannot be broken.[6] Finally Joseph is chosen by a miracle, and Mary's fears are calmed by an angel who promises her that Joseph will protect her virginity.[7]

In the following story of the Annunciation the biblical account is greatly elaborated. After her conception Mary was so radiant that neither Joseph nor any other man could look upon her,[8] an idea taken from the *Glossa Ordinaria* of Anselm of Laon, dating from the beginning of the twelfth century.[9]

---

[1] 1, 488ff.   [2] 1, 625ff.   [3] 1, 665ff.   [4] 1, 765ff.   [5] 881ff.
[6] 968ff.   [7] 1, 1340ff.   [8] 2, 1702ff.   [9] *In Matth.*, 1, 25 (*PL*, 114, 72).

Extensive use is made of the apocryphal Gospel of St. James, the miraculous elements of which are exaggerated in the most extravagant manner. A certain amount of theological teaching is given in a lengthy conversation between Jesus and Mary, who asks her Son questions about his incarnation and the Trinity, which he answers in detail.[1] Book 3 is filled with the deeds of Christ, including the apocryphal Letter of Abgar. In the Passion story Mary plays a very important, and, to modern readers, highly embarrassing role. Instead of the dignity of the sorrowful Mother who "stood" under the Cross, as St. John presents her, we are here shown a woman who has completely lost control of herself and raves hysterically. As soon as she is told that Jesus has been arrested she faints. When she comes to, she breaks out into the most extravagant lamentations. When Mary Magdalen tells her that Jesus has been scourged she falls into a deathlike swoon. She then watches Jesus carrying his cross to Golgotha and screams, tears her hair and scratches her cheeks. Jesus consoles her, foretelling his resurrection, but this has no effect;[2] under the Cross Mary continues her lamentations, alternately swooning and screaming and tearing her clothes. After Jesus has died there are further outbreaks; Mary weeps tears of blood and finally lies in a dead faint across her Son's body.[3] Book 4 treats of the Resurrection and the Assumption. The risen Christ appears to his mother, who is now so happy that she remembers nothing of her former sorrow.[4] She asks her Son to preserve her body from the fury of the Jews so that she shall not suffer any ignominy, which he promises her. After his ascension she remains in Jerusalem in the care of St. John, frequently visited by angels, who provide her with heavenly food, for she no longer takes earthly nourishment. Her garments, which are kept miraculously ever-clean and new, are those of a medieval nun, and she follows a religious rule of

[1] 2, 3450ff.   [2] 3, 4818ff.   [3] 5004 to the end of Book 3.   [4] 6130ff.

life, dividing her days between psalmody, contemplation and good works.[1] She performs many miracles, casts out devils and instructs new converts, including St. Paul, in the Faith.[2] Finally, her death and assumption are described in great detail, making full use of the apocryphal sources. Her resurrection on the third day is revealed to St. Thomas, she ascends through the various heavens, being greeted by each of the nine choirs of angels individually who salute her as the "Empress of Heaven, the mediatress of angels, men and God",[3] because "through you our [apparently the angels'] fall and ruin has been made good".[4] After that she is greeted by all the Old- and New-Testament saints, and finally by each of the three persons of the Trinity.

This *Life of Mary* had a tremendous success and was the source of the first and most popular German life of the period, written by Wernher, the Swiss—perhaps a vagrant cleric—in 1172.[5] It follows the plan and most of the details of the Latin life, which it describes at much greater length, however, and with a quite particular stress on *minne*, the German word whose English equivalent is "courtly love". When the "bishops" tell Mary to choose one of her suitors she is very upset, because all her *minne* is for God, who is so beautiful and noble and whose house is so magnificent; indeed, she is made to speak about him like a girl pointing out the advantages of her human lover.[6] For in his house is lovely music and the noble cherubim dance to it, there all is joy and feasting—like a medieval palace; she cannot be married to another, because she wears his engagement ring in her heart, and God himself is full of *minne* for her.[7] After the Annunciation Mary, who is represented as a noble medieval maiden, calls together her parents and her servants and tells them of the angel's message; later, when Joseph doubts her virtue, she calls her maidens to

---

[1] 6480ff.   [2] 6742ff.   [3] 7504f.   [4] 7511.
[5] *Das Marienleben des Schweizers Wernher*, ed. M. Päpke und A. Hübner, Berlin (1920).
[6] I, 1341ff.   [7] 1410ff.

bear witness to prove her innocence.[1] In Egypt, she is venerated as a goddess.[2]

Like his Latin pattern, Wernher, too, describes Mary's
lamentations during the Passion in the most extravagant
terms and in even greater detail. What caused this change from
the restraint of the Gospel account and the whole patristic and
early medieval literature to the descriptions of distraught grief
presented by these popular "Lives" and by a whole literature
entirely devoted to this particular subject, the so-called
"Laments of Mary" (*Marienklagen*), which were highly
popular from the twelfth to the fourteenth centuries?[3] As
Lipphardt points out, these laments have developed from the
medieval Passion plays; they are also influenced by the
staurotheotokia of the Byzantines, liturgical verses taking the
place of the ordinary *theotokia* in Passiontide and expressing
the sorrow of the Theotokos under the Cross (Greek *stauros*).
Nevertheless, these are far more restrained than the descriptions of Wernher and the various *Marienklagen*; they simply
present very gently the suffering of the Virgin Mother without
any of the extravagances of the Western lamentations. Lipp-
hard traces—I think quite rightly—these latter to the
Germanic lamentations over the dead such as they occur for
example in *Beowulf*[4] and in the *Edda* and the *Nibelungenlied*,
when Gudrun (called Kriemhild in the latter) gives free rein
to her sorrow for Sigurd-Siegfried. "Something unheard-of
happened", says Lipphardt, "when the words and gestures
of these laments were applied also to Mary"[5]—indeed, even
the short description of them given above will have struck the
reader as pagan rather than Christian. Never before had the
sorrow of the Mother of Christ been depicted as bordering on
despair and momentary insanity. Thus the intimate union
between Mary and the Church, so clearly seen by the Fathers

[1] 2, 2281ff.   [2] 2, 4463.
[3] See W. Lipphardt, "Studien zu den Marienklagen", in *Beiträge zur Geschichte der deutschen Sprache und Literatur*, 58 (1934), 390–444.
[4] *vv.* 1117f. and 3150–56.   [5] p. 407.

and still in the earlier Middle Ages, was increasingly replaced by the view of Mary as an individual—whether as the despairing Mother under the Cross or the Queen reigning in heaven. This development from the objective to the subjective, noticeable also in other departments of theology, becomes even more evident in the following centuries, leading to a decadence that finally induced the Reformers to turn altogether away from Marian devotion.

Before, however, tracing this development, mention must be made of a charming piece, not on the sorrows, but the joys of Mary, a devotion specially propagated in England, by the Yorkshire Cistercian Stephen of Salley (d. 1252). Each of his meditations is divided into a meditation proper, a "joy" and a petition, anticipating a style usually believed to have originated only in the sixteenth century.[1] There are fifteen meditations grouped into three sections of five each—the similarity to the later Dominican Rosary is remarkable—the first group taking the reader from the birth of Mary to that of Christ, the second from there to the Cross, the third from the Passion to the Assumption. The meditations are touchingly simple, without the exaggerations so frequent at that time, and Mary is seen almost entirely in her function as Mother of Christ. The meditations end with the bodily assumption and glorification of Mary at the side of her Son, where she rules as the mistress of the world, the empress of the angels and the hope and propitiation of sinners, "a faithful mediatress for the salvation of those who belong to her".[2] The simplicity and devotion of this little gem of Marian literature contrast strangely with the exaggerations which became fashionable in the latter half of the century, though after the recent discoveries of scholars the great schoolmen themselves can no longer be held responsible for them.

[1] See A. Wilmart, *Auteurs spirituels et textes dévots du moyen-age latin*, Paris (1932), p. 324. The text itself is edited in the same work, pp. 339–58.
[2] p. 356.

FROM THE RISE OF THE MENDICANT ORDERS TO THE EVE OF THE REFORMATION

THE WESTERN CHURCH

IN the twelfth century Mariology was chiefly developed by the Cistercians; in the thirteenth, on the other hand, the monastic orders receded into the background, to give place to the newly founded mendicant orders, especially the Dominicans and the Franciscans. It was they who developed the scholastic method initiated by Anselm of Canterbury and who were mainly responsible also for halting the progress of belief in the Immaculate Conception, now no longer opposed by the authority of St. Bernard but by that of Peter Lombard. (d. 1160.) Between 1148 and 1150 he had written his famous *Sentences*, a work on Christian doctrine which is mostly a compilation of the Latin Fathers and St. John of Damascus, until then very little known in the West. The *Sentences* had made hardly any impact in the twelfth century; they were attacked by Joachim of Fiore early in the thirteenth, but pronounced orthodox at the Lateran Council in 1215. After that they became the standard theological textbook on which nearly all the thirteenth-century school-men wrote commentaries. The passage that especially concerns Mariology occurs in the third book of the work, which discusses the Incarnation and in this context asks the question whether the flesh of Christ, taken from the Virgin, was subject to sin. He answers that it was, just as "the other flesh of the Virgin", but that it was purified by the Holy Spirit in such a way that it was united to the Word without any contagion of sin,[1] and that from then on Mary herself was wholly without

[1] Lib. 3, dist. 3, c. 1.

sin.[1] Thus, basing themselves on the authority of Peter Lombard, all the great schoolmen of the thirteenth century denied the Immaculate Conception until Duns Scotus initiated a new way of looking at the question.

WORKS FALSELY ATTRIBUTED TO ALBERT THE GREAT

The fame of the learned Dominican St. Albert the Great as a Marian teacher has been in great measure due to two works formerly wrongly attributed to him, Richard of St. Laurent's *De Laudibus Sanctae Mariae*,[2] believed to be a work of St. Albert till 1625, and the famous *Mariale Super Missus Est*, which was first discovered to be spurious in 1952. Owing to the reputation of St. Albert these two works, especially the latter, had an enormous influence on later Mariology and were scarcely criticized, even though, as we shall see, they contained a good deal of questionable material besides much that remains valuable.

Richard of St. Laurent (d. after 1245) was Dean of the Metropolitan Chapter of Rouen and wrote this Marian work between 1239 and 1245, perhaps even a little later.[3] In this work, which the author himself intended to be a compendium of Marian doctrine and devotion, Mary is seen above all as the Mother of Men, and she is placed in constant parallel to Christ and even to God the Father. So Richard does not hesitate to apply the *Our Father* to her, and can write: "Our Mother who art in heaven, give us our daily bread,"[4] and: "Mary so loved the world, that is, sinners, that she gave her only-begotten Son for the salvation of the world."[5] She imitates Christ when "after the example of her Son, she emptied herself, assuming the form of a handmaid. For which reason also God exalted her, and gave her a name that is above every name except her Son's, that in her name every

---

[1] c. 3.   [2] Inter *Opera Alberti Magni*, ed. Borgnet, Paris (1898), vol. 36.
[3] See J. Beumer, "Die Mariologie Richards von Saint-Laurent", in *FS*, 41 (1959), pp. 19–40.
[4] 10, 1, 8 (p. 451).   [5] 4, 18, 6 (p. 225).

knee should bow except that of her Son."[1] We see how the difference between the divine-human Christ and his human mother tends to be more and more obliterated; for Mary can hardly be said to have "emptied herself" like Christ unless we attribute divine pre-existence to her. The Liturgy is treated in the same way as the Scriptures; paralleling the end of the Canon of the Mass, "Through him and with him and in him is all glory to thee, God . . .", Richard says of Mary: "Through her and in her and out of her is the glory of the Father and the Son and the Holy Spirit increased."[2]

Mary's part in the Redemption is accentuated; she was not only "the most faithful helper of her Son" in giving him his human flesh, but also under the Cross, when she received in her heart all the wounds that he received in his body,[3] being, as the second Eve, a "helper like unto himself". (Gen. 2.18.) Richard counters the objection that in the passages from Isaiah, generally understood of the Passion, "I have trodden the winepress alone,"[4] a helper is explicitly excluded, by continuing the quotation, ". . . and there is not a man with me". This, he says, does not exclude a woman—Mary was with him.[5] For, he asserts in another passage, God "did not wish to save mankind only through the death of his Son" but also gave woman a share in his work, who suffered with him in her heart the pains he suffered in his body.[6] Mary is not even excluded from our Holy Communions. Since Richard sees the union between Christ and Mary almost as an identity, he says that "in the sacrament of her Son we also eat and drink her flesh and blood",[7] and again: "Mary feeds her guests . . . on her virginal flesh . . . also in the sacrament where the flesh of Christ and the flesh of Mary are consumed, since the flesh of the Mother and of the Son are one flesh"[8]—a view that is quite inadmissible.

[1] Cf. Phil. 2.7ff. 4, 1, 2 (p. 167).   [2] 2, 1, 4 (p. 60).
[3] 6, 2 (pp. 329f.).   [4] 63. 3.   [5] 62. 2.
[6] 2, 2, 2 (p. 83).   [7] 2, 2, 3 (p. 83).   [8] 12, 1, 12, 7 (p. 632).

Indeed, there is at times an unhealthy strain in Richard's spirituality, as when he devotes a whole book to the beauty of Mary, of which six pages describe her spiritual and no less than forty her physical beauty, though it must be admitted that much of this space is taken up by allegorical explanations, especially in his detailed exposition of Mary as the neck.[1] She was predestined from all eternity to be the Mother of Christ; in this context Richard applies to her God's command, "Let there be light". (Gen. 1.3.) Nevertheless, he asserts her initial subjection to original sin in very strong terms: "Mary was a daughter of Babylon when she was born [= "conceived"] in the womb, because we are all born children of wrath"; but she was sanctified immediately after her conception and born wholly pure; therefore he vigorously opposes the feast of her conception.[2] On the other hand, he affirms her bodily assumption,[3] and celebrates her power in heaven in very extravagant language. He separates neatly the justice of God from the mercy of Mary, not without frequently referring to the story of Theophilus. Indeed, he actually reverses the roles of Christ and Mary when he applies to her Colossians 2.14— "Blotting out the handwriting of the decree that was against us"—which, he says, "Mary did, her Son mediating" (". . . quod fecit Maria Filio mediante").[4] For Mary, the Mother, is more merciful than Christ, the Father: "Now, God the Father gave us his Son as our Father and King of Justice, and to moderate his justice he gave us the Mother of Pity and the Queen of Mercy. For often the mercy of this mother graciously liberates what the justice of this Father would rightly condemn."[5] The mercy of Christ disappears completely in this division of labour between him and his Mother; further, Mary actually changes the "temper" of the Godhead, if we may so express it, for Richard writes

[1] 5, 2, 39 (p. 302).   [2] 6, 5, 3; 334 and 10, 30, 9 (p. 519).
[3] 7, 3, 8 (p. 375) and 12, 7, 5, 4 (p. 836).   [4] 4, 6, 2 (p. 187).
[5] 6, 9, 5 (p. 345).

ingenuously: "Mary has so softened the Lord, and still continues to do so by her merits and prayers, that he now patiently
tolerates even great sins, whereas before he mercilessly
avenged even quite small ones."[1]

So Richard invests Mary even with omnipotence: "Thus
a special omnipotence is given her not only in the kingdom of
heaven, but also in the three realms of heaven, earth and hell,
so that in her name every knee should bow . . .",[2] and he
devotes a whole chapter (30 of Book 4) to "The Omnipotence
of Mary". "She can do all things, through the gift of her Son,
through whom, the Omnipotent, she has been made omnipotent . . . For she is the queen of that realm whose king is
her Son, and according to the laws the Queen has equal rights
with the King. Therefore the power of Mother and Son are
one and the same."[3] Her omnipotence shows itself especially
in her power to free those who are already in the hands of the
devil, whom she brings back to life so that they can do
penance. Here the influence of the many miracle stories is
quite evident.[4] Mary's power extends also to Christ himself,
who "has decreed to save the world through this mediatress",
who "can not only effectively implore him, but also command
[*imperare*] him by her maternal authority".[5] Therefore "to
honour Mary is to lay up for oneself the treasure of eternal
life",[6] for she will glorify in the next world her servants who
honour her in this.[7] And how is she to be honoured? Richard
of St. Laurent chiefly recommends external practices, and
those not always in the best of taste. The various members of
her body are to be adored (in the sense of venerated) and
blessed through genuflexions and the recitation of *Hail
Maries*,[8] and all holy desires, meditations and good works
should be addressed to her.[9]

It should quite frankly be admitted that this work, the

[1] 6, 9, 3 (p. 344).   [2] 4, 6, 2 (187).   [3] 4, 30, 1 (p. 254).
[4] 4, 30, 2 (p. 255).   [5] 1, 7, 10 (p. 55).   [6] 2, 1, 2 (p. 59).
[7] 2, 1, 42 (p. 81).   [8] 2, 5, 5 (p. 111).   [9] 12, 1, 11 (p. 628).

first fairly systematic treatise on the subject, combines a number of traits that could only have an unfortunate influence. The opposition of Mary, the Queen of mercy, to Christ as the King of justice and vengeance, the constant and undiscriminating application to her of New-Testament sayings referring to her divine Son, her share in the eucharistic elements, and other features, did considerable injury to sane Marian doctrine and devotion, all the more as the work went very soon under the name of St. Albert and so was regarded with the veneration due to that great theologian. Compared with it the other work mistakenly attributed to him, the *Mariale Super Missus Est*, is more sober, despite its exaggerations.

Until the year 1952 there had never been the slightest doubt that this *Mariale* was the work of St. Albert, and so it enjoyed a tremendous authority, being quoted by all the Mariologists with apparent approval. Laurentin, the well-known French Mariologist, writes with evident relief that today its good points as well as its faults can be discussed objectively, as it no longer occupies the pinnacle on which it had been placed under the patronage of a Doctor of the Church.[1] The first indication that the *Mariale* was not the work of St. Albert appeared in a footnote of an article in *Recherches de théologie ancienne et médiévale*.[2] It was by the German Redemptorist A. Fries, who two years later proved his discovery in another article.[3] Strangely enough, in the very same year a Franciscan theologian, B. Korošak, published a work on St. Albert's Mariology[4] in which he reached the same conclusion quite independently. The two scholars do

[1] *Court Traité*,[4] p. 67. It should, of course, be clearly understood that no work of theology should be exempt from proper critical study solely because the author is a saint and doctor of the Church.

[2] 19 (1952), p. 342.

[3] "Die unter dem Namen des Albertus Magnus überlieferten mariologischen Schriften", in *Beiträge zur Geschichte der Philosophie und Theologie des Mittelalters*, 37, Münster (1954), 4.

[4] *Mariologia Sancti Alberti Magni eiusque coaequalium*, Rome (1954).

not, however, agree on the date of the so far anonymous work. Fries places it at the end of the thirteenth century, whereas Korošak thinks it was written before the sermons of St. Bonaventure—that is, towards the middle of the same century. F. Pelster, in an article in *Scholastik*,[1] dates it similarly; he believes the author to have been a German Dominican, belonging perhaps to the circle of St. Albert. The question of date and place of the *Mariale* was resumed by A. Kolping in 1958.[2] After a painstaking analysis of the manuscript tradition of the treatise Kolping comes to the conclusion that it must have originated in the south-east of the medieval German Empire, somewhere in Austria or Bohemia, in the second half of the thirteenth century. He does not rule out the possibility of its author having been a member of one of the older orders (Benedictine or Cistercian), who had studied under the Dominicans.

Now, what is the reason for rejecting St. Albert's authorship of the *Mariale* after a 700-year-old tradition had attributed it to him? It is very simple, and it is surprising that it had never been seen before; it is that the doctrine of Albert's genuine works differs quite considerably from that of the *Mariale*. These differences are set out in detail in the article by Fries. The most striking one is that, whereas Albert has explicitly affirmed throughout his life that Christ was conceived only of the blood, not of the flesh, of Mary, the *Mariale* rejects this view and defends the conception from both the flesh and the blood of Mary.[3]

The *Mariale*—to give it its traditional name—differs from the work of Richard of St. Laurent in that it uses the strict scholastic method of questions, objections and solutions. It deals with such irrelevancies, absurd to the modern reader, as

[1] 30 (1956), "Zwei Untersuchungen über die literarischen Grundlagen für die Darstellung einer Mariologie des hl. Albert des Grossen", pp. 388–402.

[2] "Zur Frage der Textgeschichte, Herkunft und Entstehungszeit der anonymen Laus Virginis (bisher Mariale Alberts des Grossen)", *RTAM* 25, 285–328.

[3] q. 213 (ed. Borgnet, vol. 37, p. 301).

the sex, age and clothes in which the angel appeared to Mary, the colour of her complexion and her hair, and other questions hardly of interest to the serious theologian. The basic principle of the work is Mary's plenitude of grace, from which everything else is derived—a considerable departure from the traditional view which places her divine motherhood at the centre.[1] This novel concept leads the author to formulate the axiom that Mary was full of every grace in which a pure creature can share. He bases himself on a saying of St. John of Damascus[2] in the context of the birth of Mary from a hitherto barren woman, a privilege she shares with Samuel, "so that in this matter, too, she should not cede place to any of the famous". Right at the beginning of his treatise the author of the *Mariale* elevates these words into a general principle that "the most blessed Virgin does not cede place to any of the famous in any matter whatsoever",[3] that is to say, not only as regards spiritual, but also quite secular, gifts. Consequently, she received all the sacraments, even that of penance, with its sanctifying effects; the only exception is the sacrament of orders, though the author cannot bring himself to deprive her wholly of it and says that she nevertheless possesses its grace, dignity and power.[4] Though she did not have the actual Beatific Vision on earth, she had one most near (*propinquissima*) to it; furthermore her mode of knowing and her knowledge exceeded those which any creature could have on earth.[5] She had, *inter alia*, a perfect direct knowledge of the Trinity, as well as of the Incarnation and her own predestination; besides, she could see angels, souls and demons, had a perfect knowledge of Scripture and of the future as far as it concerned herself; she also enjoyed the knowledge of all created things.[6] This included canon law, mathematics, geography and astronomy—had the author lived in our own time he would no doubt have added aeronautics and nuclear

---

[1] q. 34, 1 (p. 71). [2] *De Fide Orthodoxa*, 4, 15. [3] p. 3.
[4] q. 43 (pp. 83ff.). [5] q. 61 (pp. 110f.). [6] q. 111 (p. 168).

physics—all of which she knew most perfectly—*in summo*. She further possessed all graces *gratis datae*—that is, those not needed for personal sanctification,[1] as well as the properties of all the angels; hence she is exalted above all the angelic hierarchies.[2] More, all blessings whatsoever, those of Adam and Eve, Abraham's blessing on Isaac, Jacob's various blessings on all his sons and so forth, are hers,[3] so that the author concludes: "Thus it is clear that the blessed Virgin possessed in the highest degree all individual and universal blessings of individuals individually and universal ones universally."[4] All this is deduced from the words of the angel— which, incidentally, as we saw in the first chapter, did not mean "full of grace" at all, but "highly favoured one".

The work is very explicit on Mary's share in our redemption. Whereas Christ is the Redeemer through his passion, Mary is the "helper of redemption through her compassion" ("adjutrix redemptionis per compassionem"[5]); a view which, as has been seen, had been present also in earlier authors, but in this clear and pithy formula attributed, moreover, to a Doctor of the Church, became a very generally accepted—though not defined—Mariological doctrine. The *Mariale* also teaches the bodily Assumption,[6] but denies the Immaculate Conception, subscribing to the more general contemporary view that Mary was sanctified in the womb immediately after her conception.[7] The clear teaching on Mary's com-passion is often held to be one of the merits of the work. But the author's extravagant deductions from his principle of the fullness of grace, despite his statement in the preface that he does not wish to praise the blessed Virgin with lies, justify Laurentin's remark that the work "manifests the first symptoms of decadence",[8] though Richard of St. Laurent's earlier work certainly shows them, too.

---

[1] q. 122 (p. 175).   [2] q. 161 (p. 234).   [3] q. 164 (pp. 240–43).
[4] q. 193 (p. 280).   [5] q. 150 (p. 219).   [6] q. 132 (p. 187).
[7] q. 127 (p. 180).   [8] *Court Traité*, p. 67.

ALBERT THE GREAT

With the genuine works of St. Albert we are in a very different Mariological climate.[1] In the still unedited *Tractatus de Natura Boni*, written before 1240, the saint establishes her as mediatress, because she gave birth to the Redeemer and because she prays for us in heaven. Her "fullness" surpasses that of all the saints, but is below that of Christ, which is a plenitude of nature. He affirms her bodily assumption as a pious belief (*pie creditur*). Albert, too, sees her not only as the Mother but as the Bride of the Son, who has received all the gifts of the Spirit and whose inner life was perfectly well ordered. She is the mother of all the faithful, who owe their virtues and merits to her intercession.[2]

The recently discovered treatise *On the Incarnation*[3] contains a special section "On the Annunciation". Thus Albert was the first to give Mariology its definite place within Christology, which it has retained through the centuries.[4] The questions Albert asks in this context are completely different from those of the *Mariale*; there is nothing about such fatuous subjects as the angel's garments, but only about the angelic order to which he belonged.[5] Albert, too, denies the Immaculate Conception, but believes that Mary was sanctified in her mother's womb.[6]

In his treatise *On the Resurrection* (vol. 26), Albert affirms again Mary's bodily assumption into heaven; but she was not, as the *Mariale* says, taken up into the "heaven of the Trinity",[7] which according to Albert, belongs to God alone, but to the so-called *empyreum*, like all the other saints and together with

[1] See A. Fries, *Die Gedanken des hl. Albertus Magnus über die Gottesmutter*, Freiburg (Switzerland), 1958.

[2] Fries, pp. 10–20.

[3] Published in the new edition of his works under the auspices of the Albertus Magnus Institut in Cologne, vol. 26 (1958).

[4] See A. Fries, *Lexikon der Marienkunde*, col. 112, s.v. "Albertus".

[5] q. 1, art. 3; pp. 174f.   [6] q. 2, art.3; p. 183.   [7] q. 151 (p. 223).

the humanity of Christ, though below it.[1] Albert always emphasizes the infinite difference between Mary and her Son, so often neglected by other authors of his time. In his commentary on the *Sentences*,[2] he affirms that though Mary is exalted above the choirs of the angels, she is nevertheless immeasurably far removed from the divine sublimity.[3] He also modifies the view, so widely held, that whatever is said in honour of Mary redounds to the honour of Christ. True, he says, the blessed Virgin is to be venerated with *hyperdoulia* (a veneration above that of the saints), but not with the worship (*latria*) due to God: "For even though the honour of the Mother is the honour of the King, yet, because he had a different generation through his Godhead, she has no claim to divine honours, because her Son did not receive his divinity from her."[4] Albert also denies her any share in the Redemption: "In the Church", he says, "there is only the Head and the members. The work of redemption belongs only to the Head. Hence being redeemed belongs to the members. Since, therefore, the blessed Virgin was a member, it is fitting for her to be redeemed."[5] He expresses the same view in his *Postilla Super Isaiam*,[6] when treating of her compassion under the Cross, which he regards as quite personal, without reference to the Redemption.[7] When Christ was making straight what was bent in man, he was the cause, Mary the exemplar, who contributed to his work only by her intercession. This means that her co-operation in our salvation is restricted to her example and her prayer.[8] Mary is thus always subordinated to her Son; there is no question in St. Albert's works of Christ condemning while Mary exercises mercy. As in the Latin Fathers, Mary is the figure of the

[1] q. 9, art. 4, 5 (pp. 287f.).   [2] Ed. Borgnet, vols. 25-8.
[3] *In I Sent.*, dist. 44, art. 5 (Borgnet, vol. 26, p. 397).
[4] *In III Sent.*, dist. 9, art. 9 (Borgnet, vol. 28, p. 182).
[5] *In III Sent.*, dist. 3, art. 3, ad primum (p. 45).
[6] Cologne ed., vol. 19.   [7] Isa. 11.1 (Cologne ed., vol. 19, p. 110, l. 49).
[8] Isa. 11.1 (vol. 19, p. 165, 3ff.).

Church,[1] and like the Church, she is the mother of all good things.[2] But, as Fries comments: "In the view of Albert Mary's com-passion has no inner relation to the rebirth of men through the death of the Lord on the Cross. She has not conceived the children of the Church through her com-passion. She is the type of the Church . . . but not the Mother of the Church."[3] In the *Mariale*, on the other hand, Mary has become "the spiritual mother of the whole human race" through her "birth-pains" under the Cross.[4]

Albert's most important Mariological teaching is given in his *Commentary on Luke*,[5] which was written between 1260 and 1274. In his preface he deliberately rejects the "frivolous" apocryphal writings.[6] He, too, applies Col. 2.9 to Mary, but, characteristically, with very careful explanations; the fullness of the Godhead dwelt in her bodily only because Christ dwelt in her, and through him alone she becomes for us a source and aqueduct of grace.[7] Her mediation of grace is in-direct, through her divine motherhood, which gave her an "exuberance" of grace, so that through her it can overflow to men.[8] Albert, too, says that God came to Mary before the angel—not, however, because he was so enamoured by her beauty, as Amadeus of Lausanne had written, but so that the Virgin should be prepared to believe the word of the angel.[9] The great schoolman has no time for imaginary detail; his exposition is always in accordance with theological truth; his whole tenor of mind is entirely different from that of the author of the *Mariale*. Because in heaven the Virgin both contemplates God and intercedes for us, combining the offices of Mary and Martha, we should salute her frequently and wisely—which means that we should not only honour her with words but should try to imitate her virtues as far as we can.

---

[1] p. 163, 22ff.
[2] Isa. 66.7 (p. 624, 45).
[3] *Die Gedanken des hl. Albertus*, p. 160.
[4] q. 29, 3 (Borgnet ed., vol. 36, p. 62).
[5] Vols. 22 and 23 in Borgnet.
[6] Borgnet, vol. 22, p. 5.
[7] Luke 1.28 (vol. 22, p. 61).
[8] Luke 1.28 (vol. 22, p. 62).
[9] Vol. 22, p. 64.

It is significant that St. Albert sees Mary in heaven not only as turned to the world, but before that as turned to God in contemplating him—a truth which is only too frequently lost sight of by many medieval (and also modern) authors, who depict her as wholly turned towards men and exclusively occupied with their concerns.

In this later work, too, Albert asserts that Jesus was formed from the blood, not the flesh, of Mary; [1] he left her womb like a bridegroom, "not violating her as a mother, but consecrating her like a spouse without stain or wrinkle", [2] following the medieval and modern custom of designating her as *sponsa*. The fourfold interpretation of the name of Mary as illuminatress, star of the sea, bitter sea and mistress, provides him with an occasion to address her personally: "Therefore, O blessed Virgin, show yourself an enlightener, and by your consent [to the Incarnation] enlighten those who sit in the shadow of death . . . Prove yourself to be the pole star, leading us to your port . . . For when we were all in bitterness, you, like a bitter sea, made the bitterness of us all your own . . . And finally you are the mistress of us all." [3] Albert, too, regards Mary as our spiritual mother, not, however, through her suffering under the Cross, but because "she conceived us in her heart at the same time as she conceived the divine Word in her womb". [4]

Despite his opposition to apocryphal stories even Albert quotes the famous Theophilus legend as an example of Mary's goodness reaching even to hell and as an encouragement for sinners to repent, while "the blessed refer their glory to her as the cause of their beatitude", [5] which, as Fries comments, "involves perhaps not only the indirect mediation through her divine maternity, but also the direct mediation through her

[1] 1.35 (vol. 22, p. 102).   [2] 1.35 (vol. 22, p. 103f.).
[3] 1.38 (vol. 22, p. 112).   [4] Luke 10.42 (vol. 23, p. 90).
[5] Luke 1.49 (vol. 22, p. 130).
10*

heavenly intercession". [1] In this work, too, Albert compares Mary with the Church, whose beauty she equals; for both are the hope of sinners and a guide in the storms of temptation; both illuminate contemplatives and protect those in trouble. [2] Indeed, every grace in the Church derives from Mary's merits, all the light of the blessed in heaven is referred to her—and again the Christological cause: because she is the Mother of the Redeemer, who has opened the gate of the heavenly kingdom. [3] St. Albert teaches the bodily Assumption. He knows very well that (Pseudo-) Jerome did not accept it, but he follows (Pseudo-) Augustine in affirming that it would not be right if Mary, from whom Christ's body was taken, were not where he is. He also quotes the ancient *Veneranda* prayer and goes on to say that she is above all angels, transcending the knowledge even of the cherubim and the charity of the seraphim. This, of course, refers only to Mary's glorified life in heaven, not to her earthly knowledge, as in the *Mariale*. She, who is teacher as well as Virgin and Martyr (through her compassion under the Cross), is crowned with all heavenly light, and, for the honour of her Son, every knee, of those that are in heaven, on earth and under the earth, bows before her, and every tongue confesses that she is the Mistress of Majesty in the glory of her Son Jesus Christ. [4] So Albert, too, applies to her this verse of Philippians—but always with reference to her Son. The cause of her veneration, of her glorification, is not her own person, but Christ; because he is God, she is the Mother of God, because he is worshipped, she is venerated above all other creatures; her glory reflects his as the moon reflects the light of the sun. Her queenship, too, depends on Christ's kingship; [5] through her we have access to her Son, and through him to the Father, as Jacob was introduced to Isaac through Rebecca. [6]

[1] *Die Gedanken*, p. 279.
[2] Luke 2.16f. (vol. 22, p. 216).
[3] Luke 10.38 (vol. 23, p. 72).
[4] Luke 10. 42 (vol. 23, pp. 90f.).
[5] Vol. 23, p. 90.
[6] Luke 11.27 (vol. 23, p. 163).

THOMAS AQUINAS

So Albert's genuine works reflect invariably the authentic Mariological tradition, without the fanciful exaggerations and details of Richard of St. Laurent and the *Mariale*. His great disciple St. Thomas Aquinas is even more reticent. His opposition to the Immaculate Conception is well known. In the third part of the *Summa Theologiae* he discusses the matter and asserts that Mary was sanctified in the womb[1] but not before animation, since in this case she would not have needed to be redeemed by Christ. He knows quite well that certain Churches celebrate the feast of her conception; but Rome does not; however, since she tolerates this celebration it is not altogether to be rejected. Yet this does not imply that the conception itself was holy; "but, since the time when she was sanctified is unknown the feast of her sanctification rather than of her conception is celebrated on the day of her conception."[2] He agrees that the state of original justice such as it existed in Adam before the Fall "seems to pertain to the Virgin Mother"; nevertheless, "it in some way impairs the dignity of Christ", who is the Saviour of all without any exception;[3] for if she had not been conceived in sin she would not have needed him.[4] On the other hand, the blessed Virgin has never committed any sin whatsoever, whether mortal or venial, for "she would not have been capable of being the Mother of God if she had ever committed a sin . . . for she had a particular affinity to Christ, who received his flesh from her . . . Further, the Son of God, who is the Wisdom of God, had dwelt in a special way not only in her soul, but even in her womb; now, it is said in Wisd. 1.4, 'For wisdom will not enter into a malicious soul, nor dwell in a body subject to sins.'"[5] St. Thomas affirms that Mary's dignity is in a certain manner

[1] q. 27, a. 1. [2] q. 27, a. 2. [3] q. 27, art. 3.
[4] *Compendium Theologiae*, 459; in *Opuscula Theologica*, Marietti ed., vol. 1 (1954).
[5] Art. 4.

infinite, because it is from God, the infinite Good,[1] and that she was established in justice by a special privilege.[2] Moreover her sanctification in the womb was far more complete than that of the other saints, such as Jeremiah or St. John the Baptist, for her sensual appetites were always completely under the control of reason.[3] He teaches the virginity *in partu*, using the traditional comparison with the risen Christ's entry through closed doors.[4] Following Aristotle's biological views, he considers that Mary only "ministered the matter to the conception of the Son of God, and therefore must be said the true Mother of the Son of God. For it does not belong to a mother that the matter she has ministered should by some power be formed by her"[5]—a view no longer tenable today.

St. Thomas is extremely careful on the subject of Mary as a mediatress of grace. Christ, being the Son of God, "had such a plenitude of grace that it overflowed on all, according to John 1.16: 'Of his fullness we have all received.' But the blessed Virgin obtained such a plenitude of grace that she was nearest to the author of grace, so that she received into herself him who is full of all grace, and, by giving birth to him, she drew in some way grace down to all."[6] So St. Thomas relates her mediation of grace strictly to the Incarnation and even so she mediates grace only "in some way" (*quodam-modo*), that is to say her mediation is not direct at all. Her intercession in heaven is not touched upon, much less her association with the Redemption under the Cross. Thus B. H. Merkelbach[7] concludes that (in contrast to most other theologians of his time) St. Thomas has not treated the doctrine of Mary's mediation either in his theological or in his exegetical works.

[1] Ia, q. 25, art. 6, ad 4 um.   [2] Ia, q. 100, art. 2 corp.
[3] *Comp. Theol.*, 461f.   [4] *Comp. Theol.*, 469.
[5] *Comp. Theol.*, 453.   [6] IIIa, q. 27, art. 5, ad primum.
[7] "Quid senserit S. Thomas de mediatione Beatae Mariae Virginis", in *Xenia Thomistica*, 2 (1925), p. 521.

Thus it is not surprising that he should have had no sympathy whatever with the various fanciful Marian speculations that were rife among the religious of his age. An excellent example of the absurd questions that were being discussed and St. Thomas' attitude to them is his *Responsio ad Lectorem Bisuntinum.*[1] Friar Gerard, a fellow Dominican, has asked Thomas whether it was true that the blessed Virgin repeated the words "a sword shall pierce your own soul" (Luke 2.35) with the greatest grief seven times a day from her purification till the Resurrection. Thomas replies that such a thing can be as easily affirmed as denied, since it is quite unsupported by any authority. "In my opinion," he concludes, "such frivolities ought not to be preached, seeing there are so many subjects for preaching that are absolutely true." This question throws an interesting sidelight on the kind of sermons that were obviously preached on the blessed Virgin at that time—the Reformers' battlecry "Back to the Bible" 250 years later is more easily understood if we remember that the Friars Gerard were very much more plentiful than the Friars Thomas.

BONAVENTURE

The Dominican Doctor's Mariological teaching was far more austere than that of his friend and opposite number in the Franciscan Order, St. Bonaventure (d. 1274). This is found chiefly in his *Commentary on the Sentences*, his treatise on the Gifts of the Holy Spirit and his sermons, at least one of which, however, Sermon 6 on the Assumption, is spurious.[2] Like all his contemporaries, Bonaventure, too, denies the

---

[1] Written A.D. 1271 in *Opuscula Theologica*, no. 939, Marietti ed., vol. 1, pp. 243f.

[2] This has been proved by J. Beumer, "Eine dem heiligen Bonaventura zu Unrecht zugeschriebene Marienpredigt?" in *FS*, 42 (1960), pp. 1–26. See also V. Plesser, "Die Lehre des heiligen Bonaventura über die Mittlerschaft Mariens", *FS*, 23 (1936), pp. 353–89, in which the sermon is still considered genuine.

282 MARY: A HISTORY OF DOCTRINE AND DEVOTION

Immaculate Conception, quoting St. Bernard's famous letter and giving a variety of reasons, among them the one of St. Thomas that if she had not contracted original sin she could not have been redeemed and that therefore the honour of her Son, the Redeemer of all men without exception, would be diminished.[1] For Bonaventure refused to interpret the axiom that the honour given to the Mother refers back to the Son in such a sense as to affirm that every honour that is attributed to the Son should also be attributed to the Mother, because, he says, "this would not be to honour the Son, but rather to dishonour him, in that an honour due to him alone would be attributed to someone else". For though we must greatly honour the Mother, we must nevertheless far more venerate her Son, through whom all honour and glory comes to her.[2] Though Mary was subject to original sin by nature, she was nevertheless free from it in her soul, and this places her between us and her Son because "she is the mediatress between us and Christ, as Christ is between us and God",[3] quoting the general opinion—incidentally, the only time the term "mediatress" is found in his works. Though Bonaventure cannot see his way to exempting her altogether from original sin—the combination of Augustine–Bernard–Lombard was too strong even for him —he minimizes the hold it had on her as much as possible. While "others were raised up after the Fall, the blessed Virgin was held so that she should not fall, as it were, in the Fall itself",[4] and in the next question he affirms that the infusion of grace took place immediately after the infusion of her soul, so that she was pure from all actual sin,[5] for "this befitted the advocate of the human race, that she should have no sin which would lie on her conscience", she who was the spouse of God and the resting-place of the whole Trinity.[6]

[1] *Comm. Sent.*, dist. 3, pt. 1, "On the Sanctification of the Blessed Virgin Mary", art. 1, q. 1, Quaracchi ed., vol. 3, p. 62.
[2] q. 2 (p. 68).   [3] q. 2 (p. 67).
[4] q. 2 (p. 67).   [5] q. 3, arts. 1 and 2 (p. 71f.).
[6] art. 2 (p. 73).

Her purification, however, did not take place all at once, but in two stages. In the first she was conformed to other saints, when she was given the faculty to avoid all sin, both mortal and venial, and in the second, from the moment of the Incarnation, this was increased to the impossibility of falling into any sin.[1] The conception of the Son of God not only completes Mary's purification, it is also the foundation of all her merits.[2] Through it "she merited the reconciliation of the whole human race; and therefore she deserves the fervent devotion of all Christians".[3] However, Bonaventure makes a very clear distinction between the veneration, *hyperdoulia*, due to her—that is, a veneration greater than that due to the saints, which is *doulia* only—and the divine honour, *latria*, due to her Son; if this were to be given to Mary it would mean idolatry. He is also very careful in circumscribing her dominion, which, as we have seen, some preachers thought coextensive with that of God himself. God has, indeed, given Mary a certain authority; but it is the dominion of *praesidentia*, such as is accorded to the governor of a province, not one of majesty and omnipotence; these God does not communicate to any creature. For though the flesh of Mary is the same as that of Christ as regards his human nature, it is not, like his, united to the Godhead. Thus Christ himself honours his Mother and wants her to be honoured as the Mother of God, but not with his own honour, because "the person of the Mother is infinitely below the person of the Son"; therefore "she is also to be infinitely less venerated and loved than her Son, according to the law of justice and right order", but "in so far as she is Mother of God, she is to be placed above all the other creatures."[4] She is both above and beside us: above through the grace of Christ's most exalted conception, beside us because of her human nature.[5]

[1] q. 3, art. 2 (p. 77).   [2] dist. 4, art. 2, q. 2 (p. 107).   [3] q. 3 (p. 113).
[4] *Sent. III*, dist. 9, art. 1, q. 3 (p. 206).
[5] *Sent. III*, dist. 28, dub. 2 (p. 634).

This is the language of the sound theologian who repudiates the false principle "like Mother, like Son", which takes no account of the infinite difference between the divine person of Christ and the human person of his Mother. This does not mean that Bonaventure in any way minimizes the glory of Mary; he only sees it in the right proportion. In the sixth book of his treatise on the Gifts of the Holy Spirit he writes: "Whoever wants to be a saint must follow the glorious Virgin."[1] For "Eve expels us from paradise and sells us [scil., into sin], she brings us back and 'buys' us [emit]."[2] This Mary does by her acceptance of the cross of Christ; but it is a passive, not an active, contribution to redemption, as Bonaventure explains in the next chapter, commenting on Prov. 31.10, "Who shall find a valiant woman? Far and from the uttermost coasts is the price of her." Using the allegorical method of interpretation, so popular in the Middle Ages, the Franciscan doctor explains: "She [Mary] paid this price as the valiant and pious woman; for when Christ suffered on the Cross in order to pay this price, that he might . . . redeem us, the blessed Virgin was present, accepting and consenting to the divine will."[3] He further explains the matter in the following chapters. Christ is, indeed, the sole Redeemer, for "no-one but Christ could give back to God the honour that had been withheld from God", but the blessed Virgin contributes to it "by consenting, as his Mother, that Christ should be offered as the price . . . the blessed Virgin offered her Son to be sacrified".[4] She paid the price by her compassion with Christ; since she had suffered no pains in giving birth to him she did so now, even though, in the higher part of her being, she was glad that he should suffer the Cross because through it he redeemed us.[5] Bonaventure strongly affirms that Mary herself profited from the Passion: "The devil fashioned the sword with which the soul of the Virgin was transfixed; and

---

[1] Ch. 12 (Quaracchi ed., vol. 6, p. 485).   [2] 14 (p. 486).
[3] 15 (p. 486).   [4] 17 (p. 486).   [5] 18f. (p. 487).

she herself was healed [*curata est*], and the devil was defeated."[1]
Like the Latin Fathers, he does not say that she became our
mother under the Cross, but at the birth of Christ. For grace
descended to us through the incarnate Word, through the
crucified Word, and through the in-breathed Word (*Verbum
inspiratum*); and because the Word was incarnate in Mary,
therefore the Apostle Paul advises those who would obtain
grace "to go to the throne of grace [Heb. 4.16], that is, the
glorious Virgin"[2]—an exegesis which is certainly not
"literal". Bonaventure distinguishes the various degrees of
"fullness of grace". The lowest is that of sufficiency, which is
in every just man; the next the fullness of abundance, which
is in perfect men only; then the fullness of excellence, which
is the privilege of Mary, and highest, the fullness of "super-
effluence", which is in Christ alone, from whose fullness we
have all received.[3]

We find the same teaching in his genuine sermons. As has
been said before, Sermon 6 on the Assumption[4] has now
been established to be spurious. Indeed, after reading
the Mariological statements in the definitely authentic
works just discussed it seems incredible that this sermon
should have been considered genuine for so long; Father
Beumer's arguments for its spuriousness are completely convincing. In the same article the author says that further
research may show some other sermons also to be spurious,
and we may perhaps at least remove one passage from a
sermon with a very bad manuscript tradition, which seems
to contradict the teaching of St. Bonaventure's genuine
works.

Most other Marian sermons reflect this teaching quite
faithfully. In his first sermon on the Purification Bonaventure
states that Mary needed baptismal grace, because she had
contracted original sin, but not penitential grace, because she

---

[1] 23 (p. 488).   [2] 1, 5 (p. 458); cf. also 6, 20 (p. 487).
[3] *Comment. on Jo.*, 1.3, vol. 6, p. 538.   [4] Quaracchi ed., vol. 9, pp. 700–06.

never committed an actual sin.[1] He interprets her name as "bitter sea", "illuminatress" and "mistress", corresponding to the threefold way of purgation, illumination and perfection, the first being interpreted of her suffering under the Cross. But the principal interpretation is that of Star of the Sea, and as such she purifies, illuminates and perfects those who are in this world.[2] In his second sermon on the same feast he stresses man's need for asking her intercession and imitating her virtues;[3] she can truly be said to be the "diffusive principle of sanctification", because Christ, who is holiness itself, was born from her, because the Church was sanctified through her Son, and finally because she obtains our sanctification from him by her prayers[4]—again the stress on Christ as the first source, which we have noticed also in Bonaventure's other genuine works. There is a similar argumentation in Sermon 4 on the Purification, where Bonaventure first explains that Christ is the mercy of God and Mary has received him into her womb and then continues: "Therefore we must fly to the mercy of the Virgin Mary as to the port of our salvation."[5] He almost goes out of his way to explain the various popular invocations of Mary with reference to her Son, as also in Sermon 2 on the Annunciation, when he says that Mary is called "liberator of captives" because Christ is our liberation,[6] and in an interesting passage from Sermon 4 on the same feast: "Therefore the Creator of all things reposed in the tabernacle of the virginal womb, for there he made for himself a nuptial chamber, so that he might become our brother; he prepared a royal throne, so that he should be our Ruler; he assumed priestly vestments, so that he should be our High Priest. By reason of the nuptials the Virgin Mary is the Mother of God; because of the royal throne she is the Queen of Heaven; because of the priestly vestments she is the advocate of the human race."[7] This is quite compatible with

[1] Vol. 9, p. 634.   [2] p. 636.   [3] p. 641.   [4] p. 642.   [5] p. 651.
[6] p. 665.   [7] p. 672.

Bonaventure's usual teaching, but what follows seems doubtful, for he reproduces Hermann of Tournai's strange idea that "through the Virgin Mother, God has become our Father" (p. 672), applies to her without restrictions Phil. 2.10—". . . that in her honour every knee should bow"—and puts her on a level with Christ when he says, ". . . that not only he, but she, too, should be our advocate, so that we should have the most powerful support from two persons [*personas*] whom it is impossible to repel, namely the Son and the Mother."[1] It is difficult to believe that Bonaventure, who elsewhere so carefully guards the difference between the human person of Mary and the divine person of her Son, should have placed both on the same level as is done here. As this sermon is extant in various versions, some shorter and some longer, it would seem that the passage just discussed might well be an interpolation or rest on a misunderstanding, since these sermons were taken down by members of the congregation.

In the next sermon the Franciscan doctor states explicitly that, though the grace of the blessed Virgin is sufficient for all, it is nevertheless efficacious only for those who make themselves worthy of it.[2] Sermon 6 on the Annunciation presents Mary under the Cross. In striking contrast to the popular Laments Bonaventure emphasizes the dignity of her grief, which was borne with "perfect virility. For it is greater to bear a wound with equanimity than to inflict a wound, and to will to see one's own Son suspended from the Cross than to kill the enemy with one's own hand."[3] In Sermon 2 on Mary's nativity Bonaventure again insists on linking her prerogatives to Christ. St. Bernard had simply exclaimed: "Take away Mary, this star of the sea . . . what else is left but surrounding gloom?" Bonaventure considers it necessary to explain: "For if you take away the Mother of God, you also take away the Incarnate Word."[4]

[1] p. 673.   [2] pp. 679f.; so also in Sermon 2 on her nativity, p. 711.
[3] p. 684.   [4] p. 709.

In the five apparently largely genuine sermons on the Assumption, the Franciscan doctor is equally sober; the application of Phil. 2.10 to Mary occurs in Sermon 4, where the manuscript tradition is bad,[1] and there are a few other passages which sound doubtful.[2] Mary is certain to be in heaven, because she gave Christ his body, and her beatitude would not be perfect if she were not in heaven with her whole person (*personaliter*), which is a compound of both body and soul.[3] She is, indeed, a fountain of grace, but only in dependence on Christ, who in his turn has received it from God the Father, the primary Source of all good things.[4] The whole tenor of these five sermons, apart from the few doubtful passages, is quite remarkably free from any exaggerations so often connected with this particular subject; for example, in Sermon 3 he censures the principle that whatever is said in praise of the blessed Virgin is too little rather than too much. "Such sayings", he comments, "are perhaps admissible in sermons, but seem exaggerated to us in Marian theology."[5]

A SPURIOUS SERMON

When we come to Sermon 6, the picture changes abruptly. Beumer considers as the most cogent proof of its non-authenticity its assertion of Mary's perfect sanctification in the womb,[6] whereas Bonaventure assumes in all his works a remaining *fomes peccati* ("fuel of sin");[7] for example, in Sermon 5 on the Purification, where he says that this was extinguished only when the Holy Spirit overshadowed her.[8] But the sermon under discussion is full of other ideas quite incompatible with the doctrine not only of Bonaventure but of any sound theologian. For example, the author of the

---

[1] p. 698.
[2] The Quaracchi edition of Bonaventure does not always come up to contemporary critical standards.
[3] Sermon 1 (p. 690).   [4] Sermon 4 (p. 696).   [5] p. 693.
[6] p. 701.   [7] Beumer, "Eine ... Marienpredigt", p. 21.
[8] Quarracchi ed., vol. 9, p. 654.

sermon, in explaining that Mary had chosen the best part, states: "The part of the creatures, who had the Lord Jesus Christ as their God, was good; the part of God the Father, who had him as his Son, was better; but she, who had him as her Son as well as her God, chose the best." So God the Father has to take second place after Mary, as also the Holy Spirit; for the Spirit proceeded from the Son, but not the Son from the Spirit, whereas the blessed Virgin proceeded from the Son as well as the Son from her.[1] It is really astonishing that such theological nonsense should have been attributed to a Doctor of the Church for seven centuries. The author further states that as God is called our Lord absolutely because of his excellence, so Mary, too, is called our Lady absolutely; and the proof of this excellence is "that the Lord has communicated to her every honour which he himself had on earth"[2]—a statement in direct contradiction with Bonaventure's constantly repeated doctrine of the infinte distance between Mary and her divine Son. Further, the sermon subscribes to what Beumer calls "a very odd idea, which probably originated in popular devotion but which can hardly be approved theologically".[3] It is the division between the realm of mercy and the realm of justice, which we have met before, but which Pseudo-Bonaventure expresses in a particularly striking and misleading way: "The blessed Virgin," he says, "chose the best part, because she was made Queen of Mercy, while her Son remained King of Justice; and mercy is better than justice . . ."[4] The consequences of such teaching, especially as regards popular devotion, are not difficult to imagine. Father Beumer comments: "The most important thing is doubtless the fundamental realization that scholastic theology at its zenith embraces two currents which are relatively independent of each other, and certainly more so than in the twelfth century. The one of these is scholarly,

---

[1] p. 703.   [2] p. 705.   [3] "Eine . . . Marienpredigt", p. 7.
[4] Quarracchi ed., vol. 9, p. 703.

the other more directly concerned with devotional practice and popular piety. If we are not mistaken, popular Mariology especially has been the first to become detached from the whole of Christian doctrine, until then still quite homogeneous, and to become fairly independent."[1]

If, as seems undeniable, this sermon is spurious, Bonaventure can no longer be quoted as a witnes to Mary's direct part in the Redemption, which is affirmed here[2] but nowhere in the saint's genuine works. The sermon also asserts her universal mediation in the strongest possible terms: "No-one enters heaven except through her . . . hence the Lord never receives anyone without her mediation."[3] For Mary is not only the mother of all spiritual men but also "the mother of the whole world [*machinae mundialis*] and the mother of the reparation of the angels".[4] As Beumer says, with this sermon removed from the works of Bonaventure, his Mariology is taken out of the popular current and brought much closer to that of St. Albert, whereas the sermon itself joins the trend represented by Richard of St. Laurent, the *Mariale* and Engelbert of Admont, though the interdependence between all these works is not yet clear and scholars disagree on the respective priorities.

SOME LESSER FIGURES

CONRAD OF SAXONY

Another Marian treatise wrongly attributed to St. Bonaventure, but which really belongs to the Franciscan Conrad of Saxony (d. 1279), is the *Speculum Beatae Mariae Virginis*[5] which explains the *Ave Maria* in eighteen lessons. It quotes extensively from Bede, Anselm, Bernard and other authorities and though following the general opinion of the time in denying the Immaculate Conception, it attributes the highest

---

[1] "Eine . . . Marienpredigt", p. 26.   [2] Quarracchi ed., vol. 9, pp. 704f.
[3] p. 705.   [4] p. 706.
[5] Ed. in *Bibl. Franc. Ascet. Med. Aevi*, Quaracchi (1904), vol. 2.

graces to the Mother of God, who is called the "universal Mother of all the faithful".[1] As such "she prevents her Son from striking sinners; for before Mary there was no one who dared thus hold back the Lord",[2] a view which we have met before during this period. As the Lord is the universal Master of all, so he has made Mary the universal mistress of heaven and earth, who even has divine properties, because God is with her.[3] "For the most blessed Virgin Mary is the red morning sky [*aurora*], the best mediatress between unjust man and the just God, the best appeaser of his wrath,"[4] who placates God by her prayers as Abigail reconciled David to Nabal.[5] The *Speculum* was extremely popular in the later Middle Ages, as is proved by the 173 manuscripts of it (between the thirteenth and fifteenth centuries) still extant.

PETER JOHN OLIVI

Peter John Olivi (d. 1298) was another pupil of St. Bonaventure, but he belonged to the strictest interpreters of the Franciscan rule of poverty, called the "Spirituals", and was involved in bitter disputes with his superiors. He had long been forgotten, until the discovery of his works in the twentieth century proved him to have been a great schoolman and theologian. His *Four Questions on Our Lady*[6] considerably influenced Bernardine of Siena, who took over almost literally the First Question, on the Virgin's consent to the Annunciation, into sermons 5 and 6 of his treatise on the blessed Virgin. Olivi holds that Mary's consent was of greater merit and virtue than any action of any other saint: for to pass from the state of virginity to that of the divine motherhood was like a death to her. As our old man is crucified in baptism, "how much more was the Virgin crucified with Christ in the hour of his conception"[7]—an idea which I have not found elsewhere before. She bore us all in her womb, as a true mother bears

---

[1] 10 (p. 135).   [2] 7 (p. 105).   [3] 8 (p. 113).   [4] 11 (p. 155).
[5] 14 (p. 203).   [6] Ed. D. Pacetti, Quaracchi (1954).   [7] p. 12.

her children,[1] and though Olivi subscribes to the current view
that she was conceived in original sin, he holds that she
received the highest wisdom and exact counsel of what to do
and what to avoid from her earliest years.[2] The second
question treats of twelve victories in twelve temptations, by
which Mary defeated the devil in a twelvefold way. Though
Scripture says nothing about these, it is certain that she
sustained as many as was expedient for her crown of glory, for
she had to share the temptations of her Son. Thus, quoting
Hebrews (4.15), as we have a High Priest who has "compassion on our infirmities", being tempted in all things as we are,
"so we have also a Mother experienced in infirmities and temptations, so that she can have compassion on our infirmities".[3]

Question 3 is devoted to the excellence and perfection of the
blessed Virgin, who "stands to the whole celestial court in the
relation of queen and mistress to her servants and hand-
maids", because she is the Mother of God, which is a higher
position than that of being mistress of God's creatures; the
latter grows out of the former as a branch grows out of its
root: "Hence it is to be regarded as certain that she herself is
above all the orders of angels, as by herself constituting one
total and integral state to which, according to right reason, no
other person can be rightly added . . . the grace of the Mother
being conformed to that of Christ as Man."[4] The last
question considers the sorrow of the blessed Virgin during the
passion of Christ and opposes a view, sometimes held in
scholastic circles, that Mary had more joy in it than sorrow, on
account of our salvation; on the contrary, Olivi says, she was
"crucified with" Christ (*concrucifixa*).[5]

UBERTINO OF CASALE

In 1305, a few years after Olivi's death, while Dante was
writing his *Paradiso*, another Franciscan Spiritual, Ubertino
of Casale (d. c. 1330), wrote his very influential *Tree of the*

[1] p. 14.   [2] p. 22.   [3] pp. 23-43.   [4] pp. 44-6.   [5] pp. 65-8.

Crucified Life of Jesus,[1] from which Bernardine of Siena took forty-seven chapters nearly literally. Like most of his contemporaries Ubertino, too, teaches that Mary was completely purified of the *fomes peccati* only at the Annunciation.[2] He uses the language of the Canticle when he describes how the Father desired her and the Son asked him to let him descend into her garden; the Father being compared to a loving spouse, whilst the Son is her only-begotten. Mary herself gave her consent to the Incarnation "in the place of the whole human nature".[3] When she had done so, she received all the perfections which a creature not hypostatically united to God could receive, especially the constant highest contemplation; all ignorance, which is a consequence of original sin, was taken away from her, and her freewill continued to function even in sleep, so that she could continue her contemplation, and thus her meriting, even then.[4] At the Annunciation, moreover, the Father took her as his spouse and communicated his paternal fecundity to her, making her "the mother of all the elect" and the "mother and associate" (*socia genitrix*) of his Son. No grace is given which she does not dispense.[5]

At the Presentation of Christ in the Temple she, "as the most generous mother, gives her only-begotten to all the sons of grace"—for he could be offered only by her—and herself as an advocate, mother, protectress and defender of all men; for as the guilty flee to the church for sanctuary, so sinners flee to Mary.[6] The following chapter contains a beautiful description of Mary's love for Joseph, a subject not often mentioned in the literature of the time. Chapter 7 of Book 2 has an interesting discussion of New-Testament passages

---

[1] *Arbor Vitae Crucifixae Jesu*; I quote from the Venice edition of 1485 in the Bodleian Library, Oxford, which has no pagination, by book and chapter; see also C. Balić, "Die Corredemptrixfrage innerhalb der franziskanischen Theologie", *FS*, 39 (1957), pp. 218–87, and E. Gurney-Salter in *Franciscan Essays*, 1, Aberdeen (1912), pp. 108–23.

[2] 1, 8.   [3] 1, 7.   [4] 1, 8.   [5] 1, 9.   [6] 2, 5.

which might imply a criticism of Mary by her Son. Ubertino does not shirk the issue, but explains that the cult of the eternal Father must come first, and that Christ meant to set an example to men that they must leave even their parents for the sake of God.

In the true Franciscan tradition Ubertino lays special emphasis on Mary's part in the passion of her Son, who "wished to associate his Mother with his pain"[1] and gave her the "primacy of compassion".[2] For he was crucified not only on the Cross, he was crucified also in the heart of Mary, who thus became the advocate of the world as he was its redeemer. Ubertino, too, quotes the passage from Genesis that it is not good for man to be alone—so she became a helper of Christ in his passion.[3] Mary's lament under the Cross is a fine piece of medieval poetry[4] and the association of the Mother with her Son in the work of redemption is expressed in the words of Christ himself, spoken from the Cross: "One thing is necessary, that I, Jesus your Son, should die in atrocious pain, that you, my Mother, should die with me in similar manner and that the world should be generously redeemed."[5] Though the term "co-redemptress" is not yet used, the idea is clearly already there.

ENGELBERT OF ADMONT

With Engelbert, a Benedictine abbot (d. 1331), we return to the atmosphere of Pseudo-Albert's *Mariale*. He wrote his long *Treatise on the Graces and Virtues of the Blessed Virgin Mary* some time between 1283 and 1325, probably in the earlier part of this period.[6] The treatise is divided into four parts: the first deals with what can be gathered about the life and virtues of Mary from the Gospels, the second with her active life as known from the works of the saints, the third with her contemplative life, and the fourth with her passing from

---

[1] 4, 11.   [2] 4, 14.   [3] 4, 15.   [4] 4, 25.   [5] 4, 38.
[6] B. Pez in *Thesaurus Anecdotum*, vol. 1, pt. 1 (1721), cols. 505–761.

this life and her glorification in heaven. Like all other Continental authors of the period, Engelbert does not assume the Immaculate Conception, but a threefold purification. She was indeed sanctified in the womb at the same time as the soul was infused in the foetus, and so the original guilt was taken away by infused grace, but the "fuel" of sin, the *fomes peccati*, which is the cause of moral weakness, was not wholly extinguished. It was further diminished at the Annunciation, but its complete destruction took place only when Christ actually dwelt in her womb.[1] Nevertheless, the feast of her conception, which became increasingly popular, might be celebrated on December 8, since it could be considered not so much as commemorating the carnal act but the actual beginning of man's salvation.[2] In Part 3 Engelbert discusses Mary's special virtues and graces in a way very similar to the Pseudo-Albert. Like him, he quotes and elevates into a general principle John of Damascus' saying that Mary is in nothing inferior to any of the "illustrious".[3] So she had all the graces of the seven sacraments, including the spiritual power, ministerial dignity and even the actual execution of the priesthood, because she fashioned the body of Christ not from bread and wine but from her own flesh and blood.[4] While still on earth she possessed all the virtues, fruits of the Spirit and beatitudes not only perfectly in conformity with this life, but also relatively (*secundum quid*) as they are in the next, so that she was actually living between the two states of earthly and heavenly existence.[5] Thus she not only knew perfectly all she needed to know, but (again, a similarity to the teaching of Pseudo-Albert) she knew perfectly how and for what purpose the world had been made, even though the author makes the typically medieval remark, that to ask and find out how the world is made is more a matter of curiosity than of utility—the kind of view that prevented scientific and technological

[1] Pt. 4, ch. 6 (708A–709B).   [2] 4, 3ff. (706).   [3] 43 (682D).
[4] Chs. 4–6 (599C–603D).   [5] Ch. 7 (608A, B).

progress for many centuries. Mary's supernatural knowledge
included the vision of the mystery of the Trinity face to face
(in this life), as well as that of all the angels, the mystery of the
Incarnation and of her own predestination; finally, she knew
in her contemplation all existing creatures and the constitution
and government of the whole world and of the Church and the
ultimate consummation of all things.[1] So it is not surprising
that Engelbert calls the blessed Virgin without qualification
the most learned and prudent of all human beings.[2]

Under the Cross Mary was the associate of the Passion
(*socia passionis*), just as she had been the minister of the Incarnation, and thus she was "the assistant of the whole work
of our Redemption",[3] and Christ himself received consolation from her compassion.[4] Mary was sixty-five years old at
the Passion, because at the time of Christ's birth she was
thirty-one—an age conflicting with the Gospel story, which
depicts her as a young girl just engaged, and with the general
opinion based on this narrative. Engelbert arrived at this odd
result by a computation typical of declining scholasticism:
At the time of Christ's conception Mary must have been
perfect both in body and age. Now, as the first term when
women are capable of childbearing is the age of twelve and the
last the age of fifty, and the middle between two terms is the
most perfect, therefore she must have been thirty-one, which
is the exact mean between these two ages![5] She died at the age
of seventy-two, seven years after the Passion,[6] without pain
and with the greatest joy.[7]

Engelbert accepts the bodily Assumption though he knows
about the difference of opinion between (Pseudo-) Jerome and
(Pseudo-) Augustine on the matter.[8] He proves that this view
is in harmony with the "sobriety of the Church", for it is
consonant with the dignity of Mary and—a very important

---

[1] 44 (684C–686A).   [2] Pt. 1, ch. 29 (547B).   [3] 1, 33 (556D).
[4] 30 (551B).   [5] Pt. 3, ch. 46 (690B).   [6] 47 (691A, B).
[7] Pt. 4, ch. 16 (722C).   [8] 4, 18ff. (724Bff.).

point for the medieval mind—with her office of mercy towards us.[1] Again and again we find that the blessed Virgin is hardly ever seen as the perfect adorer of God, but almost always, to put it quite crudely but exactly, as a kind of "universal aunt" exclusively occupied with all the needs of her clients; for she procures largesse to those in need, co-operates in all our affairs, is the most prudent adviser in all our difficulties, helps most promptly in dangers, is the most efficacious intercessor for our sins, a wonderful comforter in sorrow; she heals the sick, restores those who have fallen, liberates the oppressed, reconciles the desperate, and is the most faithful mediatress of grace.[2] Her perfect worship of God as the Second Eve, so prominent in the patristic age, is scarcely considered; instead, in this more popular literature she is elevated almost to the level of God, but on the tacit or openly stated condition that her whole raison d'être in heaven is to be concerned with the affairs of men. That she is *also* concerned with them, and far more universally than any other saint, is, of course, quite true; but to see her entirely from this point of view to the exclusion of her office as the perfect human adorer of the triune Godhead and the heavenly Christ, has robbed Mariology of a whole dimension and led to the decline so obvious in the following centuries. For if she is placed on the same level as her Son, this adoration is no longer possible, and Engelbert, like others before him, sees her as the perfect equal of her Son: "As the King of France and the Queen of France receive these titles from the same kingdom, so also the King and the Queen of the heavenly court." Thus there is an "*equal* participation of the royal glory";[3] and he repeats the same argument "that the Queen is properly so called from the same seat of authority as the King" in a later chapter,[4] emphasizing, moreover, how useful this is for us, because she is the Queen of Christ's kingdom of mercy. He does not, however, like the Pseudo-Bonaventure, divide the Kingdom of

[1] Ch. 23 (731). [2] Pt. 2, ch. 11 (579f.). [3] 4, 26 (738A, B). [4] 30 (743B).

Heaven into that of justice and that of mercy, but lets Christ and his mother rule conjointly over the latter. In herself Mary constitutes a special hierarchy, the fourth, between the one divine and the two angelic-human hierarchies: "Singly and alone by herself she is seated and reigns in the fourth hierarchy, being placed immediately below God and above every creature",[1] which actually takes her out of the mystical body of Christ, whose principal member she is, and makes her a mythical creature between God and the angels. For though, through the grace of her divine motherhood, Mary is exalted above the angels, this does not raise her into a single hierarchy by herself but leaves her completely in the human "hierarchy". We see to what extraordinary results the uncontrolled desire to heap more and more privileges on the blessed Virgin can lead. The irony of all this is that this desire missed precisely that privilege which really belonged to her: the Immaculate Conception. The study of this was reserved to the country surrounded by the sea, once severely reprimanded by Peter of Celle, where the Franciscan theologian William of Ware took up the question so dear to the heart of Eadmer almost 200 years before.

THE IMMACULATE CONCEPTION:
WILLIAM OF WARE AND DUNS SCOTUS

William taught before 1300 in the Oxford house of studies of the Friars Minor, and apparently also for a time in Paris. According to him the Immaculate Conception had been defended also by Robert Grosseteste (1175–1253) and Alexander Neckham (d. 1217).[2] After giving a summary of the

[1] 46f. (757C–758D).
[2] *Quaestio Gulielmi Guarrae, Utrum Beata Virgo concepta fuerit in peccato originali*, ed. in *Bibliotheca Franciscana Scholastica Medii Aevi*, vol. 3, Quaracchi (1904), p. 6; but this is rejected by F. M. Mildner, "The Oxford Theologians of the Thirteenth Century and the Immaculate Conception", *MM*, 2, p. 291, for Neckham, whom, he says, William misquotes. Of Grosseteste Mildner says that "he was well on the way to explaining the doctrine of the Immaculate Conception in a correct manner" (*MM*, 2, p. 299).

contrary opinions, William asserts that he wishes to defend the Immaculate Conception, because, if he should be mistaken, he would rather be mistaken in giving the blessed Virgin too much than in giving her too little,[1] a principle later expressed by Duns Scotus in a more precise form. He works according to the axiom first employed by Eadmer—*Potuit, decuit, fecit*—though he does not use Anselm's negative definition of original sin. According to William it was possible for God to preserve the substance out of which Mary was formed from the infection of original sin inasmuch as it was destined to become the body of the Virgin, even though it was infected on the part of those who produced it. He counters the objection that the immaculate conception of Mary would impair the uniqueness of Christ, with the argument that the Son was conceived pure from the pure, but his Mother pure from the impure, and he adduces a reason of fittingness (congruity) for it that God "made his Mother as pure as he was able, and thus not only cleansed her, but preserved her from all uncleanness",[2] quoting Anselm about Mary's purity, than which nothing could be greater except only God. Against the overwhelming authority of St. Bernard he adduces the story of the laybrother's vision, and to the argument that the Immaculate Conception would limit the universality of the Redemption he replies that "all the purity of the Mother came to her through her Son; therefore she needed the passion of Christ not because of the sin that was in her, but of that which would have been in her, if her Son himself had not preserved her through faith".[3]

Some modern theologians, for example J. Lechner[4] and E. Longpré,[5] have doubted the priority of William of Ware and have alleged that he owed his teaching to the influence of his pupil, Duns Scotus. But as Emmen[6] points out, in comparison

[1] p. 4. [2] pp. 5f. [3] p. 10.
[4] *Franziskanische Studien*, 19 (1932), pp. 1–12 and 99–127.
[5] *La Vierge Immaculée*, p. 11.
[6] "Die Bedeutung der Franziskanerschule für die Mariologie", in *FS*, 36 (1954), p. 405.

with the doctrine of Ware the discussions of Duns Scotus show such tremendous progress that it is highly unlikely that the former should have owed his doctrine to the latter. And thus "William of Ware is and remains the first theologian (at least of those so far known) to dare to give the pious opinion of the 'simple people' a hearing in the lecture rooms and to defend it in a commentary on the *Sentences* of Peter Lombard. This was at that time a grave theological risk."[1]

Duns Scotus (d. 1308) developed and systematized what his master had begun and thus earned the title *Doctor Marianus* besides being *Doctor Subtilis*; and his Mariology is, indeed, very subtle. He, too, discussed the matter when commenting, like all the schoolmen, on the *Sentences* of Peter Lombard.[2] Duns Scotus had begun to teach in Oxford, where he had entered the Franciscan Order, in 1289; in 1300 he succeeded William of Ware in the chair of theology and in 1304 he went to Paris. In both universities he commented on the *Sentences*, and it is significant that in the *Oxford Opus* (now called *Ordinatio*, according to the critical Vatican edition) he made his position on the question of the Immaculate Conception much clearer than in Paris, where the atmosphere was completely hostile to this subject. The main objection to the Immaculate Conception was, of course, the idea that it was incompatible with the universality of the Redemption. The "Subtle Doctor" refuted this by asserting that the new doctrine implied the exact opposite. Christ, he said, was, indeed, the most perfect Redeemer. But a redemption that preserves from sin is more perfect than one that frees from it. As regards actual sin, this is generally admitted, since all theologians believe Mary to be completely sinless. But Christ's work is in the first place concerned with wiping out original sin, only in the second place with actual sin. Hence the

[1] Emmen, "Einführung in die Mariologie der Oxforder Franziskanerschule", *FS*, 39 (1957), p. 108.
[2] I quote from C. Balič, *Theologiae Marianae Elementa* (1933), in which all Duns Scotus' Marian passages are collected and critically edited.

universal Redeemer prevents original sin more perfectly and directly than actual sin, and as he is the most perfect Redeemer, it is only to be expected that he would exercise this most perfect act at least once.[1] And thus Duns Scotus remarks in the *Oxford Opus* that Christ would not have reconciled the Trinity perfectly, if he had not prevented the triune God from being offended in the case of at least one human being.[2]

The Immaculate Conception does not mean that Mary is under no obligation to her Son; quite the contrary: "A person is not in the highest degree indebted to the mediator, if he does not have from him the greatest good which he can have through this mediator. Now, this innocence, namely the preservation from a guilt contracted or still to be contracted, can be had through the mediator; hence no person is in the highest manner obliged to Christ as mediator, if he has preserved no one from original sin."[3] If many owe Christ grace and glory, why should not one person, at least, owe him innocence? Duns Scotus can ask this question, because he follows Anselm in his view of original sin as a privation, not as inescapably linked to concupiscence, as was the prevailing Augustinian view. Hence it was quite possible that "God could infuse into the soul of such a person in the first instant as great a grace as into another soul in circumcision or baptism".[4] And this person would have been Mary, for, as Scotus says, giving his master's principle a more precise form: "If it does not contradict the authority of the Church or of Scripture, it seems probable that to Mary the more excellent thing should be attributed."[5]

Far from exempting Mary from the Redemption, her immaculate conception implies an even greater dependence on it than the lesser perfection of the redemption of the baptised. Thus the first great breach was made into the general opposition to the "pious opinion", even though Duns

[1] *Elementa*, 22, 6ff. in *Op. Ox.* and p. 48 in *Op. Par.*   [2] p. 24, 11ff.
[3] p. 26.   [4] pp. 27-9.   [5] p. 31.

11+

Scotus was very careful in his expressions and suggested also the other, more generally accepted, view of sanctification in the womb. He was nevertheless regarded by both friends and opponents as a convinced defender of the doctrine, and this makes it highly probable that he had expressed his opinion more forcefully on some other occasion, apart from the extant texts.[1]

Duns Scotus was a philosopher and theologian, not a preacher or a devotional writer, hence he has no time for the absurdities of a Pseudo-Albert and other popular authors. He denied that the blessed Virgin, sinless as she was, had ever gone to confession, and that she had received the graces of the priesthood; nor could he accept that she could give orders to God: "The blessed Virgin", he writes, "has authority to intercede by prayer, not to command"—"habet auctoritatem impetrandi, non imperandi."[2]

OTHER FRANCISCAN DEFENDERS OF THE IMMACULATE CONCEPTION

PETER ORIOL

The Franciscan Order followed its great Doctor almost at once in accepting the doctrine of the Immaculate Conception. The most famous of his disciples was Peter Oriol (Aureolus; d. 1322), who had most probably studied under him in Paris and who later taught there himself, first in the house of his order (1316), then at the university.[3] He was an intimate friend of John XXII. His treatise on the Immaculate Conception[4] was written in 1314–15 and had a great influence on

[1] See K. Koser, "Die Immakulatelehre des Johannes Duns Scotus", in *FS*, 36 (1954), p. 345.

[2] *Elementa*, pp. 171f.

[3] Cf. N. Valois, "Pierre Auriol, Frère Mineur", in *Histoire littéraire de la France*, 33 (1906), pp. 479–527; also A. Maier, "Litterarhistorische Notizen über P. Aureoli etc.", in *Gregorianum* 29 (1948), 213–51, and L. Rosato, *Doctrina de Immaculata Beatae Virginis Mariae Conceptione*, Rome (1959).

[4] *Nondum Erant Abyssi*, ed. in *Quaestiones Disputatae de Immaculata Conceptione*, Quaracchi (1904), pp. 23–94.

the evolution of the dogma; Rosato does not hesitate to say that Oriol has written the first scholastic treatise on the subject.[1] The work is divided into six parts. In the first he quotes the authorities of Scripture and of the saints which would seem to contradict the teaching; in the second he makes a very important distinction: It is quite possible, he says, that someone might contract original sin *de jure*, that is to say, from the necessity of nature, through being conceived in the normal human way, and yet not *de facto*, in actual fact, by a special grace.[2] That Mary should actually have been a "vessel of wrath", even for a moment, is "something horrible for pious ears and devout souls".[3] This distinction made a further breach in the arguments of the opponents of the "pious opinion" and helped considerably to establish the doctrine. In Chapter 3 Oriol affirms that God could certainly preserve Mary's soul from original sin, else he would not be omnipotent,[4] and in the next he uses his master's arguments of Christ as the most perfect Redeemer and preservation from original sin as the most perfect act of redemption. He also argues from Mary's divine motherhood, which is a far greater grace than the Immaculate Conception, which it really involves, and from the absolutely sinless flesh of Christ to the equally sinless flesh of Mary. As no-one doubts that God *could* preserve her in the first instant of her creation from original sin, why should he have been so cruel and lacking in filial feeling as not to have done it?[5]

Peter Oriol's argumentation is very convincing; only in one place does it become evident that he belongs to the period which saw the decline of scholasticism, when he affirms that "the Virgin Mary was chosen to be in some way the principle [*principium*] of the Holy Spirit, inasmuch as she is the principle of his principle, the Mother of the Son, from whom the Spirit himself proceeds".[6] This is an inadmissible

---

[1] *Doctrina*, p. 106. [2] *Doctrina*, p. 47. [3] *Doctrina*, p. 48.
[4] pp. 49ff. [5] Ch. 4, pp. 54–63. [6] p. 68.

introduction of Mary into the inner-Trinitarian relations, into which no creature, not even the most exalted one, can penetrate. For though she is truly the Mother of God, because her Son was true God, she can never be his "principle"—this is only the Father.

FRANCIS OF MAYRONIS

Francis of Mayronis (d. 1328), a close friend and protégé of Pope John XXII, was another influential Franciscan defender of the Immaculate Conception. His views are discussed in an article by J. Jurič, "Franciscus de Mayronis, Immaculatae Conceptionis Eximius Vindex,"[1] which is based on his commentary on Book 3 of the *Sentences*. (I quote from Jurič, as the work itself was inaccessible to me.) According to Jurič, Francis of Mayronis links the doctrine with the Scotist view that Christ would have been incarnate even if man had not sinned; hence Mary was foreseen as his Mother before the fall of Adam.[2] He further argues that Mary could not possibly have been subject to original sin, because in that case she would have suffered a greater loss than the pains of hell[3] and the angels would have been purer than she; moreover, Christ would not have been the perfect Mediator.[4] Hence, by right of being his Mother, Mary was not subject to original sin.[5] In his sermons on the feast,[6] he discusses all the reasons for and against at great length, applying especially the verse from the Canticle "Tota pulchra es . . . et macula non est in te", as well as the principle that it is better to believe too much about Mary than too little. He further applies the words from the Creation narrative, "Let there be light", to her soul[7] and defends the belief in her bodily Assumption. In this context he places her as a separate hierarchy between God and the highest angels.[8]

---

[1] *Studi francescani*, 51 (1954), pp. 224–63.   [2] p. 261, *n.* 1.

[3] p. 251.   [4] p. 253.   [5] p. 255.

[6] I quote from *Sermones de Laudibus Sanctorum*, ed. of 1498, fols. 153–62.

[7] Fol. 159ff.   [8] Fol. 101 r⁰.

WILLIAM OF NOTTINGHAM

Yet another English Franciscan, William of Nottingham (d. 1336), followed William of Ware and Duns Scotus in defending the Immaculate Conception, though he expressed himself far more carefully than Mayronis, who seems to have been the first to affirm the doctrine apodictically. William of Nottingham's relevant article from his *Commentary on the Sentences* was first published by A. Emmen.[1]

The controversy about the Immaculate Conception went on for the rest of the fourteenth century and well into the fifteenth and after. The most important opponents of the doctrine were the Dominicans, not because they begrudged the Mother of God this privilege, but because their great doctor, Thomas Aquinas, had opposed it and they would therefore not accept the "preserving Redemption" of Duns Scotus and his followers.

CARMELITES

Besides the two great mendicant orders of Dominicans and Franciscans, now ranged on opposite sides of the fence, other thirteenth-century orders entered the lists, mostly as defenders of the doctrine. The Carmelites, who claimed from the beginning to be under the special protection of the Mother of God, came to accept it as the official teaching of their order after John Baconthorp, yet another Englishman, had taught it. Baconthorp (d. 1348), a native of Norfolk, the greatest Carmelite theologian of the time, had at first rejected the arguments of Ware, Scotus and Oriol in his *Commentary on the Sentences*, written about 1320–25. In another work, written in 1330 (*Quodlibet*, 3, q. 12 (137)), he tried to compromise by teaching that, as a daughter of Adam, she had indeed contracted original sin, but as the predestined Mother of God she had not done so—an impossible idea which he only

[1] *MM*, 5 (1943), pp. 220–60.

put forward because he believed he had read both opinions in St. Anselm, since Eadmer's work was circulating under Anselm's name. Under the influence of the former, as well as of recent legislation about the feast, Baconthorp came finally to accept the doctrine unequivocally about 1340,[1] and his whole order followed him almost immediately.

Apart from his defence of the Immaculate Conception, Baconthorp was also the first to write about Mary's special relation with his order in two treatises. In one, the *Treatise on the Rule of the Carmelite Order* (written c. 1335; both were published in *Speculum Carmelitanum*, Antwerp (1680)), he sought to prove, with much imaginary detail, that the rule of the Carmelites was in many points similar to Mary's own life; in the other, he expounded the assertion of its title, *Speculum de Institutione Ordinis ad Venerationem Virginis Deiparae*, that his order was specially instituted for the veneration of the Mother of God.[2]

SERVITES

This privilege was not only claimed by the Carmelites. Another mendicant order, the Servites of Mary, founded in the late thirteenth century, asserted that our Lady herself was their true and only founder, who established them "for her service, her glory and her glorification", as says Peter of Todi, General of the Order from 1314 to 1355, in his Legend on their origin.[3]

DEVOTION TO THE SORROWS OF MARY

Their special devotion was the sorrows of Mary, which had developed from the *Planctus Mariae* and was further elaborated during the fourteenth century, when it was given a more

[1] *In IV Sent.*, dist. 2, qs. 3 and 4.
[2] On Baconthorp see B. F. M. Xiberta, "De Magistro Johanne Baconthorp, O. Carm." in *Analecta Ordinis Carmelitarum*, vol. 6, Rome (1927); also *Bibliothèque de la revue d'hist. eccl.*, fasc. 6, Louvain (1931).
[3] See *Maria*, 2, pp. 885–907.

literary form. A. Wilmart has published a fine piece, or rather a collection of four pieces, called *Dolours, Hours, Swords* and *Sorrows* which were attached to the highly popular *Mirror of Human Salvation* which originated most probably at Strasbourg in 1324.[1] At this time the number was already fixed at seven: Simeon's prophecy, the flight into Egypt, the loss of Jesus in the Temple, his arrest and the outrages following it, his crucifixion and death, his deposition into Mary's arms and their separation at his burial; though the seventh sorrow is sometimes taken together with the sixth, and the seventh is her sorrowful waiting afterwards. The *Dolours, Hours* and *Swords* are miniature Marian offices. The Hours of the Dolours begin with the *Sub tuum praesidium* as antiphon, followed by "Lady, hear my prayer, and let my cry come unto thee", and ending with a prayer to Mary, which varies according to the Hours and asks her by her sufferings during the Passion to help the sinner who is praying to her. The realistic descriptions of the sufferings of Jesus recall the crucifixes of the time, and great stress is laid on the compassionate sorrow that pierces his Mother's heart. The *Horae* begin with the *Ave Maria* as far as *benedictus fructus tuus*, to which is added the suffering that is being contemplated, for example, "cruelly treated", "crucified", "dying", followed by a prayer to Mary for knowledge of one's sins, penitence and so forth. The prayers of the *Sword* ask the sorrowful Mother to give us a share in her sufferings; she is variously addressed as Mirror of Eternity, Bower of the Divinity, Daughter of the omnipotent Father, Spouse of the Holy Spirit, Resting-place of the Holy Trinity. The fourth part, the *Sorrows*, is written in a different form and style, not as an office but as a meditation. The author tells of a Dominican Friar who received a private revelation on the sufferings of Jesus and Mary, which inspired the following meditations. Each of the seven sorrows begins with the same prayer: "Hail Mary, merciful Mother of Christ, heavenly

[1] *Auteurs spirituels et textes dévots du moyen-âge latin* (1932), pp. 522–36.

Empress. You, divine Virgin, are the gentle comforter of those who sorrow in this life." The simple rhymed meditations are a touching expression of medieval Marian piety, devoid of jarring exaggerations.

THE ANGELUS

About this time, the Angelus became a popular devotion, though in a more primitive form than today. Its practice originated with the Franciscans; at their general chapter, held at Assisi in 1269, the preachers were instructed to tell the people to say the *Hail Mary*—still in its short form—in the evening, at the threefold ringing of the bell. In 1317 the Dominicans at Frankfurt recommended the same practice, and in 1327 John XXII ordered the *Ave* bells to be rung at Rome. The practice, enriched with indulgences, soon spread throughout the Church.[1]

THE LATER FOURTEENTH CENTURY

The later fourteenth century was, on the whole, a time of decline. Scholasticism deteriorated into barren, hair-splitting nominalism; the popes were in exile at Avignon, and after their return to Rome began the scandal of the Great Schism. Italy was torn by the struggles between her city states; England and France were locked in the Hundred Years' War; Wycliffe preached reform as well as rebellion in England; in Germany the ideal of the knight was fast declining, and general insecurity prevailed. On the other hand, mysticism flourished, but mostly in its speculative form, as in Master Eckhart, Tauler, *The Cloud of Unknowing*, in which the humanity of Christ, and thus also the blessed Virgin, played only a negligible part. St. Bridget of Sweden is an exception; indeed, her Revelations reflect very faithfully the Marian teaching and devotion of her time.

[1] See S. Beissel, *Geschichte der Verehrung Mariens im 16. und 17. Jahrhundert*, p. 18.

ST. BRIDGET

As Bridget was a member of the Third Order of St. Francis she followed the Franciscan teaching on the Immaculate Conception, placing its affirmation on the lips of Mary herself,[1] and she emphasized especially her sorrows under the Cross. Bridget does not, however, accept the traditional number of seven, but has a quite different conception and enumeration. She assumes six sorrows: the sorrows of knowledge, because Mary foreknew the Passion, of hearing, when she heard her Son insulted, of sight, when she saw him crucified (Bridget reproduces the popular idea that Mary fainted), of touch, when she wrapped him in the grave-clothes, of desire, when she wanted to accompany him to heaven at the Ascension, and of compassion, in the tribulations of the Apostles.[2] At the death of Christ, which is described most realistically, her heart was pierced by five swords.[3] In heaven Mary defends Christians against the devil,[4] and—a very strange idea—shortens the life of sinners so that their sufferings in hell will be less than they would have been had they lived longer.[5] Bridget affirms unequivocally and without the necessary theological safeguards Mary's share in the objective redemption of mankind, once speaking in the person of Christ—"And therefore I can well say that my Mother and I have saved man as it were with one heart, I by suffering in my heart and flesh, she in the sorrow and love of her heart"[6]—another time in the person of Mary herself: "As Adam and Eve sold the world for one apple, so my Son and I have redeemed the world as it were with one heart."[7] She is even called "saviour" (*salvatrix*).[8] This implies naturally that all graces come to us through Mary (cf. *Revel.*, 1, 50 and frequently elsewhere). Bridget's *Sermo Angelicus de Virginis*

---

[1] *Revelationes*, 6, 49, ed. Turrecremata, Rome (1628).   [2] *Rev.*, 6, 57.
[3] 1, 27.
[4] *Revelaciones Extravagantes*, ed. L. Hollman, Uppsala (1956), ch. 89, 2.
[5] 89, 10ff.   [6] 3, 5.   [7] *Revelationes*, 1, 35.   [8] *Extravagantes*, 56, 14.

11*

Excellentia [1] is, as the title implies, wholly devoted to Mary; it was the night Office she composed for the order she had founded (Bridgettines, or Order of the Most Holy Saviour). It presents the blessed Virgin in the plan of God, in divine thought before the creation of the world, in the thought of the angels, of Adam and the Patriarchs, as the Mother of Wisdom who illumines our ignorance, and traces her life from her birth to her bodily assumption into heaven.

THE CONTROVERSY ABOUT THE IMMACULATE CONCEPTION CONTINUED

While the people prayed to the Virgin, made pilgrimages to her shrines and found consolation in their trust in the heavenly Mother for the many ills that beset them, the controversy about the Immaculate Conception continued. It came to a head in 1387, when a Catalan Dominican, John de Montesono (or Monzon), publicly declared the doctrine to be against the Faith. Called upon to retract by the faculty of theology in Paris, he refused, and the case was brought before the Bishop of Paris. He formally condemned Montesono and sentenced him to prison if he could be caught. The Dominicans supported him, as he was defending the teaching of St. Thomas, and appealed to the anti-Pope in Avignon—an action that cost them much of their popularity in France. A Franciscan, John Vitalis, composed a *Defensorium*, in which he once more stated the doctrine and summed up the controversy. This work was used by Pierre d'Ailly (d. 1420), the Chancellor of the University and later a cardinal, when he asserted that both bishops and the theological faculty of Paris had the right to condemn heretical propositions. Montesono was finally condemned and excommunicated, not because he opposed the Immaculate Conception, which at that time was still under discussion, but because he declared it to be heretical. Nicholas Eymeric, General Inquisitor of Aragon,

[1] In vol. 2 of the Turrecremata edition of 1628.

supported Montesono and was exiled by Juan I of Aragon in 1393.[1]

The opposition of the Dominicans at that stage was not altogether without foundation, if we consider that the doctrine was frequently proposed as an outcome of devotion rather than of theological considerations, as was, for example, stated at the end of the treatise of Peter of Candia (later Pope Alexander V) on the subject: "I say without prejudice to the decision of Mother Church, if this matter should be settled at some future date, that, not compelled by any reason, but solely by the purest devotion, I believe firmly and confess simply, that the most blessed Virgin Mary, Mother of God, who is exalted above the angels, was never attacked by the stain of original sin . . . And I exhort all the faithful to believe this, for if I should deviate from the truth through ignorance, I would rather err by an excess of praise than of blame."[2] It is not surprising that such a principle, which is based on the emotions rather than the intellect, should have been rejected by the disciples of St. Thomas—even though Duns Scotus and Mayronis based their teaching on quite different premises.

JOHN GERSON

But the opponents of the Immaculate Conception were not the only ones to plead for sound theological principles in the matter of Mariology. The famous mystical theologian John Gerson (d. 1429), Chancellor of the University of Paris and as such bound by oath to defend the privilege of Mary, laid down some very pertinent rules on the subject,[3] which are

[1] Cf. I. Brady, "The Development of the Doctrine of the Immaculate Conception in the Fourteenth Century after Aureoli", in *Franciscan Studies*, 15 (1955), pp. 198f.

[2] *Tractatus de Immaculata Deiparae Conceptione*, ed. by A. Emmen, *Tractatus Quatuor* (1954), p. 334.

[3] I quote from the Du Pin edition of his works, 1706, as at the time of writing the new critical edition had not progressed beyond vol. 1, containing only his letters. See also A. Combes, "La doctrine mariale du Chancelier Jean Gerson", in *Maria*, 2, p. 865ff.

contained in his treatise "On the Assumption of the Humanity of Christ".[1] After reproducing the argument of Duns Scotus for the Immaculate Conception, about Christ as the most perfect Redeemer and Mary as the most perfectly redeemed creature, which he qualifies as a "probable opinion", he goes on to say that this does not imply Mary's equality with her Son.[2] Christ, he explains, gave his Mother, both at the beginning and in her later life, those graces which were suited to her, "according to the order of his wisdom". He could, indeed, have given both to her and to his own humanity many other graces which would also have been "fitting"; he could, for example, have caused her to be born in perfect felicity, and this might have been fitting, because it would have honoured his Mother, but in actual fact he did not do so, and to draw such a conclusion would be heretical.[3] Gerson then castigates some of the absurd ideas of his time, many of which we have already encountered. It is not true, he says that Christ communicated to his Mother as soon as she had been conceived or born the perfect use of reason, even though he could have done so, and if he had done it, it would have been fitting. "To assert the opposite either in writing or in preaching is decidedly rash [temerarium], also that she had never slept, or that even in her sleep she always actually contemplated God." Christ could also have given his Mother a perfect foreknowledge of her own and her Son's life; again, it would have been fitting if he had done so—but in fact he did not do this.[4] In short, Gerson demolishes Eadmer's principle of potuit, decuit, fecit, which had become so popular in the later Middle Ages, by showing to what absurdities it could and did lead. But, some people ask, why did Christ honour his Mother with certain graces and not with others? Gerson replies with a strong affirmation of the divine transcendence, so often forgotten in the desire to explain everything, even the deepest mysteries: "Who are you, man, that

[1] Du Pin, 1, pp. 450–57.   [2] 451C.   [3] 452B–453A.   [4] 453A.

you investigate the mind of the Lord? . . . Rather place your finger on your talkative mouth and recognize your limitations." Nevertheless, pious imagination may supplement the scanty data of Scripture, as long as these are not contradicted.[1]

Gerson himself made use of this concession when he wrote his long treatise on the *Magnificat*,[2] a fine document of his ardent devotion to the Mother of God as well as of his great learning. For him, too, as for most Western Christians of the time, Mary is above all the Mother of Mercy; indeed, he reproduces the view of Pseudo-Albert of the division of the Kingdom of God into one of justice and one of mercy, the latter being the part of Mary, though he qualifies his statement by the word *quodammodo*—in a certain way.[3] In her all the beauties of creation are concentrated; though Gerson stresses her spiritual rather than her physical beauty.[4] He sees her especially in relation to the Redemption. This is worked out in various parts of the treatise. Her part in our salvation rests on the fact that she, who was most beloved by Christ, without doubt conformed herself most thoroughly to his will "so that she voluntarily consented that her Son should be crucified for our redemption, which she desired more than anyone except her Son himself".[5] Therefore she had a certain share in the priesthood. Wherever she may have been at the Last Supper, when she ate the Passover she received Christ spiritually; and "on the same Thursday night, though she was not invested with the character of the priestly office . . . she nevertheless was now, and before and afterwards, anointed into the Royal Priesthood, not indeed to consecrate, but to offer this pure Victim . . . on the altar of her heart."[6] Therefore she may be called the "Mother of the Eucharist",[7] for she is the "Mother of good grace" and "the key-bearer of the wine-cellars of the King of Peace"[8]; therefore Gerson thanks her, who has offered such a Victim for us.[9] He, too, uses the

---

[1] 453B–D.   [2] Du Pin, 4, pp. 235–512.   [3] 286A, B.   [4] 3 (265A).
[5] 6 (314D).   [6] 2 9 (397A, B).   [7] 418A and 451A.   [8] 418B.   [9] 419B.

metaphor of the neck, because Mary connects the members of the Church with Christ, their head, from whom she is the first to receive the rivers of life which she passes on in her turn.[1] Just because Gerson had a profound mystical devotion to the blessed Virgin, he opposed the puerile fancies to which many of his contemporaries were addicted, but, on the other hand, he held that "those generations of men who do not devoutly venerate Mary, are to be considered degenerate."[2] He himself invoked her in his sermon at the Council of Constance (1414–18) convened to heal the Great Schism and bring about reforms in the Church, in words filled with filial confidence in her spiritual presence at the assembly: "For you are indeed present, even if perhaps not in the bodily dimension . . . You are present by your spiritual influence and regard . . . imploring the advent of the Holy Spirit . . . by your mediation, most merciful Virgin, whom this Holy Spirit has filled not only sufficiently or even abundantly, but to a most exuberant overflowing as from a fountain, so that you may communicate this fullness also to us."[3]

THE COUNCIL OF BASLE

Though the Council healed the Schism, it did not effect the reform of the Church which was so greatly needed. Only thirteen years later another Council had to be called, the ill-fated Council of Basle (1431–49), on the agenda of which was also the controversial question of the Immaculate Conception. In December 1431, almost exactly a thousand years after Ephesus, the Fathers of the Council celebrated the feast and commissioned Cardinal Louis d'Aleman to collect all the available material on the question. The real discussion began only after the official dissolution of the Council, in May 1438. Once again the Dominicans, especially the Spanish papal theologian (cardinal in 1439) John of Torquemada, were the foremost opponents of the doctrine, its chief defender being

[1] 427C.   [2] 5 (300A).   [3] Du Pin, 3, 1234C.

the Franciscan John of Segovia. On 15 September 1438 the decree on the feast and the doctrine was approved, but as the Council had no longer legal authority the decree had no binding force, and the definition had to wait over four centuries longer to become a dogma of the universal Church.

BERNARDINE OF SIENA

The Council of Basle was continued at Ferrara (1438–9) and Florence (1439–42), with the special object of effecting the reunion with the Orthodox Church; this was actively supported by one of the most popular Franciscan preachers of the age, Bernardine of Siena (d. 1444), who also holds a special place in the Marian devotion of the time. Unfortunately he did not subscribe to the sane caution of John Gerson, but let his enthusiasm carry him to astonishing lengths. If we here criticize some of his more extravagant statements this is in no way meant to belittle his sanctity; but it would be dishonest, in a work tracing the development of Marian doctrine and devotion, to bypass such deformations if we would understand both the popular "Mariolatry" of the late Middle Ages and the subsequent Protestant reaction to it.[1] A great deal of the material contained in these sermons is taken almost literally from earlier sources, especially from authors of Bernardine's own order, such as Olivi and Ubertino of Casale. This, of course, will not be again discussed in the following pages.

Strangely enough, Bernardine did not teach the Immaculate Conception, because, as he said himself, he did not want to concern himself with the disputes of the schools. He would only affirm Mary's unique sanctification in view of her divine motherhood,[2] because Christ came especially to redeem

---

[1] I quote from the critical Quaracchi edition of the Latin sermons—the basis for his popular Italian sermons—especially from the "Treatise on the Blessed Virgin" which is made up of these sermons, most of which are contained in vol. 6 (1959), supplemented by material from other volumes.

[2] *Sermons on Feasts of the Blessed Virgin*, 4 (vol. 4, p. 538).

Mary, rather than any other creature.[1] After that begin the pious exaggerations, not to say absurdities. For even while still in the womb, he says, Mary had the use of her freewill, complete understanding and a more perfect gift of contemplation while asleep than any other saint while awake.[2] From the Annunciation she knew most perfectly everything pertaining to the mystery of the Incarnation, and by her consent to the conception of the Son of God she merited more than all other creatures, both angels and men, together in all their actions and thoughts. For through this assent she merited the dominion of the whole world, the plenitude of all graces and all knowledge.[3] For Bernardine sees Mary more and more as independent of Christ, and does not hesitate to say: "Even if she had not been the Mother of God, she would nevertheless have been the mistress of the world."[4] It is this sermon that contains the most extraordinary statements, which can hardly be dismissed as "occasional exaggerations" for which this enthusiastic client of Mary could hardly be blamed—as is done, for example, by O. Stegmüller.[5] For here Bernardine attempts to prove nothing less than that the blessed Virgin is in some respects superior to God himself. As this statement may seem incredible, I propose to give a literal translation of the relevant passages.

The blessed Virgin could do more concerning God than God could do concerning himself. For there were certain oppositions and contradictions between God and the Virgin which were reconciled when God approached the Virgin. Namely, first, it was impossible for God not to generate; it was impossible for the Virgin to give birth.

[1] *Sermons on Feasts*, 3, 3 (557).
[2] 1, 2 (p. 541); also 3, 3 (557) and elsewhere.
[3] 3, 1 (552); so also vol. 2, p. 374.
[4] Serm. 8 (= Serm. 61 for Wednesday after Easter), "On the Superadmirable Grace and Glory of the Mother of God", vol. 2, ch. 7, p. 377.
[5] *Lexikon der Marienkunde*, s.v. "Bernardinus v. Siena".

Secondly, it was impossible for God to generate anyone who was not God; it was impossible for the Virgin to generate God. Further, it was impossible for God to generate with another person; it was impossible for the Virgin to give birth without another person. Now, God came to the Virgin, and it was necessary for the Virgin to give birth, and to none other than God, and not by any other than God. Now, God could only generate God from himself; and yet the Virgin made a Man. God could only generate someone infinite, immortal, eternal, impassible, impalpable, invisible, in the form of God; but the Virgin made him finite, mortal, poor, temporal, palpable, sentient, visible, in the form of a servant, in a created nature . . . O the unthinkable power of the Virgin Mother! . . . One Hebrew woman invaded the house of the eternal King; one girl, I do not know by what caresses, pledges or violence, seduced, deceived and, if I may say so, wounded and enraptured the divine heart and ensnared the Wisdom of God . . . Surely it was quite impossible for God to do such a thing by himself. Therefore this is the prerogative of the Virgin that, since God could not do it, he did not concede this to any other creature.[1]

This extraordinary description, which surely sounds more like the legends of Jupiter than the mystery of the Incarnation, can scarcely be excused by a perfervid poetic imagination, and it is certainly not permissible in a preacher. How could an illiterate congregation (for the Latin sermons were Bernardine's foundations of his Italian ones) still distinguish between the divine Father and the human Mother of God when they were told that Mary could do more than God? Nor is this the only passage which seems to place Mary on a level with, or even above, God. For he insists that the Virgin "has added certain perfections to the Maker of the universe, namely, a beginning to the eternal principle, a period of time to the divine eternity,

[1] 1, 4 (vol. 2, p. 357).

corporeal quantity to the immense infinity, a new beauty to the eternal loveliness".[1] St. Paul had seen in the Incarnation a self-emptying of the Godhead, not an addition to the divine perfections, and until then this had been the doctrine of the Church and her theologians; we can hardly doubt that the Mother of God would herself be the first to repudiate such fancies, which have no foundation either in Scripture or in tradition and can only bring the Catholic religion into disrepute, however great the personal sanctity of the preacher and his beneficial influence in other spheres.

But even with these praises Bernardine has not yet said enough; he now wants to prove that "only the blessed Virgin Mary has done more for God, or just as much, as God has done for all mankind"; for "God fashioned man from the soil, but Mary formed him from her pure blood; God impressed on man his image, but Mary impressed hers on God ... God taught man wisdom, but Mary taught Christ to flee from the hurtful and follow her; God nourished man with the fruits of paradise, but she nourished him with her most holy milk." Therefore Mary did more for God than God did for man, "so that I may say this for our consolation, that because of the blessed Virgin, whom, however, God made himself, he is in some way under a greater obligation to us than we to him".[2]

It is characteristic that the fact that the blessed Virgin herself was made by God occurs to Bernardine almost as an afterthought; for all along he seems to have considered her as an independent personage conferring favours on him. Enough has been quoted to show that the Mariology of pre-Reformation times had really in many cases become Mariolatry, and needed to be pruned from excesses which could only lead to a debased form of Christianity among the people who were thus encouraged to place the blessed Virgin beside or even above God.

[1] I, 9, p. 380.   [2] I, 11, p. 380f.

THE LATER FIFTEENTH CENTURY

ANTONINUS OF FLORENCE

The more scholarly minds of the period avoided the worst of these exaggerations. Antoninus, the Dominican Archbishop of Florence (d. 1458), while reproducing the teaching of his predecessors, insisted particularly on Mary's part in the Redemption. The long Titulus XV in the Fourth Part of his *Summa Theologica* is entirely devoted to Mariology and greatly indebted to the *Mariale* of Pseudo-Albert.[1] Mary communicated to us her greatest good when offering Jesus in the Temple,[2] and was associated with the Father of mercies in his greatest work of mercy, when she shared in the passion of her Son "and thus became the helper of our redemption and the Mother of our spiritual generation".[3] She is even called "the priestess of justice [*sacerdotissa*], because she did not spare her own Son", but stood by the Cross, "prepared to offer the Son of God for the salvation of the world",[4] a view that has contributed to the later discussion of Mary's priestly function. Antoninus even writes that "through her Son she has absolved us from our guilt and punishment",[5] a bold expression, but which probably struck the saint's contemporaries less forcibly than it does us.

DIONYSIUS THE CARTHUSIAN

One of the most influential and fertile authors of this last century before the Reformation split European Christendom was Dionysius the Carthusian (d. 1471), a mystic and ecstatic, who had a special love of the blessed Virgin from his earliest youth.[6] He affirms her immaculate conception in his later works, after the Council of Basle had defined it—for example, in his *Commentary on the Sentences*.[7] He sings Mary's praises

[1] I have used the 1480 edition, the more recent ones being inaccessible to me.
[2] 26, 1.   [3] 14, 2.   [4] 3, 3.   [5] 16, 2.
[6] See vol. 35, 484D of his collected works, 44 volumes, 1896–1935.
[7] Vol. 23, 93A, 97C and 98D.

especially in his two treatises on the subject, "On the Praise and Dignity of Mary"[1] and "On the Dignity and Praises of the Blessed Virgin Mary".[2] Dionysius strongly affirms Mary's position as mediatress between her Son and men;[3] indeed he does not hesitate to call her "Redemptress of the world",[4] though with some safeguards. Using the traditional Eve–Mary parallel, he says that as woman had a share in the Fall, so also "a Man redeemed the world not without woman as an additional cause [*nec absque concausante muliere*]". This does not mean that Christ would not have sufficed; nevertheless, for many reasons, "Mary is considered the 'Saviouress' of the world because she co-operated with Christ." She could be called *salvatrix*, even though she was not herself the cause of salvation or of grace, but "because of her help [*propter subventionem*], for through her prayer she obtains for us grace and felicity", and many despairing men have been "redeemed" by her,[5] since her com-passion under the Cross renders her Son more willing to help us than he would otherwise have been. Being himself a mystic, Dionysius sees Mary particularly as a contemplative. Even before the Incarnation she had a perfect knowledge of the Trinity,[6] and later Christ taught her the most perfect mystical theology.[7] In a certain way she saw the essence of God even in this life, though not continuously,[8] and after the coming of the Holy Spirit the Apostles came to her with their problems to be instructed.[9]

BERNARDINE OF BUSTI

The whole Mariology of this time is summed up in the enormous *Mariale* (c. 1478) of the Franciscan Bernardine of Busti (d. 1515), which had a tremendous success. "One realizes the decadence of the period", writes Laurentin,[10]

---

[1] Vol. 35, 479–574.   [2] Vol. 36, 13–174.
[3] *On the Praise*, 1, 21 (vol. 35, 492).   [4] 2, 8 (516).
[5] 2, 9 (516f.).   [6] 2, 14 (519ff.).   [7] 2, 17 (522ff.).
[8] 2, 18.   [9] 2, 24 (529).   [10] *Court Traité*[4], pp.69f.

"which has established the reputation of this compilation whose sometimes excellent ideas are only too often drowned in a mass of extreme or inconsistent opinions." To give an idea of this now quite forgotten work,[1] I shall just quote some of the author's statements, though very few of them are original. Bernardine is particularly anxious to prove the Immaculate Conception, basing himself especially on authors of his own order, such as Duns Scotus, Francis de Mayronis and Peter Oriol, and inveighs in unmeasured terms against its opponents. He even quotes St. Thomas Aquinas as a defender, on the grounds that he appeared to someone in a vision and explained that when he wrote the relevant passage in the *Summa* he only meant to refer to the divine ordinance according to which the blessed Virgin would have contracted original sin if her Son had not preserved her from it,[2] and this story is followed by a series of miracles confirming the doctrine. At her birth Mary did not cry like other children, but chanted with the angels,[3] and he repeats the idea of Pseudo-Albert that she knew rhetoric, logic, physics, metaphysics and all other possible departments of knowledge to perfection; for if anyone else had this knowledge, God must have given it in a much higher degree to his Spouse.[4] At the age of three she was as wise as a woman of thirty;[5] she is the mistress of the world, because if a son dies without issue his mother succeeds him.[6] In the last sermons, on Mary's coronation, Bernardine follows his namesake of Siena in asserting that God could only generate an eternal and immortal Son, while Mary made him finite and mortal,[7] and he finally affirms Mary's jurisdiction of grace, so that no grace or virtue comes to man that is not dispensed by Mary.[8]

[1] Over a thousand double-column pages in the third volume of the edition of 1588 of Bernardine's works, which I have used.
[2] Sermon 7, on the Conception, p. 79.
[3] Sermon 1 on the nativity of the blessed Virgin Mary, p. 133.
[4] Serm. 5 on the same feast, p. 186.   [5] p. 262.   [6] p. 949.
[7] p. 967.   [8] p. 970.

The wildest legends and the most exaggerated claims are mixed up with sound Mariological statements in a hodge-podge of a book whose style is as impossible as its contents. As Laurentin says: "A purification was necessary."[1] But before approaching the age of the Reformers, we must throw a glance at the developments in the Greek Church, before the catastrophe of the fall of Constantinople in 1453.

THE EASTERN CHURCH

While in the West Marian doctrine and devotion developed considerably between the eleventh and fifteenth centuries, in the East they remained in some respects more static. For here the three influences that largely determined Western developments were absent: the Augustinian doctrine of original sin, which played such a decisive part in the controversy about the Immaculate Conception; an illiterate and often still semi-barbarian laity; and scholasticism. Most of the authors who will now be considered extolled Mary's purity in the highest terms and are therefore frequently cited as witnesses for the Immaculate Conception by Latin theologians, so for example by M. Jugie in his book *L'Immaculée Conception dans l'Écriture sainte et dans la tradition orientale*.[2] In order to avoid too many repetitions I shall state at once that it seems to me that the whole question was seen by the Greeks in an altogether different light from that in which it was considered by Western theologians. In the Greek Church original sin had never played the same preponderant part as in post-Augustinian Western thought. From very early times it had been assumed as an indisputable fact that Mary was the purest creature imaginable, the highest angels not excepted. St. John of Damascus had even considered her active conception to have been without sin, but as he did not share the Augustinian view of original sin as an inherited guilt transmitted through the sexual act, the problem never presented itself to

[1] *Court traité*, p. 69.   [2] Rome (1952).

him in the way it did to Latin theologians. For the Greeks saw original sin far more as mortality with all its implications, and as the Theotokos was subject to this, they did not exempt her from it.[1] On the other hand, though they affirmed Mary's complete purity, they were less interested than the Western theologians in the question of the precise moment when this had been established. We might almost say that the Latins considered the question from the historical, the Greeks from the metaphysical, point of view; the former were concerned about when this purity had begun, the latter were only interested in the fact that it existed. For this reason I do not think one can claim these Greek authors for the Immaculate Conception. They would without a doubt all have agreed with St. Anselm, that "it was fitting that this Virgin should shine with a degree of purity than which no greater can be imagined apart from God"[2]—but this did not prevent the saint of Canterbury from firmly asserting that Mary was conceived in sin. Hence we can hardly assert that the same or similar expressions in the works of the Greek authors must necessarily imply belief in the doctrine in the sense of the later definition.

JOHN MAUROPOUS

John Mauropous (d. before 1079), Metropolitan of Euchaites, a city of Pontus, was both a preacher and a poet, who wrote a sermon on the Dormition[3] in which he continued the Greek tradition of the double assumption; for he stated that Mary's body followed after her soul, but said nothing of the two being reunited.[4] She, the Virgin foretold by many signs (*polysymbolos*),[5] is above the cherubim;[6] in heaven she intercedes for men, providing for the needs of the Church and increasing our hope; for she will propitiate her Son, himself

---

[1] For this whole question see especially D. T. Strotmann, "La Théotokos, Premices des Justifiés", in *Irenikon*, 27 (1954), pp. 122–41, and J. Meyendorff, *Introduction à l'étude de Grégoire Palamas*, Paris (1959), pp. 317–22.

[2] *Cur Deus Homo*, 2, 18.   [3] *PG*, 120, 1075–1115.

[4] 20, 1097A.   [5] 27 (1104B).   [6] 28 (1105A).

the Father of Mercies (there is no division between Christ's realm of justice and Mary's kingdom of mercy as in some Latin writers), from whom she will obtain good things for us.[1]

MICHAEL PSELLOS

Michael Psellos (d. c. 1078), a typical Byzantine "polyhistor", courtier and philosopher, wrote a homily on the Annunciation[2] in which he praises Mary's purity in the highest terms. Her soul, which was most akin to God, shone in her stainless body and contained it rather than was contained by it, enhancing its splendour. Indeed, though she trod the earth she rather seemed a god with a body (this, of course, is a typical Byzantine form of speech, in which "god" does not mean the Christian Creator). Though still on earth she was never far removed from the Trinity, and even before conceiving him she saw God more clearly than the seraphim. Her body was made of the finest elements and prepared like a sanctuary for her soul. She is the ladder by which God descended to us and we ascend to him; but though this may sound like St. Bernard's image of the aqueduct its meaning is different; it refers, not to the individual who reaches God through his devotion to Mary, but to the human nature that was elevated through her childbearing.[3] As Eve's transgression was followed by a curse, so Mary's obedience to the Commandments procured a blessing. For our race had inherited the curse until the Virgin appeared, who became a rampart against the flood of evil, because she had not eaten from the Tree of Knowledge, hence had not sinned like Eve—a highly symbolic mode of expression which certainly cannot be interpreted as referring to the Immaculate Conception in the Western sense, as it seems rather to imply a personal decision.[4]

[1] 32 (1109D–1111A).   [2] PO, 16, 517–25.   [3] 4 (pp. 520f.).
[4] 5 (p. 522).

THEOPHYLACT

Theophylact (d. after 1092), a disciple of Psellos, was a deacon of the Hagia Sophia in Constantinople and tutor of the Emperor Michael VII's son, who later became Archbishop of Achrida in Bulgaria, where he suffered greatly from the absence of the Byzantine civilization to which he was accustomed. An interesting instance of how far language can influence doctrine is his exegesis of *kecharitomene*, mistranslated in the Vulgate as *gratia plena*, an expression from which the Latin authors deduced all the effects of Mary's fullness of grace discussed in the preceding pages. Theophylact sees in the word no more than that Mary was pleasing to God—grace does not come into his interpretation at all.[1] This, however, does not mean that he does not attribute the highest sanctity to her, which surpasses all creation.[2] As in most of these later Marian homilies, great stress is laid on her— apocryphal—introduction into the Holy of Holies; she was placed there because, Theophylact asserts, the High Priest realized that what was said in the Old Testament about the Ark actually referred to the Mother of God, who was worthy to live in the place where even the High Priest was allowed to enter only once a year, because she was of a purity that transcended all nature and "justified from the womb"[3]— which Jugie thinks implies the Immaculate Conception.[4] But this is no more than the opponents of the Immaculate Conception in the West, too, would admit, and the author goes on to say that Christ broke down the partition and gave all the baptized access to the Holy of Holies, and it was for this reason that the blessed Virgin was first received into it, since another woman, Eve, had caused us to be expelled from paradise.[5] The whole is a mystical interpretation of the

---

[1] *Comm. on Luke*, 1, 26ff. (*PG*, 123, 701D).
[2] *Homily on the Presentation*, 1 (*PG*, 126, 129B). [3] 7 (136D–137A).
[4] *L'Immaculée Conception*, p. 200. [5] 7 (138A)–8 (140A).

apocryphal story, which can hardly be taken to prove the author's belief in the Western doctrine.

JOHN PHOURNAS

At the beginning of the twelfth century there seems to have been a fairly strong reaction against the idea of the double assumption, as appears from the work of a little-known theologian, John Phournas.[1] He opposes "certain people" who think to honour the body of Mary by transferring it from one place to another while it had still to wait for the final resurrection like that of the other saints.[2] Phournas, on the contrary, affirms that Mary, like her Son, rose again on the third day; for as the bodies of both Adam and Eve had undergone corruption so "now the two bodies [of Jesus and Mary], having first shaken off corruption, have become the first-fruits of the hoped-for incorruption";[3] for Christ glorified the Theotokos together with himself, because he had taken his body from her—an argumentation which had also been used by Cosmas Vestitor. The same opinion is stated in almost the same words by a later writer, Michael Glykas (d. 1204), in his *Annals*.[4]

NEOPHYTUS THE RECLUSE

Neophytus the Recluse (d. c. 1220), a priest-monk and self-taught scholar, wrote two Marian sermons,[5] the first of which has an interesting illustration of Mary's purity, but which, again, I do not think refers to the Immaculate Conception. He says that just as in our Lord's parable a woman mixed leaven into three measures of flour, so also the Creator

---

[1] His "Discourse on the Translation of the Most Venerable Body of the Theotokos" was published in an appendix to the *Homilies of Theophanes Kerameus*, Jerusalem (1860), pp. 271-6.

[2] p. 271.   [3] p. 273.   [4] 3 (*PG*, 158, 440C).

[5] Ed. Jugie in *PO*, 16, one on the Nativity of Mary, pp. 528-32, the other on the Presentation, pp. 533-8.

has fashioned and renewed our aged paste through the divinely fashioned and pure leaven. For this is the astounding miracle, that the most pure Baker has mixed himself in ineffable manner with this most pure leaven and has thus refashioned the whole dough from it.[1] Surely Mary could be called a "pure leaven" also if she had only been sanctified in the womb? Later in the sermon she is praised as the Mistress of the World—an expression as popular in the East as in the West—predestined before the ages to be the dwelling-place of the Word. She is the Queen of Queens, the animated temple of the Trinity, the palace of the King of Glory, the heaven where God dwells. The Byzantine preachers evidently saw her far more in relation to God and less as "useful" for men than their Latin contemporaries, though Neophytus also gives her such epithets as "Hope of the Faithful", and at the end of his sermons asks for her intercession, but again in much simpler terms than most Western authors of the period.[2] In his Sermon on the Presentation, which, naturally, repeats the apocryphal story and the implications of Mary's sojourn in the Holy of Holies, she is called, as in the West, "the mediatress between God and sinners".[3]

GERMANUS II

Germanus II (d. 1240) was a deacon at St. Sophia when the Latin Crusaders occupied Constantinople in 1204 and treated the Christians there as if they were the infidels from whom they wanted to free the holy places in Palestine. He subsequently retired to a monastery and became patriarch of his city in 1222. In view of the experiences of his youth it is perhaps not so very surprising that he should have violently opposed the reunion negotiations which preceded the Council of Lyons (1245). He rivalled his earlier namesake in his devotion to the Theotokos, which is expressed especially in his long *Sermon on the Annunciation*.[4] He can, however, be no

[1] 3 (530).   [2] 531f.   [3] 537.   [4] *PG*, 140, 677–736.

more considered a witness to the Immaculate Conception
than the other Byzantine theologians. It is interesting that one
of the later proof passages of the Latins, Gen. 3.15, which has
been discussed in the first chapter of this book, is quoted in
this sermon, but with reference to Christ, since Germanus, of
course, read the text in the Greek translation. There the seed
is referred to as *autos*, "he" (not, as in the Hebrew, as "it"),
and thus understood of Christ, but not, as in the Vulgate, as
"she". Therefore the Greek theologians could not establish a
relation of this particular text to our Lady, as the Latins did
later,[1] though Germanus naturally continued to emphasize the
ancient parallel Eve–Mary: "Eve was cursed, while Mary
found favour."[2] In the true Byzantine tradition, Germanus
did not see Mary so much in the context of sin and salvation,
which must be presupposed in order to understand the later
definition of her immaculate conception, as did the Latins; he
considered her in the whole "economy" that set man, become
mortal through Adam's transgression, once more on the road
to immortality and "deification". One passage is typical of
his, and indeed of most Byzantine thought about Mary:
"The Virgin, being human because she is their [the first
parents'] daughter, does indeed bear certain slight characteristics of their life. For she is endowed with a mortal body and
surrounded by what is perishable, yet far superior and more
divine. For she has anticipated the pledge of incorruption and
has ascended to the immaterial existence of the angels even
whilst living among men; she is known as the ladder reaching
to heaven . . . even though her base was on earth."[3] Everything about her is worthy of the great mystery of the Incarnation, even though she was a daughter of Eve and had put
on the garments of skin. Yet the thickness of the skins was not
in her—that is to say, the turbulence of life and its untimely
worries (again, no mention of guilt, only of the consequences
of the Fall), for she was consecrated to God when she was

[1] cf. 7 (684C).   [2] 8 (684D).   [3] 12 (689B).

three years old.[1] Later in the sermon Germanus reverts to the biblical image of the ladder, which seems at first sight similar to the Western "neck" or "aqueduct"; its meaning, however, is different; for whereas the Latin images are meant to express Mary's position as mediating between God and man by her intercession, the "ladder" of Germanus refers to her position as Theotokos, in whose womb the divine and the human natures were united.[2] Thus also her surpassing purity is not attached to her own conception, but to the conception of Christ. For when Germanus says that her completely purified mind is inaccessible to any impure approach whatsoever, that she is surrounded by a fiery sword and guarded in every way from the fraudulent serpent, this refers not to the moment of her conception but to the moment of the Incarnation, because Eve's surrender to the serpent is contrasted with Mary's being overshadowed by the Spirit.[3] Then Germanus asks her to tear up the *chirographon*, the writ issued against us, with her immaculate hands, which have carried Christ, for she carried him for just this purpose, that the debts of mankind should be paid.[4] The patriarch ends his long sermon with the request that Mary should introduce all who confess her to be Theotokos into the heavenly Kingdom, for her mediation is our anchor of hope after God.[5]

THEODORE HYRTACENUS

An otherwise little-known theologian, Theodore Hyrtacenus,[6] who, like many others, also calls Mary truly the Mistress of Creation,[7] has an interesting passage on her as helper of Christ; for as a woman was implicated in the Fall, so it was also fitting that when God destroyed the common enemy and restored man's former nobility "a virgin should

[1] 13 (692A, B).   [2] 34 (717B).   [3] 44 (728C).   [4] 51 (736A).   [5] 736B.
[6] Ed. by J. F. Boissonade, in *Anecdota Graeca*, 3 (1831), pp. 1–58.
[7] p. 21.

have been taken as helper in the great mystery, so that whence the weed of destruction had grown up, thence the healing herb of salvation should have sprouted afresh".[1]

FOURTEENTH-CENTURY AUTHORS

NICEPHORUS CALLISTUS

The fourteenth century was especially rich in Marian literature in the East, though much has so far remained in manuscript. Nicephorus Callistus (c. 1335) is of particular interest, as he had many contacts with the West and was aware of the controversy on the Immaculate Conception. He is best known for his Church History; some of his poems were edited in *Byzantion*,[2] and Jugie quotes manuscript material in his book on the Immaculate Conception. He considers him the first Eastern theologian to have explicitly denied it;[3] but as we have seen that his predecessors were very far from affirming it, this denial is probably only due to the fact that he knew exactly what the Western theologians meant by it; there is little doubt that other Eastern theologians would also have taken exception to it had they been acquainted with the Latin opinion. The relevant passage, quoted by Jugie, reads: "She therefore did not bring forth through corruption, but through the word of the archangel Gabriel, after the Holy Spirit had come upon her and had removed the original pollution, if such was then still present."[4] But the view that her final purification occurred at the Annunciation had been held from early times in the Eastern Church; it is not surprising that Nicephorus should have subscribed to it. What is particularly interesting is that, though he was very anti-Western, the doctrine of the Immaculate Conception must have made quite an impression on him, for at the end of the same work he asks Mary to be propitious to him if he should have strayed from

[1] p. 21.　[2] Vol. 5 (1929), pp. 362–90.　[3] *L'Immaculée Conception*, p. 219.
[4] Jugie, p. 218.

the right way when "choosing to attribute the stain to the all-pure".[1] In his poems he expresses himself in the traditional terms. The Theotokos is his firm hope, for she is an abyss of mercies and the mistress and mediatress of the world,[2] which she has reconciled to God;[3] and the poet asks her to save him from the eternal fire.[4] In this context it may be interesting to note that, though the Theophilus story originated in the East, the Byzantines seem to have made no use of it in their sermons; the rather crude tale seems to have appealed to the naïve and credulous young peoples of the West rather than to their more sophisticated fellow-Christians of the East.

MATTHEW CANTACUZENUS

Matthew Cantacuzenus (d. 1356), who was Emperor for a time but ended his days in a monastery, is particularly interesting because he wrote a commentary on the Canticle which he largely interpreted with reference to Mary; but, in contrast with many Western authors on the same subject, he did not interpret everything of her, and his work is free from the eroticism so noticeable in his Latin contemporaries, for the bridal imagery is mostly applied to the Church, not to the Theotokos. Like all the Byzantines, Matthew praises her sublime purity, which always remained inaccessible to the wiles of the Evil One[5]—once more, an expression that cannot be pressed into meaning freedom from original sin. In fact, if we were to press the much looser language of the Eastern authors as Jugie and other Latin theologians do in order to find the Immaculate Conception in them, we should say that Cantacuzenus definitely teaches the reverse, because he writes: "And she, too, as the daughter of Eve, has received bitterness";[6] though this may just as well refer only to the sorrows that were the result of the Fall and which she shared.

[1] Jugie, p. 219. [2] No. 1, *Byzantion*, vol. 5 (1929), pp. 362f.
[3] No. 5, pp. 374f. [4] No. 8, p. 381. [5] Comm., 4.3 (*PG*, 152, 1036D).
[6] 4.13-15 (1044A).

She was the first to escape the snares of the demon; but again, there is no suggestion that she did so in a way different from the baptized Christians who followed her.[1] She is venerated not for her own sake, but because she received Christ the King in her womb,[2] and sin receded before her, because the Sun of Justice made her his tabernacle.[3] All Mary's blessings are referred to her divine motherhood; for she is the vine that has brought forth for us Christ, the Grape;[4] therefore she is now enthroned above the seraphim, holding the Creator of all in her arms.[5]

GREGORY PALAMAS

By far the most influential theologian and mystic of the Orthodox Church of the Middle Ages was Gregory Palamas (d. 1359), the famous exponent of Hesychasm. This was a system of mysticism evolved by the monks of Mount Athos, which claimed to lead to the vision of the uncreated light of the Godhead. As J. Meyendorff points out,[6] Gregory does not refer to the Theotokos in his spiritual writings, which are wholly centred in Christ, but he is well aware of "the educational value of Marian preaching for the introduction of the Christian people to the mystery of the Incarnation. This is certainly the reason why he shows his devotion to the Mother of God only in his homilies."[7] Jugie would like to claim Palamas, too, for the Immaculate Conception, and Meyendorff agrees that, "if he had shared the Western notion of original sin his outstanding Marian piety would have led him to accept it", but the point is precisely that, like all Greek

---

[1] 4.8 (1040D).   [2] 4.19 (1044C).   [3] 6.9 (1064B).
[4] 7.7-9 (1072B).   [5] 8.6f. (1077C).
[6] *Introduction à l'étude de Grégoire Palamas*, Paris (1959), pp. 317-22.
[7] *Introduction*, p. 317. These homilies are partly edited in *PG*, 151 and partly by Sophocles Oikonomos, Athens (1861). This extremely rare edition has unfortunately not been accessible to me, and I can therefore only quote certain passages reproduced in Meyendorff and in Jugie's work on the Immaculate Conception.

theologians, he equated original sin with man's mortal nature, which leads him into sin but which is not in itself sin. Indeed, he almost goes out of his way to make it quite clear that in his view Christ alone was not subject to it. In his homily on the Incarnation[1] he says that if Christ had been conceived from human seed (as Mary undoubtedly was), he could not have been a New Man and could not have redeemed us. The whole passage was reproduced verbatim in Gregory's homily on the Presentation[2] and also in that on the Annunciation,[3] as if to rule out the Western idea, which otherwise might be deduced from certain of his expressions.

For Palamas speaks of Mary in the very highest terms. Before the ages God had chosen her for his Mother and judged her worthy of a greater grace than he gave to any other human being; he made her a saint among the saints even before her marvellous childbirth.[4] All events, both before and after her earthly life, point to her; she is the thought of the Prophets, the support of the martyrs, the foundation of the Doctors;[5] the whole divinely inspired Scripture was written because of the Virgin who was to bring forth God.[6] For Palamas sees her always in relation to Christ; her divine motherhood is her raison d'être and the cause of all her surpassing graces. Unlike the Latins, Palamas interprets her name only as "Mistress", not for example also as "Star of the Sea". She is Mistress of all things, because she has virginally conceived and given birth to God, thus being the source and the root of freedom for the human race, and she stands in the middle between created and uncreated nature.[7] In his homily on the Presentation Palamas indulges in the exaggerations so common in the West. He assures his hearers that the Virgin had the most discerning mind even before her birth, which she displayed clearly long before she reached womanhood. She

---

[1] 16 (*PG*, 193B).   [2] Oikonomos, no. 52, p. 124.   [3] *PG*, 169B, C.
[4] *Hom. 52* (Oikonomos, p. 123).   [5] *Hom. 53* (p. 162).
[6] *Hom. 57* (p. 216).   [7] *Hom. 14* (*PG*, 151, 172A–177B).

12

had all the charismata and all natural gifts from her mother's womb (though Gregory does not, like Pseudo-Albert, specify that she knew astronomy, canon law etc.) so that she needed no education.[1] At her Presentation, when she was three years old, she offered herself to God by her own free will, and her life in the Temple is described in terms of Hesychasm, "practising tranquillity [*hesychasasa*] in a marvellous way".[2]

Palamas clearly teaches the bodily Assumption. If the death of the saints is to be honoured, how much more the death of her through whom they have their sanctity.[3] For she co-operated in the self-emptying of the Word (unlike Bernardine of Siena, Palamas does not imagine that the Incarnation added something to him); therefore she now also shares his glory, standing between God and mankind, and sending splendours and graces from her place in heaven down to men. Her assumption was fitting, because of her divine mother-hood. As God came from her to us, so also in future no revelations and charismata are given without her;[4] for, as Palamas says in another homily, through her all treasures have been opened to us.[5]

THEOPHANES OF NICAEA

Mary's mediation of grace is elaborated even more strikingly in a very remarkable work by a disciple of Palamas, Theophanes of Nicaea (d. c. 1381), in his *Sermo in Sanctissimam Deiparam*.[6] This treatise places the Theotokos within a cosmic setting, in which all creation is subjected to the Incarnation; without this there would have been no creation. For all things are destined for a twofold being: being simply as such (*to haplos einai*) and well-being (*to eu einai*), which Theophanes equates with the patristic concept of deification, which was brought about by the Incarnation. In the prologue

---

[1] Oikonomos, p. 150.   [2] Oikonomos, p. 171.
[3] *Hom. 37 on the Assumption* (*PG*, 461A).   [4] 464B–472D.
[5] *Hom. 18* (*PG*, 241C).   [6] Ed. M. Jugie in *Lateranum*, 1, nov. ser. (1935).

to his work the author expresses his great love for the royal Maiden, the Queen of all creation whose dignity surpasses that of cherubim and seraphim, and in whom are hidden all the treasures of wisdom and knowledge—once more the Pauline passage that referred to Christ (Col. 2.3) is applied to his Mother.[1] She is likened to the earth, because Christ's flesh was taken from her, therefore she is the source of benediction for all men,[2] and she herself is the centre that unites all creatures with one another and with God. For she has borne her Son and God in her motherly womb; therefore she is the receptacle of the divine fullness, from which God's gifts and graces flow out to all rational creatures. She alone has access to all these treasures, because Christ can be approached only through her.[3] For she is the Holy of Holies, which the High Priest of the good things to come has entered, and as no-one can come to the Father except through the Son, so also no-one can come to the Son except through his Mother, who is the inner sanctuary from which God speaks to all creatures.[4]

This mediation is universal; it extends also to the angels. Here Theophanes follows the hierarchical order of the Pseudo-Dionysius (especially of the *Celestial Hierarchies*), according to which all good things flow from God through all the angelic orders down to man. But unlike Dionysius and like his Latin contemporaries, Theophanes places the Theotokos as an hierarchy in herself between Christ and the highest angelic order. According to him all the graces flow undivided from God to the human nature of Christ, and from there, still undivided, into Mary. They become divided only after being passed on from Mary to the seraphim, because the seraphim are many, whereas Mary is one. For Mary gave the Word his human nature, therefore his divinity, too, is given through her; she mediates always, for she is the light cloud

[1] 1, 2 (Jugie, pp. 2–12).   [2] 4 (pp. 18ff.).   [3] 5 (pp. 22–8).
[4] 8 (pp. 38–40).

through which the rays of the otherwise inaccessible sun come to all creatures.[1] This mediation of Mary extends also to the sacraments. Indeed, Theophanes does not hesitate to speak of Mary in the technical language of ordination. He says that she is ordained (*cheirotoneitai*) by God to be the perfectress and teacher of the episcopal (*hierarchike*) grace and knowledge for cherubim, seraphim and thrones, whom she enlightens and perfects, thus causing them to do the same in their turn for the ranks beneath them; for she is established after Christ, the first bishop (*hierarches*, the term Dionysius uses instead of the usual *episkopos*), as a second bishop between God and the angels. For because she is the Mother of the incarnate God according to his flesh, she is also the Mother of all those who are "deified" by grace; and since in heaven there is neither male nor female, Theophanes even calls her their "father".[2] "Deification" is a common term of Greek mystical theology (cf. John 10.34f.), meaning union between God and his creatures, of which Mary is the mediatress. She mediates it also to angels; indeed, she may herself be called an angel, because she represents the divine beauty even more than the highest of them. Quoting once more Dionysius, who asserted that all the powers above us reflect divine properties, Theophanes says that Mary, being above the angels, must also reflect divine omnipotence, domination, wisdom and so forth. So she presides over both the angelic and the physical natures "as the archetype of the primary creation and the inimitable imitation of the divine beauty".[3] Hence the author gives her all the divine names, even those of God, Lord, and King of Kings. She owes these, of course, to her divine motherhood, but this itself was given her only because God foresaw that she would attain to the highest sanctity of her own freewill, only with the ordinary assistance of grace. This shows how far the author was from the Latin view of the Immaculate Conception; indeed, his opinion is open to

[1] 9f. (pp. 50–58).   [2] 11 (pp. 60–64).   [3] 13f. (pp. 68–82).

precisely the objection which the great Latin theologians of the thirteenth century invariably made; it exempts Mary from the universality of Christ's redemption. And indeed, if a creature were capable of raising herself to such a position by her own free will only with the ordinary assistance of grace (which, apparently, Theophanes thought was available even without the Incarnation), it is hard to see why Christ should have had to die at all. Theophanes goes even further. Mary only became human because of the Incarnation; if this had not taken place she would have been the first in the order of seraphim.[1] It is hardly possible to fit such a statement into an orthodox Christian theology; it could only be explained by Origen's idea of the pre-existence of souls and their "fall" into bodies. But even so, Origen saw this fall as a punishment, which could not possibly have fitted the Theotokos, who is higher than the highest angels. However that may be, the idea that Mary was really a kind of incarnate seraph borders on the ludicrous; if later Western authors were sometimes inclined to attribute anthropomorphic features to the relations between God and Mary, the Greeks fell into the opposite danger of robbing her of her humanity.

Strangely enough, however, there is one typically Latin idea to be found in Theophanes, and it is difficult to believe that there should have been no direct influence from the West. For the author, like Hermann of Tournai and others before him, compares Mary to a neck, because she directly connects Christ, the Head, with the rest of the Body and is herself second only to the Head. No member of the body can receive the good things of the head except through this neck.[2] The whole metaphor is set in the context of the Canticle, exactly as in the Latin authors, whom Theophanes must have studied fairly thoroughly, as he also wrote controversial works about the procession of the Holy Spirit against them. Another idea he elaborates, also found in the medieval Latin

[1] 16 (pp. 86–96).   [2] 22f. (pp. 126–130).

authors, is that Mary has her Son in common with the Father, but he deduces from this consequences very typical of the speculative Greek mind. He thinks that even in his earthly life Christ was far more intimately united to Mary than she was to her own heart, because he was God and therefore formed one "operation" (*energeia*) with her. In fact, he remained in her heart even after having been born from her, just as he remained with the Father also after the Incarnation; for, having entered into her once and having prepared her heart as an altar which was to receive both Priest and Victim, he remained with her for ever. More, Christ's union with his Mother was in a way as intimate as his union with the Father; and, quoting St. Basil, he even compares it to the divine circumincession, that is to say the interpenetration of the divine persons. As in the divine relations the Father penetrates wholly into the Son while yet remaining in himself, so it is also in the Incarnation; after Mary had given birth to Christ her substance went wholly into her Son even though she remained in her own person and property. So there is a complete identity between Mother and Son.[1] Thus the later Greek theologians tend to identify the Theotokos with her divine Son just as much as their Latin contemporaries, but the former give this identification a more speculative flavour by equating it with the doctrine of the circuminsession (*perichoresis*)—an intrusion of the trinitarian relations into Mariology which the earlier Fathers would certainly have rejected. Theophanes uses the same questionable method when applying to Christ and Mary the Christological *communicatio idiomatum*, according to which the attributes of Christ's humanity may also be predicated of his divinity and vice versa because of the union of his two natures in his one divine person. In his view the union between Christ and his Mother is so close that whatever is said of him may also be said of her, for she received from him the characteristics of his

[1] 24–6 (pp. 142–54).

Godhead, which she integrated to such a degree that those worthy of such contemplation perceive them even better through her than through him, just as when he lived on earth he appeared as man only in the flesh of his mother. Thus either appropriated the characteristics of the other.[1] Again, this is hardly sound theology; for the *communicatio idiomatum* is based on the hypostatic union of the two natures of Christ in his one person, whereas for all Mary's closeness to her Son, she was certainly not one and the same person with him.

Like his Western contemporaries, the author also emphasizes Mary's motherly solicitude for men, whom she loves as selflessly as she loved Christ. Therefore she suffers with the sorrowing and is glad with the joyful; indeed, even the greatest possible love of an earthly mother for her children is but a very faint reflection of Mary's love for us. For our natural mother gives us only our mere being (again *to haplos einai*) but the Theotokos gives all of us our well-being (*to eu einai*), and whereas the former makes us mortal by nature, Mary makes us immortal by grace and distributes God's gifts to us as if we were her own sons.[2]

NICHOLAS CABASILAS

Nicholas Cabasilas, an author about whose life very little is known—even the year of his death is doubtful; it may have been about 1380—wrote an *Explanation of the Divine Liturgy* and a *Life in Christ*, two entirely Christocentric works, and his three Marian homilies[3] reflect this outlook and are free from certain exaggerations of the writer just discussed. He sees Mary wholly as the Theotokos, even though he reflects what seems to have been the general opinion of the Greek theologians at this time, that her purity was attained by her own efforts. That he says in his sermon on her nativity that nature

[1] 27, 29 (pp. 158–74).   [2] 34 (pp. 198–204).
[3] Ed. Jugie (*PO*, 19, 456–510).

could not contribute anything to her birth, God, whom her
parents had invoked, having done all, can hardly refer to her
immaculate conception but obviously to the apocryphal story
of her birth from a sterile couple.[1] For he writes in another
passage that the stainless Virgin who came forth from the
earth in the same way as all others, from the fallen race,
alone of all human beings opposed all evil and gave back her
God-given beauty unsullied, for through her love of God and
her fortitude she overcame all sin.[2] In the next chapter he
enlarges further on this theme; he argues that her sinlessness
is all the more remarkable, because she did not live before all
other men, nor receive a nature free from evil, nor live after
Christ, the New Man. For if Adam, who lived in paradise,
had been without sin it would not have been very surprising,
nor if Christians after the Incarnation had remained
so; yet, if it is so difficult for men to remain without sin
even in these favourable circumstances, how greatly must we
admire the Virgin, who lived neither before the Fall nor after
Christ had redeemed us, but in the heyday of evils, in a
nature which had always learned to be defeated, in a body
which was subject to death—and yet kept her soul free from
all stain! She gained this tremendous victory by using all her
faculties for the good.[3]

Two things are quite clear from this passage: in the view of
Cabasilas Mary had not been conceived immaculate, for she
had the same human nature that had always been defeated;
on the other hand, she gained this victory over it by her own
moral efforts. As D. T. Strotmann[4] rightly says, "For a
Western ear some of his expressions have a semi-Pelagian or
even a Pelagian sound"; but we have met this tendency also
in other contemporary Eastern authors. Indeed Cabasilas
insists on the fact that the Mother of God was given no more

[1] 4 (PO, 19, 469).   [2] 6, 47.   [3] 7 (472–4).
[4] "La Théotokos, Prémices des Justifiés", in Irénikon 27 (1954) 131. Cf.
also M. Lot-Borodine, Un Maître de la spiritualité byzantine au XIVᵉ siècle
(1958).

help than others to avoid sin,[1] surely a view quite incompatible
with her immaculate conception, of which Jugie wants to make
him an exponent.[2] The Stainless One, the author goes on to
say, made this crown by her own powers; though God
assisted her no more than anyone else, she added to his gifts
so much of her own that it sufficed not only for her own glory,
but also for that of many others.[3] For all men had the power to
resist sin; but they would not use this innate goodness as they
ought; Mary was the only one who did so.[4] Nothing could
express more clearly the difference between the Eastern and
the Western views of original sin, hence the idea of an
immaculate conception simply would not make sense to a man
like Cabasilas. Indeed, he considers it necessary for Mary to
have avoided all sin by her own efforts. For, apart from its
being fitting that the Mother of the Sinless One should herself
have been like him in this respect, it was also necessary that
one human being should rise superior to sin by herself; for it
had to be shown what unspoilt human nature was. For
Christ, being God, could not sin; but Mary, being able to sin
because of her purely human nature, yet did not sin, and so
manifested man in his paradisal integrity.[5] Cabasilas uses the
Eve–Mary parallel also for showing the Theotokos as the
helper of God, but not, like most Latins, as that of her Son,
but as that of the Father; for owing to his Christocentric
outlook he refers everything to the Incarnation. Christ
reconciled man perfectly to the Father by his death on the
Cross, Mary contributed to this reconciliation by having
attracted the Mediator to man.[6] Only once does he refer to
her own part in the Passion, which she had because she shared
with her Son all that belonged to our salvation. As she had
given him her flesh and been given his graces in return, so
also his suffering. And so she was the first to become

[1] 8 (475).   [2] *L'Immaculée Conception*, 246–63.
[3] 9 (*PO*, 19, 475).   [4] 4 (471).
[5] 14 and 16 (480, 482).   [6] *On the Assumption*, 6 (*PO*, 19, 501).

13+

conformable to his death (cf. Phil. 3.10), and therefore also shared the Resurrection before all others;[1] but this does not involve a share in the Redemption, which she only had through being the instrument of the Incarnation.

In his sermon on the Annunciation Cabasilas presents Mary as man's "paraclete" with God before the coming of the Paraclete;[2] for if she had not prepared herself for the Incarnation (again the stress on her voluntary moral contribution) we should not have been saved. So the Incarnation is not only the work of the Trinity, but also of the faith and will of the Virgin.[3] Indeed, God was in a way compelled to make her his Mother, for as she possessed all the proper qualities it would have been unjust of him to have withheld this dignity from her.[4] In his sermon on the Assumption the author once more breaks out into praise of her purity, through which she made a new heaven and a new earth; or rather, she is herself the new earth and the new heaven; earth, because she comes from here below, heaven, because she did not inherit the old leaven (in view of what has been said before this refers to her victory over actual, not to her freedom from original, sin); she is a new paste and has initiated a new race. She is also a new heaven, because she bore God. If she were not the link between God and men, those below could have no share in the things above;[5] she is men's guide to God, the way to the Saviour, and through her blood (which she gave to her Son) we are saved.[6]

ISIDORE GLABAS

Despite his Christocentric outlook Cabasilas was nevertheless not free from Pelagianism; the blessed Virgin attains to her incomparable moral and spiritual height by her own efforts; the grace of God is hardly mentioned. With Isidore Glabas (d. c. 1397) we are once more in the sphere of

[1] *Assumption*, 12 (508).   [2] 3 (*PO*, 19, 486).
[3] 4 (487f.).   [4] 9 (494).   [5] 4 (498f.).   [6] 13 (510).

unrestrained rhetoric.[1] Indeed, I sympathize with Jugie, who says that "Isidore's eyes are so unswervingly fixed on the Mother that he seems to forget the Son",[2] and his language would at times be more applicable to a pagan goddess than to the human Mother of Jesus Christ. In his sermon on her nativity Isidore asks why the Virgin was not created before all else; and he answers that at the beginning creation would have been too weak to sustain her surpassing beauty, or, alternatively, that all other created things, heaven, earth and sea, were needed by the Creator to produce this masterpiece; though he hastens to assure us that she needed no creatures for her existence—on the contrary, she was the cause both of their creation and of the increase of their beauty that was to follow. So, paradoxically, what existed before her needed her to come into being; and of her alone can it be said that she brought forth her parents.[3] He also holds that Mary's beauty had so captivated the Creator that he united himself to her as closely as possible, and he adapts to her what St. Paul said of Christ (cf. Rom. 6.5): As we are made in her image, we shall also participate in her graces.[4] After creation had for a long time languished after the Fall, "a new man", that is to say, Mary, appeared, and through her man was liberated from the calamity that had befallen him, and resumed his former dignity.[5] Though this, of course, refers to Mary's divine motherhood, nevertheless Isidore's language is such that he does at times seem to forget Christ in his preoccupation with his Mother, which becomes apparent in one of the following chapters. When earth was filled with sin and unable to produce its own remedy, he writes, heaven itself had to stretch forth its hand, for "if anyone quietened that commotion [scil., of sin] . . . this wonderful physician was the Virgin."

[1] Four Marian sermons on the Nativity, the Presentation, the Annunciation and the Dormition respectively are printed in *PG*, 139, 12–164.

[2] *L'Immaculée Conception dans l'Ecriture et dans la tradition orientale*, Rome (1952), p. 265.

[3] 2 (*PG*, 139, 12D–13A).   [4] 4 (16A).   [5] 6 (17C).

Thus heaven opened and sent to earth the all-pure Virgin, who is therefore a child of heaven, notwithstanding her descent from "Adamic" parents.[1] For, like Christ, she is a "new creation";[2] and unequivocally Christological passages are applied to her. Isidore does not hesitate to write: "We have seen her glory, as the glory of the only-begotten Mother of God" (cf. John 1.14); for she is a source of light not only for those before her, but also for all future generations, therefore St. Paul's words can be applied to her: "Our life is hidden with her, and when she, our life, shall appear, we shall also appear with her in glory" (Col. 3.3f.), and even Zachary's words of the *Benedictus*: "The Orient from on high has visited us." (Luke 1.78 (9, 24A–25A).)

Mary's heavenly origin is repeatedly affirmed. In his homily on the Presentation Isidore asserts that she did not need earthly parents nor the earth to walk on, for her origin and her dwelling are above; but she had to come to earth because of the Incarnation.[3] Therefore she lived in the Holy of Holies, where she was visible only once a year, and even then only to the High Priest who was allowed to enter there.[4] In the Sermon on the Annunciation Isidore maintains that if God had not ordained that he would come to earth through her, the earth would never have borne this creature, who is above the seraphim; or if he wanted to show how great a thing he could fashion from the earth, she would indeed have descended into our world, but need not have remained long among men, with whom she had nothing in common, but would have quickly regained heaven. Only because God had to become Man to wipe out our sins did earth bear this precious jewel for so long.[5]

In fact, the author does not seem quite clear whether the Theotokos was really completely human or not; he says she is neither a human being nor an angel, but another, altogether superior, nature.[6] More, he even gives her a share in God's

---

[1] 8 (21A). [2] 12 (29A). [3] 8 (45C–48A). [4] 25 (68B). [5] 9 (81C–84A).
[6] 16 (97C).

creative work. For, he affirms, Mary is the Mother of the Word not only because she gave birth to him; she is, as it were, mother also of his creative goodness, since she is the condition and cause of its manifestation. "And, if it be not too bold, the blessed Virgin is perhaps the co-creatress [*symplástes*] with God even before she came into the world, who drew forth into being [*symparagogeis*] together with him both visible and invisible creatures . . . and gave them new beauty after her advent on earth."[1] This idea may possibly be due to the application to Mary of Prov. 8.22ff.: "The Lord possessed me in the beginning of his ways . . . I was with him forming all things"; but it is hardly possible to apply it to her quite literally. Evidently Isidore believed in her pre-existence, for he says again in a later chapter that God could have rewarded her without sending her to earth.[2] He also affirms several times that heaven, earth and man were made for Mary;[3] for when God created man he created him for her sake, because no-one else could be said to have been made in God's likeness, neither Adam himself nor any of his descendants; through her alone do we know the divine similitude.[4]

This may seem to imply that she was conceived without original sin; and again we are confronted with the difference of this concept in the thought of East and West. In the homily on the Presentation Isidore says quite plainly that she alone could say: "I was not conceived in sin", because her parents came together impelled only by God, and this is one of the great things God did for her.[5] But this concerns only the sinlessness of the "active" conception, not the consequences of it, which, as we have seen, are regarded by the Greeks not as an inherent guilt but as the fact of mortality. This is plainly stated in the sermon on the Annunciation, where Isidore says that though her soul was pure, her body was from

[1] 23 (105A).　[2] 26 (109A).　[3] *Annunciation* 22 (104A).　[4] 21 (101C, D).
[5] 13 (52C–53A).

Adam and hence subject to all the infirmities following the Fall—and this is precisely what the Greeks understood by original sin.[1] Therefore it is not so surprising as Jugie thinks that in his sermon on the Assumption the author should seem to contradict himself, when he writes: "The Virgin came forth from her own mother like a human being, and for this reason the ancient 'thickness' [*pachos*]—I mean, original sin—was born with her, which she received unwillingly, because it was impossible to escape or to transcend, of which David says, I was conceived in iniquities etc. This alone she brought into the world, but from all the other 'thickness' she remained free, and even the first she threw off"— obviously in her Assumption. For the "thickness" can only refer not to any moral stain (Augustinian view) or privation of grace (Anselm and the schoolmen following him), as original sin was understood in the West, but to the mortality of the body, the "garments of skin" with which Adam was clothed after the Fall. These are quite independent of the sinlessness of intercourse attributed by Isidore to Mary's parents. It is not, therefore, nearly so incompatible as Jugie asserts with Isidore's views expressed elsewhere, and there is no need to suppose that the passage is interpolated. Scholasticism, with its rigorous syllogistic argumentation, was never part of the Eastern tradition, and we simply cannot apply our Western logic to that tradition's exponents.

THE FIFTEENTH CENTURY

MANUEL II

The Emperor Manuel II Paleologus (d. 1425), like many of his predecessors, interested himself in theology and wrote a short treatise—rather than a sermon—on the Assumption, in thanksgiving for the deliverance from a grave illness.[2] The work reflects the traditional Mariology of the East, including

---

[1] 14 (92C–93A).   [2] *PO*, 16, 543–66.

emphasis on the Virgin's outstanding purity. But there is one passage which has led Jugie to contend that "Manuel expresses himself like a Scotist doctor of his time, like the Catholic theologians of our own day".[1] The Emperor writes: "He who foreordained her filled his Mother with his own grace at the same time as the Blessed One was born, or I might even perhaps say when she was conceived; and even before her childbirth he himself was with her ... For he was never not united to her, ever since she had her first beginning in the womb of her barren mother ... For if we know that John was full of the Holy Spirit in the womb, how can it not be right to affirm the same of the All-Pure?"[2] Quite apart from the fact that the looseness of the Emperor's language can scarcely be compared with the rigorous precision of "a Scotist doctor of his time", the comparison of Mary's sanctification at her birth *or* her conception (Manuel leaves that open) with that of John the Baptist completely rules out the unique privilege attributed to her by the Scotist theologians, and cannot be passed over cavalierly, as Jugie does when he writes: "He seems to place John the Baptist on the same level as the Mother of God and to attribute to him, too, sanctifying grace from the first moment. But this is perhaps only apparently so."[3] Sanctification in the womb has always been attributed to John the Baptist by Greek as well as by Latin theologians, and Manuel affirms only the same for Mary.

There is another passage which Jugie quotes as evidence of Manuel's belief in the Immaculate Conception. He writes that it was fitting that the blessed Virgin should be "superior to the curse ... as having become a vessel full of the blessing from which the first mother [scil., Eve] had fallen away". Jugie quotes it as far as this; he leaves out what follows immediately: "... and which the angel Gabriel came from God to bring her".[4] This is no more and no less than the

[1] *L'Immaculée Conception*, p. 286.   [2] 7 (552f.).   [3] 7 (552f.).   [4] 9 (555).

traditional Greek idea that Mary's complete purification from the curse God had pronounced on our first parents came only at the Annunciation.

GEORGE SCHOLARIOS

The case of George Scholarios, who adopted the name of Gennadius II on becoming Patriarch of Constantinople (d. after 1472), is more complicated. Scholarios is generally regarded as the most famous theologian of the Greek Church of the later Middle Ages. He was well versed in Latin theology, having studied not only St. Augustine and St. Thomas, but also later theologians like Francis of Mayronis. Though still a layman, he preached at the Court and was theological adviser to the Emperor, as whose secretary he attended the Union Council of Ferrara and Florence (1438–9) and defended the *Filioque*. But a few years later he changed his mind completely, and strongly opposed the Latins. In 1450 he left the Court to become a monk; when in 1453 the Turks conquered Constantinople they made him a slave, though in the next year Mohammed II appointed him Patriarch; but he exercised this office only for three comparatively short periods.

Mariology occupies only a small part in his works;[1] and it is interesting that the Latin notion of grace has influenced the author's thought; for, unlike his contemporaries, he does not attribute Mary's holiness entirely to her own efforts. Even though he affirms that the crown Christ wove for her consisted more of her own acts of always choosing the better part than of her divine motherhood, he admits that grace was necessary to guide and strengthen her in this, because without its influence man can do nothing; and so she is blessed because she is the Mother of God both by her own will and by nature, whose finest flower she is, because she is the beginning of those predestined to salvation as Eve was the beginning of

[1] Edited by Petit, Siderides and Jugie; I quote the Marian homilies from *PO* 16, 570–87 and *PO*, 19, 513–25.

the damned—a passage which shows the influence of St. Augustine.[1]

In his teaching on Mary's purity Scholarios follows the Byzantine tradition, but again with an emphasis on grace. The passage in question, which Jugie thinks teaches the Immaculate Conception, compares the purity of Christ with that of his Mother. Christ owed his purity to the fact that his conception (*syllepsis*) was without human seed; so he was pure by nature, having no occasion of a stain, "but to her who gave birth to him it belonged only by grace; and she was most pure *as soon as she was born*, because she was to give birth to the Most Pure One, even though she had the occasion of the stain inherent in her nature."[2] Jugie considers this a definite affirmation of the Immaculate Conception because he translates *gennetheisa euthys*, "as soon as she was born", as "dès le premier instant de sa conception"—"from the first moment of her conception". But if Scholarios had wanted to emphasize her conception, he would surely have used the unequivocal term *syllephtheisa*, not *gennetheisa*, which can, indeed, mean "beget", and thus is used of Christ as the Only-Begotten of the Father, but also means "bring forth", "give birth to" of the woman—but *not* "conceive". It is hardly probable that Scholarios should have considered the "begetting" as pure, especially as the author says in the same homily that if Christ had been conceived from human seed he could not but have shared in the stain that comes to all men from their descent;[3] besides, in the passage under discussion he constantly uses the term for "give birth"; it would be extremely misleading, to say the least, if he suddenly, in this one instance, used it for "beget" and considered as pure Mary's begetting, which he had just said could never be pure.

There is another passage on the subject in the *Treatise on the Origin of the Soul*,[4] which Jugie quotes in support of his

---

[1] *Hom. on the Presentation* 2 (515f.).   [2] 7 (577).   [3] 5 (575).
[4] 2, 20 (Petit, Siderides and Jugie, vol. 1, p. 501, 21ff.).

13*

view. But here Scholarios says explicitly that the blessed Virgin was not without a share in original sin, because she was conceived from seed—the same argumentation he used in the homily just discussed. But the grace of God completely freed her from it, as if she had come into existence without seed, and she alone among men received this privilege. Again, this is not the same as the contemporary doctrine of the Franciscans, who said precisely that Mary had no share in original sin, because God *preserved* her, not because he freed her, from it (*apellaxen*). These are, indeed, very subtle distinctions; but they are distinctions. It does not serve the cause of reunion if we in the West affirm that the Orthodox have always taught the Immaculate Conception and only stopped doing so out of sheer cussedness as soon as Rome defined it. They have, indeed, always taught the perfect purity of our Lady; but, having a quite different conception of original sin, this simply meant and means another thing to them than the Immaculate Conception means to us.

When Scholarios preached his homily on the Assumption (1464) Constantinople had fallen, the Christian Eastern Empire existed no more; soon Hagia Sophia would be turned into a mosque. He has a complete trust in the power of the Theotokos; but he also knows, what his Latin contemporaries at times tended to forget, that, far from bending the immutable will of God, her prayer is always in harmony with it: "For you would never ask him anything which you did not know he was prepared to grant."[1] Experience has taught him this; for he and his fellow-Christians have drunk the cup of ultimate wrath, so they will importune neither her nor God but be content with their fate. All they ask is that they may soon be released from this life of misery.[2]

Thus the fifteenth century is the end of an age both in the East and in the West. Constantinople has fallen; the throne of the Christian emperors is no more, and no Christian preacher

[1] 16 (586).   [2] 17 (586f.).

ascends any longer the pulpit of Chrysostom and Germanus. Many Greek Christians flee to the West, where they teach their language and thus make their own contribution to tremendous new forces about to be released; humanism, the Renaissance, the Reformation will change the face of Western Christendom almost beyond recognition. Naturally, Marian doctrine and devotion will not remain unaffected by the new era.

NOTE ON EDITIONS USED

Modern editions have been used wherever possible, otherwise Migne's *Patrologia Graeca* and *Patrologia Latina*, cited respectively as *PG* and *PL*. (A full list of abbreviations used will be found on pp. xvif.) The modern editions are quoted by page and line, but when a work is divided into brief sections it is cited only by these. The following list contains all the editions used except the two Migne Patrologies. The translations from the Latin and the Greek are my own unless otherwise indicated.

CHAPTER 2

The Apostolic Fathers, ed. Funk-Bihlmeyer (1956) (quoted by section).

Odes of Solomon, ed. and tr. J. H. Bernard, *TS*, 8, 3 (1912).

The Protoevangelium of James, quoted from E. de Stryker, *La Forme la plus ancienne du protévangile de Jacques* (1961).

Apologists (Justin), E. J. Goodspeed, *Die ältesten Apologeten*, Göttingen (1915).

Irenaeus, ed. W. W. Harvey, 1857, quoted by sections of Massuet given in the margin.

Tertullian, *CCSL*, 1 and 2.

Origen, *GCS* edition (quoted by sections and page and line where necessary).

Cyprian, *CSEL*, 3.

Methodius, *GCS*.

Peregrinatio Aetheriae, *CSEL*, 39.

Eusebius, *GCS*, vol. 4 of *Works*.

Alexander of Alexandria, *int. opp. Athanàsii*, quoted from Opitz edition and *PG*.

"Gnomai" of Nicaea, in *Studien zur Geschichte und Kultur des Altertums*, 10, 4 (1920).

Athanasius, quoted from the incomplete edition of H.-G. Opitz, *De Virginitate* from *TU*, 29, 2 (1905), otherwise from *PG*, 25–8.

Titus of Bostra, *Contra Manichaeos*, ed. P. A. de Lagarde, 1924; *Schol. in Luc.*, *TU*, 21, 1.

Lactantius, *CSEL*, 27.

Ephraem, *Carmina Nisibena*, ed. G. Bickel (1866); T. J. Lamy, *Hymni et Sermones* (1882–1902); also J. S. and S. E. Assemani, Rome edition 1732/46 (= *ER*).

Gregory of Nyssa, W. Jaeger, *Opera Ascetica* (1952), but quoted with Migne references.
Cyril of Jerusalem, *Catecheses*, ed. W. K. Reischl and J. Rupp, 2 vols., 1848/60.
Epiphanius, *GCS*.
John Chrysostom, ed. B. de Montfaucon, 13 vols., 1718–38.
Ambrose, *CSEL* and *ML*, quoted by sections.
Jerome, *CCSL* 72, 74, 78; *CSEL* 54–6, 59; also ML 22–30.
Augustine, *CSEL* and *CCSL*, *Sermo Denis*, ed. G. Morin, Rome (1930).

CHAPTER 3

Works relating to the Nestorian controversy in Schwartz, *ACO*, 1, 1, 1.
Cyril of Alexandria, *ACO*, 1, 1, 8.
Theodotus of Ancyra, *PO*, 19, 13.
Chrysippus of Jerusalem, *PO*, 19, 3.
Sedulius, *CSEL*, 10.
Leo I, *Tome* (Ep. 28) ed. C. Silva-Tarouca (1932); Sermons, *PL*, 54.
Jacob of Sarug, ed. J. B. Abbeloos (1867).
Severus of Antioch, *PO*, 8.
Narses, ed. F. Feldmann (1896).
Romanos, editions by J. B. Pitra, *Analecta Sacra*, 1 (1876) and G. Camelli, Florence (1930).
The Akathistos Hymn, ed. G. G. Meersseman (1958).
Oecumenius, ed. H. C. Hoskier (1928).
Theoteknos of Livias, ed. A. Wenger, *L'Assomption de la Très-Sainte Vierge dans la tradition byzantine du VIe au Xe siècle* (1955).
John of Thessalonica, *PO*, 19.

CHAPTER 4

Ildefonsus of Toledo, *De Virginitate B. Mariae*, ed. V. B. Garcia (1937).
Bede, *CCSL*, 1955 and 1960.
Theophilus Legend, ed. R. Petsch (1908).
Alcuin, *MGH*, *Poet. Lat.*, 1.
Paulinus of Aquileja, *MGH*, *Poet. Lat.*, 1.
Walafrid Strabo, *MGH*, *Poet. Lat.*, 2.
Milo of St. Armand, *MGH*, *Poet. Lat.*, 3.
Hincmar of Rheims, *MGH*, *Poet. Lat.*, 3.

Notker the Stammerer, ed. W. von den Steinen (1948).
Cosmas Vestitor, ed. A. Wenger, *L'Assomption* etc. (1955).
Theognostus, *PO*, 16.
Photius, ed. B. Laourdas (1959).
Euthymius, *PO*, 16.
John the Geometer, ed. Wenger, *L'Assomption* (1955); Hymns, ed.
   J. Sajdak, *Ioannis Kyriotis Geometrae Hymni in SS. Deiparam*
   (1931).
Gottschalk of Limburg, ed. G. M. Dreves (1897).

CHAPTER 5

Anselm of Canterbury, ed. F. S. Schmitt (1946–).
Eadmer, *Tractatus*, ed. Thurston-Slater (1904).
Osbert of Clare, *Letters*, ed. E. W. Williamson (1929).
Abelard, ed. V. Cousin (1836).
Amadeus of Lausanne, ed. G. Bavaud-J. Deshusses-A. Dumas in
   Sources chrétiennes (1960).
Ailred of Rievaulx, *Sermones Inediti*, ed. C. H. Talbot (1952). *De
   Institutione Inclusarum* in *Sources chrétiennes*, 76 (1961).
? Nicholas of St. Albans, ed. C. H. Talbot in *RBE* (1954).
William of Newburgh, *Commentary on the Canticle*, ed. J. C. Gorman,
   Fribourg (1960).
Vita beatae Virginis Mariae et Salvatoris Rhythmica, ed. A. Vögtlin
   (1888).
Das Marienleben des Schweizers Wernher, ed. M. Päpke and A.
   Hübner (1920).

CHAPTER 6

Albert the Great, ed. A. Borgnet, 38 vols. (1890–99) (works quoted
   by section, also by page when necessary).
Thomas Aquinas, *Opuscula Theologica*, ed. Marietti (1954).
Bonaventure, ed. Quaracchi, 10 vols. (1882–1902).
Conrad of Saxony, *Bibliotheca Franciscana Ascetica Medii Aevi*,
   vol. 2 (1904).
Peter John Olivi, ed. D. Pacetti (1954).
Ubertino of Casale, *Arbor Vitae Crucifixae Jesu*, Venice (1485).
Engelbert of Admont, ed. B. Pez in *Thesaurus Anecdotum*, vol. 1, 1
   (1721).
William of Ware, *Bibl. Franc. Schol. Med. Aevi*, 3 (1904).
Duns Scotus, ed. C. Balič, *Theologiae Marianae Elementa* (1933).
Peter Oriol, ed. in *Questiones Disputatae de Immaculata Conceptione*
   (1904).

William of Nottingham, ed. A. Emmen in *MM*, 5 (1943).
Baconthorp, in *Analecta Ordinis Carmelitarum*, 6 (1927).
St. Bridget, *Revelationes*, ed. Turrecremata (1628); *Revelaciones Extravagantes*, ed. L. Hollman (1956).
Peter of Candia, in A. Emmen, *Tractatus Quatuor de Immaculata Deiparae Conceptione* (1954).
John Gerson, ed. L. E. Du Pin, 4 vols. (1706).
Bernardine of Siena, Quaracchi edition (1955–).
Antoninus of Florence, ed. of 1480, quoted by sections.
Dionysius the Carthusian, 44 vols. (1896–1935).
Bernardine of Busti, *Mariale* (1588).
Michael Psellos, *PO*, 16.
John Phournas, Jerusalem ed. (1860).
Neophytus, *PO*, 16.
Theodore Hyrtacenus, ed. J. F. Boissonade, *Anecdota Graeca*, 3 (1831).
Nicephorous Callistus, ed. in *Byzantion*, vol. 5 (1929).
Theophanes of Nicaea, ed. M. Jugie, *Lateranum*, 1, *nov. ser.* (1935).
Nicholas Cabasilas, *PO*, 19.
Manuel Paleologus, *PO*, 16.
George Scholarios, *PO*, 16 and 19.

SELECT BIBLIOGRAPHY

(A list of abbreviations used will be found on pp. xvif.)

GENERAL WORKS

GORDILLO, M., *Mariologia Orientalis*, Rome (1954)
LAURENTIN, R., *Court Traité de théologie Mariale*, 4th ed., Paris (1959)
MANOIR, H. du, *Maria*, vols. 1–6, Paris (1949–)
MCNAMARA, K., *Mother of the Redeemer*, Dublin (1959)
NEUBERT, E., *Marie dans le dogme*, Paris (1953)
ROSCHINI, G., *Mariologia*, Rome (1947), 4 vols.
SCHMAUS, M., "Mariologia", *Katholische Dogmatik* (1955), vol. 5
STRÄTER, P., *Katholische Marienkunde*, Paderborn (1948–51), 3 vols.

CHAPTER I

ALDAMA, J. A. de, "Natus ex Maria", *GM*, 42 (1961)
AUDET, J. P., "L'Annonce à Marie", *RB*, 63 (1956)
BOISMARD, M. E., *Du Baptême à Cana*, Paris (1956)
BRAUN, F. M., *La Mère des fidèles*, Paris–Tournai (1953)
BRAUN, F. M., "La Femme vêtue du soleil", *RT*, 55 (1955)
BRAUN, F. M., "La Mère de Jésus dans l'œuvre de saint Jean", *RT*, 58 (1950), and 59 (1951)
BUSSCHE, H. van den, *L'Évangile de Jean* (1958)
CERFAUX, L., "La Vierge dans l'Apocalypse", *ETL*, 31 (1955)
COPPENS, J., "Le Protévangile. Un nouvel essai d' exégèse", *ETL*, 26 (1950), pp. 5–36
COPPENS, J., "La Prophétie de la 'Almah", *ETL* (1952)
CROSSAN, D. M., "Mary's Virginity in S. John", *MM*, 19 (1957)
DRIVER, C. R., *Canaanite Myths*, London (1925)
FEUILLET, A., "L'Heure de Jésus et le signe de Cana", *ETL*, 36 (1960)
FEUILLET, A., "Le Messie et sa mère d'après le chapitre XII de l'Apocalpyse", *RB*, 66 (1959)
FROIS, J. B. Le, *The Woman Clothed with the Sun*, Rome (1954)
GÄCHTER, P., *Maria im Erdenleben*, Innsbruck (1953)
GÄCHTER, P., "Die geistige Mutterschaft Mariens", *ZKT*, 47 (1923)

GALLUS, T., "Scholion ad mulierem Apocalypseos", *Verbum Domini*, 30 (1952)

GALOT, J., "La Virginité de Marie et la naissance de Jésus", *NRT*, 82 (1960)

JOUASSARD, G., "Deux chefs de file", *GM*, 42 (1961)

KERRIGAN, A., "John 19, 25–27 in the Light of Johannine Theology and the Old Testament", *Antonianum*, 35 (1960)

LAURENTIN, R., *Structure et théologie de Luc I–II*, Paris (1957)

LAURENTIN, R., "Le Mystère de la naissance virginale", *EM*, 10 (1960)

LAURIERS, M. L. G. des, "Mariologie et économie", *RT* (1962)

LYONNET, S. J., "Chaire kecharitomene", *BA*, 20 (1939)

MICHL, J., "Der Weibessame (Gen. 3.15) in spätjudischer und frühchristlicher Auffassung", *BA*, 33 (1952)

MITTERER, A., *Dogma und Biologie*, Vienna (1952)

RIGAUX, B., "La Femme et son lignage dans Genèse III, 14–15", *RB*, 61 (1954)

SCHEDL, C., "Femina Circumdabit Virum", *ZKT*, 83

SCHNACKENBURG, R., *Das erste Wunder Jesu, Jo. 2, 1–11* (1951)

SCHULZ, A., "'Alma'", *BZ*, 23 (1935–6), pp. 229–41

SEMMELROTH, O., "Die unbefleckte Empfängnis als heilsökonomisches Zeichen", *SK*, 29 (1954)

TRABUCCO, A., "La Donna ravvolta di sole", *MM*, 19 (1957)

CHAPTER 2

BECK, E., "Die Mariologie der echten Schriften Ephraems", *OC*, 40 (1956)

FRIEDRICH, P., *Die Mariologie des hl. Augustinus* (1907)

GARÇON, J., *La Mariologie de S. Irénée*, Lyons (1932)

HAASE, F., " Die koptischen Quellen zum Konzil von Nicaea", *Studien zur Geschichte und Kultur des Altertums*, 10, 4 (1920)

HUHN, J., *Das Geheimnis der Jungfrau-Mutter nach dem Kirchenvater Ambrosius*, Würzburg (1954)

JOUASSARD, C. G., "Le Premier-Né de la Vierge chez s. Irénée et S. Hippolyte", *RSR*, 12 (1932), pp. 378ff.

JUGIE, M., "Les Homélies mariales attribuées à Grégoire le Thaumaturge", *AB*, 43 (1925)

KOCH, H., *Adhuc Virgo*, Tübingen (1929)

KOCH, H., *Virgo Eva—Virgo Maria*, Berlin–Leipzig (1937)

NEUMANN, C. W., *The Virgin Mary in the Works of St. Ambrose* (1962)

NIESSEN, J., *Die Mariologie des hl. Hieronymus* (1913)

SOARES, E. J., "Severianus of Gabala and the Protoevangelium", *MM*, 15 (1953)

SOELL, G., "Die Mariologie der Kappadozier im Licht der Dog-mengeschichte", *TQ*, 131 (1951)

STEGMÜLLER, O., "Sub tuum Praesidium", *ZKT*, 74 (1952)

STRICKER, E., *La forme la plus ancienne du protévangile de Jacques*, Brussels (1961)

CHAPTER 3

ABBELOOS, J. B., *De Vita et Scriptis S. Jacobi* (1867)

ATTWATER, D., *The Akathistos Hymn* (1934)

BARDENHEWER, O., *Marienpredigten aus der Väterzeit*, Munich (1934)

BAUMSTARK, O., "Die leibliche Himmelfahrt der allerseligsten Jungfrau", *OC*, 4 (1904)

CHAVASSE, A., *Le Sacrementaire Gélasien* (1958)

CHEVALIER, C., "La Mariologie de Romanos", *RSR*, 28 (1938)

CHEVALIER, C., *La Mariologie de saint Jean Damascène*, Rome (1936)

EBERLE, A., *Die Mariologie des Hl. Cyrillus von Alexandrien*, Freiburg (1921)

ÉMEREAU, C., "Hymnographi Byzantini", *EO*, 21 (1922)

FELDMANN, F., *Syrische Wechsellieder von Narses* (1896)

HENNINGER, J., *Spuren christlicher Glaubenswahrheiten im Koran* (1951)

HUGLO, M., "L'Ancienne Version latine de l'hymne Acathiste", *Muséon*, 64 (1951)

JUGIE, M., *L'Immaculée Conception*, Rome (1952)

JUGIE, M., *La Mort et l'Assomption*, *ST*, 114 (1944)

JÜSSEN, K., "Die Mariologie des Hesychius von Jerusalem", in *Theol. in Gesch. u. Gegenwart* (1957)

MEERSSEMAN, G. G., *Der Hymnos Akathistos im Abendland* (1958–60), 2 vols.

ROEY, VAN, *ETL* (1955)

WELLESZ, E., *The Akathistos Hymn*, 2nd ed. (1960)

WENGER, A., *L'Assomption de la très-sainte Vierge dans la tradition byzantine du VIe au Xe siècle*, Archives de l'Orient chrétien, 5, Paris (1955)

CHAPTER 4

BEISSEL, S., *Die Geschichte der Verehrung Marias in Deutschland während des Mittelalters*, Freiburg (1909)

LECLERQ, J., "Formes anciennes de l'office marial", *Eph. Liturg.* (1960); "Te Mariam Laudamus", *Eph. Liturg.* (1961), pp. 4–5

NEFF, K., "Die Gedichte des Paulus Diakonus", *Quellen und Untersuchungen*, 35, 5 (1908)

SCHEIDWEILER, F., "Studien zu Johannes Geometres", *Byzantinische Zeitschrift*, 45 (1952)

STEINEN, W. VON DEN, *Notker der Dichter und seine geistige Welt*, Berne (1948)

WEISWEILER, H., "Das frühe Marienbild der Westkirche", *SK*, 28 (1953)

WINANDY, J., "L'Œuvre littéraire d'Ambroise Autpert", *RB*, 60 (1950)

WINANDY, J., *Ambroise Autpert, moine et théologien*, Paris (1953)

CHAPTER 5

AUBRON, P., *L'Œuvre mariale de S. Bernard*, Juvisy (1936)

AUBRON, P., "La Mariologie de saint Bernard", *RSR*, 124 (1934), pp. 543ff.

BARON, R., "La Pensée mariale de Hugues de Saint Victor", *Revue d'ascétique et de mystique*, 31 (1955)

BARRÉ, H., "Prières mariales au Xe siècle", *EM*, 10 (1960)

BARRÉ, H., "Les Premières Prières mariales de l'Occident", *MM*, 21 (1959), 128–73

BARRÉ, H., "Le *Planctus Mariae* attribué à saint Bernard", *Revue d'ascétique et de mystique*, 28 (1952)

BERNARD, P., *Saint Bernard et Notre Dame* (1953)

BEUMER, J., "Die marianische Deutung des Hohen Liedes in der Frühscholastik", *ZKT*, 76 (1954)

BEUMER, J., "Der mariologische Gehalt der Predigten Gottfried von Admonts", *SK*, 35 (1960)

BRIGHTMAN, F. E., *Eastern Liturgies* (1896)

BRUDER, J. S., *The Mariology of Saint Anselm of Canterbury*, Dayton (Ohio) (1939)

BURRIDGE, A. W., "L'Immaculée Conception dans la théologie de l'Angleterre médiévale", *Revue d'histoire ecclésiastique*, 32 (1936)

CRUM, W. L., *Coptic Ostraca*, 1902

GLORIEUX, P., "Alain de Lille, Docteur de l'Assomption", *Mélanges de science religieuse*, 8 (1951)

LIPPHARDT, W., "Studien zu den Marienklagen", *Beiträge zur Geschichte der deutschen Sprache und Literatur*, 58 (1934), pp. 390–44

MUSSAFFIA, A., *Studien zu den mittelalterlichen Marienlegenden* (1887–98)

THURSTON, H., *Familiar Prayers*, London (1953)

WILMART, A., *Auteurs spirituels et textes dévots du moyen-âge latin* (1932)

CHAPTER 6

BALIČ, K., "Die Corredemptrixfrage innerhalb der franziskanischen Theologie", *FS*, 39 (1957)

BALIČ, K., *Theologiae Marianae Elementa*, Sibehik (1933)

BEUMER, J., "Eine dem hl. Bonaventura zu Unrecht zugeschriebene Marienpredigt", *FST*, 42 (1960)

BEUMER, J., "Die Mariologie Richards von Saint-Laurent", *FS*, 41 (1959)

BRADY, I., "The Development of the Doctrine of the Immaculate Conception in the Fourteenth Century after Aureoli", *Franciscan Studies*, 15 (1955)

DESMARIS, M. M., *S. Albert le Grand, Docteur de la médiation mariale* (1935) (superseded)

EMMEN, A. "Die Bedeutung der Franziskanerschule für die Mariologie", *FS*, 36 (1954)

EMMEN, A. "Einführung in die Mariologie der Oxforder Franziskanerschule", *FS*, 39 (1957)

FRIES, A., "Die unter dem Namen des Albertus Magnus überlieferten mariologischen Schriften, Münster (1954)

FRIES, A., *Die Gedanken des hl. Albertus Magnus über die Gottesmutter*, Fribourg (1958)

HUBER, R., *The Mariology of St. Anthony of Padua* (1952)

JURIČ, J., "Franciscus de Mayronis, Immaculatae Conceptionis eximius vindex", *Studi Francescani*, 51 (1954)

KOLPING, A., "Zur Frage der Textgeschichte . . . der anonymen *Laus Virginis*", *RTAM*, 25 (1958)

KOROSAK, B., *Mariologia Sancti Alberti Magni eiusque coaequalium*, Rome (1954)

KOSER, K., "Die Immakulatalehre des Johannes Duns Scotus", *FS*, 36 (1954)

LONGPRÉ, E., *La Vierge Immaculée*.

MAREI, A., "Litterarhistorische Notizen über Petrus Aureoli", *GM* (1958)

MERKELBACH, B. H., "Quid senserit S. Thomas de mediatione Beatae Mariae Virginis", *Xenia Thomistica*, 2 (1925)

MEYENDORFF, J., *Introduction à l'étude de Grégoire Palamas* (1959)

MILDNER, F. M., "The Oxford Theologians of the Thirteenth Century and the Immaculate Conception", *MM*, 2, 291

MORGOTT, F., *Die Mariologie des hl. Thomas von Aquin* (1878)

PELSTER, F., "Zwei Untersuchungen über die literarischen Grundlagen für die Darstellung einer Mariologie des hl. Albert des Grossen", *SK*, 30 (1956)

PLESSER, V., "Die Lehre des hl. Bonaventura über die Mittlerschaft Mariens", *FS*, 23 (1936)

ROSATO, L., *Doctrina de Immaculata Beatae Virginis Mariae Conceptione* (1959)

ROSCHINI, G., *La Mariologia di San Tommaso*, Rome (1950)

STROTMANN, D. T., "La Théotokos, Prémices des Justifiés", *Irénikon*, 27 (1954)

VALOIS, N., "Pierre Auriol, Frère Mineur", in *Histoire littéraire de la France*, 33 (1906)

XIBERTA, B. F. M., "De Magistro Johanne Baconthorp", *Analecta Ordinis Carmelitarum*, 6 (1927)

SUBJECT INDEX

Adoptianism, 173
Albigensians, 256f.
Alma Redemptoris Mater, 229f.
'*Almah*, 4f., 7, 10, 37, 63f., 75, 92
Angelus, 308
Annunciation, 6–10, 139, 142, 149, 191f., 286, 324
Antidicomarianites, 70, 73
Apollinarianism (Apollinarius), 64f., 107
Arianism, Arians, 51, 64, 77ff., 118
Asceticism, 50ff.
Assumption, 72, 122f., 133–8, 141, 142f., 146ff., 155, 157ff., 161, 166, 172, 178ff., 183ff., 191, 195f., 199f., 202, 204ff., 208, 217, 222–4, 225, 233, 236, 240f., 242f., 246, 248f., 256f., 268, 273f., 278, 296, 323, 334, 342, 346
Ave Stella Maris, see *Stella Maris*

Brethren of Jesus, 13, 45, 54f., 67, 89ff.

Christology, relation to Mariology, 52, 78, 103f., 111, 117, 142, 278
Collyridians, 70, 72f.
Commemoration, Feast of, 123f, 127, 133
Communicatio idiomatum, 338f.
Compassion, see Cross
Coredemptress, see Redemption
Cross, Mary under the, 17, 24ff., 46, 63, 72, 81f., 84, 86, 96f., 114, 122, 126, 170, 189, 193, 200f., 244, 261, 273, 276, 284f., 287, 294, 296, 306f., 309, 320, 341, see also Sword of Simeon's prophecy

Death of Mary, see Assumption
Demon, 2, 25, 63f., 128, 155, 171, 205, 247, 284f., 292, 331f.
Devil, see Demon
Docetism, 16

Eve, see Second Eve
Ever-Virgin, see Virginity, perpetual

Filioque, 348

Garments of skin, 59f., 346
Gnosticism, 33, 41f., 49, 116
Grusshymnen, 231f.
Grusspsalter, 232

Hail Mary, 230f., 269, 290
Hesychasm, 332, 334
Hypapante, 48, 112f., 139, 142, 169, 286
Hyperdoulia, 73, 88, 156, 275, 283

Icon, Iconoclasm, 145, 183, 193
Immaculate Conception, xviii, 1, 57f., 64, 82f., 87, 99, 117f., 120ff., 124, 139, 148f., 151f., 154f., 163, 177, 182ff., 188, 192ff., 197, 199, 206ff., 210ff., 218–20, 224f., 227f., 234ff., 247, 250–2, 256f., 265f., 268, 273f., 279, 282, 290, 292, 295, 298–306, 309, 310f., 311, 314f., 319, 321f., 324ff., 330ff., 336f., 340, 345, 347f., 349f.
Imperfection, see under Mary, Faults
Intercession, 40, 64, 135f., 147f., 161, 168, 171, 173, 185, 190, 205, 208, 216ff., 226, 274f., 286, 297, 302, see also Mediatress
Isis, see Mother Goddess

Litanies, Litany of Loreto, 232
Little Office, see Office of Our Lady
Liturgy, 87, 111, 115, 119, 142f., 144, 168, 173, 178f., 227, 230, 241
Lives of Mary, 259–64
Lourdes, 203

Magna Mater, see Mother Goddess
Manicheans, Manicheism, 49, 54, 94, 116

NAME INDEX

Part 2

**From the Reformation
to the
Present Day**

CONTENTS

CONTENTS

FROM THE AGE OF THE REFORMATION TO THE EIGHTEENTH CENTURY

MANY things had contributed to the breaking up of the medieval order. The Hundred Years War, the Black Death, the Great Schism and the Mohammedan invasions had bled Europe white, both physically and mentally. Scholasticism had degenerated into a mere play with words which could no longer be taken seriously. The *Devotio Moderna*, which spread to the rest of Europe from the Netherlands in the fourteenth century, had provided a spiritual renewal, but its one-sided emphasis on a personal religion and its opposition to all secular interests, emphasized so strongly in its most influential literary product, the *Imitation of Christ* (c. 1418), could not satisfy a new generation which, after all the catastrophes, thirsted for another mode of life, for adventures of both mind and body and for sensual enjoyment. In the Middle Ages both art and scholarship had been completely devoted to the Christian religion; now these were freed from subservience to the Church and practised in their own right, as merely "human" activities.

Strangely enough, this new movement was not only not condemned, but even actively supported by the Church. In 1447 Pope Nicholas V had made Rome the centre of humanism, Pius II (1458–64), who had himself been a humanist of high repute before becoming pope, continued to favour the movement, and the popes of the later fifteenth and the early sixteenth centuries such as Alexander VI (1492–1503), Julius II (1503–13) and Leo X (1513–21) were all very worldly men, more interested in the arts and their own pleasures than in religion. It needed the Sack of Rome in 1527 to put an end to the paganism of the Italy of the Renaissance which had scarcely been shaken even by the religious upheavals beyond the Alps.

ERASMUS OF ROTTERDAM

The Renaissance artists depicted the Mother of God as a beautiful woman of their time, sensuous and entirely of this world. The humanists took little interest in her, as they were either not concerned with the Christian faith at all or else opposed to the popular devotion of the time which centred almost completely in Mary and the saints. This was certainly so in the case of the greatest of the humanists, Erasmus of Rotterdam (d. 1536). Erasmus is an extremely interesting and many-sided personality, and therefore very differently interpreted according to one's point of view. We are only concerned with his attitude to the blessed Virgin. Erasmus was educated by the "Brethren of the Common Life", who were exponents of the *Devotio Moderna*; later he became an Augustinian canon and was ordained priest in 1492. In 1493 he left his Order with the consent of his superiors and continued his studies in Paris. In 1499 he visited England for the first time and became the friend of Thomas More, John Colet and John Fisher. During the next twenty years he lived alternately in England, Italy and the Netherlands; in 1521 he went to Basle, but had to leave it in 1529 because he would not join the Reformers. He spent his last years at Freiburg in Germany.

In his early years Erasmus fully shared the Catholic Marian devotion of his time; he wrote a "Paean" to the Virgin Mother,[1] in which he calls her the only ornament of heaven and the most certain help of earth, with whom Christ willed to share his Kingdom, and who is invoked everywhere.[2] In a "Prayer to the Virgin Mother Mary in Misfortune" he addresses her as our only hope in our calamities[3]; and he also composed a

[1] All quotations from the Leyden edition of his works, 1703–06.
[2] 5 (1227–34).   [3] 5 (1233–40).

"Liturgy of the Virgin of Loreto" in which she is given all the usual epithets. But as he began to study the Bible and the Fathers more carefully and came into contact with the popular abuses of his time his tone changed. He reacted violently to the external practices that only too often took the place of true religion in this age of decline; and he poured his sarcasm on the superstition that was rife everywhere. He wanted to see Christ once more at the centre of Catholicism and the moral law reinstated in the place of merely external pious practices. If he not infrequently went too far in his criticisms this is due to the incredibly low standard of popular religion as well as to his ironic bent of mind.

His most biting sarcasms on contemporary Marian devotion occur in his *Familiar Colloquies*, especially in *The Shipwreck*, the *Pilgrimage for Devotion*, and *The Eating of Fish*. In the *Shipwreck* the sailors call on Mary, chanting the *Salve Regina*: "They implored the Virgin Mother, calling her Star of the Sea, Queen of Heaven, Mistress of the World, Port of Salvation and many other flattering titles which Holy Scripture nowhere applies to her." The question is then asked what Mary has to do with the sea, since she appears never to have sailed on it, and the answer comes that once Venus was the protectress of sailors, whose place has now been taken by the blessed Virgin —a reply which is not without an historical foundation. There was also an Englishman on board who promised golden mountains to the Virgin of Walsingham, which had been the most important Marian centre of pilgrimage since the eleventh century, if she were to save him from the waters. Now Erasmus was not really opposed to Marian shrines, having visited Walsingham twice in 1512 and 1514 and himself offered there a *Carmen votivum* in Greek, but he wanted to combat the superstitious idea that a vow would be invalid unless attached to a specified place where the blessed Virgin was venerated. Besides, he blames the Christians of his time that in danger they never seem to address themselves to God, but only to Our Lady and the saints.[1]

In the *Pilgrimage* Erasmus attacks the idea which we have met so often before that Christ can never deny his mother anything, in the form of a letter purporting to be written by Mary herself to Glaucoplutus, a Protestant. In this she says that she is glad that Luther has put a stop to the streams of prayer that went up to her all the time. For it is always she who is asked, as if her Son were still an infant in her arms who did not dare deny her anything for fear she might refuse him her milk. But the worst is that they often ask her such dreadful things that she cannot even mention them in writing. Then follows a description of the wishes of her clients which casts a rather lurid light on the morals of those "devout" to her, but which is not altogether exaggerated. For example, a young nun casts off her veil and asks the Mother of God to defend the reputation of her virginity which she is about to throw away; a businessman going to Spain entrusts to her the faithfulness of his concubine; soldiers planning a robbery ask for a fat haul; a prostitute for rich customers, and priests for a lucrative benefice. If she refuses, she is accused of not being the Mother of mercy, if she commits the requests to her Son she is told that he wills whatever she wills. All this, Mary says, was very distasteful to her; and she is glad to be rid of it. But this is a small blessing compared with the evils that have followed. For now she has far less honour than before, when she was called Queen of heaven and Mistress of the world, now hardly anyone will even say a *Hail Mary*. But even this she would have tolerated; however, greater things are at stake. Every saint has a weapon to avenge an injury; Peter may lock up heaven and Paul has a sword. She, Mary, has only her Son, from whom she will never be separated—so no-one can cast her out of the Church without casting him out, too.[2] This latter part of the *Letter to Glauco-*

[1] Vol. 1 (713A–714A).
[2] 775B–776B.

plutus shows clearly Erasmus' position: he only attacks an external devotion devoid of any truly religious and moral content, and on the other hand he affirms that the veneration of Mary is inescapably linked to the worship of Christ. We cannot therefore agree with C. Dillenschneider[1] when he calls this Letter an apology of the antagonists of the cult of Mary. It is not the cult itself that is attacked, quite the contrary, but the degenerate forms it had taken in the fifteenth and sixteenth centuries, of which as eminent a Mariologist as R. Laurentin writes: "One shudders to see the miserable situation in which Marian devotion found itself when the Protestant crisis broke out."[2] But then Dillenschneider had not read Erasmus himself but only the extracts published in Peter Canisius's comprehensive apologetic work *De Maria Virgine incomparabili*, from which he quotes—a none too safe procedure to ascertain the real thought of an author. In the chapter on "Ichthyophagia" (Fish-eating) Erasmus himself complains that those who oppose the exaggerations of Marian devotion are immediately suspected of heresy.[3] He is only against the constant invocation of Mary and the complete absence of prayer to the Holy Spirit, who had always been called upon by the Fathers such as Basil, Chrysostom, Ambrose, Jerome and Augustine. And he can hardly be blamed for criticizing those who are devout to the blessed Virgin with images, candles and chants but defy Christ by an impious life. They think she will be propitious to them if they sing the *Salve Regina* which they do not even understand, but offend her by spending their nights in obscenities.[4]

Erasmus was also a fine biblical scholar who did not use the Vulgate, as had been done hitherto, but the Greek original. So he translates *kecharitomene* no longer as *gratia plena*, full of grace, but as *gratiosa*, "being in favour", which is much nearer the true meaning of the Greek.[5] For this, too, he is attacked by

---

[1] *La Mariologie de St. Alphonse de Liguori* (1931), p. 15.
[2] *Maria*, 3, p. 14.   [3] 809B.
[4] 808F.   [5] *Commentary on Luke*, 1, 35; vol. 6 (223 D, 1).

Dillenschneider, who again quotes not from Erasmus himself but from Maldonatus' *Commentary on Luke*,[1] though this translation is now generally admitted by Catholic theologians. Erasmus also rightly translates *tapeinosis* in the *Magnificat* not as "humility" but as lowliness because, as he says quite rightly, it would be a strange kind of humility that was conscious of its own merit,[2] adding that theologians would be well advised to let themselves be guided by linguists—a view more easily accepted today than in his own time. He adds some further criticisms of the exaggerations we have already noted such as attributing the Beatific Vision to Mary even in this life[3] and of teaching that Christ obeys her because she is his mother. This he considers preposterous, seeing that even a father has no power over his human son who holds an office of authority in the State or the Church. How can Christ possibly be still under the authority of his mother if even civil law allows grown-up sons to marry or enter the religious life without the consent of their parents? "To me it seems a hard word to say of Christ, He owed obedience. Who owes something, sins unless he pays it. They will cry out that this offends pious ears. But what they say rather offends mine."[4] It can hardly be denied that Erasmus was justified in his opposition to the idea that even the risen Christ reigning in heaven is subject to his human mother, which, as we have seen, was so widely held in the later Middle Ages. Nevertheless, apart from his few early Marian writings, he never spoke again about the Mother of God except to criticize the excesses of devotion to her. Hence one must agree that though himself remaining a Catholic he played into the hands of the Reformers, who owed many of their arguments to him.

LUTHER

The first generation of them, however, did not yet abandon devotion to Mary completely, though their principles finally

---

[1] pp. 10f.
[2] *Commentary*, 1, 48 (225F–227B).
[3] *Commentary*, 2, 52 (238E, F).
[4] *Commentary* (239D).

led to this. For neither Luther nor Calvin would admit any contribution to salvation on the part of man. God's grace did everything, man did nothing. In Luther's view man remained a sinner whatever he did, God only imputing to him the merits of Christ; in Calvin's his salvation or damnation was immutably predestined from all eternity. If such was the case, what use was any intercession? But Luther was the less logical of the two Reformers; he would still admit that Mary could pray for us just as we can pray for each other; whereas Calvin would not allow even this. Indeed, Luther still retained a remarkable amount of Catholic teaching about her which was only jettisoned by his successors. Nevertheless, it can hardly be said of him that "his Marian piety is as strong and warm as that of the medieval clients of Mary", as R. Schimmelpfennig writes in her *History of Marian Devotion in German Protestantism*.[1] This is an unwarrantable exaggeration. Luther's whole view of Mary as a rather pathetic young girl without intrinsic sanctity or merit is opposed to Catholic teaching.

Naturally, before he broke with the Church he still accepted this teaching. In 1516 he preached a Latin sermon on the Immaculate Conception[2] and one on the Assumption[3] which hardly differ from similar contemporary sermons on the same subjects. Even in 1520, three years after he had affixed his famous Ninety-five Theses to the door of the Schlosskirche at Wittenberg he still quoted saints like Bernard and Augustine, stating that Mary had first received Christ in her soul before conceiving him in her womb.[4] But a year later, in his *Exposition of the Magnificat*, most of which was written before he went to the Diet of Worms and which he finished on the Wartburg while waiting for the development of his movement, his tone became different.[5] True, at the beginning and end of the

[1] *Die Geschichte der Marienverehrung im deutschen Protestantismus* (1952), p. 12.
[2] Weimar edition, vol. 1, pp. 106f.   [3] pp. 77–9.
[4] *Sermon on the Nativity of Christ*, vol. 7, pp. 188–93.
[5] Vol. 7, pp. 538–604.

work he still asks "the tender Mother of God" to obtain for
him the right spirit to explain the Canticle usefully and
thoroughly[1]; but this spirit differs considerably from that of the
traditional interpretation. Luther retains Mary's perfect virginity, including the virginity *in partu*,[2] and he praises her
humility and her perfect abandonment, which rule out any
pride or possessiveness about the tremendous honour that God
has done her by making her his mother. Nevertheless, in
accordance with his teaching that man can do absolutely
nothing to co-operate with God and everything is wholly due
to his grace, the Reformer stresses over and over again that
Mary has nothing of herself, indeed, she herself is but "nothingness".[3] If we would honour her we should say to her: "O
blessed Virgin and Mother of God, how utterly nothing and
despised you have been, and yet God has looked upon you so
graciously and abundantly and has done great things in you.
You have not been worthy of any of these, and the superabundant grace of God is in you far above your merit."[4] He blames
those who honour her, because they make an "idol" of her. To
honour her properly, she should "be stripped completely of
everything and only be regarded in her nothingness, afterwards
we should admire the overwhelming grace of God who looks
so graciously on such a lowly, worthless human being".[5] If, on
the other hand, she is represented as having great things of
herself we are contrasted with her and not she with God, and
so we lose all confidence in his grace. Because she was so unworthy and God nevertheless gave her so much grace, we are
encouraged to trust in him.[6] The whole Lutheran theology is
in this: man can do nothing whatsoever, everything comes
from God without any human co-operation.

Strangely, and inconsistently enough, Luther firmly believes
that Mary was completely without sin, which in itself surely

[1] p. 545.
[2] p. 549.
[3] p. 568.
[4] p. 568.
[5] p. 568.
[6] p. 569.

makes her different from us,[1] even though this is due only to grace. Apart from her physical contribution her co-operation in the divine motherhood is precisely nil. Luther does not object to the words of the *Regina caeli* "quem meruisti portare" (whom you have merited to bear), because we say the same of the Cross, which is only wood. This expression means no more than that she was suitable and foreordained to give birth to Christ, just as the wood of the Cross was suitable and foreordained to bear his body. According to Luther one must say this, "so that God's praise and honour might not be diminished by attributing too much to her. It is better to give too little to her than to the grace of God. Indeed, one can never give her too little (what a difference to the principles of medieval preachers!) since she is created from nothing like all other creatures." She may indeed be called "Queen of heaven", but this does not make her an idol (*Abgöttin*), "that she might give or help, like some people think . . . She gives nothing, but only God."[2] The comparison of Mary with the wood of the Cross is characteristic of Luther, in whose theology human free will has no place. It deprives not only Mary of the honour due to her, but every human being of his dignity.

In the next year, 1522, Luther's thought becomes even more unorthodox. In his *Sermon on Mary's Nativity*[3] he affirms that "we are just as holy as she, for that she has a greater grace is not due to her merit". We could not all be the Mother of God; but otherwise she is just the same as we are.[4] He assures his hearers that they will not be damned even if they should never honour nor even think of the Mother of God—but if they do not give alms to the poor they will, indeed, be damned, a reaction to a purely external devotion which Luther, like Erasmus, carried to extremes. Nevertheless, the Reformer still allows his followers to ask her for her intercession, like the

[1] p. 573.
[2] pp. 573f.
[3] 103, 312–31.
[4] p. 316.
[5] p. 322.

other saints, "but we will not have her for our advocate",[1] the difference between the two being that the term "advocate" implies an actual contribution to the efficacy of prayer through her merits. In the same year Luther also preached on the sorrows of Mary when he explained the loss of Jesus in the Temple and took the opportunity to criticize those who attributed omniscience to Mary: "The Virgin has no need of false, invented praise" he said—obviously a reminiscence of St Bernard.[2] He frequently insists on Mary's emptiness and lowliness nearly always with the idea that thus we may gain confidence,[3] and even believes her to have been a poor, despised little orphan,[4] an idea for which there is no evidence in Scripture. As is seen from these sermons Luther did not at once abolish the Marian feasts. In his Church Order of 1523 he wants to keep the feasts of the Purification and the Annunciation, because they are feasts of Christ, and to retain those of the Assumption and the Nativity for some time, because their abolition would have upset the people too much.[5]

It certainly cannot be said that Luther's devotion to the Blessed Virgin was as warm and tender as that of the medieval saints. In fact, W. Tappolet[6] admits that, when collecting the material for his book, the file of Luther headed "Limits of Sanctity and Errors of Marian devotion" contained more material than any of the others; and in his explanation of Jer. xi.13 the Reformer even equates the Catholic devotion to the Blessed Virgin with the cult of Baal denounced by the prophet.[7] Nevertheless, he seems to have had a real affection for the "little maiden" whose faith he deeply admired, and whose grace he never doubted. Though he believed that at the wedding of Cana Christ reproved his mother, he praised her for yet believing in his goodness and telling the servants to do his

---

[1] p. 325.   [2] Vol. 12, 413.
[3] *Sermon on the Feast of the Visitation* (1523), vol. 12, p. 614.
[4] p. 458.   [5] Vol. 12, pp. 37 and 209.
[6] *Das Marienlob der Reformatoren* (1962), p. 93.
[7] *Anmerkungen zur Bibelübersetzung*, 4, 96.

bidding.[1] In a sermon on the Annunciation (1527) he held up her faith as an example, showing his well-known hatred of reason by adding that she did not follow this.[2] He again emphasizes her littleness by explaining her name not as Lady, Star of the Sea or Bitter Sea, but as "a little drop of water".[3] He opposes the *Ave Maria* as a prayer, but admits that she is full of grace, "because the grace of God makes her full of all that is good and empty of all evil".[4] He still believes even in the Immaculate Conception in the full Catholic sense, saying that "one believes blessedly that at the very infusion of her soul she was also purified from original sin".[5] He seems to have given up this belief later on, though he still held even in 1544, two years before his death, that she was completely without sin when she conceived the Lord Jesus.[6] In another sermon on the Wedding of Cana, preached in 1528, Luther stressed Christ's anger with her even more than he had done three years before and asserted that she was in the wrong, even though he once more praised her faith. But, he continued: "At that time Christ then realized ... that in time his mother would be given greater honour ... than he himself, that is to say one would believe her to be a mediatress and an advocate between God and ourselves; in order to prevent this he addresses her very harshly not only here but also in other places in order to show that we ought not to be concerned with her but with him."[7] Luther

---

[1] 17² (65–7) preached in 1525.

[2] 17 (399f).

[3] p. 405.

[4] p. 409.

[5] 17² (288).

[6] Vol. 52, p. 39. We therefore agree with W. Tappolet (p. 32): "The assertion of H. Preuss, that from 1528 onwards Luther no longer believed in the Immaculate Conception, only because there are no explicit statements on the subject, is no less doubtful than that of R. Schimmelpfennig, according to which Luther held the same view which the Church of Rome defined as a dogma in 1854" and with his statement that, whatever Luther's later attitude to the Immaculate Conception, he believed till the end of his life that "Mary, even if she should not have been without original sin from birth, was purified from it by the Holy Spirit at the moment of the conception of Jesus". (Tappolet, text.)

[7] 21 (65).

does not, however, explain why this action of Christ had so little effect that the Blessed Virgin has nevertheless been invoked as our advocate in the whole Church from very early times.

It is significant that he himself had to admit that his followers did not replace devotion to Mary by more fervent prayer to her Son. On 25 March 1532 he complained: "Once we said so many rosaries to Mary; now we are so sleepy in prayer to Christ that we do not pray even once in a whole year. God will surely punish this indifference to the Saviour. Is it not a shame once to have elevated the Mother so highly and now completely to forget the Son?"[1] In his later years Luther preached much less about Mary, but he never wavered in his belief in her perfect virginity and her divine Motherhood, which he still vigorously affirmed in 1543.[2]

CALVIN

Calvin (d.1564) gave an even lower place to the Blessed Virgin. As K. Algermissen says in his important article on him in *Lexikon der Marienkunde*,[3] Calvin's "mariological thought, like all his other views, was determined by his central theological idea of the majesty and glory of God, before which all creaturely being and action has almost no importance whatsoever". Since everything depends solely on the will of God he rejects even the intercession of the Blessed Virgin.[4] Indeed, Calvin considers all prayer addressed to her to be against Scripture; to ask her to obtain grace for us is no less than an "execrable blasphemy", because God has predestined the measure of grace for every man from all eternity.[5] To call her our hope, life, light and other similar names is to turn her into

---

[1] 36 (152).   [2] 53, 640–43.

[3] I am indebted to this article, the first comprehensive presentation of the subject, for the following paragraphs.

[4] Ep. 1438 (op. 14, 21); Edition: *Calvini Opera omnia*, Braunschweig-Berlin (1864–1900), from which all following quotations are taken.

[5] *Art. facult.*, Paris 15 (op. 7, 44).

an idol and detract from God's honour,[1] and to regard her as our "advocate" is blasphemous, because she needed Christ as much as all other human beings.[2] The same holds good for such poetical expressions as sweetness, hope and so forth, which, Calvin alleges, are contrary to Mary's own wishes, because by applying these terms to her we praise herself, not God in her.[3] On the other hand, he fully recognizes the dignity of her divine motherhood.[4] "It cannot be denied", he writes, "that by electing and destining Mary to be the mother of his Son, God gave her the highest honour."[5] He also teaches her perpetual virginity, but ridicules the idea that she had made a formal vow; after the Annunciation all intercourse with men was excluded for ever.[6] Even though he rejects any cult, he wants his followers to venerate and praise her and regard her as a teacher who instructs them in the commandments of Christ.[7] When saying the *Magnificat* they should recognize that she was filled with many virtues and praise God after her example, that is by recognizing that we ourselves are nothing.[8] In the same French *Harmony of the Gospels* Calvin calls Mary, surprisingly, the treasurer of grace (la trésorière de la grâce), because she has preserved all things in her heart not for her own use, but for others. She is not, however, treasurer in the Catholic sense. Calvin's expression only means that she has preserved the doctrine which opens the kingdom of heaven as a good entrusted to her and we have received it through her mediation so that by means of her we might be guided to our Lord Jesus Christ. "The Spirit of God places her here like a picture, so that every man should conform himself to the reverence she has brought to the Word of God."[9]

---

[1] *Serm. 139,* op. 29, 213; and *Serm. 64* in Job, op. 34, 27.
[2] *Serm. de la proph. du Christ,* op. 35, 686f.
[3] *Harm. Ev. ad Luc.,* I, 34 (op. 45, 35).
[4] I, 34 (op. 45, 35).   [5] I, 27 (op. 45, 348).
[6] I, 34 (op. 45, 30).   [7] I, 34 (op. 45, 38).
[8] *Harmonie Evangélique Serm. 11* (op. 46, 122).
[9] Op. 46, 309f.

ZWINGLI

The third of the great Continental Reformers, Ulrich Zwingli (d. 1531), a native of the Swiss canton St. Gall, followed Luther's line. In his *Marienpredigt* of 1522[1] he emphasized, like the German Reformer, her poverty and lowliness as well as her permanent virginity. Her faith remained intact even on Calvary where she was an example of fortitude; Zwingli rightly reacts against the medieval presentations of her as swooning and lamenting under the Cross. He objects to a false trust in the recitation of *Hail Marys* without a corresponding Christian life; for, he says, Mary's greatest honour is her Son and our love for him, "and the more the honour and love of Christ Jesus grows among them, the more grows also the esteem of Mary". Nevertheless, he rejects her veneration together with the veneration of saints in general, since he does not believe that they belong to the Church.[2]

BULLINGER

Heinrich Bullinger (d. 1575), though belonging to the second generation of Protestants, was important especially through his influence on the Reformation in England. Having dedicated his *Hausbuch* to Edward VI and the Duke of Suffolk, during the persecution under Mary he harboured many of the higher English clergy who turned to him for advice when they returned home under Elizabeth I. Bullinger's *Mariology* is nearer to Catholic beliefs than that of the other Reformers. Like Zwingli, he, too, wrote a *Marienpredigt*, though his other works, for example his *Commentary on Luke*, also contain some Marian material.[3] He defends Mary's perpetual virginity, including the virginity *in partu*[4] and inveighs against the false Christians (*Scheinchristen*) who defraud her of her rightful

---

[1] Published in vol. 1, pp. 391–428 of his *Works*, Berlin 1905.
[2] Cf Tappolet, pp. 240–55.
[3] I quote the *Marienpredigt* from the comprehensive extracts given in Tappolet, pp. 263–338, the original work being inaccessible to me.
[4] pp. 277ff.

praise: "In Mary everything is extraordinary and all the more glorious as it has sprung from pure faith and burning love of God."[1] She is "the most unique and the noblest member" of the Christian community, not, however, its head or mistress.[2] He will not pronounce either on her Immaculate Conception or her bodily Assumption: "Let it suffice us", he says, "simply to believe and confess that the Virgin Mary ... completely sanctified by the grace and blood of her only Son and abundantly endowed by the gift of the Holy Spirit and preferred to all ... now lives happily with Christ in heaven and is called and remains ever-Virgin and Mother of God. ..."[3] But despite his sincere veneration for her, Bullinger rejects her invocation[4] and mediation, though this does not mean that he is hostile to her, else he would also be an enemy of Christ.[5] In his work *De origine erroris*, 16 (1568), he even professes the belief that the body of the Virgin Mother of God has been taken up to heaven by the angels, because he does not think that Elijah can have been superior to her in this respect. As Tappolet points out,[6] this sentence, still retained in the Dutch edition of 1602, was eliminated in the French edition of 1549 (Geneva).

PROTESTANT CREEDS

In contrast to the Reformers themselves the official Protestant Creeds contain next to no teaching about the Mother of God. The Confession of Augsburg (1530) drawn up by Melanchthon and approved by Luther rejects the Catholic veneration of Mary in Article 21; and the Lutheran attitude is further explained in Melanchthon's *Apologia Confessionis Augustanae* where he opposes the verse, recited frequently in the Breviary office of the time: "Mother of grace, protect us from the enemy, receive us in the hour of death." "Even though the Mother of God prays for the churches," says Melanchthon, "this is too much

[1] p. 290.   [2] p. 291.
[3] p. 292.   [4] p. 289.
[5] p. 292.   [6] p. 327.

that she should overcome death and protect us from the great power of Satan. For why should Christ be needed, if Mary could do this? For even though she is worthy of the highest praise, she nevertheless does not want to be considered equal to Christ, but would rather that we should follow the example of her faith and humility. Now it is quite obvious that through such false teaching Mary has been put in the place of Christ; she has been invoked, men have trusted in her goodness, they have wanted to reconcile Christ through her, just as if he were not the Reconciler but only a terrible Judge, desirous of revenge."[1] The Schmalkaldic Articles (1537) drawn up by Luther himself, only state that the Son was born of the pure, holy Virgin Mary.[2] The Formula of Concord (1577) is slightly more explicit; the Virgin is called highly praised (*hochgelobt*), her virginity *in partu* is affirmed as well as her true divine Motherhood and her perpetual virginity.[3]

THE ENGLISH REFORMERS

The attitude of the English Reformers was similar, though in the Book of Common Prayer, which underwent many changes between 1549 and 1662, the feasts of the Purification, Annunciation, Visitation, Nativity and even the Conception of Mary were still retained. But Article 22 of the Thirty-Nine Articles, first issued in 1563, forbade completely the "invocation of Saints" as "a fond thing vainly invented and . . . repugnant to the Word of God", and the feasts were there really only in name. All the Marian shrines, including Walsingham, were destroyed; within two generations the Mother of God had faded from the memory of Anglicans, and Puritanism did the rest to uproot devotion to her completely not only in the Free Churches but also in the Church of England in the sixteenth century.

---

[1] T. Kolbe, *Die symbolischen Bücher der evangelisch-lutherischen Kirche* (1912), p. 227, from which also the following quotations are taken.
[2] 1, 4 (p. 229).   [3] 2, 8 (p. 679).

THE COUNCIL OF TRENT

The Council of Trent (1545–63), convoked to deal with the catastrophic situation the Reformation had brought about, had too much on its hands to deal explicitly with questions of Mariology. It only declared in its decree on original sin (15th Session, 17 June 1546) that this did not include the Blessed Virgin, and in its decree on the veneration of saints (22nd Session, 3–4 December 1563) that it was good and useful to invoke them in order to obtain benefits from God through his Son Jesus Christ, without mentioning, but necessarily including, her in this general defence of prayer to the saints.

THE ROSARY

In Catholic countries, of course, the veneration of the blessed Virgin continued as before. The Rosary devotion had become particularly popular, though it had not yet acquired our stereotyped form, even among the Dominicans, its foremost popularizers since Alain de la Roche (c. 1470) founded his Rosary Confraternities. He was the first to connect St. Dominic with it, but, as H. Thurston has pointed out, he "based his revelations on the imaginary testimony of writers that never existed".[1] The devotion in its present form of the meditation of its special fifteen mysteries accompanied by 150 *Aves* and fifteen *Paters* and *Glorias* developed in the sixteenth century. The Feast of the Rosary was first instituted by the Dominican Pope St. Pius V, who attributed the naval victory over the Turks at Lepanto on Sunday, 7 October 1571, to the rosaries recited on that day by the Roman Confraternities.

---

[1] *Catholic Encyclopedia*, under Rosary. See also his articles in *The Month* (October 1900 and ff.); H. Holzapfel, *St. Dominikus und der Rosenkranz* (1903). M. Gorce, in *Les origines du Rosaire et ses antécédents historiques* (1931), still defended the legendary attribution to St. Dominic, repeated in several papal documents on the subject, though in the bull of Leo X *Pastoris Aeterni* it is still qualified by the words "as it reads in the histories", and Pius V adds "as is piously believed".

PETER CANISIUS

The Rosary devotion was also taken up by the Jesuits; one of its most ardent promoters was Peter Canisius (d. 1597), who saw in the renewal of Marian devotion the best way to make good the ravages of the Reformation. He also wrote the first important Mariological work after the Reformation in defence of the Catholic veneration of the Mother of God, *De Maria Virgine Incomparabili*, which appeared at Ingolstadt in 1577. The work is divided into five parts, dealing with Mary's origin, youth and virtues, with her perpetual virginity and sinlessness, her divine motherhood, the biblical foundations of Mariology and her Assumption and cult. The treatise quotes extensively not only from the Fathers and the medieval theologians, but also from the writings of the Reformers, and is free from most of the exaggerations of the fourteenth- and fifteenth-century authors, though it accepts the various apocryphal stories and the later legends without any attempt at criticism. Canisius reacts strongly against Luther's idea of Mary's humble origin and his interpretation of her name as a "little drop". He stresses her unique dignity, which even some Protestants acknowledge, beginning with her position as the Second Eve and discussing her Old-Testament types.[1] He affirms the Immaculate Conception, which Luther himself had still accepted for a time, but which was completely rejected by his followers,[2] and he defends against Luther the traditional inclusion of the Wisdom passages in the Marian Liturgy on the grounds that Mary had been predestined and foreseen from all eternity.[3] Though Canisius says explicitly that he will not defend the apocryphal Gospel of St. James, he nevertheless reproduces the story of her upbringing in the Temple from other authorities, without realizing that these all go back to the Gospel of St. James as their source.[4] He cannot see why it should be absurd that Mary should have been nourished by angels and quotes the *Revelations of St.*

[1] 1–3 (2–25).   [2] 1, 5ff. (33ff.).
[3] 1, 11 (75).   [4] 1, 11f. (78–84).

Bridget on the subject as well as those of other mystics.[1] In the second book Canisius defends the traditional Catholic belief in Mary's vow of virginity which she made even before the Annunciation and in her personal merit, which, of course, the Reformers had to deny because of their doctrine of justification by faith alone.[2] In book three, treating of the divine mother-hood, Canisius first discusses the angelic salutation and its use in the *Hail Mary*[3] as well as the Rosary.[4] He attacks both Erasmus and the Reformers for translating *gratiosa* instead of *gratia plena* and insists that the latter is the right rendering of the Greek—a view not shared by many other Catholic exegetes; but Canisius was at times over-conservative, as when he rejected the idea that contemporary scholars might know more than earlier ones.[5] In a fine chapter he explains Mary's supreme dignity, which is based on her divine motherhood, her nearness to the Trinity and the deep mutual love between her and her Son, and interprets the passage, "Who is my mother?" (Matt. xii.48ff.), constantly quoted by Protestants against the uniqueness of the blessed Virgin, as obviously metaphorical and in no way impairing this uniqueness.[6] On the other hand, he defends such traditions as that Christ was conceived on 25 March and born on 25 December as absolutely true.[7] In book four Canisius defends the Catholic interpretation of Marian passages in Scripture against certain Protestants who, unlike the Fathers of the Reform themselves, explained them con-sistently in the worst possible sense, alleging for example that Mary's question to the angel, "How shall this be done?", im-plied doubt, and that she therefore was an example to un-believers.[8] But he also rejects views now generally accepted by Catholic theologians, for example that she had no perfect knowledge of the mystery of the Incarnation and of the

[1] 1, 13 (90).
[2] 2, 14–16 (201–18).
[3] 3, 2 (239ff.).
[4] 3, 10 (279).
[5] 3, 4–7 (248–65).
[6] 5, 13 (294–9).
[7] 3, 22 (346).
[8] 4, 1 (356ff.).

Divinity of her Son from the beginning, as Erasmus had asserted.[1] At that moment of history the paramount need seemed to be to oppose all criticism of traditional beliefs except those that were frankly superstitions; so Canisius also blames Luther for representing Mary as occupied with household cares, whereas she was brought up in the Temple, far removed from ordinary earthly concerns; he rejects the translation of "lowliness" instead of "humility" in the *Magnificat*[2] and also the neuter in Gen. iii.15 instead of the wrong feminine, "*she* (instead of it, i.e., the seed) shall crush your head"; the mistranslation, he asserts, is consecrated by a centuries old tradition and may therefore not be abandoned.[3] Mariology, like other departments of theology, suffered from the taking up of defensive positions all along the line. This stress on defence also led to certain denials of abuses which, as we have seen, were only too widespread, even though they never affected the official teaching of the Church. For example, he attacks Luther for saying that Catholics go to Mary rather than to Christ, that they attribute to Christ the realm of justice and to Mary that of mercy and that they say Mary can command her Son.[4] But certain preachers actually did say these things; and through the attribution of their works to such authorities as St. Albert and St. Bonaventure, these ideas had a tremendous influence. For the moment they were, indeed, abandoned; but we shall see that they turned up again when the effects of the Reformation had worn off.

On the other hand, Canisius put up a very necessary defence of the Church's traditional language about Mary, which Luther, Calvin and their followers took in an absurdly literal sense. They cavilled at her being called life, sweetness, hope and similar things which, they averred, could be properly said only of God. Canisius retorts that St. Paul called even his converts his hope, joy, glory and crown (cf. 1 Thess. ii.19; Phil.

[1] 4, 2 (362ff.).   [2] 4, 7 (389).
[3] 5, 9 (594–5).   [4] 5, 11 (606ff.).

iv.1); all lovers use such expressions—so why should we not speak in such terms of the Mother of God? True, we also speak of her as our mediatress; but in her case we use this word in a quite different sense, detracting in no way from the uniqueness of Christ, the only Mediator in the exact sense of the term. The same is true of the *Salve Regina*, so severely censured by the Protestants; for she is truly called queen and mother of mercy, because she is the Mother of God and obtains spiritual life for us by her prayers; and we call her our hope and even our salvation (salvatrix), because she intercedes for us.[1] He admits that certain abuses have, indeed, infiltrated into her cult; but, fallen men being what they are, this is not surprising, since they have even penetrated into the worship of God Himself. All this was rectified at the Council of Trent.[2] The work ends with a defence of Marian miracles, which one should not be too quick to reject if they seem probable and edifying, of Marian images, pilgrimages (he accepts the legend of the Holy House of Loreto) and other practices of devotion.[3]

The work shows the great erudition of its author and became a mine of information for later writers on the subject; as we have seen, even Dillenschneider still relied on it for his presentation of the thought of Erasmus. It was first and foremost a work of controversy and apologetics, not a systematic presentation of Catholic Marian doctrine. To produce this was left to another Jesuit, the Spanish theologian Francis Suarez (d. 1617).

FRANCIS SUAREZ

Suarez incorporated his Mariology in his tratise *De mysteriis vitae Christi*,[4] in close relation with Christology; his work became the basis of most later presentations of the subject. Mary was elected from all eternity to become the Mother of God, even—following Duns Scotus—before God foresaw the fall of

[1] 5, 13 (615–22).   [2] 5, 15 (641f.).
[3] chs. 18–31 (673–762).
[4] (1952); Paris edition (1856–78), vol. 19.

men.[1] He emphasizes her noble parentage against Luther[2] and, again following Scotus, teaches that she was redeemed by Christ through being sanctified and preserved from original sin in the first instant of her conception, since she would have been subject to it because of her origin.[3] Suarez affirms that she had the use of her reason from the first instant of her conception, because John the Baptist had it, who leapt in the womb of his mother when Mary approached her, and the Blessed Virgin could not be inferior to him in this respect[4]; from the same moment she also had the firm proposal to preserve her virginity.[5] For, Suarez argues, Mary received every grace that could be given to a pure creature, and the mysteries of her graces cannot be measured by ordinary laws.[6] According to him, the grace given to Mary in her first sanctification was more intense than the supreme final grace of angels and men,[7] and after this first sanctification her every single act merited an increase of charity, grace and glory, because all her actions were deliberate and all were, of course, good. For she never voluntarily averted her mind from divine contemplation, and even the brief sleep she allowed herself was often interrupted by divine thoughts. Thus, at the end of her life, her grace was "almost immeasurable".[8] "It follows that at the end of her life the Blessed Virgin could by one act merit as many degrees of grace as she had obtained in the whole course of her former life by all her acts together; it is probable that her final grace was greater than that of all angels and saints combined, and it is possible that she had such grace even from the moment of the Incarnation",[9] a view shared by later authors. Against several medieval authors Suarez holds that she did not receive the sacraments of order, penance and matrimony, but he re-

---

[1] *Disputatio*, I, 3, 2 and 4.
[2] 2, I, 2f.
[3] 3, 2, I–3, 5, 8.
[4] 4, 7, 2f.
[5] 6, I, 3.
[6] 3, 5, 30f.
[7] 4, I, 4.
[8] 18, 2, 2–4, 2.
[9] 18, 4, 6–9.

gards it as certain that she was baptized by Christ and frequently received the Eucharist. She also received the sacrament of Confirmation in some way; but whether she received Extreme Unction is not sure, because she had never sinned.[1] Christ loved his mother more than all other saints, and Suarez approves Bernardine of Siena's idea that he had come more to redeem Mary than all other men.[2] "The blessed Virgin frequently merited more by her single acts than individual saints by all the acts of their life"; nevertheless, "it is certain that she merited nothing *de condigno* which is the proper privilege of Christ, but by meriting the Incarnation *de congruo* she merited a great good for us, and while she lived she could also merit many other good things".[3]

Disputatio, 19 is devoted to her knowledge. Suarez quotes Bernardine of Siena and Pseudo-Albert on the subject, but is more careful than they. He considers it more probable that Mary had a supernatural and directly infused knowledge of the supernatural objects of faith, because many of her privileges, for example the Immaculate Conception, would seem to require it; he also thinks that she had theological wisdom, by which the mysteries of faith as well as the truths of conclusions contained in them are known more distinctly; for she was the teacher of the Apostles. Moreover, he holds that from the beginning she had perfect knowledge of all things pertaining to the Divinity and the Trinity in particular, and from the moment of the Incarnation or at least from the birth of Christ she also knew all that belonged to the mystery of the Redemption[4]; but he regards it as more probable that she had no special knowledge of the natural world.[5] She had, however, many revelations; and it is probable that she even at times saw clearly the divine essence.[6] Suarez teaches the bodily Assumption which, he thinks, took place three days after her death,

[1] 18, 3, 2–5. [2] 18, 4, 10.
[3] 18, 4, 14. [4] 19, 3, 3–5.
[5] 19, 5, 1. [6] 6 19, 4, 2.

which was due to love.[1] The perfection of her beatitude, her beatific knowledge and vision surpass those of all angels and saints; for she sees in the Word all that God sees, excepting only what belongs to Christ and to the inner thoughts of his soul, which she is prevented from seeing because she is far inferior to him in dignity and beatitude. But, apart from this deficiency, "Under Christ the Blessed Virgin is as it were the universal cause most intimately connected with him; hence it belongs to her position to comprehend in the Word the whole universe and the state of all the blessed and the damned."[2] *Disputatio*, 22 discusses her part in the Redemption. Just as Christ is our King because he has redeemed us, so Mary is called the Mother of all men, because she has contributed in a special way to our redemption by providing her own substance and voluntarily offering him for us and desiring and providing for our salvation in a unique manner.[3] Her cult is not the cult of *latria*, and the language used of her, for example in the *Salve Regina*, must be properly understood. He explains carefully—as was necessary in view of Protestant accusations—in what sense she was called the hope of sinners, the joy and salvation of the world, or even reparatrix and mediatress. These expressions are not used of her in the same sense as they are of God; for him we ask to do things for us, her to intercede.[4]

ROBERT BELLARMINE

Robert Bellarmine (d. 1621), a contemporary of Suarez and also a Jesuit who was declared a doctor of the Church in 1931, did not treat our subject systematically; his Mariological teaching is scattered throughout his works. As against most of the theologians of his time, especially those of his own order, he did not think that the Immaculate Conception could be defined, because it had no clear basis in Scripture (session of the Holy Office of 31 August 1617); but he personally believed in

[1] 21, 1, 4–11.   [2] 21, 3, 5.
[3] 22, 2, 4.   [4] 22, 3, 1f.

it, as is quite clear from his sermon on the Feast; indeed, he
considers Mary's greatest grace that she was prevented from
contracting original sin by the merits of Christ's passion.[1] He
teaches the same in his *Conciones Lovanienses*, 42 (Naples
edition, 1872ff.), on the nativity of Mary, in which he attacks
Luther for saying that all Christians are as holy as Mary. The
Church, he says, has always followed the *via media* between
the ancient Collyridian heresy, which made her a goddess, and
the Reformers, who consider her equal to all other human
beings. Catholics venerate Mary as the noblest member of the
Church, because all graces come from Christ as the Head and
flow through her as the neck, which is one of his favourite
metaphors. In one of his sermons, *Super Missus est*,[2] he interprets her name as *gutta maris*, a drop of the sea, as Luther had
done, but he adds that she was this only in her own humble
view, whereas God's grace made her the most glorious star,
greater than the whole sea, so that all men look up to her. She
is "full of grace" in a twofold sense; on the one hand she possessed all the effects of grace in the highest degree and therefore was *gratiosissima*, as the Greek text has it, and on the other
she was full of the grace required for her special office of the
divine motherhood, and therefore *plena gratia*, according to
the Latin translation—thus combining both the new and the
old renderings of the text. He insists, as Catholic theologians
did more and more after the Reformation, that she derived her
special graces not from her own power or merits, but from God
whom it had pleased to elect her before all others.[3] She did not
intend to become the Mother of God and Queen of angels, but
she led such a perfect life that she made herself worthy of this
honour,[4] a view slightly at variance with what has just been
said, explained perhaps by the fact that the sermon in which

[1] *Opera Oratoria Postuma*, Rome (1942), p. 62.
[2] *Op. Or. Postuma*, vol. 1, p. 265.
[3] *Op. Or. Postuma*, vol. 1, pp. 266f.
[4] *Op. Or. Postuma*, vol. 1, p. 303.

Bellarmine expressed it was preached several years later than the former.

In his treatise on the Seven Words of Christ from the Cross he rejects the idea that Mary was beside herself with grief. Though the sword of sorrow transfixed her, she stood under the Cross firmly (*constantiae plena*), for though she loved the flesh of her Son she loved even more the honour of the Father and the salvation of the world. In the same passage he writes that Christ gave his mother three lives: human life, when he created her, the life of grace at the same moment, and the life of glory when he exalted her above the angels; and so he gave her more than he received from her—the sane theological view, as opposed to the imaginings of a Bernardine of Siena. Bellarmine, too, defended the *Salve Regina* against the Reformers.[1] There is no reason why she should not be called Queen, seeing she was the Mother of the King, nor why she should not be addressed as Mother of mercy, since she gave birth to Christ, from whom we have received mercy. We call her our life not because she is life by essence, which is God, or its principal source, which is Christ, "but because she gave birth to Christ and through him is made the Mother of all who live by the spiritual life".

The Jesuits were also responsible for the spread of Marian devotion among the laity through the establishment of the Marian Congregations, founded by Johannes Leunis (1535–84). He had formed an élite of his pupils into a group who undertook to hear Mass and say either the Little Office of the Blessed Virgin or the Rosary every day. In 1564 he formally placed this group under the protection of the Mother of God with the title "Maria Annuntiata", and in 1584, shortly after the death of Father Leunis, Gregory XIII made this association the principal Marian congregation, which was to be established in all the colleges of the Jesuit Order.

[1] *De Reparatione Gratiae*, I, 15.

LAWRENCE OF BRINDISI

While the Jesuits were working out a Marian doctrine considerably sobered up after the objections of the Reformers, the Franciscans largely continued their immediate pre-Reformation tradition. Its most important representative is the Capuchin Lawrence of Brindisi (d. 1619), whose *Mariale* constitutes the first volume of the critical edition of his Works (1927). The first part of it treats of the Praises and Invocation of the Virgin Mother of God, the second of her feasts. St. Lawrence considers Mary less as the Mother of God than as his bride, and emphasizes again and again her similarity to Christ—a point of view which is not without its dangers. He constantly compares Mary and Christ to Eve and Adam or Esther and Ahasuerus without any suggestion of the fundamental difference between Christ and Mary on account of the Hypostatic Union of Christ's human nature to his divine Person. So he can state quite baldly: "Christ the Man (who, after all, cannot be separated from his Divinity) and the Virgin Mother of God are alike in nature, grace, virtue, dignity and glory",[1] which is certainly not true of the last four qualities. He says the same in his interpretation of the *Magnificat*[2]; in his sermons on the Immaculate Conception, which he established following Duns Scotus,[3] he asserts that Mary "has reached the sanctity of Christ",[4] for she is as like Christ as Eve was like Adam.[5] In his description of Mary's "marriage" to God he follows Bernardine of Siena, but occasionally in terms which are even more objectionable than those of his predecessor. She is "the woman ... who is united (*copulata*) to God" in "a divine marriage"[6]; she possesses God as her Bridegroom, for to "overshadow" (Luke i.35) means to "act as a husband".[7] Hers is a "true

---

[1] 1, 6 (*Super Fundamenta eius*, 5, 6).
[2] 9, 3.   [3] 11, 2f.
[4] 9, 5.   [5] *Super Fundamenta*, 2, 6.
[6] *In Visionem S. Ioannis Evangelistae*, Serm. 1, 7 and 2, 4.
[7] 3, 4f.

betrothal and marriage with God, from which followed the conception of Christ". "God required her free consent to contract matrimony through the heavenly paranymphus (similar to the English best man, bridegroom's friend) Gabriel; thus the Virgin was conjoined and copulated with God in a legitimate and true marriage",[1] a very strange idea, seeing that most theologians consider Mary's marriage to Joseph, though never physically consummated, to have been a true and legitimate marriage. Lawrence follows Bernardine in teaching that the Incarnation was caused by God's love for Mary, and consequently "amends" John iii.6 to read: "God so loved Mary that he gave his only-begotten Son".[2] Indeed, her grace and beauty have drawn him from paradise as the magnet draws iron, and "as Jacob was captivated by love for Rachel . . . so God was captivated by love of you".[3] But even this is not enough, and in his sermons on the Angelic Salutation he actually writes: "Great is the might and power a beautiful woman has over a man who is in love with her . . . she causes him to rave (*insanire*), and causes the lover to go out of his mind (*amantem amentem reddit*) even with the mere glance of her eyes. But the Virgin could do this with God himself, hence he says: 'Avert thine eyes from me.' (Cant. vi.4.) She has caused God in some way to rave so that, having left his majesty behind, He took on the form of a servant." For "She could turn God from a lion into the gentlest lamb and make God most loving to man, indeed, make him Man . . . as Queen Esther made King Ahasuerus most favourable to the Jews . . . O wonderful power!"[4] Even the greatest and sincerest lovers of the blessed Virgin will probably agree that this description of God as an infatuated husband tamed by Mary is nothing less than blasphemous, however much allowance we may make for the enthusiasm of the preacher and the fact that he is, of course, speaking metaphorically. Nevertheless, good taste alone should

[1] 5, 4.
[2] *Super Missus est*, 8, 5.
[3] 12, 3.
[4] *In Salut. Angel.*, 5, 5.

have forbidden him to use such unsuitable terms. It is such exaggerated language which had infuriated the Reformers and which was very soon to produce another controversy; and if we quote these unpleasant products of a not altogether healthy devotion we do so to make understandable the following reactions which were not, as is so often maintained, the outcome of irrational dislike of the Mother of God but of well-founded concern for a sane and balanced Marian doctrine and piety.

Lawrence interprets Rev. xii entirely of the blessed Virgin without any reference to the Church. Commenting on St. John's description of the woman as clothed with the sun he asserts that Mary appears here in greater glory than that in which Christ or even God himself have ever appeared, giving as the reason that she is so much more lavishly adorned because of her sex, just as a queen wears more jewellery than a king.[1] So he can also write that "her kingdom and empire is no less than the Kingdom of God and the Empire of Christ".[2] Therefore her cult, too, should be similar to that of Christ: "Because Mary is similar to Christ as Eve to Adam . . . the invocation of the Virgin must be similar to the invocation of Christ, the honour and cult given to her must be similar to the honour and cult of Christ",[3] a very strange idea, seeing that the Church distinguishes very carefully between the worship, *latria*, due to God and Christ alone, and *hyperdoulia*, the special veneration given to Mary. If popular preachers said such things in their sermons, Protestants could hardly be blamed for accusing Catholics that they were giving Mary the honour due to God alone. In the same work he alleges that Mary is more inclined to mercy than Christ, which he proves by her intervention at Cana.[4] He teaches the Immaculate Conception which he considers even more admirable than the virginal conception of her Son because, he argues, it is more extraordinary that she should be conceived holy from sinful parents than that Christ should

---

[1] *In Visionem* 1, 5.   [2] 2, 6.
[3] *Super (Salve Regina*, 1, 1).   [4] 3, 3.

have been conceived equally holy from the holy Virgin.[1] Mary is also associated on an equal footing with her Son in the forgiveness of sins. For as the first parents would have communicated the indwelling of the Holy Spirit, purity from sin and charity with all the other gifts of the Spirit to their children had they not sinned, "so Christ and Mary have obtained these three from us by their merits and together confer the remission of sins, the resurrection of the flesh and eternal life".[2] There is no sign of Mary's subjection to her divine Son, indeed, some passages sound as if she were greater than he, for according to Lawrence Mary truly constituted him heir of the Davidic Kingdom,[3] and through her he received the new kingdom of the Church as Jacob was blessed by Isaac through the intervention of his mother.[4] She is also closely associated with his sacrifice and his priesthood: "The spirit of Mary was a spiritual priest (*spiritualis sacerdos*), as the Cross was the altar and Christ the sacrifice, even though the spirit of Christ himself was the principal priest, but the spirit of Mary was one with the spirit of Christ ... Therefore the spirit of Mary performed the priestly office together with the Spirit of Christ at the altar of the Cross and offered the sacrifice of Christ to the eternal God for the salvation of the world", so that one can truly say of her, as of God, to whom she was most like in spirit, that she so loved the world that she gave her only-begotten Son.[5] The identification of Mary with Christ could hardly go further, and it is hardly surprising that the saint thinks that "even the tongue of the Holy Spirit is scarcely sufficient to celebrate her praises worthily".[6] For she is the "Socia Dei"[7] and most like God in power, wisdom and goodness.[8] It must be said in fairness that Lawrence affirms several times that Mary has all her graces

---

[1] *In. Conc. Imm.*, 5, 4.
[2] *In Salut. Angel.*, 4, 3.
[3] *In Salut. Angel.*, 10, 3.
[4] 10, 2.
[5] *In Salut. Angel.*, 3, 5.
[6] *In Ass.*, 1, 8.
[7] *Super Missus est*, 13, 5.
[8] 13, 8.

and glory from God, not from herself[1]; but, as this discussion has surely shown, his language is mostly so exaggerated that it is hard to understand how his *Mariale* can be called not only "one of the most eloquent works of praise" but also one of "the best founded in doctrine".[2] Among other books of the period there is the work of the Canon of the Lateran, J. Guarini, *Of the Sacred Empire of the Virgin Mary* (1600), the very title of which is characteristic of the contemporary attitude to the Mother of God.

THE "ÉCOLE FRANÇAISE"

The seventeenth century was a period of unrest for central Europe, ravaged by the Thirty Years' War, while French Catholicism was exposed to the influence of Jansenism, this stern quasi-heretical party which was inspired by an exaggerated Augustinian pessimism. Even orthodox French writers of the time were not entirely free from it; it shows itself for example in the emphasis on the vileness of fallen human nature and even on the humiliation of the impersonal human nature of Christ, which is one of the chief characteristics of Pierre de Bérulle.

1. BÉRULLE

Bérulle (d. 1629), the founder of the French Oratory, was educated by the Jesuits and studied theology at the Sorbonne; he greatly admired the mystic teaching of St. Teresa and introduced her reformed Carmelites to France. His own spirituality, however, differed considerably from that of the Spanish mystics; it centred in the interior "states" (*états intérieurs*) of the Incarnate Word as the pattern of the spiritual life of the Christian. This emphasis on the Incarnation naturally includes the Mother of the Word made Man who, in Bérulle's view, is

---

[1] e.g., *De Virginis Deiparae Doloribus*, 6, 2 and *In Conc. Imm.*, 3, 3.

[2] Jean de Dieu in his article "La Vierge et l'Ordre des Frères Mineurs", in *Maria*, 2, 814.

as intimately united to Jesus as the Father is to the Son.[1] He even goes so far as to say that Mary's fiat in assenting to the Incarnation is "much more powerful in its issue and effect than that God pronounced when creating the universe. For if by this latter he once made the world, the other now produces the author of the world",[2] one of those extraordinary statements the consideration of Mary's assent to the Incarnation produces in certain minds. It is further elaborated when Bérulle asserts that Mary gives a greater life to Jesus than he gave to her; for Jesus made her only the Mother of God, whereas she has conceived, incarnated and brought forth the Son of God.[3] He also reproduces the medieval idea that by reason of her divine motherhood Mary constitutes an order by herself between God and the highest angels,[4] and he repeats the story of her upbringing in the Temple.[5] His main concern, however, and herein lies his originality, is with the interior states of the Virgin both before and after the Annunciation. He describes her constant growth in grace which is hidden from her by her humility,[6] because "Almah" means hidden.[7] Before the angel came to her she was in a state of admirable elevation, while at that moment the Trinity in heaven were in consultation, the angels waiting outside for the outcome of their deliberations— an extraordinarily anthropomorphic description, obviously inspired by the proceedings of the French court. While the angel was on his journey to Nazareth God himself prepared Mary's soul, who was sighing for the sins of the universe and longing for the coming of the Messiah.[8] The angel surprised her in this heavenly state, and when he spoke to her she entered into another, permanent state: the state of the Mother of God. Before that she was alone (Bérulle apparently takes no notice of Joseph), because Jesus alone was worthy to keep her company;

[1] *Vie de Jésus*, 28.   [2] *Grandeurs de Jésus*, 11, 10.
[3] 11, 12.   [4] 11, 11.
[5] *Vie de Jésus*, 5, 1.   [6] 5, 2.
[7] 6, 2.   [8] 6, 7.

and he again compares her fiat with the fiat of creation.[1] He describes the Incarnation with great delicacy, without the extraordinary fancies of a Lawrence of Brindisi: as the Father unites his paternity to Mary, "the Son proceeding from the Father finds himself proceeding from the Virgin".[2]

In the later chapters Bérulle discourses at length on the relation of Mary to Jesus in her womb—a subject dear to the École Française and perpetuated in the prayer of St. Sulpice: "O Jesu vivens in Maria." Bérulle enlarges on Christ's complete dependence on Mary in his state before his birth, when the two hearts of Jesus and Mary are so near to each other and his first occupation is with the Father, while his second is with her. In this state Mary is in a "perpetual ravishment", of which she alone was capable while on earth.[3] While Jesus was in her womb Mary penetrated perfectly the mystery of the Incarnation, she was occupied with the first actions of his soul treating with his Father; this ravished her, "who was holily occupied with her Son and his states and exercises". For though she had not the divine light which manifested the divine Essence to her, she enjoyed the angelic light, which showed her all the actions of his soul. So she contemplated his life and occupations in herself and entered into his interior life, while he drew her into his own knowledge of the Father, for she was too near to him not to know his states and secrets—statements evidently not in accordance with the first chapters of Luke's Gospel. She also knew his quality of victim, "through this quality Jesus bore a humiliating state in a divine state. And this humiliation pierces the heart of the Mother and humiliates her, too".[4] In his Discours de la visitation (Œuvres de piété, 35, 6) he again considers the state of Jesus in the womb of Mary—a somewhat embarrassing preoccupation which is present also in his letters, as he frequently recommends it as a subject for meditation.[5]

[1] 15f.   [2] 20.
[3] ch. 28.   [4] 29, 2.
[5] e.g., Ep. 100 and Ep. 2 to Carmelites.

2*

He also emphasizes Mary's maternal authority over Jesus. She has a right of property in him which belongs to her alone, and so also has a special power to give Jesus to souls—a thought that will be elaborated especially by Grignion of Montfort.[1] Bérulle, too, recommended the much discussed vow of slavery to Mary. The idea was probably inspired by the Confraternities of Slaves of the Virgin which existed in Spain at the beginning of the seventeenth century.[2] In Bérulle's version it reads: "To the perpetual honour of the Mother and the Son I wish to be in the state and quality of servitude with regard to her who has the state and quality of the Mother of my God ... and I give myself to her in the quality of a slave ... I renounce the power and liberty I have of disposing of myself and my actions, and place myself entirely in her hands."[3] This vow of servitude—expressed externally in the wearing of small chains—soon aroused strong opposition in which the jealousy between the Carmelite Fathers and the Oratorians also played a considerable part. The question was decided by the Holy Office which, in 1621, refused to approve the vow but allowed the "servitude" to Mary as a private devotion.

Despite such exaggerations, however, Bérulle's Mariology has the great merit of being completely dependent on Christ. As H. Bremond,[4] A. Molien[5] and others have remarked, the founder of the French Oratory renewed devotion to the Blessed Virgin in more than one respect by spiritualizing and freeing it from many superstitious accretions, so that for the École Française "devotion to the Virgin is but one with devotion to the Incarnate Word".[6]

---

[1] Ep. 2 to Carm.
[2] Cf. A. Molien, *Le Cardinal de Bérulle* (1947), 2, 54–61.
[3] Molien, 2, 248.
[4] *Histoire littéraire du sentiment religieux en France*, 3 (1921), pp. 88f.
[5] Article "Bérulle" in *Dictionnaire de Spiritualité*, vol. 1, col. 1559.
[6] Bremond, p. 97.

2. OLIER

Jean-Jacques Olier (d. 1657), the founder of the famous seminary of St. Sulpice and author of the prayer "O Jesu vivens in Maria", continued the line of Bérulle, but in a far less sober spirit.[1] Having in his youth been subject to psychological disturbances for several years, some of his later spiritual experiences such as the fifteen-year-old Mary's presence in his soul may well have been, as Bremond believes, the psychological reaction against his former neurotic ideas of pride,[2] and Pourrat holds that many Marian visions and revelations he had in later years were probably no more than his own pious thoughts.[3] This accounts no doubt for many of his exaggerations.

The following analysis of Olier's Mariology is based on the aforementioned edition of the *Vie intérieure*. When God the Father wanted to make his Son Man, "He chose the most holy Virgin as his help and spouse. For God the Father ... wills that in the mystery of the Incarnation Mary should be his spouse, in this sense that the Father, who is the principle of the generation of the Word according to his Divinity, destines the holy Virgin to become the principle of the generation of this same Word according to his humanity."[4] For this he wants Mary's consent; for "God the Father, as a holy and faithful husband, wants to unite the most holy Virgin to himself and give her the perfect possession of his Person, his treasures, his glory and all his goods".[5] So Olier considers the relation between the Father and the blessed Virgin as a real marriage in which the person and possessions of the husband belong to the

---

[1] I regret not having been able to use E. M. Faillon's very rare edition of his *Vie intérieure de la très sainte Vierge*, Rome 1866, but only the somewhat expurgated version of 1875. The Migne edition of his other works (1856) has also been inaccessible to me. See also the works of P. Pourrat, *Jean-Jacques Olier*, Paris (1932); id. in *Maria* 3; Laurentin, *Maria, Ecclesia, Sacerdotium* (1952); C. Dillenschneider, *La Mariologie de St. Alphonse* 1, 234–38; G. M. de Fruges, *Jean-Jacques Olier* (Paris), n.d.; Bremond, 3, pp. 419–507.

[2] Bremond, p. 447. [3] Bremond, p. 202.

[4] ch. 1, 1 (p. 2). [5] 1, 2 (p. 6).

wife. And not only that. When God predestined us "his holy
spouse was (already) present to his spirit. He saw ... what she
would have desired for each of us had she been already in the
world, and *he acted according to the intentions, the desires and
the prayers of Mary*, which he foresaw."[1] Surely this can mean
no less than that God has arranged our salvation according to
the views of Mary—that he is no longer the First Cause of all
things, but that his will depends on hers.

Mary's youth is described according to the apocryphal story
of her upbringing in the temple, where, as a child of three,
"she renews her vows of victim and servant with an even
greater love ... than she had done in the sacred temple of
Anne's womb".[2] In the temple of Jerusalem she assisted at the
sacrifices of the Old Covenant and, "more enlightened than
the priests ... saw, adored and contemplated Jesus Christ under
all these symbols"[3] since "she was already without knowing it
performing the holy functions of the priesthood which she
would have to exercise on Calvary".[4] For there the Father
"associates her with Jesus Christ, priest of the exalted sacrifice
which she must offer with him on Calvary ... and communicates to her the priestly spirit in an eminent manner".[5]

Though she is so closely associated with her Son, Olier allows
her no active share whatsoever in the formation of his human
body—though he had called her the principle of his humanity.
"The most holy Virgin," he writes, "in whom admirable and
incomprehensible things came to pass, was completely passive
in this operation, everything only taking place in her presence
and her person",[6] no doubt because he subscribed to the idea
that anything to do with childbirth was unclean, not realizing
that without actively contributing to the formation of Christ
Mary could not be truly his mother. He goes further: "Mary
did not conceive a child, but a perfect man. When God the

---

[1] p. 8 (my italics).
[2] 3, 1 (43ff.).
[3] 3, 2 (49).
[4] 3, 3 (50).
[5] 2, 2 (30).
[6] 5, 1 (77).

Father engendered the incarnate Word, he made at this very moment a perfect Man; that is to say as perfect in the light of his reason and as advanced in wisdom as he will be at the age of thirty-three",[1] a view impossible to reconcile with Luke ii.52: "And Jesus advanced in wisdom and age..."

Another extraordinary idea, though in line with the preoccupation of the École Française, is Olier's view that Christ's sojourn in the womb of his mother was the most important time of his life; for he says "the Church... gives us more time to adore this mystery than she gives us to adore all the other mysteries together. Sometimes we have only one day... or even forty, as for the Resurrection; whereas to honour Jesus hidden in the womb of his mother... she gives us six whole months, from the Visitation to Christmas."[2] For Mary holds the middle between the cursed creatures of earth and the sanctity of heaven—another indication of the fundamental pessimism of the École Française—and so the time spent in her womb tempers his shock of meeting the sinful world; therefore Jesus stays there as long as he can and only leaves it at the last moment decreed by his Father.[3] Mary herself "was destined to form with her divine Son but one victim of expiation and one same sacrifice of praise".[4] Her intervention at Cana shows "that he gives nothing to his Church except in consequence of Mary's desires".[5] That from then on the disciples believed in Christ (John ii.11) "was one of the supernatural effects the most holy Virgin wanted to obtain"; at the same time she also secured the Eucharist for the Church,[6] for this was what she really desired when intervening at Cana. By so quickly acceding to Mary's request Christ's "intention is to show us that he has only accorded his Church this great sacrament... in consequence of Mary's desires and that, by the dominion of love she has over

---

[1] 5, 1 (78).
[2] *Explication du Magnificat*, 3 (p. 107).
[3] 8, 1 (118).   [4] 9, 5 (179).
[5] 10, 1 (189).   [6] 10, 3 (195).

his heart, she disposes of his divine power according to her liking in favour of men".[1] Though she was absent from the Last Supper, Jesus instituted the Sacrament "for love of her and out of his personal regard for her".

Olier's view of Mary's relation to her Son on Calvary is even stranger. He thinks that there Jesus, being in the place of sinners, drew down the Father's wrath on himself. Seeing himself abandoned by God, He then "seeks, in the tenderness of his mother, what he no longer finds in that of his eternal Father".[2] But instead of consoling him, Mary caused him more pain by her sufferings than all his other sufferings together.[3] And so "in her quality of the New Eve, while the universal sacrifice is offered on the Cross in the person of Jesus Christ, the most holy Virgin offering on her part this divine victim for men, feels herself, too, charged with their sins and obliged to make satisfaction for their crimes" for as the New Eve she had to contribute to our reconciliation with the Father.[4] After this idea of Mary making "satisfaction" (a view, we would stress, which has never been countenanced by serious theologians let alone by the authority of the Church) it is scarcely surprising to read that Christ has ceded all the rights to his infinite merits to Mary, who is now their mistress, distributing them as she sees fit.[5] At his resurrection he unites himself to her "and becomes with her one principle of divine generation for the whole body of the Church".[6]

Olier places the blessed Virgin far above the Church; for "all that appears in the Church is small in comparison with the eminent participation of himself Jesus Christ gives to his holy mother", who now is not only the spouse of the Father, but also becomes that of the glorified Christ and thus "the dispenser of all their treasures".[7] For "there has always been in the Mother and the Son but one and the same interior life, one

---

[1] 10, 4.   [2] 12, 2 (219).
[3] 12, 2 (220).   [4] 12, 3 (221f.).
[5] 12, 4 (225).   [6] 13, 2 (241).   [7] 13, 3 (p. 243).

and the same spirit, which diffuses in both the same lights and the same sentiments", so that after Pentecost she becomes "the guide (*directrice*) of the whole world",[1] and God contemplates in her his own perfections as in a spotless mirror.[2] "After the Ascension Mary has guided the whole Church... and told each of the Apostles what he had to do",[3] and now, in heaven "it seems to me that Jesus and Mary are wholly consummated into one and are but one thing".[4] Therefore Christ, "being Lord of the whole world, gives her full possession of all he is and all he has; and in her he possesses all things with greater pleasure than if he possessed them only in himself. In him the power of Mary extends to all creatures.... Similarly, as spouse of the eternal Father, she has also all power with him through her prayers; he wills what she wills; he does good to everyone to whom she wants it done. She has only to will and everything is done.... The power of the most holy Virgin as spouse is measured by the omnipotence of God, who gives her the use of all his goods; thus she is all-powerful to give everything"[5]; "she is like a queen reigning on the throne of God".[6] Therefore she is "the sure refuge of sinners and criminals from the rigour of the wrath and vengeance of Jesus Christ... which she appeases and soothes".[7] For after falling into grave sin "it is difficult to change Christ from his quality of Judge to that of Advocate.... This is what the most holy Virgin does"; for she "does not turn away from anyone for any reason whatsoever; the most wicked and the greatest criminals find in her the sure place of their penance".[8] "Our Lord as God places his omnipotence in the hands of his mother to use it as she wishes ... on the one hand she uses this power to do good; on the other she binds the power of Jesus Christ to prevent the evil he would do to the guilty."[9]

[1] 14, 1 (253-5).   [2] 15, 4 (278).
[3] 17, 1 (308).   [4] 18, 1 (315).
[5] 18, 2 (319f.).   [6] 18, 3 (320).
[7] 18, 3 (328).   [8] 20, 1 (351, 355).   [9] 20, 2 (356).

He elaborates the traditional parallel of Mary and Esther. "Her incomparable beauty . . . which gave her so much power over the heart of Ahasuerus . . . was a figure of the so powerful charms which Mary's penitence and tears have over the heart of God. . . . Hence, as soon as Mary presents herself to God and appears before him full of tears . . . his heart is touched and he dries the tears of his spouse, he forgives men's sins. . . . It is she who stops the arm of God's justice, power and revenge by the force of her mercy and love."[1] If it might seem that Christ himself thus disappears behind Mary this is just what he wants; for Olier writes: "Such is the nature of the holy love Jesus bears his divine mother that he would like to see her everywhere and always to hear her spoken of. . . . He wants Mary to be like a circle that surrounds him, through which one must pass in order to go to him; for he is delighted thus to remain surrounded, enveloped and hidden under his mother, in order that she should be loved, invoked and sought by all who want to reach him."[2]

Olier has been quoted so extensively because, as founder of St. Sulpice and an immensely popular missionary, he had an enormous influence on French Catholicism. Whatever beneficial effects his devotion to the blessed Virgin—which, in his case, was matched by an intense love of Christ—may have had on himself and those who knew how to interpret his fervent tirades in an orthodox way, it is hardly surprising that ordinary people should have placed the blessed Virgin by the side or even above God and that even well-meaning Protestants should have been scandalized. This at least was the experience of Henri Boudon (d. 1702), himself not only a disciple of Olier but also the author of several books on the blessed Virgin and an exponent of the dubious *esclavage* (*slavery*) to her. When visiting the diocese of Evreux in his capacity of archdeacon he found that "frequently, when interrogating people on the subject,

[1] 20, 2 (356f.)   [2] 19, 1 (339).

they answered that the holy Virgin is as much as, or more than God himself", and he adds that "certain extraordinary ways of speaking" about her used by some saints "which could serve as an occasion for people to fall into error and for heretics to be scandalized" ought to be explained properly.[1] But if preachers and missionaries speak about the blessed Virgin in such misleading terms, who is to give the necessary explanations?

3. JEAN EUDES

Jean Eudes (d. 1680), another exponent of the École Française, was an Oratorian before he founded his own Congregation of Jesus and Mary (1643). His Bérullian devotion to the interior of Christ and his mother centred in their two hearts. His principal works on Marian spirituality are *La Vie et le royaume de Jésus*[2] and *Le Cœur admirable de la très sainte Mère de Dieu* (1681).[3] Like Olier, who was influenced by him, being seven years his junior, he saw Mary as the spouse of the priest; indeed, at the age of sixty-seven he drew up a formal contract of marriage with her and henceforth wore a ring, like Alain de la Roche, the propagator of the Rosary, though he had consecrated himself to her much earlier. In *La Vie et le royaume* he writes: "Mother of grace and mercy, I choose you for the Mother of my soul.... I accept and recognize you as my sovereign, and in this position I give you all the power over my soul and my life that is possible under God. O holy Virgin, regard me as something that belongs to you, and by your goodness treat me as the subject of your authority"[4]—language befitting the age of absolutism, soon to be represented by the *Roi Soleil*. As for all the École Française, Mary and Christ are but one: he who sees Jesus sees Mary; for "Jesus and Mary are the first two

---

[1] *Œuvres*, ed. Migne (1856), vol. 2, cols. 326 and 331; quoted from Dillenschneider, *Mariologie*, p. 130.

[2] 1637, which I have read in the Lyons edition of 1679, the *Œuvres complètes*, Varnes 1905–11 being inaccessible to me.

[3] Cf. also C. Lebrun, *La Spiritualité de S. Jean Eudes*, 1933; Eng. tr. 1934.

[4] p. 64.

foundations of the Christian religion, the two living sources of all our blessings", though he hastens to add that "for herself Mary is nothing, her Son Jesus is all in her".[1] We must adore him in her and make ourselves dependent on her as our mother and our sovereign, to whom we should subject ourselves as slaves; we must make this gift to her every day and more especially once a week or at least once a month.[2] Eudes recommends meditation on her states and mysteries, emphasizing such non-scriptural subjects as her sojourn in the womb of her mother, her birth, the day when she was given her name, her presentation, the state of her childhood, her sojourn in the Temple, her espousals; further her establishment in the dignity of Mother of God at the age of fifteen, the sojourn of Jesus in her womb and her travels with him all through his public life, the latter subject being certainly opposed to the scriptural account and due to the principle of the École Française that Christ should never be considered without his mother.[3] It is characteristic that Eudes, too, prefers to meditate on Jesus "captive in the womb of his mother".[4]

In his later work, Le Cœur admirable finished just before his death (not accessible to me), he defended the cult of the Heart of Mary, as distinct from the Heart of Jesus, by a wealth of quotations, attempting to trace the devotion to the beginnings of Christianity. The work is divided into twelve books, books 4 and 5 describing how the divine Word imprinted on Mary's heart a perfect reproduction of the divine attributes and a share in the properties of each of the Three Persons of the Trinity. (See Lebrun, Spiritualité.) For "the heart of the glorious Virgin is a marvellous expression of the wisdom of God"[5]; it is "the living image of the divine mercy"[6] and "with the Son of God, is the source of all the good things that proceed from the mystery of the Incarnation", quoting Prov. viii.30, "I was with

[1] p. 322f.
[2] pp. 324f.
[3] pp. 327f.
[4] pp. 421ff. and 441ff.
[5] Vol. 1, bk. 4, ch. 6 (quoted Maria, 6, 792).
[6] 5, 1.

him forming all things".[1] It was this idea of Mary as the *source* rather than the recipient of grace which had, not without some reason, so much infuriated the Reformers, and which Eudes attributes to the Church—not simply to individual preachers or liturgical poetry—when he writes: "The Church gives to her names and qualities which belong only to God" and interprets Luke ii.19 as meaning that she preserved in her heart the immense treasures of the divine mercy, the inexhaustible sources of the divine Wisdom[2]; though he certainly did not think of her as the primary, but only as the secondary source of grace. Though in 1669 The Roman Congregation of Rites had refused to approve the Office and Mass which Eudes had composed for a liturgical feast of the Most Holy Heart of the Virgin Mary, the new devotion soon became popular, especially as Clement X approved it (1670–76).

OTHER TRENDS OF SEVENTEENTH-CENTURY MARIOLOGY

Apart from the Immaculate Conception Mary's part in the Redemption was a frequently discussed subject of Mariology, a term which seems to have been first used by Nicolas Nigido, who published his *Summa sacrae Mariologiae* in 1602.[3] The Jesuit Chirino de Salazar, who was rescued from oblivion by Laurentin, treated the problem of Mary's priesthood particularly in his *Commentary on Proverbs*, in which he uses extraordinarily strong language. "To offer Christ to and for us", he asserts, "is the right solely of the Virgin and of no-one else . . ." the Virgin offers him undoubtedly as something that belongs to her (*aliquid quod suum est*)[4]; for Mary had a real "dominium" over her Son, who was "constituted under her parental power"[5]; he even goes so far as to say that Mary herself sacrificed her Son: "If,—to assume the impossible—the will of the

---

[1] 5, 11.   [2] 5, 13.

[3] This information and that on Chirino de Salazar are taken from R. Laurentin, *Maria, Ecclesia, Sacerdotium* (1952), p. 211; on Salazar, pp. 232ff.

[4] Prov. 8, n. 215 (1, 624C, quoted in Laurentin, p. 244).

[5] no. 208 (1, 622A, Laurentin, p. 245).

Father had not intervened and the Mother alone had desired and decreed that her Son should die for men, this would have sufficed that Christ, obedient to his Mother, should have freely accepted his death."[1]

Another Jesuit, Theophilus Raynaud (d. 1663), also associates Mary with the Redemption, but in far more measured terms.[2] He follows the traditional view according to which the divine motherhood is the source and principle of all Mary's perfections; hence she received whatever graces were necessary for that, but not all she would have been capable of receiving.[3] In his *Nomenclator Marianus*, Lyons (1639), after giving a comprehensive glossary of Marian epithets taken from the Fathers, the medieval theologians and the Liturgy, he defended the application to Mary of names properly belonging to Christ, such as Cause of Salvation, our Hope, and so forth, by pointing out that she was all this only in dependence on Christ. The same held good for the title "mediatrix", which was never meant to detract from the unique mediation of Christ. Though Raynaud criticized certain excesses of Marian piety he defended the authenticity of the Carmelite Brown Scapular (*Scapulare Partheno–Carmeliticum*, Paris (1654). This devotion seems to have spread only in the fifteenth century, though, according to the legend our Lady herself had given it to St. Simon Stock (d. 1265) and promised its devout wearers to free them from Purgatory on the Saturday following their death. This, the so-called Sabbatine Privilege, was supposed to have been confirmed by a bull of John XXII in 1322. Though Raynaud considered the story authentic and praised the devotion, later members of his Order, such as the Bollandist, D. Papebroch, in 1696 and H. Thurston in his articles in *The Month* (1927), attacked the story, which today is no longer defended by serious scholars.

[1] Ibid., no. 225 (224D, p. 246).
[2] *Diptycha Mariana*, 1643; I am using the Lyons edition of 1665, p. 224.
[3] pp. 11f.

The Dominican Vincent Contenson (d.1674) developed his Mariological views in volume 6 of his *Theologia Mentis et Cordis*, Lyons (1681), basing his teaching on the growing belief in the inseparable union of Mother and Son. So he quotes with approval contemporary thinkers who believe that in every man something (physical) of what he had received in the womb remains unchanged until death, hence something of Mary's substance remained always in Christ, and so he claims that "the Fathers frequently affirm that we are fed in the Eucharist with the substance of Mary". Therefore there is between Christ and Mary "a certain species of identity".[1] Though he will not enter into the dispute whether grace was infused into Mary at the first or second instant of her conception, as he himself says, "because of the reverence due to the constitutions of the Apostolic See", he thinks that the first grace of Mary was more perfect and intense than all other graces of men and angels from the beginning to the end of the world.[2] For Mary's glory begins where that of other saints ends. Contenson subscribes to the medieval view that the Virgin constitutes a hierarchy by herself, below Christ and above the highest angels; moreover, she is the principal instrument of predestination,[3] "through whom, as through a channel, God directs the streams of grace to all the faithful".[4] For Mary's beauty has wounded the heart of God; therefore "he is hardly to be considered a Christian, and certainly not a Catholic, who is not a Marian (*Marianus*) in his heart" and to love Mary is necessary for salvation.[5] Because she has a certain "consanguinity" with God, she is extremely close to the hypostatic order[6]; indeed, he dares to say that "the Mother of God is the complement of the Trinity", because through her the Trinity, who was unknown before, was made manifest. For as the Mother of God she proceeds in some way from the Trinity; the works of the Trinity *ad extra*

[1] Contenson, 816.   [2] Contenson, 773.
[3] 795.   [4] 810.
[5] 812.   [6] 815.

being completed by her. All things were, indeed, made by the Word, but they were not remade without the Mother of the Word; and because she has given us the Redeemer she can in a certain way herself be called Redemptress,[1] and being the Mother of God "she has dominion and power over Christ".[2]

It can hardly be said that Contenson imitated the sobriety of St. Thomas who never used such language. On one point, however, Contenson was very firm: he stressed repeatedly that mere external devotion to the blessed Virgin is not enough to secure salvation.[3] She must not be honoured with the lips alone while the heart is far from her, and men are very much deceived if they think they will go to heaven merely by giving their name to a Marian Confraternity or by wearing a scapular. "All these sacred observances", he warns, "are worth nothing unless they spring from the source of charity and have solid virtues attached to them."[4] This may seem self-evident to us today; unfortunately it was not so in the seventeenth century. It is very probable that the Dominican's warnings have some connection with the controversy aroused by Letter 9 of Pascal's *Provinciales* (1656/57).

The Controversies Around Pascal and Widenfeld

I. *LETTRES PROVINCIALES*, NO. 9

As is well known, Pascal (d. 1662) had close relations to Port-Royal and hence to the first exponents of Jansenism, that rigorist party of seventeenth-century French Catholicism which professed an exaggerated Augustinianism and was particularly opposed to the Jesuits' doctrine of grace and morals. In Letter 9 Pascal attacked a now long-forgotten Jesuit Père Barry, who had written a book entitled *Paradise opened to Philagie by a hundred easily practised devotions to the Mother of God*.[5]

---

[1] 840–43.   [2] 818.
[3] 846.   [4] 868–70.
[5] *Le Paradis ouvert à Philagie par cent dévotions à la Mère de Dieu, aisées à pratiquer.*

Pascal's quotations from this strange book fully justify his wrath; today it seems almost incredible that it could ever have been allowed to be published. Here are just a few examples from Pascal's quotations that will help us to understand the controversies that followed.

"The devotions to the Mother of God you will find in this book are as many keys to heaven which will open all paradise provided you practise them." Indeed, it is sufficient to practise even but one of them. Among them are: saluting the Virgin when seeing her images; frequently pronouncing the name of Mary; commissioning angels to salute her on our behalf; wishing to build her more churches than all the monarchs of the world together; saying every day a *Hail Mary* in honour of her heart, though it is not necessary to give her one's own heart if this be too much attached to the things of this world; simply carrying a rosary or an image of her on one's person. It is expressly stated that the efficacy of these devotions does not presuppose a Christian life; for the author tells the story of a woman who had lived and died in mortal sin, but had daily saluted Mary's image. As a consequence, Christ resurrected her after her death so that she could do penance. This proves that anyone who practises one or more of these little devotions will never be lost!

It is scarcely necessary to point out that such teaching is diametrically opposed to the New Testament as well as to the Church's teaching on sin and repentance. On the other hand, human nature being what it is, it was only too popular.[1]

Pascal's perfectly justified attack on a superstitious and purely external cult of the blessed Virgin roused a considerable controversy and was frequently misrepresented as an attack on the

---

[1] Pascal held the Jesuits responsible for the spread of such false devotion. But, as H. Bremond points out in his *Histoire littéraire du sentiment religieux en France*, vol. 9 pp. 252f., other members of the Order, such as Raynaud, had different views. However, the very fact that such a book as Barry's could be written and published shows the low standard of morality in general and of Marian devotion in particular in certain circles at this time.

Marian cult as such, which was laid at the door of Jansenism. As Paul Hoffer, in his well-balanced book on the devotion to Mary at the decline of the seventeenth century points out:[1] "One has never been able to convict an authentic Jansenist of having attacked the dogma of the invocation of saints and of the Virgin, or of having knowingly turned one of the faithful against devotion to Mary. . . . This famous Jansenist conspiracy against the Virgin has never existed anywhere but in the imagination of their opponents." Indeed, the nuns of Port-Royal were especially devout to her, even calling her "our great mediatress",[2] which is not surprising, since God and Christ were being represented to them as such stern Judges that Mary remained their only refuge. What the Jansenists did attack was the unwarranted trust in Mary's intercession on behalf of unrepentant sinners as well as current absurd little devotions like those to her left foot or the soles of her shoes.[3]

2. THE AVIS SALUTAIRES

The Jansenist troubles were at their height when, in November 1673, there appeared a little booklet of sixteen pages which at any other time would probably have attracted no attention whatsoever. It was called *Monita salutaria*, better known under its French title *Avis salutaires de la Bienheureuse Vierge à ses dévots indiscrets*. It was published in Ghent anonymously, but with the Imprimatur. In view of the ensuing extremely bitter controversy it is essential to summarize its contents.[4] 1. "Those who persevere in sin love me in vain. . . . Do not imagine that I am the refuge of impenitent sinners." 2. One should not accept stories of her apparitions and revelations too easily. 3. "Love of

---

[1] *La dévotion à Marie au déclin du XVI* siècle (1938), pp. 75f.

[2] Marie-Claire Arnaud, *Lettres,* ed. Faugère, Paris (1858), quoted Hoffer, pp. 83f.

[3] See Hoffer, p. 114.

[4] I am using the Latin original with section numbers; there is also an English translation of 1687 which appeared under the title: *Wholsome Advices from the Blessed Virgin to her Indiscreet Worshippers.*

me is not beautiful without charity towards God who created me." 4. Opposes the idea that Mary frees impenitent sinners from hell through membership in confraternities. This is a ruse of the devil of which men should beware. 6. Praise of Mary should end in God, not in herself. 8. "Do not worship me as if there were no access to God through Christ without me." 9. Mary is not mediatress and advocate in the same sense as Christ. 10. "If you love and venerate me as your patroness with God you do well, for my prayers are of great value. . . . But do not call me omnipotent, Saviouress or Co-redemptress. . . . Do not say that it is possible to appeal from the divine tribunal to mine." 11. She is not to be put in the same category as God or Christ. 12. "Do not say that Christ is a severe Judge, but I am the Mother of Mercy", for "God is an inexhaustible source of mercy and grace." 15. is directed against Marian slavery (*esclavage*), 16. against decking Mary's statues with precious jewels while letting the poor go hungry, and 17. against the belief that there are different Madonnas in different localities.

As Hoffer rightly says, the doctrine of these *Avis* is perfectly orthodox.[1] Nor did the author attack imaginary abuses; the devotional teaching and practices, as we saw when discussing Olier, Barry and others were often very dubious; indeed, just about this time many writings on the subject had to be placed on the Index.[2] Even Dillenschneider must admit the existence of abuses in Marian devotion[3]; nevertheless, he blames the *Avis* for opposing the idea that "Mary snatches her devout clients from hell and defends them before the tribunal of God"[4] and for saying that he who displeases God displeases also Mary. "Who does not see", Dillenschneider comments, "to what extreme despair such assertions must lead".[5] This can only mean that Mary's attitude to sinners is opposed to God's, and

---

[1] Hoffer, pp. 266–313.
[2] Hoffer, pp. 315f.
[3] *La Mariologie*, etc. I, 5.
[4] I, 48.   [5] I, 51.

who does not see that this makes nonsense of the words of Christ himself: "The Son of man is come to seek and to save that which was lost" (Luke xix.10) and indeed of the whole teaching of the New Testament?[1]

Despite the Imprimatur the *Avis* was immediately attacked in unmeasured terms, and the people, who could not read Latin, were made to believe that it contained the most horrible blasphemies against the blessed Virgin. Sermons were preached against it in which the author and his friends were called wild beasts, and soon the traditional antagonism between regular and secular clergy came into play; the religious Orders' confraternities of the Scapular, the Rosary and others attacked the Censor who had given the Nihil Obstat, and the Jesuits held processions of the Virgin in reparation. Only a few months after its publication (November 1673) the book had caused a tremendous stir all over Europe and its author looked around for defenders. Peter of Walenburch, suffragan Bishop of Cologne, stated that he could discover nothing against faith or morals in the little work, but this did not pacify its detractors, who soon accused it of Jansenism—and this quite unwarranted accusation decided its fate. Though Choiseul, the Bishop of Tournai, considered it very good and had it translated into French, and though the Archbishop of Cologne approved it, too, the religious Orders obtained a condemnation from Rome and it was placed on the Index in June 1674 as tainted with Jansenism. Only then did its author become known, and this made things worse, for he was a layman, Adam Widenfeld, an advocate of Cologne, who was very rich and devoted part of his time and fortune to explaining Catholicism to the Protestants—as Hoffer points out, he would today no doubt have been applauded as a great lay ecumenist.[2] After the condemnation

[1] We cannot but agree with G. Miegge, pp. 151ff., that this form of Marian piety was caused by the medieval and later misconception of Christ as an inhuman Judge: "On one side a divinity all severity and all justice: and on the other a compassion that is all human and without justice."

[2] Hoffer, pp. 184.

the attacks on the book and its author became even more violent. The opponents took not the slightest notice either of its contents or of the good intentions of the author. Most of the pamphlets appeared anonymously, but they usually betrayed their origin by reflecting the preoccupations of the Orders from which they emanated, and which were particularly incensed at the idea that a layman dared give advice to clerics.[1] One of the publications which was not anonymous but was written by the Benedictine Vicar-General of the Bishop of Paderborn, stated that the Church had never defined that the admirable Mother was *not* the refuge also of impenitent sinners: "Therefore the great and admirable Mother remains and shall remain as long as the world stands, the refuge even of impenitent sinners, according to the mind of the Holy Fathers and the Church."[2] It cannot be stressed sufficiently that neither the Fathers nor the authorities of the Church have ever said anything of the kind, which would indeed make nonsense of the teaching of Christ and the Apostles.

JEAN CRASSET

Fortunately, the more sober opponents of Widenfeld never taught such a pernicious doctrine, such as for example the Jesuit Jean Crasset (d. 1692) in his work *La véritable dévotion envers la sainte Vierge établie et défendue*.[3] He affirms most strongly that "the Virgin has no other will than that of God, she loves all that he loves and hates all that he hates; hence she wants to save all men just as he does".[4] When Widenfeld had said that Mary does not love sinners he meant, of course, impenitent ones. We have seen that many of his adversaries (including even modern authors like Dillenschneider) opposed

---

[1] Cf. Hoffer, pp. 208ff.

[2] Quoted Hoffer, p. 222; L. Dript, *Statera et examen libelli cui titulus Monita salutaria* (1675), p. 36.

[3] (1679); I quote from the second edition (1687).

[4] quest. 9 (p. 93).

him for this, whereas others, such as Crasset himself, misinterpreted him as meaning all sinners. For Crasset teaches emphatically that: "Those who live badly in the hope that the Virgin will obtain pardon for their crimes have never been devout to her but rather her greatest enemies, bearing on their forehead the sign of their reprobation ... there is nothing more opposed to her spirit than a presumptuous trust in her mercy."[1] The next section deals with the question: "Whether to be saved it suffices to be devout to the Virgin"—which most other opponents of Widenfeld answered in the affirmative. Crasset is quite certain that they are wrong: "This proposition is untenable", he says, "for it is a truth of faith that to be saved it is not enough to serve the holy Virgin, nor to wear her scapular, nor to belong to all her confraternities: but one must still do penance and keep God's commandments." Further, "it is not reasonable to believe that devotion to the holy Virgin is a more powerful means of salvation than that to her Son", "for according to all the rules of reason and of faith it is certain that the love of Jesus Christ is more powerful to save us than the love of Mary". On the Day of Judgement Mary will say, like her Son, "I do not know you" to those who have been only externally devout to her without the practice of good works.[2] According to Dillenschneider and others Crasset, too, would lead sinners to despair! He also strongly reacts against opposing like Olier Mary's mercy to God's wrath; on the contrary, "Even though she is a Mother of mercy, she has not nearly as much tenderness for us as God, who is Goodness Itself."[3] If the unfortunate Widenfeld had written these words, he would no doubt have been accused of blasphemy, whereas, in fact, the opposite view is an insult to God who, according to St. John, is himself love. (1 John ix.8.) Crasset goes even further and says: "Let us love her as the Mother of love, let us fear her as the Mother of justice."[4]

[1] q. 13 (pp. 153f.).
[2] q. 14 (pp. 158–60).
[3] q. 4 (p. 31).
[4] q. 14 (p. 162).

Despite his very balanced views Crasset was violently attacked by some Protestants, among them a "Mr. Fleetwood", an English layman who wrote *An Account of the Life and Death of the Blessed Virgin according to Romish Writers* (1687). He wrongly accused him of teaching that a man could be saved merely by some devotion to Mary, because Crasset repeats some stories including the famous Theophilus legend according to which the Virgin saved some men from hell and holds—following the majority of medieval and contemporary authors—that she can "in some way change the first decisions of Providence", as is proved by her intervention at Cana.[1] On the other hand, one cannot but sympathize with Mr. Fleetwood when he asks: "Would one believe that a Jesuit should have the confidence to furbish up such ridiculous things as these (e.g., also the story of a statue of Mary kneeling down before the Child she holds to save a soldier praying to her), at this time of day, in such an age as ours?"[2] We shall see that unfortunately such stories continued to be repeated by Catholic authors in support of their teaching on Mary's all-powerful intercession, an attitude that did much damage to the Catholic cause in the following century.

MARY D'AGREDA

One of the most popular, but from this point of view most damaging publications was the *Mystical City of God. The Divine History and Life of the Virgin Mother of God*, written by Mary d'Agreda, a Spanish Franciscan nun (d. 1665) and published posthumously (1670). She claimed that God had given her six angels who, after purifying her, had led her into the divine Presence. He revealed the deepest mysteries to her and then ordered her to describe the beauties of Mary. The whole book is a hodgepodge of apocryphal stories and her own fertile imagination. To give only a few samples: From the beginning of the world Mary was exempt from the fall of

---

[1] q. 3 (p. 21).   [2] Fleetwood, p. 34.

Adam—which would mean she did not need to be redeemed.[1] Mary, like Christ, preceded Adam[2] and was present at the creation of the world, because the Incarnate Christ was already there.[3] Chapter 15 gives a detailed account of her conception, at which God ordered a thousand angels to be present for her defence and to serve her like vassals. Anne was forty-four years of age when Mary was conceived and could no longer bear a child without a miracle, whilst her husband was seventy; there follows a long discussion of all sorts of factors that intervened to make the conception as miraculous—and therefore as perfect—as possible; for Anne's sterility remained and she and her husband had no pleasure in the conception. Yet somehow some matter was miraculously produced from which Mary's body was formed in such a way that all the "four humours" were admirably mixed in it. We are further told that her body was formed on a Sunday and the soul infused the following Saturday, so God made Mary in seven days, as he had made the world. She received the use of reason at the moment of her conception, and from that same moment she began to destroy sin. In the following chapter we are told that from this time also she possessed quasi-omniscience: for she knew all about creation and the fall of the angels as well as the first state of Adam and Eve, the order of nature, stars and planets, purgatory, limbo and hell as well as the mysteries of the Incarnation, and from this first moment of her conception she made acts of the most heroic virtue. Thus she is the special mirror of the Deity and the *unique* (!) mediatress of mankind, therefore God revenges specially every wrong that is done to her. On the other hand, she would show herself grateful if the doctrine of the Immaculate Conception were to be defined.[4] At the moment of her birth she was in a divine ecstasy, and she, who surpassed the angels in wisdom and knowledge, was treated like a child.[5]

[1] Bk. 1, ch. 4, n. 48.   [2] 1, 5, 54.
[3] 1, 11 (133).   [4] 1, 19.
[5] 1, 21.

Enough will have been quoted to show the tenor of the book, which was forbidden by Innocent XI; but this decision was revoked at the insistence of the King of Spain. In 1696 the book was condemned again as containing many rash statements and hallucinations apt to expose the Catholic religion to ridicule. It was placed on the Index in 1704, but removed from it a year later. It was popular reading throughout the eighteenth century.

Bossuet

One of the most determined opponents of Mary d'Agreda's revelations was Jacques-Bénigne Bossuet (d. 1704), the celebrated French preacher and Bishop of Meaux. Though a disciple of Bérulle and the École Française his views on the blessed Virgin are far less exaggerated than those of the former, let alone those of Olier. He never loses sight of the infinite difference between the transcendent Creator and the human Mother of God.[1] He states his Mariological principles in his Sermon for the Day of the Scapular, also called "On Devotion to the Blessed Virgin". What he wants to give is "A completely Christian doctrine which will establish devotion for the holy Virgin not on dubious stories, nor on apocryphal revelations, nor on uncertain reasonings, nor on indiscreet exaggerations, but on solid maxims based on the Gospel."[2] Bossuet teaches both the Immaculate Conception[3] and the bodily Assumption.[4] In his famous *Elevations on the Mysteries* he asserts the vow of virginity, saying that God himself will take the place of her husband and unite himself to her body, by extending the

[1] I quote from F. Lachat's edition of the *Œuvres complètes*, Paris (1862). Cf. also E. Janssens, *La dévotion mariale de Bossuet*, Liege (1946). There is an English edition of the relevant texts by F. M. Capes, *Bossuet on Devotion to the Blessed Virgin* (1899).

[2] Bossuet, vol. 11, 364.

[3] *Catéchisme des Fêtes*, vol. 5, 183 and elsewhere.

[4] Vol. 5, 190f.

eternal generation of the Son to her. There are no fanciful details, which Bossuet vigorously rejected in his "Remarks on the Mystical City of God", but only respect for the great dignity of the Mother of God and the "chaste mysteries of Christianity".[1] Bossuet bases himself particularly on the traditional Eve–Mary parallel on which he establishes the blessed Virgin's share in our redemption: "This is the solid foundation of the great devotion the Church has always had for the holy Virgin. She has the same part in our salvation as Eve had in our ruin: this is a doctrine received by the whole Catholic Church through a tradition going back to the origin of Christianity."[2]

This share in our salvation is founded on the two scriptural facts of the Incarnation itself and of Mary's presence on Calvary. For as God has once given us Christ through her this order cannot be changed; as we have once received the principle of grace through her, so we now receive through her also its applications.[3] Later she had to stand under the Cross so that she should not only be immolated with her Son but also be associated with the whole mystery of the Redemption. She died with him, as it were, in perfect submission, and so Christ communicated to her his own fecundity by saying, "Behold thy son"; and through these words she became the Mother of his children. For it was her destiny to join the Eternal Father in giving her consent to the death of their Son, and so, when John is given her in the place of Christ "she becomes the Mother of Christians in the stress of an affliction without measure."[4] He reiterates this teaching in his second sermon on the same subject. But Mary's love for men does not differ from God's, as so many of Bossuet's contemporaries asserted, but she orders her love on that of the Father.[5] Therefore Bossuet, too, emphasizes most strongly that true devotion to Mary can be practised

[1] Twelfth Week, third Elevation (vol. 7, 201–03).
[2] Elev. 5, 205.
[3] *Sermons for the Feasts of the Holy Virgin*, vol. 11, p. 44.
[4] *On the Compassion of the Blessed Virgin*, 1, vol. 9, pp. 500–20.
[5] P. 547.

only in the context of an authentic Christian life, that it is mere superstition to believe she will help us if we only practise a few little devotions, but make no effort to improve our morals. Whoever behaves in this way, "let him know that, since his heart is far from Jesus, Mary abhors his prayers". In vain do such people call her mother; for she is ashamed of them. If a person is to be her son he must resemble Jesus, else she will reject him.[1] This is stronger language even than Widenfeld's but, *quod licet Jovi, non licet bovi*, and what was true Christian doctrine in the pulpit of the "Eagle of Meaux" became Jansenist error under the pen of the jurist of Cologne.

GRIGNION DE MONTFORT

Louis-Marie Grignion de Montfort (d. 1716), whom Bremond calls "the master *par excellence* of Marian devotion ... who is both the last of the great Bérullians and an outstanding missionary"[2] is the author of two Marian treatises, *L'Amour de la Sagesse éternelle* and the far more popular *True Devotion to the Blessed Virgin*.[3] *The True Devotion* was lost for about a century and only rediscovered in 1842, when the revival of Marian spirituality after its decline in the Age of Enlightenment brought the book a tremendous success. Grignion's Marian thought has many admirers as well as critics; for many of his ideas are controversial. The basis on which Grignion builds his Marian edifice is that, "It is more perfect, because it is more humble, not to approach God of ourselves without taking a mediator",[4] for "to draw near to his holiness directly, and without any recommendation, is to fail in humility", just as we would not approach an earthly king without an introduction.[5] It is clear, then, where this idea comes from: it is the attitude of the subject of an absolute king, who does not dare

---

[1] p. 548.   [2] Bremond, vol. 9, p. 271.
[3] Modern edition of the former (1932) inaccessible to me; Eng. tr. of the latter by Faber, which I quote from the ed. of 1937.
[4] p. 49.   [5] p. 50.

approach the Roi Soleil or his successors without a recommendation. But can this be the attitude of a Christian nourished
on the Gospel? The Lord's own prayer is the *Our Father*, by
which he has taught us to go to God direct; and in his great
high-priestly prayer he tells his disciples: "In that day, you
shall ask in my name, and I say not to you that I will ask the
Father for you. For the Father himself loveth you, because you
have loved me." (John xvi.26f.) But Grignion goes so far as to
blame those who counsel devotion to Christ rather than to
Mary.[1] It is a sign of heresy to say only the *Our Father*, but not
the Rosary or the *Hail Mary*[2]—but what about those well over
twelve hundred years of Christianity when neither of these
prayers was known?

One of the least pleasant features of the book is the author's
intolerance of all who do not share his views. He calls anyone
who criticizes his language as extravagant a carnal man and a
worldling,[3] and all those who do not surrender themselves to
Mary "reprobates".[4] It is extreme blindness if we do not consecrate ourselves to her and do not depend on her to go to God,[5]
for by depending on her "we acknowledge ourselves unworthy
and unfit to approach his Infinite Majesty by ourselves"—a
rather Jansenist attitude, though the Jansenists themselves were
violently opposed to Grignion. On the other hand, if Christians
follow his teaching he promises them wonderful rewards. For
this devotion is "an easy way of arriving at union with our
Lord",[6] it is a way all of honey and roses, because Mary covers
all crosses with sugar so that her servants swallow them gaily.[7]
Further, no faithful client of Mary will ever fall into heresy[8]
and our good works are more capable of converting sinners and
comforting souls in purgatory if they pass through Mary's
hands than if they do not,[9] and she keeps our treasures safe for

[1] pp. 34ff.
[2] p. 166.
[3] p. 117.
[4] p. 127.
[5] p. 87.
[6] p. 94.
[7] p. 95f.
[8] p. 106.
[9] p. 110.

us.[1] For Mary "is so full of inventions that she knows all the secret ways of gaining the heart of God", she dresses our bodies and souls—like Rebecca the two kids—for the taste of God and by going to her we make sure "that the value of all our good works shall be employed for the greatest glory of God".[2] For if we offer Jesus anything by ourselves he will examine the offering and frequently reject it, because it is stained by self-love, whereas, if we present our works through Mary "we take him by his weak side" and so he does not consider the gift so much as the Mother who presents it.[3]

Grignion, of course, subscribes to the medieval idea that Christ always obeys his mother. "The greatness of her power", he writes, "*which she exercises even over God himself*, is incomprehensible.[4] For Christ was subject to her for thirty years, and by this subjection has given more glory to God than if he had converted the whole world by his miracles, and in her womb (note again the preoccupation of the École Française) he was a "captive and loving slave".[5] "Jesus in his mother's womb" is "an abridgment of all mysteries".[6]

What, then, is this new devotion Grignion preaches, which, he says, is "a mystery of grace unknown even to the wisest and most spiritual Christians"? It is that the Holy Spirit produces Jesus Christ in his members through Mary.[7] For when he has found Mary in a soul he flies there[8]—though it may surely be argued that the Holy Spirit is infused into the soul at baptism and that this Marian devotion is quite secondary to the indwelling of the Holy Trinity. One of the reasons why the Holy Spirit does not do greater wonders in souls is because he does not find Mary there. Now if she is to make her dwelling in a soul she must be given dominion over it.[9] This is done by interior as well as external practices. The former consist in honouring her,

---

[1] 114.   [2] p. 93.
[3] p. 92.   [4] Introduction, my italics.
[5] p. 85.   [6] p. 163.
[7] p. 5.   [8] p. 14.   [9] p. 14.

mediating on her, making acts of love, praise and gratitude to her and such like; while the latter comprise enrolling in her confraternities, joining her religious congregations, wearing the rosary, the scapular or small chains.[1] But he has never heard of any practice at all equal to the one he is about to reveal, which in its perfection will be practised only by a select minority. This practice is nothing else but "a perfect renewal of the vows and promises of Holy Baptism", made in the form of a complete consecration to our Lady by which we must give her our own body with all its senses and members, our soul and its powers, our external goods present and to come as well as our interior and spiritual goods, including all the merits acquired by our good works.[2] Moreover, we should never dare to approach Christ on our own, "however sweet and merciful he may be, but always avail ourselves of the intercession of our blessed Lady".[3] Then "the soul of our Lady will communicate itself to you . . . her spirit will enter into the place of yours". He longs for the time when "souls breathe Mary as the body breathes air", and he prays: "Adveniat regnum Mariae".[4] For Mary is the mould into which souls must be poured to be formed in her spirit, easily and without too much effort. "By this practice", he concludes, "faithfully observed, you will give Jesus more glory in a month than by any other practice, however difficult, in many years", because thus Christians abandon their own intentions and lose themselves in those of the blessed Virgin, who gave more glory to God by threading her needle than all other saints by all their heroic acts put together.[5] For "we cannot approach Jesus but by Mary, we can only see Jesus and speak to him by her intercession. . . . It is in Mary that Jesus Christ has calmed his Father, irritated against men."[6]

This necessity to approach Jesus through Mary extends even to the Eucharist. Before Holy Communion we should ask

[1] pp. 68ff.   [2] pp. 74f.
[3] p. 89.   [4] pp. 145f.
[5] pp. 147-9.   [6] p. 164.

Mary to lend us her heart and "represent to her that it touches her Son's glory to be put into a heart so sullied and inconstant as yours, which would not fail either to lessen his glory or destroy it". At Holy Communion itself we are to tell Jesus that he should not regard us, but only Mary who is acting for us. Grignion then gives several forms of spending the time after Communion: "You will introduce Jesus into the heart of Mary," he suggests, "or you will sit like a slave at the gate of the king's palace, where he is speaking with the queen ... they talk one to the other without need of you"; for "the more you leave Mary to act in your Communion, the more Jesus will be glorified".[1] It seems at least arguable that just this Act of Holy Communion, in which Christ wants to be most intimately united to man, had better be left to spontaneous reaction instead of being encumbered with such artificial little practices.[2]

Nevertheless, these practices are not the real preoccupation of Grignion. Through his devotion to Mary he wants to lead the Christian to devotion to Christ; he is convinced that this is the shortest way to achieve great sanctity. For his thought is decidedly eschatological; he is sure that "the formation and education of the great saints who shall come at the end of the world are reserved for Mary".[3] This end is near, and the great

[1] pp. 177–81.
[2] On this subject E. Raitz von Frentz, S.J., says in his article, "Die Vollkommene Andacht zu Maria des hl. L. M. Grignion de Montfort", in Sträter, *Katholische Marienkunde* (1951), 3, 190–94: "It may be questioned whether such a conscious surrender is necessary to the perfect veneration of Mary, and even more to perfect sanctity. This will have to be denied.... Thus it can hardly be said that it (the devotion of Grignion) is possible and suitable for all Christians.... In the case of many Christ would be relegated too much to the background of their religious life.... This difficulty is felt especially in contemporary piety, which is largely based on the mysteries of the Trinity, of the historical and the glorified Christ, and of the mystical body of Christ, and which demands that the central doctrines, God and Christ, should also have their central position in the human consciousness.... Even during the examination of the book in the eighteen-forties it was felt that the demand to offer everything to God only through Mary was dogmatically difficult, since the acts of *latria*, especially the sacrifice of the Mass, are offered to God directly."   [3] p. 13.

saints of these times will be "nourished by her milk ... sheltered under her protection".[1] In the early times of the Church Mary had remained hidden, because people might have attached themselves too grossly to her, "because of the admirable charms which the Most High had bestowed even upon her exterior". But in the Second Coming of Jesus Christ Mary must be revealed by the Holy Spirit so that Christ might be made known; she must shine forth in power against the enemies of God, for in some way the devil fears her more than God himself.[2]

With Grignion we have reached the apogee of the Marian devotion of the École Française. Far from assuming that some small token of love for the blessed Virgin is enough for salvation, he demands the complete interior surrender to her so as to be entirely formed by her—an office which, in former centuries, had been attributed to the Holy Spirit, as the hymn "Veni Creator Spiritus" makes abundantly clear.

CONTINENTAL PROTESTANTISM AND THE CHURCH OF ENGLAND IN THE SEVENTEENTH CENTURY

The generations succeeding the Reformers increasingly neglected or even despised the Mother of Christ, though in the seventeenth century a new current made itself felt which, though rejecting Catholic teaching about her, nevertheless stressed her personal holiness, as for example Johann Arndt (1621), a mystical writer who influenced German Pietism,[3] and V. Herberger.[4] Jacob Böhme (d. 1624), the mystical shoemaker of Silesia, incorporated Mary in his theosophical system by associating her with the divine Wisdom, a gnostic concept. This Wisdom, which is a "heavenly virgin"—a kind of Gnostic aeon—descends into the earthly body of Mary at the Incarna-

---

[1] p. 19.   [2] pp. 21–4.
[3] e.g. *Lehr-und Trostbüchlein* (1621), p. 243; quoted Schimmelpfennig, p. 52.
[4] *Evangelische Herz Postille* (1697), 1, 120 and elsewhere; quoted Schimmelpfennig, pp. 52, 57.

tion.[1] "In this way the corrupted soul of Adam in the body of Mary was again placed within the eternal (incorrupt) humanity."[2] Mary is, indeed, greater than any daughter of Adam, but only because she was united to this heavenly virgin[3]; for the living essence, that is to say the heavenly Wisdom, entered the half-dead essence of Mary.[4] She herself was not free from original sin though she was purer than any other human being because of the holiness of her parents.[5] Therefore she died according to her external life, "but she lives according to the benediction in God's essence and also in her own essence".[6] These strange speculations have little to do with orthodox Christian thought, but they exercised a strong influence on the Sophiology of nineteenth- and twentieth-century authors such as Solovieff and Bulgakov.

The Anglican theologians of the seventeenth century, the so-called Caroline divines, have far more to say about the blessed Virgin.[7] William Forbes (d. 1634), Bishop of Edinburgh, whose *Considerationes modestae et pacificae controversiarum*[8] was published posthumously, states that: "It was merely the religious adoration of the blessed Virgin... that St. Epiphanius sharply reproves... in the Collyridians, but neither he nor any other of the Fathers find fault with the bare addressing of her that by her prayers she would help us before the Lord."[9] Anthony Stafford (d. ?1645), a layman, wrote a book entitled *The Femall* [sic!] *Glory or The Life, and Death of Our Blessed Lady, the Holy Virgin Mary, God's Own Immaculate Mother* (1635) which carried an Imprimatur by Archbishop

---

[1] *Von den drei Principien göttliches Wesens*, 22, 74; *Von der Menschwerdung Jesu Christi*, 1, 8, 4; 1, 9, 14.
[2] *Vom dreyfachen Leben des Menschen*, 8, 80.
[3] *Menschwerdung*, 1, 9, 20.   [4] 1, 9, 22.
[5] *Drei Principien*, 22, 80.   [6] *Menschwerdung*, 1, 9, 19.
[7] Cf. R. Bickersteth, *The Blessed Virgin and Anglican Divines* (1907), and A. M. Allchin in *The Blessed Virgin Mary*, ed. E. L. Mascall and H. S. Box.
[8] Ed. in the *Library of Anglo-Catholic Theology*.
[9] Vol. 2, p. 241.

Laud.[1] The book aroused the fury of the Puritans, which is not surprising since it reproduces a remarkable amount of Catholic teaching. He praises both Mary's external and internal beauty, though he rejects such expressions as that she was in no way inferior to her Son according to the flesh, and his partner in the sacrifice of Calvary: "Neither her modesty nor mine will admit of this blasphemous flattery. I willingly allow her to be the *vessel*, but not the *fountain* of grace."[2] In the chapter on her youth he records, with some reservations, the stories about her upbringing in the temple, though he concludes: "These curiosities, and bold conjectures, let us rather believe than contest... for it is wisdom to grant what we cannot refute."[3] Quoting not only the Fathers, but also such medieval authors as St. Bernard and Damian, he holds that "she understood that her consent was not only required to be the *parent* of the Almighty, but the *spouse* also of the Holy Spirit.... She clearly foresaw, that she was not only chosen to conceive the Son of God, to bring forth, to nurse and govern him, but also... to yield him up... to... persecution, and lastly to the cursed death of the Cross."[4] He opposes, however, the amorous descriptions found in some authors which compare "God to a woer, the angel to a solicitor and Mary to the beloved", which go further "than either the divine will or human modesty permit".[5] On the other hand, he is broadminded about attributing to secondary causes actions properly due to the First Cause, "and in this way we may impute to Mary what work soever God, with her co-operating, has wrought".[6] Stafford also shows her under the Cross, standing "with the affection of a mother, the passion of a woman, but with the constancy and fortitude of a man in beholding her own blood spilt, her own flesh rent, and mangled before her face".[7] He reserves judgement on her bodily Assumption,[8] but

---

[1] I use the facsimile edition by O. Shipley, 1869.
[2] p. 10 (his italics).
[3] p. 19f.
[4] pp. 35f.
[5] p. 72.
[6] pp. 86f.
[7] p. 142.
[8] p. 160.

shows her as "a transcendent creature ... a being not to be considered as a mere woman, but as a type, or an idea of an accomplished piety" and inveighs against the Puritans who dishonour her and allege that Christ himself dishonoured her—which he could not have done without breaking his own commandment.[1]

Stafford was a High Churchman; but in the Low Church her praise was not unknown either. Joseph Hall (d. 1656), Bishop of Norwich, who was persecuted by the Puritans, wrote about her in his *Contemplations*, ed. P. Wynter, Oxford (1863). Though he takes strong exception to the *Hail Mary* as a prayer, which he considers attributes to her the honour due only to God, he has no objection to praising her, indeed he writes: "How gladly do we second the angel in the praise of her which was more ours than his! How justly do we bless her whom the angel pronounceth blessed ... O blessed Mary, he cannot bless thee, he cannot honour thee too much, that deifies thee not"[2]— a sentiment that could be shared by any Catholic, with only this decisive reservation, that the Catholic like the Orthodox Church does not equate prayer to Mary with her deification. Bishop Hall has no doubts about the greatness of the honour done to the Mother of God. "No mortal creature", he writes, "was ever thus graced that he should take part of her nature that was the God of nature ... that her womb should yield that flesh which was personally united to the Godhead!"[3] The Incarnation in Mary was "an exaltation of the creature beyond all example ... Here was a double conception; one in the womb of her body, the other of the soul ... For what womb can conceive thee and not partake of thee? ... How fit was her womb to conceive the flesh of the Son of God ... whose breast had so soon by the power of the same Spirit conceived an assent to the will of God?"[4] Hall also describes very touchingly the scene under the Cross, when she remembered the prophecies of Simeon and Anna, "and, laying all these together, with the

[1] pp. 168–70.   [2] Vol. 2, p. 302.
[3] p. 303.   [4] pp. 304f.

3*

miserable infirmities of his Passion, how wert thou crucified with him!" but "Lo, that faith of thine in his ensuing Resurrection, and in his triumph over death, gives thee life, and cheers up thy drooping soul, and bids it in an holy confidence to triumph over all thy fears and sorrows!"[1]

Mark Frank (d. 1664), Treasurer of Pembroke Hall who was deprived of his office from 1644 to 1660 because he refused to subscribe to the Puritan "League and Covenant", preached a sermon on the Annunciation[2] in which he says that he would not have chosen this particular theme "but that I see it is time to do it, when our Lord is wounded through our Lady's sides; both our Lord and the Mother of our Lord, most vilely spoken of by a new generation of wicked men who, because the Romanists make little less of her than a goddess, they make not so much of her as a good woman . . ." He will not give her any other titles than those the Scriptures give her, but includes the traditional translations of her name such as Star of the Sea, Domina, "a Lady, a name yet retained, and given to her by all Christians", and Holy Mountain.[3] For "The Mother of God is above the greatest we here meet with upon the earth", no-one is more filled than she with sanctifying grace, God only excepted. Frank asserts her perpetual virginity, including the virginity *in partu*; but "they do her wrong as well as God, that give his glory unto her, who will not give his glory to another, though [= not even] to his mother, because she is but his earthly mother—a thing infinitely distant from the heavenly Father". Nevertheless, "God has styled her 'blessed' by the angel, by Elizabeth; commanded all generations to call her so, and they hitherto have done it, and let us do it too. Indeed, some of late have overdone it; yet let us not therefore underdo it."[4]

The well-known devotional writer, Bishop Jeremy Taylor (d. 1667), also presented Mary as an example of holiness, especi-

[1] pp. 671.
[2] *Libr. Angl. Cath. Theol.*, vol. 2, pp. 35f.
[3] pp. 39f.   [4] pp. 45–50.

ally in his *Life of Our Blessed Lord and Saviour Jesus Christ*.[1]
He described her early retired life in constant converse with
angels, according to tradition[2]; indeed she was so holy "that
she drove away temptations and impure visits and all unclean
purposes" from her surroundings,[3] and her motherly care
should be an example to all mothers.[4] He, too, admired her
fortitude under the Cross, where she stood "sad, silent, and
with a modest grief, deep as the waters of the abyss . . . full of
love, and patience, and sorrow, and hope . . . she passed from
the griefs of the Passion to the expectation of the Resurrection
. . . and though her grief was great enough to swallow her up,
yet her love was greater, and did swallow up her grief".[5] The
works of others, such as of George Bull, Bishop of St. David's
(d. 1710),[6] and George Hickes (d. 1715),[7] whilst also admitting
Mary's holiness, are mainly concerned to repudiate Catholic
"exaggerations". In general it may be said of these Caroline
divines, that though they defend a personal veneration of
Christ's mother, they nevertheless reject a public cult, and we
agree with Bickersteth that one of the main causes "for the
virtual dethronement of our blessed Lady from her rightful
place in the hearts and minds of Anglicans lies in the fact that,
as a consequence of the changes of the sixteenth century, she
passed almost entirely out of the daily devotional life of the
Church [of England]". Thus, "not all the glowing language of the Caroline divines availed to keep alive in the breasts
of Anglicans a true appreciation of our Lady's part in God's
scheme of grace".[8]

[1] *Works*, ed. Heber and Eden (1847), vol. 1.
[2] Part 3, section 1, 3 (p. 50).   [3] 1, 2, 5 (p. 57).
[4] 1, 3, 3 (p. 67).   [5] 3, 15, 12 (p. 710).
[6] Ed. E. Burton (1827), vol. 1, Sermon 4 on "The Blessed Virgin's Low and
Exalted Condition", pp. 83–112.
[7] *Speculum Beatae Virginis*, 2nd ed. (1686).
[8] Hickes, pp. 46–8.

8

FROM THE AGE OF ENLIGHTENMENT TO THE PRESENT

The Eighteenth Century

THE eighteenth century is generally known as the age of rationalism and "enlightenment". Human reason claimed its rights in a way it had not been able to do before, and with it came both valid criticism and exaggerated trust in its ability to solve all human problems. Many representatives of the Church took up a hostile attitude to the new mentality, seeing exclusively its negative side which was, indeed, very prominent; and at first those who attempted to come to terms with it were easily suspected of heresy.

Ketwigh

At the beginning of the century the Mariological positions of the past were once more defended in a large work, called rather militantly *Panoplia Mariana* (*Full Marian Armour*), by the Flemish Dominican John Baptist van Ketwigh, which was published in 1720. As Dillenschneider has rescued it from, it seems to us, well-deserved oblivion, calling it "the book of a master which constitutes a Mariology of the very first rank"[1] and as this judgement has been repeated without verification, for example by E. Böminghaus in *Maria in der Offenbarung*,[2] we would give a brief analysis of the work. First of all, it consists almost entirely of quotations, mostly of medieval and later

[1] *La Mariologie* etc, I, 145.
[2] In Sträter, *Marienkunde* I², p. 360, where Dillenschneider's language is even exaggerated and it is said that this work "surpasses in theological acumen and depth all former apologies and has, indeed, to be regarded as a masterpiece of scholastic theology in the sense of St. Thomas".

writers such as the pseudo-Albert, Dionysius the Carthusian, Bernardine of Busti and a large number of others, many of them quite forgotten today. These serve to substantiate the author's theses well known to us from previous chapters. He affirms for example that "it may be said in an orthodox sense that the most worthy Virgin Mother of God has a quasi-parental power over Christ her Son and a measure of ordering and commanding him, who was voluntarily subject to his mother", though this subjection was not one of necessity but of filial piety.[1] Further, it may be said that God is in a certain sense Mary's debtor, even though she has everything from her divine Son.[2] She is especially the Mother of the souls in purgatory, for "having, humanly speaking, the keys of purgatory, she closes it to the living who are devout to her so that they do not enter, and opens it to the dead".[3] He defends the application of certain attributes properly divine to Mary, though with some restrictions. He says, for example: "In the Catholic sense . . . this is true: Mary is the omnipotent Mother and the Virgin of unlimited power, not, indeed, of an omnipotence which is the attribute of God but of an intercessory omnipotence that can obtain all things from God."[4] This omnipotence extends even to hell, for "she can mercifully free men certain of their damnation, and who have already died in the state of damnation, while the divine sentence remains suspended".[5] Ketwigh defends the title of Co-redemptress because she has given birth to the Redeemer, has offered him hanging on the Cross for our redemption, and has obtained by her prayers and merits that Christ's passion should be applied to men. In Section 3 he asserts most emphatically that all good things pass through Mary's hands, and that the prayers of individual saints can obtain nothing for us unless Mary joins hers

[1] Sect. 1, princ. 1, prop. 4.
[2] Sect. 1, princ. 1, prop. 5.
[3] Sect. 1, princ. 1, prop. 7.
[4] 2, 2, 1.   [5] 2, 2, 2.

to theirs. Devotion to her is necessary for salvation, a sign of eternal predestination, and neglect of it is a sign of eternal damnation.[1] In Section 4 he establishes that the blessed Virgin is the queen and mistress of every creature: "To do all to the glory of the most holy Virgin Mother of God, to consecrate oneself to her as her servant or slave and to want to die for her honour . . . is just, praiseworthy and acceptable to God."[2] He sanctions the idea that Mary has been given the realm of mercy whilst Christ reserved to himself the kingdom of justice, though adding that "in actual fact the kingdom of God is indivisible, and the tribunal of Christ and Mary are really one".[3] Nevertheless, "It is a perfectly correct and genuinely Catholic advice to give to the faithful to appeal (the word to be taken in a less rigorous sense) or recur from the tribunal of divine justice to the Curia of Mary's mercy."[4] He reiterates the same in the next proposition, where he says that it is permitted throughout life and in death so to appeal from God's tribunal of justice to Mary's tribunal of mercy—obviously an idea very dear to him. He also defends the view of Eadmer (quoted as Anselm) that we often obtain something more quickly by the intercession of Mary than from Christ direct.[5] As this is so, it is not surprising that Christians should pray more to Mary than to Christ, a practice Ketwigh defends in a somewhat roundabout way: "Because the faithful are taught that the most blessed Mother of God has everything she can do and give from God, it follows that, when they invoke her, God himself is implicitly invoked and honoured."[6] He concludes: "We shall not cease to have recourse first and more frequently to the most clement and powerful Mother of God as our primary Mediatress in all our tribulation and need, than to her Lord and Son, the Judge of us all"[7]—surely a teaching that cannot fail to harm men's love of Christ and their trust in his mercy. Against authors like

---

[1] 3, 3, 5f.   [2] 4, 4, 3.
[3] 5, 5, 1.   [4] 5, 5, 2.
[5] 5, 5, 4.   [6] 5, 5, 4.   [7] 5, 5, 4 (p. 271).

Bossuet and Crasset Ketwigh defends the view "never repudiated by any of the faithful" that Mary is particularly "the
refuge of obstinate and despairing sinners". But here he is
begging the question. He inveighs against Widenfeld who
writes: "Do not imagine that I am the refuge of impenitent
sinners", and he comments: "As if this could not happen,
that through Mary's mediation the obstinate and impenitent
heart could not be taken away and a new heart be given which
makes them penitent"[1]—but this, surely, is not the point. No
one doubts that—with or without the blessed Virgin's special
intercession—God can give a new heart to sinners, even obdur-
ate ones. What Widenfeld—and many others—were up against
was the idea that Mary could somehow save even impenitent
sinners only because they practised some external devotion to
her. This point Ketwigh simply avoids.

In Section 8 the Dominican discusses the honour God has
done to Mary, asserting that Christ served and obeyed her for
thirty years, "that we should see that Christ preferred the
honour of his Mother to the salvation of the universe",[2] and
concluding that the whole Trinity "honours, praises and glori-
fies" her.[3] Indeed, only God can praise Mary adequately and
according to her merits[4]; and so he considers any excess in her
service far better than a deficiency and defends such propositions as that Mary's throne equals that of Christ, and that she
is by right the Mistress of the whole world and has jurisdiction
over it.[5] In the next "proposition" he vigorously denounces
any criticisms of exaggerated Marian devotion from the pulpit,
including Crasset (without naming him) in his censures and
defending even the most extravagant Marian miracles reported
by such unreliable writers as Alain de la Roche.

Enough will have been said to show whether this wholly
uncritical compilation can really be called "a Mariology of the
very first rank". It seems to have been directed not only against

[1] 5, 5, 4 (p. 291).   [2] 8, 8 (p. 328).
[3] 8, 8 (p. 332).   [4] 9, 9, 1.   [5] 9, 9, 2.

Widenfeld but also against contemporary defenders of a more critical approach such as L. A. Muratori (d. 1750).

MURATORI

He was a fine scholar, librarian to the Duke of Modena, with a critical mind open to contemporary ideas, so his theological writings were often attacked as unorthodox. He was protected, however, by no less a person than Benedict XIV (Pope from 1740 to 1758), himself very learned and not given to credulity, as his great work on beatification and canonization amply proves. In 1714 Muratori published a treatise on *Moderation in Matters of Religion* under the pseudonym Lamindus Pritanius, no doubt aware of the opposition any critical attitude to the subject was bound to arouse in the Italy of his day. In this work he discusses the Immaculate Conception (I quote from the Arezzo edition of his *Works* [1770]), which, he says, the Church has every right to define if it can be deduced from Scripture or established by the constant tradition of the Fathers.[1] What aroused the wrath of his opponents was his attitude to the so-called *vœu sanguinaire*. This was a vow, made by some upholders of the Immaculate Conception, to defend this opinion —which, let it be stressed, was at that time not yet a dogma of the Church—even unto death. Muratori pointed out that it was certainly an act of piety to defend this opinion in writing and by arguments, but he could not see how one could bind oneself by oath to shed one's blood for it whenever the occasion offered. "This", he wrote, "is certainly a novel kind of martyrdom, of which our ancestors have never dreamed, and which our descendants, if they are sensible, will never approve ... For one's blood should be shed not for our opinions, but for the divine revelations and holy laws."[2] This very sensible attitude provoked an enormous controversy carried on largely under

---

[1] 1, 17 (pp. 151f.).   [2] 2, 6 (p. 268).

pseudonyms.[1] Muratori was attacked, because this opinion, his opponents said, was not a private view but actually the teaching of the Church. He replied to his critics in a much later work, *De superstitione vitanda*.[2] Indeed, considering dispassionately this vow of giving even one's life in defence of the Immaculate Conception, it seems not only undesirable, as at that time the opinion was not a doctrine of the Church even though it was very widely held, but also quite unreal; for who would have wanted to kill anyone only for holding this belief? Surely even the most enraged Dominican would not have dreamt of taking the life of a Franciscan for opposing the view of St. Thomas, and Protestants blamed the Church for a good many other things, while no pagan would have understood what the controversy was all about. Therefore this "vow" appears to posterity rather like a kind of peculiar devotion than a real issue of life and death. Muratori once more stated his views in a book on the properly regulated devotion of Christians[3] which was examined by the Congregation of the Index in 1753 but found to be completely orthodox. Our subject is treated especially in chapter 22. Muratori reminds Christians that Mary is not a divinity; she should be venerated as our advocate, but she has not the right to forgive sins and she cannot save us. One often says that she gives orders in heaven; but such expressions should not be taken seriously: her office is to pray, not to command. He carefully analyses the sense in which Mary may be said to mediate grace without prejudice to Christ; he does not accept her universal mediation. He condemns as a

[1] See J. Stricher, *Le vœu du sang en faveur de l'Immaculée Conception*, 1960.

[2] (17740), Arezzo ed., vol. 5. It is interesting to note that X. le Bachelet, in his treatise on the Immaculate Conception in *Dict. théol. cath.*, cols. 1180–85 attacks Muratori for his views, while E. Amann, in his article in the same *Dictionnaire*, says it is pure calumny to say that Muratori attacked belief in the Immaculate Conception, finishing with the words: "Truly, few men have deserved so well of the Church and of religion." (*Dict. théol. cath.*, under Muratori, col. 2553.)

[3] *Della regolata divozione de Cristiani* (1949), vol. 6 of the Arezzo edition.

superstition that if one is devout to Mary without leading a virtuous life one will never be damned, and he regrets the endless multiplication of Marian feasts which far exceeded those of Christ.

ALPHONSUS LIGUORI

In the year of Muratori's death there appeared a work which once more gathered up all the Marian teaching and legends of the past and was destined to become the most popular of all modern books on the subject, the *Glories of Mary* of Alphonsus Liguori (1786). The founder of the Redemptorists owes his title of "Doctor of the Church" to his work on moral theology, not to his spiritual writings. This must be emphasized, for his book on Marian devotion, though showing immense industry, is neither a work of true erudition nor of independent thought and research. As Alphonsus himself says in his introduction it is meant for the "devout reader" especially for the preacher, to whom it is to furnish material for sermons and meditation. The work is divided into two main parts, the first being an interpretation of the *Salve Regina*, the second containing discourses on various mysteries and feasts such as the Annunciation, the Assumption, the Sorrows of Mary and similar subjects.

St. Alphonsus is anxious to establish as a fact that all graces pass through the hands of Mary, and so to encourage the faithful to have unbounded confidence in her. He regards it as certain that "all graces that God gives to men pass through the hands of Mary"[1] and from this he deduces that her intercession is necessary for our salvation.[2] For Christ surrendered all the riches of his mercy to his mother, who was given to the world so that they might descend from heaven only through her.[3] Thus the saint also reiterates the medieval idea that God's kingdom is that of justice, Mary's that of mercy: "As angels

---

[1] *Salve Regina*, 2, 2.
[2] *Salve Regina*, 5, 1 is dedicated to the proof of this.
[3] Visitation point 2.

and men, and all things that are in heaven and on earth, are
subject to the empire of God, so they are also under the
dominion of Mary... Mary, then, is a queen: but for our
common consolation... she is a queen so sweet... that the
holy Church wills that we should salute her... under the title
of Queen of Mercy", whereas "the Eternal Father made Jesus
Christ King of justice, and consequently universal Judge of the
world", and he quotes with approval the words of an earlier
author (Ernest, Archbishop of Prague) to the effect "that the
Eternal Father gave the office of judge and avenger to the Son,
and that of showing mercy and relieving the necessitous to the
Mother", which appears to be more effective than the office of
Christ, because "each of her prayers is, as it were, an established law for our Lord".[1] So, "if God is angry with a sinner,
and Mary takes him under her protection, she withholds the
avenging arm of her Son, and saves him".[2] In fact: "Mary...
knows so well how, by her tender and soothing prayers, to
appease the divine justice, that God himself blesses her for it
and, as it were, thanks her for having prevented him from
abandoning and chastising them as they deserved."[3] So the
blessed Virgin is here depicted as a kind of wise wife and God
as an irate husband who might have done something violent
which he would have regretted later if she had not prevented
him. Indeed, "the chief office given to Mary, on being placed
in this world, was to raise up souls that had fallen from divine
grace and to reconcile them with God",[4] and one cannot help
wondering what, then, was the office of Christ. According to
the *Glories of Mary* this seems to have been hardly more than
the physical side of redeeming men by dying, and even to do
this Jesus had to have his mother's permission,[5] a view he reiterates later in the same work when he writes that the Father
"willed that Jesus should not sacrifice his life for the salvation

[1] *Salve Regina*, 1, 1.
[2] 3, 2.   [3] 6, 2.
[4] 6, 3.   [5] 1, 3.

of men without the concurrent assent of Mary . . . by which she should spontaneously offer him to death".[1] And so Alphonsus can pray: "O compassionate Mother . . . I do not even fear thy Son, though justly irritated against me, for at a word of thine he will be appeased. I only fear lest . . . I may cease to recommend myself to thee, and thus be lost."[2] Can Protestants really be blamed if they accuse Catholics of putting Mary in the place of God, if such is the teaching of one of the most influential modern saints? More, Alphonsus also attributes omnipotence to her—not, of course, an omnipotence of nature but of grace, "Since the Mother", he writes, "should have the same power as the Son, rightly has Jesus, who is omnipotent, made Mary also omnipotent",[3] and she is omnipotent "because by her prayers she obtains whatever she wills"[4] which, as is clear from what has been said above, does not always coincide with what God wills. In fact "Mary has only to speak, and her Son executes all".[5] For, says Alphonsus, Mary has given Christ his human nature, and in exchange He gives her his divine nature (!), "that is, omnipotence, by which thou mayest be able to help to save all whomsoever thou pleasest".[6] The Catholic people could surely be excused if, after hearing sermons based on the *Glories*, they were not certain whether Mary was really divine or not, especially as the saint enforced his teaching by stating that "God . . . made himself one and the same thing with her",[7] and that "Jesus and Mary . . . both offered one and the same sacrifice".[8]

Enough will have been quoted to show that the *Glories of Mary* abounds with statements which require a lot of explaining away, if they are not to be understood by the unprejudiced reader as being detrimental to the omnipotence of God and the mercy of Christ. The saint's teaching is supported by a wealth

[1] *Disc. on Purific.*
[2] *Salve Regina*, 2, 2.
[3] *Salve Regina*, 6. 1.
[4] *Salve Regina*, 6. 1.
[5] *Salve Regina*, 6, 1.
[6] *Salve Regina*, 7, 1.
[7] *Disc. on Annunc.*
[8] *Disc. on Purific.*

of quotations and "examples" from the most disparate authors, from St. Thomas Aquinas (hardly anything of him, though!) to some quite unknown visionaries; St. Bridget's *Revelations* are special favourites, and are reproduced as incontrovertible facts, as are the many miracles stories (most of them quite incredible), which are used to substantiate the claims of Mary's unfailing assistance. If Miegge calls the book "devoid of the most elementary critical sense"[1] Catholic readers will find it difficult to contradict him.

The *Glories of Mary* was meant to be a counterblast to the rationalism of the time; to revive devotion to the Mother of God in an age that had little use for supernatural realities. It evidently was what the devout wanted and has edified countless millions of the simple faithful who had in any case remained untouched by the tenets of Enlightenment. But it would seem only reasonable to conjecture that those who had been affected, however lightly, by the spirit of the age must have been estranged even more from the Church in general and Marian devotion in particular by the extravagances of the work.[2]

"ENLIGHTENMENT"

In the latter part of the century, as rationalism had made considerable headway, it did not remain confined to the world outside the Church, but penetrated deeply also into the clergy, especially in Germany and France. It affected, of course, the veneration of the saints and especially Marian devotion which, as we have seen, had frequently been lacking in balance. Now

[1] Miegge, p. 146.
[2] According to Dillenschneider, vol. 1, pp. 264ff. the work had a great vogue in nineteenth-century France; but there was also opposition, especially in Germany, where I. Doellinger, one of the principal opponents of the definition of papal infallibility, criticized the *Glorie* for its absurd (*abenteuerlich*) legends and defective quotations (Doellinger-Reusch, *Geschichte der Moralstreitigkeiten in der römisch-katholischen Kirche seit dem 16. Jahrhundert*, 1889, pp. 390f. and 404f.). In England the reception was cool, though Manning liked it; but neither its flowery style nor its teaching could be expected to appeal to the Anglo-Saxon mind.

there was an outcry to get back to the essentials of Christianity and to primitive teaching, and thus there was the danger of going to the opposite extreme and sacrificing also legitimate developments. Mariology was completely neglected, many local breviaries had the Marian feasts reduced to the minimum of the Annunciation, the Purification, the Visitation and the Assumption; the *Hail Mary* was scorned and the Rosary was rejected as nothing but vain repetitions. Many Marian shrines were abolished, and some bishops ordered the removal of votive images, scapulars and rosaries which the faithful had hung on statues of the blessed Virgin. There were also frequent attacks on the Marian confraternities; and the suppression in 1773 of the Jesuit Order, by Clement XIV under pressure from the governments of France, Spain, Portugal and a number of Italian states, struck a further blow at Marian devotion, which the Order had so consistently fostered. Apart from very few and unimportant publications, serious Marian literature simply ceased to exist, though there remained a certain amount of popular devotion not unmixed with superstition, which was catered for by sermons and popular tracts put out by the Orders and Congregations particularly devoted to the Mother of God. The anti-ecclesiastical legislation of Joseph II (Holy Roman Emperor from 1765 to 1790) with its stress on reform, religious toleration and the rights of the civil power over the Church, contributed further to a slackening of spiritual fervour in general and of Marian devotion in particular. The French Revolution, which enthroned the goddess of reason in Notre Dame de Paris, and the consequences of which spread throughout Europe, did the rest. The Church reached the low-water mark of its influence, and with it also Mary, its type and most eminent member.

THE DEFINITION OF THE IMMACULATE CONCEPTION

It is a frequently observed tendency of history that when one development has reached its saturation point its antithesis begins to appear or to reappear. With the French Revolution rationalism had overreached itself; it was followed by the emergence of "romanticism", an attitude of mind that was favourable once more to irrational and suprarational influences, to emotional as well as mystical experiences. In Germany Joseph von Görres wrote a history of Christian mysticism (1836–42) and Clemens Brentano published the revelations of Anna Katharine Emmerich (d. 1824) in 1833. Marian teaching and devotion profited from this new mood: one doctrinal definition and three widely publicized apparitions gave both an impetus which carried them forward on one tremendous wave of enthusiasm that did not spend itself for over a century.

As we have seen, the question of the Immaculate Conception had been discussed for centuries. Public interest in it was stirred by Catherine Labouré's vision of the Miraculous Medal, to be discussed in the following section, and several theologians wrote treatises on the subject, among them the Jesuit Giovanni Perrone, whose work *De Immaculato Beatae Virginis Mariae Conceptu* was published in 1847 and went through ten editions within five years. By this time the doctrine had been accepted by all Orders, and in 1847 even the Dominicans petitioned Rome to be allowed to celebrate the feast, like the others, with an octave and with the word "immaculate" added to the mention of Mary's conception. Permission was given, and they were assured that this in no way affected their oath to teach the doctrine of St. Thomas.

Nevertheless, there remained a certain amount of opposition, especially from the liberal Catholics of Germany, but also from certain circles in France and England, which prevented Gregory XVI from defining the doctrine. With the accession of Pius IX, however, the situation changed. The new Pope was personally devoted to the cause of the Immaculate Conception; in 1848 he ordered the formation of a special theological consulta and a pontifical commission to investigate the question; the majority of the former, seventeen as against three members,

declared themselves favourable to a definition. In the next year
Pius asked the bishops through an encyclical to report on the
sentiments in their dioceses with regard to the proposal of a
definition; of the 603 bishops asked only 56 were against it,
among them the Archbishop of Paris, who considered the doctrine neither definable nor opportune. But since more than
nine-tenths of the bishops were in favour, the Pope formed a
special congregation with the task of drawing up the bull.

The dogma of the Immaculate Conception of the Blessed
Virgin Mary was proclaimed by the Constitution *Ineffabilis
Deus* on 8 December 1854. It begins with the statement that
God prepared for himself a mother whom he loved above all
other creatures, and therefore gave her incomparably more gifts
than to any other creature, human or angelic. That original
innocence was closely linked to her great dignity of Mother of
God, the Catholic Church had inculcated ever more clearly, and
this doctrine had been admitted from earliest times. Therefore
her Conception had always been presented as something ex-
ceptional, and the Church had applied to it in her Liturgy the
texts referring to the divine Wisdom. The Constitution then
gives an account of the history of the doctrine, the institution
and approval of the feast by various popes, the enrichment of
the cult by indulgences, the permissions granted to cities and
kingdoms to place themselves under the protection of Mary
under the title of the Immaculate Conception, the approval of
confraternities and religious congregations dedicated to the
same mystery, and finally its inclusion in the litanies and the
Preface of the Mass. The Pope goes on to say that his predecessors had never allowed this doctrine to be criticized and
he quotes especially Alexander VII who in his constitution,
Sollicitudo omnium ecclesiarum, of 8 December 1661, had condemned the opinion contrary to the Immaculate Conception
and had forbidden any negative discussion as well as any books
denying it. He quotes, as the weightiest authority, the Council
of Trent, which had excluded Mary explicitly from original

sin. This doctrine, which had always existed in the Church, had become progressively clearer. "The Church", continues the Pope, "has regarded it as a sacred deposit received from the ancient fathers and stamped with the glorious impress of revealed doctrine. Of this the monuments of antiquity . . . in the Eastern as well as the Western Church, bear the strongest testimony." As biblical evidence he then quotes Gen. iii.15: "Wherefore, as Christ, the mediator between God and man, has . . . blotted out the handwriting of the decree of condemnation against us . . . so, in like manner, the most holy Virgin linked to him in the closest and most indissoluble bonds, in union with him and through him, waging eternal hostilities against the poisonous serpent, and obtaining a decisive triumph over him, completely crushed his head under her immaculate heel." He further gives an account of the traditional images and epithets praising her perfect purity. As the second biblical evidence the Pope mentions the "gratia plena", a "unique and solemn salutation" never applied to anyone else. After comparing Mary with Eve before she had fallen he gives another string of images applied to her such as "lily among thorns", "incorruptible wood" and so forth. Hence it is no wonder that bishops and other churchmen, religious Orders and even kings and emperors should have petitioned the Holy See to define the doctrine. After briefly rehearsing the final steps taken by the Pope, he then pronounces the formal definition of the dogma:

To the honour of the holy and undivided Trinity, to the glory and adornment of the Virgin Mother of God, to the exaltation of the Catholic faith, and the increase of the Catholic religion, We, by the authority of Jesus Christ our Lord, of the blessed Apostles, Peter and Paul, and by our own, declare, pronounce and define that the doctrine which holds that the blessed Virgin Mary, at the first instant of her Conception, by a singular privilege and grace of the omnipotent God, in consideration of the merits of Jesus Christ, the Saviour of mankind, was preserved free from all stain of original sin, has been revealed by God, and therefore is to be firmly and constantly believed by all the faithful.

Of course the only part of the bull which is infallible is the definition itself, because some of the historical matter may be open to criticism. The question is: does this definition flatly contradict the teaching of St. Anselm, St. Bernard, St. Thomas, St. Bonaventure and so many other authoritative theologians who held Mary to have been conceived in sin? It does not seem so, because the two great objections which had formerly prevented the acceptance of the doctrine in the Western Church were solved by the definition itself, which is partly based on the teaching of Duns Scotus. The one objection was that every normal conception, being accompanied by concupiscence, is therefore sinful. Hence, as Mary was not born from a virgin, she could not but be subject to original sin. Now the definition does not envisage this, the "active" conception, at all. What it says is that Mary's own state at the moment of her conception, her "passive" conception, was sinless. The second objection was that if Mary was conceived immaculate she would have no need of a redeemer. This objection was ruled out by the explicit statement that she was conceived immaculate "in consideration of the merits of Jesus Christ", and we have seen that Duns Scotus regarded this as a more perfect mode of redemption than the ordinary one, after original sin has been contracted. So the definition says neither that the act by which Mary was conceived was without sin nor that she had no need of a redeemer, and thus it is not surprising that the Catholic world should have accepted it very quietly, with far fewer defections than the opponents of the definition had anticipated.

Naturally, reactions outside the Catholic Church were different, especially as the actual import of the definition was frequently misunderstood. As we have seen, the orthodox theologians' idea of original sin differed considerably from that of the Western Church; moreover, they frequently assumed that the dogma envisaged the active conception. In England Samuel Wilberforce preached against it as "heretical", because not contained in Scripture, and Pusey, in his *Eirenicon*, foresaw that it would be a further obstacle to reunion.

After the definition studies on the subject multiplied. The most important were the three-volume work by the Jesuit Carlo Passaglia, *De Immaculato Deiparae Semper Virginis Conceptu Commentarius*,[1] A. Ballerini's *Sylloge Monumentorum ad Mysterium Conceptionis Immaculatae Virginis Deiparae Illustrandum*[2] and the more popular work by Bishop W. B. Ullathorne, *The Immaculate Conception of the Mother of God*, which appeared in 1855.

MARIAN APPARITIONS

I. *GENERAL OBSERVATIONS*

The Immaculate Conception was not only the business of theologians; the interest of the devout laity in it received a tremendous impetus from two Marian apparitions, the one before, the other after the definition of the dogma. Now, before discussing these events we would briefly state what is their position in the Church and in how far they impose themselves on the acceptance of Catholics.

First of all, however much approved by the Church, these apparitions do not belong to what is called the "deposit of faith", hence Christians will not give the same assent of faith to them as they give to the doctrines of the Church. They will only give them the same merely human credence as they give to any other statement they hold to be true. They are not, however, *obliged* to give such an assent if, after mature reflection, they feel unable to believe in the apparition in question, even

[1] Rome (1854–5).   [2] Rome (1854–6).

though it may have the approval of the Church. As Father E. Schillebeeckx, OP, points out in his book *Mary, Mother of the Redemption*[1]:

> The Church's approbation of an apparition or private revelation is . . . never an infallible proof of its historical truth and authenticity. It is merely an official confirmation of the fact that sufficient evidence has emerged from the investigation to enable us to be cautiously certain in our acceptance of the divine authenticity of the apparition on rational grounds. It would perhaps be more precise to say that it is ultimately only a question of an authoritative opinion concerning our cautious approval. To all intents and purposes, the Church does no more than give her official permission that Mary may be venerated in a special way at the place where the apparition has occurred. [The author goes on to quote the Acts of the Fifth Provincial Council of Malines (1938), to the effect that] in the opinion of the Church, it is in no way necessary for all the faithful to believe in these matters. All that the Church declares is that, in her judgement, they are in no way contrary to faith and morals and that there are sufficient indications for their pious and cautious approval by human faith.[2]

Hence, belief in or rejection of a certain apparition or private revelation is left to the conscience of the individual Catholic, though respect for the authority of the Church will certainly lead him to refrain from openly attacking or ridiculing an officially approved phenomenon, although it is permissible to point out certain features of a revelation which lead one personally to reject it. It should, moreover, be remembered that in private revelations just as much as in mystical experiences the personality of the recipient plays an important part and is

[1] *Sheed and Ward*, London (1964).
[2] pp. 197f.

bound to colour even the most authentic supernatural experiences. All these observations must be kept in mind also when approaching the Marian apparitions of the nineteenth and twentieth centuries. Unfortunately, only one of them, the apparitions of Lourdes, has been critically examined; for the others we have to rely on more or less popular accounts.

2. THE MIRACULOUS MEDAL

The first among them, which had a considerable influence on general interest in the Immaculate Conception preceding the definition of the dogma, is the vision of the so-called Miraculous Medal of Catherine Labouré (1806–76).

Catherine was a simple peasant girl, who entered the novitiate of the Daughters of Charity of St. Vincent de Paul in the rue du Bac in Paris, in April 1830. She was obviously a "visionary type", for immediately after joining the novitiate she had various visions, for example of the heart of St. Vincent, of our Lord in the blessed Sacrament and of Christ the King. Of her famous visions of the blessed Virgin, which she communicated only to her confessor, there exists an account written by herself, but only many years after the event. In this she writes that on the eve of the feast of St. Vincent, in the night from the 18th to the 19th of July 1830, she had a great desire to see the blessed Virgin. Before going to sleep, she swallowed a small piece of linen, a relic of St. Vincent, hoping that the saint would obtain for her the grace of seeing the Mother of God.

Her desire was fulfilled: About half-past-eleven at night she heard a voice calling her and saw a child dressed in white, about four or five years old, who told her to go into the chapel, where the Blessed Virgin was awaiting her. As she was afraid that someone might hear her get up, the child told her that everybody was asleep; so she dressed and went through the corridors of the convent, where all the lights had been put on, and into the chapel, which was also illuminated as for the

Midnight Mass at Christmas. Catherine had to wait for some time; then the child, whom she took to be her guardian angel, told her that the Virgin was coming. She heard a rustle like that of a silk dress and saw Mary sitting in a chair by the altar. Catherine ran towards her, knelt down and put her hands on the Virgin's knees. Then Mary gave her instructions about her conduct in various matters and explained to her all the things she had seen.

The vision of the Miraculous Medal took place in November of the same year, during the evening meditation. Again Catherine heard the rustle of silk, and this time the Virgin appeared to her standing, dressed in a white silk robe, her head covered with a white veil falling down to her feet, which rested on a white ball. There was also a serpent of greenish colour with yellow specks. The hands of the vision were lifted up, holding a golden ball surmounted by a small golden cross. Catherine also noticed that the vision had three rings on each of her fingers, adorned with wonderful stones which emitted brilliant rays. She then heard a voice saying: "This ball which you see represents the whole world, particularly France, and every person in particular." She was further told that the rays from the rings symbolized the graces Mary gave to all who asked her, while some stones, from which no rays went forth, were the graces men forgot to ask her for.

At this moment, Catherine told her confessor, an oval frame appeared round the Virgin, inside which was written in gold letters: "O Mary, conceived without sin, pray for us who have recourse to you." Then the golden ball in Mary's hands disappeared and the hands themselves remained outstretched, continuing to emit the rays, while a voice was heard telling Catherine to have a medal struck according to this model, which would obtain great graces for all those who wore it with confidence.

After that the picture seemed to turn round and show on the reverse side of the medal an "M" surmounted by a cross, and below it the two hearts of Jesus and Mary, one surrounded by a crown of thorns, the other pierced by a sword. On disappearing, Mary told the sister that henceforth she would see her no more, but she would hear her voice in her prayers.

The tremendous success of the Miraculous Medal is well known. After the Archbishop of Paris had given his permission it was first struck in 1832 and was soon distributed all over the world in millions. Catherine herself, however, remained completely unknown, for both she and her confessor kept the secret of her identity. Only six months before her death she revealed it to her superior.

During the official enquiries into the circumstances of the revelation of the Miraculous Medal Catherine herself was not summoned at all, a very unusual procedure, due to her persistent refusal to appear before the authorities. Moreover, she suffered from strange periods of amnesia, when she could not remember any details of what she had seen even when questioned by her confessor.

The story of Catherine Labouré and the Miraculous Medal differs considerably from the Marian apparitions that followed it. First, the vision happened to a grown-up person, not to a child. Secondly, Catherine had fervently prayed to see the blessed Virgin, and consequently knew at once who the apparition was; finally, the vision did not demand a new sanctuary or a pilgrimage, but a medal. The tremendous popularity of the Medal, to which soon numerous miracles were attributed, had also a great influence on the definition of the Immaculate Conception, as it impressed the doctrine on the consciousness of Catholic people and led to a growing demand to have it solemnly defined.

3. THE APPARITIONS OF LOURDES

Four years after this definition, another series of Marian apparitions took place, which increased the popularity of the dogma still further, and led to the establishment of a Marian shrine that has become the most frequented place of pilgrimage in modern times. These, of course, are the apparitions of the blessed Virgin to Bernadette Soubirous at Lourdes. Our account of the events is based on the immense documentation presented by R. Laurentin,[1] supplemented by the work of A. M. Olphe-Galliard.[2]

Bernadette Soubirous (1844–79) was the eldest daughter of a miller. Her parents were very poor, largely through their own fault, as they were shiftless and, according to the testimony of their neighbours, also fond of the bottle. They were both illiterate, and so was Bernadette until, in her late teens, she learned to read and write. She was a very small and sickly child, who had cholera when she was eleven, as a consequence of which she suffered from asthma for the rest of her life. Shortly before her illness her father had to give up the mill and became a day labourer, while her mother worked in the fields and the children had to contribute to the household by collecting rags and bones. There were only two beds for the whole family of parents and four children, who had to live in one very unhealthy room in an old disused prison which was infected with vermin. They were so desperately poor that Bernadette's small brother was found eating candle wax in church. Though not particularly devout, the Soubirous were ordinary practising Catholics, and Bernadette knew the *Our Father*, *Hail Mary* and *Creed* as well as the prayer of the Miraculous Medal, "O Mary conceived without sin."

In September 1857 Bernadette was sent to Bartrès near Lourdes to help her former wet nurse. There she was over-worked and, moreover, had to interrupt her catechism instructions for her first Holy Communion. In January 1858, therefore, her father took her home, though conditions there had

---

[1] *Lourdes. Histoire authentique des apparitions* (1958ff.).

[2] Léonard Cros, SJ, *Lourdes 1858. Témoins de l'Evénement. Documents présentés par le P. M. Olphe-Galliard*, Paris (1957).

gone from bad to worse, her father being out of work and lying in bed all day while the children were almost starving.

Then, on 11 February, began the series of events that has made the names of Lourdes and Bernadette famous throughout the Christian world. On this morning Bernadette, her small sister and one of her friends had been sent out to gather firewood. An old woman directed them to the grotto of Massabielle; there was a canal near the grotto through which the other children waded after having taken off their clogs, because there was more wood on the other side. Bernadette, however, who was wearing stockings because of her asthma, asked her friends to throw stones into the canal so that she would be able to jump from one to the other without having to wade through. But they only laughed at her and told her to follow their example.

Bernadette had just begun to take off her stockings when she heard a noise as of a gust of wind, but noticed that the leaves on the trees did not move. She turned towards the grotto, from where the sound seemed to come, and there she saw what she described two days later to her confessor, Abbé Pomian, as "something white in the shape of a girl". Throughout the interrogations that followed she would always call the apparition "Aqueró", a dialect term meaning "this thing". On this first day she instinctively put her hand in her pocket, produced her rosary and knelt down to pray, while the vision, who also carried a rosary with a large shining cross, moved the beads with her fingers, but did not move her lips. When the rosary was finished the vision disappeared, and Bernadette's companions returned, making fun of her, because she had been praying out of doors instead of helping them. She interrupted them with the question whether they had not seen anything, but refused to reveal her own vision. Later, however, she gave in to the persistent questions of her sister, who in her turn told their mother about it. Soon all Bernadette's small friends knew

4+ II

that she had seen a mysterious lady in the grotto, and on Sunday, 14 February, they urged Bernadette to go there again.

After having received permission from Bernadette's father, about a dozen girls set out to the grotto, taking a bottle of holy water with them. Soon Bernadette announced that the lady was there, smiling at her and saluting her, and to make sure that the vision was not from the devil she threw holy water at it, but the lady only smiled. Then Bernadette fell into an ecstasy, her face grew pale, and she no longer moved. This frightened the other children, who tried to pull her away. They finally fetched a miller from the neighbourhood and succeeded in getting her to the mill, where she at last woke up from her trance and told them that she had seen "a pretty young girl with a rosary over her arm". There was a crowd of people at the mill, and when Bernadette's mother arrived, very angry that her daughter had become such a centre of excitement, she was told that Bernadette had looked like an angel in her ecstasy. The sisters at the convent school at Lourdes, however, were sceptical, and on the following Monday Bernadette was questioned at length and ridiculed.

On Thursday, 18 February, she went again to the grotto, accompanied by two devout ladies. One of them had been sufficiently naïve to bring with her writing materials, and when Bernadette said that the lady was there she was handed pen and paper and told to ask the vision to write down what she wanted. When Bernadette did so, "Aqueró" simply laughed; then she spoke for the first time—in Bernadette's patois—saying: "This is not necessary." The vision then asked the girl: "Will you do me the favour to come here for a fortnight?" following up her request with the words: "I do not promise to make you happy in this world, but in the next." What struck Bernadette particularly was the extraordinary politeness of the lady, who did not address her with the familiar "tu" (thou), like everybody else, but with the polite "vous", and further requested her to visit the grotto as a favour.

The Thursday on which this decisive apparition occurred was market day in Lourdes, and so it is not surprising that the tale of Bernadette's strange experiences should have spread throughout the countryside like wildfire. Within the fortnight the number of people arriving at the grotto increased from day to day: on 20 February there were about thirty, the next day a hundred, on the 24th between two and three hundred, on 2 March there were sixteen hundred and fifty, and on 4 March between seven and eight thousand, for on that day, the last of the fortnight, a miracle was expected to happen, though this did not take place.

Nothing much happened on 19 February, for Bernadette's aunt, who accompanied the girl, was so frightened by her pallor when she was in ecstasy that she gripped her arm and screamed. This day Bernadette had taken a candle, and afterwards she was also given a medal to take with her, most probably the Miraculous Medal. On the next day she was in ecstasy for about a quarter of an hour, smiling and saluting the vision.

The 21st was a Sunday, and though Bernadette went to the grotto as early as six o'clock in the morning, there were already large crowds waiting for her. They were delighted to see her in ecstasy and assured each other that the little one saw the blessed Virgin. Later she had to recite her experiences to a priest, and after this she was summoned to Monsieur Jacomet, the police inspector. People tried to frighten her by telling her that she might be put in prison, but she replied with great spirit: "If they put me there, they will have to let me out again." In fact, Jacomet was very courteous to her, made her sit down and asked her her age, which she did not know. Asked to describe "Aqueró", she replied that she was "like a little girl". She was dressed in a white robe held together by a blue girdle, had a white veil on her head and a yellow rose on each foot; she held a rosary in her hand. Thus, in answer to the many questions put to her, Bernadette's description was now much more detailed than at her first interview with her confessor, when she had simply said she had seen "something white in the shape of a girl".

Jacomet wanted her to promise not to go to the grotto any more, but she refused. When, at the end of the interview, Bernadette's father arrived, the policeman exacted an undertaking from him not to let his daughter go to the grotto again.

Despite this prohibition Bernadette visited the grotto the very next day, but she had no vision and was extremely sad, saying tearfully: "I do not know in what way I have failed this lady", but later expressed the opinion that there had been no vision because people had touched the wild rose bush on which the lady appeared to stand. As Abbé Pomian, however, stated that no-one had the right to forbid Bernadette to visit the grotto, Bernadette's father withdrew his prohibition, and the following day, in the presence of about a hundred spectators, Bernadette had her vision—and not only that, but on this day she herself seems to have spoken to the lady for the first time, for she was seen to nod, shake her head and laugh.[1]

While the inhabitants of Lourdes and its surroundings were divided between enthusiastic belief, perplexity and downright

---

[1] Laurentin interprets the absence of the vision on 22 February as a special tactic of our Lady: "The spectacle of this little humiliated girl . . . changes the dispositions of those immediately responsible. . . . The triumph of the Virgin passes through the suffering of Bernadette." (*Lourdes*, "La Quinzaine des apparitions, première semaine", p. 161.) This, of course, is possible. However, there might also be a more natural explanation. The realization that by going to the grotto Bernadette was disobeying her father may have troubled her, so that she was not sufficiently calm to be able to concentrate on a supernatural experience. For we would submit that even in the apparitions of Lourdes there are certain features that point to the personal—if subconscious —activities of the visionary. For example, the vision is very small, no taller than Bernadette herself, who was undersized, and she addresses the little girl with "vous", which may quite well be a compensation for the general contempt in which the "little idiot" had been held until then. For all her humility, it does seem that Bernadette was not altogether indifferent to suddenly being the centre of interest—as was only natural, for she was certainly not yet a saint. For example, one of the pious ladies accompanying her was somewhat taken aback when on her arrival Bernadette said a little peremptorily: "Let me pass, let me pass." (Léonard Cros, p. 102.)

opposition, the phenomena at the grotto entered a new phase. When Bernadette arrived there on 24 February, she cast an astonished glance at the crowd numbering between two and three hundred. She lit her candle as usual and began to recite her rosary. After the first decade the vision appeared, but, instead of smiling as usual, Bernadette's face became sad and at times even angry. She seemed to be looking for someone, going backwards and forwards between the interior and the entrance of the grotto. Then she made two steps on her knees. When she seemed to fall over, her aunt Lucille cried out in alarm, which causd Bernadette to look round, telling her aunt not to upset herself. When she once more turned towards the grotto, the vision had disappeared. On her way back the girl told her aunt that she was not to accompany her another time.

When Bernadette was asked whether the lady talked to her she was quite astonished that no-one else had heard their conversation, which she believed to have been carried on in a normal voice: "She speaks to me in patois", said Bernadette, adding proudly: "She says 'vous' to me." She later explained that Aqueró had said "Penitence" and told her to pray for the conversion of sinners; when asking her to go on her knees and kiss the ground, the vision had politely asked her whether this would trouble her, whereupon Bernadette had answered: "O no, (I will do it) with all my heart."

According to the investigations of Laurentin the discovery of the spring took place during the ninth apparition, on 25 February. The first visitors had come to the grotto at two o'clock in the morning. Later Bernadette arrived, accompanied by three aunts and followed by an escort, for by that time the police had received orders to control the crowds and prevent accidents. Bernadette recited her Rosary, but was not in ecstasy, for soon she gave her candle to one of her aunts to hold and herself went on her knees to the back of the grotto, while kissing the ground at the same time. Again she went backwards and forwards, looking for something; finally she went once more to the back of the grotto and looked with an expression of distaste at the moist ground under her feet. Finally she bent down and scratched the soil, formed a piece of mud into a ball and tried to put it in her mouth. After rejecting it three times in disgust, she at last collected a little muddy water in her hand and swallowed it, then took some more and smeared it over her face. After that she ate some of the herbs growing in the mud.

Not surprisingly, the spectators were disappointed and even disgusted with this strange behaviour, thinking Bernadette had gone out of her mind, though some imitated her and swallowed water from the same muddy spot. Afterwards she was questioned by several people, including one of the parish priests, Abbé Pène, and explained that Aqueró had told her to drink and wash at the source. Not seeing any water, she had turned first to the River Gave, which was quite near, but was then directed by the vision to the spot from which she had actually drunk. She was then summoned to Monsieur Dutour, the Imperial Procurator, who began the interrogation by asking what the vision was like. She replied: "Like nothing." When he insisted that she should indicate what it resembled most she said: "The blessed Virgin of the parish church for the face and the clothes . . . but alive and surrounded by light."[1] This is very important, because it is sometimes stated that Bernadette's vision was responsible for a new artistic type of the blessed Virgin, whereas this did not differ substantially from Murillo's (1617–82) paintings of the Immaculate Conception, to which both the image of the Miraculous Medal and one of the Marian statues in Bernadette's parish church bore a striking resemblance. The Procurator then ordered her not to return to the grotto; but she again refused to give such an undertaking, because she felt drawn to the grotto "by an irresistible force".

Thus the next day, 26 February, she again set out for Massabielle, despite the opposition of her mother, but the same thing

[1] Laurentin, *Lourdes*, p. 438.

happened as when she had gone before without permission: there was no apparition. However, she did her penitential exercises, moving on her knees and kissing the ground, and people filled bottles with water from the spring, which gradually grew larger as the crowds were scratching the earth around it. The same happened on Saturday, 27 February, but there was a vision. The next day it was estimated that about eleven hundred and fifty persons had come to the grotto, and there was a large number of policemen. The apparition lasted a long time, and afterwards Bernadette was again questioned, this time by Monsieur Ribes, the *juge d'instruction*. He threatened her with prison, but she replied: "I am ready, put me there, but make it solid and well locked, or I shall escape." She also told the Judge that next Thursday would be the last day of the apparitions.

These interrogations added to the general excitement, and on Monday, 1 March, fifteen hundred people went to the grotto, and soldiers had to make a way for Bernadette. On this morning a strange incident happened. She took a rosary from her pocket and held it up to the grotto, then put it back and produced another one. All sorts of tales spread around this simple movement, but Bernadette herself explained that a sick woman had given her her rosary to present to the lady; when she took it out Aqueró seemed to be angry, and so she exchanged it for her own.

On Tuesday, 2 March, there were even more people. On this day the apparition asked Bernadette to tell the priests that there should be a procession and a chapel should be built. So Bernadette went to Abbé Pomian, of whom she was less afraid than of the Curé, Peyramale, but Monsieur Pomian was doubtful, since he had examined her on the catechism the week before and had found her very ignorant. He sent her to the Curé, who treated her very roughly. She denied claiming to have seen the blessed Virgin, but told him that Aqueró had asked for a procession to the grotto. When asked on which day the procession was to be she could not remember, and under his fierce cross-questioning she even told him she was not quite sure whether the vision had actually asked for one. Only after she had left did she remember that she ought also to have mentioned the building of a chapel. So she returned in the evening, accompanied by a devout lady, gave her message, and was told she ought to ask the apparition her name.

In the meantime the police had to take stringent security measures, as the crowds increased each day; on 3 March there were between three and four thousand.

Bernadette arrived at seven o'clock, accompanied by her mother and an aunt. She knelt down to say her Rosary, but nothing happened, and in the general rush her candle was broken. She was very disappointed, but returned secretly in the afternoon when there were only about a hundred people there; and now the lady appeared, confirmed that she wanted a chapel, but only smiled when Bernadette asked her her name. In the evening she reported to the Curé, who told her that if the Lady wanted a chapel she should say her name and cause the rose bush at the grotto to bloom.

On 4 March, the last day of the fortnight, the gendarmes kept the crowds moving, having inspected the grotto during the night to make sure there was no hidden apparatus there which might account for the miracle that was confidently expected to happen on that day. Bernadette was late, because three doctors had arrived from Bordeaux to examine her. She was accompanied by her family and by her cousin Jeanne, whom she promised to stay close to when she (Bernadette) was in ecstasy. Many people presented their rosaries for her to touch, which she did in order to be rid of them. When she had finally arrived at her customary place in front of the grotto she had become separated from her cousin, and suddenly a loud voice was heard: "The little one demands one of her cousins", who was then conducted to her by two policemen.

Bernadette began to recite her Rosary, while the crowds waited in breathless excitement. But they were to be disappointed, for nothing else happened but that Bernadette entered into ecstasy, smiled and saluted the invisible lady, went into the interior of the grotto and back again, and finally extinguished her candle and went home. On her way back she met a blind girl whom she had already noticed before; she ran to her and embraced her. Bernadette may have expected a miraculous cure, but nothing happened. Nevertheless, the crowds accompanied her to her house, surging forward and trying to touch and kiss her, as if she had miraculous powers.

In the evening Bernadette presented herself once more before the Curé, telling him that she had asked the lady her name and also begged her to make the rose bush blossom, but she had answered both requests with a smile. However, she still wanted a chapel.

So the fortnight of the apparitions was over, and the vision had not revealed her name; nor had there been a miracle, for the discovery of the source cannot be regarded as one, since its existence was well known to shepherds and fishermen. When more and more people dug around it to draw water it naturally expanded.

Nevertheless, on 24 March Bernadette let it be known that she was again going to Massabielle on the following day, the feast of the Annunciation, so there was a small crowd, estimated at between fifty and a hundred people, waiting at the grotto. Once more Bernadette entered into ecstasy; once more she asked the vision her name. She had to repeat the question three times before the lady finally answered, again in dialect: "I am the Immaculate Conception." On her way to the priest Bernadette repeated these words over and over again, for she believed she had never heard them before, and as she had a very bad memory she was afraid to forget them.[1]

[1] Bernadette's own assertion has been accepted by all Catholic writers on the subject, and there is no reason to doubt her subjective veracity. But is it to be believed possible that in the year 1858, four years after the definition of the Immaculate Conception, a girl who went to church regularly, who attended catechism classes, and who had, moreover, been constantly questioned both

4*

After this Bernadette saw the blessed Virgin only twice more: on 7 April, when the apparition repeated her demand to have a chapel built on the site of the grotto, and on 16 July, the feast of Our Lady of Mount Carmel. Then all her visions ceased. She was ill for a long time and also suffered much from constant interrogations. On 21 May, 1866, she had the joy of attending the first Mass celebrated at the grotto, and in July of the same year she entered the convent of the Sisters of Notre Dame at Nevers, where she stayed until her death, having still much to suffer both physically and spiritually.

The shrine, which her visions had initiated, flourished despite much early opposition, and despite a sudden epidemic of false visionaries who disturbed Lourdes and the surrounding countryside with their antics, calling forth the intervention of the police. These, and the crowds which continued to visit the grotto after miracles had been reported, caused the authorities to forbid access to it and to remove the candles, rosaries and other pious objects with which it had been adorned. But in October 1858 all these measures were revoked, and the flow of pilgrims continued to increase each year. For by then the ecclesiastical authorities had taken charge, and the Bishop of Tarbes had ordered an investigation, the result of which was published in January 1862, confirming that the blessed Virgin had really appeared to Bernadette, authorizing the cult of Our Lady of Lourdes for the diocese, and proposing to build a sanctuary on the territory of the grotto. Two years later the statue was blessed—a sculpture which, incidentally, was not approved

---

by priests and lay people during the preceding weeks, should never have heard the words: "the Immaculate Conception"? She may neither have heard nor, of course, understood them consciously; but there seems a strong possibility that she had heard these words before and that they had sunk into her subconscious, from which they emerged when she was in trance. This does not mean that there was no objective truth in the apparition and the revelation of its name; we would only point out that there are, as has been suggested in a previous note, certain features in the events of Lourdes which are not necessarily quite so miraculous as they are generally held to be.

by Bernadette herself—and in 1866 the crypt was inaugurated. The Church of the Immaculate Conception was finished in 1872, and in the same year the first torchlight procession took place. Soon national, and later international, pilgrimages began; in 1884 the Medical Bureau was set up to investigate reported miracles; six years later the Feast of Our Lady of Lourdes was instituted for certain dioceses, and extended to the whole Church in 1907. Bernadette was canonized in 1933, and in 1958 the centenary of the apparitions was celebrated with great enthusiasm and splendour.

The story of the poor peasant girl to whom the blessed Virgin revealed herself as the Immaculate Conception has gripped the imagination of the whole Catholic world and beyond, for it was celebrated even by the German Jewish writer Franz Werfel in his famous *Song of Bernadette*, and the film based on the book made it known to an even wider public. It may be said without exaggeration that Lourdes has become the modern centre of Marian devotion throughout Christendom, which no other shrine has as yet eclipsed.

4. LA SALETTE

In 1846, between Catherine Labouré's vision of the Miraculous Medal and the event of Lourdes, another Marian vision had been reported, alleged to have been seen by two children, Melanie and Maximin, aged fourteen-and-a-half and eleven years respectively. Like Bernadette, Melanie Calvat (1831–1904) and Maximin Giraud (1835–75) both came from poor and shiftless families and were illiterate. In September 1846 they met for the first time when they were temporarily employed as cowherds.

In the afternoon of the 19th of the same month they had gone to sleep for an hour; on waking they looked for the cows, which had disappeared, found them at some distance and turned back to collect their satchels, which they had left on some stones by a spring. Suddenly Melanie saw a light and then a lady sitting on one of the stones, with her elbows on her knees and her face in her hands. She called to Maximin, who was a little distance behind her, and he asserted that he, too, saw the figure, suggesting that they should defend themselves with a stick if she should do anything to them. Then the lady rose, folding her hands on her breast, and told the children not to be afraid, but to approach her: "I am here to tell you great news." The children came near and the lady walked with them a few steps, one child on either side of her. She then said to them: "If my people will not submit, I shall be forced to let go the arm of my son; it is so heavy and oppressive that I can no longer restrain it."

The children said they thought it might be a mother whom her children had beaten and who had escaped to the mountains, an idea which fits in ill with the description they gave of the lady. For she wore a white, large-sleeved dress sewn with pearls; her shoes were white, with gold buckles, edged with roses and pearls. A kind of golden apron hung from her waist and a white shawl, also edged with roses, from her shoulders. Besides, she wore two golden chains, a large one next to her shawl and a smaller one round her neck, from which hung a long cross with the figure of Christ and on either arm of the cross was a hammer and a pair of pincers respectively. She wore further a kind of white cap with a garland of many-coloured roses. The whole apparition was one of unearthly light; besides, it was transparent and surrounded by a brilliant halo.

That the children should have mistaken this extraordinary figure for an ordinary woman fleeing from her family certainly taxes one's credulity.

The vision, which was weeping throughout the conversation with the children, then embarked on a long complaint delivered in French, which the children did not understand very well but nevertheless reported. She told them that she had suffered for them a long time and that they would never be able to reward her for what she had done for them. She—the children insisted that this was what the lady had said—had given them six days for work and reserved the seventh for herself (!), but no one would grant her that. Further, the cart drivers always used her Son's name when swearing: these two things were weighing down the arm of her Son.[1]

The apparition then outlined the punishments that would overtake the people for these sins. The harvest would fail, and they would only have enough potatoes till Christmas. At this point the two children did not understand, and now the lady changed from French into the local patois, repeated the matter of the potatoes and prophesied a great famine, when nuts and grapes would rot.

After that Melanie ceased to hear the lady's voice for some time, while Maximin was listening; after that Maximin no longer heard it, but it became audible again to Melanie. The children asserted that during this time each of them had been told a secret, which they were not to divulge to anyone. Then the voice became once more audible to both, and the lady said that if people were converted, the stones and rocks would turn into wheat and the fields would sow themselves with potatoes. This was followed by the vision's demand to the children to say their prayers better. Then she returned to the matter of the bad harvest, recalling to them what Maximin's father had said about it. Finally she told the children to "spread this message among all my people". Then the apparition turned, and after repeating her injunction hovered above the ground and began to melt away. It was only then, the children asserted, that they realized that they had not spoken to an ordinary woman.

Melanie and Maximin then returned to their cows and

---

[1] It should be noted that just these sins, prevalent especially among the poor, seem to have been generally condemned from the pulpits in those days, as evidenced by the complaints of the Curé d'Ars, for example. Nothing is said by the apparition about such much graver matters as flagrant social injustice, mere superficial religious observance and lack of charity, which were prevalent at the time—sins condemned in the Gospels far more vigorously than the desecration of the Sabbath and taking the Lord's name in vain.

discussed their experience. When they came home in the evening they told the story to their parents and other relatives, who decided that it was a matter for the parish priest. He believed at once that the children had seen the blessed Virgin and told his congregation so on the following Sunday, on which day, strange to say, Maximin failed to go to Mass. On the same day some neighbours wrote down the message of the lady as Melanie reported it, and on Monday Maximin was questioned and told the same story.

The apparition of La Salette was approved by the diocesan, the Bishop of Grenoble, in 1851. It was at first taken up enthusiastically by the Curé d'Ars, but after a visit from Maximin in September 1850 he turned against it, saying that Maximin had told him he had actually seen nothing. This statement, however, is supposed to have been due either to a misunderstanding or to a prank played by Maximin. In any case, after eight years of doubt the Curé demanded and obtained a sign from heaven which caused him to return to his original belief. La Salette became a place of pilgrimage, though a far less frequented one than Lourdes, and both miracles and conversions have been attributed to it.

The subsequent career of the child visionaries, however, is not very reassuring. Melanie tried her vocation in various convents and claimed to receive many visions and revelations, most of them with an apocalyptic content; she also published a book, *The Apparition of the Most Blessed Virgin on the Mountain of La Salette*, in which she divulged the "secret" the apparition had communicated to her; this book was later placed on the Index and the revelation of the secret forbidden to be discussed. Maximin, on the other hand, had no further visions. He tried to be a priest but failed; he had various jobs (among others he sold a liqueur called Salettine with his name on the label which, understandably, caused much scandal) he was always in debt and died of a heart disease after a pilgrimage to La Salette.

There exists no critical account based on first-hand sources, as in the case of Lourdes. But, apart from the difficulties already pointed out, there are others. The fussy and minute description of the lady's appearance is one. Much graver is the theologically inaccurate, but very popular idea that Mary restrains her Son from punishing his people. The long discourse of the apparition, too, seems very improbable, especially as its contents are, as the well-known Jesuit historian H. Delehaye has pointed out[1], remarkably similar to those of a "Letter fallen from heaven", which circulated at the time. For a proper evaluation of the experiences of the children at La Salette we should have to know much more not only about the circulation of this letter, but also about the various conversations they overheard and the sermons they attended. Such knowledge is obviously impossible to acquire at this late date; but in the opinion of the present writer there seems to be nothing either in the description of the apparition or in its discourses that points unmistakably to a supernatural origin. The so-called "secrets", too, which have been solemnly forbidden to be published by the Church authorities, seem to have contained nothing more than vague apocalyptic threats. That both miracles and conversions are believed to have taken place at La Salette is no cogent proof of the authenticity of the original apparitions. God answers the trusting prayers of the faithful in many places which, through these very prayers and, of course, the sanctuaries built on their site, acquire a holiness of their own, regardless of their origin.

5. PONTMAIN

The last officially approved Marian apparition of the nineteenth century took place also in France, and again it was children who claimed to have seen the blessed Virgin. In the evening of 17 January, 1871 (that is, towards the end of the Franco-German War), the twelve-year-old Eugène Barbadette walked out of the barn where the animals were being fed "to

[1] in Mélanges Grandmaison, February-April number of *Recherches de Science religieuse* (1928).

see what the weather was like". Looking at the sky, he saw
there a beautiful lady dressed in a blue robe adorned with
golden stars which fell, unbelted, to her feet, shod with blue
sandals that had a golden ribbon tied into a rosette over the
instep. Her head was covered with a black veil and she wore a
golden crown with a red border round the centre. When an
old woman came out of the barn Eugène asked her whether
she saw anything, but she saw nothing. Then his father and
his ten-year-old brother Joseph came out. The father saw
nothing, but Joseph claimed to see the same as his brother. The
boys' mother immediately thought the vision was the blessed
Virgin.

Soon the neighbours gathered and a nun who was teaching
the children was called and arrived with another sister, but
neither could see the apparition. The nun went to fetch three
other children, two of whom immediately claimed also to see
the beautiful lady. By the time the parish priest arrived on the
scene, accompanied by his old housekeeper, most of the villagers
were assembled, and he ordered the Rosary to be recited. The
children now saw something else: an oval frame, of the same
colour as the lady's robe, surrounded her, within which there
were four candles, two at a level with her knees, the other two
at a level with her shoulders; besides, a small red cross appeared
on her breast.

While the people were praying the apparition doubled in size
and the stars on her robe multiplied. When the *Magnificat*
was intoned, there slowly appeared writing in block letters
beneath the lady's feet reading: "But pray, my children".
During the litanies this was followed by the words: "God will
answer you in a short time." During the *Salve Regina* the
writing finished with the words: "My Son lets himself be
moved"—referring, as is generally believed, to the end of the
war.

So far the lady had appeared in the posture of the Miraculous
Medal; she then raised her hands to shoulder level, the writing

vanished and a large red cross appeared, while the candles lit themselves. When the people sang the *Ave Maris Stella* the red cross disappeared and a small white cross was seen on either shoulder. Finally the parish priest had evening prayers said, during which a white veil covered the lady, beginning at her feet, and the apparition was over.

It is interesting to note that an author who believes completely in the authenticity of the apparition, H. Maréchal, O.P.,[1] himself points out various details which should justify grave doubts. For example, the chaplet recited was the small red rosary in honour of the twenty-six Japanese martyrs, which would account for the unusual colour of the crosses and the crucifix. As regards the white crosses, the Curé had caused crosses to be erected all over the parish. Further, the oval frame would have been suggested by niches over the principal entrance of the houses at Pontmain where the Curé had asked his parishioners to install statues of Our Lady. The four candles had their material counterpart in four candles which the same Curé himself always lit during the war after Sunday Vespers before the image of the Immaculate Conception. Finally, the blue robe studded with stars was no doubt inspired by the roof of the church, which was painted in this way. It is very suggestive, too, that whereas before the arrival of the Curé the children had only seen the lady, as soon as he came on the scene the vision became much more elaborate: the frame and the candles, the crosses and the writing appeared only after his arrival.

The episcopal approbation of the apparition was given in 1872; the basilica of Pontmain was blessed five years later.

It is not surprising that this series of apparitions, which were accompanied by miracles like those of Lourdes, should have greatly increased popular Marian devotion. Indeed, so strong was the influence of both the new dogma and the apparitions within the Catholic Church that these events are often regarded

[1] *Mémorial des Apparitions de la Vierge dans l'Eglise*, Paris (1957), pp. 122f.

as having ushered in a new epoch in its life, which has come to be called the "Marian Age".

THE OXFORD MOVEMENT—NEWMAN AND PUSEY'S *EIRENICON*

The revival of Marian devotion was not confined to the Catholic Church. In England the Oxford Movement, whose chief exponents were John Keble (d. 1866), E. B. Pusey (d. 1882) and John Henry Newman (d. 1890), revived especially Patristic studies, and so was quite naturally led to a fresh appreciation of the role of the *Theotokos* in the Christian dispensation. In 1823 Keble had written the first stanzas of his famous hymn *Ave Maria*, inspired by his mother's death, which was published in his immensely popular *Christian Year* (publ. 1827) for "The Annunciation of the Blessed Virgin Mary". In it the preacher of the celebrated sermon on National Apostasy of 1833 addressed Mary as the "blessèd Maid, Lily of Eden's fragrant shade ... whose name all but adoring love may claim", accents which had not been heard in the Church of England since the seventeenth century. In 1832, thirteen years before his conversion, Newman preached a sermon on the Annunciation in which he praised Mary's transcendent purity in such terms that he was accused of teaching the Immaculate Conception.[1] In 1843, in a sermon on "The Theory of Developments in Religious Doctrine" for the feast of the Purification,[2] he called Mary "our pattern of Faith, both in the reception and in the study of divine truth" who "symbolizes to us, not only the Faith of the unlearned, but of the Doctors of the Church also, who have to investigate, and weigh, and define, as well as to profess the Gospel". Nevertheless, he rendered her no personal cult, and even three years before his conversion he still regarded her public veneration as incompatible with the worship of God. Only after he had become a Catholic did he realize that the

[1] *Parochial and Plain Sermons*, vol. 2, p. 132.
[2] *Oxford University Sermons* No. 15 (1843).

Marian doctrine he had professed even as an Anglican could not be separated from devotion.

One of Newman's first sermons preached as a Catholic priest at St. Chad's Cathedral in Birmingham in 1848 was devoted to "Our Lady in the Gospel".[1] Though in it he told his congregation "that if you cannot enter into the warmth of foreign books of devotion, it is a deficiency in you",[2] a view which later he was emphatically to renounce, his language is very different from that of the Catholic preachers who have been considered in the preceding sections of this book. He was too steeped in Scripture and the Fathers—and also, as will be seen presently, too ignorant of later Catholic Marian writings—to have any inclination to pious exaggerations. Thus, in this sermon, he explains very carefully the seemingly derogatory Gospel passages on the blessed Virgin so often adduced in inter-denominational controversy, once again praises her perfect purity, and tells his hearers: "Depend upon it, the way to enter into the sufferings of the Son is to enter into the sufferings of the Mother."[3]

Of his *Discourses to Mixed Congregations*, his first work published as an Oratorian (1849), two sermons are devoted to Mary, the first, Discourse 17, being called characteristically "The Glories of Mary for the Sake of her Son", the second "On the Fitness of the Glories of Mary". Though the titles recall the work of St. Alphonsus Liguori, nothing could be farther from its spirit than their sobriety and absence of legendary material except for one short passage on Mary's youth in the Temple.[4] In the first Discourse Newman affirms that devotion to Mary is "integral to the worship of Christ ... that the glories of Mary are for the sake of Jesus; and that we praise and bless her as the first of creatures, that we may duly confess him as our sole Creator".[5] For "Mary is exalted for the sake of Jesus",[6] because

[1] *Catholic Sermons of Cardinal Newman*, London (1957), pp. 92–104.
[2] p. 103.   [3] p. 103.
[4] Disc. 18, p. 370.
[5] P. 344.   [6] p. 348.

"A mother without a home in the Church, without dignity, without gifts, would have been, as far as the defence of the Incarnation goes, no mother at all.... If she is to witness and remind the world that God became man, she must be on a high and eminent station for the purpose." It is already the pen of a master which places the exaltation of Mary in and by the Church unmistakably on its only true foundation: the divinity of her Son. "Why should she have such prerogatives, we ask, unless he be God? And what must he be by nature, when she is so high by grace? This is why she has other prerogatives besides, namely, the gifts of personal purity and intercessory power, distinct from her maternity; she is personally endowed that she may perform her office well; she is exalted in herself that she may minister to Christ."[1]

Five years before the definition of the Immaculate Conception Newman taught the doctrine in unmistakable terms. "Mary, then", he writes, "is a specimen, and more than a specimen, in the purity of her soul and body, of what man was before his fall, and what he would have been, had he risen to his full perfection."[2] "As grace was infused into Adam from the first moment of his creation, so that he never had experience of his natural poverty, till sin reduced him to it; so was grace given from the first in still ampler measure to Mary, and she never incurred, in fact, Adam's deprivation. She began where others end, whether in knowledge or in love... Such is her prerogative of sinless perfection, and it is, as her maternity, for the sake of Emmanuel." The same applies to her "intercessory power", the subject he had found most difficult in his Anglican days. After enumerating many Old Testament examples of intercession, "why should we wonder at hearing that Mary, the only spotless child of Adam's seed, has a transcendent influence with the God of grace? And if the Gentiles at Jerusalem sought Philip, because he was an Apostle, when they desired access to Jesus... is it strange that the Mother should

[1] p. 350.   [2] p. 352.

have power with the Son, distinct in kind from that of the purest angel and the most triumphant saint? If we have faith to admit the Incarnation itself, we must admit its fullness"—and this, of course, includes the Mother of the incarnate God. Newman never removes the *Theotokos* from the Christological setting in which all her privileges find their proper place and reason. On the other hand, he does not present her as a teacher of the Apostles, as some late medieval and post-Tridentine preachers had done; for "she interfered not with his work, and even when he was gone up on high, yet she, a woman, went not out to preach or teach, she seated not herself in the apostolic chair . . . she did but humbly seek her Son in the daily Mass of those who, though her ministers in heaven, were her superiors in the Church on earth".[1] Nor did she shine forth in the earliest Church, when her Son had first to be proclaimed, but later, "when heretics said that God was not incarnate, then was the time for her own honours" and so she "has grown into her place in the Church by a tranquil influence and a natural process'.[2]

In the second sermon, "On the Fitness of the Glories of Mary", he formally teaches the Assumption on the grounds of "the *fitness* of this termination of her earthly course . . . without which Catholic teaching would have a character of incompleteness",[3] "rather as a point of doctrine than as a theme for devotion",[4] thus anticipating the formal definition by almost exactly a century.

The most explicit statement of Newman's Mariology is contained in a much later work, "A Letter Addressed to the Rev. E. B. Pusey on Occasion of his *Eirenicon*", which forms part of the second volume of *Certain Difficulties Felt by Anglicans in Catholic Teaching*.[5] But to appreciate this we have first to discuss Pusey's *Eirenicon*, written in 1865 in the form of a

[1] pp. 354-6. [2] p. 357.
[3] p. 361. [4] p. 370.
[5] I quote from the new edition (1892).

letter addressed to Keble, in which he considered, among other things, "that vast system as to the blessed Virgin" as "the special 'crux' of the Roman system" and one of the principal obstacles to reunion. He takes his materials chiefly from Liguori, but also from Grignion de Montfort, both of whom had shortly before been translated into English; he quotes further a German Mariology by Oswald which had appeared in 1850 but had been placed on the Index, a fact Pusey did not know at the time. In the *Eirenicon* he attacked the recently defined dogma of the Immaculate Conception as a further obstacle to reunion, though he misunderstood it so as to include the active conception. He gave a painstaking and very interesting analysis of the opinions of the minority of bishops who opposed the definition, regretting that they were overruled and that there had not been a council to decide the matter.[1] But his chief quarrel is with the large number of statements on the blessed Virgin to be found in late medieval and post-Tridentine authors, so many of which were quoted with approval in *The Glories of Mary* which he had carefully excerpted. As all of them have been quoted in earlier sections of this book there is no need to go into them in detail. Pusey's chief objections are directed against the view that Mary is mediatress of all graces whose intercession is in some way necessary to salvation,[2] that her mercy is opposed to Christ's vengeance, that she is Co-Redemptress,[3] that she has authority over Christ,[4] that she produces Christ in souls[5] and so forth. He also objects to St. Alphonsus' habit of adducing the *Revelations of St. Bridget* as evidence of his doctrine, especially of the Immaculate Conception, which leads him to the strange idea that the Church herself had accepted these revelations to support the dogma.[6]

In his *Letter to Pusey* (1866) Newman first blames him for having given a very one-sided presentation of Catholic teaching

[1] pp. 121, 126, 146.   [2] pp. 101–3.
[3] p. 152.   [4] p. 160.
[5] p. 160.   [6] pp. 172f.

on the Blessed Virgin[1] and then proceeds to outline his own
views squarely based on the teaching of the Fathers who, he
says, "are enough for me. I do not wish to say more than they
suggest to me, and will not say less."[2] First of all he makes a
"distinction between faith and devotion": "I fully grant that
devotion towards the blessed Virgin has increased among
Catholics with the progress of centuries; I do not allow that
the *doctrine* concerning her has undergone a growth, for I
believe that it has been in substance one and the same from the
beginning." He bases his exposition of Catholic belief on the
earliest Christian teaching about Mary as the Second Eve, as it
is found especially in St. Justin, Tertullian and Irenaeus.[3]
"What is especially noticeable in these three writers", he says,
"is that they do not speak of the blessed Virgin merely as the
physical instrument of our Lord's taking flesh, but as an intelli-
gent, responsible cause of it; her faith and obedience being acces-
sories to the Incarnation, and gaining it as her reward."[4] In this
he opposes Pusey, whom Newman accuses of considering Mary
only as "a physical instrument of our redemption",[5] an interpretation of his view which Pusey repudiated later. Newman
shows that the doctrine of Mary as the Second Eve must have
gone even beyond Justin to the age of the Apostles themselves[6]
and remained an unbroken tradition in the Church. Having
established this he proceeds to develop in masterly fashion the
doctrine of the Immaculate Conception from this earliest view
of Mary as the Second Eve. "Have you any intention to deny",
he asks, "that Mary was as fully endowed as Eve? Is it any
violent inference that she, who was to co-operate in the redemption of the world (Newman means, of course, through the
Incarnation), at least was not less endowed with power from on
high than she who ... did ... but co-operate ... for its ruin?
If Eve was raised above human nature by that indwelling moral

[1] p. 8.   [2] p. 25.
[3] pp. 31–5.   [4] p. 35.
[5] p. 36.   [6] p. 38.

gift which we call grace, is it rash to say that Mary had even a greater grace? ... And if Eve had this supernatural inward gift given her from the first moment of her personal existence, is it possible to deny that Mary too had this gift from the very first moment of her personal existence? ... Well, this is simply and literally the doctrine of the Immaculate Conception ... and it really does seem to me bound up in the doctrine of the Fathers, that Mary is the Second Eve ... Mary may be called, as it were, a daughter of Eve unfallen."[1]

After basing the Immaculate Conception on the Patristic doctrine of the Second Eve, Newman proposes to "find the doctrine of our Lady's present exaltation in Scripture".[2] This he does in Chapter 12 of the Apocalypse. He knows very well, of course, that the Woman clothed with the Sun signifies the Church: "But what I would maintain is this, that the Holy Apostle would not have spoken of the Church under this particular image, *unless* there had existed a blessed Virgin Mary, who was exalted on high and the object of veneration to all the faithful. No one doubts that the 'man-child' spoken of is an allusion to our Lord; why then is not 'the Woman' an allusion to his mother?"[3] Newman links this scriptural image to "the paintings of the catacombs. Mary is there drawn with the Divine Infant in her lap, she with hands extended in prayer, he with his hand in the attitude of blessing. No representation can more forcibly convey the doctrine of the high dignity of the Mother, and I will add, of her influence with her Son."[4] So the power of Mary's intercession is not a modern idea, as his Anglican friends were maintaining, but very ancient—indeed, we have seen clear evidence of it in the papyrus fragment of the prayer *Sub tuum praesidium*.

After this Newman approaches the subject of the *Theotokos*. This title, he says, "has nothing else but a well-weighted, grave, dogmatic sense, which corresponds and is adequate to

[1] pp. 45-7.   [2] p. 53.
[3] p. 58.   [4] p. 55.

its sound". It signifies that "in one respect she surpasses all even possible creations, viz., that she is Mother of her Creator . . . It is the issue of her sanctity; it is the origin of her greatness".[1] He links it to her Immaculate Conception as well as to her Assumption and follows it up by a string of quotations from early Christian authors, concluding: "This being the faith of the Fathers about the blessed Virgin, we need not wonder that it should in no long time be transmuted into devotion."[2] "As then these ideas of her sanctity and dignity gradually penetrated the mind of Christendom, so did that of her intercessory prayer follow close upon them and with them", for "the weapon of the Second Eve and Mother of God is prayer".[3] This is her principal office—an office which it is particularly necessary to emphasize in our own time—for "She is the great exemplar of prayer in a generation which emphatically denies the power of prayer *in toto*, which determines that fatal laws govern the universe, that there cannot be any direct communication between earth and heaven, that God cannot visit his own earth, and that man cannot influence his providence"—words which are as applicable today as they were a hundred years ago.

After tracing Marian doctrine and devotion to the first Christian centuries Newman defends the language in which this devotion has sometimes expressed itself on the grounds of his doctrine of development, for:

living things grow into their perfection, into their decline, into their death. No rule of art will suffice to stop the operation of this natural law, whether in the material world or in the human mind. We can indeed encounter disorders, when they occur, by external antagonism and remedies; but we cannot eradicate the process itself, out of which they arise . . . If what I have been saying be true of energetic ideas generally, much more is it the case in matters of religion. Religion

---

[1] p. 62.   [2] p. 65.   [3] p. 73.

acts on the affections; who is to hinder these, when once roused, from gathering in their strength and running wild?...And of all passions love is the most unmanageable; nay more, I would not give much for that love which is never extravagant...So it is with devotional feelings. Burning thoughts and words are as open to criticism as they are beyond it. What is abstractedly extravagant, may in particular persons be becoming and beautiful, and only fall under blame when it is found in others to imitate them.[1]

But, after saying that much, Newman goes on to circumscribe the office of Mary and to define it in contrast with that of her Son: "He alone has an entrance into our soul, reads our secret thoughts, speaks to our heart, applies to us spiritual pardon and strength. On him we solely depend. He alone is our inward life...In this sense he may be called, as in nature, so in grace, our real Father. Mary is only our mother by divine appointment, given us from the Cross; her presence is above, not on earth; her office is external, not within us...her power is indirect. It is her prayers that avail, and her prayers are effectual by the *fiat* of him who is our all in all. Nor need she hear us by any innate power, or any personal gift; but by his manifestation to her of the prayers which we make to her... He who charges us with making Mary a divinity, is thereby denying the divinity of Jesus. Such a man does not know what divinity is. Our Lord cannot pray for us, as a creature prays, as Mary prays...To her belongs, as being a creature, a natural claim on our sympathy and familiarity, in that she is nothing else than our fellow...We look to her without any fear, any remorse, any consciousness that she is able to read us, judge us, punish us."[2]

There are in this description of Mary's office three features which distinguish it from much that had been written before. First, Mary's prayer depends entirely on her Son. Indeed, it is

[1] p. 79f.   [2] pp. 84f.

not she who makes our needs manifest to him—as had so often been said—but he who makes them known to her. God as the First Cause of all things and all knowledge is kept ever before Newman's eyes. Secondly, Mary remains external to us, precisely because she is a creature, even though the most exalted one. God alone sees the heart, God alone can indwell souls. And, thirdly, we look towards her without fear because she is not able to punish or judge us—not because she could turn God's wrath away from us or in any way interfere with his judgement, but because she is and always remains a creature, "nothing else than our fellow", without the divine power of judging or its necessary corollary of saving in the strict sense of the word.

Such is the admirably balanced Mariology of Newman himself; he then deals with the excesses of which Pusey had accused the Church Newman had joined. He had one immense disadvantage there: he did not know the authors Pusey had quoted. He had never read Liguori's *Glories of Mary* and had never so much as heard the names of Grignion de Montfort and Bernardine of Busti. "One thing, however, is clear about all these writers", says Newman, "that not one of them is an Englishman ... they are foreigners; we are not answerable for their particular devotions ... If the Catholic faith spreads in England, these peculiarities will not spread with it."[1] This sudden somewhat narrow nationalism is surprising in such a great mind as Newman's was; perhaps it may be attributed to the fact that he was, on this point, very much on the defensive, and Pusey had no difficulty in refuting him. For in his *First Letter to the Very Rev. J. H. Newman* (1869), Pusey assured his correspondent that "in three instances only ... I went to any book not in use in England"; most of his quotations were taken from the *Glories of Mary*, the third edition of the English translation of which had come into Pusey's hands in 1841. It is even more surprising that Newman should not even have

[1] pp. 98–100.

heard the name of Grignion de Montfort, because his *True Devotion* had been translated by Newman's own fellow Oratorian F. W. Faber and been published in 1863, three years before Newman's reply to Pusey's *Eirenicon*. However, without knowing these authors Newman judged their extravagances very severely, and we will quote his words in full, for we are glad to have the support of the greatest theologian of the nineteenth century for the critical remarks that have been made from time to time in the course of our presentation of the subject:

> Coming to the statements...which offend you in works written in her honour, I will allow that I like some of those which you quote as little as you do...they affected me with grief and almost anger; for they seemed to me to ascribe to the blessed Virgin a power of "searching the reins and hearts", which is the attribute of God alone; and I said to myself, how can we any longer prove our Lord's divinity from Scripture, if those cardinal passages which invest him with divine prerogatives, after all invest him with nothing beyond what his mother shares with him? And how, again, is there anything of incommunicable greatness in his death and passion, if he who was alone in the garden, alone upon the Cross, alone in the Resurrection, after all is not alone, but shared his solitary work with his blessed mother...if I hate those perverse sayings so much, how much more must she, in proportion to her love of him? And how do we show our love for her, by wounding her in the very apple of her eye?...[1]

And he continues:

> I put away from me...without any hesitation, as matters in which my heart and reason can have no part...such

[1] p. 703.

sentences and phrases, as these: that the mercy of Mary is infinite; that God has resigned into her hands his omnipotence; that it is safer to seek her than to seek her Son ... that our Lord is subject to her command; that his present disposition towards sinners, as well as his Father's, is to reject them, while the blessed Mary takes his place as an advocate with Father and Son . . . that Mary is the only refuge of those with whom God is angry ... that it would have sufficed for the salvation of men if our Lord had died, not in order to obey his Father, but to defer to the decree of his mother ... that, as the Incarnate God bore the image of his Father, so he bore the image of his mother ... that elect souls are born of God and Mary; that the Holy Ghost brings his action into fruitfulness by her, producing in her and by her Jesus Christ in his members ... that she and the Holy Ghost produce in the soul extraordinary things; and that when the Holy Ghost finds Mary in a soul he flies there. Sentiments such as these I freely surrender to your animadversion; I never knew of them till I read your book ... They seem to me like a bad dream. I could not have conceived them to be said. I know not to what authority to go for them ... They defy all the *loci theologici* ... They do but scare and confuse me ... I should but be guilty of fullsome frigid flattery towards the most upright and noble of God's creatures, if I professed them ... I will say plainly that I had rather believe (which is impossible) that there is no God at all, than that Mary is greater than God. I will have nothing to do with statements, which can only be explained, by being explained away ... I consider them calculated to prejudice inquirers, to frighten the unlearned, to unsettle consciences, to provoke blasphemy, and to work the loss of souls.[1]

Such is Newman's judgement on the Marian teaching of, for

[1] pp. 113-15.

example, Bernardine of Siena, Alphonsus of Liguori and Grignion of Montfort.

SCHEEBEN

Matthias Joseph Scheeben (d. 1888), a professor of dogma at the seminary at Cologne, has been called by C. Feckes the "theologian of modern Mariology."[1] He wrote a *Manual of Catholic Dogmatics*,[2] the third part of which contains his Mariology. Scheeben's aim was to present a strictly scientific doctrine, situated in the whole context of theology between the treatise on Christ and that on the Church, and based upon Scripture and the Fathers. As Feckes points out,[3] on certain points his exegesis is no longer valid, for example his argumentation from the Canticle and the Wisdom books. Nevertheless his work, which during forty years lay almost forgotten, has exercised an increasing influence since the nineteen-twenties. Like Newman, Scheeben based his doctrine on the concepts of the New Eve and of the divine motherhood, but his use of the former was very different from that of Newman. For whereas Newman contented himself with the Patristic view, which saw the Virgin Mary as opposed to the Virgin Eve on account of her obedience, Scheeben used the medieval idea of Mary as the helper of Christ. The parallel Eve–Mary in relation to Adam–Christ was not used by the Fathers, because Adam was Eve's husband, whereas Mary was the Mother of Christ; moreover, the *adjutorium simile sibi* could not strictly be applied to Mary as it was to Eve, because Mary, being completely human, was not so similar to her divine Son as Eve was to Adam. Scheeben overcame the first difficulty by regarding Mary not only as the Mother, but also as the bride of Christ, and the second by stating that:

---

[1] In *Maria*, 3, pp. 555–71.

[2] *Handbuch der katholischen Dogmatik*, 1882 (the edition from which I quote).

[3] *Maria*, 3, p. 563.

in her transcendent position Mary appears, through the grace of her divine motherhood, in such eminent way as image and similitude of God, beside, with, and next to Christ that the Church does not hesitate to apply to her the scriptural descriptions of the eternal Wisdom.... Thus there is in Mary, analogously to Christ, a communication in the glory and virtue of the divine Persons, a certain *communicatio idiomatum divinorum* in a unique form such as happens in no other creature.... True, we may not therefore attribute to the Mother of God the predicate of *Dea*, goddess ... nevertheless there is in her quality of being a child of God also a specific reflex of the divine daughtership of the eternal Wisdom towards God the Father.... The name of "daughter of God" which is based on this reflection of the daughtership of the eternal Wisdom ... is the most sublime ... divine predicate with which the supra-creaturely glory of Mary can be described.[1]

We are far from the sobriety of Newman who considered Mary as "nothing else than our fellow".

Scheeben lays particular stress on his idea of Mary's bridal relationship to her Son, and this for a reason that can hardly recommend itself to ecumenically interested theologians. He says that Protestants admit that "Mary is indeed the Mother of God, but not the bride of God", hence "the formula of the *gottesbräutliche Mutterschaft* (an untranslatable expression, meaning a motherhood that involves the fact that she is the bride of God) is of great value for doctrinal controversy"; though it has also "considerable constructive theological value for the scientific development of Mary's privileges." Indeed, Scheeben considers this notion of bridal motherhood "the key to all Mariology".[2] According to him, Mary was "placed in a true and actual spiritually-matrimonial relationship to God from the beginning", which he calls a "divine marriage", so

[1] *n.* 1618. [2] *n.* 1592.

"that Mary's existence is formally effected only as the existence of the Bride of God", "she proceeds from his creative act and power ... as the Bride of God"[1] Scheeben thus describes this divine marriage:

> The factor that really forms the *personal character* in the divine motherhood and ... represents *the grace of the divine motherhood* is a *supernatural, spiritual union of the person of Mary with the divine Person of her Son, which is effected by the will and power of God* (his italics). ... The simplest, most precise and most natural description of this union with the divine Person is the term *matrimonium divinum* or *conubium Verbi* in the strictest sense of the word ... and which therefore is just as much the most perfect image of the Hypostatic Union of a created nature with God as human marriage is the image of the union of the body with the spiritual soul. Seen in this way, this union, according to the nature of marriage, involves a togetherness of both persons in one organic whole, in which they are grown together, and a mutual belonging, in which Mary is joined to the Logos and completely possessed by him, whilst the Logos, as being infused into her ... gives himself to her and receives her as his companion and help into the most intimate, complete and permanent communion. That Mary's divine motherhood really includes such a *matrimonium divinum* follows from the nature of the case as necessarily as every properly established human motherhood ... presupposes a *matrimonium humanum*.[2]

Scheeben rejects the idea that Mary has a maternal authority over Christ, "through which she would be *domina Christi* ... since the maternal authority even over purely human beings is not a real *dominium*". In the case of Christ we can only speak of a "belonging of Christ to Mary, on which rests her part in

[1] *nn.* 159f.   [2] *nn.* 1588f.

his possessions and her *dominium* over his subjects as a *condominium*. This belonging and this *condominium* have exactly the form of the claims which the bride has on her bridegroom through his acceptance of her and her performance of bridal services."[1] Thus Mary is the secondary principle of the supernatural life of grace and that "member of humanity which reaches upwards into a higher order". Thus "she may even be called the mystical head of humanity in a relative sense, insofar as she is not regarded as one Body with Christ but as the Bride of Christ opposed to him".[2] Nevertheless, Christ is the true Head; but Mary is the spiritual Mother of men, "sub- and co-ordinated to her Son as their spiritual Father and as such occupies... an intermediary position between them and Christ similar to that of a natural mother between father and children".[3] In the same way she may be designated "in and with Christ as the *corner-stone* of the spiritual edifice" of the Church, but most adequately as the *heart* of the mystical Body, an image Scheeben prefers to that of the "neck".[4] Because the Mother of God "has a share in the peculiarly transcendent and immanent position of Christ", she also shares in his position as Mediator between creatures and God; hence "she must be regarded as the Mediatress in an analogous sense as Christ is the Mediator", being "in herself a substantial link... which binds creatures to God."[5] Scheeben is careful, however, to distinguish her mediation from that of Christ, which is not in any way diminished through hers, "but presupposed or rather elevated", for her mediation rests wholly on that of her Son, who is the direct Mediator towards God, whereas she is only Mediatress to Christ and only through him to God. Nevertheless, her mediation of grace is "so perfect and universal, that Mary is active not only by interceding in the distribution of it, but also in preparing the reception of the principle of grace in the Incarnation and

[1] *n.* 1623.   [2] *n.* 1626.   [3] *n.* 1627.
[4] *nn.* 1628f.   [5] *n.* 1630.

co-operating in the acquisition of it through the sacrifice of Christ".[1]

Scheeben goes on to explain his view of the veneration of Mary by *hyperdoulia,* which he regards as different not only in degree but in kind from the ordinary *doulia* due to the saints. In his opinion "the dignity of the divine Maternity involves... for all creatures a relation of formal dependence on and subjection to Mary as the Mistress of creation and the Queen and Mother of the realm of grace... a true relation of subjects (*Untertanenverhältnis*)".[2]

After a long discussion of the Immaculate Conception and a shorter one of the Assumption Scheeben explains Mary's part in the redemptive work of her Son. He bases it on the grace of the divine maternity, which is "the principle of a supernatural activity specifically proper to her in a similar way as the grace of union is for the humanity of Christ, and which gives her activity a quite peculiar dignity and force.... This activity belongs... to a creature, who is united to Christ and God only as a bride." Therefore she is "an organ of the Holy Spirit working in and through her analogously as the humanity of Christ is the organ of the Logos",[3] and so she is truly the Bride of the Logos and the bearer of the Holy Spirit.[4] Hence "the effects of the redemptive work of Christ can and must be attributed also to his mother as their principle in a very true sense", which, he says, is an "explicit dogma, based on the ecclesiastical reading of the Protoevangelium according to the Vulgate: *ipsa conteret caput tuum.*... Thus she is the middle cause (*Mittelursache*) of all the effects of salvation in all, including pre-Christian, humanity, especially in our first parents themselves ... and the mediatress of the production and acquisition of these fruits".[5] However, she is completely subordinated to Christ, and therefore Scheeben dislikes the expression "co-redemptress". For "instead of stressing the ministering subjection

[1] *n.* 1631.   [2] *n.* 1632.   [3] *n.* 1764.
[4] *n.* 1766.   [5] *n.* 1771.

and dependence of Mary, [this term], taken by itself, suggests so strongly a co-ordination with Christ . . . that it ought only to be used with an *express restriction* such as 'in a certain sense' " (his italics). Scheeben himself wishes to call her activity "bridal co-operation", which corresponds to the "adiutorium simile sibi". He also rejects a too exact parallelism between the process of the fall and that of the redemption, because this might lead to a defective or even entirely mistaken idea of the economy of salvation,[1] since Eve had an independent role in the fall, which is not the case in Mary's relation to the redemption. More, Scheeben rejects the idea, so often found especially in sermons on the Annunciation, that without Mary's *fiat* there would have been no redemption: "This co-operation [through her assent]" he says, "involves a true dependence of the whole work of redemption on her will, but only in such a way that it was willed and ordered by God and in no way endangered the accomplishment of the work, because God ordered together with the dependence also the actuality of the consent. Hence it is not proper to emphasize this assent to such an extent as to say: if Mary had not given her assent the redemption would not have taken place; for this suggests that God had no absolute will to effect the redemption or had not the power to secure Mary's consent; it means, in fact, that Mary had been as independent in assenting to God's will as one man is from another." Hence it is "quite incorrect to say that through this act, by which she gained the Redeemer, she merited in a strict sense all the effects of the redemption".[2]

This, however, is not to say that Mary did not co-operate in the redemption, but Scheeben reiterates that this co-operation was a "bridal" one, by which "the physical Mother of Christ co-operated with him as her spiritual Bridegroom in the most intimate spiritual communion".[3] Scheeben also defines very carefully Mary's share in the redemptive sacrifice of Christ. "It must be pointed out", he writes, "that solely the sacrifice of

[1] *n.* 1782.   [2] *n.* 1788.   [3] *n.* 1788.

Christ ... is an independently effective sacrifice, whereas the sacrifice of Mary, being a purely affective one, is joined to it only as a secondary, accompanying sacrifice, or rather ... is only a reflexion of it." Hence Mary may, indeed, be called "*co-operatrix Redemptoris*, but not *corredemptrix*, because by her action she in no wise gives or pays herself the price of redemption".[1] Once again, hers is a "bridal co-operation",[2] which Scheeben further defines by saying that "Mary co-operated in the truest and fullest sense of the word as offerer of the sacrifice (*Opferbringerin*), which she offered with Christ as her sacrifice, so that through this mode of offering the redemptive sacrifice came from, and belonged to humanity perfectly and in every way". It did so because it was taken from her own flesh and blood, because she disposed of this God-given offering, and because she consented to his death by giving up her own will, thus participating in his sacrifice "in such a way that the passion of Christ was also her passion in the fullest sense of the word".[3] So Scheeben calls her the "deaconess at the priestly sacrifice of Christ". "In this way Mary is accorded a true co-operation in the sacrifice of Christ, which also belongs to the subjective integrity of the sacrificial action, without in the least way impairing the independence and hegemony of the sacrificial activity of Christ".[4] Thus, "through the mediation of Mary Christ is offered as a sacrifice not only by mankind and from mankind, but also in mankind, so that he lives in it, and mankind on its part is sacrificed in him through loving compassion with his passion".[5]

Scheeben draws far-reaching conclusions from Mary's compassion. For through it "she has co-effected ... all the effects of Christ's sacrifice. ... Therefore we can say that, through co-operating with him, Mary has made satisfaction for sin with him, merited grace and hence redeemed the world by paying the price of redemption ... but only ... with the express addi-

[1] n. 1793.   [2] n. 1795.   [3] n. 1796.
[4] n. 1797.   [5] n. 1799.

tion: in Christ and through Christ". In this sense Mary is core-demptress, "as *diacona sacerdotis* and *ara sacrificii*", as the deaconess of the priest and the altar of sacrifice. This "co-operation of Mary with the sacrifice of Christ [must] be regarded as theologically certain and on no account only as a pious opinion".[1] From this it follows that through her co-operation Mary "has received and appropriated for all mankind all the merit of the redemptive sacrifice ... and with it all saving graces ... and that mankind has taken possession of the merit of Christ's sacrifice only through and in Mary. ... The consent of Mary to the sacrifice of Christ was ... *the* mediating act by which the merits of the sacrifice were given to all other men."[2] "As Christ by his passion ... generates the new humanity as a father ... so Mary by her compassion as a mother."[3] Therefore she "is the spiritual mother of mankind in a higher way than even the Church", for she is united to Christ as the spiritual Father of mankind in such a way "that she herself mediates his union with the Church and so is also the Mother of the Church; further, she co-operates fundamentally in establishing and acquiring the rebirth of all mankind, whereas the Church is active only in applying the completed work of redemption to individuals".[4] She was therefore also the protectress and comforter of the young Church, left by Christ to the orphaned Apostles "together with the Holy Spirit, whose special image and organ she is".[5] She has also a special relation to the Eucharist, insofar as "in the eucharistic communion she enters into a substantially organic relation with her children through the flesh and blood of Christ which was taken from herself", though he rejects any pseudo-mystical conclusions from this which had been condemned, for example, in the book of Oswald which had been quoted in Pusey's *Eirenicon*.

In the distribution of graces "Mary's co-operation is to be confined to the form of her glorious intercession",[6] terms like

[1] *n.* 1809. [2] *n.* 1810. [3] *n.* 1813.
[4] *n.* 1818. [5] *n.* 1824. [6] *n.* 1828.

Mary "commanding" in heaven are "hyperbolical figures of speech ... which may be admitted only before a well-instructed and devout public".[1] Finally Scheeben elucidates the true meaning of the proposition that Mary is the mediatress of all graces. It does not mean "that we receive no grace unless we ourselves ask Mary for her intercession; it only affirms that no prayer of ours is answered without the help of Mary's intercession. ... It does not mean either that Mary's intercession is generally necessary to induce Christ to make his intercession, as if he were not prepared to do so on his own account; the doctrine only implies that ... the intercession of Christ is not to profit anyone without the concurring intercession of Mary, and that consequently every grace is given only as one that is also co-impetrated by her."[2] For Mary's "constant co-operation with Christ ... must be considered as natural as that of the heart with the head in its influence on the life of the other members of the body".[3]

The logical concatenation of Scheeben's teaching is impressive. Though his idea of the bridal relationship between Christ and his mother has not been widely accepted, his influence on twentieth-century Mariology has been considerable and seems to be still in the ascendant.

GROWING DEVOTION

While Newman and Scheeben were writing their carefully considered Mariological treatises, Catholic devotion to the Immaculate Virgin expressed itself in many ways. A growing number of congregations were dedicated to her; for example the Society of Missionaries of Mary, founded by Grignion de Montfort, was finally approved in 1853; the Prêtres de Sainte Marie had been founded two years before, the Congregation of Marie Réparatrice was established in the same year as the dogma of the Immaculate Conception was defined, and in

[1] n. 1832.   [2] n. 1835.   [3] n. 1838.

England the Little Companions of Mary were founded at Nottingham in 1877. The public veneration of the Heart of Mary, promoted by St. Jean Eudes, was recognized in 1804, and received a new Mass and Office "Of the Most Pure Heart of Mary" allowed in "certain places" in 1855; May devotions, which had become popular in Italy in the eighteenth century, now spread throughout the whole Church. Lourdes became an ever more popular place of pilgrimage renowned for its miracles, and La Salette, where two children had claimed to have seen the blessed Virgin in 1846, also increased in fame. It seemed as if Mary was making her influence felt at a time when the Church was beset by enemies from without as well as from within. For after the definition of Papal Infallibility in 1870 Bismarck had begun his *Kulturkampf* against German Catholicism; the rising working classes became estranged from the Church especially in France; in Italy the national movement of the Risorgimento had resulted in the destruction of the temporal power of the Papacy. When, in 1878, Leo XIII succeeded Pius IX the problems confronting the new Pope were enormous.

Papal Teaching in the Late Nineteenth and Early Twentieth Centuries

Leo XIII is most widely known for his social teaching; his Marian doctrine is expressed particularly in his encyclicals on the Rosary, a devotion which he recommended very strongly in those bad times when the Church and especially the Pope were so violently attacked.[1] In *Octobri Mense* of September 22, 1891, the Pope affirms that no grace comes to us except through Mary, "so that, as no one can come to the highest Father except through the Son, so hardly anyone can come to the Son except through the Mother". Though Christ is, indeed, our most loving Saviour, nevertheless we also fear him as our inexorable

[1] *Acta Leonis Papae XIII*, Bruges (1898), vol. 5, 7–18.

Judge, therefore we go to Mary who is only loving and who was given to mankind under the Cross.[1] In another encyclical on the same subject, *Fidentem piumque*,[2] the Pope explains in what way she can be called a mediatress: "Undoubtedly," he says, "the name and attributes of the absolute mediator belong to no other than Christ... yet there is no reason why certain others should not be called in a certain way mediators between God and man... especially has the blessed Virgin a claim to the glory of this title. For no single individual can ever be imagined who has ever contributed or ever will contribute so much toward reconciling man with God. She it is from whom Jesus is born. She is therefore truly his mother and for this reason a worthy and acceptable mediatress to the Mediator."[3]

Leo's successor St. Pius X (Pope 1903–14) celebrated the half-centenary of the definition of the Immaculate Conception by another Marian encyclical, *Ad diem illum* of 1904.[4] On his accession to the Papacy he had taken as his motto "To restore all things in Christ", and in the encyclical he explains Mary's part in this work of restoration; for, he says, "Can anyone fail to see that there is no surer or more direct road than by Mary for uniting all mankind in Christ?"[5] For on her, the noblest foundation after Christ, rests the edifice of the Faith, and "no one can ever be more competent as a guide and teacher in the knowledge of Christ". For she shared in his sufferings under the Cross, and thus, quoting Eadmer's treatise *On the Excellence of the Virgin Mary*, c. 9, "she merited to become most worthily the Reparatrix of the lost world and Dispensatrix of all the gifts Our Saviour bought for us". The Pope is careful, however, to point out "that the dispensation of these treasures is properly the peculiar right of Jesus Christ, for they are the exclusive fruit of his Death and he of His own power is the

---

[1] p. 10.
[2] *Acta Papae Leonis XIII*, vol. 6, 211–17.
[3] pp. 214f.
[4] I quote from the official English translation.   [5] n. 2.

mediator between God and man. Nevertheless, by this afore-mentioned companionship in sorrow and suffering between the Mother and the Son, it has been granted to the sublime Virgin to be the most powerful mediatress and advocate of the whole world with her divine Son."[1] Thus she is also "the most sure and efficacious assistance to us for arriving at the knowledge and love of Jesus Christ". The Pope goes on to give very definite teaching on right devotion to the Mother of God, decisively rejecting the idea we have met several times that it does not necessarily include moral amendment. "Sincere devotion to the Virgin", he says, "is only that which springs from the heart; and acts of the body have here neither utility nor value, if the acts of the soul have no part in them. Now these latter can only have one object, which is that we should fully carry out what the divine Son of Mary commands. . . . Let each one fully convince himself of this, that if his piety towards the Blessed Virgin does not hinder him from sinning, or does not move his will to amend his evil life, it is a piety deceptive and lying, barren of its proper and natural fruit." (n.3.)[2]

In these papal encyclicals two subjects are touched upon which were to be canvassed in innumerable publications throughout the twentieth century: the Marian mediation of all graces and the coredemption. Mary's bodily Assumption into heaven was also being discussed; indeed, it had been so widely and consistently believed that Newman took it for granted, and that its definition had been demanded at the First Vatican Council. But before summarizing the latest development in the Catholic Church recent trends in some of the churches separated from Rome indicating a growing *rapprochement* have to be considered.

[1] Ibid.

[2] Cf. Against this Dillenschneider, who says that such teaching "discourages the sinner . . . by representing to him the uselessness of his prayers as long as he has not turned away from sin" (*Mariologie*, 1, 47)—only his reference is to the unfortunate Widenfeld, not to Pope Pius X!

RUSSIAN ORTHODOXY

The Greek Orthodox Church has remained true to its tradition, but has rejected the dogma of the Immaculate Conception. We have seen before that this difference between East and West rests on the different view of original sin. Moreover, the actual content of the Catholic dogma was widely misunderstood; a passage from Sergius Bulgakov (d. 1944) is evidence of this. He holds that the Immaculate Conception "distinguishes the Mother of God from the rest of mankind and seems consequently to render her incapable of imparting to her divine Son the authentic manhood of the old Adam, with its need of redemption. The blessed Virgin, since she is truly human, shares with humanity both its original sin and also that inherent infirmity of human nature, which finds its extreme expression in ... natural death ... However, the force of original sin, which varies greatly from man to man, is in her reduced to the point of a mere possibility, never actualized. In other words, the blessed Virgin knows no personal sin, *she was manifestly sanctified by the Holy Ghost from the very moment of her conception.*"[1] Surely this last sentence expresses almost exactly the meaning of the Catholic dogma? We note again that original sin is equated here with mortality and all its concomitants, hence the inability of the Orthodox to admit its absence in Mary. One cannot help wishing that this difference in the concept of original sin might be cleared up sufficiently to allow a better mutual understanding of the positions on both sides. For Bulgakov's Marian teaching is in most respects indistinguishable from Catholic doctrine, a fact which is all the more important since he played a considerable part in the Ecumenical Movement. In the special number of *Die Hochkirche*, the organ of Friedrich Heiler's High Church Movement in Germany, dedicated to the commemoration of the fifteenth centenary of the Council of Ephesus in 1931, Bulgakov

---

[1] *The Wisdom of God* (1937), p. 173 (my italics).

wrote: "As long as there exists this mysterious antipathy against any Marian devotion on the part of Protestantism a true reunion of the churches is impossible", for "a correct doctrine of the Church is impossible without a Mariology. The Mother of God is the personal head of the Church (though certainly in a different sense from Jesus Christ himself), namely as the head of mankind, as the creaturely centre. She has given her Son his humanity, and his humanity is hers. She is the Church in its creaturely-human aspect. The Mother of God is also the Mother of humanity ... To the blessed Virgin belongs the perfection of the Church, its very principle, and in this sense she is venerated and glorified as the highest creature, higher not only than any human being, but also than any angel."[1]

Bulgakov elaborates his teaching in *The Wisdom of God*, in which he summarizes what he had written on the subject in his larger works, especially *The Burning Bush* (1927). In complete accord with Catholic teaching he affirms that "the birth of Christ from the Virgin is not merely an isolated event in time; it establishes an eternally abiding bond between Mother and Son". Under the Cross she died a spiritual death with Christ; she received the Holy Spirit "in superabundant fullness" at Pentecost, and, "although following the law of human nature, she tasted natural death, yet 'death could not detain her', for her humanity is at the same time that of Christ himself, who is the well of life".[2] She is "midway between creation and the heaven of God ... The Mother of God, since she gave to her Son the manhood of the second Adam, is also the mother of the race of man ... the spiritual centre of the whole creation, the heart of the world. In her, creation is ... completely divinized"; she is "in relation to the Word, Mother and Bride", and she 'presents her petitions for the world, for which we unceasingly solicit her". For "she is the appointed

[1] pp. 244f.   [2] pp. 176–8.

intercessor for the human race, blessing them with her protect-
ing veil in a peculiar sense, otherwise than do the saints in general".[1] "She has arrived at the fullness of the godlike life of
grace which for the rest of creation remains to be revealed.
Therefore the Mother of God remains inaccessible to the world,
for she is above the world, and if she appears to it, that is only
in virtue of her loving condescension."[2] Hence, "to separate
Christ from his mother (still more to forget her, as historical
Protestantism has done) is in effect an attempted violation of
the Incarnation in its innermost shrine ... Yet veneration of
the Virgin extends not merely to her divine maternity, but
also to herself". She is "as it were a personification of the
Church".[3] This is the traditional Catholic teaching that unites
East and West in their common devotion to the *Theotokos*,
and it is encouraging that Heiler himself, who had once been
a Catholic but later joined the Swedish Lutheran Church and
founded the German High Church Movement, could write:
"A Church which does not honour the Mother of the Lord is
neither faithful to the New Testament, nor ecumenical, nor
German."[4]

Bulgakov, however, further developed his Marian teaching
on what he calls "sophiological" lines. Regretting that the
theme of *Sophia*, Wisdom, has hardly been touched on in the
West, he wished to purify it from the gnostic and other unorthodox accretions it had received at the hands of Vladimir
Soloviev (d. 1900), who was partly influenced by Jacob
Boehme, whose works had made a great impression in Russia.
Bulgakov distinguishes between uncreated Wisdom—that is,
Christ as worshipped by the Greeks, for example in the church
of *Hagia Sophia* in Constantinople—and the Mariological interpretation Wisdom received in Russia, where "there even
exists a proper office of Sophia, the Wisdom of God, which is
combined with the office of the Dormition".[5] "The Christo-

[1] pp. 180f.   [2] pp. 182.   [3] pp. 184f.
[4] *Hochkirche* (1931), p. 202.   [5] *Wisdom*, p. 187.

Sophianic and the Mario-Sophianic interpretation", he explains, "are there simultaneously present." Mary is connected with Wisdom for two reasons. First "in so far as she is the Spirit-bearer, in virtue of the personal descent on her of the Holy Ghost"[1]; in this capacity she is not venerated personally, but the veneration is directed to the Holy Spirit. "But besides this we find another meaning attached to the veneration of our Lady, in so far as it is directed to *created* Wisdom. She *is* created Wisdom for she is creation glorified. In her is realized the purpose of creation, the complete penetration of the creature by Wisdom."[2] "According to the sophiological interpretation of the definition of Chalcedon", writes Bulgakov, "the two natures in Christ correspond to the two forms of *Sophia*, the divine and the created. The created humanity of Christ... came to him from the Mother of God. It belongs to her. In a true sense it is possible to say that she herself personally is this created manhood of Christ, that she is the created *Sophia*. The manhood of Christ belongs at once to him, since it is one of his two natures, and to her, in whom it personally subsists. And it is in this sense, as sharing the human nature of the God-man that his holy mother is the created *Sophia*."[3] Though these speculations will probably not commend themselves to Catholic theologians, they show nevertheless the tremendous veneration in which the blessed Virgin is held in modern orthodox thought, even though her Immaculate Conception is often more clearly denied than in Bulgakov's works.

THE CHURCH OF ENGLAND

As is well known, the established Church does not speak with one voice, and while Broad Churchmen may even deny the divinity of Christ with all that this denial implies for his mother, the High Church, especially its Anglo-Catholic section, often approaches the Catholic position in doctrine as well as in

[1] p. 187.   [2] p. 188.   [3] p. 189.

devotion. A lady chapel exists in most Anglican churches; even pictures or statues of our Lady of Lourdes are not unknown in some of them. The shrine of Walsingham, which had been destroyed in 1538, was restored in the early twentieth century, and is now a place of pilgrimage for Anglicans as well as for Catholics, the Rosary being recited there by both. The Rosary is also recommended in the *Anglo-Catholic Prayer Book* of 1931, which contains a number of other Marian devotions such as the Angelus, the Regina Coeli, the Litany of Loreto and special prayers for Marian feasts. Several books on the Mother of God written by Anglican theologians are also very Catholic in outlook, for example Bede Frost's *Mystery of Mary* (1938) and the symposium *The Mother of God* (1948) edited by B. E. Mascall, who contributed to it the chapter on "The Dogmatic Theology of the Mother of God". There he emphasizes the traditional doctrines of Mary as the Mother of God and also of her as the Mother of the Church; moreover, he accepts her virginity *in partu* and *post partum*, her Immaculate Conception and her bodily Assumption, though he does not think any of these doctrines ought to be imposed as of faith. T. Parker, in his contribution on "Devotion to the Mother of God" in the same work, considers that the Eastern Church has been more faithful to Mariological tradition than the West, because it stresses the honour due to her more emphatically than her power of intercession, which came to take the first place in the Latin Church.[1]

CONTINENTAL PROTESTANTISM

The position of Continental Protestantism is far more negative. As R. Schimmelpfennig rightly says[2]: "The further New Testament criticism and research into the history of religions progress, the more is the Gospel voided of its content." She

[1] See also G. M. Corr, "La Doctrine mariale et la pensée Anglicane contemporaine" in *Maria*, 3, 713–31.
[2] Op. cit., p. 115.

mentions, however, a few evangelical pastors who have written about the blessed Virgin, though, of course, in a very different style from that of Catholic authors, keeping entirely within the limits of the Gospel story.[1] Besides, there are now two movements among German Evangelicals that foster greater devotion to Mary than has been known since the Reformation: the *Berneuchener* (so called from the estate on which there have been annual gatherings of clergy and laymen since 1923) and the *Hochkirchliche Bewegung* founded by F. Heiler. The latter especially has consistently propagated devotion to Mary, as is evidenced by the many articles on the subject in its periodical *Hochkirche*.

Calvinism, however, has always been far more opposed to the veneration of Mary than Lutheranism, and Karl Barth, its greatest contemporary exponent, though accepting the term "mother of God" as "permitted and necessary as an auxiliary Christological statement" despite its being "burdened" (*Belastung*) by Roman-Catholic Mariology, nevertheless regards the latter as a "pathological growth of theological thought" which ought to be cut out.[2] Indeed, he says "Where Mary is 'venerated' . . . the Church of Christ does not exist"[3]—a statement which implicitly rejects both the Catholic and the Orthodox Churches, as well as Monophysites and other surviving ancient Christian bodies.

From the First World War to the Present

The first half of the twentieth century offers a striking parallel to that of the nineteenth. For in our time, too, there

---

[1] She mentions H. Fleming, *Maria die Mutter unseres Heilandes* (1930), Adolf Schlatter (d. 1938), "one of the few more recent evangelical theologians who often kindly remember the Mother of God in their writings and sermons" (p. 121) and H. Lamparter, who wrote *Die Magd des Herrn* (1949), "in which the author wanted to draw a truly evangelical picture of Mary so that protest against the cult of Mary should not remain entirely negative" (p. 122).

[2] *Die kirchliche Dogmatik*, 2. Halbband, 3rd ed. pp. 151-3.

[3] Ibid., 153f.

have been several Marian apparitions, and the still growing devotion and Mariological research have culminated in another definition.

According to C. M. Staehlin,[1] thirty series of apparitions with about three hundred individual visions were investigated in Western Europe between 1930 and 1950 alone, all experienced by children. Only three twentieth-century apparitions have so far (1965) been approved by ecclesiastical authority, the most famous of them being the apparitions of Fatima.

I. FATIMA

Up to the present no critical edition of the Fatima material exists, and the issue is further complicated by the fact that the principal visionary, Lucia dos Santos, now the Carmelite Sister Mary Lucy of the Immaculate Heart, has from time to time published further visions as well as additions to the original reports. These, which are somewhat dubious, are left out of the following account.

According to the early records, on 13 May 1917, Lucia, aged ten, accompanied by her two cousins, Francisco (aged nine) and Jacinta Martos (aged seven), went to tend her parents' flock in the Cova da Iria, a kind of vale more than a mile distant from the Portuguese village of Fatima, the children's home. They were all three illiterate, and none of them was particularly pious; for they had been told to say their Rosary every day, but acquitted themselves of this duty by saying only the first two words of the *Our Father* and the *Hail Mary*.

They were playing near their flock when they suddenly saw what seemed a flash of lightning in the clear sky. They ran for shelter to a tree; then there was another flash, and while they were running to another tree the two girls suddenly stopped, because they saw "a pretty little lady" standing above it. The vision told them not to be afraid, and when Lucia asked her

---

[1] *Apariciones*, Madrid (1954), p. 12; quoted from Karl Rahner, SJ, *Visions and Prophecies*, 3rd German ed. (1960), p. 10.

where she came from she replied: "From heaven." She further told the children that she wanted them to come to the same place on the 13th of each month for the next six months: "Then I will tell you who I am and what I want, and I will come back here a seventh time." To Lucia's question whether she and Jacinta would go to heaven the lady replied in the affirmative; Francisco, too, would go to heaven, "but he will have to say many rosaries". Lucia then asked about the fate of two other children, who had died. The lady answered that one of them was in heaven, but the other was in purgatory "till the end of the world"—an unbelievable fate for a small child, hence in many books this answer has been suppressed. Francisco did not see the vision in the beginning, and he never heard any words; Jacinta both saw and heard, but never spoke to the lady herself.

Lucia ordered her cousins to say nothing about their experience, but Jacinta could not keep silent, and soon the whole village knew the story. On 13 June about sixty people went to the Cova. The vision told Lucia to learn to read and, in reply to a question from the girl, said that a sick man would be cured in the course of the year if he were converted. After this the children were questioned by many people and the parish priest suggested that the apparitions might be due to the devil.

On 13 July the crowds who went to the Cova had increased to between two and three thousand. Lucia asked the vision to work a miracle. The lady repeated her demand that the children should come to the same place each thirteenth of the month; in October she would tell them who she was and what she wanted. In the meantime they should say the Rosary every day in honour of our Lady of the Rosary to obtain peace. They should also add a special prayer after each decade: "My Jesus, forgive us; save us from the fire of hell; raise all souls to heaven, especially those who need it most." At one moment during the vision Lucia went pale and cried out in terror. This seems to have been the point at which the children saw a vision of hell,

6*

which Lucia described at a later date in the conventional terms of fire and black demons.

At this period anticlericalism was rife in Portugal, and the secular authorities feared a religious revival. The local administrator, Arturo de Oliveira Santos, was a particularly enraged atheist; and on 13 August he abducted the children, put them in prison for a night and terrorized them with threats of frying them in boiling oil. But in spite of his threats the children insisted that their story was true; they were released after two days.

On 19 August the children went to a place called Valhinhos, and there the lady appeared unexpectedly. In answer to Lucia's question what was to be done with some money that had been left at the Cova, the vision replied that two processional stands should be made, to be carried, the first by Lucia, Jacinta and two other girls, the second by Francisco and three small boys, all dressed in white, on the feast of our Lady of the Rosary. Whatever was left over should be used to build a small chapel. The apparition further said that she would work a miracle on 13 October, but it would be less impressive than originally planned, because of the kidnapping of the children.

On 12 September thousands of people, including for the first time some clergy, came to Cova. When the children arrived at noon the following day, some of the spectators believed to see a dimming of the light, which was supposed always to precede the apparition, while others saw nothing. One of the priests, the future Vicar-general of Leiria, recalled fifteen years later to another priest that they had seen a "globe of light coming from the east". On 27 September a Canon Formigao conducted an interrogation. The lady was described as wearing a white dress with gold borders which was tied at the neck with a golden cord, and a white veil. A white Rosary hung over her right hand; she also wore small gold earrings. She had promised to come on 13 October with St. Joseph and the Holy Child, and soon afterwards there would be peace.

The story of the expected miracle spread like wildfire; in the morning of 13 October there were about seventy thousand people at the Cova, though it was pouring with rain. Lucia's mother was terrified lest the expected miracle should not happen and the people take their revenge on the family. The crowds were highly excited; according to Canon Formigao thousands went down on their knees, weeping and praying to the Queen of Heaven for her motherly protection.[1] The lady appeared, telling Lucia that she was the lady of the Rosary; the war was ending that day and the soldiers would soon return home (in fact the armistice was not declared until thirteen months later). Then the lady disappeared. Suddenly Lucia cried out: "Look at the sun !", where she claimed to see successively our Lady of Sorrows, our Lady of Mount Carmel, St. Joseph with the Holy Child and our Lord (did she think the Holy Child and our Lord were two different persons?). By this time the rain had stopped, and when the crowds obeyed Lucia's demand and looked into the sun they saw various phenomena which have been described in different ways: the sun rotated three times, giving out multi-coloured rays; it seemed to approach the earth, a red light was seen and there was an intense heat; it zigzagged from east to west; it appeared to fall from the sky; later it zigzagged up again.

One thing about this "miracle" is certain: the sun cannot possibly have executed these movements, for this would have meant the end of the solar system. How else are the phenomena—which, it must be stressed, were not observed by all those present—to be explained? There is, first of all, the fact known to us all that if we stare into the sun we see all sorts of colours. Further, there are many phenomena that occur in the atmosphere after a heavy rain—these, of course, would have been seen by everyone, but this was not the case. Thirdly—and this explanation seems to cover many of the phenomena given in the various accounts—mass suggestion produced by Lucia's

[1] See K. Rahner, *Visions and Prophecies*, 3rd German ed., p. 40.

cry "Look at the sun!" and the fervent expectation of a miracle by the crowds may account for the "dance of the sun". These difficulties, combined with the error about the end of the war have caused a certain amount of doubt about the authenticity of the apparitions.

Nevertheless, Fatima has been approved by the ecclesiastical authorities, even though rather slowly. In 1919 the parish priest of Fatima sent his report to Lisbon, at the same time giving up his parish on the grounds that it had become too burdensome for him. In the same year Francisco died during an influenza epidemic, in 1920 Jacinta. In 1922 an episcopal commission began the canonical enquiry into the phenomena of Fatima, after the bishop had authorized the celebration of mass at the Cova da Iria and bought the surrounding land. The commission finished its report in 1929, and in the following year the bishop proclaimed the apparitions worthy of belief. Pius XI granted indulgences for visits to the shrine. Pius XII contributed much to the cult. In 1942, on the twenty-fifth anniversary of the apparitions he sent a radio message to the Catholics of Portugal in which he published the text of his consecration of the world to the Immaculate Heart of Mary, and in 1952 he fulfilled the desire of Lucia who had claimed that the blessed Virgin demanded a special consecration of Russia to the same. If this were done, Lucia affirmed, the conversion of Russia was promised *unconditionally*. It is hard to see why a formal act of consecration should have such a tremendous effect; as Father Martindale pointed out, "the conversion of the world was not unconditionally attached to Calvary itself". Indeed, so far the promised effects of this consecration have not become apparent.

2. BEAURAING

Fifteen years after Fatima, towards the end of 1932, no fewer than five children claimed to have seen the blessed Virgin at Beauraing, a small Belgian town near the French border. They were two sisters, Andrée and Gilberte Degeimbre, fourteen and nine years of age respectively, and two sisters and a brother, Fernande (fifteen), Gilberte (thirteen) and Albert Voisin (eleven). They were normally naughty children, who liked to ring door bells and run away and to play similar pranks. On 29 November four of them went to the school of the Sisters of Christian Doctrine to collect Gilberte Voisin and accompany her home. Having rung the bell of the convent school door Albert turned round and exclaimed that he saw a light. When a nun opened the door the children told her that they saw a white form in the air. The sister thought they were up to their usual pranks and shut the door in their face.

The next day they claimed to see the same form at the same time and place. The same happened on 1 December, when the children were accompanied by Andrée's mother. On the following day the children returned to the spot in the evening, this time accompanied by several relatives and neighbours. They went down on their knees at once, stating that our Lady had appeared and Albert asked her whether she was the immaculate Virgin, at which the vision nodded. She told the children to be very good and they then went home. On 4 December they asked the vision to cure two chronic invalids they had brought with them; they did not, however, wait for an answer but went on to ask when they were to return, to which the vision replied: "On the day of the Immaculate Conception." They then asked whether a chapel should be built on the spot, to which she replied in the affirmative. On 5 December the children asked the vision to perform as many miracles as possible, but received no answer.

On 8 December there were unprecedented crowds, estimated at between ten and fifteen thousand people, including several doctors, on the site of the apparitions. The expected miracles, however, did not happen, though two invalids asked the blessed Virgin for a cure and the children said that the apparition was there. The doctors carried out some experiments, testing the sensitivity of the children to light and touch; some of the children responded, some appeared to feel nothing.[1]

On 17 December the blessed Virgin appeared again and, at the request of the clergy, the children asked her what she wanted, to which she replied: "A chapel." Not much happened on the following days; there was no apparition on Christmas Day nor on the 26th. On 28 December the vision said: "It will soon be my last appearance." On 29 December Fernande reported that the vision had opened her arms and that she had seen a golden heart. On the following day the other children said they had seen it, too. On 2 January the vision said that, on the next day, she would speak to each of the children in private. On that day at first all the children except Fernande Voisin had a vision. Suddenly Fernande fell to the ground, said "Yes, yes", and started to sob. On their way back home all the children were in tears. Later Andrée said that the blessed Virgin had told her that she was the Mother of God, the Queen of heaven, and asked her to pray always, "farewell". Gilberte Voisin reported that the vision had told her a secret and then said: "I will convert all sinners, farewell." To both Albert Voisin and Gilberte Degeimbre she had also told a secret and said "farewell". Fernande she had asked whether she loved her Son, to which the child had replied: "Yes." The vision had then asked: "Do you love me?", and when Fernande had answered in the affirmative the blessed Virgin told her to sacrifice herself for her, the Virgin, which the girl understood to mean that she should become a nun. In fact, however, Fernande never became a nun but married and had many children.

After much controversy Beauraing was recognized by the Bishop of Namur in 1943 and again in 1949 with the permis-

---

[1] It should be noted that these experiments tell us nothing about the authenticity or otherwise of the apparitions, since persons in trance or under hypnosis do not react to external stimuli, regardless of the cause which induces these states.

sion of the Holy See which itself, however, refrained from authorizing the apparitions.

3. BANNEUX

Banneux, too, is situated in Belgium; it is a small hamlet in the Ardennes. The apparitions there took place between 15 January and 2 March 1933. The visionary was the nearly twelve-year-old Mariette Beco. She had gone to catechism classes very irregularly since May 1931 and had taken in hardly anything. From October 1932 she no longer attended either catechism or Mass. On 15 January, at seven o'clock in the evening, she looked out of the window into the garden and saw a beautiful, luminous lady who smiled at her. The girl turned at once to tell her mother, then continued to look at the vision, who made a sign to her and then disappeared. She was dressed in white with a blue belt, had a rosary over her arm and a rose on her right foot. Mariette told her parents and then a school friend, who in turn informed the parish priest. He smiled and said that Mariette had probably heard about the children at Beauraing.

On 18 January Mariette went out into the garden despite the cold and knelt down to say the Rosary. The vision appeared, hovering on a cloud a little above the ground. She was luminous and her head was surrounded by a brilliant halo. Then the vision beckoned to Mariette and receded, Mariette following her, till she came to a little brook. The vision ordered the girl to put her hands in the water, telling her that this stream was reserved for herself: "Bonsoir. Au revoir."

The next night Mariette went again into the garden; the lady appeared and told her she was the Virgin of the Poor. Then she led the girl again to the brook and told her that it was for all the people for the relief of the sick, and that she would pray for Mariette. On the following day, 20 January, the vision appeared again at the same time and, making the sign of the Cross, said she wanted a small chapel. After this

Mariette fell down unconscious and had to be carried into the house. For more than three weeks she continued to go into the garden at night, but nothing happened until 11 February, incidentally the Feast of Our Lady of Lourdes. On that night the vision reappeared, led the girl to the brook and said: "I shall relieve suffering. Au revoir." After that Mariette asked to be given Holy Communion and received it for the first time. On 15 February, at the request of the priest, she asked the vision for a sign and received the reply: "Believe in me, I shall believe in you." Then she was told a secret, and after that the vision exhorted her to pray much, an injunction repeated on 20 February. The final vision occurred on 2 March, when the girl was told: "I am the mother of the Saviour, Mother of God. Pray much. Adieu." Once again Mariette became unconscious and had to be carried into the house.

In 1937 the episcopal commission declared that the reality of the apparitions of the blessed Virgin to Mariette Beco "is at least probable". The decision was confirmed again, as for Beauraing, by episcopal authority without engaging the Holy See, but with its permission, in 1949.

All these modern Marian apparitions, from La Salette in 1846 to Banneux in 1933, have one feature in common: they all happened to children or adolescents. Must this be necessarily attributed to the blessed Virgin's preference for children to be her messengers, or is there no possibility of a psychological explanation?

Those who believe in the authenticity of all these apparitions invariably point out that it is very unlikely that the children, who were frequently threatened or bribed, should have stuck to their stories if they were lying. This is certainly true. But the presupposition behind this opinion is that there is only one alternative: either lies or authentic apparitions (for diabolic intervention can be ruled out). There is, however, another possibility, which is only too frequently overlooked or discarded *a priori*: the psychological explanation.[1] For it is a commonplace of child psychology that both children and adolescents have considerable eidetic gifts and are able to visualize as outside themselves objects that present themselves to their conscious—or subconscious—imagination. These need not be regarded as hallucinations, for they will often occur in perfectly normal children. In his book on *Visions and Prophecies* Karl Rahner mentions a very illuminating experiment reported by C. M. Staehlin.[2] Staehlin tested the suggestibility of six boys between fifteen and eighteen years of age, letting appear to them by suggestion a battle of medieval warriors above a single tree. Of these six boys two saw nothing, two only saw the battle, and two both saw and heard the noise, including the shouts of individual knights. The boys were strictly controlled and unable to communicate with one another before each of them had reported what he had seen and heard. Then, very surprisingly, even the two who had both seen and heard agreed with each other in all the details.

This, surely, was a very remarkable experiment. The possibility of applying its results to such phenomena as the agreement of the children of La Salette, Fatima and Beauraing is obvious. Hence it does seem that, before accepting the authenticity of the various apparitions, those who have doubts may— while respecting the judgement of the ecclesiastical authorities —prudently reserve their own judgement until the psychological background of all these occurrences has been more fully investigated.

A further development, arising from the apparitions, was the crowning of Marian statues, as was done by Leo XIII for the statue of La Salette and by Pius XII for that of Fatima. Recently Marian statues, usually those of Fatima, have made

---

[1] This seems to me enforced by the "secrets" which most of the children claimed to have been told, which would enhance still further their own importance in the eyes of the adults, and which became a standing feature of these apparitions from La Salette onwards.

[2] *Apariciones*, Madrid (1954), pp. 389f.

"pilgrimages", that is they have been carried in solemn procession from one town to another.

PAPAL TEACHING

Pope Pius XI continued the line of Leo XIII when, in 1937, he issued his encyclical *Ingravescentibus malis*, in which he urged the recitation of the Rosary as a remedy for the evils of the time: for it was the age of National Socialism, well-established communism and the imminence of another world war. Six years before he had sanctioned a new Marian feast, that of the divine motherhood, for the whole Church, with its own mass and office.

PIUS XII

The Second World War broke out in 1939. Pius XI died in the same year and was succeeded by Pius XII, himself a member of the Marian congregations, who has done more for the spread of Marian devotion than any pope before him except perhaps Pius IX. In his prayer on the occasion of his consecration of the world to the Immaculate Heart of Mary in 1942 the Pope asked the blessed Virgin under the appellations of Queen of the Rosary and Help of Christians for effective assistance in the present calamities, "entrusting ourselves to your Immaculate Heart in this fateful hour of human history". At the end of his important encyclical on *The Mystical Body of Christ* (1944) he referred again to this consecration as well as to her reign, not yet defined, in heaven both in body and soul. This definition came in the jubilee year, 1950, in the Apostolic Constitution, *Munificentissimus Deus*. As in Pius IX's *Ineffabilis Deus* the definition is preceded by an historical part, which, in its exact quotations and references shows the tremendous progress of research during the ninety-six years separating the two constitutions. In Section Seven the Pope gives his reasons for considering the solemn definition as opportune; not only does he hope for a still greater increase in Marian devotion, but "likewise it is to be hoped that from meditation on the glorious example of Mary men may come to realize more and more the value of a human life entirely dedicated to fulfilling the will of the Heavenly Father and to caring for the welfare of others. We also hope that, while materialistic theories and the moral corruption arising from them are threatening to extinguish the light of virtue, and by stirring up strife, to destroy the lives of men, the exalted destiny of both our soul and body may in this striking manner be brought clearly to the notice of all men. Finally, it is our hope that faith in the bodily Assumption of Mary into heaven may make our faith in our own resurrection both stronger and more active."[1]

Then follows the actual definition, which declares "it to be a dogma revealed by God that the Immaculate Mother of God, Mary ever Virgin, when the course of her earthly life was finished, was taken up body and soul into the glory of heaven". It will be seen that the terms of the definition are studiously vague. It does not even make it clear that Mary died, nor does it say at what exact date she was taken up to heaven, for "when her earthly life was finished" leaves this question entirely open. So Mascall, though deploring the definition itself because he does not consider belief in the Assumption necessary for salvation, admits that if it had to be defined it could not have been done in more satisfactory terms.[2] His view seems to be fairly representative of Anglo-Catholicism, for it was shared by Bishop Mortimer of Exeter who discussed the definition in similar terms at a diocesan conference in October 1950. The Protestant reaction was, of course, negative,[3] while the Orthodox could hardly oppose the definition of a belief that had been held in their Church for over a thousand years, as is admitted for example by P. Spasskij.[4]

[1] nn. 49–51.
[2] In Das neue Mariendogma im Lichte der Geschichte und im Urteil der Oekumene (1951), ed. by F. Heiler.
[3] Heiler, passim.
[4] Heiler, p. 149.

The solemn definition of the Assumption was followed four
years later by the proclamation of a Marian Year in honour of
the centenary of the Immaculate Conception. It was announced
by Pius XII's encyclical *Fulgens Corona*, in which the Pope,
after recapitulating the doctrine of the Immaculate Conception
and linking it to that of the Assumption exhorted the bishops
to encourage a new flowering of Marian devotion everywhere,
expressing itself particularly in Marian sermons and pilgrimages to the various shrines, especially to Lourdes. The
Marian Year ended with another encyclical, *Ad Caeli
Reginam*, establishing the royal dignity of Mary and the feast
of her queenship. The Pope's intention was to renew the
ancient devotion to Mary as Queen, whose royal dignity rests
on her divine motherhood[1] and who "plays a unique part in
the work of our eternal salvation".[2] Without calling her Co-
Redemptress, the Pope explained that she was associated with
Christ "in a way parallel to the way in which Eve was
associated with Adam . . . So just as the human race was committed to death through a virgin, it is saved by means of a
virgin".[3] Therefore "she, too, shares in his Kingship, although
she does so in an analogous and attenuated fashion".[4] "For this
reason, let all loyal followers of Christ take pride in being subject to the rule of the Virgin Mother of God."[5] The Pope adds,
however, that, while we should beware "of a too constricted
attitude of mind in face of the . . . sublime . . . dignity" of
Mary, men should also "guard against unfounded opinions
and exaggerated expressions"[6]

It would be impossible to discuss all the papal pronounce-
ments on the subject of Mary that have emerged during the
nineteenth and twentieth centuries; but in view of the fact that
these are frequently quoted in the relevant literature as almost
infallible teaching it should be of interest to mention certain
observations of the foremost contemporary mariologist, René

[1] 26.   [2] 27.   [3] 28.
[4] 29.   [5] 31.   [6] 32.

Laurentin, in his book, *Mary's Place in the Church*.[1] He states that in papal encyclicals, as in every other branch of literature, it is essential to consider the literary *genre* of the various documents: "For lack of an enlightened method of exegesis," Laurentin writes, "papal teaching is interpreted in the most varied and conflicting ways." He gives as an example a letter of thanks by Pope Pius IX to the author of a book on the Marian priesthood, in which the Pope wrote: "The Mother of God... is so closely united to the sacrifice of her divine Son that she has been called the *Virgin Priest* by the Fathers of the Church." Laurentin comments: "Certain partisans of the Marian priesthood[2] were overjoyed at these words, seeing them as the seal of the 'infallible pope' on the doctrine. It was indeed the infallible pope who signed the document in question, but it was a document which in no way involved his infallibility... What is more, it is a fact that no Father of the Church ever used the expression 'Virgin Priest'!"

"The most widely misunderstood consideration in this connection", Laurentin continues, "is that the majority of the Marian documents issued by the papal magisterium in the last century have had to do with devotional matters, notably the rosary. Though they may indeed contain important doctrinal considerations... they are not, for all that, dogmatic constitutions. The intention behind them is not so much to define a body of doctrine, as to bring forward considerations calculated to nourish and enlighten devotional fervour. For this reason their style is better classed as homiletic, and the language tends to be oratorical, full of images, and sometimes more generous than rigorous... It would be a bad mistake if one were to take pastoral utterances of this kind and turn them into dogmatic theses."

[1] Eng. trans. Burns and Oates, London (1965).
[2] Which was censured by the Holy Office by decree of 29 March, 1916, and again in 1927. See P. Sträter, *Katholische Marienkunde*, Paderborn (1952), vol. 2, pp. 296f.

As a further example Laurentin quotes Benedict XV to the effect that Mary "abdicated her maternal rights over her Son for the sake of the salvation of the world", commenting that no mother has a right over her Son's life and that the Pope here spoke metaphorically, as he did when he added "that Mary sacrificed her Son in so real a way that it is perfectly justifiable to say that she herself redeemed the human race with Christ". " 'Generosity' with the use of vocabulary is here in control", Laurentin writes, "and this is a very typical echo of the Italian piety of the age."[1]

He adds in his notes that "Italian Mariology is tender, laudatory and eloquent...Its verbosity and its fairly general maximalism depend on a criterion proper to Italy, but in Italy often invoked even by official theologians—that of 'generosity with the Madonna'... The Mariology of the popes, from Pius IX to Pius XII chiefly, is penetrated through and through with this national tendency, even though it does, by all the breadth of its universal catholicity, rise above it."[2]

This tendency, though it has noticeably decreased since the death of Pius XII, still made itself felt in the proclamation of Paul VI, at the end of the Third Session of Vatican II (1964) of Mary as the Mother of the Church, despite the rejection of any new official Marian titles by the Council. This proclamation, of course, has not the force of an infallible definition.

MARIAN ASSOCIATIONS

Apart from the traditional Marian organizations, such as the congregations and confraternities which have continued to flourish, there has appeared, in the present century, another type of lay groups designed to carry out a Marian-orientated apostolate with, strangely enough, a distinctly militant flavour. Such is, for example, the "Militia Immaculatae", founded by

[1] *Marie*, pp. 97–100.
[2] *Marie*, p. 158.

the Polish Franciscan martyr Maximilian Kolbe in 1917. Among other apostolic works it publishes Marian literature with a view to sanctifying Christians in all walks of life by example, prayer, suffering and work, and a complete consecration to Mary Immaculate. It has now over two million members.

In 1921 Frank Duff, an Irish layman, founded the Legion of Mary which, according to its official handbook (1959) "is an association of Catholics, who, with the sanction of the Church and under the powerful leadership of Mary Immaculate... have formed themselves into a Legion for service in this warfare which is perpetually waged by the Church against the world and its evil powers. The Legion of Mary is therefore organized on the model of an army, principally on that of the army of ancient Rome..." It is inspired by Grignion de Montfort, and legionaries are obliged to enter "into a compact with Mary, whereby one gives her one's whole self, with all its thoughts and deeds and possessions... without the reservation of the smallest part or slightest little thing". It means that the legionary is a slave of Mary, committing absolutely everything to her. The Miraculous Medal is the special badge of the Legion and their particular prayers include the *Magnificat*.

The German Schönstatt Movement has a slightly different character; its terminology is somewhat commercial rather than militant, and it has its own sanctuary at Schönstatt in West Germany (a chapel which had been dedicated in 1914 and was destined to become a place of pilgrimage) where Mary is venerated as *Mater ter admirabilis*, the thrice admirable Mother. The members of Schönstatt, which was recognized as a Secular Institute in 1948, give Mary a blank cheque (*Blankovollmacht*), that is to say they surrender themselves to her unconditionally, exchange hearts with her and henceforth "live by the *Blankovollmacht*" in complete dependence on the thrice admirable Mother.

MARIAN CONFERENCES AND PUBLICATIONS

In the second third of this century there also began the publication of periodicals entirely devoted to Marian research and spirituality, such as *Mariale Dagen* (Tongerloo) in 1931, the popular *Marianist* (Dayton, Ohio) in 1942, the *Marian Studies* (U.S.A.) in 1950 and the strictly theological *Marianum* (Rome) in 1938 and *Ephemerides mariologicae* (Madrid) in 1951, to name only a few. Besides, both national and international Marian congresses were held throughout the world, which published their proceedings in many volumes: for example, the one held in Rome in 1950 under the title *Alma socia Christi*, and that held at Lourdes in 1958 called *Maria et Ecclesia*. Indeed, the Marian literature of our century is so overwhelming that it is quite impossible to give even the most superficial survey of it. To quote once more Laurentin[1]: "Never has so much been written about our Lady." Father Besutti in his specialized bibliographies cites the following figures[2]: 982 titles in 1948-9; 2209 titles in 1950-1; 5758 titles in 1952-7. In round figures this is a thousand a year, and it does not include more popular non-scientific periodicals. In spite of this omission the author confesses frankly that he is overwhelmed by this material, which, as he writes, "knows no limits".

CONCLUSION

We have seen how, roughly within the last century and a half, the so-called Marian movement has gathered momentum until it reached its peak in the pontificate of Pius XII. But with the *aggiornamento* of John XXIII and the Second Vatican Council it seems that the crest of the wave is passed; it seems unlikely that there will be any new Marian definitions in the near future, such as that of the mediation of all graces and the co-redemption. Both the biblical and the ecumenical move-

[1] *Mary's Place in the Church*, p. 11.
[2] *Bibliografia Mariana, 1950/1*, Rome (1952), p. 5.

ments will play their part in keeping Marian doctrine and devotion within the limits of sound theology and practice.

For Mariology follows the trend of theology as a whole, which today turns increasingly to its biblical and patristic sources in a movement of renewal and adaptation. In this the Mother of God, too, will play her part, as she has done from the beginning of Christianity, when the angel first greeted her as the new Daughter of Sion with his *"chaire kecharitomene"*.

BIBLIOGRAPHY

AGREDA, MARY d', *The Mystical City of God*, first Spanish ed. (1670)

ALGERMISSEN, K., see under Calvin in *Lexikon der Marienkunde*

ALLCHIN, A. M., "Our Lady in Seventeenth-century Anglican Devotion and Theology", in Mascall and Box, q.v.

ALPHONSUS LIGUORI, *The Glories of Mary*, Eng. ed.

BALLERINI, A., *Sylloge Monumentorum ad Mysterium Conceptionis Immaculatae Virginis Deiparae Illustrandum*, Rome (1854–6)

BARTH, K., *Die kirchliche Dogmatik*, 2. Halbband, 3rd ed.

BAUMANN, B., *Maria mater nostra spiritualis. Eine theologische Untersuchung . . . in den Äusserungen der Päpste vom Tridentinum bis heute (1563–1947)*, Brixen (1948)

BEEVERS, J., *The Sun her Mantle*, Dublin (1953)

BELLARMINE, R., *Conciones Lovanienses 42*, Naples (1872ff.)

BELLARMINE, R., *Opera Oratoria Postuma*, Rome (1942)

BENNET, V. and WINCH, R., *The Assumption of Our Lady and Catholic Theology* (1950)

BÉRULLE, P. de, *Works*, ed. J. P. Migne, Paris (1856)

BICKERSTETH, R., *The Blessed Virgin and Anglican Divines* (1907)

BOEHME, J., *Works*, ed. K. W. Schiebler (1922); Eng. tr. by J. Ellistone and J. Sparrow (1644–62; re-edited 1762–84)

BOSSUET, J.-B., *Œuvres complètes*, ed. F. Lachat (1862)

BREMOND, H., *Histoire littéraire du sentiment religieux en France*, III (1921)

BULGAKOV, S., *The Burning Bush* (1927)

BULGAKOV, S., *The Wisdom of God* (1937)

BULL, G., Sermon 4 on "The Blessed Virgin's Low and Exalted Condition", in *Works* ed. E. Burton (1827), vol. 1, pp. 83–112

BULLINGER, H., *Marienpredigt*; extracts in Tappolet, q.v.

CALVIN, J., *Opera Omnia*, Braunschweig-Berlin (1864–1900)

CANISIUS, P., *De Virgine Incomparabili*, Ingolstadt (1577)

CAPES, F. M., *Bossuet on Devotion to the Blessed Virgin* (1899)

CHEVALIER, *La Médaille miraculeuse* (1878)

CONTENSON, V., *Theologia Mentis et Cordis* (1681)

CRASSET, J., *La Véritable Dévotion envers la sainte Vierge établie et défendue* (1679)

CROS, L., Lourdes 1858. *Témoins de l'Evénement. Documents présentés par le P. M. Olphe-Galliard*, Paris (1957)

DELIUS, W., *Geschichte der Marienverehrung* (1963)

DILLENSCHNEIDER, C., *La Mariologie de St Alphonse de Liguori*, 2 vols. (1931)

DILLENSCHNEIDER, C., *Le Sens de la foi et le progrès dogmatique du mystère marial* (1954)

DOELLINGER, I., Reusch, *Geschichte der Moralstreitigkeiten in der römischkatholischen Kirche seit dem sechzehnten Jahrhundert* (1889)

DRIPT, L., *Statera et examen libelli cui titulus Monita Salutaria* (1675)

ERASMUS OF ROTTERDAM, *Opera*, Leyden (1703–06)

EUDES, JEAN, *Œuvres complètes*, Varnes (1905–11)

EVEN, M., *Notre-Dame de Pontmain* (1946)

FLEETWOOD, *An Account of the Life and Death of the Blessed Virgin according to Romish Writers* (1687)

FLEMING, H., *Maria die Mutter unseres Heilandes* (1930)

FORBES, W., *Considerationes modestae et pacificae controversiarum*, ed. with an Eng. tr. in the *Library of Anglo-Catholic Theology*, 2 vols. (1850–56)

FRANK, M., *Sermon on the Annunciation, Library of Anglo-Catholic Theology*, vol. 2

FRIEDEL, E. J., *The Mariology of Cardinal Newman*, New York (1928)

FROST, B., *The Mystery of Mary* (1938)

FRUGES, G. M. de, *Jean-Jacques Olier*, Paris, n.d.

GORCE, M., *Les Origines du Rosaire et ses antécédents historiques* (1931)

GREEF, DE and ROUVROY, *Les Faits Mystérieux de Beauraing* (1933)

GRIGNION DE MONFORT, L.-M., *L'Amour de la Sagesse éternelle* (1932)

GRIGNION DE MONFORT, L.-M., *True Devotion to the Blessed Virgin*, Eng. translation by F. W. Faber, new ed. (1937)

GUARINI, J., *Of the Sacred Empire of the Virgin Mary* (1600)

HALL, J., *Contemplations*, ed. P. Wynter, Oxford (1863)

HEILER, F., ed., *Das neue Mariendogma im Lichte der Geschichte und im Urteil der Oekumene* (1951)

HICKES, *Speculum Beatae Virginis*, 2nd ed. (1686)

HOFFER, P., *La Dévotion à Marie au déclin du XVII siècle* (1938)

HOLZAPFEL, H., *St Dominikus und der Rosenkranz* (1903)

JANSSENS, *La Dévotion Mariale de Bossuet* (1946)

JAOUEN, J., *La Grâce de La Salette* (1946)

KERKOFS, L. J., *Notre-Dame de Banneux* (1950)

KETWIGH, J. B. van, *Panoplia Mariana* (1720)

KOLBE, T., *Die symbolischen Bücher der evangelisch-lutherischen Kirche* (1921)

LAMPARTER, H., *Die Magd des Herrn* (1949)

LAURENTIN, R., *Marie, l'Eglise et le sacerdoce* (1953)

LAURENTIN, R., *Lourdes. Historie authentique des apparitions* (1958ff). (This monumental work has superseded all previous publications on the subject)

LAURENTIN, R., *La Question Mariale* (1963). Eng. translation *Mary's Place in the Church* (1965)

LAWRENCE OF BRINDISI, *Mariale*, vol. 1 of the new Franciscan edition of his *Works* (1927)

LEBRUN, C., *La spiritualité de S. Jean Eudes* (1933). Eng. translation (1934)

LEO XIII, *Acta Papae Leonis XIII*, vols. 5 and 6

LOCHET, L., *Muttergotteserscheinungen* (1957)

LUTHER, M., *Werke*, Weimar edition, ed. J. C. F. Knaake and others (1883ff)

MARÉCHAL, H., *Mémorial des apparitions de la Vierge dans l'Eglise* (1957)

MARTINDALE, C. C., *The Message of Fatima* (1950)

MASCALL, E. L. and Box, H. S., edd. *The Blessed Virgin Mary. Essays by Anglicans* (1963)

MIEGGE, C., *The Virgin Mary. The Roman-Catholic Marian Doctrine*, Eng. translation (1955)

MOLIIEN, A., *Le Cardinal de Bérulle* (1947)

MONIN, A., *Notre-Dame de Beauraing* (1949)

MULLER, A., *Ecclesia-Maria*, Fribourg, 2 (1955)

MURATORI, L. A., *Works*, ed. Venice, 48 vols. (1790–1800)

NEWMAN, J. H., *Parochial and Plain Sermons*, vol. 2

NEWMAN, J. H., *Oxford University Sermons No. 15* (1843)

NEWMAN, J. H., *Catholic Sermons of Cardinal Newman* (1957)

NEWMAN, J. H., *Discourses to Mixed Congregations* (1849)

NEWMAN, J. H., "A Letter Addressed to the Rev. E. B. Pusey on Occasion of his *Eirenicon*", in *Certain Difficulties Felt by Anglicans*, new ed. (1892)

NIGIDO, N., *Summa sacrae Mariologiae* (1602)

OLIER, J.-J., *Works* ed. Migne (1856)

OLIER, J.-J., *Vie intérieure de la très sainte Vierge*, Rome (1866 and 1875)

PASCAL, B., *Lettres Provinciales* (No. 9), ed. H. F. Stewart, Manchester University Press (1920)

PASSAGLIA, *De Immaculatae Deiparae Semper Virginis Conceptu Commentarius* (1854f.)

PERRONE, G., *De Immaculato Beatae Virginis Mariae Conceptu* (1847)

PIUS IX, *Ineffabilis Deus* (1854)

PIUS X, *Ad Diem Illum* (1904)

PIUS XI, *Ingravescentibus malis* (1937)

PIUS XII, *Munificentissimus Deus* (1950)

PIUS XII, *Fulgens Corona* (1953)

PIUS XII, *Ad Caeli Reginam* (1954)

POURRAT, P., *Jean-Jacques Olier* (1932)

PREUSS, H. D., "Maria bei Luther", in *Schriften des Vereins für Reformationsgeschichte* (1954)

PUSEY, E. B., *Eirenicon* (1865)

PUSEY, E. B., *First Letter to the Very Rev. J. H. Newman* (1869)

RAHNER, K., *Visions and Prophecies*, Eng. translation (1964)

RAYNAUD, T., *Nomenclator Marianus* (1639)

RAYNAUD, T., *Diptycha Mariana* (1643)

RAYNAUD, T., *Scapulare Partheno-Carmeliticum* (1654)

SCHEEBEN, M. J., *Handbuch der katholischen Dogmatik* (1882)

SCHILLEBEECKX, E., *Mary, Mother of the Redemption*, London, Sheed and Ward (1964)

SCHIMMELPFENNIG, R., *Die Geschichte der Marienverehung im deutschen Protestantismus* (1952)

SEMMELROTH, A., *Urbild der Kirche. Organischer Aufbau des Mariengeheimnisses* (1950)

STAEHLIN, C. M., *Apariciones*, Madrid (1954)

STAFFORD, A., *The Femall* [sic] *Glory*, ed. O. Shipley (1869)

STRICHER, J., *Le Vœu du sang en faveur de l'Immaculée Conception* (1960)

SUAREZ, F., *De mysteriis vitae Christi*, Paris ed. (1856–78), vol. 19

TAPPOLET, W., *Das Marienlob der Reformatoren* (1962)

TAYLOR, J., "Life of Our Lord and Saviour Jesus Christ", in *Works* 1, ed. Heber and Eden (1847)

THURSTON, E., articles on the Rosary in *The Month* (1900ff.)

ULLATHORNE, W. B., *The Immaculate Conception of the Mother of God* (1855)

WIDENFELD, A., *Avis salutaires* (1673), Eng. translation 1687

ZWINGLI, U., "Marienpredigt", in *Works*, vol. 1, 391–428, Berlin (1905)

SUBJECT INDEX